# SOVIET POLITICAL THOUGHT

# SOVIET POLITICAL THOUGHT

## An Anthology

*Selected, Translated, and Edited by*
Michael Jaworskyj

The Johns Hopkins Press, Baltimore, Maryland

# Preface ∽

This volume is an anthology of Soviet political thought. It traces the evolution of Soviet thought from the Bolshevik Revolution of 1917 to the Twenty-second Congress of the Communist Party in 1961. The span of time covers three phases of Soviet intellectual history. First, the revolutionary twenties, which were characterized by a radically new social engineering and by intellectual ferment, optimism, and impatience. Second, the period of Stalin's authoritarianism, in which political authority sought to impose ideological uniformity, yet failed to fully eliminate dissension. Third, the post-Stalin years, distinguished by increasing attempts to re-examine the ideological inheritance from the earlier periods.

For the purpose of presenting a comprehensive picture of the evolution of Soviet political thought, the author has chosen not to pursue the popular approach, which is restricted to studying "classics," that is, the views of Marx, Engels, Lenin, Stalin, and Khrushchev. While the popular approach has its merits, it nevertheless suffers from immanent liabilities in that it merely reveals "official" Soviet political thinking. Proponents of this approach have succumbed to what may be called a hero-interpretation of Soviet thought by creating the impression that after the Bolshevik Revolution the production of political thought became a monopoly of the political leaders—Lenin, Stalin, Khrushchev, etc. Consequently, the popular approach has resulted in an inaccurate picture of the scope, aims, and content of Soviet political thought.

For example, proponents of the popular approach have neglected the body of political thought produced during the 1920's. Yet this was a dynamic and prolific period in the history of Soviet social thought. The literature of this period—produced by political and legal theorists, economists, philosophers, historians, and ideologists—is diverse, original, and full of cognitive content; and the range of both theoretical and practical problems discussed is indeed impressive. Soviet social thinkers in the twenties took these problems seriously, much more so than did their Western counterparts, for they were engaged in a new type of social engineering. They considered themselves to be the builders of a new, "rational" social order founded on principles presumably never before applied.

Western proponents of the hero-approach in studying Soviet political thought commit a similar fallacy with regard to the "Stalin period." It has become fashionable in the West to assert that during Stalin's regime only his views prevailed. But this is far from the truth. First, many of the philosophical and political views attributed to Stalin had been discussed in the early twenties before he assumed dictatorial power. Second, despite the wholehearted determination of Stalin and his lieutenants to superimpose an official set of views, they failed to bring about complete uniformity. Moreover, Stalin, who enjoyed a monopoly over interpretation of the basic tenets of Marxism-Leninism, reversed himself on several occasions, the last of which took place in connection with the "Linguistic Controversy" in 1950. The effect of Stalin's pronouncements on this and other controversies amounted to a direct condemnation of the principal tenets of dialectical and historical materialism in Marx's, Engels', and Lenin's formulation, and, indeed, in Stalin's own earlier interpretation.

The popular hero-approach has even less validity in studying Soviet political thought after Stalin's death. There are no more heroes in the Soviet Union who could singlehandedly control the thought processes of social theorists. Indeed, since Stalin's death, but especially since the Twentieth Party Congress, there has been a tendency on the part of the Party leaders to abstain from making binding pronouncements of a general doctrinal or philosophical nature, as had been the case under Stalin. Rather, the Party has restricted itself to the formulation of short-run and long-run social objectives, and of the means necessary for their attainment, which are periodically presented in the form of Party programs. The "theoretical" elaboration of the Party's policies, as well as of various philosophical, political, and economic problems that fall under the label of Marxism-Leninism, are being left increasingly to professional social thinkers who are associated with institutions of higher learning. Therefore, exclusive reliance upon "official" Party pronouncements for the purpose of presenting Soviet political thought necessarily results in an incomplete picture.

To avoid the shortcomings of the popular approach, the author decided to use the writings of professional Soviet social thinkers—philosophers, political theorists, historians, legal theorists, economists, sociologists, and Party ideologists. The main stream of Soviet political thought, with all its currents and undercurrents, is more accurately reflected in their writings than in the Party programs or in the "official" writings of Lenin, Stalin, or Khrushchev. At the same time, concentration upon the writings of social theorists will account for the "official aspects" of Soviet political thought, because the views of Marx, Engels, Lenin, Stalin, and other Party leaders are frequently referred to and liberally quoted in these writings.

The main body of the book consists of translations of Soviet materials until now unavailable in Western languages. These materials—representing the views of more than fifty Soviet social thinkers—were selected for their intellectual value and historical relevance. The author has sought to avoid presenting merely small fragments of the original materials. His aim has been to present complete arguments, which unfortunately necessitated some duplication.

The translated materials are presented in chronological order. This form of presentation makes it possible for the reader to follow the flow of arguments and counterarguments. However, for the convenience of the reader, the translated materials are divided into three parts reflecting major phases in the development of Soviet political thought. Each part is preceded by an introduction indicating the principal features that distinguish one phase from another.

The entire body of translations is preceded by an Introduction, in which the philosophical and methodological assumptions underlying Soviet political thought are discussed. These assumptions were stated in the works of Marx, Engels, Lenin, and Stalin, and are frequently referred to by Soviet writers. It is hoped that the discussion of these assumptions will bring some clarity to the maze of ideas underlying Soviet political thought and will facilitate the reader's understanding of the translated materials.

A word of explanation is necessary concerning the problem of rendering Russian titles in English. The system of transliteration used is that of the Library of Congress, with diacritical marks and ligatures eliminated. In transliterating the titles of books and articles, the English style of capitalization was adopted.

It should be noted that the omission of sections of the articles has been indicated by the symbol . . . . . . .

Another problem that should be mentioned concerns the footnotes in the translated Soviet materials. Soviet authors frequently furnish merely general information as to the sources they used, without indicating edition, place, and date of publication, and page numbers. In most cases, for the reader's benefit, the missing information has been provided.

At this point I wish to express my gratitude to Professor Robert W. Tucker, of The Johns Hopkins University. As my teacher, Professor

Tucker instilled in me lasting interest and critical insight in social ideas. As a friend, he contributed greatly to the completion and the publication of the manuscript.

I am also grateful to Miss Elaine Paul, Miss Ruth Macniven, and Miss Ksenia Horoshak for their typing and editing assistance.

My final expression of thanks goes to Jack G. Goellner, editorial director of The Johns Hopkins Press, for his encouraging interest in the manuscript, and to Miss Penny James for her endurance and efficiency in editing the manuscript.

*New York*                                                MICHAEL JAWORSKYJ
*January,* 1967

# TABLE OF CONTENTS

## PART II

### STALINIST AUTHORITARIANISM

## PART III

### IN SEARCH OF MARXIST IDENTITY

# SOVIET POLITICAL THOUGHT

# Introduction ∾ Philosophical Assumptions Underlying Soviet Political Thought

## THE SCOPE AND NATURE OF THE MARXIST DIALECTICAL METHOD

An understanding of Soviet political thought is greatly facilitated by a familiarity with the various philosophical, methodological, and epistemological assumptions underlying it. These assumptions were stated in the works of Marx, Engels, Lenin, and Stalin. Soviet social thinkers view these assumptions as constituting a specific *method,* which they claim to be using constantly in the process of elaborating their theories. This method is designated most commonly as the Marxist dialectical method. However, frequently it appears under different labels, such as the Marxist, the Marxist-Leninist, the materialist or revolutionary method.

Whatever its label, the Marxist dialectical method is acclaimed by Soviet writers to be "the sole strictly scientific method." It is supposedly grounded on propositions that have the character of "objective" or "absolute" truth; consequently, it is purported to be superior to all other methods ever used. It is this method that presumably is responsible for the scientific character of Soviet social theory.

In the judgment of Soviet writers, the Marxist dialectical method is not merely a scientific method in the strict meaning of the term. In addition to being the ultimate method for studying social phenomena, it represents at the same time a most advanced theory of cognition, a most progressive political ideology, a method for the revolutionary transformation of old social orders into new ones, a method for the conduct of domestic and international policies, and finally, a method for foreseeing and predicting the future.[1]

In other words, the Marxist dialectical method is purportedly a method of science and of politics at the same time: it is as suited for the purpose of determining and executing policy objectives as it is for the purpose of scientific investigation. In view of this assumption, Soviet writers vehemently reject the contention of some Western theorists that the nature of science is distinct from that of politics

[1] See, for example, P. Fedoseev, "Znachenie Marksistsko-Leninskoi Teorii Poznaniya dla Obshchestvennykh Nauk" (The Significance of the Marxist-Leninist Theory of Cognition to the Social Sciences), *Kommunist,* No. 8 (1955), pp. 21–34.

and that, consequently, the method used in politics is inapplicable to the field of science. They reject with equal vehemence the view that a scientific method cannot be simultaneously a political ideology. They argue that the outstanding peculiarity of the Marxist dialectical method—a peculiarity that makes it superior to all methods used by "bourgeois" social scientists—lies in the fact that it succeeds in blending all these qualities. Soviet writers contend that the Marxist dialectical method is diametrically opposed to all methods ever employed by "bourgeois" social scientists, especially to the Humean, Kantian, and neo-Kantian methodology, to Hegelian idealism and mechanistic materialism, to Comtian socialological positivism, to pragmatism, empiricism, intuitionism, logical positivism, and operationalism. In their judgment, all "bourgeois" methods are "artificial," "abstract," or "formal," in the sense that they represent merely a set of operational rules free of value content, or, if they provide for such a content, then it is based on "false" or "subjective" values. In contrast, the Marxist dialectical method is presumably neither artificial nor formal, because its principles are deduced from "real life" and the values it comprises are "true," that is, "objectively" existing values.

The Marxist dialectical method covers a broad spectrum of problems that in Soviet literature appear under the labels of *philosophical, dialectical,* and *historical materialism.* Following Lenin, who maintained that Marxism is "cast from a single piece of steel," Soviet writers assert that the various doctrines constituting the Marxist dialectical method represent not only a logically consistent but also an "organically" unified system of thought.

It will be seen, however, that this contention is of doubtful validity, for the various problems subsumed under the labels of philosophical, dialectical, and historical materialism are at times either unrelated or simply logically incompatible. This fact is rather significant because Soviet political thought is the product of the Marxist dialectical method and consequently it reflects all its inconsistencies. In view of this, an attempt will be made to determine the content of philosophical, dialectical, and historical materialism; to find out what, if anything, they have in common; and to point out their relationship to Soviet political thought.


PHILOSOPHICAL MATERIALISM

As indicated earlier, Soviet writers identify the Marxist dialectical method with philosophical, dialectical, and historical materialism. In turn, philosophical materialism, as a constituent part of this method, is depicted by them as an epistemological basis of dialectical and historical materialism. In other words, philosophical materialism presumably integrates components of the Marxist method into a closed, univocal system based on monistic assumptions.

In discussing the subject matter of philosophical materialism, Soviet writers traditionally refer to Engels' views as stated in *Ludwig Feuerbach* and *Anti-Dühring,* to Marx's indirect pronouncements on this subject scattered throughout his works, and to the interpretations of these views advanced by Lenin and Stalin. Engels', Marx's, Lenin's, and Stalin's views, which Soviet writers identify with philosophical materialism, were couched in the cumbersome language of Hegelian idealism. However, stripped of the obsolete philosophical verbiage, it becomes apparent that philosophical materialism deals essentially with two basic problems.

The first problem is the one concerning the relationship between "Spirit" and "matter." That is to say, Engels and Marx were confronted with the traditional theological and Hegelian philosophical claim that the Spirit, or what Hegel called "the Idea," was *prior* to matter. The theological notion of the Spirit and Hegel's notion of the Idea coincide with one another: both of them were intended to signify a *non-material* phenomenon, a phenomenon existing in the form of *thought.* Hence the question of priority of spirit over matter raises, in effect, the question concerning *the priority of thought over matter.* Such was also Engels' understanding of this problem. In his words,

The great basic question of all, and especially of recent philosophy, is the question of the relationship between thought and existence, between spirit and nature. . . . Which is prior to the other: spirit or nature? Philosophers are divided into two great camps, according to the way in which they have answered this question. Those who declare that spirit existed before nature . . . have formed the idealist camp. The others, who regard nature as primary, belong to the various schools of materialism.[2]

Engels, Marx, Lenin, and Stalin were materialists because they recognized the priority of matter over thought. In recognizing matter's priority over thought, they committed themselves to a view diametrically opposed to the theological and idealist theses that assert priority of thought over matter. At the same time, however, they committed the same error as theologians and idealists. The question concerning the priority of thought over matter is of a religious origin. This fact has been recognized quite clearly by Engels, though it is frequently overlooked by his Soviet followers. In Engels' words,

[2] *Ludwig Feuerbach,* cited by Lenin, *Collected Works* (New York, 1930), XXIII, 21–22.

Thus the question of the relation of thinking to being, the relation of spirit to nature—the paramount question of the whole philosophy—has, no less than all religion, its roots in the narrow-minded and ignorant notions of savagery. But this question could for the first time be put forward in its whole acuteness, could achieve its full significance, only after European society had awakened from the long hibernation of the Christian Middle Ages. The question of the position of thinking in relation to being, a question which, by the way, had played a great part also in the scholasticism of the Middle Ages, the question: which is primary, spirit or nature—that question, in relation to the Church, was sharpened into this: "Did god create the world or has the world been in existence eternally?"[3]

Engels' error lies in his assumption that a theological question —a question that, as he correctly stated, has "its roots in the narrow-minded and ignorant notions of savagery"—raises a rational problem and that consequently it can be answered scientifically. His line of reasoning was as follows: theologians were right in raising the question concerning the relationship between thought (spirit, God) and matter (nature, being) but they failed to answer it correctly. Only now, with the development of a "scientific" approach represented by Engels and Marx, could it be answered. The "scientifically correct" answer to this question is that matter was prior to thought.

What Engels did was to accept uncritically the theological assumption that an understanding of thought and matter is impossible without first answering the "paramount question." His error lies precisely in the acceptance of this assumption. For the question "Which is primary, spirit or nature?" is analogical to the question "Which was first, the chicken or the egg?" It stands to reason that science is able to bring about an understanding of the structure and the properties of chickens and eggs and also of the causal relationship between them, without answering the question of their absolute priority. Indeed, science does it without even raising such a question. It could be argued that even if it were possible to ascertain scientifically the priority of chickens or eggs, this would not add anything to our knowledge, which science obtained without raising the question. The same applies to the question concerning the priority of thought or matter.

Although scientifically irrelevant, the presupposition of the temporal priority of thought over matter, or vice versa, is of great significance to theology and to materialism in Engels' and Marx's interpretation. According to the theological view, God as the non-material spiritual entity is the creator of the material world which

[3] *Ludwig Feuerbach* (New York, 1941), p. 21.

he controls by virtue of being its creator. Similarly, according to the proponents of philosophical materialism, matter, being prior to thought, controls thought by virtue of its temporal priority.

The assumption that matter controls thought underlies the materialist theory of cognition, which is known as the "reflection theory of knowledge." According to this theory, the function performed by the human mind in the process of cognition is that of "reflecting," "copying," or "photographing" the external reality.[4] From the viewpoint of this theory, man's mind does not appear as a creative and hence interpretive instrument, but rather as a passive camera-like or mirror-like instrument, confined to mechanical copying of the reality surrounding it. The most obvious implication of the reflection theory of knowledge is that the ideas entertained by man (and this includes scientific, philosophical, etc., ideas) are not the product of his mind. The mind does not create them; it finds them, so to speak, ready-made in nature, and then reflects them.

It is customary among Soviet writers to describe the reflection theory of knowledge as the only consistent and scientific one. Under closer analysis, however, it is rather apparent that it is burdened by insurmountable difficulties. Its principal deficiency is a failure to provide standards for judging the accuracy of reflection. As long as such standards are not furnished, the assumption that the mind's reflections represent an accurate, undistorted picture of reality remains an article of faith. Soviet theorists find the proof of the accuracy of the mind's reflections in the classics, that is, in the writings of Engels, Marx, Lenin, and Stalin. But their views on this subject constitute optimistic declarations to the effect that man's mind, being a part of nature, must reflect nature accurately. To quote Engels: "But if . . . the question of what thought and consciousness really are and where they came from is raised, it becomes apparent that they are products of the human brain and that man himself is a product of nature, a product which has been developed in and along with its environment; *hence it is self-evident that the products of the human brain, being in the last analysis also products of nature, do not contradict the rest of nature but are in correspondence with it.*"[5]

Similarly, according to Lenin, the picture of matter reflected in

---

[4] Vladimir I. Lenin, *Sochineniya* [Works] (4th ed.; Moscow, 1941–50), Vol. 14 (1947), p. 252.

[5] *Anti-Dühring* (2nd ed.; Moscow, 1959), p. 55 (italics added). A similar but more strongly stated view on this subject appeared in Engels' notes to the second German edition of *Anti-Dühring*. There he wrote the following: "The fact that our subjective thought and the objective world are subject to the same laws, and hence, too, that in the final analysis they cannot contradict each other in their results, but must coincide, governs absolutely our whole theoretical thought" (p. 504).

mind is a "true picture of . . . objective reality,"[6] or "an approximately true (adequate, ideally exact) reflection of it."[7] Mind reflects
accurately because it is "a piece of nature reflecting other pieces of
nature."[8]

These contentions represent a *naturalistic* aspect of the reflection
theory discussed within the framework of philosophical materialism.
Within this framework *man's* mind appears in its "natural purity";
it is viewed as an element of nature unaffected by the "corrupting"
influences of *man's* social experience. It is because of its natural
purity that the mind's reflections of "objective reality" are accurate.
And since in actuality these reflections assume the form of ideas or
statements about "objective reality," it follows that all statements
are equally objective and hence equally valid. From the viewpoint
of philosophical materialism it is impossible to make a distinction
between true and false statements, for all statements appear to be
accurate reflections of reality. In other words, however contradictory
and absurd our views of reality may be, they must be accepted on
their own merit as self-evident truths.

The reflection theory of knowledge has a serious bearing upon the
theory of society and politics. The assumption that man's ideas are
reflected from nature leads to an entirely different conception of
society from the assumption that ideas are creations of the human
mind.

Since according to the reflection theory of knowledge all of man's
ideas are reflections of nature, it is reasonable to conclude—as Soviet social theorists do—that the laws governing man's social behavior are also deduced from nature. But if it is true that man's social
life is governed by laws derived from nature, and, in addition, if it is
assumed that these are the same laws that govern nature, then
social order cannot be considered to be man's creation. On the contrary, social order appears then to be an extension or a replica of
natural order—a more or less perfect replica, depending upon the
accuracy of nature's reflections taken by the human mind.

On the other hand, the assumption that ideas are the creation
of the human mind leads to a diametrically opposed conclusion—to
an activist conception of society. One can speak validly of social
order, as distinct from natural order, only if it is assumed that social
order is founded on principles, laws, or, in brief, on ideas that are of
man's creation. For only if man is capable of creating his own ideas
can he succeed in creating a social order distinct from that of nature.

It is rather apparent that the reflection theory of knowledge ulti-

---

[6] *Sochineniya*, Vol. 14, p. 116.          [7] *Ibid.*, p. 312.
[8] *Ibid.*, Vol. 19 (1948), p. 61.

mately leads to an anti-activist, naturalistic conception of society. Its most obvious implication is that the social values entertained by man are not of his own making, that they have an objective existence independent of man's volition, and that man mirrors them from nature. The most obvious weakness of the reflection theory is that it cannot account for the fact that men living in various societies entertain mutually incompatible values. The explanation implied by the reflection theory is that this is merely a reflection of the fact that nature is permeated by conflicting values. But such an implication is too fantastic to be fully accepted even by Soviet exponents of the reflection theory of knowledge. Consequently, it will be seen that within the framework of historical materialism they modify the reflection theory of knowledge in a way that permits them to speak of "true" and "false" values.

## DIALECTICAL MATERIALISM

In contrast to philosophical materialism, which represents essentially a theory of cognition, dialectical materialism may best be described as a general theory of *nature*. The expression "nature" is used here in its broadest, all-inclusive sense, encompassing the material world, the social world, and the world of ideas. This is significant, for if dialectical materialism were concerned only with nature in the narrow meaning of the term—designating only the material world—there would be no need to deal with it in a study of Soviet political thought. The fact is, however, that dialectical materialism is based on the assumption that the material world, the social world, and the world of ideas are integral parts of a universal process of "motion" and "development." Another assumption underlying dialectical materialism is that the universal process of motion—and hence the process of development of all its constituent parts: nature, society, and ideas—is governed *by the same laws,* namely, by "dialectical" or "natural" laws.

It is these laws that constitute the principal object of investigation within the framework of dialectical materialism. Soviet theorists contend that dialectical materialism succeeded in furnishing "scientific" answers to such questions as the character of these laws, their sphere of operation, and their relationship to the material world, to man's actions and to his thought. In doing this, they follow Engels, who described dialectical materialism, or what he called "dialectics," as "the science of the general laws of motion and the development of nature, human society, and thought."[9]

[9] *Anti-Dühring,* p. 194.

According to Soviet theorists, "the science of the general laws of motion" was developed by Engels and further expounded by his disciples, Lenin and Stalin. However, there are gross discrepancies between Engels', Lenin's, and Stalin's interpretations of dialectical materialism. Consequently, it is desirable to discuss them separately.

*Engels' Interpretation of Dialectical Laws*

According to Engels, "the science of the general laws of motion" is based on a "dialectical" conception of nature. He derived this conception of nature from the "new German philosophy" which "culminated in the Hegelian system." In his words, "In this system—and herein is its great merit—for the first time the whole world, natural, historical, intellectual, is represented as a process, i.e., as in constant motion, change, transformation, development; and the attempt is made to trace out the internal connections that make a continuous whole of all this movement and development."[10]

The process of motion in which "the whole world, natural, historical, intellectual" is involved is not simply a mechanical one. The process represents a "progressive development," a development that, as stated by Hegel and frequently repeated by Marx and Engels, proceeds from "lower" to "higher" levels.[11] It is a self-improving process, presumably directed toward the attainment of physical, intellectual, and moral perfection.

The process of progressive development is fully predictable, for, in Engels' judgment, it is dominated by natural laws. These laws exist independent of man's volition and are beyond his control. They determine, with an "iron necessity," the behavior of the elements of nature, man's social behavior, and his thought.

As admitted by Engels, these natural laws were discovered by Hegel, but Hegel failed to understand them correctly. It is Engels and in part Marx who succeeded in explaining the "true" nature of these laws and their effect upon man's actions and thought. Following Hegel, Engels contended that "the whole world, natural, historical, intellectual" is governed by three laws.

The first law cited by him is *"the law of the transformation of quantity into quality and vice versa,"*[12] which in the Soviet literature is also known as the law of "precipitated" or "leap-like" development. The discovery of this law has presumably invalidated the traditional view asserting that the process of development proceeds in a gradual, evolutionary manner. According to Engels, the gradualness in the development of nature and society is frequently disrupted

---

[10] *Ibid.*, p. 37.     [11] Engels, *Feuerbach*, p. 44.
[12] *Dialectics of Nature* (Moscow, 1954), p. 83.

by "qualitative leaps," that is, by a "sudden," "precipitated," "revolutionary" change of quantity into quality and vice versa.

In support of this view, Engels referred to a celebrated illustration of "quantitative leaps" given by Hegel. Hegel argued that, given a certain quantity of water at 0° C., the "slightest shock is sufficient for it suddenly to become hard," which means that the slightest lowering of temperature below this point will transform water into ice "suddenly." This sudden transformation presumably represents "an interruption in gradualness," that is, a "precipitated" or a "revolutionary" change into a new quality.

The "sudden leaps" that are responsible for the precipitation of social development are the revolutions. Revolution—the employment of physical force for the purpose of changing the existing social system—appears as a necessary and unavoidable condition of social development. From Engels' point of view, revolutions appear as natural, not social, events; they appear as being superimposed upon man by the laws of nature and hence as beyond his control. In brief, the law of the transformation of quantity into quality and vice versa justifies revolutions as being both morally desirable and naturally necessary.

The second law advanced by Engels is *"the law of the interpenetration of opposites,"* known in Soviet literature as "the law of contradictions." This law attempts to explain the fundamental assumption of dialectical materialism asserting that everything in existence—nature, society, thought—is in a process of motion and development. It asserts that motion and development are possible because of the clash of opposites, or contradictions, that is, the conflict between opposite elements constituting nature, society, and thought.

In society, the opposites or contradictions assume the form of social classes, one struggling against another. From the viewpoint of the law of the interpenetration of opposites, the class struggle constitutes an unavoidable and necessary condition of social development. And, like revolutions, the class struggle appears as an event brought about by natural law and therefore beyond human control.

The law of the interpenetration of opposites also has bearing upon the rules of formal logic. The rule of logical non-contradiction, as pointed out by Aristotle, asserts that "the same attribute cannot at the same time belong and not belong to the same subject and in the same respect."[13] According to this rule, for example, the two statements "A is here" and "A is not here" are logically contradictory

---

[13] "Metaphysics," in *The Basic Works of Aristotle,* ed. Richard P. McKeon (New York, 1941), p. 166.

and thus mutually exclusive; both of them cannot at the same time be true.

Engels maintained that this rule is invalid because it does not correspond to "objective reality." In his judgment, contradictions are "objectively present in things and processes."[14] Hence, he concluded—in conformity with the reflection theory of knowledge—that contradictions inherent in nature not only should but must be reflected in human thought and reasoning.

The third law, *"the law of the negation of the negation,"* has been characterized by Engels as "an extremely general—and for this reason extremely far-reaching and important—law of the development of nature, history, and thought, a law which . . . holds good in the animal and plant kingdoms, in geology, in mathematics, in history and in philosophy. . . ."[15] This law covers "a very simple process which is taking place everywhere and every day, which any child can understand as soon as it is stripped of the veil of mystery in which it was enveloped by the old idealist philosophy."[16]

As an illustration of this "simple process" in nature, Engels pointed out a germinating grain of barley which "negates" itself in growth and ultimately "negates its negation" by producing a new seed. The illustrations from history are the various stages of man's social development, each "negating" another: the primitive community, the slave-holding community, feudalism, capitalism, socialism, and communism. In "human thought, . . . primitive, natural materialism" was "negated by idealism," and the latter in turn "was negated by modern materialism."[17]

In brief, the law of negation of negation is based on the assumption that the past, the present, and the future of nature, of man's social life, and of man's thought constitute an endless process of development taking place independent of man's volition. This process evolves through certain stages, one contradictory to another, and hence one eventually superseding another, but at the same time each stage being a necessary condition for the stage following it. Taken together, all these stages represent a process of development in the sense that the transformation of one stage into another is presumably irreversible and that each stage appears to be higher, both intellectually and morally, than the stage preceding it.

### Lenin's Interpretation of Dialectical Laws

In recent years it has become fashionable among Soviet theorists to give almost exclusive credit to Lenin for the advancement of dia-

[14] *Anti-Dühring*, p. 166.    [15] *Ibid.*, p. 193.    [16] *Ibid.*, p. 186.
[17] *Ibid.*, p. 190.

lectical materialism. In fact, however, Lenin's contribution to the clarification of the problems that fall within the scope of dialectical materialism is not very impressive. His works, to be sure, are full of scattered notes on dialectical materialism, but some of these notes (especially those in his *Philosophical Notebooks*) are almost unintelligible to one who is not thoroughly familiar with his mode of thinking.

In contrast to Stalin, who modified dialectical materialism almost beyond recognition, Lenin was primarily concerned with corroborating Engels' theory of dialectical laws and with defending it from its critics. In the process of doing this, however, he somewhat extended the meaning of dialectical laws.

To begin with, Lenin unquestionably accepted Engels' contention that everything in the universe is in the process of development and that this development is governed by three dialectical laws. Furthermore, he acknowledged that these laws are "the laws of nature."[18] Moreover, he accepted Engels' view that these laws are deterministic in character, in the sense that they absolutely dominate man's actions and thoughts.

However, on various occasions, Lenin spoke of dialectical materialism—of which natural laws are an essential part—as representing a "new," dialectical "logic" or "method." Thus, in his *Philosophical Notebooks,* these laws are no longer treated as the laws of nature but rather as methodological principles to be used for the purpose of a scientific investigation.[19]

But it is doubtful that they can be used for such a purpose. A description of nature, of social reality, or of man's intellectual activity, rendered in conformity with these principles, can hardly add anything new to the assertions comprised in them. In all probability such a description would constitute merely a reassertion of the original principles, and hence would add nothing new to the object under study. The results of using the three laws as methodological principles would be similar to the use of a theological view—that man's actions are determined by God—as a methodological principle. A description of man's actions in conformity with such a principle would merely reassert the original premise. The application of such a method to the study of social reality would eventually lead to pure dogmatism. And it will be seen that this is frequently the case with the interpretation of social reality advanced by Soviet theorists.

Another interesting point in Lenin's treatment of dialectical materialism is his interpretation of the law of the interpenetration of

[18] *Sochineniya,* Vol. 14, p. 175.
[19] *Collected Works* (Moscow, 1961), Vol. 38, pp. 319, 359–62.

opposites. Lenin attached a greater significance to this law than to others. In expounding the thesis that motion and development in nature and society are possible only because of the opposites or contradictions, Lenin advanced a peculiar interpretation of the relationship between them. On the one hand, he developed what is known as the "theory of the unity of opposites," while on the other, he advanced the "theory of the struggle of opposites."

It is quite apparent that the idea of the unity of opposites plays a crucial role in Lenin's understanding of motion and development. For example, on one occasion Lenin asserted that "in brief, dialectics can be defined as a doctrine of the unity of opposites. This embodies the essence of dialectics. . . ."[20] In another place, Lenin stated that "*dialectics* is the teaching which shows how *opposites* can be and how they happen to be (how they become) *identical*. . . ."[21] Furthermore, according to Lenin, "The identity of opposites (it would be more correct, perhaps, to say their 'unity' . . . ) is the recognition (discovery) of the contradictory, *mutually exclusive,* opposite tendencies in *all* phenomena and processes of nature (including mind and society). The condition for the knowledge of all processes of the world in their 'self-movement,' in their spontaneous development, in their real life, is the knowledge of them as a unity of opposites."[22]

Lenin, indeed, was right in assuming that if opposites are responsible for motion, then they must somehow be united in the sense that there must be something holding them together, restraining them from disintegrating into a state of chaotic behavior, and preventing them from reciprocal destruction. There must be a force restraining the opposites, especially in view of Lenin's assumption that the motion and development for which they are responsible is directed toward the attainment of a definite end. Such a motion is conceivable only if the opposites are held in check and properly balanced against each other. And since, according to Lenin, these opposites in society are represented by social classes, it follows that the maintenance of a balance between the classes is indispensable for social development; otherwise, classes may destroy each other and put an end to the development.

This, in part, was the view of Bukharin, who took the idea of the unity of opposites seriously and developed it to its logical end, in what came to be known as the equilibrium theory. With Stalin's ascendance to power in the late 1920's, Bukharin was stigmatized as an opportunist, for his theory asserted not only a possibility but a necessity for the reconciliation of class antagonism between the pro-

---

[20] *Ibid.,* p. 223.          [21] *Ibid.,* p. 109.          [22] *Ibid.,* pp. 359–60.

letariat and the peasantry. Stalin, on the other hand, maintained that social progress could be assured only through "the struggle of contradictions," that is, through the "intensification of the class struggle" and the ultimate liquidation of the peasantry by the proletariat.

Stalin's position was in conformity with Lenin's theory of the struggle of opposites. While depicting the unity of opposites as a necessary condition of natural and social development, Lenin at the same time fully accepted Marx's class-struggle theory of society. Under the influence of Marx's theory, Lenin argued that "development is the 'struggle' of opposites. . . . The unity (coincidence, identity, equal action) of opposites is conditional, temporary, transitory, relative. The struggle of mutually exclusive opposites is absolute, just as development and motion are absolute."[23]

The result is a complete reversal of the roles played by the unity and the struggle of opposites. Previously, the unity of opposites appeared as a permanent foundation in whose framework the struggle of opposites evolved. Now, it is the other way around; the struggle of opposites appears as an absolute condition, while the unity of opposites becomes a transitory occurrence. But if the struggle of opposites is an absolute one, unbound by time, then it will never end. Consequently, there will be no end to class struggles.

The implications of Lenin's theory of the struggle of opposites are clearly incompatible with the idea of communism. According to Marx, Engels, and Lenin himself, communism will be a classless society, a society without opposites and hence without struggle. If Lenin's theory of the struggle of opposites is correct, then communism is unattainable. The attainment of communism presupposes the disappearance of classes. But, taking the viewpoint of the law of the interpenetration of opposites, this is impossible, for classes constitute the instruments through which this law operates in society.

*Stalin's Interpretation of Dialectical Materialism*

In advancing his interpretation of dialectical materialism, Stalin claimed to have taken into account not only the views of Engels, Marx, and Lenin, but also "the experience of the proletariat" as "the ruling class" in the Soviet Union. It was presumably this experience of the proletariat (as interpreted by Stalin) that was responsible for the drastic revision of the original tenets of dialectical materialism.

It will be recalled that Engels viewed dialectical materialism as "the science of the general laws of motion and the development of

23 *Ibid.,* p. 360.

nature, human society, and thought." Lenin accepted this view un-conditionally. He also accepted Engels' conclusion that the develop-ment of nature, society, and thought is governed by three natural laws. However, at the same time, Lenin considered these natural laws to be methodological principles that could be used for the purpose of scientific investigation. In contrast to Engels and Lenin, Stalin tended to regard dialectical materialism almost exclusively as a method, that is, as the "Marxist dialectical method." This method presumably is applicable to the study of both natural and social phenomena. If "properly" applied, it can furnish "scientific" answers to questions concerning the historical past, the present, and the future.

Stalin stated his views on dialectical materialism in 1938, in his *History of the Communist Party of the Soviet Union (Bolshevik)*— *Short Course.* One of the most conspicuous features in his formula-tion of dialectical materialism is the absence of the law of negation of negation, which Engels considered to be one of the principal laws of nature. Stalin simply discarded this law without giving an explana-tion. It was only after his death that Soviet theorists raised the ques-tion concerning its status.

In conformity with his understanding of dialectical materialism as a method, Stalin argued that it comprises four "principal features." The first feature asserts that everything in the universe is interre-lated: "Contrary to metaphysics, dialectics does not regard nature as an accidental agglomeration of things, of phenomena, unconnected with, isolated from, and independent of each other, but as a con-nected and integral whole, in which things, phenomena, are organi-cally connected with, dependent on, and determined by each other."[24]

From this view, Stalin deduced a conclusion concerning the method to be used for studying natural and social phenomena, a conclusion asserting that the study of any phenomenon taken by itself is "mean-ingless," and that if it is to be understood and explained it must be "considered in its inseparable connection with surrounding phenom-ena as one conditioned by surrounding phenomena."[25]

The second feature of dialectical materialism is, in effect, a brief summary of Engels' concept of nature in motion, as discussed pre-viously: "Contrary to metaphysics, dialectics holds that nature is not in a state of rest and immobility, stagnation and immutability, but rather in a state of continuous movement and change, of continuous renewal and development, where something is always arising and developing, . . . something always disintegrating and dying away."[26]

---

[24] *Problems of Leninism* (Moscow, 1954), p. 714.
[25] *Ibid.,* p. 715.          [26] *Ibid.*

From this interpretation of nature Stalin came to two conclusions, one concerning the method of study for natural and social phenomena, the other pertaining to the conduct of domestic and international politics. With regard to the former, Stalin maintained that natural and social phenomena "should not be considered solely from the standpoint of their connection and interdependence but also from the standpoint of their movement, their change, their development, their coming into being and going out of being."[27] In respect to domestic and foreign policy he concluded the following: "The dialectical method regards as important primarily not that which at the given moment seems to be durable and yet is already beginning to die away, but that which is arising and developing, even though at the given moment it may appear to be not durable, for the dialectical method considers invincible only that which is arising and developing."[28]

As an illustration of this principle, Stalin referred to the fact that in the late eighties Marxists "based their orientation on the proletariat," who then constituted an insignificant minority, and not on *Narodniki* and peasants, who then constituted the vast majority of the population. "And they were not mistaken," continued Stalin, "for, as we know, the proletariat subsequently grew from an insignificant force into a first-rate historical and political force."[29] Supported by this fact, Stalin formulated a general principle for the conduct of policy: "Hence, in order not to err in policy, one must look forward, not backward."[30] He elucidated this principle, though in equally general terms: "Hence we must not base our orientation on the strata of society which are no longer developing, even though they at present constitute the predominant force, but on those strata which are developing and have a future before them, even though they at present do not constitute the predominant force."[31]

The third feature of dialectical materialism corresponds to what Engels referred to as "the law of the transformation of quantity into quality," which in Soviet literature is also known as the law of precipitated or leap-like development. Stalin defined it in the following manner: "Contrary to metaphysics, dialectics does not regard the process of development as a simple process of growth, where quantitative changes do not lead to qualitative changes, but as a development which passes from insignificant and imperceptible quantitative changes to open, fundamental changes, to qualitative changes; a development in which the qualitative changes occur not gradually, but rapidly and abruptly, taking the form of a leap from one state to

[27] *Ibid.*     [28] *Ibid.*     [29] *Ibid.*, p. 719.     [30] *Ibid.*     [31] *Ibid.*

another; they occur not accidentally but as the natural result of an accumulation of imperceptible and gradual quantitative changes."[32]

Supporting his views with Engels' opinion that "in the last analysis nature's process is dialectical and not metaphysical," Stalin argued that "the dialectical method therefore holds that the process of development should be understood not as a movement in a circle, not as a simple repetition of what has already occurred, but as an onward and upward movement, as a transition from an old qualitative state to a new qualitative state, as a development from the simple to the complex, from the lower to the higher."[33]

From the interpretation of nature as a progressing and self-perfecting process, Stalin deduced conclusions pertaining to society. He argued that if everything is progressing and "if the dying away of the old and the upgrowth of the new is a law of development," then it follows that nothing is "immutable," that there can be neither "immutable social systems" nor "eternal principles of private property."[34] Furthermore, according to Stalin, since precipitated, leap-like changes are the necessary conditions of the natural and social process of development, "revolutions made by oppressed classes are quite natural and inevitable phenomena."[35] Both of these conclusions are significant for they assert that no social system is immutable, an assertion that can be interpreted to mean that neither a socialist nor a communist system is exempt from the law of precipitated development, and that, consequently, both of them are subject to leap-like changes by means of revolution.

The fourth principal feature of dialectical materialism, in Stalin's interpretation, is identical with Engels' law of the interpenetration of opposites, or the so-called law of contradictions. Stalin formulated it in the following way: "Contrary to metaphysics, dialectics holds that internal contradictions are inherent in all things and phenomena of nature, for they all have their negative and positive sides, a past and a future, something dying away and something developing; and that the struggle between these opposites, the struggle between the old and the new, between that which is dying away and that which is being born, between that which is disappearing and that which is developing, constitutes the internal content of the process of development, the internal content of the transformation of quantitative changes into qualitative changes."[36]

In support of this view Stalin quoted Lenin as saying that "in its proper meaning, dialectics is the study of the contradictions *within the very essence of things*" and that natural and social development

---

[32] *Ibid.*, pp. 715–16.        [33] *Ibid.*, p. 716.        [34] *Ibid.*, p. 719.
[35] *Ibid.*, p. 720.        [36] *Ibid.*, p. 717.

takes place only because of the "struggle of opposites."[37] Accordingly, he argued that "the dialectical method therefore holds that the process of development from the lower to the higher takes place not as a harmonious unfolding of phenomena, but as a disclosure of the contradictions inherent in things and phenomena, as a 'struggle' of opposite tendencies which operate on the basis of these contradictions."[38]

From this conception of natural development Stalin derived three conclusions, none of them following logically from the premise. First, he maintained that since any development presupposes contradictions, or "opposite forces," social development is dependent upon "class struggle" and, therefore, "it is clear that the class struggle of the proletariat is a quite natural and inevitable phenomenon."[39] The second conclusion, concerning the method of studying society, asserts that because of the contradictions inherent in society "we must not cover up the contradictions of the capitalist system but disclose and unravel them."[40] The final conclusion at which Stalin arrived refers to the conduct of policy. It states that since the class struggle is a natural prerequisite of social development, "we must not try to check the class struggle but carry it to its conclusions."[41] Hence, continued Stalin, "in order not to err in policy, one must pursue an uncompromising proletarian class policy, not a reformist policy of harmony of the interests of the proletariat and the bourgeoisie, not a compromiser's policy of 'the growing of capitalism into socialism.' "[42]

Dialectical materialism was subjected to a further revision in 1950, in connection with the famous linguistic controversy. The principal issue underlying the linguistic controversy was whether or not the development of language is governed by the law of the transformation of quantity into quality. Stalin answered the question negatively and at the same time pointed out that this law is in general inapplicable to the social conditions existing in the Soviet Union:

> Marxism holds that the transition of a language from an old quality to a new does not take place by way of an explosion, by the destruction of an existing language and the creation of a new one, but by the gradual accumulation of the elements of the new quality, and, hence, by the gradual dying away of the elements of the old quality.
> It should be said in general for the benefit of comrades who have an infatuation for such explosions that the law of transition from an old quality to a new by means of an explosion is inapplicable not only to the history of the development of language; it is not always applicable to some other social phenomena of a basal or superstructural character. It is com-

[37] *Ibid.*, p. 718.     [38] *Ibid.*, pp. 717–18.     [39] *Ibid.*, p. 720.
[40] *Ibid.*     [41] *Ibid.*     [42] *Ibid.*

pulsory for a society divided into hostile classes. But it is not at all compulsory for a society which has no hostile classes.[43]

He illustrated this new thesis with the following example:

> In a period of eight to ten years we effected a transition in the agri-
> culture of our country from the bourgeois individual-peasant system to
> the socialist, collective-farm system. This was a revolution which
> eliminated the old bourgeois economic system in the countryside and
> created a new, socialist system. But this revolution did not take place by
> means of an explosion, that is, by the overthrow of the existing power
> and the creation of a new power, but by a gradual transition from the
> old bourgeois system of the countryside to a new system. And we suc-
> ceeded in doing this because it was a revolution from above, because
> the revolution was accomplished on the initiative of the existing power
> with the support of the overwhelming mass of the peasantry.[44]

Stalin's thesis that the law of the transformation of quantity into
quality is inoperative in Soviet society implied a complete negation of the previously held deterministic conception of society. Soviet
society no longer appears to be dominated by natural laws. The Soviet government appears now to be capable of devising and pursuing
its own policies, including the revolutions from above, independently
and in spite of natural laws. The law that Engels presumed to be
dominating nature, society, and thought, has been subordinated to
the Soviet state.

Stalin's new thesis in combination with his earlier pronouncements also served as a justification for the revision of the law of
contradictions. In 1939, at the Eighteenth Party Congress, he implied that the law of contradictions was inoperative in the Soviet
Union. This implication was contained in his description of the
class relationship in Soviet society.

> The feature that distinguishes Soviet society today from any capitalist
> society is that it no longer contains antagonistic, hostile classes; that the
> exploiting classes have been eliminated, while the workers, peasants and
> intellectuals, who make up Soviet society, live and work in friendly
> collaboration. Whereas capitalist society is torn by irreconcilable antag-
> onisms between workers and capitalists and between peasants and land-
> lords—resulting in its internal instability—Soviet society, liberated from
> the yoke of exploitation, knows no such antagonisms, is free of class con-
> flicts, and presents a picture of friendly collaboration between workers,
> peasants and intellectuals. It is this community of interests which has
> formed the basis for the development of such motive forces as the moral
> and political unity of Soviet society, the mutual friendship of the nations
> of the U.S.S.R., and Soviet patriotism.[45]

The view that the law of the interpenetration of opposites was no

---

[43] *Marxism and Linguistics* (New York, 1951), p. 27.
[44] *Ibid.,* pp. 27–28.           [45] *Problems,* pp. 777–78.

longer applicable to Soviet society became generally accepted by Soviet theorists only after the publication of Stalin's *Marxism and Problems of Linguistics*. V. P. Chertkov, a philosopher, advanced a typical argument in support of the new interpretation of the law of contradictions. First, he gave his understanding of this law to be "that all objects and phenomena of nature are intrinsically contradictory, and that these inner contradictions, the inner struggle of the new with the old in the objects and phenomena, constitute the source of self-development, of self-motion of nature and society."[46] But the same author continued,

> Under socialism we find something else. The basic contradiction that exists under capitalism is absent under socialism. Under socialism, principally different laws operate: relations of production are not contradictory but correspond completely to the forces of production in society. . . . It is precisely this "complete correspondence," discovered by J. V. Stalin, that accounts for the fact that in its development socialism does not take the course of disintegration but, on the contrary, the course of constantly increasing consolidation of its forces.
> . . . These new laws and motive forces, discovered by J. V. Stalin, show very resolutely that the basic law of dialectics (the law of contradictions) manifests itself differently in the conditions of the Soviet socialist system than in conditions of a society divided into antagonistic classes.[47]

The contention that under Soviet conditions the law of contradictions manifests itself differently than in the capitalist countries was in line with Stalin's revision of the law of the transformation of quantity into quality. The latter law asserted that an explosion, that is, a revolution, is a necessary and inescapable condition of social development. Such an explosion was assumed by Engels, Marx, Lenin, and originally by Stalin, to be an inevitable result of the operation of the law of contradictions. The recognition of the universal validity of these laws implied that even the Soviet regime must eventually be overthrown and replaced by a more progressive one. Among other things, it was this politically undesirable implication that made Stalin deny the effectiveness of dialectical laws in the Soviet Union.

## HISTORICAL MATERIALISM

Historical materialism is most commonly described by Soviet theorists as "the science of the general laws of the development of

[46] V. P. Chertkov, "Nekotorye Voprosy Dialektiki v Svete Truda I. V. Stalina" [Some Problems of Dialectics in Stalin's Work], Akademiya Nauk SSSR, Institut Filosofii, *Voprosy Dialekticheskogo i Istoricheskogo Materializma v Trude I. V. Stalina "Marksizm i Voprosy Yazikoznaninya"* [Problems of Dialectical and Historical Materialism in Stalin's Work "Marxism and Problems of Linguistics"] (Moscow, 1951), p. 316.
[47] *Ibid.*, pp. 319–20.

society."[48] According to Stalin, "Historical materialism is the extension of the principles of dialectical materialism to the study of social life, an application of the principles of dialectical materialism to the phenomena of the life of society, to the study of society and of its history."[49] Similarly, according to Lenin, historical materialism is "the consistent extension" of dialectical and philosophical materialism "to the domain of society."[50] Following Lenin, Soviet theorists contend that historical materialism is "one of the greatest achievements of scientific thought" and that it constitutes "a strikingly integral and harmonious scientific theory."[51]

The major problems to be discussed within the scope of historical materialism are the following: (1) the materialist theory of history; (2) the theory of necessity and freedom; (3) the theory of basis and superstructure; (4) the nature of ideology; (5) the Marxist conception of social classes; and (6) the principle of partisanship.

*The Materialist Theory of History*

Following Marx and Engels, Soviet theorists attached an enormous significance to history because of the assumption that knowledge of the past makes it possible to predict the future. It is in view of this assumption that Marx and Engels were preoccupied with tracing the history of man's social development. Primarily, however, they were interested in finding out the *causes* underlying man's social actions: are man's actions "spontaneous," that is, are they an expression of man's desires, fears, and intentions, or are they determined by "forces" beyond his control? Stated differently, Marx and Engels were interested mainly in the question "Does man make his own history, or is history made for him?" To this question they offered different answers.

In various places Marx and Engels seem to have committed themselves to a distinctly *activist* view of history. For example, in *Ludwig Feuerbach,* Engels argued that "the history of the development of society proves to be essentially different from that of nature. . . . In nature . . . there are only blind unconscious agencies acting one upon another. . . . Nothing of all that happens . . . is attained as a consciously desired aim. In the history of society, on the other hand, the actors are all endowed with consciousness, are men acting with deliberation or passion, working toward definite goals; nothing happens without a conscious purpose, without an intended aim."[52]

A similar activist view was stated by Engels in *Dialectics of Na-*

48 See, for example, Collective Authorship, *Osnovy Marksizma-Leninizma* [The Foundations of Marxism-Leninism] (Moscow, 1960), p. 150.
49 *Problems,* p. 713.          50 *Sochineniya,* Vol. 21 (1948), p. 40.
51 *Ibid.,* Vol. 19, p. 5.          52 P. 48.

*ture:* "With man we enter *history.* Animals also have a history. . . . This history, however, is made for them. . . . On the other hand, the more that human beings become removed from animals in the narrow sense of the word, the more they make their history themselves, consciously, the less becomes the influence of unforeseen effects and uncontrolled forces on this history, and the more accurately does the historical result correspond to the aim laid down in advance."[53]

An even more activist view of history was implied by Marx and Engels in *The Holy Family,* in which they took issue against Bruno Bauer who conceived of history as something superimposed upon man: *"History* does nothing; it 'does *not* possess immense riches,' it 'does *not* fight battles.' It is *men,* real, living men, who do all this, who possess things and fight battles. It is not 'history' which uses man as a means of achieving—as if it were an individual person—its own ends. History is *nothing* but the activity of men in pursuit of their ends."[54]

It is debatable, however, whether these activist views on history were intended by Marx and Engels to be taken seriously. These views appear primarily in their earlier works and are incompatible with the assumptions underlying dialectical materialism which they developed later.

The view of history that appears most frequently in Marx's and Engels' writings is clearly deterministic. It ensues directly from the propositions of dialectical materialism, which have been discussed earlier. Stated briefly, Marx and Engels viewed history as representing a process of development, a process governed by natural laws that operate independent of man's volition.[55] This process of development is "progressive," or self-perfecting, in the sense that it proceeds through inevitable stages, each stage being morally, intellectually, economically, politically, etc., "superior" to those preceding it. It started with a primitive community and proceeded through a slave-holding community, feudalism, capitalism, socialism, toward communism.

In contrast to dialectical materialism—in whose scope the process of natural and historical development appeared to be infinite—the view of history advanced within the framework of historical materialism is based on an assumption that the process of historical development will eventually come to an end. The highest stage of this

[53] P. 48.
[54] Cited by T. B. Bottomore and M. Rubel (eds.), *Karl Marx: Selected Writings in Sociology and Social Philosophy* (London, 1956), p. 63.
[55] See, for example, Engels' *Feuerbach,* pp. 47, 48, 49, and *Anti-Dühring,* p. 17.

development, and hence presumably the end point of historical development, will be the stage of *communism*.

It will be the stage in which man's action is no longer dominated by natural laws. Man at this stage of development will become free, for the forces that dominated him in the past will be subordinated to his will. From that point on, man will be able to make his own history. In Engels' words, "The laws of his own action, hitherto standing face to face with man as laws of nature foreign to and dominating him, will then be used with full understanding, and so mastered by him. Man's own social organization, hitherto confronting him as a necessity imposed by nature and history, now becomes the result of his own free action. The extraneous objective forces that have hitherto governed history pass under the control of man himself. Only from that time will man himself, more and more consciously, make his own history. . . . It is the ascent of man from the kingdom of necessity to the kingdom of freedom."[56]

*Necessity and Freedom*

The problem of necessity and freedom concerns the relationship between man and natural laws. It has been seen earlier that, according to dialectical materialism, everything in the universe is dominated by natural laws. The same view found expression in Marx's and Engels' deterministic interpretation of history. They assumed that the process of historical development is governed by natural laws independent of man's volition. According to Marx, these laws are "working with iron necessity toward inevitable results."[57] This could only be interpreted to mean that history is not made *by* man but rather that it is made *for* man.

If it is assumed that history—meaning man's actions and thoughts—is determined by natural laws, then it seems reasonable to conclude that the relationship between natural laws and man expresses natural necessity. It does this in the sense that man, confronted with these laws, appears to be incapable of alternative behavior; he must behave in one specific way, namely, the way determined by these laws. But if man must always act in the way determined by natural laws, then it is impossible to speak of him as being free. For it would be just as meaningless as to say that a piece of iron exposed to heat is free to expand or not to expand.

This, however, is not the view of Marx, Engels, and their Soviet followers. They contend that the fact that man's behavior is dominated by natural laws is compatible with the idea of freedom. In their

[56] *Socialism: Utopian and Scientific* (New York, 1935), p. 45.
[57] *Capital* (New York, 1936), p. 13.

judgment, these laws express a "blind necessity" only as long as man *is not cognizant* of the fact that they are dominating his behavior. Once man comes to know this fact—and especially after he acquires the understanding of the nature of their operation—he becomes free. Then, to use Engels' expression, necessity becomes transformed into freedom: the laws that previously dominated man become subordinated to his will.[58]

As indicated earlier, such a transformation of necessity into freedom will take place under communism. Under the latter conditions "there can be talk of real human freedom, of an existence in harmony with the laws of nature that have become known."[59] There, "The laws of his own social action, hitherto standing face to face with man as laws of nature foreign to and dominating him, will then be used with full understanding, and so mastered by him."[60]

It is quite apparent that "real human freedom" raises a metasocial problem, a problem that is distinct from social or "civil" freedom. Freedom as a social problem concerns the relationship between individuals and, in turn, their relationship to the existing political authority. On the other hand, the freedom with which Engels and Marx were preoccupied concerns man's relationship to natural laws. But man's relationship to natural laws (whether presupposed or actually existing) has as little to do with man's social freedom as the theologian's concern with man's relationship to God. Man can be free from natural laws or God, yet be socially enslaved. Conversely, man can be dominated by both natural laws and God, yet be socially free. Man's social freedom is not contingent upon his relationship to natural laws; it depends upon his relationship to other individuals and to social authority.

This, however, is not the way Soviet thinkers are accustomed to viewing the problems of freedom. They argue that social freedom—expressed in the form of legal rights—is a sham. In this respect they follow Engels, whom they quote as having stated that "political freedom is a false freedom, worse than the worst type of slavery; it is an illusory freedom and, consequently, a true slavery."[61] Soviet social thinkers are interested in "true" freedom, that is, in freedom

[58] *Anti-Dühring*, p. 157; Lenin, *Sochineniya*, Vol. 14, p. 177. For a critical discussion of freedom as recognition of necessity, see A. J. Ayer, *Philosophical Essays* (London, 1954), pp. 277–78; Sidney Hook, *The Hero in History* (Boston, 1955), pp. 247–48; Max Eastman, *Marxism: Is It Science?* (New York, 1940), pp. 64–72; and H. B. Mayo, *Democracy and Marxism* (New York, 1955), pp. 175–81.
[59] *Anti-Dühring*, p. 158.
[60] *Ibid.*, p. 390.
[61] *Die Neue Zeit*, XXVIII, 428, cited by I. Podvolotskii, *Marksistskaya Teoriya Prava* [The Marxist Theory of Law] (Moscow, 1923), p. 109.

from natural laws which presumably dominate man's thought and actions.

Their preoccupation with "true" freedom is responsible for an almost complete de-emphasis of the problem of civil freedom in Soviet political thought. Furthermore, it gives rise to the claim that there is "real freedom" in Soviet society, a claim that was advanced even at the height of Stalin's autocratic rule.

A Soviet philosopher, P. Yudin, advanced a typical argument along those lines. He first indicated that *"the laws of historical necessity will remain in existence forever, but men will more and more get to know and to master them. [Consequently,] the results of social development will more and more coincide with the will, desires, and aims of men."*[62] According to Yudin, though, such developments are bound to take place only under socialism. In fact, in his judgment, "The victory of socialism in the U.S.S.R. has brought about victory over the natural forces of the social laws of development, over the blind forces of historical necessity. *A leap took place* from the realm of necessity into the realm of freedom."[63]

This is in contrast to conditions "under capitalism," where, in Yudin's opinion, "the laws of social development confront men as alien and hostile forces" and where they "impose themselves upon men as natural calamities."[64] The "victory over natural forces . . . and historical necessity" under socialism was possible because the Communist Party adhered to Engels' "indisputable scientific conclusion" that "freedom consists in acting and behaving in conformity with the laws of nature and the laws of society."[65] The party formulated its policies on the basis of a "thorough study" of natural and historical laws. Consequently, its actions are always in conformity with natural necessity. In doing this the party "transforms necessity into freedom."[66] In other words, the party assumes the role of an agent of nature.

## The Theory of Basis and Superstructure

Another problem that occupies a prominent place in the scope of historical materialism is the theory of basis and superstructure. In effect, this theory represents an *economic* interpretation of society, and as such is logically unrelated to the naturalistic propositions of dialectical materialism. The term "basis" (or "foundation") designates a certain type of social phenomena, broadly called economic,

---

[62] *"Svoboda i Neobkhodimost"* [Freedom and Necessity], *Kommunist*, No. 14 (1939), p. 83.
[63] *Ibid.*        [64] *Ibid.*, p. 82.        [65] *Ibid.*, p. 78.        [66] *Ibid.*, pp. 80–81.

while the term "superstructure" is used as a designation for all remaining social phenomena.

The principal question that this theory raises is one concerning the *causal* relationship between basis and superstructure, that is between economic and non-economic social phenomena. This question is not as clear and simple as it would appear on the surface. Soviet social thinkers are in agreement that Marx and Engels elaborated the theory of basis and superstructure. Furthermore, they also agree that this theory is crucial to the Marxist understanding of society. They disagree, however, about the relationship between basis and superstructure. The ground for their disagreement is to be found in Marx's and Engels' conflicting interpretations of that relationship.

According to Marx, the economic basis, or "the mode of production," determines all non-economic, superstructural phenomena: "The mode of production in material life determines the general character of social, political and spiritual processes of life. It is not the consciousness of men that determines their existence but, on the contrary, their social existence determines their consciousness."[67]

Apart from occasional discrepancies concerning the social phenomena that constitute the economic basis,[68] Marx consistently maintained that basis and superstructure stand one to another as a cause to an effect, the former always dominating the latter. The superstructure was frequently described by Marx as being "ideological," meaning that it is causally ineffective vis-à-vis the economic basis.

Before Marx's death, Engels concurred with him that "the ultimate explanation of the whole superstructure"—that is, of "juridical and political institutions as well as of the religious, philosophical, and other ideas of a given historical period"—must be sought in the economic basis.[69] Furthermore, Engels agreed with Marx that basis and superstructure stand one to another as cause to effect. Basis dominates superstructure; consequently, each change in basis brings about a corresponding change in superstructure.

[67] *A Contribution to the Critique of Political Economy* (Chicago, 1904), pp. 11–12.

[68] As indicated earlier, Marx most frequently identified the economic basis with "the mode of production" or "the forces of production." However, he also spoke of "the relations of production" as constituting "the economic structure of society, the real foundation" (*ibid,* p. 11). Ironically, the same "relations of production" were described by Marx as legal relations and hence as properly belonging to the causally passive superstructure. For a thorough discussion of the relations of production and their relationship to the forces of production, see John Plamenatz, *German Marxism and Russian Communism* (London–New York–Toronto, 1954), pp. 21–35.

[69] *Anti-Dühring,* p. 41.

This interpretation of the relationship between basis and super-structure is of utmost significance to social theory in general and to political and legal theory in particular. Its most obvious implication is that superstructural phenomena, such as social, political, religious, and philosophical ideas, juridical and political institutions, and positive law, are causally ineffective. Being merely ideological reflec-tions of the basis, superstructural phenomena appear to be passive, that is, unable to act upon the basis.

This interpretation of the relationship between basis and super-structure represents an extreme case of *economic determinism,* in the sense that causal capability is attributed exclusively to the eco-nomic basis while fully denied to the superstructure. As such, this interpretation conforms to the monistic assumption underlying philo-sophical materialism which states that matter was prior to thought and therefore determines thought. Applied to man's social sphere of existence, this assumption resulted in the conclusion that economics are prior to, and hence determine, all other aspects of man's life.

To be sure, after Marx's death, Engels revised his own and Marx's original interpretation of the relationship between basis and super-structure. First, in a letter to Bloch (September 12, 1890), he con-tended that their views had been misinterpreted.[70] Then, in a letter to Mehring (July 14, 1893), Engels admitted his mistake in attributing an exclusive causal capability to the basis while denying it to the superstructure.[71] One of the latest and presumably the most authori-tative statements on basis and superstructure was made by Engels in a letter to Starkenburg (January 25, 1894). In it, as in the previous letters, he argued that there is a *causal interaction* between basis and superstructure: "Political, juridical, philosophical, religious, literary, artistic, etc., development is based on economic development. But all these react upon one another and also upon the economic base. It is not that the economic position is the *cause and alone active,* while everything else has a passive effect. There is, rather, interaction on the basis of the economic necessity, which *ultimately* always asserts itself."[72]

The effect of Engels' new interpretation was a clear modification if not a renunciation of economic determinism. The deterministic view of the relationship between basis and superstructure was con-sistently rejected by Stalin. Even in his early lectures on "The Foundations of Leninism," Stalin denounced Kautsky for his adher-ence to "the productive forces theory." This theory, in Stalin's judg-

---

[70] Karl Marx and Friedrich Engels, *Correspondence 1846–1895* (New York, ca. 1935–36), p. 475.

[71] *Ibid.,* pp. 510–12.        [72] *Ibid.,* p. 517.

ment, leads to political fatalism, for it asserts that the productive forces—the economic basis of society—determine all aspects of man's social life independent of his will. In other words, "the productive forces theory" denies the ability of the superstructural phenomena, among them political ideas and organized movements, to act upon the basis. According to this theory, man cannot act contrary to the "level of the productive forces" existing at a given time. Whatever happens in society, "The 'productive forces' are 'to blame.' That is the precise explanation vouchsafed to 'us' by Mr. Kautsky's 'theory of the productive forces.' And whoever does not believe in that 'theory' is not a Marxist. The role of the parties? Their importance for the movement? But what can a party do against so decisive a factor as the 'level of the productive forces?' "[73]

Stalin reiterated his antideterministic views in his essay on "Dialectical and Historical Materialism."[74] Finally, he assigned an even more active and independent role to the superstructure in an essay written in connection with the linguistic controversy in 1950.[75] There he stated that "the base is the economic structure of society at a given stage of its development."[76] On the other hand,

. . . The superstructure consists of the political, legal, religious, artistic, and philosophical views of society and the political, legal, and other institutions corresponding to them. . . .[77]

Furthermore, the superstructure is a product of the base; but this does not mean that it merely reflects the base, that it is passive, neutral, indifferent to the fate of its base, to the fate of the classes, to the character of the system. On the contrary, no sooner does it arise than it becomes an exceedingly active force, actively assisting its base to take shape and consolidate itself, and doing everything it can to help the new system finish off and eliminate the old base and the old classes.[78]

Stalin's emphasis upon superstructure as "an exceedingly active force" sought to liquidate the remnants of "vulgar materialism" which

[73] Stalin, *Problems,* p. 34.

[74] *Ibid.,* p. 727.

[75] The linguistic controversy—which Stalin claimed to have resolved in his *Marksizm i Voprosy Yazykoznaniya* [Marxism and Problems of Linguistics], (Moscow, 1950)—concerned the question of whether language belongs to the basis or the superstructure. Stalin argued that such phenomena as language belong neither to the basis nor to the superstructure: "Language is not a product of one or another base, old or new, within the given society, but of the whole course of the history of society and the history of bases throughout centuries. . . . Language . . . is the product of a whole number of epochs, in the course of which it takes shape, is enriched, develops, and is polished. A language therefore exists immeasurably longer than any base or any superstructure" (*Marxism and Linguistics,* pp. 11–12).

[76] *Ibid.,* p. 9.

[77] *Ibid.*

[78] *Ibid.,* p. 10.

"ignores the mobilizing, organizational, and reformist role of progressive theory."[79] In other words, he aimed at putting an end to the views of many Soviet thinkers who argued that social ideas and institutions are merely a passive reflection of the economic basis and hence are deprived of an independent causal ability.

Stalin's activist view of superstructure was in conformity with his reinterpretation of dialectical laws (which were discussed earlier). In his treatment, man no longer appears as a blind instrument in the hands of certain presupposed natural or economic forces. Rather, man appears as an active being, capable of shaping his social life in conformity with his own subjective desires. However ironical it may sound, Stalin himself laid the doctrinal foundations for social activism and individualism which have been on the upsurge since the "de-Stalinization" of the Soviet Union.

### The Nature of Ideology

The problem of ideology is related to the reflection theory of knowledge, which was discussed in the preceding section on philosophical materialism. One of the assumptions underlying philosophical materialism is that the function performed by the human mind is one of reflecting "natural reality." What is significant is that in the scope of philosophical materialism man's mind is viewed as an intrinsic part of nature and consequently as reflecting it faithfully.

Like philosophical materialism, historical materialism—or rather one of its parts, namely, the theory of basis and superstructure—also deals with the problem of the ability of the human mind to reflect the world surrounding it. However, in contrast to philosophical materialism, which views man and the world surrounding him in their natural purity, historical materialism deals with a socially "corrupted" mind, a mind whose reflecting function is affected by its social surroundings. Marx and Engels maintained that the reflections of external reality taken by a socially corrupted mind have an *ideological* character.

These mental reflections are ideological in the sense that the picture of natural and social reality appears in them in an *inverted* form. In Engels' words, "In all ideology men and their circumstances appear upside down as in a *camera obscura*": the cause appears as an effect, the superstructure as the basis.[80] Under certain social conditions such an inversion takes place in practically all spheres of man's existence. For example, an inversion of cause and effect takes place in

[79] *Ibid.,* p. 33.
[80] Karl Marx and Friedrich Engels, *The German Ideology* (New York, 1960), p. 14.

a "money-market economy," that is, in a capitalist system of economy: "Economic, political and other reflections are just like those in the human eye, they pass through a condensing lens and therefore appear upside down, standing on their heads. Only the nervous system which would put them on their feet again for representation is lacking. The money-market man sees only the movement of industry and of the world market in the inverted reflection of the money and stock market, and so effect becomes cause to him."[81]

Marx used the treatment accorded commodities as an illustration of an inversion of cause and effect. A commodity, in his judgment, is a product of the labor process at a certain stage of social development. Economists, however, have assumed that commodities lie at the basis of the labor process. In their interpretation, commodities acquire an existence independent of the labor process and of the men engaged in their production.[82]

Another example of inversion, given by Engels, is the conflict between the social classes: "Just as the movement of the industrial market is . . . reflected in the money market and, of course, in inverted form, so the struggle between the classes already existing and already in conflict with one another is reflected in the struggle between government and opposition, but also in inverted form, no longer directly but indirectly, not as a class struggle but as a fight for political principles, and so distorted that it has taken us thousands of years to get behind it again."[83] Legal principles, according to Engels, represent another case of an inverted reflection of economic reality: "The reflection of economic relations as legal principles is necessarily also a topsy turvy one: it happens without the person who is acting being conscious of it; the jurist imagines he is operating with a priori principles, whereas they are really only economic reflexes; so everything is upside down."[84] Finally, Engels cited religion and philosophy as examples of ideologies "which soar still higher in the air,"[85] in the sense that their connection with the economic basis becomes almost entirely lost: "Still higher ideologies, that is, such as are still further removed from the material, economic basis, take the form of philosophy and religion. Here the interconnection between the ideas and their material conditions of existence becomes more and more complicated, more and more obscured by intermediate links. But the interconnection exists."[86]

---

[81] Letter to Conrad Schmidt, October 27, 1890, in Marx and Engels, *Correspondence*, p. 478.

[82] *Capital*, p. 83.

[83] Letter to Schmidt, October 27, 1890, in Marx and Engels, *Correspondence*, p. 480.

[84] *Ibid.*, p. 482.     [85] *Ibid.*     [86] *Feuerbach*, p. 55.

Why does social reality become inverted in the reflections taken by the human mind? Or, why do man's ideas of social reality have an ideological character? Is it a matter of choice or of necessity? To these questions Marx and Engels gave contradictory answers.

According to some of their statements, the inversion of social reality does not appear to be a deliberate act on the part of man. Indeed, it seems to take place independent of man's volition: man is not even aware of the fact that he is producing an ideology. In Engels' words, "It happens without the person who is acting being conscious of it."[87] Furthermore, "The real motives impelling him remain unknown to him; otherwise it would not be an ideological process at all."[88] "If in all ideology men and their circumstances appear upside down as in a *camera obscura,* this phenomenon arises just as much from their historical life process as the inversion of objects on the retina does from their physical life process."[89]

What is responsible for the ideological character of man's ideas of social reality is the peculiar "mode of production," or "the material basis," which determines the content of "intellectual production."[90] More specifically, the picture of social reality in man's mind becomes inverted because this reality itself is inverted and contradictory. For example, speaking about religion as an ideology Marx argued that "this state, this society, produce religion which is an inverted world consciousness, because they are an inverted world."[91] Furthermore, "The fact that the worldly basis stands out against itself and an independent realm establishes itself in the skies can be explained only by the fact that the worldly basis itself is split and contradictory in itself."[92] "Consciousness"—that is, a "false" consciousness, one that inverts the picture of social reality—"must rather be explained from the contradictions of material life, from the existing conflict between the social forces of production and the material relations of production."[93]

From this point of view, the distortion of social reality in man's ideas appears not as a matter of choice but rather as a matter of necessity. Man living under certain social conditions cannot help

[87] Letter to Schmidt, October 27, 1890, in Marx and Engels, *Correspondence,* p. 482.
[88] Engels, Letter to Mehring, July 14, 1893, *ibid.,* p. 511.
[89] Marx and Engels, *Ideology,* p. 14.
[90] Marx, "Theories of Surplus Value," in Bottomore and Rubel (eds.), *Marx: Selected Writings,* p. 82.
[91] *Kritik des Hegelschen Staatsrecht,* cited by Bottomore and Rubel (eds.), *ibid.,* p. 26.
[92] Marx, *Kritik,* cited by Hans Kelsen, *The Communist Theory of Law* (New York, 1955), p. 23.
[93] *A Contribution,* p. 12.

but produce a distorted view of the reality surrounding him. He does not know, and presumably is not in a position to know, that "contradictory" social reality affects his mind in such a way that it cannot produce a true picture of this reality.

To be sure, however, Marx and Engels also advanced a diametrically opposed interpretation of the reasons underlying the ideological character of man's ideas. According to this interpretation, the inversion and hence the distortion of social reality in man's ideas does not appear as a matter of necessity but rather as a matter of choice. More specifically, the distortion appears as a deliberate act, an act of deception and justification. This view of ideology is apparent in Marx's and Engels' description of the ruling class as "the ruling intellectual force." "The ideas of the ruling class are in every epoch the ruling ideas: i.e., the class, which is the ruling force of society, is at the same time its ruling intellectual force. . . . The individuals composing the ruling class possess among other things consciousness, and therefore think. Insofar, therefore, as they rule as a class . . . , [they] rule also as thinkers, as producers of ideas, and regulate the production and distribution of the ideas of their age: thus their ideas are the ruling ideas of the epoch."[94]

The view that an ideology is the product of a rational act is even more evident in Marx's and Engels' description of the division of labor among the members of the ruling class: "The division of labor . . . manifests itself also in the ruling class as the division of mental and material labor, so that inside this class one part appears as the thinkers of the class (its active, conceptive ideologists, who make the perfection of the illusion of the class about itself their chief source of livelihood), while the other's attitude to these ideas and illusions is more passive and receptive, because they are in reality the active members of this class and have less time to make up illusions and ideas about themselves."[95]

The "thinkers" of the ruling class, in Engels' words, become "the undisguised ideologists of the bourgeoisie and the existing state."[96] Their function is to justify the rule of the bourgeoisie by presenting its subjective interests as "universal" ones: "For each new class . . . is compelled, merely in order to carry through its aim, to represent its interests as the common interest of all the members of society, put in an ideal form; it will give its ideas the form of universality and represent them as the only rational, universally valid ones."[97]

The identification of the ruling class interests with "the common interest of all the members of society" results in "idealizing phrases,

[94] *Ideology*, p. 39.   [95] *Ibid.*, pp. 39–40.   [96] *Feuerbach*, p. 60.
[97] Marx and Engels, *Ideology*, pp. 40–41.

conscious illusions, and deliberate deceits."[98] And "the more they are condemned as falsehoods, and the less they satisfy the understanding, the more dogmatically they are asserted and the more deceitful, moralizing, and spiritual becomes the language of established society."[99]

Marx's and Engels' interpretation of the reasons underlying an ideology leads to two conclusions. On the one hand, they argued that under certain conditions man's ideas of social reality must inevitably be ideological in character. Individuals entertaining these ideas assume that they are true, but the fact of the matter is that under the existing social conditions truth is inaccessible to them. On the other hand, Marx and Engels maintained that individuals living under the same social conditions are capable of knowing truth. But truth is presumably detrimental to the ruling class. Consequently, "conceptive ideologists" of the ruling class deliberately distort the picture of the existing social reality for the purpose of deceiving the exploited classes and thus justifying the ruling class.

At any rate, according to Marx and Engels, ideology occurs only under social conditions that are "contradictory," that is, conditions under which there is a conflict between the forces and the relations of production, or, in brief, in a society divided into antagonistic classes. Consequently, to get rid of ideology it is necessary to remove the conditions that produce or require it. In Marx's words, "The call to abandon their illusions about their conditions is a call to abandon a condition which requires illusions."[100] Ideology "comes to a natural end, of course, as soon as society ceases at last to be organized in the form of class rule, that is to say as soon as it is no longer necessary to represent a particular interest as general or 'the general interest' as ruling."[101]

Specifically, according to Marx and Engels, the solution to ideology will be communism, the harmonious society of the future. A communist society will be non-contradictory, for there will be no classes and the relations of production will be in full harmony with the forces of production. Consequently, it will neither produce nor require an ideology.

*The Marxist Conception of Social Classes*

The significance of the concept of social classes to Soviet social

[98] *Ibid.*, cited by Bottomore and Rubel (eds.), *Marx: Selected Writings,* p. 81.
[99] *Ibid.*
[100] *Kritik,* cited by Bottomore and Rubel (eds.), *Marx: Selected Writings,* p. 27.
[101] Marx and Engels, *Ideology,* p. 41.

theory can hardly be overstated. Marx, Engels, and their Soviet followers attribute quite a number of social consequences to the existence of classes. To begin with, classes are viewed as the media through which the laws governing the universe operate in society. Furthermore, classes appear to be the phenomena that determine the peculiar content of history, namely, the fact that *"all* history, with the exception of its primitive stages, was the history of class struggles."[102]

More specifically, classes are linked with the disintegration of the primitive community, with the rise of law and state, with the antagonism and struggle in society, with social revolutions, with the existence of peculiar forms of government, and with the rise of ideology. On the other hand, the disappearance of classes is connected with the evanescence of law and state, with the replacement of a "class morality" with a "real human morality," with the removal of economic and political inequality, conflict, and exploitation, and with the creation of a communist society.

Since Marx and Engels attributed so many social occurrences to the presence or absence of classes, it is of the utmost significance to determine what the phenomena called "classes" are, how they come into being, and what the features distinguishing them from one another are.

In *The German Ideology* Marx and Engels asserted that "separate individuals form a class only insofar as they have to carry on a common battle against another class; otherwise they are on hostile terms with each other as competitors."[103] In a polemic against Karl Heinzen, Marx argued that "classes . . . are based upon economic conditions independent of their will and are set by these conditions in a relation of mutual antagonism."[104] This view coincides with Engels' assertion that the "warring classes of society are always the product of the modes of production and exchange—in a word, of the *economic* conditions of their time."[105] In an unfinished chapter of *Capital,* Marx argued again that the answer to the question "What constitutes a class? . . . can be found by answering another question: what constitutes wage-labourers, capitalists and landlords into three great social classes?"[106] Thus, in his judgment, "The owners of mere labour-power, the owners of capital, and the landowners, whose respective sources of income are wages, profit, and rent of land, or in

---

[102] Engels, *Socialism*, p. 25.
[103] Pp. 48–49.
[104] "Moralizing Criticism and Critical Morality: A Polemic against Karl Heinzen," *Selected Essays* (New York, 1926), pp. 156–57.
[105] *Socialism*, p. 25.
[106] *Capital* (Chicago, 1909), III, 1031.

other words, wage-labourers, capitalists and landowners, form the three great classes of modern society based on the capitalist mode of production."[107]

The most obvious implication of the above quoted statement seems to be that the source of income is what distinguishes the "three great classes." In fact, Marx indicated the possibility of such an understanding by stating that "at first glance it might seem that the identity of revenues and source of revenue is responsible" for the three classes.[108] "However," he continued, "from this point of view, physicians and officials would also form two classes, for they belong to two distinct social groups, and the revenues of their members flow from the same common source."[109] But, according to Marx, neither doctors nor public officials constitute a class.[110] Hence, he concluded, the source of revenue cannot serve as a criterion for determining classes.

Another feature used by Marx and Engels for the purpose of distinguishing one class from another is the division of labor. For example, in *The German Ideology* they maintained that the division of society into classes has taken place with the rise of towns and with the subsequent development of antagonism between the towns and the country. Under these conditions, "first became manifest the division of population into two great classes, which is directly based on the division of labour and on the instruments of production."[111] The main characteristic of that division is the "subjection of the individual . . . under a definite activity forced upon him—a subjection which makes one man into a restricted town-animal, the other into a restricted country-animal, and daily creates anew the conflict between their interests."[112]

Since "country-animals" are peasants, it follows that peasants are one of the "two great classes." But speaking of the French peasants in *Eighteenth Brumaire,* Marx contended that they are not a class but merely a "vast mass." He justified the latter conclusion by stating that "in so far as millions of families live under economic conditions of existence that divide their mode of life, their interests, and their culture from those of other classes, and put them into hostile contrast to the latter, they form a class. In so far as there is merely a local interest among these small peasants, and the identity of their interests begets no unity, no national union, and no political organization, they do not form a class."[113]

The definition of classes that is most frequently quoted by Soviet

---

[107] *Ibid.*         [108] *Ibid.,* p. 1032.         [109] *Ibid.*
[110] *Ibid.*         [111] P. 44.                     [112] *Ibid.*
[113] *The Eighteenth Brumaire of Louis Bonaparte* (New York, 1964), p. 109.

writers belongs to Lenin. In his judgment, "Classes are large groups of people which differ from each other by the place they occupy in a definite historical system of social production, by their relation to the means of production, by their role in the social organization of labor, and, consequently, by the dimensions and methods of acquiring the share of social wealth that they obtain. Classes are groups of people, one of which may appropriate the labor of another, owing to the different places they occupy in the definite system of social economy."[114]

The principal weakness of Marx's and Engels' theory of classes is that they nowhere clearly define the meaning of the proletariat as a class. The importance of such a definition cannot be overemphasized because of the central role assigned to the proletariat in their social theory. The proletariat was depicted by Marx and Engels as an executor of natural and historical necessity, as a medium through which the laws of nature operate, and as an agent that will bring about a classless society. Finally, the proletariat is the class that will lead humanity out of the realm of necessity into the realm of freedom.

Marx and Engels usually spoke of the proletariat as one of "the three great classes of society," by which Marx meant "the owners of mere labour power, the owners of capital, and the landlords,"[115] and which Engels designated as "the feudal aristocracy, the bourgeoisie, and the proletariat."[116] Frequently, though, they contraposed the proletariat to the bourgeoisie only because they thought that modern society possessed a distinctive feature: "it has simplified class antagonisms" and hence "is splitting up into two great hostile camps, into two great and directly contraposed classes: bourgeoisie and proletariat."[117]

While describing the proletariat as one of the great classes, Marx failed to indicate precisely what marks the proletariat as a class. The classical ambiguity concerning the status of the proletariat as a class appears in *The Communist Manifesto*. There—after the proletariat has been depicted as a class par excellence, as a lone revolutionary class confronted with "decaying classes"—Marx and Engels declared that the "immediate aim of all the communists is the same as that of all the other proletarian parties: formation of the proletariat into a class."[118] At the same time, Marx registered a complaint that the "organization of the proletariat into a class, and

---

[114] *Sochineniya,* Vol. 29 (1950), p. 388.
[115] *Capital,* p. 1031.    [116] *Anti-Dühring,* p. 130.
[117] *The Communist Manifesto,* with Introduction and Explanatory Notes by D. Ryazanoff (New York, 1930), p. 26.
[118] *Ibid.,* pp. 42–43.

consequently into a political party, is continually being upset . . . by the competition between the workers themselves."[119]

Another description of the proletariat as a class appears in *The Critique of Hegel's Philosophy of Law*. There Marx argued that the proletariat is "a class in radical chains, a class of bourgeois society which is no class of bourgeois society, an estate which is the dissolution of all estates, a group which has a universal character because of its universal suffering, and which does not claim a particular justice because no particular injustice but the injustice *par excellence* has been imposed upon it."[120] In *The German Ideology* the proletariat was described as "a class . . . which has to bear all the burdens of society without enjoying its advantages, which, ousted from society, is forced into the most decided antagonism to all other classes; a class which forms the majority of all members of society, and from which emanates the consciousness of the necessity of a fundamental revolution, the communist consciousness, which may, of course, arise among the other classes too, through contemplation of the situation of this class."[121]

The delusive nature of the proletariat as a class is more apparent in Marx's and Engels' explanation of its revolutionary role. They maintained that the proletariat, by means of a revolution, "abolishes the rule of all classes with the classes themselves, because it is carried through by the class which no longer counts as a class in society, is not recognized as a class, and is in itself the expression of the dissolution of all classes."[122] The definition of *proletariat* is further obscured by Marx's statement that the "proletariat is recruited from all classes of the population."[123]

Judging by a letter written to Weydemeyer, Marx was aware of the inconsistencies involved in his interpretation of classes. But he disavowed responsibility for them and suggested that those who are searching for inconsistencies in his theory of classes "would do better first to acquaint themselves with bourgeois literature before they presume to yap out their contradictions of it."[124] Marx adopted the class theory of society from his "bourgeois" predecessors, who developed it and who are responsible for the contradictions inherent in it:

And now as to myself, no credit is due to me for discovering the

---

[119] *Ibid.*, pp. 37–38.

[120] In Karl Marx and Friedrich Engels, *Historish-kritische Gesamtausgabe* (1st ed.; Frankfurt am Main, 1927), Vol. 1, pp. 205–6.

[121] Marx and Engels, pp. 68–69.          [122] *Ibid.*, p. 69.

[123] Marx and Engels, *Manifesto*, p. 214.

[124] Marx, Letter to Weydemeyer, March 5, 1852, in Marx and Engels, *Correspondence*, p. 57.

existence of classes in modern society nor yet the struggle between them. Long before me, bourgeois historians had described the historical development of this class struggle and bourgeois economists anatomy of the classes. What I did that was new was to prove (1) that the *existence of classes* is only bound up with *particular, historic phases* in the development of production; (2) that the class struggle necessarily leads to the *dictatorship of the proletariat;* (3) that this dictatorship itself only constitutes the transition to the *abolition of all classes* and to a classless society.[125]

## The Principle of Partisanship

The principle of partisanship, or in the Russian language, *partiinost,* is a logical outgrowth of the assumptions underlying dialectical and historical materialism. Partisanship—i.e., the interpretation of social phenomena in conformity with the party's line—had been advocated by an earlier Soviet social theorist,[126] but it was only formulated as an exclusive "methodological principle" of "Marxist science" in the mid-forties. Since then, the principle of partisanship has become a standard and the most outstanding feature of the "Marxist-Leninist method." It constitutes a significant clue for comprehending the intricate nature of the Soviet concept of social sciences.

Briefly stated, the principle of partisanship is diametrically opposed to the rationalist view which insists on a separation of social science from politics and on an abstention from value judgments within the scope of scientific activity. It denies the possibility of a scientifically objective theory—objective in the sense that its content is not determined by certain social, e.g., political, religious, or moral, preferences.

To justify the employment of the principle of partisanship in the field of social science, Soviet writers usually refer to Lenin's views. In his lecture "On the State" Lenin maintained that there is "scarcely . . . another question that has been so confused, deliberately or not, by the representatives of bourgeois science, philosophy, jurisprudence, political economy, and journalism, as the question of the state."[127] He amplified the statement in the following way:

[125] *Ibid.*
[126] See, for example, E. Pashukanis, *Za Markso-Leninskuyu Teoriyu Gosudarstva i Prava* [For a Marxist-Leninist Theory of State and Law] (Moscow-Leningrad, 1931), pp. 37–38. In his opinion, "A close link of the theoretical work with the class struggle, with the political tasks of the proletariat and its party, and with the practice of the socialist construction, carrying out partisanship (*partiinost*) in our science, the introduction of collectivism in our work, the renunciation of individualism, of working alone—this is the path we should choose" (p. 37).
[127] *Sochineniya,* Vol. 29, pp. 434–35.

This question has been so confused and complicated because it affects the interests of the ruling classes more than any other (yielding in this respect only to the foundations of economic science). The theory of state serves as a justification of social privilege, a justification of the existence of exploitation, a justification of the existence of capitalism. And that is why it would be the greatest mistake to expect impartiality on this question, to approach this question in the belief that people who claim to be scientific can give you a purely scientific view on the subject. When you have become familiar with this question and have gone into it deeply enough, you will always discern in the question of the state, in the doctrine of the state, in the theory of the state, the mutual struggle of different classes, a struggle that is reflected or expressed in the conflict of views on the state, in the estimate of the role and significance of the state.[128]

Arguing along similar lines in *Materialism and Empirio-Criticism,* Lenin denounced bourgeois philosophers, economists, and "bourgeois professors" in general for the partisan character of the assumptions underlying their theories.

*Not a single one* of these professors, who are capable of making very valuable contributions in the special fields of chemistry, history, or physics, *can be trusted one iota* when it comes to philosophy. Why? For the same reason that *not a single* professor of political economy, who may be capable of very valuable contributions in the field of factual and specialized investigation, *can be trusted one iota* when it comes to the general theory of political economy. For in modern society the latter is as much a *partisan* science as is epistemology. Taken as a whole, the professors of economics are nothing but scientific salesman of the capitalist class, while the professors of philosophy are scientific salesmen of the theologians.[129]

Lenin stated a similar view in an essay on "The Three Sources and the Three Component Parts of Marxism":

Throughout the civilized world the teachings of Marx evoke the utmost hostility and hatred of all bourgeois science (both official and liberal), which regards Marxism as a kind of "pernicious sect." And no other attitude is to be expected, for there can be no "impartial" social science in a society based on class struggle. In one way or another, *all* official and liberal science *defends* wage-slavery, whereas Marxism has declared relentless war on wage-slavery. To expect science to be impartial in a wage-slave society is as silly and naive as to expect impartiality from manufacturers on the question whether workers' wages should be increased by decreasing the profits of capital.[130]

128 *Ibid.,* p. 435.
129 *Ibid.,* Vol. 14, pp. 327–28.
130 *Selected Works* (2 vols.; Moscow, 1947), I, 59–60.

It is evident that Lenin considered partisanship to be a major defect of bourgeois social science, philosophy, and epistemology. But nowhere in his writings did he indicate that the same might be true of Marx's and Engels' theories of society. On the contrary, he implied that their partisanship was conducive to science. For example, in his *Materialism and Empirio-Criticism* he acknowledged "partisanship" and the "partiality of Marx's theory" while at the same time asserting that the theory is "permeated throughout" with "objective truth."[131] In *Economic Content of Populism* Lenin argued that the superiority of Marx's materialism over all other theories lies in the fact that "materialism comprises, so to speak, partisanship, which enjoins the direct and open adoption of the standpoint of a definite social group in any evaluation of events."[132]

Soviet writers use these views as a justification of partisanship in their interpretations of social reality. But they disagree with Lenin on the reasons underlying partisanship. In Lenin's interpretation, partisanship in social theories appears as a deliberate act, as an act of volition and choice. Lenin does not preclude the possibility that bourgeois social thinkers can elevate themselves above partisanship. In fact, he explicitly states that they are "capable of making very valuable contributions in the special fields of chemistry, history, or physics." It is only when they identify themselves with "the interest of the ruling class" that they adopt a partisan point of view. But there are also those who do not identify themselves with the ruling class and who, consequently, are capable of producing a non-partisan, scientifically objective theory of society. That presumably was the case of Marx, Engels, and Lenin. While living under bourgeois conditions, they elevated themselves above the interest of the ruling class and produced a scientific explanation of social reality.

Such a possibility is precluded by Soviet writers. For example, M. A. Arzhanov argues that the content of social theories produced in a class society must *inevitably* be partisan. In his judgment the principle of partisanship rests on the "recognition of the inevitability of the class and partisan character of social opinions, convictions, theories, etc., in a class society."[133] Social thinkers living in a class society may be suffering from the illusion that their theories are objective, but, in fact, these theories are permeated with partisanship in favor of the ruling class.

[131] Lenin, *Sochineniya,* Vol. 14, pp. 304–5.
[132] *Ibid.,* Vol. 1 (1941), pp. 380–81.
[133] Akademiya Nauk Soyuza SSR, Institut Prava, *Teoriya Gosudarstva i Prava* [The Theory of State and Law] (Moscow, 1949), p. 22.

An objective or, what Arzhanov calls a "truly scientific theory," of society is attainable only under social conditions such as those existing in the Soviet Union. But paradoxically, in his judgment, the truly scientific theory is not bound by the prerequisite of impartiality. Partisanship is a deficiency of bourgeois theories but not of a truly scientific theory. The truly scientific theory—that is to say social theory developed by Soviet thinkers—is admittedly partisan; indeed, it is "permeated with the spirit of militant partisanship."[134]

Arzhanov justifies this paradox by asserting that Marxist theories "defend openly the principle of partisanship in science" because "the interest of truth, of science, and the interest of the working classes do not contradict one another but, on the contrary, coincide completely."[135] Or, as stated by another Soviet writer, "partisanship of the Marxist theory of state and law . . . secures a truly scientific approach toward the study of the state and law" and helps to develop "a true science, which furthers the progressive development of society."[136]

According to an editorial in *Voprosy Istorii* [Problems of History], "communist partisanship is not contradictory to, but fully complementary with, scientific objectivity because . . . the subjective class aims of the proletariat coincide with the natural laws of the development of humanity that are independent of the will and consciousness of man."[137] The same editorial stated that the principle of partisanship is "organically connected with the fundamental premises of dialectical materialism, political economy, and historical materialism, . . . three component parts of our great revolutionary theory which is transforming the world."[138]

The view that partisanship is "organically" connected with dialectical and historical materialism is indeed correct. Although neither Marx nor Engels spoke of the principle of partisanship, partisanship was implicit in their naturalistic theory of history. It will be recalled that they viewed history as a process of development governed by natural laws. This development represents a self-perfecting process in the biological as well as the *moral* sense. It started with a primitive stage and will eventually culminate with a stage of com-

---

[134] *Ibid.*, p. 25.
[135] *Ibid.*, p. 23.
[136] M. P. Kareva, S. F. Kechekyan, A. S. Fedoseev, and G. I. Fedkin, *Teoriya Gosudarstva i Prava* [The Theory of State and Law] (Moscow, 1955), pp. 14–15.
[137] Editorial, "V. I. Lenin o Partiinosti v Istoricheskoi Nauke" [Lenin on Partisanship in the Science of History], *Voprosy Istorii*, No. 4 (1958), p. 18.
[138] *Ibid.*, p. 4.

munism—the highest stage of historical development. Thus, communism, as the inevitable result of historical development, coincides with communism as the ultimate social value presupposed by Marx and Engels. History, as an impersonal process, appears to be working toward the same end as that chosen by Marx and Engels.

From a rational point of view, it might be argued that theirs is a partisanship delusively projected into history. But such is not the view of Soviet writers, who, following Marx and Engels, maintain that there are objectively existing values. These values are objective because, presumably, they exist independent of human volition; their source is nature, and their depository is history.[139] Soviet writers claim that their partisanship is based on these objectively existing values, and from this they conclude that "the partisanship of Marxist philosophy . . . secures the most thorough and the most accurate knowledge of objective truth."[140]

[139] See, for example, A. F. Shishkin, "Nauka i Moral" [Science and Morality], *Voprosy Filosofii,* No. 4 (1961).
[140] Fedoseev, "Znachenie Marksistsko-Leninskoi Teorii Poznaniya," p. 21.

# PART I ⚭ REVOLUTIONARY INTELLECTUALISM OF THE 1920's

# Introduction ∽

The 1920's in the Soviet Union represented the period of intellectual ferment, optimism, and impatience. The social forces unleashed by the Bolshevik Revolution generated an unprecedented number of problems that called for immediate solution. The solution of these problems had to conform to the requirements of immediate political expediency, yet at the same time had to be in accordance with the ultimate objectives of the Bolsheviks, namely, communism.

Bringing about such solutions was not an easy task, for the requirements of immediate expediency were frequently in conflict with ultimate ends. This is why the first attempts to formulate Soviet political theory—that is, the determination of ultimate and immediate policy objectives and the means for their materialization—were made soon after the October Revolution.

The first step in this direction was Lenin's *State and Revolution* (1917), which sought to fix the place of the proletarian revolution within the framework of general historical development, to describe its inevitable consequences, and to outline the main features of the future communist society. However, Lenin's work was too far removed from existing reality and hence could not contribute much to the solution of the immediate problems.

The political thought that affected postrevolutionary events considerably was produced by Soviet thinkers in response to the rising political problems. That is, the foundations of Soviet political thought were laid by writers who discussed theoretical issues in connection with immediate policy objectives. Among those writers were Lunacharskii, Goikhbarg, Kozlovskii, and Stuchka.

The essays by these writers are included in this book, and the reader should find them illuminating. They discuss crucial political problems with which Bolsheviks were confronted between 1917 and 1920. Each of them speaks as a Marxist, yet it is rather apparent that none of them is sufficiently familiar with the writings of Marx and Engels. Thus, to justify the creation of the "proletarian" court, Lunacharskii finds it necessary to invoke the views of such German and Russian "bourgeois" writers as Berolzheimer, Knapp, Menger, Jellinek, and Petrazhitskii. In discussing the goals and methods of the Bolshevik Revolution, Goikhbarg is clearly influenced by the French writer Leon Duguit; he even quotes Woodrow Wilson to support some of his arguments. Similarly, Stuchka uses the writings of Voltaire and Renner to support his views.

At any rate, early Soviet writers—most of whom occupied crucial positions within the governmental structure—possessed a scant familiarity with the original writings of Marx and Engels. Rather, they derived their knowledge indirectly, primarily from German interpretations of Marx and Engels. Surprisingly enough, they seemed to be unfamiliar with Lenin's writings also, for references to his works did not appear until the early twenties.

The first attempt (acknowledged by later Soviet writers) to formulate a more systematic Marxist foundation for Soviet political thought was made by Magerovskii in an essay on dialectical realism, written in 1920 but published in 1922. This essay—as its author admitted—reflects general confusion on social problems that prevailed in the minds of Soviet thinkers at that time, but especially a confusion of Marx's and Engels' philosophical assumptions with those of Hegel.

Magerovskii's controversial article gave impetus to a more thorough study of the original works of Marx and Engels. This study eventually led to the painful realization that there are definite discrepancies between Marx and Engels; it also revealed a "young" and an "old" Marx, each speaking a different philosophical language. Furthermore, there was a growing realization among Soviet thinkers that Marx and Engels had failed to provide a specific description of the period of transition to communism. It now became apparent to many of them that the Soviet government would have to improvise and that at times it would have to resort to measures that were overtly contrary to Marx's general outline of the transition period. Moreover, some writers concluded that the introduction of socialism as the indispensable transition period would be impossible for some time because of the ideological, scientific, and technological backwardness of the Soviet Union. (See Krylenko's article "The Conflict between Socialist Theory and Soviet Reality," this volume.)

The saving grace for Soviet thinkers in the early twenties was their profound faith in Marxist methodology. Following the views of Rosa Luxemburg, they maintained that "political economy as a science found its completion and its end in Marx's theory."[1] The attainment of the ultimate knowledge of economic phenomena was due, in their

---

[1] Rosa Luxemburg, *Vvedenie v Politicheskuyu Ekonomiyu* [An Introduction to Political Economy] (n.p., 1925), pp. 66–67, cited by M. Rezunov, "K Voprosu o Metode Izucheniya Prava" [On Methodological Problems in Studying Law], *Sovetskoe Pravo*, No. 3(33) (1928), p. 52.

judgment, to a peculiar method developed by Marx. This method was assumed to be grounded on propositions that had the character of "eternal" truth.[2] If properly applied, this method would furnish correct solutions to scientific and political problems.

The anticipated results failed to materialize, however. The application of the Marxist method to the study of various social phenomena produced mutually incompatible interpretations. At first there was a tendency to attribute the failure to the misapplication of the method, but gradually Soviet social thinkers became aware of the deficiencies inherent in the method itself. This awareness led them to a searching re-examination of their earlier attitude, which resulted in endless methodological controversies. Eventually, by the end of the twenties, methodological problems were relegated to professional philosophers.

The methodological controversies were reflected in the treatment accorded by Soviet writers to various social problems, especially law and the state. Law and the state occupied the most prominent positions in Soviet political thought from its very inception. The preoccupation with these social phenomena on the part of Soviet thinkers was quite natural in view of their commitment to communism as the ultimate social value. Communism—conceived of as the morally most desirable and the historically inevitable end—was to be an entirely new social order; it was to be based on principles diametrically opposed to those underlying all previous social orders. Negatively speaking, communism was supposed to represent a classless, lawless, and stateless society. In terms of its positive content, communism was variously described by Soviet thinkers as a harmonious society, as conditions of full equality and true freedom, and as conditions under which all of man's material and spiritual needs will be fully satisfied.

Apart from differences in the degree of emphasis placed upon one or another positive aspect of communism, Soviet writers were in agreement that the elimination of law and the state constitutes an indispensable condition for the advent of communism. It is in view of this consideration that they were preoccupied with the problem of law and the state, that is, with their nature and the conditions of their disappearance. Another reason for the preoccupation with law and the state in the twenties was the fact that Soviet authority—

---

[2] Ladislaus Rudas, "Preodelenie Kapitalisticheskogo Oveshchestvleniya ili Dialekticheskaya Dialektika" [The Overcoming of Capitalist Reification, or Dialectical Dialectic], *Vestnik Kommunisticheskoi Akademii,* No. 10 (1925), p. 56.

professedly committed to the liquidation of these social phenomena
—was increasingly resorting to the use of law and was taking determined measures toward strengthening the state and its bureaucratic
apparatus. Early Soviet writers were puzzled by this development, for
most of them had assumed (following the thesis of economic determinism) that law and the state would automatically and immediately
disappear after the nationalization of land and the means of production and distribution.

This assumption was soon discarded and replaced with a less optimistic one. By the mid-twenties the prevailing argument was that
while law is an *intrinsically bourgeois and hence evil* phenomenon, it
is a *necessary evil* that must be used for bringing about the transition
to communism; it would "wither away" in the future, presumably
the near future, but no one could foretell precisely when. Eventually, in the latter half of the twenties, some writers began to argue
that Soviet law had acquired a new content—that it now served the
consolidation of the proletarian revolution—and that, consequently,
it was possible to speak of proletarian law as distinct from its bourgeois predecessor. This view, in a partially implemented form, became an "official" view in the thirties.

These, and earlier-mentioned considerations, were responsible for
the intense preoccupation with law (and related problems, such as
equality, justice, civil freedom, and morality) on the part of Soviet
social thinkers during the twenties. Unable to find the answers in
the "classics" of Marx and Engels, Soviet writers began to study
Western literature on this subject. Originally, they intended to subject various Western theories of law to a Marxist analysis, hoping
that in the process they would develop a systematic Marxist theory
of law. This attempt, however, proved abortive. Its outcome was a
split among Soviet writers into various schools of thought roughly
corresponding to those in the West. Thus, there was the *sociological
school of law* (numerically the strongest and most popular) represented by P. Stuchka, A. K. Stalgevich, E. B. Pashukanis, N. V. Krylenko, A. Piontkovskii, S. Kechekyan, M. M. Isaev, N. N. Polyan-
skii, N. Totskii, F. Ksenofontov, A. Trainin, L. Uspenskii, F. D.
Kornilov, M. Dotsenko, and I. Razumovskii. Another group consisted of the proponents of the *psychological* approach to law,
namely, M. Reisner, I. Ilinskii, E. Engel, M. Cheltsov-Bebutov,
D. Dembskii, Ya. Berman, M. Rezunov, and A. Popov. The third
group known as exponents of *the social function theory,* were represented by A. Goikhbarg, S. Raevich, E. Kelman, and S. Askna-
zii. These writers were influenced by a French jurist—Leon Duguit.

Finally, there was the numerically smallest group known as the "normativists," represented by D. Magerovskii, I. Podvolotskii, I. Voitinskii, and V. Veger.

The theories of law advanced by the representatives of these groups were claimed to be "truly Marxist," yet they were at variance with one another. The fact that Soviet writers were offering conflicting theories, while presumably using the same "Marxist method," was not an indication of an anti-Soviet conspiracy as was claimed during Stalin's period. It was, rather, a reflection of the fact that during the twenties, Soviet writers were free to determine the meaning of "the Marxist method" in their own way, without political interference.

Marx and Engels had failed to present this method in a systematic form. There was an abundance of implicit and explicit observations of a methodological nature in their works, but many of these observations were mutually incompatible. Consequently, by placing emphasis upon one or another aspect of the Marxist method, Soviet writers were bound to arrive at conflicting interpretations of law and other social phenomena.

# The Revolution, Law, and the Courts*

## ◌ *A. Lunacharskii*

A society is not a unified whole. There are classes with antagonistic interests and hence with diverse mentalities and legal con-
sciousnesses. These classes are struggling in the womb of society. On
the one hand, by means of the power of the state, the ruling classes
secure for themselves privileges and punish those who encroach
upon these privileges in conformity with their own law. On the
other hand, the ruling classes infuse into the consciousness of the
people a belief that their judicial order is a manifestation of "Justice," that their judicial institutions are the basis of all social life, and
that any tampering with these institutions may bring about the destruction of the entire culture.

In addition to introducing a higher economic order, the new
class in the capitalist system, that is to say, the proletarian class,
also promulgates a law that is incomparably higher than the decaying,
ossified law of the old system—a law that served the usurpers and
exploiters as a watchdog.

As long as this new class is suppressed, however, as long as it
remains a victim of the law made by its masters, it is, naturally, deprived of the opportunity to formulate its own legal consciousness; it
cannot create its own ideal of court and legal code in a vacuum. Any
attempt of a socialist legal theorist to draft a project of a code of

* *From* "Revolutsiya i Sud" [Revolution and the Court], *Pravda*, No. 193
(December 1, 1917).

[Lunacharskii's article aimed at justifying the need for the creation of a
proletarian court and law. On the one hand, it was directed at the conservative
faction of Bolsheviks which favored the preservation of the old, prerevolutionary courts; on the other hand, it was directed at the anarchistically oriented
faction which opposed all courts on the grounds that they were incompatible
with the aims of the revolution.

Lunacharskii, then Commissar of Education, was given the task of persuading both factions of the necessity to create a proletarian court as an indispensable prerequisite for the consolidation of the revolutionary gains. His article
was credited, by later Soviet writers, for its success in appeasing the dissenting
factions and for the subsequent creation of the "People's Court."

Apart from its practical merits, Lunacharskii's article is significant to the
study of Soviet political thought because it represents the first attempt to lay
down doctrinal foundations for the Soviet judiciary, which eventually developed
into a highly complex system. The most conspicuous feature of his article is
the reliance upon the views of "bourgeois" theorists such as Berolzheimer,
Jellinek, and Petrazhitskii rather than those of Marx and Engels.]

law for the future system in advance would be nothing but an interesting science fiction like Wallace's and Bellami's novels. To be sure,
such attempts have been made. Anton Menger, a talented quasi-
bourgeois and quasi-socialist, has gained quite a reputation from
such attempts.

All such attempts are, nevertheless, merely a theoretical game.
Each class creates its law *in fact* only when it makes use of its *power,*
when it shapes social reality to its own image, i.e., in conformity with
its fundamental class interests, on the one hand, and the existing
conditions, on the other. But one class, even a class that attained
political power through the means of a harsh revolution, is not capable of creating a new world immediately. According to Marx, this
world is born covered with a membrane of the old social texture.

This should not be interpreted to mean that the revolutionary
class should move slowly and ceremoniously against the old order. Its
task is to destroy and to create. The revolutionary class brings a new
legal consciousness (i.e., the presentiment of new juridical forms and
relationships) which corresponds to the new economic conditions
created by the revolution. Furthermore, the revolutionary class
brings a new juridical consciousness as well as a new concept of
good and evil. The revolution itself is a fact of contraposing a new
law to the old one, an act of a popular mass trial over the hated
system of privilege. The creation of a new civil and criminal law, a
new state structure, new organs of power, judicial organs included,
strengthens the revolution and at the same time formulates and ma-
terializes the new revolutionary legal consciousness, which has been
brought forth by the new class interests and the new economic planning.

On October 25, the greatest revolution ever known was accomplished. For the first time, the working masses have not simply won
(this happened previously) but, unlike the March of 1917, they
have preserved the fruits of victory in their own hands. Can one
then expect that, having accomplished the revolution, having become the political and military masters of our country, the proletariat and the peasantry will tolerate the old judges and the old
laws, as did the Kerenski pseudorevolutionary government? Can we
expect that the new master of the situation, the working people,
would tolerate bourgeois verdicts that had been handed down in the
spirit of capitalism and in the name of a government overthrown
and destroyed by these working people? Could we expect the working
people to allow the Senate to make laws in the name of the overthrown regime?

Revolution was accomplished for the purpose of creating a new law and the opportunity for a new legal consciousness to be translated into reality. This is why a victorious people should immediately start building new courts and a new code, building them in practice—at first gropingly—guided by their revolutionary consciousness, but gradually formulating a new law and crystallizing new, fine, and firm forms of a true people's court.

To destroy the old court—the weapon of our enemy—and our fetters, is the first duty of revolutionaries; natural fighting spirit directs them toward this. Then to outline the foundations of the new court, even if in a most general way. Thirdly, to assign the remaining tasks to the creativity of the revolutionary people.

Like the Roman world, the bourgeoisie, which took root in feudal society, stood firmly for the absolute recognition of private property. Hence it was able to replace the law of the old regime with the available Roman law, only slightly modified to new conditions. The proletariat cannot choose such a path. The proletarian movement is a progressive one, not retrogressive; there is no precedent in history for a proletarian law. Since under capitalism the proletariat was deprived of the opportunity to develop its legal creativity, it has no choice now but to learn how to adjudicate pragmatically and create its own customary law, deducing it from the sources of the same spiritual movement that led the proletariat to the victorious revolution and that reflects its class character, its growth, and its significance in the social life. The Council of the People's Commissariat, abolishing the czarist and bourgeois courts, urges the Russian working people toward such creativity.

Let the bourgeois jurists argue that what we have said today, and what the people will do tomorrow, is unheard of, and, from the judicial point of view, monstrous. It is inadmissible only from the viewpoint of a stagnant pseudoscience that constitutes the artificial foundation and justification of the inhuman law of its masters. Even some honest and talented bourgeois scientists, who have sought to ground their juridical theories in the true sciences of biology, psychology, and sociology, have spoken our language long before our revolution as though foreseeing it.

We urge our enemies, before they begin criticizing us, to read a few paragraphs from the writings of the theorists whom they recognize as authorities in the field. These paragraphs sound as though they were written yesterday, and as though they were written specifically in defense of the type of courts that we are forced by the existing circumstances to create. We also urge our friends to listen to what such true scientists, though not "Bolsheviks," have to say about the revolutionary creation of law.

Thus, Berolzheimer speaks about an entirely new law which, though it appears in the form of a demand for a new justice, is brought forth by the fourth estate. He also speaks about the impending transition period, "in which, in an intense conflict, the last remnants of the old, disappearing system and the first elements of the new system will meet."[1] Menger has even made an attempt to formulate this law, which is rooted in the consciousness of the new rising class, and which will be materialized in a new, popular workers' state.[2]

Also, Jellinek, a master professor, quite flatly recognizes the existence of law that is engendered in the womb of the bourgeois state, and that is not produced by means of juridical methods. For example, he speaks about "norms," which on the social, though not judicial, level function as written law, despite the fact that they were not created in a formal legislative order.[3]

Knapp, a student of the great Feuerbach, has grasped quite distinctly the difference between the new and as yet unrealized law (under whose banner the new class accomplishes the revolution in order to concretize this law) and the dominant, written law. This jurist writes the following concerning the revolutionary epoch: "The problem of right is frequently decided in the revolutionary street battles or in hardships of a world war; the right always appeals to an objective might, which alone can secure the *external right.*" This is exactly the problem we are confronted with: following the transfer of power into the hands of a new class, we must transform the inner legal consciousness into a young, mighty law.

Professor Petrazhitskii, in whom official Russian science takes pride as one of the greatest authorities in Europe, has described most vividly the relationships between the "positive," i.e., written law, and the "intuitive" law of the new social forces, i.e., their ideal of justice. To quote Petrazhitskii, "The simultaneous existence and functioning of the positive (written) law with the intuitive law (with the ideal of the new classes) is possible only if there is a general agreement between them; if the discord reaches a certain degree, then the disintegration of the positive law becomes inescapable; in a case of opposi-

[1] Fritz Berolzheimer, *System der Rechts-und Wirtschaftsphilosophie* (Munich, 1907), II, 483.

[2] Anton Menger, *Neue Staatslehre* (Jena, 1904).

[3] Georg Jellinek, *Verfassungsänderung und Verfassungswandlung* (n.p., n.d.), p. 3.

tion, the disintegration is brought about through a social revolution."

Such a revolution took place on October 25. It would be beyond comprehension if bourgeois positive law continued to exist by some miracle even after the Revolution—especially since the Revolution had been aroused by the craving to destroy it!

Petrazhitskii describes in detail how the new legal ideal grows among the lower classes . . . under the influence of changing conditions. He states that the sense of justice becomes even more offended when it encounters opposition, then "it reaches a fanatical hatred of the existing order with its laws, and ultimately it arouses an explosion—the Revolution."[4]

Petrazhitskii is not frightened by even such manifestations of the new, popular, and revolutionary legal consciousness, which, of course, will never accompany the proletarian revolution: "However repulsive the guillotines of the Revolution and the destruction of the cultural centers are, they are an inescapable result of the insulted popular sense, a spontaneous vengeance for the suppression of rights, i.e., people's inner legal consciousness."

The conclusion is obvious: the people engender a new intuitive law, which calls, first of all, for the destruction of all organs of the old law that are perceived by them as complete injustices. This intuitive law (reflecting class interests of the masses, and corresponding to the new rising social structure) can be distinctly formulated only in the process of a direct, revolutionary legal creativity. Such is the law of revolution, especially great revolutions that have no precedents.

Down with the courts-mummies, with the altars of the dead law! Down with the judges-vampires, who are ready to drink the blood of the living on the fresh grave of tyrannical, capitalist rule! Long live the people who create a new law in their courts, which are boiling and fermenting like a new wine: a just law for all, a law of the great fraternity and equality of the workingman!

---

[4] L. Petrazhitskii, *Teoriya Prava i Gosudarstva v Svyazi s Teoriei Nravstvennosti* [The Theory of Law and State in Connection with the Theory of Morality] (Petersburg, 1909).

# The Goals and Methods of the Proletarian Revolution*

## ♋ A. G. Goikhbarg

The proletarian revolution—proletarian not only in terms of forces that brought it about, but also in terms of the goals pursued instinctively or consciously by the masses carrying it out—aims at replacing sooner or later the old bourgeois individualistic system with a socialist collectivist system. With a complete socialization of production and exchange first, and then of consumption, and with the elimination of any and all struggle between men in the process of acquiring the material means of existence, full opportunity will be opened for the *unhindered,* thorough development of man, of man's personality, not as a separate individual but as an organic part of the organic whole that is called humanity.

Then the struggle from the sphere of relationships between men will be carried over into the sphere of relationships between humanity and nature: in a persistent struggle with nature, men will wring from it . . . more secrets, learn new forces of nature, master these forces, adapt them to the growing needs of mankind, and transform themselves from slaves of unintelligible and elemental forces into their conscious masters.

At the present time it is difficult to foresee the end of man's struggle in the sphere of conquering natural forces, which is aimed at creating a beautiful, diversified, and free life for mankind. But this long struggle, perhaps the struggle of generations, will be a struggle between neither men nor groups of men divided by geographical, state, or class boundaries, but will be the struggle between humanity and nature. Then the period of struggle and wars between men will become a legend; men as harmonious parts of a single integral organism—of humanity—will combine their powers for the common good and will not direct them for defeating, conquering, oppressing, or enslaving one another. The source of coercion will disappear in the relationships between men. Also, the *law,* which is called forth by the constant struggle of men as separate individuals, groups, states, etc., will then disappear as an organization of coercion in the sphere of human relationships.

* *From* "Proletarskaya Revolutsiya i Grazhdanskoe Pravo" [Proletarian Revolution and Civil Law], *Proletarskaya Revolutsiya i Pravo,* No. 1 (1918), pp. 9–20.

Not only will civil law disappear with the consolidation of collectivism, but also law in general. The harmonious coexistence of men will be based not on the principle of social coercion and social necessity or, in other words, on law, but on the principle of complete social freedom. Then, for the first time, humanity will need no *guarantees* against the freedom or even the arbitrariness of its separate organic parts, i.e., of the individuals comprising it. Completely changed conditions of human existence will bring about such a regeneration of social psychology that the individual arbitrariness, which disturbs the harmony of humanity's life, will become such an infrequent anomaly that it can either be disregarded or eliminated by means other than the contemporary legal guarantees.

But, if such will be the end result of the creation of the socialist system, does it mean that immediately after the outbreak of the proletarian revolution, which is confined to only one country, *decrees* can be issued *abrogating* the whole previous bourgeois legal structure, and that the creation of new socialist relationships can be left to the "natural" course of events? Is an *unregulated* transition from the anarchistic arbitrariness of the bourgeois individualistic system toward the harmonious freedom of the socialist social system possible?

The questions themselves imply that the negative answer is self-evident. It is self-evident that during the transition period some spheres of law will be blossoming, will attain unprecedented intensity, whereas, at the same time, other spheres of law will fall into decay, fade, shrink, approach the non-being, or finally disappear. Thereby the changes will assume a more violent character in the sphere of legislation than in the sphere of operative law which comprised the nucleus of the new system in the past.

But the decrees by themselves do not provide for the final solution of the problem. Decrees—which in brief but harsh statements have abolished survivals of the past, have untied old fetters that bound men and hindered their activity, and thus have given to individuals a complete freedom of action, while assuming or hypocritically pretending that the clash of free egos would produce general well-being—were appropriate and have attained their goal in the period of the exemplary French *bourgeois* Revolution, which aimed at creating a system of *anarchistic individualism* in the sphere of economic relations. But the proletarian revolution, which pursues entirely different goals and which faces the task of constructing and consolidating a diametrically opposed system of *regulated collectivism,* cannot, obviously, limit itself to the mere negative activity of issuing decrees. The *positive* task of regulating relationships, which should replace the previous chaotic system, is of great significance in the legal sphere of the transition period.

Concerning this subject, we find the thoughts of a most prominent "young" Marxist, Karl Renner, to be quite deep and interesting in a recently published work.[1] In one of the chapters dealing with the differences between the bourgeois and the proletarian revolutions, K. Renner develops the following thoughts.[2]

What the bourgeois revolutions do in the economic sphere is very simple and relatively quickly attainable: they untie and free men and material elements of production from all traditional, feudal, or class fetters and leave them alone. In the name of these revolutions, the state tells man: "From now on you are a person, and economically you are free to do whatever you desire; your higher and fundamental right in this sphere is to be entirely independent of me." In exactly the same way, the state addresses itself to material things: "From now on you are nothing but commodities, regardless of whether you are plots of land, fruits, animals, products of labor, or anything else; I see no difference between you. You have the right to be in circulation without my help. Persons and commodities, you have to act on the basis of free contract; my task is merely to provide coercion for the fulfillment of your contracts."

It is quite obvious that such non-interference requires no creative economic activity from the state and that it can be accomplished at any time by simple decrees. Regardless of the amount of time that passed before the feudal society became disorganized to the degree that it began to conceive of itself as a simple society of commodity possessors, and regardless of the political efforts that had to be spent by the bourgeoisie in gathering political power, formally the bourgeois revolution was accomplished by means of decree, declaring: "Men and commodities, move. You are free!" No additional organizational work was to be done by the bourgeois revolution, with the exception of the creation of a justly arbitrating state, of a *Rechtsstaat,* of the highest realization of the bourgeois ideal of social life, above which even such great bourgeois minds as that of Kant were unable to see, and which Ferdinand Lassalle ironically called a night guardian.

It would be absurd to assume that the proletarian revolution will become a copy of a bourgeois revolution, that it will perform the same function, and that it will adhere to the same forms. On the contrary,

---

[1] *Marxismus, Krieg und Internationale* (Stuttgart, 1917).
[2] *Ibid.,* pp. 20–26.

since it represents a recent and a higher historical formation, the bourgeois form of revolution and its formulas are reactionary in comparison to the proletarian revolution. The non-limitation of men and things which bourgeois ideology calls freedom is an anarchy from the viewpoint of the proletarian revolution and thus is something reactionary. The proletarian revolution foresees a new system in the future; in place of the capitalist system it sees a socialist economic and social system.

Living in this bourgeois world, whose anarchistic character was so clearly described by Friedrich Engels, Marx stated the following: "What you call absence of restraint and freedom is, in fact, universal social dependence." Having failed to consciously create a social order for yourselves, you fell under the material law of capital which dominates all participants of production; you are the slaves of things but, as persons, you assume that you are free. But this law of capital compels you to unite, and one day it will even force society to dethrone it, to replace it with conscious social guidance, and to create conditions in which the economy would not dominate the society but society would dominate the economy, in which the bourgeoisie would not dominate the state but the state would dominate the bourgeoisie until organized society would finally dissolve the bourgeoisie. Capitalism gives birth to its own grave digger, namely, socialism. In this sense, socialism means a conscious domination of organized society over economy.

An organized society is not an anarchistic conglomeration of individuals but their merging into one general will. Unfortunately, this merging can be brought about neither by decree nor in one day. Ask any political representative of any locality, or any representative of the local labor union, how much time, effort, and adroitness is needed to lead a few hundred people to one thought and will, to uproot from their minds bourgeois prejudices of anarchistic free "individuality," and to replace them with the awareness that it is better to be a free member of a free society. Take a look at our professional, cooperative, and political organizations and you will see that years and decades will be needed for the psychological regeneration of the proletarian upheaval, and that it will be achieved not by means of violence or decrees but by means of work and education.

Having taken all this into consideration, one can understand the deep contrast between the bourgeois and the proletarian world: the essence of a bourgeois system is the juridical title, property; the essence of a proletarian system is work, a protracted process of work that cannot be replaced with any ingenious invention; the virtue of a bourgeois system is the sovereignty of the individual; the virtue of a proletarian system is a disciplined incorporation into the general will, into the organization.

The organized society takes rule over the economy into its own hands; such is the material task of the new proletarian formation. The domination over economy is a feature that not only distinguishes it from the bourgeois state system but makes it diametrically opposed to it. The bourgeois system constitutes a domination over men by means of law, in other words, by means of command and obedience or, in brief, by means of legal enactments; the organ of this system is the jurist; its higher form is legislation.

At the present time, during the war, even a layman sees that simple legislation is powerless, and especially powerless in coping with the economy. In fact, domination over the economy has already ceased to be domination; it consists of drafting and fulfilling plans of work, of technical ideas and technical work. This demonstrates the tremendous difference. The bourgeois law declares: "You, subjects of bourgeois law, may or should build houses with such and such legal limitations." Such an order is issued with one stroke of the pen. On the other hand, the social, general will proclaims: "We will build accommodations for everyone." The latter law is no longer an order but a program of work.

After the passage of decrees on August 4, which was the culmination point of the French Revolution, the free citizens could begin to dance blissfully on the plazas of Paris; they were free persons, they were unrestrained proprietors, and the commodities circulated freely (or, at least, were supposed to circulate freely) in all markets; the development of the capitalist mode of production could now begin. However, the moment the proletariat establishes its rule in this state, work, not dancing, will begin. Years will pass, indeed—years rich in work—until, for example, each member of society is furnished with worthy accommodations.

A correct understanding of the form and content of the proletarian upheaval can be acquired by examining the measures taken by the bourgeoisie in anticipation of this upheaval. The bourgeoisie, desiring to obtain the greatest possible exploitation of work, could not wait for each worker to privately acquire the training necessary for the production process by means of free competition between the private teachers and educators; it created the public schools, thus adopting in this sphere methods that are available to the socialist system and that are the only suitable methods. At first the bourgeoisie carried out its decision by means of law. Thus, for example, in 1869, a public school law was issued in Austria. But law is simply a word, and, in addition, a word that is not at all similar to the biblical words used during the six days of creation: "let it be"—and "it became"! Let the school building be; let the school teachers be! As a true social law, this law was a program of work: we wish to build schools; we wish to create teachers' colleges; we wish to develop methods of teaching and school facilities; we wish to give each child an education in eight years. Almost half a century has passed since this law was issued, yet not all school buildings are yet erected; the preparation of teachers is still unsatisfactory; school equipment is still unavailable. None of these school needs will ever be attained, because time rushes forward, and the government merely follows, far behind, in satisfying the needs: in their very nature, all the tasks of the government are endless.

Equally endless will be the economic tasks of socialism; it may suffice to mention only one example, namely, the task of organizing agricultural production. Each step uncovers new problems during this process. Nothing is more dangerous than injecting into the proletariat the faith in decrees which prevailed during the French Revolution; nothing is more dangerous than to expect miracles from socialism like those that took place in the days of the creation: "let it be"— and "it became." The day the proletariat establishes a dictatorship over the economy the phantom of the state will disappear and the work of the administration will begin. Indeed, this work will be free of any private interests; it will be capable of producing faster and more efficiently and will precipitate social development. Miracles, however, will not take place.

The temple of bourgeois authority is legislation and its fetish is the law; the temple of the socialist world system is administration and its divine service is work. It is by no accident that the political ideals of the bourgeoisie are embodied in parliamentarianism and the *Rechtsstaat,* whereas, the socialist community is, in its very nature, primarily a community of administration.

A socialist and Marxist, K. Renner is not the only one to notice the transition from legislation to administration. He merely depicts, in a most salient and bold manner, the distinctions between the bourgeois and the proletarian methods. In the works of many bourgeois scientists one can also find references to the fact that sovereignty, commands, and legislation begin to play the secondary role even in bourgeois society and give way to the direct satisfaction of communal needs, administration, and economic management. For example, Duguit, a French professor, has devoted a whole book to this question.[3] In part, the same thoughts can be noted in the book published in the past century by the present American president, Woodrow Wilson. In his book, for example, we find the following lines:

> . . . The legislative power is but a part of government. Legislation is but the oil of government. It lubricates its channels and speeds its wheels; it lessens the friction and so eases the movement. . . . It is even more important to know how the house is being built than to know how the plans were conceived by the architects and how the necessary materials were figured out. It is better to have skillful work—stout walls, reliable arches, unbending rafters, and windows sure to "expel the winter's flaw"—than a drawing on paper which is the admiration of all the artists in the country.[4]

The tasks of the proletarian revolution can be carried out neither by means of decrees nor by means of legislative acts that provide for juridical titles and procedures through which certain rights *can* be acquired. Even more so, they cannot be carried out by means of norms, which are based on the premise that the corresponding relationships should be regulated by voluntary private contracts, and which begin to function only when the persons who have entered into certain relationships forget or overlook some details of these relationships. These tasks will be carried out, not by rejecting the interference of the state, but, on the contrary, by organized administration, by economic management, by accommodating the material, spiritual, and cultural needs of the population. Naturally, the outlining of these tasks and the drafting of such plans will also be done at first in the form of decisions that, on the surface, may resemble previously written laws. But will the legislation dealing with civil rights, as they have been understood earlier (in German: *bürgerliches Recht,* bourgeois right), be included in this system of legislation as its independent part? Or, will we have to admit that civil law is to be abolished? Or, more precisely, that the relationships that previously were regulated by civil law should be regulated by norms of an entirely different type, not the bourgeois-individualist but the organizational-social type?

But what, in fact, is the nature of civil law? The disputes concerning the limits of civil and public law and the essential features distin-

---

[3] *Les transformations du droit public* (Paris, 1913).

[4] *Gosudarstvennyi Stroi Soedinennykh Shtatov* [The Political System of the United States] (n.p., n.d.), a Russian translation of Wilson's *Congressional Government* (1885), pp. 257–58.

guishing civil law from public law are far from being resolved in Western European literature. The same is true of our country, despite the fact that since 1864 a rule has existed asserting that all controversies concerning *civil rights* are subject to judicial decision. In general, however, one can accept the explanation of the nature of the public law . . . given by Professor I. A. Pokrovskii as the most satisfactory:

> *The method of juridical centralization* constitutes the essential feature of civil law. . . . Different methods are employed in the domains in which law is regarded as belonging to the *private* or *civil sphere.* In the latter case, the state authority abstains, *as a rule,* from a direct regulation of relationships: it does not put itself in the position of an exclusive regulating center but, on the contrary, leaves the regulation to a multitude of other small centers which, like other independent social units, are conceived of as legal subjects. In the majority of cases, such legal subjects are individuals, men. . . . All these small centers are assumed to have their own will and initiative and consequently are responsible for the regulation of the relationships between themselves. The state does not determine these relationships in any way; it merely assumes the role of an organ protecting that which has been determined by others. The state does not prescribe to a private person to become a proprietor, an heir, or a husband; all this depends upon the private person himself or upon several private persons (parties to a contract); but state authority will protect relationships established by private will. As a general rule, the state authority resorts to action only if for any reason private persons do not fulfill their obligations. . . . Thus, for example, in the case of the absence of a will, the state determines the order of inheritance in conformity with law. Consequently, as a rule, the norms of private law do not have a coercive but merely a subsidiary or supplementary character and can be abrogated or replaced by private decisions. . . . Thus, whereas public law is a system of centralized juridical relationships, civil law, on the contrary, is a system of *juridical decentralization:* its very existence presupposes the existence of a great number of self-determining centers.[5]

But can the proletarian state authority, established for carrying out the tasks of the proletarian revolution, play a neutral, Pilate-like role in relation to the economy while accommodating the material and spiritual needs of the people? Can it, "as a rule, abstain from the direct regulation" of relationships that play the decisive role? Can it tolerate the situation under which the sphere of material private relationships would be based on the principle of freedom to trade in private property? Can it tolerate the situation under which the sphere

[5] I. A. Pokrovskii, *Osnovnye Problemy Grazhdanskogo Prava* [Basic Problems of Civil Law] (n.p., 1916), pp. 11–12.

of legal relationships would rest on the principle of freedom of contracts and agreements? Can it tolerate the situation under which the sphere of post-mortem proprietary relationships would rest on the principle of the freedom of wills?

The proletarian state authority—i.e., the class authority whose life depends upon the organization, unification, centralization, but not the atomization and decentralization of work—cannot do this. That could not be done even by bourgeois authority, which was forced, by the development of economic relationships, to take care of the regulation of some material, civil, and hereditary relationships. But was the unlimited freedom of property, contracts, agreements, and wills really preserved in bourgeois legal systems?

Even the most extreme individualists, for example, Professor I. A. Pokrovskii, are forced to acknowledge the possibility of a different regulation of the relationships that at times were regulated (or, rather, remained unregulated) by civil law.[6]

Is it conceivable, especially at the present time, in view of problems raised by war and starvation and the transformations that either have been or soon will be accomplished, that the state authority will, as a matter of principle, abstain from direct interference in the sphere of relationships regulated by the private law? Can one really argue that the right to own belongs to the sphere of the civil law discussed earlier, especially since not only the property right has been limited but the main object of the private law, the land, has been withdrawn from arbitrary private domination and regulation. . . . Can one speak . . . of freedom of contracts and agreements when the hiring of labor and the renting of lodgings is regulated by the state authority; when the latter determines the profit limit of both individual and collective enterprises; when the main part of production and exchange have become nationalized; and when general labor conscription is in preparation?[7]

. . . We have seen that the relationships that originally were exempt from the interference of the bourgeois state authority (which was true only of the period of simple commodity production) became the objects of an increasing state interference even before the proletarian revolution. The interference will be intensified . . . further by the state authority, which is an instrument of the proletariat, and which is responsible for the transition toward full collectivism.

[6] *Ibid.,* pp. 14–15.

[7] It should be noted that for people who did not possess private property, general labor conscription existed in the bourgeois society not only factually but also juridically. This conscription was sanctioned either by the threat of starvation or by punishment for stealing, vagrancy, or beggary.

The private, civil, bourgeois law, which is based on the individualistic principle of *laissez faire, laissez passer,* is in the process of decay
everywhere. At the time of the proletarian revolution, this law is in a
state of agony and will be replaced with the social law of the transition period, a law that is based on planned and centralized accounting
and whose aim will be the satisfaction of the material and spiritual
needs of men, members of the great and constantly expanding collective.


Individualistic civil law dies away finally in the period of the proletarian revolution and is replaced by an entirely different law, social
law. From this point of view, it may appear that the proletarian revolution is confronted in this sphere with two independent tasks, the
task of abolishing and the task of creating, and that the former task
is very easy and identical with the abolishing function of the bourgeois, e.g., the French Revolution. This is not, in fact, the case. The
abolishing aspect of the proletarian revolution's task is fundamentally
different from the abolishing task of a bourgeois revolution and is
carried out with tremendous difficulties that are not encountered in
the materialization of the legal tasks of the bourgeois revolution. The
abolishing aspect of the proletarian revolution is indissolubly connected with its creative part. *Not only are the old relationships abolished,* but also the *mode* of regulating new relationships is changed in
the most radical and unusually complicated manner; the non-organi-
zational mode of regulation is replaced by an organizational one.
    . . . For example, the carrying out of the abolishing task in the
sphere of the inheritance law would be quite easy if it consisted only
in abolishing, in the non-recognition of property relations of the deceased person, if it were decided that the property belonging to the
dead person during his life should cease to be attached to, or connected with, anyone, that his debts should be cancelled, that all his
claims be terminated, and that his personal property be free and accessible to anyone. The difficulties arise, however, when the task is
different, when the previous *order* for regulating the property relations of the deceased person is abolished and replaced with another
more complicated one, when . . . the state authority . . . must determine all details concerning the disposal of the property of the deceased.
    But these difficulties are of a different nature from those indicated
by the critics of the abolishment of the private inheritance law. Thus,
the previously mentioned Professor I. A. Pokrovskii, among others,
argues in the following way:

As long as the economic system is based on the principle of private initiative, the abolition of the right to dispose of one's property in case of a death will lead to a number of difficult negative consequences. If people were deprived of the right, in case of their death, to take care of close persons, who are not legal heirs, or to give their property for any other purposes that were dear to them during their life, people would lose the most effective stimulus for the development of their economic energy and initiative. Instead, at the end of the life the tendency toward useless waste and squandering of money may develop.[8]

All these fears are rather more apparent than real. First, when we are confronted with the task of abrogating wills and the private right of inheritance, the economic system is not any longer based on the principle of private initiative. Second, no one can know, not even approximately, when his life is approaching the end. Third, even the critics admit that at the present time the stoppage or discontinuance of enterprise does not depend upon man's will.[9] Fourth, in most cases, the useless waste and squandering of money does not imply the destruction of property but its transfer into other hands. Finally, . . . it is quite conceivable that the desire to take care of the needy and to work for the general good, i.e., for the state, may become a stimulus for the intensification of one's initiative. In fact, bourgeois thought leans toward the acceptance of this view. . . .

. . . Our difficulties are to be sought somewhere else. The abolishment of part of the decree, that part which repeals inheritance, is indissolubly connected with the creative part. The property, i.e., all property remaining after . . . a person's death, should remain intact, should be registered, and instead of being used for the satisfaction of individual and arbitrary wishes and claims, it should be used for a standardized security for the needy people and for the purpose of general welfare, i.e., for the needs of the state. For this is needed: the creation of organizations that would account for such property, of organizations for the investigation of such property that would determine satisfactory methods for urgent, temporary, and final satisfaction of needy people, and, finally, of an appropriate organization for the managing of such property. All this work requires much time. But, above all, social law, which is directed at restraining individual

---

[8] *Osnovnye Problemy,* pp. 265–66.

[9] See Werner Sombart's assertion (*ibid.,* pp. 275–76): "*Everywhere we encounter a peculiar form of psychological coercion: frequently the entrepreneur does not wish to go further but he must.* Contemporary economic man is victim of the production line in his enterprise. There is no place for his personal virtues, because they became subordinated . . . to the latter. The speed of the enterprise determines his own speed; he cannot afford to be lazy as the worker at a perpetually working machine cannot."

tendencies, aspirations, and claims in favor of society, calls for time and struggle if it is to materialize. Hence, generally speaking, the struggle takes place not only for the creation of a new law but also for the materialization of existing laws; both the struggles *de lege ferenda* and *de lege lata* are in existence.[10] Frequently, a much greater part of the struggle is wasted on the implementation of the law than on its creation (for example, the law limiting working time or the law protecting child labor). This calls for a constant and energetic defense of the law by interested persons. In particular, concerning the law abrogating inheritance, it is indispensable that interested persons and institutions, political organs, and members of the community should regularly and energetically defend the norms of this law; not only should they abstain from evading it, but they should act against attempts by others to do so.

The law finds itself and asserts itself only in struggle. The abolishing and the creative tasks of the proletarian revolution both require energetic and practical work for their materialization. At the same time, the carrying out of these tasks constitutes the materialization of the program of work, practical everyday work, sociopsychological regeneration. The decrees merely furnish the stimuli that accelerate movement in this direction.

[10] See Renner, *Marxismus*, pp. 235–36.

# Law and Crime: Their Origin and the Conditions of Their Elimination*  ‿  M. Kozlovskii

Among ideologies, by means of which the ruling classes hold the oppressed masses in the sphere of their influence, law deserves an especially honorable place. Since its duty was to protect the relations of production and to secure the exploitation of labor by the capitalists, law had to be transformed into a higher mystical authority—into a fetish. . . . Official theories have been explaining the origin of law from the very moment of its birth until now in a metaphysical way. At the dawn of the history of class society the establishment of law was attributed to the deity. . . . Later . . . its origin was attributed to other mystical forces or metaphysical beings, such as "nature," "national spirit," "objective spirit," "general will," "collective will," the "will of the state," "reason," and similar fictions.

. . . Marx, the great proletarian thinker, removed the veil of mystery from this sacred, bourgeois phenomenon. He demonstrated that law is a social relationship; that it grows from the relations of production; that it is brought about by, and corresponds to, the relations of production; that it changes, develops, and dies away with them. All that was needed to ascertain the moment of the birth of law was to lay bare the roots of social relationships.

. . . The "naturally progressive process of the development of law" can be reduced to the following brief formula: A communist system knows of no law. Law comes into being together with economic inequality, with the split of the population into classes. The legal system of antiquity reflected the exploitation of slave labor. Feudal law —up to the nineteenth century—reflected the exploitation of serfs. Bourgeois law—since the French revolution—has represented a reflection of the exploitation of "free" labor by the capitalists. The transition period from capitalism to socialism (which for the first time in this world is being experienced in Russia after the October Revolution) brings forth a law never known before. It is no longer a law in the proper meaning of the term (signifying a system of suppression of the majority by the minority). It is a proletarian law, but a law nevertheless, in the sense that it serves as a means of suppressing

* *From* "Proletarskaya Revolutsiya i Ugolovne Pravo" [The Proletarian Revolution and Criminal Law], *Proletarskaya Revolutsiya*, No. 1 (1918), pp. 21–27.

the resistance of the minority by the working classes. (In this period law is no longer a written code; the armed people are fighting their class opponents without any special rules.)

Law, as an external protection of the relations of production, continues to function in a socialist society, but it gradually withers away, and, with the transition into communism (which precludes an economic inequality), it completely disappears. Having originated in economic inequality (after primitive communism), in the future communist society law dies away together with economic inequality. Such is the life process of law. Mankind has already gone through the major part of this process. At present, our country is experiencing the epoch of proletarian law. What is its destiny?

. . . With the final suppression of the bourgeoisie the function of proletarian "law" will gradually diminish and be replaced by the organizational rules of economic life—production, distribution, and consumption. The organs of law will be transformed into economic, administrative organs. Judges will be replaced increasingly by workers, overseers, and bookkeepers.

Proponents of the so-called sociological school of law (Menger among them) are in agreement with the view . . . that the legal order will be transformed gradually into an economic organization, but they refuse to accept the view that law will disappear completely. In defense of this scientifically hopeless position, they advance arguments taken from the field of criminal law, that is, from the sphere of crimes.

Menger argues that . . . regardless of the type of society . . . the possibility of the disappearance of crime is inconceivable because of the basic instincts of man's nature. He admits only the possibility that crime will become a less frequent occurrence.

. . . It is evident that . . . his argument is based on a fetishist view of law as something eternal.

We know that the prerequisite of the state, law, and crime is economic inequality, which arose because of the division of society into classes. Consequently, with the disappearance of the class system and the subsequent disappearance of inequality, all these, including crime, will disappear. To a Marxist, crime is a product of the irreconcilability of class antagonism. The anarchy in capitalist production (which generates instability in man's existence . . . ) gives rise to excesses, extremism, and crime, indeed, most atrocious crimes. Exploitation of the masses produces want, misery, ignorance, savagery, and vice. . . . These manifestations will vanish only in the more advanced phase of communism but will remain in the transition toward communism in the form of rudimentary remnants of the past.

Mankind cannot emancipate itself at once from this bloody legacy of centuries-long servitude. It will hound us for a long time, until finally humanity "will transform conditions of necessity into conditions of freedom."

The transition system toward socialism (brought about in Russia through the October Revolution) received an unusually great inheritance of criminality from imperialism, which is responsible for the unheard-of slaughter of the peoples, for famine, and brutality. The proletarian government is confronted with an extraordinarily difficult task—to take care of this evil. What are the measures it will have to take for fighting this evil during the transition period?

To begin with, our punitive policy will put an end to the principle of retribution, for the reason alone that we do not assume that the offender is in possession of a "free" will or simply a "will." Being determinists, we accept as axiomatic the proposition that an offender is a product of the social milieu and that his actions and motives are independent of his own and our "will." It would be absurd to give him "his due" for something of which he is not guilty. Torture and cruel punishment should be rejected. We think that the attempts to reform a criminal are futile. . . . At best, we can only laugh at the sentimental methods of re-education that are being practiced in some countries abroad, such as high calorie diets, long walks, massages, bathing, calisthenics, etc. In conformity with our view of the causes underlying criminality, the only aim of the imposed punishment should be self-defense or the protection of society against encroachments, in which case the government will have to take decisive, surgical measures, that is, measures of terror and isolation.

There is no need to think about general preventive measures, because life itself will be working for us, bringing us closer to communism, where there will be no crime, no violence, and hence no punishment and no law. In the meantime, however, as long as we . . . cannot yet proclaim *"pereat Iustitia, fiat mundus,"* our work in the punitive sector will be directed . . . by our class interests—it will be a rigid suppression of encroachments against society on the part of the parasitic minority in conformity with the interests of the working masses of the population.

To work out a detailed plan of the measures to be used in the struggle against criminality and to put it into the form of a legal code would be tantamount, at present, to inventing a more or less ingenious utopian system. What is necessary now is to give the revolutionary masses an opportunity to demonstrate their own law creativity. . . . The healthy class instinct of the workers will point the proper way to them.

# "Law and Right Are Inherited Like an Eternal Disease"* ∞ *P. Stuchka*

If, in considering the law, we have in mind only its bourgeois meaning, then we cannot speak of a proletarian law, for the goal of the socialist revolution is to abolish law and to replace it with a new socialist order. To a bourgeois legal theorist, the term "law" is indissolubly tied in with the idea of the state as an organ of protection and as an instrument of coercion in the hands of the ruling class. With the fall or rather the *dying away* of the state, law in the bourgeois meaning of the term also *dies away*. When we speak of a proletarian law, we have in mind *law of the transition period,* law in the period of the dictatorship of the proletariat, or law of a socialist society, law in a completely new meaning of the term. For, with the abolition of the state as an organ of oppression in the hands of one class or another, the relationships between men, the social order, will be regulated not by means of coercion but by means of the conscious good will of the workers, that is, the will of the entire new society.

In this respect the tasks of bourgeois revolutions were considerably easier than the task of a socialist revolution. Voltaire's revolutionary statement is well known: "If you intend to have good laws, then burn the old and create new ones." We know that this requirement was not fulfilled by any bourgeois upheaval, not even by the great French Revolution. The latter mercilessly burned feudal castles and the titles to these castles, liquidated privileges and the holders of these privileges, and replaced the feudal system with a bourgeois one. Notwithstanding, the oppression of man by man survived, and some old laws remained unburned and binding. The legal monument of the French Revolution—Napoleon's *Civil Code*—came into being only ten years after the Revolution (1804), and only after the victory of the counterrevolution.

In one of his earlier writings (1843), Marx vividly outlined the basic difference between bourgeois and socialist revolutions: "A bourgeois revolution dissolves old feudal forms of organization through the political emancipation of independent persons, without tying and subordinating them to a new economic form. . . . It divides the person into man and citizen, whereby all the socioeconomic rela-

---

* *From* "Proletarskoe Pravo" [Proletarian Law], *Oktyabrskii Perevorot i Diktatura Proletariata* [The October Upheaval and the Dictatorship of the Proletariat], a collection of essays (Moscow, 1919), pp. 24–28.

tionships of citizens belong to the sphere of their private affairs which are of no interest to the state. . . . Man appears to be leading a double life, a heavenly and an earthly life, in the political community, where he is a *citizen,* and in a bourgeois society, where he acts as a *private person* and either looks upon other men as means, or lowers himself to a means or a toy in the hands of others." *Private* interests are indifferent, for, regardless of whether a man in bourgeois society is satisfied or hungry, whether he is physically fit or incapacitated, whether he has time to satisfy his spiritual needs, this is his private affair, the egoistic interest of each separate person, with which the state does not interfere. "The state can be turned into a free state without turning man into a free man."

What the bourgeois revolutions did was merely to put into power a new class in place of the old one, or along with the old, and to change the form of the organization of state power. The mode of oppression was freely changed without changing the text of old laws. The continuity of law seems to be the essence of the stability of human society, which is based on the principle of exploitation of man by man. Thus, the laws of slaveholding Rome survived not only the feudal system but even all phases in the development of capitalism, imperialism included:

*Es erben sich, Gesetz und Recht*
*Wie eine ewige Krankheit fort.*[1]

Bourgeois revolution did not always adhere to Voltaire's words; it did not burn old laws as resolutely as it should, and when it burned them it failed to eradicate them from the minds of the people. As pointed out by Renner, "The human mind is a reliable storehouse in which Moses' stone tables with his commandments are as real as any recent decree issued by the government; in it the ancient historical elements are interwoven with contemporary elements into a single reality." This is the source of all theories of the *divine* origin of such institutions as sacred property, the "inborn" character of class privileges, the "natural right" of the master to the services of the worker, etc.

Whereas socialist theory is a merciless critique of everything in existence, the proletarian revolution is a merciless destroyer of the existing state and social system. . . . As in other fields, in the field of law the proletarian revolution is first to fulfill the prerequisites of true democracy. It translates Voltaire's words into reality and solemnly throws into the fire the sixteen volumes of *The Collection of Laws of*

---

[1] "Law and right are inherited like an eternal disease."

*the Russian Empire* together with its empire and its imperialism. Some of our revolutionaries tried in vain to preserve some of its parts spared by fire . . . , instead of creating new, truly revolutionary law.

The proletarian revolution calls for creativity. It must be courageous, not only in a destructive work, but also in a law-creating role. It may seem that the references to the old law in the decrees of the Workers-Peasants government are highly inappropriate, for the laws of the earlier governments should have been burned. But the socialist upheaval is not simply a leap into the unknown. It is a protracted, more or less long process of civil war, a process that results in the transformation of the bourgeois social system, with its division into classes of oppressors and oppressed, into a socialist system. This transition period requires a special transitional law, in part because the bourgeois system cannot be transformed into a socialist system instantly, and in part because the old system remains in existence in people's minds as a past tradition. This feeling prevails also among all strata of the proletariat, which are merely awakening now and still "whirl in the traditional ideology and nourish themselves with the intellectual leavings of the bourgeoisie."

The Workers-Peasants Revolution found a formula that correctly solves this problem. The Decree on Court (No. 1) asserts that new courts are "guided in their decisions and verdicts by laws of the overthrown government *only if* they were not repealed by the Revolution and are not contradictory to revolutionary conscience and revolutionary law consciousness." This, on the one hand, was an answer to the attempts to retain old laws that, although burned, were still living in people's minds. On the other hand, this was an answer to our right-wing Marxists, who reproached us for having anarchistic tendencies, namely, for our rejection of the laws of earlier governments. I then gave the following answer to our opponents:

Gentlemen, what do you understand under the protection of the rule of law? The protection of the law which belongs to the past social epoch, law that was made by the representatives of social interests that are no longer in existence or are passing away, interests that are contradictory to the needs of society? Social system is not based on law. This is a juridical prejudice. On the contrary, law should be based on the existing social system . . . , law inevitably changes with the changing conditions of life. Protection of old law at the expense of the needs and demands of social development is in essence nothing but a protection of obsolete separate interests at the expense of the present-day interests of the entire society. Such defenders of the rule of law proclaim as governing the interests that in fact are no longer governing. Such a defense thrusts upon society laws that are contradictory to the conditions of life and even to the mode of production. . . . Such phrases about the rule of law constitute either a conscious deception or an unconscious self-deception.

What was the reaction to my answer? Some Marxists stigmatized my answer as anarchistic, and I had to reveal the secret that it was taken literally from Karl Marx's famous speech, delivered to a trial jury in Cologne. No, we are not anarchists; we assign a great, and at times perhaps even too great a significance to law, but only to law of the new system.

. . . Like any state, the Workers-Peasants Soviet Republic is a class state, but its task is not the oppression of the poor in the interest of a clique of the rich; on the contrary, its task is the dictatorship of the poor, i.e., the overwhelming majority, for "the suppression of an insignificant minority, that is, the bourgeoisie, with the aim to liquidate the exploitation of man by man and to establish socialism under which there will be no division into classes and no state authority." A unification of the working citizen and the workingman into a whole takes place in the Soviet Republic.

All revolutions begin with the destruction of Montesquieu's theory of the division of powers. . . . The Soviet authority, which came into being in the R.S.F.S.R., on October 25, 1917, *is at the same time legislative, executive, and judicial authority.* It does not reject a technical division of labor, but it rejects the hypocritical theory of the independence of one branch from another. The dictatorship of the proletariat and of the poor peasants constitutes a single power.

. . . We[2] are told that even today, two years after the October Revolution, we do not yet have a written proletarian law. We could answer that the great French Revolution came into possession of the *Civil Code* only fifteen years after the Revolution, and only after the victory of the counterrevolution. But, as always, we are frank and therefore we state directly that such a written proletarian code will never come into existence in our country. When we speak of the proletarian law, we have in mind a transient law.

Our great achievement in the revolution of law is a clear understanding of the meaning of law and court. "Law is a system or an order of social relationships, corresponding to the interests of the ruling class and protected by an organized force." Hence, without classes, there will be no class organization (the state), no law, and no courts.

---

[2] The following part is taken from P. Stuchka, "Nizverzhenie Prava" [The Overthrow of Law], published at the end of 1919 and reprinted in P. Stuchka, *13 Let Borby za Revolutsionno-Marksistskuyu Teoriyu Prava* [Thirteen years of Struggle for the Revolutionary Marxist Theory of Law] (Moscow, 1931), pp. 227–28.

# "Dialectical Realism" as a Method of Cognition of Social Phenomena*  ↺  *D. Magerovskii*

To an unenlightened man whose thinking is disorganized, the problem of being is nonexistent. The stream of his psychic experiences, in which his "ego" is emersed, is taken by him for the true being. A chaos of sensations and sensory images constitutes the world of his experience. A credulous acceptance of anything that appears in his consciousness and a superficiality in ascertaining facts, the causes generating them, and their significance are the features characteristic of the man whose thinking is undisciplined. His picture of the world surrounding him is unstable and contradictory. Indeed, one could argue that a picture of the world is nonexistent for him; for him there are only separate, disjointed facts, facts that are contradictory, at times meaningless because of their isolation from the whole, and colored with the sensory experiences of both the cognizing subject and his environs. Living in this "distorted" world, in the world of sensory phantasmata and contradictory facts, man acts, i.e., strives to change the existing reality, but fails to attain desired results; the world of objective being refuses to subordinate itself to him.

A mastery over the world is attainable only through organized thinking, which alone is in a position to organize the existence with which it is confronted. The real world does not directly manifest itself to man's consciousness. Man's experience is a product of protracted sedulous work and of a specifically refined and wrought technique of thinking.

That being determines consciousness . . . is a truth that constitutes the cornerstone of any realistic philosophy, and in particular the philosophy of dialectical materialism. As stated by F. Engels, "A

* *From* "Sotsialnoe Bytie i Nauka Prava" [Social Existence and the Science of Law], *Nauchnye Izvestiya* (Moscow, 1922), Vol. 1, pp. 1–33.

[This article was written and accepted for publication in 1920, but, for reasons of "technical nature," was not published until two years later. Magerovskii cautions the reader that a number of propositions presented in the article are not correct and that he consented to publish it in its original form for the following reasons: "(1) it contains a number of propositions advanced in science for the first time . . . ; (2) this article represents a definite stage in my philosophical and scientific development, namely, the transition from objective idealism to dialectical materialism, and this change in my world outlook is but a reflection of what is characteristic of our contemporary social thought, and because of this it is of objective interest" (p. 1).]

method has been found to explain man's knowing by his being, instead of, as heretofore, his being by his knowing."[1] Thus, from the point of view of the philosophy of realism, our consciousness and our experience are deeply rooted in being, are determined by it, and find in it the supreme criterion of their truthfulness. "In practice," says K. Marx, "man must prove the truth, i.e., the reality and power, the this-sidedness of his thinking."[2] This is what distinguishes the philosophy of realism from psychologism, from relativism, and from subjective idealism.

Consciousness is determined by being, but at the same time consciousness is not a passive object mechanically reflecting this being; man's cognitive experience is the product of the activity of the consciousness and of its attitude toward being.[3] An act of contemplation is not contradictory to practice; it is a species of the same genus, of purposive activity. Consciousness is a purposive activity aimed at revealing being, whereas practice is a purposive activity aimed at changing being. Both these activities are closely related, complementary one to the other and each dependent upon the other.

Speaking of the general nature of cognitive activity, we should distinguish three basic phases. The first phase does not constitute an act of cognition, yet at the same time it is an indispensable prerequisite of cognition. It is a life with objects. Living with objects . . . we are with them in a condition of mutual penetration, but, being penetrated by objects, we do not know them. Our cognitive activity, which produces an abstract knowledge, begins to work in this initial stage of penetration. In the second phase of cognition a split in the initial life with objects takes place: we contrapose ourselves to objects. Only on the ground of contraposition of one's self to objects is any knowledge possible. But abstract knowledge is still deficient, because it splits the whole object into separate objects of cognition. Only in the third phase . . . do we attain the real goal of cognition: the contemplation of the true object. From the point of view of real knowledge, the preceding phases are merely instruments in its attainment. The contemplation of the real object is the ultimate aim of our cognitive activity.

The above-mentioned second and third phases of cognition are not temporal phases but logical phases, i.e., they are elements of cognition that appear jointly. By contraposing myself to an object I in-

---

[1] Friedrich Engels, *Anti-Dyuring* [Anti-Dühring] (4th ed.; Petersburg, 1917), pp. 18–19.
[2] Friedrich Engels, *Lyudvig Feierbakh* [Ludwig Feuerbach] (Petersburg, 1906), Appendix: Marx's Theses on Feuerbach, Thesis 2.
[3] *Ibid.*, Thesis 1.

stantly begin to contemplate it, but it appears as something that is covered with the haze of vagueness; only through the differentiation of individual objects does the haze begin to disappear, and my contemplation approaches its goal—the true contemplation of the crystal-clear living object.

The dependence of thinking upon being demonstrates a close dependence of a method of cognition upon the nature of the object of cognition. The methodological principles uncover the object of our cognition and, because of this, blend the gnosiological element with the ontological element. Methodological principles, being a definite point of view on the object of our experience, make possible for us the direct contemplation of this object. The directness of contemplating the object of cognition by means of a methodological principle fosters an illusion of creation of this object by the subject. The history of the idealist system brilliantly demonstrates this constantly recurring cognitional illusion. One of the most vigorous attempts to overcome this idealistic self-deception of the nineteenth century was the creation of the philosophy of dialectical materialism. The idealism, represented by Hegel, aspired to overcome the closed circle of subjective thought by means of objectivizing and identifying it with the world process. But Hegel's thought, arrested in itself, was incapable of resolving itself into the living, real world. "The dialectic of the concept itself," says F. Engels, "now became merely the conscious reflection of the dialectical motion of the real world, and Hegel's dialectic standing on its head was placed upon its feet again."[4] The world, revealed by organized consciousness, is a world of organic unity, is a non-contradictory system purified from sensuous elements. Interrelatedness, interaction, unity, and development are the features characteristic of the organic nature of true being.

Looking from the point of view of the history of the development of human thought, we see that human consciousness succeeded in revealing the specific aspects of being only gradually. . . . At first, only the crude world, the most noticeable world, the world directly affecting man's sensory organs, i.e., only the world of physical being, was revealed to human consciousness. Concepts of space and time, characteristic of this type of being, were regarded for a long time as being indispensable for any being. But gradually a new type of being revealed itself to human consciousness, a type of being in which the concept of space is not inherent. This new type is the world of psychological being. For a long time human consciousness rested on the discovery of these two types of being, attempting to attribute all ex-

4 *Anti-Dyuring*, pp. 32–33.

periences either to the physical or to the psychological being. But the concept of causality and power, characteristic of these two worlds, cannot account for the multiformity of the unfolding world; new facts call for new generalizations, for new points of view. Finally, the conception of a supraspatial being comes into existence, that is, the conception of the teleological or ideal being (the world of numbers, ethical norms, ethical values, cultural values, etc.).

Because of the habit of contemplating separate spheres of being in their isolation and in their specific exclusiveness, human consciousness becomes incapable of comprehending the living objects that constitute the various spheres of being. This inability of philosophical idealism to comprehend the living, organically united, interacting, and developing being was noted by the founders of dialectical materialism. They characterized it as a metaphysical or a mechanistic mode of thinking and contraposed to it organic, dialectic, and realistic thinking. As stated by Engels, investigation in the field of natural science has brought about a few positive results, "but this method of work has also left us as a legacy the habit of observing natural objects and processes in isolation, apart from their connection with the vast whole; of observing them in repose, not in motion; as constants, not as essentially variables; in their death, not in their life."[5] Furthermore, Engels continued, "The metaphysical mode of thought reaches a limit, beyond which it becomes one-sided, restricted, abstract, and lost in insoluble contradictions. In the contemplation of individual things, it forgets the connection between them; in the contemplation of their existence, it forgets the beginning and end of that existence; of their repose, it forgets their motion."[6]

In contrast to the metaphysical mode of thought, the cognitive task of dialectical realism or materialism is the concrete, living totality of being, contemplated in its formation and change. But some followers of dialectical materialism have either simplified or distorted it. For example, some regard the idea as something alien to being, as a product of the brain's transformation of the sensations and the feelings that man receives from the external world. Such a view, on the one hand, simplifies and vulgarizes reality by depriving it of its teleological element, and on the other hand, it separates thinking from being. In their numerous writings, the founders of dialectical materialism have indicated that the ideal has an existential nature, that thought is fused with real or material being. For example, K. Marx asserted: "From idealism, which, by the way, I have equated with Kant's and Fichte's idealism, I arrived at the conclusion that

[5] *Ibid.,* p. 14.    [6] *Ibid.,* p. 15.

*the idea is to be sought in the reality."*[7] Furthermore, "It is not enough that thought strives to be translated into reality; what is necessary is that reality itself should lead to thought."[8] In the writings of F. Engels we find the following view: "Without making blunders, thought can bring together into a unity only those elements of consciousness in which or in whose real prototypes this unity . . . existed before."[9] The view that idea is not abstracted from being itself, that it is a product of man's psyche leads to a dichotomy between thinking and being, to the very dualism that dialectical materialism seeks to overcome, and in fact overcomes, by *finding the idea in reality itself.*

The fundamental features of being are universal: the worlds of cosmic, biological, and social life comprise an organic whole, interconnectedness, interaction, and dialectical development; the idea dissolves itself in all forms of being and permeates the concrete, living reality. To the unity of being corresponds the unity of methodological principles, which lies at the basis of all types of scientific cognition. . . .

Most investigations conducted in the field of social phenomena have either a purely empirical or a utilitarian-applied character. Knowledge of the nature of social being in its organic totality is a result of protracted development of scientific social thought. Law, politics, economics, ideology, etc., have been studied for a long time in isolation from total social life; instead of being studied as functions of the whole, they were studied as independent and isolated phenomena.

All nineteenth- and twentieth-century ventures to study the world of social life as a *sui generis* being fall into two types: (1) studies from the point of view of the law of causality; (2) studies from the non-behavioral, teleological, value point of view. Ventures of the first type were conducted under various sociological banners; ventures of the second type were conducted under sociophilosophical banners.

For a long time, researchers of both integrated social life and its individual manifestations sought to reduce them to the spheres of the earlier-discovered being—either to the sphere of physical being (geographical, biological, ethnological, etc., schools) or to the sphere of psychic being (individual-psychological, collective-psychological, individualistic, etc., schools). Finally, however, the truth has been grasped that the physical and psychic factors merely condition social

---

[7] Marx's letters to Ruge, 1837–38, *Die Neue Zeit,* XVI, 4.

[8] Karl Marx, *Vvedenie k Kritike Filosofii Prava Gegela* [An Introduction to the Critique of Hegel's Philosophy of Right] (Petrograd, 1906), p. 42.

[9] *Anti-Dyuring,* p. 31.

being but do not constitute its *specificum*. As pointed out by Baldwin, "The banks are not the river; chemistry is indispensable to life but is not life; environmental forces are indispensable to evolution but they are not the vital forces; life processes are indispensable to consciousness but they themselves are not psychic processes; consciousness is indispensable to society but not every consciousness is a social consciousness."[10]

In approaching social being and its phenomena as a *sui generis* being, sociological schools have, for the most part, dwelt only on its causal and power aspects without noticing the ideas by which social being is penetrated. Furthermore, they have failed to notice its organizational-volitional nature, as well as the living, organic totality of this multiform being. The object of study was completely beyond their ideological grasp, and all their attempts to contemplate and to act upon social being failed, because social being is not exhausted by the mere mechanics of power.

We indicated earlier that the second type of studies of social being and its phenomena was conducted under the banner of philosophy, that is, the philosophy of history, law, ethics, aesthetics, etc. In the writings of Kant, Fichte, Hegel, and, at the present time, in the writings of Cohen and Rickert, we find examinations of social being and its phenomena. Whereas the first type of theorist treats the object of study as belonging to the sphere of causal-power being, the second type of theorists investigates the object of study from the point of view of a non-behavioral, teleological, value being. Arrested forms, abstract schemes, and lifeless objects, which replace the concrete, living, social being, are frequently the results of such an approach.

The nature of social being requires that it should be contemplated both in the sphere of causality and power and in the sphere of values and teleology. Overcoming the narrowness of each of these two modes of thinking is indispensable for a social scientist. . . . Value and power are blended in social reality. Hence, the true task of social science is to study their confluence in the various spheres of social life.

. . . Only one who regards theory as a prelude to action is capable of grasping the nature of social being, for social being is a continuous action. K. Marx, the great social theorist, applied to the study of social being the same principles that he applied to the study of nature. The organic totality of social being is the first axiom of Marxism. According to Marx, "Man is not an abstract being inhabiting the outer

[10] James M. Baldwin, *Dukhovnoe Razvitie s Sotsiologicheskoi i Eticheskoi Tochki Zreniya* [Spiritual Development from the Sociological and Ethical Viewpoints] (n.p., 1913), Vol. 1, p. 9, translation of *Social and Ethical Interpretations in Mental Development* (New York–London, 1897).

world; man's world is society, the state."[11] "Human essence is no abstraction inherent in each single individual. In its reality it is an aggregate of social relations."[12] The *interdependence* of the subjects of social life was thus declared to be the first and the fundamental feature of social being. Again, according to Engels, "It is not a question so much of the motives of single individuals, however eminent, as of those motives that set in motion great masses, whole peoples, and whole classes of the people; and here, too, not the transient flaring up of a straw fire which quickly dies down, but a lasting action resulting in a great historical transformation."[13] Furthermore, "In the history of society all acting forces are endowed with consciousness, and are acting with deliberation and passion, working toward definite goals. But this distinction, important as it is for historical investigations, particularly of single epochs and events, cannot alter the fact that the course of history is governed by general inner laws."[14] Though stressing the inner laws of historical process, F. Engels has cautioned that it is not a mechanical, automatic process: "Men make their own history, whatever its outcome may be, in that each person follows his own consciously desired ends, and it is precisely the resultant of these many wills operating in different directions and of their manifold effects upon the outer world which constitutes history."[15] Similarly, K. Marx reproached both Feuerbach, for not viewing human activity as an objective activity, and the materialistic doctrine, which asserts that men are products of circumstances and upbringing, and which neglects the fact that circumstances are changed precisely by men and that the educator must himself be educated.[16]

In noting the totality, interdependence, and activism of social being, Marxism deems it to be its principal task to discover inner tendencies of social being, tendencies that determine and condition the activity of men, classes, and people. By knowing the inner laws of social development, man will be able to master social being to the same extent that he is capable of mastering cosmic and organic forces. Knowing the nature of social being, man will be capable of changing it, thus helping the basic inner tendencies of social development to assert themselves. As pointed out by K. Marx, "The philosophers have interpreted the world in various ways; the point, however, is to change it."[17]

[11] *Vvedenie*, p. 31.
[12] Marx's Theses on Feuerbach, Thesis 6, cited in Engels' *Feierbakh*, pp. 51–52.
[13] *Ibid.*, p. 39.        [14] *Ibid.*, p. 37.        [15] *Ibid.*
[16] Marx's Theses on Feuerbach, Thesis 3.
[17] Marx's Theses on Feuerbach, Thesis 11.

Thus we see that an aggregate of actions of interdependent social subjects constitutes the substance of social life. Owing to this, social action is the central concept in investigating the nature of social being. Action in general is a purposive activity aimed at changing being.[18] If the action of a social subject is examined apart from the actions of other social subjects, it does not lead us to the process of social life.

. . . Purposive moment in social action has been stressed by K. Marx, who described it as an inevitable element of man's social life: "What distinguishes the worst architect from the best of bees is this, that the architect raises his structure in imagination before he erects it in reality. At the end of every labor process, we get a result that already existed in the imagination of the laborer at its commencement, that existed, so to speak, ideally. Man not only effects a change of form in the material given by nature, but he also projects into this material his own conscious goal which, like the law, determines his mode of operation, and to which he must subordinate his will."[19]

Social actions may be directed either directly toward the attainment of social ends, or toward the actions of other people. In both cases the attainment of the ends intended by social action necessitates definite rules that would promote their attainment: in the former case, methodological, aesthetic, technical, etc., rules are necessary; in the latter case, legal norms are necessary. Legal norms are rules demarcating, coordinating, and directing actions of social subjects; thereby the directing property of legal norms may either promote or bring to a stop definite actions of social subejcts. To put it differently, law channels and shapes spontaneous social actions. Law connects organically all actions of social subjects. In directing social actions, law itself is subject to change, either directly during its application, or under the influence of the principal inner forces of social life, which, in the final analysis, determine the actions of social subjects.

. . . Just as the conduct of one individual is evaluated by another individual . . . , the conduct of individual members of a society is evaluated from the point of view of the norms governing that society. A legal norm states how a given member of a given society ought to behave. The totality of all legal norms in a society stipulates conditions under which all members of society ought to behave in a specific way, that is, it teaches *how the society in which they live should be organized.*

. . . Thus the question arises, "What is the source of norms?" In

---

[18] An action is distinct from a movement in that the former pursues a goal whereas the movement changes being independent of any goal.

[19] *Kapital* [Capital], ed. Struve (Petrograd, 1899), I, 127.

answering this question, we encounter complex economic, ideological, and political forces that give rise to norms. At times we see human actions that cannot be brought under a common denominator, uncoordinated actions seeking to attain common goals. The forces of the developing collective give rise to norms that demarcate and coordinate the actions of social subjects, i.e., *organize* previously unsystematized actions. Concentrating on our environment, but especially on the class struggle and, in general, on the conflicts between social groups, we begin to discern the delicately woven pattern of social forces and causative and purposive interactions that give rise to social norms and to social organization. . . .

Now, penetrating the real nature of law, we shall examine conditions that determine human actions. According to Engels, "Everything that sets men in motion must go through their minds; but what form it will take in the mind will depend very much upon the circumstances."[20] The actions of every man are determined by the necessities generated by his existence. "Thus it is a question of what the many individuals desire,"[21] though, since we study social being, we should not deal with individual persons but with collectives; hence, of special interest to us are the necessities of collectives. "It is not a question so much of the motives of single individuals, however eminent, as of those motives that set in motion great masses, whole peoples, and whole classes of the people; and here, too, not the transient flaring up of a straw fire which quickly dies down, but a lasting action resulting in a great historical transformation."[22] Human necessities are of two types: economic and ideological. In examining the development of social being, we notice that the relationship between human necessities is governed by a definite law. The primary necessities of the collective life, which must be satisfied before any other, are economic. Only after the minimum of economic necessities has been satisfied does man turn to the satisfaction of ideological necessities. The development and the satisfaction of the ideological necessities of the masses take place on a basis nurtured by economic stimuli and lead the masses to action. The foregoing leads us to the conclusion that the ideological side of social existence is historically conditioned, that is, is conditioned by its economic side. Nevertheless, it would be wrong to establish a constant law of causal dependence of the ideological being upon the economic. Economic phenomena precede, condition, determine, but do not engender ideological phenomena. All changes in economic phenomena are reflected in ideological phenomena, which makes us conclude that there is a *functional*

[20] *Feierbakh*, p. 39.          [21] *Ibid.*, p. 37.          [22] *Ibid.*, p. 39.

*dependence* between economic and ideological phenomena. Nevertheless, the functional dependence between economic and ideological
phenomena is not an exclusive and sole principle of the development
of social existence. At a certain point of their development, ideological phenomena, which have grown on the foundation of economic
structure, begin to exert influence and to condition the economic side
of social life.[23]

The law of dependence of the ideological side of social existence on
its economic side has a historical, not an absolute meaning. It has
been effective in history till now, but its force will be *surmounted* in
the course of development of social exstence. *From economic necessity toward ideological freedom*—this is the social ideal that the
masses should strive to realize. In other words, when humanity has
mastered nature, has decreased labor waste, has completely satisfied
economic necessities, it will, owing to perfection of technology and
collectivist organization of production and distribution, arrive at a
point at which it will make a leap from the realm of necessity into the
realm of freedom.[24] This will be a society of creative people or, to
use Marx's words, it will be an "association in which free development of each is the condition for free development of all."[25]

But the future, free human society is being born in the pangs of
historical process. Economic necessities of the collective give rise to
its economic organization. Historical process reveals great social antagonisms in the system of economic organization, which is shaped
and secured by the corresponding legal organization. The social process of producing economic values is at the same time a process of the
disintegration of the collective into antagonistic groups. . . .

The class structure of society makes an imprint upon the entire
legal organization of society as well as upon the goals pursued and
materialized by social authority. This is so because the economically
dominant class holds in its hands the state authority, and the legal
system is geared toward reflecting in its norms the ideals of the ruling
class. . . .

The science of law should not limit itself to the study of the social
forces that gave rise to legal orders. . . . It should also point out the
ways for the creation of a new legal order. A legal theorist cannot be
a passive observer of social life; he must be its active builder; he
should be a social technician in the full meaning of the term.

. . . The science of law, the objective of which is the study of the

[23] See Plekhanov, *Osnovnye Voprosy Marksizma* [The Fundamental Problems of Marxism] (Moscow, 1920), pp. 36–37.
[24] See Engels, *Feierbakh*, p. 237.
[25] *Kommunisticheskii Manifest* [The Communist Manifesto] (n.p., n.d.).

nature and types of social organization, is a mighty instrument in the struggle of classes and political parties. The ability to organize one's class or party and to disorganize one's opponent is the prerequisite for a quick and lasting victory. At all times the ruling classes have recognized the significance of jurists as social organizers of the legal system which strengthens the authority of these classes. The ruling class has assigned a task, and jurists, through their interpretation of the application of legal norms, have found the most elastic and expedient forms for the materialization of the policy of the ruling class. The jurist has become accustomed to this policy and to the forms of its materialization to the degree that the entire system of positive norms and institutions has become his second nature. His mentality was developed and permeated by the spirit of the positive law. Jurists always have been the most valuable servants and agents of the ruling classes. Being brought up on the positive law and being permeated by its ideology, they have been the most conservative element in revolutionary movements. A new class arising in the arena of social life would find in them most savage and uncompromising enemies: they would be incapable of being permeated by the spirit and the form of new law. As members of new institutions, they would fail for the most part in adapting themselves to the spirit and activity of these institutions, even if they wanted to: the defunct institutions still would be alive in their consciousness and would persist in governing their will.

Therefore, the task of a new class, of a class asserting its authority, is to create new jurists, new social technicians, who would build new institutions and direct their transforming activity. The proletariat is entering the arena of world domination. Its task could be expressed in the following slogan: not death to all law and all jurists, but death to old law and its old servants; life to the education of new social technicians, of new jurists. The proletariat should advance future jurists from its own womb, for its class consciousness should be the departure point of its legal practice. The science of law has been a mighty instrument in the hands of monarchy and bourgeoisie; the working class should exploit the science of law for the construction of the organs of its own dictatorship. However, the builders of the organs of the proletarian dictatorship should be aware that they are specialists merely for a brief period. The dictatorship of the proletariat is transitional, and the time is near when it will be transformed into labor cooperation, in which everyone will be a participant and a builder of free forms in a creative life.

# The Marxist Class Theory of Law* ∽ *P. Stuchka*

Had I to write for a Marxist journal on the Marxist understanding of mathematics, astronomy, or religion, I would feel much better than when writing on law; for who will read an article on law and a theoretical one at that? We are more interested in the questions of our relationship to distant planets or to even more distant gods than in the question of relationships between men.

. . . Were we asked . . . about our Marxist understanding of law, then, I am afraid, it would become apparent that we do not have, and cannot have, such an understanding; for, on the question of law —as on many other questions—we think in a purely bourgeois manner. I might add that this is quite understandable and natural.

In an introductory lecture to the courses for people's judges delivered in 1918, I happened to use the following phrase: *"At the moment we are not so much in need of jurists as of communists."* In saying this I had in mind, of course, old bourgeois jurists whom I contraposed to communists with the revolutionary legal consciousness. I did not realize at that time that my contraposition had been presaged at one time by Engels. In the process of writing my work on the Marxist theory of law I encountered an interesting editorial in *Die Neue Zeit* (1887) directed against "Juridical Socialism." This editorial, I found . . . , had been written jointly by Engels and Kautsky, who stated: "Religious banners waved for the last time in England in the seventeenth century, and hardly fifty years later a new world outlook appeared, undisguised, in France. This new world outlook was destined *to become the classical outlook of the bourgeoisie: the juristic world outlook.* . . . It was a secularization of the theological outlook. Man-made law took the place of the dogma of divine law; the state took the place of the church."

Since Engels opposed the Christian world outlook to the *juridical* or bourgeois world outlooks (treating the latter two as identical), we ought, quite legitimately, after the victory of the proletariat, to oppose the bourgeois or *juridical* world outlook to the proletarian or the *communist* world outlook. To be able to oppose such a new world outlook, however, it must be formulated, for it does not exist in nature in a ready-made form. And, as long as we have not yet formu-

* *From* "Marksistskoe Ponimanie Prava" [The Marxist Understanding of Law], *Kommunisticheskaya Revolutsiya*, No. 13–14 (37–38) (November, 1922), reprinted in P. Stuchka, *13 Let Borby za Revolutsionno-Marksistskuyu Teoriyu Prava* [Thirteen Years of Struggle for the Revolutionary Marxist Theory of Law] (Moscow, 1931), pp. 67–76.

lated it, the old, i.e., *bourgeois or juridical, world outlook* will prevail, unnoticed, in our minds as before.

. . . If we intend to expand our understanding of Marx and Marxism (and such an expansion is vital), and if we do not want to arrive at the point of full degeneration, then the problem of law (i.e., the problem of the definite order of human relations) must assume one of the prominent places in historical materialism . . . together with the problem of social classes and the class struggle.

## CLASS AND LAW

I place the problem of law in the forefront to stress the fact that I am not as concerned with legal problems as with class problems, i.e., with the fundamental problems of the Marxist world outlook, and ultimately, with communism. Still, not long ago, we were unable to comprehend adequately the problem of the classes and class struggle; however, to be able to explain the idea of a class law and the class protection of this law (i.e., class judiciary), we must have, primarily, a clear view of the idea of classes and the class struggle.

Certainly it is not an accident that Kautsky . . . contended that a class "represents not only a common source of income but also, arising from the latter, common interests and a common antagonism toward other classes, each seeking to use the source of income of another for its own enrichment." Should *class* be defined according to the distribution of income, however, then the class struggle is reduced to the struggle for income of one class at the expense of another; i.e., for the distribution of products, this would mean that the struggle is reduced to an economic struggle of the classes, all of them tied together by this common goal. Such an explanation would be acceptable to any Scheidemannist, especially with the stipulation given by Kautsky that a similar antagonism of interests also exists between the individual subdivisions within these classes.

Marx explicitly stated that the principal factors responsible for the division of people into social classes is the *distribution of the people in production* and the distribution of the means of production among them, and that in its turn the process of production determines the process of distribution of products. Fin-Enotaevskii gave a reply to Kautsky in 1906 in which he proved, by quoting Marx's words, that "classes are determined by the distribution of the elements of production" and that "classes are determined by their role and their relationship in the process of production." The revolutionary class struggle is, consequently, nothing but *the struggle for a role in production,* for the distribution of the means of production. Hence, since the distribution of the means of production is expressed and secured in the law of private property, the struggle for the role in production becomes the struggle for or against the right of private ownership for these means of production. The revolutionary class struggle is thus *a struggle conducted around the law,* because of the law, and *in the name of one's own class law. . . .*

If, under law, we understand *a definite order of social relationships* (i.e., the interrelationships of the people in production and exchange —and this is the understanding at which even bourgeois science, namely, the sociological school, arrived), then it becomes obvious to us that such an order cannot be eternal or immutable, that, in fact, it changes with the victory of the classes. Since it is a product of the class struggle, law always has a class character. Bourgeois science failed to arrive at such a conclusion and, therefore, even its finest representatives find themselves in an impasse from which there is no escape. Socialists, not excluding Marxists, keep company with bourgeois scientists. Thus, we are accustomed to speaking of *class judiciary;* however, prior to the Revolution of 1917 we opposed it in favor of an independent, impartial judiciary. The same is still being done by all socialists who either have forgotten—or are unfamiliar with—Marx's words: "What an unreal illusion a nonpartisan court is when the legislator himself is partisan; of what value is an impartial judicial decision when the law is partial?" They also spoke about the *class state* but compared it to a pure, genuine democracy. Even communists—who recognize the class character of all states and who oppose the bourgeois class judiciary to the class judiciary of the proletariat—have failed to understand the idea of *class law.* Could there be, in fact, a class law and a class justice?

At this point we shall not argue with the proponents of the idea of eternal, sacred, divine, etc., law . . . however, we shall take, as an example, a Marxist scientist who plays an outstanding role in the theory of Soviet law. In Comrade Magerovskii's article[1] the following is to be found: "Among the totality of social relationships and, in particular, among economic relationships, some stand out that are *fixed by the collective,* through means of social norms, as *relationships* externally binding to all members and *safeguarded by society* against violation. *This system of externally binding social norms, supported and protected by society against violation, is, precisely, the law,* and the social relationships regulated and organized by this law are *legal relationships."*

It is evident that Magerovskii's views closely approximate our definition of law. He speaks of the legal relationships and of the system

---

[1] D. Magerovskii, "Sovetskoe Pravo i Metody Ego Izucheniya" [Soviet Law and Methods of Its Study], *Sovetskoe Pravo,* No. 1 (1922), pp. 24–32.

of social relationships. But, while we assert that the system of social relationships is supported and protected, by the class state, i.e., by a class, he maintains that it is supported and protected by *society,* or, as he states elsewhere, by a *collective.* This means that the *social will* or the *social contract* is the source of law. As a result, *law appears not as a class but as a social institution.*

We read further that "as long as we are studying the law of a class society, the socioclass point of view . . . has an unconditional validity for us, and *the law of this society* will constitute a system of externally binding social norms, *supported and protected against violations by the economically ruling class of this society.*" Something is incorrect here, for, according to one definition, law is a product of the whole society and is protected by the whole society, while, according to another definition, it is protected merely by a class. Hence it would appear that Comrade Magerovskii has failed to find one definition of law: *in one case* it is a *social* law (in a preclass or postclass society) while *in another case* it is a *class* law (i.e., in a class society).

Were we to follow the valuable acquisition of the bourgeois sociological school (for example, Professor Murovtsev), who states that law is not simply an aggregate of norms (we shall not argue at this point whether these norms are of an "internal" or "external" use) but is a system, i.e., an order of social relations, then it will become clear to those of us who recognize the theory of revolutionary class struggle that this order is an object or a result of the class struggle or rather a result of the victory in this struggle of one or another class: which is to say that the law in this society is a class law.

. . . The ideas of "class" and "law"—especially at the present time —are inseparable. We use the term law for defining the distribution of people in production, i.e., the distribution of the means of production (private property) and the role of people in production, protected by the state power of a class state. This is precisely the society that is known as a *legal* order or a *Rechtsstaat.* The class struggle is reduced now to all-out protection of this legal order on the one hand, and to an attempt to overthrow this state and social order on the other.

WHAT IS THE LAW?

My book *The Revolutionary Role of Law and State* demonstrates that the bourgeoisie could not find a scientific definition of law and also of state, because it failed to adopt the class point of view. Indeed, it could not afford to adopt this point of view since it would have been tantamount to the recognition of the proletarian revolution. I have shown in the preceding section that law is purely a class idea.

First, our definition of law asserts that law is "a *system* or an *order of social relationships;"* secondly, that the determining element of this order or this system is the *interest* of the ruling class; thirdly, that this system or this order of social relationships is maintained in an *organized way,* i.e., that it is supported and protected against violations by the *organization of the ruling class*—the state. Hence, in law we distinguish *its content* (social relationships) and *the form* of its regulation and protection (the state power, statutes, etc.). Such a distinction was made by Marx (see the Introduction to his *Critique of Political Economy*) when he spoke (1) of "property" and (2) of "forms" for securing this property (courts, police, etc.). It was in the famous Preface to his *Critique* that he spoke of "relations of production or—*speaking juridically—property relations."* In another instance he illustrated that any mode of production, that is to say any society, has its own specific type of "property" (mode of appropriation). Therefore, taking into account the achievements of the sociological "science of law," we are able to define law as a system or an order of social relationships (i.e., relations of production and exchange—briefly, property relations).

. . . While we place at the *basis of law its content* (the "system of social relationships") some writers place at its basis the *form of law,* i.e., *the system or the aggregate of norms* or, more specifically, of social norms, which are manifestations of the will of neither a society, a people, nor a class. In other words, they commit the same error as the bourgeois jurists who, speaking of *law in the objective sense,* had in mind an aggregate of written laws. In turn, the relationships regulated by this objective law are conceived by the bourgeoisie as law in the subjective sense. Here we see clearly the dividing line between us and the bourgeois world outlook—the world outlook of a society of goods producers. We designate social relationships as *the objective content* of law; the bourgeois jurists designate the form of law, the *manifestation of a will,* or, simply, a *will.* We consider the form (the will) to be a *subjective element,* while the bourgeoisie attributes "subjectivity" to the *content* of law (to social relationships). Bourgeois jurists consider the form, the subjective element, as the basis, and the content or the objective element as the superstructure. In this respect law constitutes no exception. That is why, if we desire to remain Marxists, we must break off with the volitional theory of bourgeois science, because it does not lend itself to the adaptation to Marxism. At the same time the interest theory of bourgeois jurisprudence is a direct forerunner of the Marxist conception of law; one has only to introduce the class point of view.

. . . In our judgment the decisive role belongs to the objective element, to the interest,[2] which determines the will of the individual and, to an even greater degree, class consciousness. In the aggregate of norms (written, legal norms; customs; judicial practice; etc.) we see merely the form of law, its subjective element. Hence, to be able to put an end to all idealist survivals, we must break off once and for all from the volitional theory of law.

The volitional theory of law had a real meaning when people believed in the will of a higher being or in the creative force of an absolute idea. . . .

. . . But volitional theory is also being connected with the teleological theory. According to this theory, the purpose of law is merely a part of the world's and humanity's purpose. In this category belongs the ultimate purpose of the eloquent, idle-talking Stammler, who is quite popular in our country. His "unconditional, final purpose of human society is an ideal unity. . . . It will be a society of free-willing people (*frei wollender Menschen*)."

. . . To be sure, we do recognize goals, and in issuing written laws we seek to achieve them. That is why some contend that our class will, the aggregate of our decrees, is our class law. But this proves precisely the contrary. The aggregate of our decrees has never embraced, and does not now embrace, the entire sphere of legal relationships; that is why we introduced the idea of a revolutionary legal consciousness. At the time when we were threatening speculators with severe punishment, they were celebrating at Sukharovka and elsewhere the orgies of their profiteering relations. And the fact that today we are legalizing some of these orgies hardly corresponds to the free will of the proletarian class. No, the will of a statute is not the single creator of law; this will is powerless *against* the economic "laws of nature." Shchedrinski's pompadour in vain issued *ukazes* to stop the flow of water in the rivers. As long as we were guided by the laws of economic development in issuing our decrees, we hastened the advance of history. What is the point, then, to speak about will as the decisive element when it is merely *a reflection of the true consciousness of the class interest.*

We should not be blamed for disregarding law in general. On the contrary, at times we have placed too great a trust in the force of decrees. . . . We will be on the right path when we adopt our scientific definition of law, according to which law is a system, an order, of social relationships or, in other words, *a system of organized protection of the class* interests. . . .

---

[2] Ihering, a bourgeois scientist, says: "Even logic is subordinated to interest."

# Law, Socialism, and State Capitalism in the Transition
# Period* ∞ *D. Magerovskii*

Law is a sphere of social life to which Marxist thought, and in particular the founders of dialectical materialism, paid little attention. While adequate attention was given by them to the study of philosophy, of economy, and even to the study of the state—a phenomenon closely connected with law—the nature of law remained beyond the scope of their study. The theory of state in the transition period from capitalism to communism was carefully developed by K. Marx in a number of his works, but of law in the transition period we know little.

. . . Law exists not only in societies divided into social classes; there were, and there will be, classless societies that had, and will have, law (primitive society and socialist society). At the present time there are societies existing within the framework of a class (for example, associations of employers and labor unions) which also employ law. Law is necessitated not only by inner class contradictions in a society but also by a society's relation to nature and to other antagonistic societies. Law existed in a primitive communist society because there man depended extensively upon external nature, which necessitated the creation of an extraordinarily rigid legal order, an order that would insure the possibility of the physical existence of society. Law has also existed, and is existing, in all class societies; it organizes the dominant class economically, subordinates to its will the exploited class, and thereby prevents society from disintegrating. Law will also exist in a classless socialist society; only in the communist society, when man has subordinated to his will not only social forces but also natural forces, can he forsake an externally binding order of social relationships of any kind; and law will die away because of uselessness, as the state dies away in the preceding period (in socialist society). But as long as there is a class society there is law, and . . . the law of this society constitutes a *system of externally binding social norms, supported and protected against violations by the economically dominant class of this society.*

". . . Between the capitalist and the communist society lies the pe-

* *From* "Sovetskoe Pravo i Metody Ego Izucheniya" [Soviet Law and Methods of Its Study], *Sovetskoe Pravo*, No. 1 (1922), pp. 24–32.

riod of revolutionary transformation from one to the other. There corresponds to this also a political transition period in which the state can be nothing but the revolutionary dictatorship of the proletariat."[1] These are the views of the great founder of scientific socialism, who deduced an exact, though abstract, formula for the future transition period between capitalism and communism from his analysis of social reality. The period between 1917 and 1921 reveals to us the concrete content of the political form of this transition period, namely, the form of a Soviet republic.

The law of the R.S.F.S.R. offers a most vivid and typical example of a regime of the revolutionary dictatorship of the proletariat. The great monument to the Revolution is the law that has been brought forth by the Revolution. . . . The October Revolution overthrew the bourgeois system of Russia as well as the entire system of legal relationships, which supported and organized the class rule of Russian landlords and capitalists. After the victorious Revolution, the proletariat brilliantly exploited the organizational force of legal norms. . . . The developing social struggle forced the class that took the power into its hands to create a simple and elastic, but nevertheless militant, organizational apparatus. The preservation of victory required the ability to organize oneself and to disorganize the ranks of the class enemy. Soviet law, engendered in the womb of the proletarian spirit, has brought about an unprecedented system of social organization. It sought to accomplish simultaneously and collaterally two tasks: to create a powerful apparatus for the class struggle directed against both the Russian and the international bourgeoisie and to prepare conditions for the construction of a socialist society. The "Declaration of the Rights of the Working and Exploited People" proclaims that the principal goal of Soviet Russia is the "merciless liquidation of the exploiters" as well as "the establishment of the socialist organization in society."[2]

Recognizing that the system of state power rests on the system of economic organization and on the form of economic power, and, furthermore, recognizing that he who holds economic wealth also holds political power, the Russian proletariat has proclaimed socialization of land, nationalization of forests and natural resources, nationalization of banks, and workers' control over production as the first step toward transferring the means of production into the hands of the Soviet Republic.

[1] Karl Marx, *Kritika Gotskoi Programmy* [Critique of the Gotha Program] (Petrograd, 1919), p. 32.
[2] R.S.F.S.R., Constitution (1918), Art. 3.

In the bourgeois state the state authority was the center for guiding the network of capitalist organizations. Having seized the state authority, the proletariat accomplishes two goals: (1) it smashes into pieces the organizational center of the bourgeoisie; (2) it builds up a most powerful apparatus for guiding the organizations of the workers and the exploited. The class struggle, after the proletariat's seizure of the state authority, enters a new phase of its development; all aspects of the struggle acquire an unprecedented systematic character. However, in contrast to the bourgeoisie, which took power into its hands for the purpose of securing the principle of private property "forever," and of creating an "immutable" order of the exploitation of man by man, the proletariat seizes power with the aim of "destroying the exploitation of man by man and building up socialism, in which there will be no classes and no state authority."[3]

In studying Soviet law, we note, before anything else, its dual nature. On the one hand, it is still directed toward the past, toward bourgeois society; it still comprises elements of bourgeois law. On the other hand, it is directed toward the future, toward a socialist society, and, owing to this, it comprises elements of socialist law. Soviet law has a dual nature because of the nature of social relationships, but, in particular, because of the *production relationships* in the Soviet system, which determine both the form and the content of law. The Soviet system does not destroy the bourgeoisie; it remains in existence as a class. In *The Communist Manifesto* Marx stated the following: "The proletariat will use its political power to wrest, *by degree,* all capital from the bourgeoisie, to centralize all instruments of production in the hands of the state, i.e., in the hands of the proletariat organized as the ruling class; and to increase the total amount of productive forces as rapidly as possible." Following this statement, Marx enumerated the significant measures that will be introduced by the proletariat, which has elevated itself to the dominant class in the most advanced countries. These measures are: abolition of private ownership of land and application of all rents of land to public purpose, a heavy progressive or graduated income tax, abolition of all right of inheritance, confiscation of the property of all emigrants and rebels, centralization of the means of communication and transport in the hands of the state, and centralization of credit in the hands of the state. Marx thought that even in the most advanced countries the bourgeoisie, removed from political power and restricted in its property rights, would continue to exist, though in a framework deter-

[3] *Ibid.,* Art. 9.

96                                    SOVIET POLITICAL THOUGHT

mined by the proletariat, to the moment "when, in the course of development, class distinctions have disappeared and all production
has been concentrated in the hands of the united members of society."[4]

In its "Declaration of the Rights of Workers and Exploited People," the Constitution of the R.S.F.S.R. proclaims the main goals
and tasks of the Soviet Republic and enumerates the measures that
will create the economic foundation for the political authority of the
proletariat, and which, essentially, correspond to the measures outlined in The Communist Manifesto. However, among these measures,
neither the state monopoly of the instruments of agricultural production nor the state monopoly of domestic commerce is listed; nor is
the inevitability of a complete nationalization of production mentioned. In the chapter devoted to Soviet electoral law the various
categories of citizens who are deprived of electoral rights are listed;
this demonstrates that the bourgeoisie and bourgeois relationships
will continue to exist in the Soviet regime. From this we deduce that
neither The Communist Manifesto nor the Soviet Constitution presupposed that the measures we took in the epoch of so-called "war
communism" were absolutely necessary. The New Economic Policy,
functioning within the existing framework, neither deprives the Soviet
Constitution of its economic basis nor restrains it.

Mention should be made in this context of the principle of equalization of wages advanced in the "epoch of war communism." In
Critique of the Gotha Program Marx stated that even in a socialist
society (or, to use Marx's expression, in the "first phase of communist society"), in which class distinctions are absent, "the same principle prevails in the distribution of products among producers as "in
the exchange of commodity equivalents: a given amount of labor in
one form is exchanged for an equal amount of labor in another
form."[5] The "rights of the producers are proportional to the labor
they supply; the equality consists in the fact that the measurement is
made with an equal, standard labor."[6] This right "tacitly recognizes
unequal individual endowments and, thus, unequal individual productive capacities as natural privileges."[7] "But these defects," Marx continued, "are as inevitable in the first phase of communist society as
they are when they have just emerged after prolonged birth pangs

---

[4] Kommunisticheskii Manifest [The Communist Manifesto] (n.p., n.d.).
[5] Kritika Gotskoi Programmy [Critique of the Gotha Program] (Petrograd,
1892), p. 16.
[6] Ibid., p. 17.
[7] Ibid.

from capitalist society. Rights can never be higher than the economic structure of society and its cultural development conditioned thereby."[8] Only in a communist society, when man has subordinated natural forces, and when, owing to this, the quantity of products has reached such abundance that each man can be satisfied according to his needs, does the law become useless and die away.[9] Economic necessity (the degree of the development of the production force) forces Soviet law to apply the principle of individual and collective interestedness in remunerating the producers, that is, the principle of the bourgeois law.

Thus, we see the following features of the Soviet system: (1) the bourgeoisie remains in existence; (2) the economic rights of the bourgeoisie are restricted by the proletariat; (3) the bourgeoisie is cast away from the apparatus of state power; (4) the proletariat holds power in its own hands through the nationalization of land, banks, transportation, and individual branches of heavy industry; (5) the personal interest of the workers regulates the intensiveness of labor. The enumerated factors describe a part of the real social relationships that constitute the basis of Soviet law. These relationships of production, and along with them the relationships of exchange, constitute the *peculiar relationships of state capitalism*. They are peculiar because state capitalism under the dictatorship of the bourgeoisie is a system of the expanded economic power of the bourgeoisie, whereas state capitalism under the dictatorship of the proletariat is a system of the restricted economic power of the bourgeoisie. The old relationships of production have not yet been destroyed by the proletariat, which became the ruling class, but are changing in the following ways: (1) the proletariat has confined them to a definite framework; (2) the proletariat determines economic goals that the bourgeoisie must inescapably materialize. Indeed, the bourgeoisie remains as a bourgeoisie, but now it serves the aims of the proletariat. This is the meaning of state capitalism under the dictatorship of the proletariat.

The remaining . . . relationships of production which constitute the basis of the Soviet law are the *peculiar relationships of the agrarian étatisme*. Their peculiarity consists in that agrarian *étatisme* under the dictatorship of both the bourgeoisie and the landed class constitutes a system of expanded power of these classes, whereas, under the dictatorship of the proletariat, agrarian *étatisme* expands the power

---

[8] *Ibid.*, p. 18.
[9] *Ibid.*

of the proletariat in its union with the peasantry. Social relationships
of agrarian *étatisme* under the dictatorship of the proletariat have the
following features: (1) the private ownership of land has been abolished and, owing to this, the class of landlords has been destroyed;
(2) the ownership of land is in the hands of the state; (3) the state
power is in the hands of the proletariat in conjunction with the
peasantry; (4) the peasantry has the right both to use the land and to
devise the forms of its use; (5) the proletariat, as a result of its
monopoly of credit and foreign commerce and of its leading role in
industry, regulates agricultural production.

. . . The significance of Soviet law in consolidating the dictatorship
of the proletariat is obvious. Unfortunately, inadequate recognition
of this fact is quite widespread, both among the party workers and
among Soviet workers in general. This is detrimental to attempts to
set up a Soviet apparatus, to regulate social life, and to conduct a
desirable policy. Law is a very sensitive instrument; an unskillful
handling of law may backfire upon the one who uses it.

# Inconsistencies in the Marxist Theory of Basis and Superstructure*   ᔆᕦᕱ   P. Stuchka

Marx used the contraposition of basis and superstructure as a *figurative expression;* but he did not invent it (see his *Theories of Surplus Value*). Neither his nor Engels' use of this picture was especially consistent. In the *Critique of Political Economy* Marx spoke about the economic structure of society (the sum total of the relations of production) as the real basis above which rise juridical and political superstructures, etc. He described this "immense superstructure" as juridical, political, religious, etc., in one word, ideological forms of "man's *consciousness and struggle."* In *Eighteenth Brumaire* he stated the following: *"Above the various forms of property,* above social conditions of existence, rises *the whole superstructure* of various and peculiarly made-up sensations, illusions, and views on society."

In his *Theories of Surplus Value* . . . we encounter the phrase "that contradictions in material production made necessary *a superstructure of various strata of ideologists."* In *Anti-Dühring* Engels spoke of the "investigation of human living conditions, *social relations, legal and state forms, together with their ideological superstructures."* At any rate, it is difficult to believe that Marx and Engels had in mind a Philistine architectural picture of a multistoried building with the first, second, etc., floors rising above the solid "foundation."

It seems to me that Marx had in mind simply a figurative expression of his philosophical views on being and consciousness, nothing more nor less. Nevertheless, economic relations, and legal relations as their concrete legal expressions, i.e., *as a concrete system of social relations among men,* belong to the basis, while their abstract form (written law, ideology, etc.) belongs to the superstructure.

* *From* "Materialisticheskoe ili Idealisticheskoe Ponimanie Prava?" [Materialist or Idealist Understanding of Law?], *Pod Znamenem Marksizma*, No. 1 (1923), pp. 177–78.

# A Normative Conception of Law: Podvolotskii versus Stuchka* ∾ *I. Podvolotskii*

## LAW—A SYSTEM OF NORMS OR A SYSTEM OF SOCIAL RELATIONSHIPS?

We have advanced the view that law is a system of norms, determined by the economic relationships and interests of the dominant class. These norms sanction existing relationships and make them compulsory for society as a whole. Economic relationships, secured by legal norms, acquire a form of legal relationships.

This, however, is not the view of Comrade Stuchka. In his opinion, law is precisely a system of social or production relationships. Those who view law as a system of norms are stigmatized by Stuchka as bourgeois jurists. In view of this, we shall point out the difference between our conception of law and that of the bourgeoisie.

We have indicated on numerous occasions that, according to bourgeois jurists, law develops by itself, and that its existence is independent of social conditions. For example, R. Stammler asserts that we do not deduce external social norms from an objective reality but find them a priori.[1] Thus, it appears that "economic" relationships are being formed by a presupposed external norm and that presupposed norms determine social life, instead of vice versa. According to our view, . . . social and production relationships bring forth legal norms; legal norms are their juridical expression. Furthermore, bourgeois jurists identify legal norms with the "general will," with the will of the people, whereas we assert that they are class norms reflecting the interests of the dominant class. Hoping that Comrade Stuchka will see the difference between our concepts and bourgeois concepts, we shall continue our analysis. . . .

At the very outset we raise the question: "If social relationships and law are identical, why use two designations?" Why, then, do we speak of law at all? The designation "system of social relationships"

---

* From *Marksistskaya Teoriya Prava,* s Predisloviem N. Bukharina [The Marxist Theory of Law, with an Introduction by N. Bukharin] (Moscow-Petrograd, 1923), pp. 163–87.
[1] R. Stammler, *Khozyaistvo i Pravo* [Economy and Law] (Petersburg, 1907), Vol. 1(?), translation of *Wirtschaft und Recht nach der materialistischen Geschichtsauffassung: Eine sozialphilosophische Untersuchung* (Leipzig, 1896).

is completely sufficient. It stands to reason, though, that Comrade Stuchka knows that these two phenomena are not identical; otherwise, he would have had to cease to speak of law. Or, if these phenomena are distinct, why does Comrade Stuchka attribute to them the same meaning?

It is evident that Comrade Stuchka's position is indefensible. If the law and the system of production and other social relationships are the same, we are justified to use these expressions alternately. For example, the statement "production relationships determine classes" should then be identical with "law determines classes." The statement "social relationships determine the state" should be identical with "law determines the state." Naturally, the results following the identification of law with production or social relationships are very non-Marxist. Therefore, one should not assert that law is a system of social relationships, i.e., one should not transpose them.

But what is law? If we look at the surface of the phenomena in social relationships, both production and other social relationships appear in their legal uniforms. Here law blends with social relationships. Indeed, the same is true of the process of man's social life, which appears as a single process. But in order to comprehend it, we divide this single process, by means of analysis and abstraction, into its component parts. Without doing this, scientific knowledge of social life would be unattainable. Without an analysis and abstraction we would continue to see merely the surface of these phenomena without acquiring knowledge of the mechanism that motivates them. Comrade Stuchka has done exactly this, he took a look at the surface of the phenomena and began to paint the portrait of law, instead of examining them analytically, part by part. . . .

For example, we shall examine the act of "sale and purchase," of which Comrade Stuchka speaks. The question is whether this act is a legal or an economic act. Indeed, it is both a legal and an economic act. But does this mean that law is an economic relationship? At first glance one could deduce such a conclusion, and, in our opinion, that is what Comrade Stuchka did.

The history of Roman law demonstrates that at the time when the act of "sale and purchase" arose as an economic fact because of the necessities of economic development, it was neither recognized nor sanctioned by society. There was no guarantee that an acquired article could not be taken away. In other words . . . the new forms of barter were not yet recognized as relationships compulsory to society. But eventually these new forms asserted themselves and were recognized and sanctioned by the economically dominant class as relationships compulsory to the whole society. *This recognition, this sanctioning by society (i.e., by the dominant class), is the law.*

Thus, on the one hand, *the act of sale and purchase is an economic act* while, on the other hand, *it has also a juridical side—its recognition by the class in power, which is the law. And an economic act, protected by law, is a legal act.*

Of course, barter came into being, not because it was recognized by law, but, on the contrary, the law came into being because, prior to it, barter existed as an economic, non-legal phenomenon. The same is true of the system of economic relationships taken as a whole. On one hand, *there is a system of economic relationships;* on the other hand, the dominant class makes this system *compulsory* to everyone, makes a law reflecting this system which, having received legal sanction, becomes a legal system. Therefore, laws are coercive norms, making the existing system of relationships compulsory.

We demonstrated earlier that Marx and Engels have also comprehended law as a system of norms established by the dominant class for the purpose of sanctioning existing relationships. To quote Marx again, "Both political and civil legislation *have always merely expressed recorded demands of economic relationships."* Another quotation from Marx gives us an even more vivid description of the nature of law: *"Law does nothing but sanction existing relationships."* Again, Marx stated in *The Communist Manifesto, "Your law is the will of your class elevated to a law, a will whose content is determined by the economic conditions of the existence of your class."*

To be sure, Comrade Stuchka throws a suspicion upon Marx himself, suspecting him of idealism because of the use of the term "will." But Marx quite clearly indicates what determines the will. Hence, where is idealism? Does Comrade Stuchka not recognize the will as a factor of historical development? If not, then he should admit it openly, and we shall gladly place his name on the register of "economic materialism." Since Comrade Stuchka mistrusts Marx, we shall quote an unequivocal statement made by Engels: "State and public laws are determined by economic relationships. The same, of course, is true of civil law, the role of which is in essence to sanction the existing economic relationships between individuals, relationships that are normal under the given circumstances."[2]

The views quoted demonstrate quite clearly the substance of law and its inevitability in a class society. The production relationships as well as the social relationships have always existed in the past and will

[2] *Lyudvig Feierbakh* [Ludwig Feuerbach] (Moscow, 1918[?]), p. 68.

exist in the future. But is the same true of law? No, law will not exist forever. *Why, then, is law necessary in a class society, in addition to production relationships? Law is necessary in a class society because it is a society with antagonistic relationships and because class society is hostile to the majority. That is why the dominant class makes this system a legal system, i.e., one that is coercive and compulsory to everyone, and why it secures this system with legal norms reflecting its will and its interest.*

## BASIS AND SUPERSTRUCTURE

The principal theory of Marx, namely, the theory of basis and superstructure, suggests that law alone is a superstructure and that, consequently, it should not be confused with the basis, which is the system of economic relationships. Nevertheless, Comrade Stuchka confuses this point and, in addition, attributes it to Marx himself. According to Comrade Stuchka, Marx committed a sin in his famous preface to *Zur Kritik* . . . , when he asserted that "at a certain stage in their development, the material forces of production in society come into conflict with the existing relations of production or—juridically speaking—with the property relationships within which they are developing."

Comrade Stuchka infers from the quoted paragraph that, according to Marx, law is the relationship of production. But if this is true, then, according to Marx, the forces of production come into conflict with the law; law then appears to be the basis of society. This is tantamount to saying that Marx was not a Marxist. It is obvious that Comrade Stuchka has misinterpreted Marx.

What is the meaning of the expression "juridically speaking." In the preceding pages we have demonstrated that a juridical or legal phenomenon is an economic fact, or economic relationship, that, according to Marx, is "sanctioned," or, according to Engels, "sanctified," by legal norms. In the paragraph quoted by Comrade Stuchka, Marx intended to say that property relationships are relationships of production, i.e., economic relationships, sanctioned by law or "expressed juridically." And this means that Comrade Stuchka is completely wrong. He could have seen this by himself, had he read the lines that precede and follow the quoted paragraph. Marx has stated there the following view: *"The sum total of the relationships of production constitutes the economic structure of society, the real foundation, on which rise legal and political superstructures."* Furthermore, Marx asserted, "In considering revolutions, *the distinction should always be made between the material transformation of the economic conditions of production . . . and the juridical, and the political . . . , in short, ideological forms in which men become conscious of this conflict."*

It is evident that, contrary to Marx's suggestion, Comrade Stuchka has failed to see the "difference," and *has confused the superstructure with the basis.* There is, however, another question that should be raised in this context. Comrade Stuchka and some of his opponents . . . confuse the law with legal phenomena. We saw earlier, though, that law and legal phenomena are two entirely distinct things.

Law is a system of norms, the sanction of existing economic relationships. Law is a superstructure that grew up from certain relationships of production, i.e., from the basis, and that in turn reacts upon the basis, sanctioning it, securing it, and making it compulsory. Under the influence of the superstructure, the basis, i.e., the economic relationships, become legal relationships. Consequently *legal relationships* (phenomena, facts) *are economic relationships affected by the reaction of the superstructure, i.e., of the law. This is the result of the interaction between basis and superstructure.*

## FORM AND CONTENT

In examining law from Comrade Stuchka's point of view, we have seen that he confused the superstructure with the basis. Once he made the error of one anti-Marxist confusion, he then committed an additional mistake which is logically related to the former. That is to say, he confused the form with the content, and he stigmatized as bourgeois jurists those who do not accept this interpretation. In his *theses* on law, he asserted the following: "The answer to the question of whether law is a system, an order, of social relationships, i.e., the content of norms, or whether it is a system or an order of norms, i.e., a form of the system of relationships, depends upon the point of view we adopt in approaching this question. . . . To a bourgeois jurist, law, in its objective meaning, is the form, i.e., the sum total of norms; to a Marxist, on the contrary, law is the system of relationships, the content of norms."[3]

It is beyond any doubt that the economic relationships constitute the basis, the foundation. The law, according to Marx, does not belong to the basis; it is merely a *superstructure* that enables the basis

---

[3] P. Stuchka, "Zametki o Klassovoi Teorii Prava" [Notes on the Class Theory of Law], *Sovetskoe Pravo,* No. 3 (1922).

to function legally. Thereby, law does not become the content of legal phenomena; it remains always merely the form, the uniform, in which the economic facts are clothed. According to Marx, "The juridical forms, in which economic transactions appear as acts of the will of interested persons, as expressions of their common will and of their obligations, simply as forms, cannot determine the content of transactions but merely express it."[4]

The quoted views brilliantly reveal the full nature of law. Marx demonstrates that laws are coercive norms used by the state for securing certain economic relationships, that law is merely a sanction of the existing economic relationships, that law is merely the form of these relationships. Since the content of these relationships is determined by the economy, the norms merely formulate ("express") it.

Marx's view fully reveals the falsity of Comrade Stuchka's views, which are based on his confusion of superstructure with basis and of form with content. We do not doubt that Comrade Stuchka had good intentions. He intended to smash to pieces the normative theories of the law of the bourgeois jurists; however, he exaggerated the significance of the economy to the degree that . . . he became incapable of solving the problem correctly. First of all, he failed to notice that legal norms are not self-developing, are not universal norms, as it is contended by bourgeois jurists. Second, and even more serious, he placed the superstructure (law) on the same level as the basis, or, stated more precisely, he confused them. In doing this, Comrade Stuchka performed a bad service for historical materialism. Instead of strengthening materialism (which he sincerely intended), he reinforced idealism by declaring the superstructure (law) to be the basis of society. Very truly, everything has its own dialectic!

P.S. Our manuscript was completed when we became acquainted with a new article by Comrade Stuchka, "Materialist or Idealist Understanding of Law?"[5] Our pessimistic fears were justified. Comrade Stuchka has arrived at the logical end. In his new article he not only places law on the same level as economy but declares the system of economic relationships to be part of this law: "The system of relationships is the material element of law, whereas the system of norms is the ideal, idealistic, element of law."[6]

Thus, the system of relationships is merely an *element* of law . . . , or to put it differently, the basis is a part of the superstructure. Com-

[4] *Kapital* [Capital] (n.p., n.d.), III, Part 1, 324.
[5] *Pod Znamenem Marksizma*, No. 1 (1923).
[6] *Ibid.*, p. 168.

rade Stuchka's mistake is too obvious . . . , but he remains undis-
turbed. He deliberately turns Marxism inside out, and in full serious-
ness contends that *"Marx used the contraposition of the basis and
the superstructure as a figurative expression."*[7]

Everything is very clear and simple: the old man, Marx, took a
fancy to the expressions "basis" and "superstructure"; he simply
blurted them out. And prior to Comrade Stuchka's revelation, we,
the sinful, thought that the concept of basis and superstructure constituted the foundation of the materialist theory of history. Indeed,
Comrade Stuchka is free to place law as the basis of society and to
declare production and other relationships to be "elements" of law,
but he has no right to attribute this view to Marx.

Having depicted law as all inclusive, as embracing all elements of
man's social existence and consciousness, Comrade Stuchka at the
same time contends that law appears in three forms: (1) "the concrete form of social relationships"; (2) "an abstraction of social relationships," i.e., "the legal form of a social phenomenon"; and (3)
"the intuitive form," i.e., man's legal experiences.[8]

. . . Translated into Marxist language, Comrade Stuchka's juridical
conceptions mean the following: (1) the first form of law is *economy*
(or economy sanctified by law); (2) the second form is the *sanctioning* of the economy by the power of the dominant class, i.e., *legal
norms or law;* (3) the third form is legal consciousness (class, group,
individual, consciousness).

To be sure, however, neither the first form, i.e., the *economy,* nor
the third form, i.e., *legal consciousness,* is a law. Consequently, only
the second form, i.e., *the norms sanctioning the economy,* is law. In
fusing three distinct things into one concept, Comrade Stuchka introduces into the theory of law an anti-Marxist vagueness.


## REACTION OF THE LAW UPON THE ECONOMY

Comrade Stuchka's main mistake leads to some additional misunderstandings. Thus, according to Stuchka, the assumption that law
is a system of norms implies that norms regulate the economy. Such
a view, in his opinion, is unacceptable to a Marxist, for, according to
the latter, the economy determines the norms, not vice versa.

Needless to say, Comrade Stuchka's approach to the problem contains not even an element of the dialectic. It is self-evident that laws
reflect the economy through the prism of class interest. Once legal

[7] *Ibid.,* p. 177.
[8] *Ibid.,* pp. 168–69.

norms come into being they regulate economic relationships: *first,* as previously indicated, they make economic relationships legal; and *second,* they regulate the economic relationships in conformity with the will of the dominant class. We hope Comrade Stuchka does not deny the role of the classes and does not reduce everything to economy. This would be contrary to Marx.

Law not only regulates but also exerts an influence upon economy; it can hinder economy (as feudal law hindered rising bourgeois relationships) or it can secure the correct course for economic relationships by protecting and strengthening them and by providing space for their development. Finally, Comrade Stuchka should be aware of the fact that legal acts are capable of producing changes in the economy (for example, legal acts of the Soviet authority providing for the nationalization of land, property, etc.).

*Law, like any other superstructure, does not arise from the basis only, but, in its own turn, exerts influence upon the basis.* This has been unequivocally stated by Marx: *"The influence of law upon the consolidation of the relations of distribution and, owing to this, the influence upon production, is the object of a special examination."*[9]

Engels expressed himself even more strongly on the subject of the influence of law upon economy: *"Political, legal, . . . etc., development is based on economic development. But all these react one upon another and also upon the economic basis."*[10]

Indeed, Comrade Stuchka had to reject these views because he maintained that law is a system of relationships. It stands to reason, though, that this system cannot act upon itself.

## A DIFFERENT COURSE IN THE DEVELOPMENT OF LAW AND ECONOMY

Comrade Stuchka ought to know that law does not merely reflect economic relationships, but, as we have stated earlier, reflects them through the prism of the interests of the dominant class. In doing this, a distorted, an incorrect, reflection may take place. As pointed out by Engels, "In a modern state, law must not only correspond to the general economic position and be its expression but must also be an expression that is consistent in itself, and that does not, owing to inner contradictions, look glaringly inconsistent. And in order to achieve this, the faithful reflection of economic conditions is more and more infringed upon. All the more so, it rarely happens that a

[9] *Die Neue Zeit* (n.v.), p. 744.
[10] Letter to Starkenburg, January 25, 1894.

code of law is the blunt, unmitigated, unadulterated expression of the domination of a class."[11]

A true reflection, one that would vividly reveal the class nature of the law, is inconvenient for the dominant class. To be sure, however, law, like any superstructure, depends upon the course of the economy. This is a literary truth. Nevertheless, Comrade Stuchka should know that law, while being determined by the course of economy, has its own path of development (and thereby affects the course of the economy).

Earlier we have seen that, in the case of the law of private property, the same legal norms can accommodate two different economic systems. In the English case we have seen that, owing to a rapid development of economic relationships, the old legal norms are slowly changed, and a new economic content is infused into the old legal forms. The case of the Prussian land law is an example of the adaptation of the trade law to feudal relationships. Finally, the *Civil Code* offers an example of replacing an old legal system with a new one and of bringing law into step with economy. All this took place because law is not determined by economy alone; it is also determined by the relationships of class forces, by other social superstructures, and by the dynamism of the development of legal ideology. Engels stated, "The basis of the law of inheritance—assuming that the stages reached in the development of the family are equal—is an economic one. But it would be difficult to prove, for instance, that the absolute liberty of the testator in England and the severe restrictions imposed upon him in France are only due in every detail to economic causes. Both, however, react back upon the economic sphere to a very considerable extent because they influence the division of property."[12]

This problem (namely, that law has its own course of development, which does not necessarily coincide with the development of the economy) also remains incomprehensible to Comrade Stuchka. He quotes a passage from the Introduction to *Zur Kritik,* in which Marx stated the following: "A genuinely difficult problem, which should become an object of study, is the following: why do production and legal relationships pursue different courses of development? The best example of this is the relationship of Roman civil law to modern production."

Comrade Stuchka contends that this problem still remains unexplained.[13] It stands to reason, however, that only one who is not

[11] Letter to Conrad Schmidt, October 27, 1890.
[12] *Ibid.*
[13] *Sovetskoe Pravo,* p. 12.

acquainted with Marx's description of the transformation of a simple barter economy into a capitalist one can advance such a contention. . . . Indeed, looking from Comrade Stuchka's point of view, this problem must remain unexplained. If law is a system of economic relationships, then it is inconceivable that law could pursue a course of development different from that of the economic relationships. . . . What Comrade Stuchka has failed to notice is that, in the quoted passage, Marx had indicated that one *should not* confuse law with economic relationships. And that is exactly what Comrade Stuchka has done.

### THE LAW OF TWO CLASSES

There is another problem that should be mentioned. Comrade Stuchka seems to recognize, though in a vague way, the simultaneous existence of two systems of law, that is, the law of two classes existing at the same time. He illustrates this with the diarchy, where, besides the old power, there exists also a "parallel power of another class, which has the same power, or almost the same power, as the official political authority."[14] As an example of a diarchy, he cites the February revolution, "when the diarchy existed, both openly and formally, in the form of a bourgeois government side by side with the Petrograd Executive Committee, which represented the actual power of the working class and petty bourgeoisie."

Indeed, it is true that the Soviets existed along side of the Provisional government. . . . Nevertheless, looking from a class point of view, one must admit that the state machine was then in the hands of the capitalist class. . . . The "socialists," who played the leading role in the soviets, were far from being capable of resolving the tasks of the working class. The mass of the workers was not yet ready for the conquest of political power. As a result, the soviets, who had voluntarily renounced their power to the bourgeoisie, had become an appendage of the bourgeois political machine. When the masses became ready for conquest, when the soviets became transformed into organs of their will and their interest, then the Provisional government was swept away, for two governments *of two classes cannot exist at the same time.*

What about the system of law? *It is, indeed, naïve to speak about the existence of two legal systems at a time when capitalistic relationships are definitely dominant, when the government is in the*

---

[14] *Revolutsionnaya Rol Prava i Gosudarstva* [The Revolutionary Role of Law and State] (Moscow, 1921), p. 38.

*hands of the capitalist class.* Regardless of many concessions on the part of the losing class, the law remains the law of the capitalist class so long as the political power remains in its hands, i.e., as long as the capitalist system of relationships is still in existence. Only the revolution was able to put an end to class law. *Hence, looking from a class viewpoint, two systems of law cannot exist at the same time. One law is only possible, namely, the law of the ruling class.*

Apart from the above-said, the problem is quite simple if it is approached *dialectically.* The old state was in the process of disintegration. A new state was coming into being but was not yet a state. The existing class organizations of the proletariat, i.e., the soviets and the Party, were the only *potential political authorities.* Equally, the proletariat's class interests and its political program were still a *law in becoming* (a law *im Werden,* to use a German expression). They became the law only after the proletariat's conquest of power. Prior to that, the positive law was the law of the bourgeoisie.

    . . . To conclude, *laws are coercive norms, sanctioning social relationships in the interests of the ruling class.* Therefore, the law is always the law of the ruling class. Law comes into being because of the contradictions within a class society. The system of relationships within a class society is hostile to the suppressed majority of the people. Owing to this, the ruling class sanctifies the dominant relationships as binding upon the whole society and regulates them with legal norms. These legal norms reflect the existing relationships faithfully or incorrectly depending upon the needs of the class interests. The ruling class makes legal concessions, depending upon the relationships between the classes, and, in doing this, moderates the struggle. Therefore, like all superstructures, law depends upon economy, but law also has its own inner logic of development and this in turn reacts upon the economy.

# Law as an Instrument of Class Domination*

## ⌀ *I. Podvolotskii*

*Law is both a historically inevitable and a transitional phenomenon of a class society. It constitutes a system of coercive social norms that reflect the economic as well as other social relationships of a given society. It is a system of norms created and protected by the state power of the dominant class for the purpose of sanctioning, regulating, and consolidating these relationships, and, consequently, for consolidating the domination of a given class.*

. . . In a capitalist society the bourgeois system of law, which is created and protected by the power of the capitalist class, regulates and consolidates capitalist relationships and the domination of the capitalist class. This is the reason for its being a system of the bourgeois law.

. . . However, we are confronted with the question: "What type of law will exist during the period of the proletarian dictatorship?" The answer is "bourgeois law." This answer calls for a further explanation.

At first glance, it appears that the substantiation of this answer can be found in the works of Marx and Lenin. We have in mind especially Lenin's analysis of the views Marx stated in *The Critique of the Gotha Program.* Marx said that in the first phase of communism, when realization of the principle "from each according to his abilities, to each according to his needs" is not yet possible, equal pay for labor is still in fact an unequal "bourgeois law," for neither men nor their families are equal. In Marx's words, *"Indeed, we have equal law here; but it is still a 'bourgeois law,' which, like every law, presupposes inequality."*

We shall examine later the question: "Will law exist at a higher stage of communism?" However, an obvious conclusion seems to follow from the quoted views: a "bourgeois law" will exist in the transition period.

We stated earlier that, judging by their external manifestations—i.e., by their form—elements of bourgeois law will undoubtedly re-

* From *Marksistskaya Teoriya Prava,* s Predisloviem N. Bukharina [The Marxist Theory of Law, with an Introduction by N. Bukharin] (Moscow-Petrograd, 1923), pp. 192–98.

111

112                                           SOVIET POLITICAL THOUGHT

main in the transition period, for commodity relationships will still be
in existence. Will it, however, be a real bourgeois law? The answer is
*no*. What is the meaning of bourgeois law? Bourgeois law is a law of
the bourgeois class, protecting its domination through preservation
of the capitalist social system.

. . . We demonstrated earlier that our civil law does not seek to
protect and strengthen domination of the bourgeoisie. But, in addition to civil law, we also have constitutional law, i.e., *basic* law, which
quite clearly provides for the class domination of the proletariat. Furthermore, we have criminal law, which, like civil law, frequently
comprises provisions like those found in bourgeois criminal codes but
performs a completely different function. Previously, criminal law
protected the class domination of capital and, consequently, was a
capitalist law. Now these legal norms are in the service of the proletariat and, therefore, they are the proletariat's law.

The example of criminal law alone demonstrates that one should
not judge the nature of law by its form. In evaluating its nature, one
must always determine whose social system it strengthens and, consequently, whose class domination it protects. Thus, our constitutional law, criminal law, and civil law, indeed, our whole legal system, is in the service of the proletariat and is protected by the
proletariat's power. Therefore, it is a system of proletarian law. The
private law, which constitutes a part of this system, is, therefore,
proletarian law, in spite of the fact that it reflects commercial relationships and in spite of the fact that it is formally a "bourgeois law."

Following Marx and Lenin, I have placed the expression "bourgeois law" in quotation marks. I did this . . . in order to demonstrate that "bourgeois law" (in quotation marks) has an entirely different meaning from bourgeois law (without quotation marks) and
that, consequently, they should not be confused. Both of them have
the same form, but each has its peculiar *essence*. Lenin was also of
this opinion. The following statement indicates that he thought bourgeois law (without quotation marks) could exist only within a system
of capitalist relationships: *"Bourgeois law, with respect to the distribution of articles of consumption, inevitably presupposes the existence of the bourgeois state, for law is nothing without an apparatus
capable of enforcing the observance of the law."*[1]

It is quite evident that, when Lenin designates the distribution of
articles of consumption in the first phase of communism as "bourgeois law" (in quotation marks), he defines this law in terms of its

[1] *Gosudarstvo i Revolutsiya* [State and Revolution], *in Sobranie Sochinenii*
[Collected Works] (Moscow, 1921), XIV, Part 2.

form and projects into it an entirely new content. Lenin states quite clearly that bourgeois law, in terms of its content, i.e., *bourgeois law* per se, is conceivable only in a bourgeois state. Therefore, there can be no bourgeois law in the proletarian state, i.e., law reflecting the interests of capital and serving its domination. . . .

But does the proletariat need law in general? Yes, beyond any doubt. The proletariat has overthrown bourgeois authority but has not yet succeeded in destroying classes and antagonisms in society. Antagonisms still exist—not only the antagonism of the defeated class of the bourgeoisie toward the proletariat, but also conflict between the proletariat and the peasantry, as well as contradictions within the proletariat. And as long as antagonisms exist, as long as resistence is still possible, the proletariat must secure the new system of relationships with legal norms that are compulsory for all strata of society. Having suppressed an active bourgeois resistance in the struggle, the proletariat must place the bourgeoisie in a legal strait jacket—in a position where it could not interfere with the proletariat's work. Therefore, law is inevitable as an instrument of systematic siege, as an instrument for peaceful suppression of the opposition. . . . Like every law, the proletarian law also regulates the conduct of the members of the proletarian class, subordinating the will of each member to the collective will, to the interests of the whole class. . . .

. . . To be sure, this law is different from all previous forms of law. It is the law of a majority, whereas all previous law was the law of a minority exploiting the majority of society. In addition, all previous legal systems sought to secure class domination forever. The proletarian legal system seeks to secure domination by the proletariat only for the purpose of overcoming any class domination and, at the same time, for rendering law unnecessary.

# The Withering Away of Law* — *I. Podvolotskii*

"Are we also in the sphere of law growing organically into the state of the future, or should we find our own 'social law'—which would replace the bourgeois law—by means of contemplation . . .?" "Our present work is devoted to the conversion of law and, in particular, to the transformation of the bourgeois law into the social law of the future society." So reasons Karner,[1] while Magerovskii simply speaks of "socialist law."

Apart from small mistakes, such reasoning contains two colossal errors. First, we do not wait for a peaceful transformation of the bourgeois state and law; instead, we destroy them and replace them with our own proletarian class state and our own system of proletarian law. Second, after the revolution, the process of the transformation of society into communism will *not* be accompanied by the transformation of the protetarian state and proletarian law into the state and law of the future society or into the "socialist law." On the contrary, both will gradually wither away.

Regarding the state, Lenin has examined its future quite thoroughly in his book *State and Revolution*. Regarding law, we have made an attempt to state the views of Marx and Engels. According to their views, *law is a class phenomenon and, consequently, the transformation of bourgeois law into socialist law is inconceivable. Bourgeois law must be destroyed and replaced with a system of proletarian law*. Now our task is to demonstrate that *no law will exist in a communist society*.

The task of the proletarian dictatorship is to destroy classes and class antagonism in society. The proletariat cannot accomplish this task without law. Naturally, with the transfer of all means of production to the hands of society, the bourgeois class, qua class, will begin to disappear. Also, its resistance to new social order will disappear. Consequently, *law, the role of which is to sanction the existing social relationships, will not be needed as long as these relationships are observed voluntarily*.

* From *Marksistskaya Teoriya Prava*, s Predisloviem N. Bukharina [The Marxist Theory of Law, with an Introduction by N. Bukharin] (Moscow-Petrograd, 1923), pp. 198–206.

[1] *Sotsialnye Funktsii Prava* [The Social Functions of Law] (Moscow, 1923), pp. 4–6.

However, in spite of the fact that the means of production will be in the hands of society, the productivity of labor will not permit, during the first period of communism, a completely free distribution of products. The slogan "from each according to his abilities, and to each according to his needs" will not have materialized. Consequently, it will still be necessary for society to organize the distribution of products in conformity with certain principles.

Earlier, we quoted Marx as saying that, during the first period of communist society, an equal remuneration is in fact unequal and unjust, because people are unequal in terms of their abilities, family situation, etc. This is why Marx designated the equal remuneration of individuals for their work—which results in inequality—as "bourgeois law."

We indicated earlier that to both Marx and Lenin the expression "bourgeois law" had a relative meaning. We also stated that in the transition period "bourgeois law" exists only in form, not in content. The same applies to what Marx designated as "bourgeois law" in the first period of communism. In this stage of communism, *bourgeois law no longer exists; there is only "law," in quotation marks—"law" which is withering away.* It is still "law," though in very big quotation marks, because, in spite of the socialization of the means of production and, consequently, the impossibility of exploitation, the revival of opposition against the existing social relationships is still possible on the part of the previously exploiting class, which has not gotten rid of its ideology.

To be sure, however, the transformation of "law" into simple social norms is possible in the first period of communism if the antagonistic groups and class antagonisms in general disappear. Therefore, the phenomenon designated by Marx as "bourgeois law" will be neither "bourgeois law" nor law in general, because, in view of the fact that classes and class antagonisms disappear, there will be no domination by one part of humanity over another, and society will become united. These are no longer norms established by a class in its own interest, to which society must subordinate itself. These are simply norms for the distribution of products, norms established by the unified society itself. Distributed products (though not necessarily equally distributed) cannot become means for the domination of man by man, because the means of production are in the hands of society and the relationships between people are no longer disguised in a fetish-like veil. As stated by Marx and Engels, "Communism will prevent no man from appropriating the products of society; all that it does is to deprive him of the opportunity to subjugate the labor of others by means of such appropriation."[2]

Thus, while losing their legal character, the norms for the distribution of products will still remain in the first period of communist society. But, as this society develops,

in a higher phase of communist society, when the enslaving subordination of man to the division of labor, and with it the antithesis between mental and physical labor, has vanished; when labor is no longer merely a means of life but has become life's principal need; when the productive forces have also increased with all-around development of the individual and all the springs of social wealth flow more abundantly—only then will it be possible to transcend completely the narrow outlook of bourgeois law and only then will society be able to inscribe on its banners: "From each according to his ability, to each according to his needs."[3]

We indicated earlier that under "bourgeois law" Marx understood simply the norms of the distribution of products. In a completely developed communist society these norms will become obsolete and will thus wither away. Since each man will be able to get products according to his needs, the norms of distribution will be as necessary for society as the right to walk on two legs.

Naturally, we do not deny the possibility of excesses by some members of communist society; such excesses will be the behavior of defective persons, a manifestation of atavism, the eructation of the class past on the part of some persons. It is quite obvious that these singular cases will call for an attentive attitude on the part of society: medical treatment and influence, applied from case to case. But no a priori fixed, obligatory norms will be needed, as no norms prohibiting certain conduct to mental patients are now needed.

Consequently, *neither law nor any other norms will be transformed or regenerated into social norms; they wither away because of their obsolescence.* As pointed out by Marx,

Undoubtedly, it will be said, religious, moral, philosophical, political, and legal forms have been modified in the course of historical development. But religion, morality, philosophy, politics, and law constantly survived this change.

There are, besides, eternal truths, such as freedom, justice, etc., that are common to all phases of social development. But communism destroys eternal truths, it destroys all religion and morality, instead of con-

---

[2] *Kommunisticheskii Manifest* [The Communist Manifesto] (n.p., n.d.).
[3] *Kritika Gotskoi Programmy* [Critique of the Gotha Program] (n.p., n.d.).

stituting them on a new basis; it therefore acts in contradiction to all past historical development.

What does this accusation reduce itself to? The history of all past societies was founded on class contradictions, contradictions that assumed different forms in different epochs. But whatever form they may have taken, the exploitation of one part of society by the other is a fact common to all past ages. No wonder, then, that the social consciousness of past ages, despite all the multiplicity and variety it displays, moves within certain common forms, forms of consciousness, which will vanish completely only with the total disappearance of class contradictions.

The communist revolution is the most radical rupture with traditional property relations; no wonder that its development involves the most radical rupture with traditional ideas.[4]

Thus, law, which expressed interests of the ruling class attributed to the whole society, existed at all stages of class society. Hence, by its very nature, law is an instrument of suppression and inequality. In vain some quasi-Marxists think of "transforming" it into a "social" law equal for all. With the disappearance of classes and social antagonisms, when society will become a society of equals, when it will be recognized by all as such, and when social ideas will be accepted by each member of society as his own, then there will be no need for law. Then, this flower of class society, from which the fragrance of sweat and blood emanates, will fall into decay and will *die away,* because it will lose the ground on which it grew up, the ground of tears, sweat, blood, class oppression, slavery, and exploitation.

[4] *Kommunisticheskii Manifest.*

# Civil Liberties: A Bourgeois Deception*

## ∽ *I. Podvolotskii*

Imitators of Marxism exclaim self-righteously: "But what about the freedom of the individual, press, speech, assembly, etc., etc.? Are they also, in your judgment, class rights and not individual rights?"

These "freedoms" have succeeded in revealing their ungainly class nature to the extent that there is hardly anything to be said about them. But since necessity forces us to prove that black is black, we shall refer our "Marxists" to Marx himself. "For the first time," says Marx, "I used the expression 'modern mythology' as a designation for the goddesses of 'Justice, Freedom, and Equality,' who are beginning to reign once again."[1]

Thus, to Marx, all this is a mythology—a deception. Freedom, equality, are to Marx as unreal as goddesses. Nevertheless, some "Marxists" are intoxicated with "freedom," "equality," etc., and extol them as eternal and pure truths. But an abstract, eternal freedom was alien to Marx. "Be not deceived by an abstract word: *freedom.* The question is, 'Whose freedom?' *This word does not signify man's freedom from other men. It signifies the freedom of the capitalist to suppress the worker.*"[2]

This is the way Marx posed the question. To him an eternal goddess of freedom—the fetish of freedom—is nonexistent; what does exist is only freedom for a certain class. *In a capitalist society, it is the freedom of the capitalists to suppress the working class.*

. . . We shall quote a long paragraph from Marx's *The Eighteenth Brumaire* hoping that the quasi-Marxist blockheads will be able to see that freedom in a capitalist society is freedom for capitalists alone.

The inevitable general staff of the liberties of 1848, personal liberty, liberty of the press, of speech, of association, of assembly, of education and religion, etc., received a constitutional uniform which made them invulnerable. For each of these liberties is proclaimed as the *absolute* right of the French *citoyen*, but always with the marginal note that it is un-

* From *Marksistskaya Teoriya Prava,* s Predisloviem N. Bukharina [The Marxist Theory of Law, with an Introduction by N. Bukharin] (Moscow-Petrograd, 1923), pp. 102–110.
[1] Letter to Engels, August 1, 1877.
[2] Karl Marx, *Rech o Svobode Torgovli* [Speech on Freedom of Trade] (Moscow, n.d.), p. 30.

limited insofar as it is not limited by the "equal rights of others and the public safety" or by "laws" that are intended to mediate just this harmony of the individual liberties with one another and with the public safety. For example: "The citizens have the right of association, of peaceful and unarmed assembly, of petition, and of expressing their opinions, whether in the press or in any other way. *The enjoyment of these rights has no limit save the equal rights of others and the public safety.*" (Chapter II of the French Constitution, Art. 8.)—"Education is free. Freedom of education shall be *enjoyed* under the conditions fixed by law and under the supreme control of the state." (Ibidem, Art. 9.) —"The home of every citizen is inviolable *except* in the forms prescribed by law." (Chapter II, Art. 3.) Etc., etc.—The Constitution, therefore, constantly refers to future organic laws that are to put into effect those marginal notes and regulate the enjoyment of these unrestricted liberties in such manner that they will collide neither with one another nor with the public safety. And later, these organic laws were brought into being by the friends of order, and all those liberties were regulated in such a manner that the bourgeoisie in its enjoyment of them finds itself unhindered by the equal rights of the other classes. Where it forbids these liberties entirely to "the others" or permits enjoyment of them under conditions that are just so many police traps, this always happens solely in the interest of "public safety," that is, the safety of the bourgeoisie, as the Constitution prescribes. In the sequel, both sides accordingly appeal with complete justice to the Constitution: the friends of order, who abrogated all these liberties, as well as the democrats, who demanded all of them. For each paragraph of the Constitution contains its own antithesis, its own Upper and Lower Houses, namely, liberty in the general phrase, abrogation of liberty in the marginal note. Thus, so long as the *name* of freedom was respected and only its actual realization prevented—of course, in a legal way—the constitutional existence of liberty remained intact, inviolate, however mortal the blows dealt to its existence *in actual life.*

Engels' views are in full conformity with those of Marx: "The so-called rights of man . . . were in fact restricted by the bourgeois ruling class; the suppressed class has always been deprived of them either directly or indirectly."[3]

In examining social relationships, Marx and Engels have discovered that freedom in a capitalist society signifies the freedom of capitalists to protect the "social safety" of their system, and that the rights of the suppressed classes amount to nothing. But some "Marxists" consult only constitutions and find in them solemn proclamations of eternal and universal freedom. Consequently, they fail to see that this freedom does not exist in reality, for its existence would be contrary to the interests of "social safety."

There are, however, other reasons responsible for the fact that the

[3] *Proiskhozhdenie Semi, Chastnoi Sobstvennosti i Gosudarstva* [The Origin of the Family, Private Property, and the State] (Petersburg, 1920[?]), p. 54.

"freedom" of the proletariat in a capitalist system is a fiction, a deception. These reasons are independent of the fact that capitalism permits and protects only the "freedom" that does not conflict with the "social safety," i.e., with the domination of the capitalist class. *Under conditions of the economic domination of the bourgeoisie, the freedom of private property is transformed into the privilege of capital, into a right favoring the capitalist system and domination by capitalists. Equally, under the conditions of economic and political domination by capital, freedom and democracy are instruments of the bourgeoisie in suppressing the exploited classes.* As stated by Marx, "Slavery in the bourgeois society creates an appearance of full freedom, for it appears as a legal form of individual independence . . . , whereas, in fact, it is a complete enslavement and a complete rejection of man. In the bourgeois society, right took the place of privilege."[4]

*. . . The bourgeoisie possesses entire economic power, whereas the proletariat possesses nothing. Because of the economic power of the bourgeoisie, "freedom" and "democracy" remain a fraudulent claim; it is "freedom" of the bourgeoisie to exploit the working class.* As pointed out by Engels, "Political freedom is a false freedom, worse than the worst type of slavery; it is an illusory freedom and, consequently, a true slavery. The same applies to political equality."[5]

Such is the problem of freedom, seen apart from political oppression and moral enslavement. It should be kept in mind, though, that the bourgeoisie holds in its hands political power in addition to control over prisons, the army, churches, and schools. The bourgeoisie oppresses economically but it also enslaves people morally; if the latter two fail, the bourgeoisie resorts to the employment of sheer physical force. With the increase of oppression, the bourgeoisie calls on its agents in the labor movement to increase the extolling of bourgeois freedom and democracy.

The proletarian revolution will put an end to bourgeois "freedom." The dictatorship of the proletariat will destroy the bourgeois system and will bring forth a classless, communist society, a society without class antagonisms and, consequently, without the state and law. Only in a classless society, in a society without state and law, will man be free. *It is absurd to speak of freedom under the law; law is incompatible with freedom. Consequently, in a society where freedom prevails, there will be no law.*

[4] *Svyatoe Semeistvo* [The Holy Family] (n.p., n.d.), p. 255.
[5] *Die Neue Zeit*, XXVIII, 428.

# Justice, the Ideology of Law, and Revolution*

## ↶ A. G. Goikhbarg

With the grace of God, the feudal state was a religious state. On the other hand, the bourgeoisie designated its state as a *Rechtsstaat,* as a state of law. Religion and law are the ideologies of the suppressing classes, the latter gradually replacing the former. Since we must, at the present time, fiercely struggle against religious ideology, we will, in the future, have to struggle against the ideology of law to a considerably greater degree. Any conscious proletarian either knows or has heard that religion is the opium of the people. But only a few, in my opinion, know that law is an even more poisoning and stupefying opium for the people. In his *The Eighteenth Brumaire,* Karl Marx stated that "the traditions of the deceased generations haunt the minds of the living like a nightmare." The difficulty in getting rid of these stupefying traditions depends upon the degree to which these traditions have been inculcated in the minds of the present generation. The difficulties are especially great when a generation has been inculcated with more recent traditions.

Law is more recent than religion, and, therefore, the struggle against the idea of law, the idea that serves the interests of the exploiting classes, is considerably more difficult than the struggle against religious ideas. Since this struggle will be considerably more difficult, antilaw propaganda should become a more pressing task for us than antireligious propaganda. Law is the new sanctuary of the exploiting classes, a sanctuary that replaced the religious one. Having abandoned the ideology of religion, these classes seek shelter in the ideology of law. The degree to which the idea of law governs those minds that are seemingly free of the religious opium can be seen from the following example. Indeed, it is either difficult or inconceivable to imagine that a party that pretends to be a revolutionary socialist party would make the defense of religion part of its political program. It took place, though, in the case of law. In opposition to the slogan of the Social Democrats: "Proletarians of all countries unite," the Socialist Revolutionary party advanced its own slogan:

---

* *From* "Neskolko Zamechanii o Prave" [Some Notes on Law], *Sovetskoe Pravo,* No. 1(7) (1924). This article later appeared as the first and second chapters of Goikhbarg's *Osnovy Chastnogo Imushchestvennogo Prava* [Foundations of the Private Property Law] (Moscow, 1924), pp. 7–27.

121

"In the struggle you shall gain your *right*." Needless to say, if one would ask the Social Revolutionaries of what right they speak, they would answer that they are concerned not with a bad, but with a good, *true* people's right. But this answer would disclose even more lucidly the degree to which they are trapped in the captivity of the idea of law, and the degree to which the tradition of bourgeois law haunts their minds like a nightmare.

Quite a few sins of this type are committed by Communists. It may suffice to mention our "revolutionary consciousness of law," "proletarian consciousness of law," and "socialist consciousness of law." These concepts were derived from an assumption that there is a certain everlasting, immutable law, which was misapplied in the various epochs preceding the Soviet epoch. However, the great hostility and aversion that Karl Marx expressed in treating the concept of law and the very idea of "right" are well known. In describing his participation in formulating the statute of the first international society of workers (First International), Marx stated the following: "My proposals were all accepted by the subcommittee. Only, I was obliged to insert two phrases, one about 'duty' and 'right,' another about 'truth, morality, and justice.' But these are placed in such a way that they can do no harm."[1]

To be sure, however, I would like at the very beginning to remove the possibility of any misunderstandings. Speaking of the necessity to conduct antilaw propaganda, I naturally intend neither to encourage disobedience of the *rules* established by the Soviet authority, nor to encourage insubordination to what we call the Soviet law. Indeed, it would be very nice if we could do without this expression, if we could replace it with another.

The concept of law is cloaked with such a mystical veil and is associated in the minds of the "living generations" with such enigmatic experiences that it would be extremely desirable to replace it with a new concept, with a concept that would embrace the regulating norms and the organizational rules which we are forced to use in the transition period preceding the final and universal victory of communism. There are, however, some terms that, so to speak, are being suckled with mother's milk. The term "law" is one of them.

In any case, our generation, which experienced the proletarian revolution, but which was born during prerevolutionary conditions, will not relinquish this term. It will be good if future generations succeed in giving it up. It is quite possible to separate this term com-

---

[1] Marx, Letter to Engels, November 4, 1864.

pletely from the idealist mystery in which it is cloaked, to impregnate it with real content, and to give it the meaning which it should preserve for the time being: the meaning of a correct norm, of an expedient rule, a rule realizing the goal for which it was created. Thus, in such a sense, the term "right" was used by Lenin in his speech directed against the so-called freedom of the press. Arguing for the right of the Soviet authority to suppress the bourgeois press, he reminded me that after the February revolution the bourgeois authority had closed the monarchistic press, and added: "If the bourgeoisie was *right* in closing the monarchistic press, then we have the *right* to close the bourgeois press."[2] In other words, Lenin conceived of the law as being an expedient rule, a rule which we, judging from its results, were right in creating. Here the term "law" is deprived of any ideological veil, of any absolute character, of inalienability, of immutability, and of eternity.

To what degree some free minds—and even one of the founders of socialism, the leader of the German working movement, Ferdinand Lassalle—were under the influence of the idea of law, can be seen in their works. After reading Lassalle's *The System of Acquired Rights,* Engels wrote the following to Marx:

> Lassalle is full of prejudice; he still believes in the "idea of law," in the absolute law. For the most part, his statements against Hegel's philosophy of law are correct, yet his own new philosophy is far from being correct. Purely from the viewpoint of philosophy, he should have advanced to the point at which he would be able to see that the only absolute is the historical process and not the temporary results of this process; without the historical process the idea of law would not have appeared.

But, whereas Lassalle had not advanced far enough to reject the absolute character of law, the ideologists of the bourgeoisie simply identify law as a natural property of man. They speak of "our sense of law" as one of the external senses. They contend that the sense of law, the legal instinct, is innate in man. Earlier it was contended that man *is a religious being,* and that the religious sense is innate in man. Then, the same contention was advanced in connection with law: *man is a legal being.* The latter view is the essence of Petrazhitskii's theory, which attracted so many proponents among the intelligentsia, even among the revolutionary intelligentsia who called themselves Marxists. The psychological theory of law—a theory which asserts

---

[2] See John Reed, *Desyat Dnei, Kotorye Potryasly Mir* [Ten Days That Shook the World] (Moscow, 1923).

that law is spawned in man's psyche and that it constitutes an everlasting and ineradicable property of man—does not merely correspond to the interests of the bourgeoisie; it expresses the fundamental
view of a bourgeois, according to which his right to property, to the
means of production, and to pocket the fruits of other men's labor is
eternal and will never die or discontinue. This bourgeois view has
also been adopted by the representatives of non-capitalistic producers, by the representatives of petty bourgeois democracy, and by
bourgeois ideologists. But even more, this idea was adopted by the
workers. As stated by Marx, "In social conditions that are dominated
by capitalistic production, even the non-capitalistic producer is subject to capitalistic ideas."[3]

Therefore, bourgeois ideologists will not be held responsible for
the adherence to such ideas. It is not their fault, but their misfortune.
No one can (speaking of mass occurrences) separate himself from the
ideological atmosphere that surrounds him and in which he grows up
and becomes educated. As stated by Marx, "From my point of view
more than from any other, an individual cannot be held responsible
for the social conditions of which he is a product, however subjec-
tively he may strive to elevate himself above them."[4] Indeed, not even
persons who have discovered the relative, historical, and transitional
meaning of these ideas are capable of liberating themselves from
them. The best example of this is the ingenious Marxist P. Lafargue,
Marx's son-in-law. Having subjected the metaphysical ideas of justice (i.e., of law) and freedom to a devastating plebeian critique, he
stated:

Belford Bax reproaches my contemptuous attitude toward justice,
freedom, and other features of bourgeois metaphysics; he says that these
ideas are so universal and inevitable that even in my critique of their
bourgeois versions I employ certain ideals of justice and freedom.
Needless to say, neither the extremist philosopher-spiritualists nor I can
escape the influence of its ideas; each uses his own ideas as the criteria for
judging the ideas and the conduct of other people. But, whereas certain
ideas are inevitable in the social setting in which they came into being,
it does not follow that they, like mathematical axioms, are inevitable in
other social conditions.[5]

At the time when Lafargue wrote these lines, Belford Bax was a
socialist like Lafargue and belonged to the same proletarian interna-

[3] *Kapital* [Capital] in Karl Marx and Friedrich Engels, *Sobranie Sochinenii*
[Collected Works] (Moscow, 1922), VI, 13.
[4] *Kapital* [Capital] (Moscow, 1923), I, xxxiii.
[5] *Ekonomicheskii Determinizm Karla Marksa* [Karl Marx's Economic De-
terminism] (Moscow, 1923), p. 55.

tional (Second). The bourgeois ideas of justice, law, etc., appeared to him to be eternally existing. Lafargue unmasked these ideas, proved that they are not sacred and that they serve the selfish and dirty interests of the capitalist ruling class. But many leaders of the Second International, who later became outspoken servants of the bourgeoisie, were "filled with indignation" at his critique of bourgeois ideas. Lafargue answered them with penetrating irony:

> Vandervelde and other comrades are shocked by my disrespectful and rather "extremist" manner of unmasking everlasting ideas and principles. To treat Justice, Freedom, or the Fatherland as metaphysical and ethical *prostitutes being sold* in the academic and parliamentary speeches and electoral programs . . . ! This is sacrilege! Had these comrades lived at the time of the Encyclopedists, they would have thrown the same accusations at Diderot and Voltaire, who seized the aristocratic ideology and submitted it to the trial of their reason, who poked fun at the sacred principles of Christianity, at the Orleans Virgin, at the blue-blooded aristocracy, at divine law, and at other divine things.[6]

Lafargue demonstrated quite clearly that those who defend the idea of law (justice) in the bourgeois system are as reactionary as those who defended the idea of divine law in the transition period of feudal to bourgeois law. Though ideologists should not be held responsible for their ideologies, nevertheless—when our ideologists, living in the transition period from the bourgeois to the communist system, continue to advance the bourgeois idea of law as eternal truth, an idea serving the interests of the bourgeoisie—one cannot refrain from using Marx's expression in characterizing these people as a "slavish herd of imitators" (*servum pecus imitatorum*). Furthermore, one cannot refrain from stating that they became "petty peddlers of commodities produced by big foreign firms" and that they use a "method . . . that is characterized by the romanticism of other professions, whereas their theories are but popular preconceptions derived from the superficial, external appearance of things. . . ."[7]

The views asserting that man is a legal being and that a legal sense is an innate property of man are also popular preconceptions derived from the most superficial external appearance of things. In general, the social qualities of man are not natural but artificial, historically transitional properties. Marx denied that social qualities are innate in man, with the exception of man's inherent propensity to be a social being. He demonstrated that Aristotle's definition of man as a political being is invalid. Marx stated: "Man by his very nature is an

---

[6] *Ibid.*
[7] Karl, Marx, *Kapital,* in Marx and Engels, *Sobranie Sochinenii,* III, 384.

animal, 'though not a political but, in any case, a social animal.' "
To this he added: "Strictly speaking, Aristotle's definition asserts
that man, by his very nature, is the citizen of the city-republic. This
conception has been as characteristic of classical antiquity as Frank-
lin's definition of man as a tool-making animal was for the Yankee
age."

The assumption that bourgeois law is an innate quality of man is
tantamount to the eternalization of bourgeois relationships. It is for
this reason that a defense of this view is identical to supporting the
interests of the bourgeoisie. Because of this Marx severely refuted
this view: "Nature does not produce, on the one side, owners of
money or commodities, and, on the other, men possessing nothing
but their own labor power. This relationship was neither created by
nature nor is it a social relationship common to all historical periods.
It is clearly the result of past historical development, the product of
many economic revolutions, the product of the extinction of a whole
series of older formations of social production."[8] Capitalist relationships are the result of the extinction of feudal and simple commodity
relationships. Hence, capitalist law is nothing but the form of these
historically transitional relationships.

The ingenious Marxist thinker Lafargue, who mercilessly and vig-
orously struggled against any forms of bourgeois ideology, thoroughly analyzed the idea of law (justice) and revealed its true nature. A French bourgeois philosopher contends that "justice (i.e.,
law) is eternal, though it only gradually permeates man's spirit and
social reality." At the same time, however, he claims that the process
of the gradual permeation of justice has reached its culmination
point in the bourgeois system. Commenting on this view, Lafargue
ironically stated that "bourgeois society and bourgeois thought are
thus the ultimate and the highest manifestations of immanent justice." The progress of justice (law) came to an end with the establishment of the bourgeois system. As pointed out by Lafargue, "The
bourgeoisie interpreted its conquest of power as immeasurable social
progress, whereas the aristocracy interpreted it as a ruinous regressive movement." The bourgeoisie identified progress with the liquidation of the aristocracy. Following the defeat of the aristocracy . . . by
the French Revolution . . . , the bourgeois idea of progress began to
view itself as the only legitimate representative of progress. The
bourgeoisie contended, quite conscientiously, that its customs, mor-

[8] *Kapital* (1923), I, 139.

als, virtues, private and public morality, and its mode of production and exchange were the most progressive. Prior to the bourgeois revolution, ignorance, barbarism, injustice, and insanity prevailed. After the bourgeois revolution, as stated by Hegel, "for the first time the Idea began to govern the world." The social domination of the bourgeoisie became identified with the reign of reason.

This was the first step toward the theory which asserted that progress ceased with the conquest of political power by the bourgeoisie. The idea of progress and evolution was very popular in the early part of the nineteenth century, when the bourgeoisie was still intoxicated with its political victory and with the startling growth of its economic wealth. But, with the appearance of the proletariat in the political arena in England and France, the bourgeoisie became troubled with the preservation of its domination, and the idea of progress lost its original fascination for it. Since then, the idea of progress has ceased to be of importance in the ideology of the bourgeoisie. Its ideas are eternal and hence not subject to any change. Its law, too, is eternal law. Nothing is progressive for the bourgeoisie, unless it leads to its own victory. Since the aim of progressive development is the transition of the social dictatorship into the hands of the bourgeoisie, and since this aim has been achieved, progress has ceased. Assuming that the transfer of authority into its hands was the only progressive event of history, the bourgeoisie is, in fact, convinced that the seizure of power by the proletariat would be, as Herbert Spencer contended, tantamount to the return to barbarism and "serfdom." To be sure, however, the aristocracy thought the same of the bourgeoisie.

The bourgeoisie is compelled to conceal the unattractive nakedness of its system with eternal ideas, ideas of justice, of law, etc. Oscar Wilde said that, when a woman uses strong perfume, she has something to conceal. According to Lafargue, the same is true of the bourgeoisie.

No other ruling class has ever shouted so much about ideals, for no ruling class has ever been in need of concealing its actions to the same degree with an ideological twaddle. In the hands of the bourgeoisie, ideological charlatanism became the most reliable and most effective means of political and economic deception. Nevertheless, the striking conflict between word and deed prevents neither historians nor philosophers from maintaining that eternal ideas and principles are the exclusive moving forces of the history of the peoples living in a bourgeois system. Such an unheard-of error by historians and philosophers . . . serves as an indisputable proof of the immense power of ideas, and, at the same time, as a proof of the adroitness of the bourgeoisie, which succeeded in cultivating and exploiting this power for its benefit.

The idea of law (justice) most appropriately serves the interests of the exploiting class and holds the masses in subordination.

The ruling class always declares everything that serves its political and economic interests to be just and everything that is in conflict with such interests unjust. Justice, in its understanding, is realized only when its class interests are satisfied. . . . Therefore, ironically, justice is depicted with a cover over its eyes, in order to prevent it from seeing the trite and dirty interests it protects. The feudal and guild organizations, which were detrimental to the interests of the bourgeoisie, had been unjust in their opinion. Therefore, they were destroyed by immanent justice. Bourgeois historians contend that justice could not suffer the armed robbery of the feudal barons, who used robbery as the exclusive method for increasing their land holdings and augmenting their power. Nevertheless, this does not prevent venerable, immanent justice from approving armed robberies committed by a peaceful bourgeois . . . in "barbarian" countries of the new and the old world. . . . In the name of *law*, immanent justice solemnly approves and permits only economic robberies, robberies that the bourgeoisie, without any special effort, commits daily against hired labor. Economic robbery corresponds to the temperament and character of this justice, and, therefore, it willingly assumes the duty of the watch dog of the bourgeois wealth which, obviously, is nothing but a legal and just accumulation of plundered wealth.

. . . . . . .

. . . Justice, which according to philosophers governs in a bourgeois society, directs man toward a peaceful and happy future. In fact, however, it is the other way around: it is a fecund mother of diverse injustices. In the past, justice gave to slaveholders the right to possess a man as an animal; at the present time it gives the right to the capitalist to exploit proletarian children, women, and men like pack animals. Justice placed the lash in the hands of the slaveholder and kindled his hearth when he whipped the slave; now, again, justice permits the capitalist to take the surplus value, which is produced by hired labor, and it leaves his conscience at rest when he compensates labor with starvation wages, the labor that is the source of the capitalist's wealth. I use *my right,* contended the slaveholder when he whipped the slave; I use *my right,* contends the capitalist, when he openly steals the hireling's labor.[9]

The bourgeoisie is not merely unwilling to recognize the transitional character of its legal institutions, it even exempts them from the influence of simple progress, change, and development. "The bourgeoisie and its most educated representatives go even further in their attempts to restrain the course of progress; they remove from its influence a whole number of social organisms of the utmost significance. Economists, historians, and philosophers, who seek to prove that . . . the patriarchic form of the family and the individual form

---

[9] Lafargue, *Ekonomicheskii Determinizm,* pp. 49–54.

of property are not subject to change, contend that these forms were in existence at all times."[10]

I shall demonstrate in a few examples how powerful the idea of law is in the hands of the exploiting class, which by means of this idea keeps the exploited classes in check. The actions that lead to *the same socially detrimental consequences* either provoke aversion and indignation on the part of the broad masses of the people or are received in an indifferent way, depending upon whether or not they are in violation of the law. For example, an incestuous person, a man cohabiting with his daughter or mother, is subject to loathing. Incest is contrary to the "elementary principles of law." In antiquity, Xenophon explained the reasons underlying the prohibition of incestuous marriages: they produce sick children. Soon incestuous cohabitation threatens the populace with degeneration, sickness, and premature death.

It would seem, then, that whenever a certain human conduct threatens other people with degeneration, premature death, etc., such conduct should always arouse "social" indignation. . . . But when such conduct brings forth benefits to dominant groups, it is declared to be in conformity with "law," and does not arouse condemnation. The relationship of the capitalists to the workers during the entire nineteenth century, and indeed now, has entailed degeneration, an increase of the death rate, sickness, and suffering, in comparison to which incest appears to be of no significance. In his *The Situation of the Working Class in England,* Engels indicted the bourgeoisie for the mass murder of the workers. . . .

. . . Capitalists have looked quite coolly at the death and mutilations of workers, which could have been prevented with the expense of a few dollars. (See, for example, statistics cited by Marx on a flax mill where six cases of death and sixty extensive mutilations were counted, which could have been prevented by providing safety devices at the expense of a few shillings. . . .) This conduct of the capitalists is not contradictory to the "principles of law"; their behavior is in conformity with the "law"; and hence they are considered to be decent men, who are not the object of condemnation.

. . . The stealing of bourgeois private property is also contrary to the "elementary principles of law." Consequently, you can leave an average bourgeois in your apartment without any surveillance: he will not steal anything from you. But the stealing of a worker's time, of his labor—even if it is contrary to legislative acts which

---

[10] *Ibid.* I quote Lafargue so frequently because he is the only one who, with unusual vigor, has "seized by the throat" bourgeois ideology.

determine the hours and conditions of work—is not contrary to the "law," and hence is not dishonorable. . . .

. . . In contemporary bourgeois society, law plays the same role as Christianity played in the ancient world of slavery. In his *The Origin of Christianity*, Kautsky arrived at the conclusion that "the ancient world held slaves solely by means of *fear*. Christianity for the first time elevated weak-willed submissiveness to the level of a *moral obligation* that should be performed with joy!"[11] Likewise, the bourgeoisie, instead of employing naked force, prefers to entangle the exploited masses in the invisible ties of a legal ideology that is preached by philosophers and jurists for a small fee.

We refuse to see in the law a certain idea that could prove to be beneficial to the working class, to the proletariat. At a certain time this idea made sense, but at the present time it is superfluous in the ideology of the proletariat. Consequently, it is indispensable to exterminate this idea from proletarian minds. Criticizing the Gotha Program, Marx wrote in 1875:

I have dealt more extensively with "equal right" and "just distribution," in order to show what a crime it is to attempt, on the one hand, to force on our Party again, as dogmas, ideas which in a certain period had some meaning but which now have become obsolete, verbal rubbish, while again perverting, on the other hand, the realistic outlook which it cost so much effort to instill into the Party, but which has now taken root in it, by means of ideological nonsense about right and other trash so common among the democrats and French Socialists.[12]

A disclosure of the ideological and almost religious disguise of law is not alone sufficient for its realistic understanding, an understanding implicit in all teachings of Marxism. It is equally indispensable to explain the appearance and the development of legal ideas corresponding to the social relations that generated them. Looking from this point of view, it can easily be proved that at the present time these ideas are survivals of earlier periods and social conditions. In his letters to Engels (August 1, 1877) and Sorge (October 19, 1877), Marx designated these ideas of justice, equality, and freedom as "modern mythology," as a "new mythology" that some would put in the place of the materialistic basis of socialism. This, according to Marx, requires serious objective study. It is considerably easier to criticize this mythology than to explain it in terms of the economic

[11] *Proiskhozhdenie Khristianstva* [The Origin of Christianity] (Moscow, 1923), p. 351.
[12] *Kritika Gotskoi Programmy* [Critique of the Gotha Program] (Petrograd, 1919), p. 19.

relations that generated it, a procedure that is the requirement of the Marxist method. Speaking of religion, and this is applicable to all ideologies, Marx stated the following: "Indeed, it is much easier, by means of an analysis, to find the kernels of fantastic religious conceptions than it is to deduce religious forms from certain real life relationships. The latter method is materialistic and, consequently, is a scientific method."[13] The quoted view was restated by Engels in a letter to Conrad Schmidt on August 5, 1890. "In general, the word *materialistic*," writes Engels, "serves many of the younger writers in Germany as a mere phrase with which anything and everything is labeled without further study; they stick on this label and then think they have disposed of the question. But our conception of history is, above all, a guide to study, not a lever for construction after the manner of the Hegelians. All history must be studied anew; the conditions of the existence of the different formations of society must be individually examined before an attempt is made to deduce from them the political, civil-legal, aesthetic, philosophic, religious, etc., notions corresponding to them. Only a little has been done here, up to now, because only a few people have got down to it seriously. In this field we can utilize unlimited help; it is immensely big and anyone who will work seriously can achieve a lot and distinguish himself."

Hence, it is not enough to advance a critique of legal ideology. It is indispensable to determine, step by step, which living conditions gave rise to the corresponding legal ideas, and how these legal ideas were preserved as an instrument of suppression, even after they ceased to correspond to the earlier conditions. An attempt in this direction will be made in the following chapters.

In conclusion, a few words should be added on the future of law. The legal norms, which we called correct rules coercively prescribing human conduct, stripped of the halo of "sanctity," will be preserved even after all legal ideas have been exterminated from human minds. Concerning religion—the "old mythology"—Marx stated: "The religious reflection of the actual world will disappear only when the relationships of men's practical daily lives are expressed in a clear and reasonable connection between them and nature."[14] The same applies to the "new mythology," to the legal reflection of the actual world, to legal ideas and conceptions. Speaking of two types of justice, retributive and distributive, which lie at the basis of law (the former of criminal law, the latter of civil law), Lafargue noted:

[13] *Kapital* (1923), I, 349.
[14] *Ibid.*, pp. 46–47.

"The barbarian replaced spilled blood with property; property replaced man; man in a civilized society has only rights given him by property. The communist revolution, which abolishes private property and gives to everybody the same things, will free man and will regenerate the spirit of equality. Then the idea of justice which has haunted man's mind since the time of the creation of private property will disappear as an old nightmare tormenting wretched civilized humanity."[15]

With the disappearance of the idea of law, coercive rules, or what are traditionally known as legal norms, will also disappear. In the *Critique of the Gotha Program,* Marx proved that all law is an expression of inequality. Consequently, with the disappearance of all exploitation and all inequality, i.e., with the complete accession of the communist system, the necessity for coercive rules, which at the present time are called laws, will disappear completely. If, as stated by Marx in his *Critique of the Gotha Program,* "law can never elevate itself above the economic structure and the cultural development determined by this structure," then, with the advance of the economic structure of society to the level of complete communism, the high cultural development conditioned thereby will render superfluous and unnecessary any coercive regulation of human relations. The results, which in the transition period were achieved by means of coercive norms, will be attained by themselves because they will be rooted in the nature of the economic relations of that time.

From the above-said it follows that the legislation of the proletarian state should not be influenced by any presumed, eternally existing concept of law and that it can and should reject the "new mythology." In establishing definite rules, proletarian legislation must take into consideration only their expediency, i.e., the question of whether or not or to what extent these rules achieve the goals for which they were created. But bourgeois ideology in this sphere sets up invisible and dangerous traps. The "new mythology," driven out through the door, comes back through the window. We are being told that, from the political point of view, the creation of an unlimited scope of rights is inevitable. A scope as unlimited as it was at the beginning of the past century after the fall of feudalism and the establishment of the bourgeois system. We hear from different sources that instead of limiting rights it is indispensable to establish the broadest possible scope of rights, because even the smallest restriction . . . will weaken

[15] *Ekonomicheskii Determinizm,* p. 138.

the stimulus of economic activity and accumulation. They tell us that our policy—according to which our state grants rights only for the purpose of developing the forces of production and revokes them if their application produces results contradictory to the intended socioeconomic purpose . . . , and interferes, in the interest of society, with the relationships that previously were known as private—as in conflict with the sound sense of individualism innate in each man. Individualism, that is, freedom of exploitation, presented as an exclusive stimulus of man's activity, is being advanced as an eternally existing frame of mind, or truth, whose existence is not determined by social conditions and hence is not subject to extermination under changed conditions.

. . . It stands to reason, though, that individualism is not a permanent feature of human nature at all. Its origin, existence, and, consequently, its disappearance, are determined by the conditions of social life.

. . . At any rate, in the period of bourgeois trusts, cartels, syndicates, etc., individualism is not and cannot be the dominating frame of mind. Neither can it become the dominating principle, determining mass activities, in the transition period of the Soviet Union. . . .

. . . We grant private property rights only with the aim of developing the forces of production of our country. Consequently, contrary to bourgeois "legal-political principles," which aim at protecting the interests of one or another group of the exploiting class, we have established the following rule: rights are granted only if they are conducive to the development of the forces of production, i.e., to the development of the entire national economy, the objective of which is to satisfy the needs of the popular masses. This principle is clear; it does not aim at protecting the interests of the individual groups dominating the masses but, on the contrary, is willing to sacrifice the interests of individual persons for the attainment of the general goal.

. . . While living in Soviet countries . . . , in the transition period from the capitalist toward the communist system, we consciously strive for the development of the forces of production. The development of the forces of production . . . is our direct and immediate goal. Therefore, we undertake measures, establish rules, and grant "rights" within the scope dictated by our goals.

Hence, it does not mean that the character of the rights granted by us is immutable, i.e., not subject to change and not subject to restrictions and expansions. It was indicated above that the French bourgeois revolution took place almost a hundred years after the English

Revolution, and, consequently, having taken place under more mature conditions, did away with feudalism completely. That means that the English bourgeois revolution, which took place a hundred years earlier than the French Revolution and, consequently, under less mature conditions, preserved many feudal features up until the present time. The proletarian revolutions also are carried out under diverse and more or less mature conditions.

Our revolution took place earlier than in other countries, and hence under less mature conditions. In addition, it was accomplished in a most economically backward country. The forthcoming revolution in Germany will take place not only later but also under more mature economic conditions than those existing in our country six years ago. It will do away with the survivors of the bourgeois system in a more radical manner. There, the development of the forces of production will call for the granting of fewer "rights" than in our country. Even fewer "rights" will have to be granted in America. The decrease of these "rights" in our country can take place only commensurably with the development of the forces of production and the maturation of our conditions. The dynamic process of the development of the forces of production will reduce the scope of the unavoidable concessions to the previous regime. Our legislators must always take this process under consideration; otherwise, to quote Marx, this process will, by itself, "correct the arbitrary violations committed by the state authority."

# "The Narrow Horizon of Bourgeois Law"*

## ∞ E. B. Pashukanis

As Marx pointed out in his *Critique of the Gotha Program,* the transition epoch is characterized by the fact that human relations will per force be circumscribed for a certain period of time by "the narrow horizon of bourgeois law." It is interesting to ascertain what, in Marx's judgment, this narrow horizon of bourgeois law is.

Marx takes as a premise a social order wherein the means of production belong to all society and wherein producers do not exchange their products; consequently he is taking a stage higher than the New Economic Policy through which we are living. The bond of the market is replaced entirely by an organized bond, and, accordingly, "labor consumed in the manufacture of products is not manifested in the form of value (as a supposed property of the products themselves) since here—in contrast to capitalist society—the labor of the individual is part of the collective labor directly and not indirectly."[1] But even if the market and the barter of the market were completely eliminated, the new communist society, according to Marx, must for a certain time bear "in all relationships—economic, moral, and intellectual—the sharply defined imprint of the distinguishing attributes of the old society from whose innermost parts it came to light." This is stated in the principle of distribution, according to which each producer personally obtains precisely what he furnishes to society (after the making of certain deductions). Marx emphasizes that, regardless of radical changes of content and form, "the principle here dominant is the same principle as that which prevails in the barter of goods equivalents: a definite quantum of labor in one form is exchanged for the same quantum of labor in another form." Insofar as the relationships of the individual producer and society continue to retain the form of an equivalent exchange, they continue to that extent to preserve the form of law as well, for, "by its very nature, law is merely the application of a like scale." However, the natural differ-

* From *Obshchaya Teoriya Prava i Marksizm* [The General Theory of Law and Marxism] (Moscow, 1924), translated from the fourth edition (Moscow, 1928), pp. 22–24. An English translation of the whole work is available in Babb and Hazard (eds.), *Soviet Legal Philosophy* (Cambridge, Mass., 1951).
[1] *Kritika Gotskoi Programmy* [Critique of the Gotha Program] (Petrograd, 1919), p. 15.

ences of individual capacities are not taken into consideration here, wherefore, "by its content, this law—like law of every sort—is the law of inequality." Marx says nothing as to the necessity of state authority, the coercion of which would secure the fulfillment of these norms of the "unequal" law that preserves its "bourgeois limitedness," but this is perfectly obvious. Lenin drew such an inference: "As regards the distribution of products of *consumption,* bourgeois law, of course, inevitably presupposes the *bourgeois state* as well, because law is nothing without a mechanism capable of compelling the observance of legal norms. It follows that under communism not only does bourgeois law remain for a certain time but so does the bourgeois state without the bourgeoisie."[2] Once the form of an equivalent relationship is provided, this means that a form of law is provided—a form of public (i.e., state) authority—which is thereby enabled to remain in force for a certain time, even in conditions where the division into classes no longer exists. The dying out of law —and therewith of the state—will be complete, according to the view of Marx, only when "labor, having ceased to be a means of life, shall itself become the primary necessity of life," when the all-sided development of individuals shall be accompanied by an expansion of production forces, and everyone shall labor voluntarily according to his abilities, or, in the words of Lenin, "shall not make deductions after the fashion of Shylock so as not to work an extra half hour more than someone else": in a word, when an *end shall finally have been put to the form of the equivalent relationship.*

Accordingly, Marx conceived of the transition to expanded communism, not as a transition to new forms of law, but as the dying out of the juridic form in general, as liberation from this heritage of the bourgeois epoch, which was destined to outlive the bourgeoisie itself. At the same time, Marx points out the basic conditions of the existence of the legal form, a condition rooted in economics itself, namely, the unification of labor efforts on the principle of an equivalent exchange—that is to say, he reveals the profound inner connection between the form of law and the form of goods. A society that, in view of the condition of its forces of production, *is compelled* to preserve a relationship of equivalency between expenditures of labor and compensation therefor, in a form that is reminiscent (although only remotely reminiscent) of the exchange of goods values, *will be forced* to preserve also the form of law. It is only if we start from this basic element that we can understand why a whole series

[2] *Gosudarstvo i Revolutsiya* [State and Revolution].

of other social relationships takes on juridic form. On the contrary, to reason that courts and statutes will remain forever and aye, for the reason that certain crimes against personality, and so forth, will not disappear under the maximum of economic security, is to take elements that are derivative and of minor importance for the principal and basic elements. For even bourgeois advanced criminologists are convinced theoretically that the struggle against criminality may itself be regarded per se as a task of medical pedagogy, for whose solution the jurist—with his *corpus delicti,* his codes, his concept of "guilt," his "unqualified or qualified criminal responsibility," and his subtle distinctions between participation, complicity, and instigation —is entirely superfluous. And, if this theoretical conviction has not as yet led to the abolition of criminal codes and courts, this is so only because the overcoming of the form of law is connected not only with going beyond the framework of bourgeois society but also with a radical deliverance from all the survivals of that society.

# Morality, Law, and Justice* ∽ E. B. Pashukanis

This ambiguity of the ethical form is not something accidental, a kind of an external defect, caused by the specific shortcomings of capitalism. On the contrary, it is an essential feature of the ethical form as such. Elimination of the ambiguity of the ethical form means transition to a planned social economy, and this in turn means the realization of a social order in which people can form and apprehend their relationships by employing the simple and clear concepts of harm and advantage. To destroy the ambiguity of the ethical form in its most essential field, i.e., in the sphere of man's material existence, means the destruction of that form in general.

It is from this very point of view of harm and advantage that pure utilitarianism, striving to dispel the metaphysical fog surrounding the ethical theory, approaches the concepts of good and evil. This, of course, simply destroys ethics, or, more accurately, tries to destroy and to vanquish ethics. For ethical fetishes can be completely overcome in reality only if the fetishisms of commodities and of law are vanquished at the same time. People whose conduct is guided by the clear and simple concepts of harm and advantage will not require that their social relationships be expressed either in terms of value or in terms of law. Until this historical stage of development is attained by mankind, however—that is to say, until mankind is rid of the inheritance of the capitalist epoch—the struggle of theoretical thinking can only anticipate this future emancipation without the capacity to embody it in practice. We must here recall Marx's words concerning goods fetishism: "The tardy scientific discovery that the products of labor—insofar as they are values—represent only a material expression of the labor expended on their production, constitutes an epoch in the history of human development; but it is certainly far from destroying the material semblance of the social character of labor."

But it will be objected that the class morality of the proletariat is now already liberated from all fetishes. That which is morally due is that which is beneficial to the class. In this form, morality comprises

* From *Obshchaya Teoriya Prava i Marksizm* [The General Theory of Law and Marxism] (Moscow, 1924), translated from the fourth edition (Moscow, 1928), pp. 102–6. An English translation of the whole work is available in Babb and Hazard (eds.), *Soviet Legal Philosophy* (Cambridge, Mass., 1951).

nothing absolute—since what is beneficial today may cease to be beneficial tomorrow—and comprises nothing supernatural or wrapped in mystery, inasmuch as the principle of benefit is simple and a matter of reason.

There is no doubt that the morality of the proletariat—or rather of the advanced strata of the proletariat—loses its doubly fetishistic character, being liberated, let us say, from religious elements. But morality, even morality that is completely free from an alloy of religious elements, remains morality all the same, that is to say, a form of social relationship in which not everything as yet is reduced to man himself. If the living link with the class is in reality so strong that the boundaries of the ego are effaced, as it were, and the benefit of the class actually merges with individual benefit, then there is no sense in talking about the fulfillment of a moral duty; in general, the phenomenon of morality is then absent. Where such a merger has not taken place, an abstract relationship of moral duty, with all the consequences ensuing therefrom, inevitably arises. The rule, so act as to confer the greatest benefit on the class, will sound like Kant's formula, so act that the maxim of your conduct may serve as a principle of universal legislation. The whole difference is this, that in the former case we introduce a concrete limitation, we set a class framework for ethical logic.[1] But within this framework it remains in full force. The class content of ethics does not per se destroy the form of ethics. We have in view the form of the actual manifestation and not merely the logical form. Deep within the proletarian, that is to say, the class collective, we observe the means of realizing that which is morally due, means that are identical in form and that take shape from two contrasting elements: (1) on the one hand, the collective does not renounce all possible means of exerting pressure upon its members to incite them to that which is morally due; (2) on the other hand, the same collective classifies conduct as moral conduct only when this external pressure—as a motive—is concededly absent. It is for this very reason that morality and moral conduct are so closely bound up with hypocrisy in social practice. It is true that the conditions of the life of the proletariat include the prerequisites for the development of a new, loftier, and more harmonious

---

[1] Needless to say, extraclass ethics can exist only in the imagination—and in no wise in practice—in a society torn by class conflict. The worker—deciding to take part in a strike, notwithstanding the deprivations associated therewith for him personally—may formulate this decision as a moral duty to subordinate his private interests to the general interests. But it is perfectly manifest that his concept of the general interests cannot include the interests of the capitalist (*against* whom the struggle is being carried on) as well.

form of the relationship between personality and the collective, as evidenced by the facts relating to the manifestation of the class solidarity of the proletariat. But the old continues to exist alongside of the new. Side by side with the social man of the future, who merges his ego with the collective and finds therein life's highest satisfaction and meaning, the moral man continues to exist, bearing upon himself the weight of a more or less abstract duty. The victory of the first form has the force (1) of complete liberation from all the survivals of private-property relationships and (2) of the final re-education of mankind in a spirit of communism. Of course this is not at all a task purely ideological or pedagogic; the new type of relationship requires the creation and strengthening of a new material economic basis.

It must, therefore, be borne in mind that morality, law, and state are forms of bourgeois society. The fact that the proletariat may be compelled to use them by no means signifies that they can develop further in the direction of being filled with a socialist content. They have no capacity adequate to hold a socialist content and are bound to die out to the extent that it is brought into being. Nevertheless, in the present transition period the proletariat, in its class interests, must necessarily utilize in one way or another these forms that have been inherited from bourgeois society and thereby exhaust them completely. To this end, the proletariat must first and foremost have a notion of the historical origin of these forms that is perfectly clear and free from ideological haziness. Its attitude must be one of sober criticism, not only as regards the bourgeois state and bourgeois morality, but also as regards its own state and its own proletarian morality—that is to say, it must comprehend the historical necessity of their existence and of their disappearance alike.[2]

In his critique of Proudhon, Marx points out . . . that the abstract concept of morality is by no means an absolute and eternal criterion through the employment of which we could construct an ideal, i.e., a just relationship of exchange. This would mean an attempt "to reorganize chemical metabolism in conformity with 'eternal ideas,' 'special attributes,' and 'affinity,' instead of studying the actual laws

[2] Does this mean that "there will be no morality in the society of the future"? Of course not, if morality is understood in a broad sense as the development of the higher forms of humaneness and the conversion of man into a generic being (to use the expression of Marx). In the given instance, however, the concern was with something different, with the specific forms of moral consciousness and moral conduct which, having performed their historical role, will have to yield place to other and higher forms of the relationship between the individual and the collective.

of that metabolism." For the concept of justice is itself drawn from the exchange relationship and expresses nothing whatsoever outside that relationship. Strictly speaking, the very concept of justice comprises nothing essentially new, as compared with the concept of human equality which we have analyzed earlier. Therefore, it is ridiculous to see any independent and absolute criterion in the idea of justice. Indeed, cleverly employed, the idea affords greater possibilities for interpreting inequality as equality and is therefore particularly suitable for concealing the ambiguity of the ethical form. On the other hand, justice is the step whereby ethics descends to law. Moral conduct must be "free," but justice can be constrained. Constraint of moral behavior tends to negate its own existence, while justice is "rendered" to man openly; it admits of external effectuation and of active and egoistic interestedness.

# Toward a Marxist Conception of Law and State*

## ᢙ N. V. Krylenko

I think that, of all the ventures of bourgeois science to comprehend the meaning of social life and to give a scientific explanation of social phenomena, the ventures directed at explaining the phenomenon called law have been the most hopeless. Social life in general, that is, social relationships, have always been to bourgeois science a mystery which it cannot grasp. And comprehension of the true nature of the social relationships that go under the name of legal phenomena has been an absolutely insoluble task for bourgeois society. It has been an insoluble task primarily because law—as we know it in its coming into being, in its development, and in its history—is, as it always has been, a definite system of ideas and prescriptions of custom and statutes (both written and unwritten) which are constantly changing along with the development of society. In order to know the meaning of legal phenomena, in the broad sense of the term, bourgeois scientists would have to discover the reasons responsible for the constant change of legal phenomena, as well as the reasons why legal ideas are in a constant state of flux.

. . . But, when a bourgeois scientist raises the question concerning the source of those changes, he instantly answers that they originate "in the mind." By giving such an answer—namely, that legal ideas, the system of law, and legal relationships originate in the mind—he commits the first and fundamental error, because in fact it is the other way around. *Legal phenomena, like all other expressions of social relationships, do not originate in the mind; on the contrary, they come to the mind from other sources.* We shall see later how this takes place. The bourgeois scientist's trouble consists in that, when confronted with the question of the genesis—of the sources—of law, he instantly commits the basic methodological error which prevents him from seeing that end meets end. To be sure, a bourgeois scientist is not capable of avoiding such an error; this we shall see soon.

Following the first erroneous answer that law originates in the mind, he commits a second inescapable error. To be more specific, having

* From *Besedy o Prave i Gosudarstve* [Discourse on Law and State] (Moscow, 1924), pp. 3–16.

asserted that law is a product of the mind, i.e., that it is a product of the ideological function of consciousness, he involuntarily poses the question: "Whose consciousness?" In answering this question he commits a second error. His answer is that it is the consciousness of the nation, of the people, or of brilliant individuals. His first error, namely, the formulation of the origin of legal phenomena as a result of the ideological function of the consciousness, leads to a second error, to an incorrect formulation of the question of to whom the consciousness belongs. The answers given to this question by pre-bourgeois theorists were even more primitive and naïve. Thus, some contended that consciousness is a manifestation of the "natural law" or of the "lord God."

All these various answers have one thing in common. They are based on the assumption that law is a product of the function of the brain, consciousness, and ideology, which are presumably not only separate but even independent of the immediate social, political, and economic conditions in which they and the law come into being, develop, and become active. This is a fundamental methodological error, an error that predetermines the answer to the question: "What is the law?"

Our main task, then, is to place the object of our study—that is, the law—in its real, kindred social setting, in which it came into being. However, prior to doing this, we intend to examine several bourgeois theories as examples of the fact that incorrectly posed questions lead to absolutely false answers. Furthermore, we intend to demonstrate why a bourgeois thinks incorrectly and why he cannot think differently.

The aforesaid should not be interpreted to mean that we reject fully all bourgeois works on law. Nothing is further from the truth. A few great thinkers of the bourgeois school of law have made a considerable contribution to the science of law. Some of them, as we shall see, approached quite closely the essence of the question but failed to solve it. In the process of revealing the nature of legal phenomena, we shall keep in mind the historical conditioning and inescapability of the fact that bourgeois jurists have not, and could not, furnish a correct definition of law. Or, to put it differently, we shall answer Kant's question: "Why are jurists still searching for the definition of law?" In order to answer this question, we shall examine some bourgeois theories. . . .

Professor Korkunov, the "reactionary free thinker," as he has been characterized by Stuchka, defined law as a system of "the delimitation of interests." We must admit that to a certain extent this definition is better than any other. But is it true that, in fact, law is the delimitation of interests? We would like to supplement this definition: law is the delimitation of interests *from the viewpoint of the preservation of the ruling class's interests*. Our amplification offers a specific point of view which will illuminate quite a few confused questions. Without the amplification, Korkunov's definition is worthless, for it instantly raises in our minds several questions: "What is the meaning of the delimitation of interests?" "From what point of view are the interests delimited?" "By whom and where are the interests delimited?" "In what direction are they delimited?" and "What methods are used in delimiting the interests?" Are the interests delimited from the point of view of "ultimate justice" or from the point of view of the ruling class? Reticence brings Korkunov's definition to naught. Nevertheless, Korkunov noted correctly some aspects of legal relationships, namely, that *all legal disputes involve conflicts of interests*. He failed, though, to answer the questions: "What type of interests?" and "Whose interests?" Consequently, his definition, although it is one of the oldest and most closely approaching the essence of the problems, is incomplete.

A question arises in this context: "Is a bourgeois scientist capable of answering these questions . . . ?" One would assume that, proceeding with the definition of law as the delimitation of interests, he should be capable of answering the practical question: "From what point of view does the law delimitate interests?" That is, he should be capable of giving a true answer, namely, that law delimitates interests from the point of view of the interests of a given class: for example, in a bourgeois society, from the point of view of the bourgeois class. Or he should be capable of telling a lie: for example, that law delimitates interests from the point of view of the "interests of the state," the social interests of the whole "people," "higher interests," "ultimate justice," or anything else. One would assume that in the latter case he should be able to invent a fiction, a fetish, or a clever expression in order *to slur over the essence of the matter*. The fact is, however, that neither the bourgeois state nor bourgeois scientists are capable of telling the truth. This is not due to their unwillingness to tell the truth; it is due to the fact that as the representatives of the ruling class their minds fail even to conceive of such a formulation of the problem. They are thoroughly convinced that the delimitation of interests is done from the point of view of the interests of the people, ultimate justice, etc., etc. And this means that the principal defect of their formulation of the problem is to be sought in the absence of *the class point of view*. The class point of view was entirely inconceivable, for it would have revealed the class nature of the state in its very nakedness. . . .

The next theory to be examined is that of Professor Petrazhitskii. In his opinion, law is an emotion, that is, a certain sensation peculiar to each man. When a man says "This is mine," he expresses his sensation. There are two types of sensations. . . . First, a legal sensation, which finds its expression in a binding, coercive norm, statute, or custom; second, a moral sensation, which is not expressed in coercive norms.

We need not examine Petrazhitskii's theory in detail. The gist of this theory is that the source of law is transferred from a pure intellectual sphere into a psychological sphere. Man no longer "invents" the legal system by means of his "mind." The source of law is now the emotional depth of human perceptions: man's "ego," with its inner sensations and emotions. To be sure, however, Petrazhitskii has failed to raise the crucial question: *"What is the source of human emotions?"* We are told that legal norms are legal emotions, that legal norms are rooted in the depth of the human psyche, but we do not know what the source of the latter is. Petrazhitskii did not raise the question, because it leads to economic materialism. According to the latter, only class psychology exists; everything is determined by class interests and by the class struggle. . . . A bourgeois scientist cannot raise the question, because he would have to admit that legal emotions are derivative from the interests of a given social class; that these interests vary from class to class; that the variety of interests leads to a struggle; and that the dominant system of legal relationships has a class character because it always constitutes an objective reflection of the interests of the dominant class, either in writing or in consciousness. The bourgeois scientist obviously cannot afford to do this, for it would be tantamount to committing public suicide.

The next problem that we intend to examine is the definition of law offered by a German scientist, Jellinek. If I recall correctly, Jellinek asserts that law is an expression of the "ethical minimum, reflected in a written form, at a given time." Like others, Jellinek has failed to raise the essential questions: "Is there only one ethic?" "Are ethical views always the same?" We know for sure that ethical ideas are not immutable, that, at any time, two diametrically opposed ethical views on the same subject can exist. But a bourgeois scientist cannot admit this, because this would be tantamount to undermining the very basis of the bourgeois system. The following example may serve as an illustration of our view. The peasants have seized the land from the landlords. The question arises: "Did they commit an ethical or an unethical act?" Naturally, any peasant will answer that, indeed, it was an ethical act. On the other hand, the landlord will say that this act has nothing to do with ethics, that it was an act of robbery. To be sure, the landlord is right from his point of view. These are two diametrically opposed views of the same fact, clearly demonstrating the class nature of ethical ideas. What do we mean when we say "This is violence," "This is an arbitrary rule"? The meaning of these statements is that we appeal to certain common principles that are presumably binding upon everyone. In fact, however, this means that we appeal to principles that we presuppose to be universal but that might not be recognized as such by our class enemies. This is why Jellinek's definition of law does not withstand criticism.

The next definition of law belongs to a German scientist, Ihering. According to Ihering's theory, which reflected the history of Germany in the 1870's and 1880's, "power creates law; law is the politics of power." To put it differently, law is the embodiment, the legitimization of power in a written form. Ihering approached the problem correctly, but he, too, failed to raise the questions: "What type of power?" "Whose power?" and "Under what conditions is the power employed?"

Thus, following the examination of the various definitions, it becomes obvious that . . . an analysis of any social phenomenon must take into account the class point of view. But the raising of the class problem by a bourgeois scientist would be tantamount to recognition of the class nature of the state, of society, and of any legislation. This, however, would amount to telling the truth, which is antithetical to him and to his class nature. Therefore, it is obvious that, even if they were willing, the bourgeois scientists are organically incapable of either positing or correctly answering these questions.

In order to show how far-reaching is the inability to carry an analysis to its very end, even among non-bourgeois scientists, I would like to cite an example given by Comrade Podvolotskii. In the discussion of Reisner's theory, Podvolotskii indicates that "Reisner, too, is filled with indignation at the attempts to interpret the law as an instrument of exploitation." According to Reisner,

It is impossible not to notice the striking fact that we, in tune with bourgeois theorists, are ready to confuse the state with the law as two phenomena inevitably and inescapably related to one another. If the state is an organization of the proprietary classes directed against the indigent classes, then all law, as an inescapable ally of the state, appears as though tainted with the same exploitative aim. And if the state is ultimately doomed to disappear together with all other attributes of the contemporary class state, then the law is threatened with the same destiny.

This is Reisner's protest against the view that *all law is class law.* But is there any other law? Why does Reisner think that it is so terrible when we assert that all law is the law of exploitation? What is the meaning of the exploitative law? The law is an instrument by means of which a class protects its interests. When the interests of a landlord require enslavement of peasants' labor, he issues a law that says that the serf is a slave, is his property, which he can exploit, sell, deposit, kill, etc. In the paragraph quoted by Podvolotskii, Reisner stated that "law appears as though tainted with one and the same exploitative aim." What a strange fear of words! If the entire burden of taxation in the Workers-Peasants state falls upon the proprietary class, then the questions arise: "What is it?" "Is it a norm, a law?" "Is it or is it not an exploitative norm?" Why not admit that it is an exploitative norm? Is there anything silly in that? I see absolutely nothing terrible in such a formulation of the problem. Yes, we exploit our class enemies whenever it is necessary. Indeed, our enemies are not the only ones we exploit. For example, we have issued a law on the apportionment of products and, in conformity with this law, we took everything away from the peasants with the exception of what was necessary to satisfy their bare necessities. With the food collected by means of violence, we fed the city and the army. Was this not exploitation of peasants' labor in favor of a definite minority of the population? Indeed, it was exploitation, but I see nothing terrible in that. . . . We resorted to such action because we had to feed the army, which was defending the state. . . .

From Reisner's point of view it follows that the law in itself, that is to say, the "pure" law, is not an instrument of exploitation. I would like to see at least one norm that has not an exploitative character. I would be willing to prove that every norm serves as an instrument for the protection of the ruling class's interests. As long as classes exist— as long as they have not yet died away—every norm has an exploitative, compulsory, class character in relation to another class.

The aforesaid is an example of the fact that scientists, even those who call themselves Communists, cannot cut the umbilical cord that ties them to the bourgeois system and bourgeois theories. Thus, Podvolotskii also reproaches Comrade Stuchka for committing the same sin: for not carrying out the class point of view to its logical end. He quotes Stuchka as saying: "The system of relationships is the material element of law, whereas the system of norms is the ideal, ideological element of law." Podvolotskii intends to demonstrate that even Stuchka has not yet broken off with the bourgeois conception of law as a pure ideological product. . . . How right Podvolotskii is, we shall see later. Nevertheless, the fact is that even one of our most consistent theorists is reproached for committing the same sin.

This is why, prior to the examination of law, one must establish some general principles, general theses, from which we should not and cannot deviate under any circumstances. . . . These principles are the following: First, *every society* is a class society, and, therefore, all facts and occurrences of social life in a class society are nothing but the form, the reflection, the manifestation of the class struggle. Consequently, all social institutions, *without any exception*—the state in its totality as well as an individual legal norm—are class institutions reflecting the interests of the ruling class. . . .

Because of the class struggle, the legal norms in a class society constitute a middle line, a watershed, at which the struggle comes to a stop, for it has found its expression in written norms. But neither the class character of the norms nor their class origin is thereby affected. Moreover, the purpose of the legal norm is always to preserve the existing social order—its uninterrupted functioning—and that means to *protect the interests of the dominant class*. Looking from this point of view, every norm is rooted in the class nature of society and reflects the interests of the dominant class. Therefore, we shall always reject the attempts, regardless of by whom made, to separate the essence of legal phenomena from the class struggle and class interests.

We would like to give another and final example that will demonstrate in a most obvious way the errors stemming from inconsistency in this field. Presumably, we all are familiar with Lassalle's *The Nature of the Constitution* and *Workers' Program*. These books were published in 1863 and 1865 respectively. In one of these books Lassalle raises the question: "What is a constitution?" A constitution, he answers, is guns, prisons, and bayonets. In other words, he . . . conceives of a constitution as material force. The gun is a constitution, he asserts, because a gun constitutes power, is an instrument of coercion. . . . Nevertheless, having correctly formulated the problem, Lassalle concludes his *Workers' Program* in the following way: "Universal electoral rights—this is the banner that will lead us to the victory; of another banner we cannot conceive." He develops the following argument in support of this view. Each class, he states, fills the state system with its own contents: the feudal class, or the first estate, filled it with its content; the bourgeois class filled it with "its own idea." The fourth estate (or proletariat) should infuse into the state its own ideas, namely, "solidarity of interests, universality, and mutuality in development." According to Lassalle, the proletariat should accomplish this by means of a universal electoral law. The state and the guns will then serve the working class. In his opinion, "Through the universal electoral right, the elected representatives will finally become a faithful and accurate reflection of the people who elected them."

To be sure, Marx was very critical of such an approach. In his famous *Critique of the Gotha Program,* he openly spoke about the "struggle against the Lassallian faith in state miracles." The gist of the controversy is that, while Lassalle correctly formulated the problem of the nature of state machinery as an instrument of compulsion and exploitation, he separated this state machinery as something entirely independent from social class relationships. Furthermore, he assumed the possibility that the working class, having conquered the state machinery, will infuse into the state its own ideas and will compel the state to serve its class interests. To put it differently, the state appears as being suspended in the air, torn away from class interests, from society, and from the living people who comprise this machine. A false interpretation of the nature of social relationships led Lassalle to the creation of a political program that asserted that all efforts of the working class should be directed toward the conquest of the state machinery only by means of universal electoral suffrage.

This is why our task is the following. The cited examples should help us to comprehend the methodological errors of our opponents, and to prevent them from committing such errors in the future. First, the law, in its rise, development, and content, is not an independent phenomenon. Second, the law is always derivative in its rise, development, and content. The law is always derivative from the existing social relationships, and its content always reflects the interests of the dominant class. The law expresses the interests of the dominant class, this is our third thesis. As such, the law is a result of the class struggle; it is the point at which the clashes of the class struggle come to a stop. This is the proper approach. If we deviate from this approach even one iota, we shall make errors that may have grave practical consequences. . . . If we adhere to this approach, then our answers will always be correct.

# The Affinity between Some Bourgeois and Marxist Theories of Law*  ∽  *A. S. Rubinshtein*

In our recent legal literature one encounters frequent and valid references to the similarity of some bourgeois legal theories to the fundamental assumptions of the Marxist theory of law.[1] So far as we know, however, no one has thus far undertaken a thorough study of this curious phenomenon, perhaps because of the fact that the Marxist theory of law itself has not yet been scientifically worked out.

We have in existence at the present time several independent and valuable works devoted to an explanation of the Marxist theory of law. These greatly facilitate a comparison of Marxist and bourgeois theories of law. Without intending to exhaust the problem, our aim is to show the principal points at which the similarity of bourgeois jurisprudence and Marxism is most vivid.

The closeness of certain bourgeois theories to the principles of the Marxist theory of law manifests itself primarily in the question of the nature and significance of law. We encounter in the philosophical system of Marxism, if not two distinct theories of law, then at least two formulations of the same theory, one of which is increasingly attracting the attention of revolutionary Marxists. Specifically, this is the theory that underlies the official definition of law, the definition advanced at one time by the Collegium of the People's Commissariat of Justice of the R.S.F.S.R.

"Law"—this formula declares—"is an order of social relations, established in the interests of the ruling class and protected by its organized power." Of special interest, undoubtedly, is the *first* part of the definition: "Law is *an order of social relations.*" Law is conceived here not as a stupefied, ossified "rule of conduct," not as a "system of written laws," but as a *living social force, as an organization of social relations,* as a "stream of life itself."[2]

* *From* "Novye Idei Burzhuaznoi Yurisprudentsii i Marksistskaya Teoriya Prava" [New Ideas in Bourgeois Jurisprudence and the Marxist Theory of Law], *Vestnik Sovetskoi Yustitsii* [Organ of the People's Commissariat of Justice of the Ukranian S.S.R. and the Ukranian Juridical Society], No. 20 (30) (1924), pp. 653–65.

[1] See Podvolotskii, *Marksistskaya Teoriya Prava* [The Marxist Theory of Law] (Moscow, 1923), and Stuchka, *Obshchee Uchenie o Prave* [The General Theory of Law] (Moscow, 1921), p. 105.

[2] The last expression taken from Veresov, "Klassovyi Pravoporyadok" [Class Legal Order], *Sovetskoe Stroitelstvo* (Odessa, 1920), No. 3–4.

It is precisely such a materialist conception of law (as opposed to an idealist, "normative" conception) that is becoming increasingly popular in current bourgeois jurisprudence. It is most fashionable in bourgeois *jurisprudence* to approach law as a *living, real organization of reality,* that is, as *reality itself,* looked upon from a specific *point of view.* In this connection it is of interest to quote E. Ehrlich, who is one of the most famous modern bourgeois jurists: "Law," says Ehrlich, "is the real foundation of human society; it is a skeleton of human society."[3]

. . . Now law is no longer regarded as a categorical command directed at society with the purpose of *reforming* the social system; no, law is a simple *reflection,* an *expression* of those economic relationships that arise and develop independent of the *direct will* of the legislator. As stated by Marx, "Society is not based on law. This is a fantasy of jurists. On the contrary, law should be based on society; it should be an expression of society's general interests and needs, arising from the existing material mode of production."[4] Kantorovich (Gnaeus Flavius), who is one of the acknowledged representatives of bourgeois jurisprudence, adheres to a similar point of view. While drawing a distinction between the so-called free law as a real organization of social relationships and the official law as a reflection of this organization in legal codes, Kantorovich asserts that the "free law is the *soil* from which the official law springs and to which it should always conform."[5]

Hence, society does not serve law; law should serve, and factually always does serve, society. That is the meaning of the *"instrumental"* character of law. But the idea of the *instrumental* character of law is still alien to our jurists. We had an opportunity to witness this during the discussion of Comrade Malitskii's paper on the inheritance law. . . . His critics asked him a "devastating" question; was he speaking about *de lege lata* or *de lege ferenda?* In answering the question . . . , Comrade Malitskii stated that "if a given law is . . . expedient and necessary, then it should not be prevented from being translated into reality in defiance of the interest of the whole society."[6]

From the point of view of the *instrumental* character of law—which is increasingly attracting attention from bourgeois jurists and

---

[3] *Freie Rechtsbindung und Rechtswissenschaft* (n.p., n.d.), p. 9; see also Spiegel, *Gesetz und Recht* (n.p., n.d.), pp. 27, 119.

[4] Marx, *Rech na Kelnskom Protsesse* [Speech at a Cologne Trial] (Moscow, 1923), p. 29.

[5] Gnaeus Flavius, *Der Kampf um die Rechtswissenschaft* (1st ed.; n.p., 1906), p. 14.

[6] *Vestnik Sovetskoi Yustitsii,* No. 15 (25), p. 481.

which is solely acceptable for the Marxist theory of law—a strict differentiation of *lex lata* and *lex ferenda* is meaningless. *Lex lata* that is, the law acting in the interests of society, is the *lex ferenda,* that is, the law that *ought* to act in the interests of society. If a law is not acting in the interests of society, then it is not a law but a dead letter that neither should be—nor is—applied by the courts.

What remains is the question of what happens when a written law does not express—that is, does not correspond (or ceases to correspond) to—the interests and the needs of society. This question brings us to the very essence of the new ideas in bourgeois jurisprudence and to the principles on which modern bourgeois legal systems are based.

We shall note initially that law can fail to express the needs of society either under all conditions or only *"under certain concrete conditions."* Almost all legal orders have a group of norms that, although sanctioned by the legislator, are never applied to life. The prerevolutionary Russian, in particular, knew many such "ineffective laws" that were made void through judicial decisions. All these norms were not applied to life, because, in general, they had ceased to correspond to the interests and needs of society. Such norms, however, are not many and are almost completely absent in modern legal systems, particularly in our legal system.

Of considerably greater interest are the norms that do not correspond to the interests and the needs of society "under certain concrete conditions." To this group belong all norms of all legal systems ever in existence. One could say without any exaggeration that each of these norms may not correspond to the interests and the needs of society under certain conditions, depending upon the character of the specific and unique social relationship to which it applies. In this case, what is the role of "truly effective norms"?

Also in cases of "concrete" non-correspondence to the needs of society, an effective norm is not applied to life; thus, for a while, it remains, in effect, outside the legal life of society. In the conditions of a capitalist society, the theory of the "interpretation of law" serves as a justification for such a "concrete" non-application of an effective norm. According to Radbruch, "The essence of this theory is that an appearance is created that law is being interpreted, while in fact it is being misinterpreted." The aim of the bourgeois theory of the interpretation of law was precisely to misinterpret the law at the proper moment. But this process of misinterpretation of law (that is the "distortion" of its "true" meaning) was carefully concealed by bourgeois theorists. Only the instrumental and the Marxist theories of law admit its existence.

At times, however, bourgeois jurists spoke of it quite openly. Mittelstädt, a German jurist and former member of the *Reichstag*, revealed the "secret" of bourgeois justice by stating the following: ". . . since our criminal law was not especially designed to serve as a weapon against the Social Democrats, it should be transformed into such a weapon through a subtle and refined interpretation of the positive norms."

The Marxist theory of law, as well as some recent trends in bourgeois jurisprudence (in particular the so-called *school of free law*), do not resort to such doubtful connivances in defending the legitimate interests of the ruling class. Both of these theories tear the mask from the traditional theory of "interpretation" and proclaim that the guardian of the interests of society is not the law, which under certain conditions may not correspond to these interests, but the living personality of a judge.

We could continue to present the similarities between the Marxist theory of law and some recent trends in bourgeois jurisprudence. There is a great abundance of material in this field. . . . However, the above-said is sufficient to arrive at the following conclusion: What differentiates the Marxist theory of law from its bourgeois counterparts is its philosophical depth, consistency, and completeness, but the main difference is its class principle, which is not always adhered to by bourgeois jurists. At the same time, however, the corresponding trends in bourgeois jurisprudence remain of interest to us; they reveal a deep, almost insoluble crisis in jurisprudence (not only of bourgeois jurisprudence), a crisis that is developing under the direct influence of Marxism.

# The Law and Communism*  ⌒  *N. V. Krylenko*

So far we have stated that law is a derivative of socioeconomic relationships. Furthermore, we have asserted that, judging by its content, the law is a system of norms the task of which it is to justify or to protect (or, at first to protect and then to justify) the existing legal order. That is to say, its task is to protect the exising legal order by means of police, prisons, and armies and to justify it by means of universities.

The remaining question concerns the future of the law. We have stated previously that law is a class phenomenon and that, consequently, a non-class law, a supraclass law, a law that is not connected with the interests of a class, is inconceivable. Moreover, we have argued that there is no law without coercion. From the above-said follows the inescapable conclusion that *without classes there will be no law*. But is this conclusion correct? There is disagreement among our theorists concerning this conclusion. Logic tells us that, assuming that law is always a class phenomenon, without classes there will be no law. On the other hand, our inner feelings are revolting against such an answer: how could we live "without any law"? In addition, if it is true, as contended by Stuchka, that law is a "system of social relationships," does it then follow that social relationships will also disappear? Or, if social relationships are to stay, does it mean then that law will not disappear? The problem needs clarification.

Obviously, social relationships as such will not disappear. But will law as a coercive norm, as a norm supported by the force of compulsion, as an instrument of the state's coercion, disappear? The answer is quite obvious. We have always thought, at least until now, that at the moment of the disappearance of classes the state would die away, that the functions of the state would gradually wither away, i.e., they would fall off. Police, army, courts, and other institutions that rule with rods of iron would disappear, would die away, would fall off. Owing to this, the law, as a written norm, with all its elements of coercion and with its class content, would also disappear. But what will remain? Our answer is, *anything you like, but not law*.

Some writers contend, however, that only the coercive function, the coercive character of legal norms, will disappear, whereas law itself, without coercion, will remain. To restate it: they contend that

* From *Besedy o Prave i Gosudarstve* [Discourse on Law and State] (Moscow, 1924), pp. 30–33.

it will be a new law, a law that has lost its class character. In our opinion, this view is absurd. The proponents of this view commit a common fallacy, namely, *they identify law with something that it is not.* We declare openly that legal norms are inconceivable without compulsion. *Such norms will disappear* following the disappearance of compulsion. Secondly, as we have stated earlier, all norms that ever existed pursued the task of exploitation, suppression, and domination of one class by another. *Such norms will also disappear.* Thus, law in the real meaning of the term, *law as we have known it through all centuries,* will disappear. However, the question of what will remain arises. To this question we give the following answer: social relationships will remain, not law. Social relationships will go through an evolution and will experience altruistic moments that will be stronger, perhaps, than egotistic ones. *Social relationships, however, must never be confused with law as we know it.* Anyone who confuses them falls into Petrazhitskii's trap and is caught in a quagmire of idealism. Idealists seek to separate the historical substance of law from their "concept" of law, from the "idea of law," and from the "pure" law. They do this in order to show that law is not evil, in order to justify the existing, real, historical law as well as their contemporary philosophy of law. This is why Reisner commits a fallacy by asserting that law does not always have an exploitative character. Stuchka also commits an error by asserting that law is a system of social relationships, for social relationships will continue to exist, even though they are of a new type. These new social relationships should not be confused with the existing ones (with their present form), that is to say, with the real historical law. There is no other law, no abstract law; law has always been a class phenomenon and, therefore, it is indissolubly connected, first, with the class principle and, second, with compulsion. Thus, we say the following of the future of law: law, as a class law, will disappear at the moment of the disappearance of classes. It will disappear as an instrument of exploitation and coercion at the moment when exploitation and coercion disappear. It will be replaced by something else, with new social relationships, with new experiences, which we shall designate by a name other than law. We know law as it is. Law is either an expression of a statute in a written form or an expression of customary law in an unwritten form; it is an expression of the social relationships that were brought forth by the production relationships of society for the purpose of regulating these relationships in the interest of the economically dominant class; these relationships are protected by the coercive force of law.

# Bourgeois and Marxist Conceptions of State*

## ∾ F. Ksenofontov

There are, in fact, as many theories of state as there are lawyers in the United States. Nevertheless, none of these theories is capable of ascertaining its meaning. Some of them cloak it with a philosophical fog; some "search" for its juridical nature; some speak of it without even attempting to define it. Here are examples of these theories.

According to Lorentz Stein, "The state, like an individual's *Ego*, is neither a result nor a prerequisite of law; it is neither an ethical form nor a logical conception. The state is a higher material form of individuality. Its nature lies in that it is self-sufficient. Like an individual's *Ego*, the state can neither be proven nor justified. It exists in itself. The state's *Ego*, like an individual's *Ego*, cannot be derived from something else. The state is a great fact which demonstrates that the people's unity has its own peculiar, independent, and self-acting existence, and that it exists outside and above the will of society." Needless to say, one needs iron patience to be able to read this idealistic gibberish to the end. Another definition of state appears in Magaziner's writings:

> Judging by its tasks, the state authority should stand above the class struggle; formally, the state authority was an umpire in the class struggle; it created the rules of this struggle. This was the most significant task of the state.
> . . . this means that according to law, the subjective task of the state is to protect the general interest whereas, in fact, its objectively existing task is to protect the class interest. Normally, class interest coincides with the general interest, though, at times, it may be in conflict with it. . . . The protection of a class to the detriment of society is tantamount to distorting the legal role of the state.[1]

A third definition was advanced by Professor Lehning. He contended that "the fundamental and most general concepts underlying the science of state are very difficult to comprehend and probably will forever remain beyond our comprehension."[2]

---

* From *Gosudarstvo i Pravo* [The State and Law] (Moscow, 1924), pp. 79–84.

[1] *Obshchee Uchenie o Gosudarstve* [The General Theory of State] (2nd ed.; Petersburg, 1922), pp. 10–11.

[2] Cited by P. Stuchka.

We would fail to get a full picture of the bourgeois juridical science without becoming acquainted with the following view: "According to law, the state is an impartial umpire between the struggling classes; it must keep the scales of justice in its hands without disturbing their balance. The nature of the state could be comprehended correctly only from the juridical point of view."[3]

These are the pearls of the bourgeois science of state. Their worthlessness is evident even to some bourgeois professors who are "revolting" against them. For example, a French professor, L. Duguit, has stated the following in his lectures: "Not without some apprehension do I begin my lectures fearing that I may become embroiled with orthodox jurists. I am not at all capable of understanding their contention that there is a difference between a factual and a juridical truth. In my opinion, all juridical constructions based on this view are worthless. We should accept the facts as they are: the state is neither a juridical person nor law. The state is a superior power, a coercive force of those who govern, of the governing over the governed."[4]

An original answer to the quoted theories was given by a Russian cadet scientist, Petrazhitskii. However, Petrazhitskii committed the absurd mistake of denying the existence of the state as a real thing and of asserting that the state exists only as an *"idea in man's mind."* The state, according to him, is not a real thing but a *phantasm.* All this demonstrates the worthlessness of bourgeois science in general and juridical science in particular.

Now we shall deal with the Marxist approach to the question of the existence of the state. As we have indicated earlier, according to our view, the state is primarily a definite *social relationship* of men; it is a social phenomenon. "Marxism examines all social phenomena in their connection and interaction whereby each series of these phenomena constitutes a link in the chain of causes that either preserve and develop or destroy a definite type of production relationship, a definite structure of society."[5] Only with such an approach could a correct understanding of social phenomena and hence of the state be brought about. This was also Marx's view, which he stated as follows:

Legal relations as well as forms of state (and hence the state itself—

[3] Magaziner, *Obshchee Uchenie,* p. 9.
[4] *Sotsialnoe Pravo, Individualnoe Pravo i Preobrazovanie Gosudarstva* [Social Law, Individual Right, and the Transformation of the State] (Moscow, 1909), p. 16.
[5] N. Bukharin, *Teoriya Istoricheskogo Materializma* [The Theory of Historical Materialism] (Moscow, 1922), p. 18 (?).

F.K.) can neither be understood by themselves nor explained by the so-called general progress of the human mind; they are rooted in the material conditions of life which are summed up by Hegel under the name "civil society"; the anatomy of civil society should be sought in political economy. This anatomy may be formulated briefly as follows: In the social production that men carry on they enter into definite relations that are indispensable and *independent* of their will; these relations of production correspond to a definite state of development of their material forces of production. The totality of these relations of production constitutes the economic structure of society, the real basis on which legal and political superstructures arise. . . . The mode of production of material life determines the general character of the social, political, and spiritual processes of life. With the change of economic foundation the entire immense superstructure is rapidly transformed.[6]

To this remarkable outline of the materialist conception of the historical process should be added another excerpt from Marx's *The German Ideology*: "The class struggle is the content of history. The struggle for democracy, aristocracy, monarchy, and for electoral right is merely a deceptive form of a genuine war between classes. The class struggling for power presents its own interest as a general one. The state is precisely the form within which the ruling class realizes its interests."

These quoted paragraphs . . . give the key to the Marxist conception of state. We can safely conclude that the state is not an independent entity, but a *definite political organization which arose as a "superstructure," on a particular "basis," under particular conditions*. The state is a definite relationship between men, that is to say, a relationship of domination and subordination, a relationship between classes. Marx and Engels regarded the state as a "political expression of a broad socioeconomic category: the class society."[7]

The state arose as a result of the division of society into classes, and, like classes, it is a *legitimate child* of the economic development of society. The state is neither an "illegitimate child," nor an entity imposed upon society from "outside"; it is neither a reflection nor a realization of a reason nor is it a moral idea; it is a reflection and a realization of a class society; it has a *class nature*. The state, being a product of class society, constitutes its organization. As stated by Engels, the state demonstrates the fact that society has split into classes with contradictory and irreconcilable interests; it demonstrates that society has entered into conflict with itself and that an organiza-

[6] *K Kritike Politicheskoi Ekonomii* [A Critique of Political Economy] (Moscow, 1922), p. 32.
[7] N. Bukharin, *Teoriya Proletarskoi Diktatury* [The Theory of Proletarian Dictatorship] (n.p., n.d.).

tion, *power* (not abstractions or ideas in man's mind!), is needed, which could prevent society from disintegrating because of the class struggle. For the preservation of society, for its future life, a new organization is necessary. In brief, a human organization, an organization for *governing the people* is necessary. The state is such an organization. The state, which arose out of the categorical needs of a class society, keeps class contradictions in check. But the state was born at the height of the class struggle and, owing to this, it became an organization of the economically strongest class, the ruling class; it secured its political rule. Having at its disposal the state apparatus, the state controls a colossal instrument of suppression and uses it for the exploitation of the have-not classes. This was true of the ancient state . . . , of the feudal state . . . , and it is equally true of the modern state, which is an instrument of the exploitation of hired labor by the capitalists. The modern state, according to Engels, is in fact a capitalist machine, a state of capitalists, a collective capitalist.

. . . The ruling class is unwilling to admit that the state is its own class organization; it is interested in concealing the true nature of the state. . . . In the ancient world as well as in the feudal age, a divine origin and divine authority were attributed to the state; these were advantageous to slaveholders and feudal lords. Under capitalism, this "supernatural" power lost its divine nature but remained to be connected with the "moral ideal," with the "general will," with the "idea of law," which are elusive to simple, ordinary people. This is why the state was endowed with all the features of a living and abstract person, of a conscious being acting independently of the people. This is advantageous to the bourgeoisie.

We shall return now to the contention of bourgeois juridical science that the state is representative of the entire society. To be sure, Marxism also regards the state as representative of the society, as its most extensive organization embracing the entire class society. But there is a tremendous difference between our conception of the state as a "representative of society" and the conception of bourgeois professors. To them, the state is a "representative of society" in the literal meaning of the term, whereas to us it has a relative meaning. As pointed out by Engels in *Anti-Dühring,* "The state was the official representative of society as a whole; but it was this only insofar as it was the state of that class which itself represented for the time being society as a whole—in ancient times the state of slave-owning citizens; in the Middle Ages the feudal lords; in our own time the bourgeoisie. When at last the state becomes the real representative of society, it renders itself unnecessary."

# Anarchism and Marxism*   ௸   *V. Veger*

Anarchists intend to organize autonomous economic factories on the principle of the self-determination of the workers. They urge the workers to take over the industrial plants and reorganize them in conformity with this principle. They spurn a centralized organization in the administration of economic enterprises. An anarchist is a bold advocate of unlimited freedom. In order to assure the greatest possible degree of freedom to an individual person, he is in favor of abolishing an industrial organization based on the principle of subordination. He advocates the establishment of artels, of petty labor unions at individual plants, and of communes. The anarchists' economic views are grounded in their conception of personal freedom, in their insistence that the individual be provided with the greatest possible degree of autonomy. This leads to the rejection of both management and subordination in economic enterprises.

In addition to rejecting economic authority and centralized organization in the industry, anarchists also reject political authority. . . . They see in the state one of the greatest evils, and contend that the oppressive state authority as well as the entire state apparatus must be destroyed. According to anarchist theory, the destruction of the state is the main task of the workers. The state should be destroyed immediately, today, this very minute. Having destroyed the power of the bourgeoisie, the workers should immediately abolish the state, the apparatus of coercion, as well as all other authorities. Confronted with these views, we ask the anarchists: Can all authority really be destroyed immediately? If you destroy authority immediately, how will you organize the new administration? If the bourgeoisie decides to revolt against you, how will you fight it back? Anarchists give no satisfactory answers to these questions. They assert that the workingmen constitute the overwhelming majority; once the power of the insignificant minority has been overthrown by the workers, it will be unable to re-establish its power. Concerning the question of the administration of the economy and the organization of society, anarchists assert that the people themselves will resolve the problem. Most likely, this problem will be resolved by means of unions, artels, and communes.

* From *Pravo i Gosudarstvo Perekhodovogo Vremeni* [Law and State in the Transition Period] (2nd ed.; Moscow, 1924), pp. 46–48.

Anarchists insist upon the destruction of the state, whereas Marxists assert that after the victory of the proletariat and after a period of the proletarian dictatorship the state will wither away. At this point, at the point concerning the future of the state, anarchists and Marxists are in agreement. However, anarchists insist upon an immediate destruction of the state, whereas Marxists assert that the social revolution, i.e., liberation from the bourgeoisie, will be accomplished through the dictatorship of the proletariat. On this point the difference is quite substantial. Marxists and anarchists are essentially in agreement concerning the past and the present status of the state, but they disagree completely on the dictatorship of the proletariat. Marxism asserts that the proletarian state, which entails a long period of an organized proletarian domination over its enemies, is indispensable for the transition toward the communist free society.

Nevertheless, some socialists have contended that . . . what distinguishes anarchism from socialism is that the anarchists are enemies of the state, whereas Socialists are proponents of the state. Such a view is contradictory to Marxist theory. Marx and Engels asserted that the state is a class society and that it will inevitably disappear after the dictatorship of the proletariat. With the liquidation of classes the state will cease to exist. Indeed, in *The Communist Manifesto,* Marx and Engels spoke of the proletariat as a dominant class, as a class that will centralize the means of production in its own hands. But these remarks refer to the dictatorship of the proletariat in the transition period. They refer to the period of time when a power apparatus is still necessary for the defense against violators and for the struggle against the international bourgeoisie, which has at its disposal a tremendous military force and which can be fought only by force.

# The Conflict between Socialist Theory and Soviet

# Reality* ᏜᏜ N. V. Krylenko

The task to be pursued in our last discourse is twofold. On the one hand, we shall complete our general theoretical examination of the nature and essence of the state and make an attempt to outline those communal forms that will be adopted by the new society, which we would no longer call a state. This is one task. The second task of our last discourse is . . . to examine the question of what should be done right now with . . . our state machinery, which came into being as a result of the seven-year-old construction of the state and the seven-year-old dictatorship of the proletariat; or, to put it differently, what should be our present-day practical task in translating theory into practice. The latter task has proved much more complex and more difficult than it seemed to us in 1917. So far, not only have we failed to cope with this task, but in many respects we have simply retreated from it.

The last statement needs some elucidation. The Soviet state . . . was born in storm and stress. . . . Its theoretical foundations became known in general only on the eve of its creation. (Lenin's *State and Revolution* was written in August, and published in November, 1917.) For the most part, the Soviet state was the result of a spontaneous activity of the masses rather than the result of a well-thought-out plan drafted by the revolutionary party in a time of peace. Such a state of affairs was bound to affect its future destiny. It was easy to destroy the old machine. But to build a new one in an atmosphere of fighting and civil war, without any practical experience and with hardly any theoretical knowledge, was difficult, to say the least. Consequently, the old became interwoven with the new; and the old revived once again. This is why, six years after the overthrow, in March, 1923, Lenin was forced . . . to write the following prophetic lines apropos the Soviet, proletarian state: "The conditions in our state apparatus are to such a degree grievous, if not shocking, that we must begin to think all over again of how to struggle against its deficiencies." Furthermore, "Already for five years we have been fussing about the improvement of our state apparatus, but it is pure

* From *Besedy o Prave i Gosudarstve* [Discourse on Law and State] (Moscow, 1924), pp. 140–76.

fussiness that, after five years, proved to have been futile or even useless and harmful."

The trouble lies in the fact that—as he stated in his article . . . of January, 1923—"with the exception of the People's Commissariat of Foreign Affairs, our state apparatus for the most part represents a survival of the past; only to a very small degree was it subjected to any serious changes. It is only slightly retouched at the top and in all other respects remains most typical of our old state apparatus."

This was Lenin's characterization of the conditions of the state apparatus in the sixth year of the dictatorship of the proletariat, i.e., the condition of the instrument by means of which the proletariat was materializing its dictatorship. At any rate, such a characterization of the instrument of the dictatorship should be taken as suggesting apprehension for the very dictatorship itself. This, however, is only one side of the problem. The trouble is even more serious. Because of the fact that the traditions, the habits, the system, and the methods of administration, and to a considerable degree even the personnel were, and remain, borrowed by our state apparatus from the old one, our apparatus became transformed in part into those "special cadres of men specializing in administration" which, as Engels stated, "having at their disposal the public force and the right to exact taxes, stand as organs of society *above society.*"

The new society—which, according to Engels, should "organize production anew on the basis of a free and equal association of the producers and *put the whole state machine where it then belongs: in the museum of antiquities, side by side with the spinning wheel and the bronze ax"*—found itself dominated by the state, which is beginning to subordinate *to its influence even the new leaders.*

The situation that arose in connection with the state apparatus . . . is vividly and clearly described in the resolution of the Twelfth Party Congress, which considers it to be a principal political problem. The problem is how to again draw our state closer to its initial point of departure, when it served as an organ of the dictatorship and self-activity of the masses. We shall answer this basic question first.

Lenin raised the question concerning the new form of the state for the first time in his "Theses" in April, 1917. He requested then the creation of a "state-commune" in which "there would be no police, no army, and no bureaucracy," and in which the state would be founded "on the principle of electiveness and recall of all officials at any time, with their wages not exceeding those of an average good worker." At the same time he issued several instructions concerning what the working class *should not* do during the construction of its state.

In his *State and Revolution,* dated August, 1917, while analyzing this "state-commune" and its nature, Lenin emphasized that its distinctive objective feature lies in that it should be built in such a way *as to render objectively impossible the recurrence of the old state of affairs and the old bureaucratic order.*

Lenin had the following to say about the destruction of this old state order, of the old state machine, as the *principal* task of the revolution: "In fact," he wrote, disagreeing with Kautsky, "it is the other way around. Marx's idea is that the working class itself must break up, shatter the ready-made state machine, and not confine itself merely to taking possession of it." Furthermore, Lenin continued, "In these words, 'to break up the bureaucratic and military machine,' is contained, briefly stated, *the principal lesson of Marxism on the task of the proletariat* in relation to the state during a revolution. It is just this lesson which has not only been forgotten but downright *distorted* by the prevailing Kautskyist 'interpretation' of Marxism."

Lenin repeated these views on several occasions, in many places: "Bureaucratic military machinery oppresses, crushes, exploits. . . . To shatter this machine, to break it up—this is the true interest of the people, of its majority of workers and peasants; this is the preliminary condition of free union of the poorest peasantry with the proletarians; without such a union, democracy is unstable and socialist reorganization is impossible."

So wrote Lenin. By *breaking up* he meant precisely what he said, in the most direct and literal sense of the word. And this is quite different from merely replacing the old bureaucratic machine with a new one made in its image, with the only difference that the individual administrative branches of this . . . machine are headed by Communists. Such a view, according to Lenin, is a direct distortion of Marxism. To break up, to smash, to *destroy*—this is what Lenin was striving for.

In another place he wrote: "Particular attention should be given to Marx's profound remark that the destruction of the military and bureaucratic machine is *the prerequisite* for any real revolution of the people." This is the first instruction. But what should be put in place of the destroyed old machine? Lenin offered the following answer: "There is not even a grain of utopia in Marx's view of the new society in the sense that he either invented it or dreamed it up. . . ." "He regards the birth of the new society from the old one and the forms of transition from the latter to the former as a natural-historical process. *He takes into account* the experience of the proletarian mass movement and seeks to deduce from it a practical lesson. He *learns* from the Commune, for no great revolutionary thinker is afraid to learn from the experience of the great movements of the oppressed class."

The new society is not invented; *it is brought forth by the revolution. . . .* What has our revolution brought about for us? Even prior to our revolution, Lenin attempted to find out the peculiar features of the new society and the new state from the experience of the Paris Commune and from Marx's writings. The experience of the Russian Revolution reproduced these features on an even vaster historical scale. In analyzing the Commune, Marx stated: "The commune was the only political form within which economic emancipation of the proletariat was objectively possible." Lenin raised additional questions: What is the meaning of the "objective" form of the proletarian socialist republic? What will be the type of state that is being created by the proletariat? Having noted the initial destructive work of the Commune with respect to the means of coercion—army, police, etc. —Marx continued:

The Commune was formed of municipal councilors chosen by universal suffrage in various wards in Paris. They were responsible and revocable at short terms. The majority of its members were naturally workingmen, or acknowledged representatives of the working class. . . . So were the officials of all other branches of the administration. From the members of the Commune downward, public service had to be done at workman's wages. The vested interests and the representation allowances of the high dignitaries of state disappeared along with the high dignitaries themselves. . . . The judicial functionaries were divested of their sham independence. . . . They were to be elective, responsible, and revocable. . . . The Commune has freed the peasant from police, field guards, priests, lawyers, notary publics, and other leeches of the capitalist system.

In this destruction of officialdom with its hierarchy, and in the equalization of the wages of all officials, Lenin saw the image of the *new form,* which *in itself* would make the regeneration of the old *conditions* impossible and would become the foundation of the *new* system. To quote Lenin, "All officials, without exception, elected and subject to recall at any time, their salaries reduced to the 'workingmen's wages'—these simple and 'self-evident' democratic measures completely uniting the interests of the workers and the majority of the peasants, at the same time serve as a bridge leading from capitalism to socialism. These measures refer to the state, to the purely political reconstruction of society."

Both Marx and Lenin saw in these measures objective guarantees against the possibility of the re-establishment of the old machine which, in Lenin's words, "as special cadres of men separated from the popular masses, stands above the masses." In its first stage, the Russian Revolution fully adhered to these precepts. The Councils of Workers' Deputies, as the fundamental cells of both the state and social systems, were placed at the head of the governing units. From this ensued the corresponding solution of all remaining problems . . . : first, the problem concerning the system and the methods of administering individual communes, or individual city, district, or village councils; second, the problem concerning the methods and the systems of coordinating the activity of the communes or councils; third, the problem concerning the construction and the function of a central authority.

The Commune furnished an example of both how to build the state in Paris and how to establish a state system on the entire territory of France. However, Marx devoted only brief observation to this problem: "In this brief period of national organization, in which the Commune had no time to develop, it was understood quite clearly that the commune would . . . become the political form of even the smallest village." "The communes would elect a 'national delegation' to Paris."

Our revolution produced more. The principal foundations of our Soviet state system lie in the fact that the councils are the basic cells in all villages (however remote), that the councils rather than the population at large elect national delegates to Moscow—to the All-Russian Congress of Councils. They also have the authority to elect and to remove any public official at any time. In this respect our revolution, led by Lenin, has acted in conformity with the precepts of the Paris Commune and in conformity with Marx's outline. This experience of the Russian proletarian revolution, which was not available to Marx, found its theoretical expression in Lenin's writings. . . . The question of what should be the basis of the unification of individual communes into a state in the absence of "commanding authority," Lenin answered with another question:

But will it not be centralism if the proletariat and poorest peasantry take the power of the state into their own hands, organize themselves freely into communes, and if they *unite the action of all the communes* in striking at capital, in crushing the resistence of the capitalists, in transferring private property in railways, factories, land, and so forth, to the *entire* nation, to the whole society? Will that not be the most consistent democratic centralism? And proletarian centralism at that?

Bernstein simply cannot conceive of the possibility of a *voluntary centralism*, of a voluntary union of the communes into a nation, of voluntary fusion of the proletarian communes in the process of destroying bourgeois supremacy and the bourgeois state machine. Like all Philistines, Bernstein can imagine centralism only as something from above, to be imposed and maintained solely by means of bureaucracy and militarism.

This was Lenin's answer to the question, and seven years of experience have proved its validity. Our system of the Soviet state has realized fully this voluntary unification of communes into a nation. This was accomplished in 1917 and 1918 without special cadres of men organized especially for the purpose of suppressing those who did not desire to subordinate themselves to the central authority.

It should be noted that we were forced neither to search for nor to invent new forms. The new forms *were produced by the Revolution* and were accepted and adopted as such. Since October, 1917, the proletarian revolution has been building the system of state administration of such a voluntary centralism and continues to do so now.

The question concerning the functions of the authority has proved to be considerably more complicated. As a matter of fact, this is the most complicated question. Moreover, it is a question that concerns the techniques and the essence of state administration. The big question was: "How should we administer our society from the bottom up?" This was the question on which our theory and practice split. Therefore, we shall subject this question to a thorough analysis, indicating at what points our practice diverges from the theory. As we have seen, the principal thing that the Revolution did was to abolish parliamentarianism in its old form. Instead of every three years electing to parliament deputies who would "represent and suppress" the people, the communes now elect deputies *to work*.

Commune, or council, taken as a local cell, became a self-governing unit during the first period of the Revolution. The population of this unit governed itself in the manner of a "primitive democracy," *without any* directives from the central organs of the government. This was the correct answer of the Revolution. As pointed out by Marx, "The very existence of the commune involved, as a matter of course, local municipal liberty, but no longer as a check upon the now superseded state power." An identical demand was once advanced by Engels: "A complete self-government of provinces, districts, or communes, through officials elected by universal suffrage; *abolition of all local and provincial authorities that were set up by the state.*"

According to Lenin, "In Engels' opinion, centralism does not exclude in the least such wide, local self-government that combines voluntary defense of the unity of the state by the communes and districts *with the complete abolition of all bureaucracy and all commanding from above.*"

Such was the basic type of administration brought about by the proletarian revolution. Lenin described it exhaustively in the following way:

Having conquered political power, the workers will break up the old bureaucratic apparatus; they will shatter it to its very foundation, until no stone is left upon another; and they will replace it with a new one consisting of these same workers and employees, *against* whose transformation into bureaucrats measures will at once be undertaken, as pointed out in detail by Marx and Engels; (1) not only electiveness but also instant recall; (2) payment no higher than that of ordinary workers; (3) immediate transition to a state of affairs where all fulfill the functions of control and superintendence so that *all become bureaucrats for a time, and no one, therefore, can become a bureaucrat.*

These were Lenin's views, but until now they seemed to us somehow unrealizable, despite the fact that they had been both theoretically and practically verified. Experience has shown that this program *proved to be practically realizable at the moment of the Revolution and is being realized up to the present day.* It is being realized . . . in the overwhelming majority of our villages, where simple and uncomplicated functions of state government are carried out by the villagers *in rotation* and where the bigger and more serious problems of social life are resolved at the village meetings by means of a "primitive democracy," or, to use a scientific expression, by means of "direct democracy."

This new "type" was produced by the Revolution. . . . It constitutes a great achievement . . . and it represents the most ideal form of people's democracy. Marx had the following to say on this subject: "The Commune was no longer a state in the proper meaning of the term. . . ." Similarly, according to Lenin, "Once the Commune smashed the bourgeois state machine, the special force for suppression of the population gave way to the population itself."

. . . The question arises, though, whether or not it is possible to create such a state apparatus *in which the organs of the central government would be based on the same principles as the administrative organs of small communes.* With the exception of an indication that some functions would remain in the hands of the central government, we have seen that Marx has nothing else to say. However . . . , this question has been treated in detail by Lenin. Since our practice in this respect *deviates* completely from theory, we shall first raise the theoretical problem.

According to Lenin, the principle that should underlie the methods of administration of the central government is identical with the method (engendered by the Revolution) of constructing local cells. Lenin first examined a simple case in municipal government. In particular, in a chapter devoted to the housing question, he analyzed the mechanics of this branch of administration . . . and stated the following: "The renting out to separate families of houses belonging to the whole people presupposes the collection of rent, a certain amount of control, and some rules regulating the allotment of houses. All this demands a certain form of state, but it does not at all demand a special military and bureaucratic apparatus with officials occupying especially privileged positions."

. . . The housing question is, however, an elementary branch of administration. In a chapter dealing with "Kautsky's Polemic against the Opportunists," we find a paragraph dealing with the complex administration of railways, which presumably cannot be effectively managed without the old bureaucratic system of administration based on the principle of appointments, centralization, and a special bureaucratic hierarchy. Speaking on this subject, Lenin stated the following:

So far as this assumed necessity of bureaucratic organization is concerned, there is no difference whatever between railways and any other enterprise of large-scale machine industry, any factory, any large store, or large-scale capitalist agricultural enterprise. The technique of all such enterprises requires the very strictest discipline, the greatest accuracy by everyone in carrying out the work alloted to him, because of the peril of stoppage of the whole business or damage to mechanism or product. In all such enterprises the workers will, of course, "elect delegates" who form *"something in the nature of a parliament."*
But here is the crux of the matter: this "something in the nature of a parliament" will not be a parliament in the sense of bourgeois parliamentary institutions; it will not merely "determine the conditions of work and supervise the management of the bureaucratic apparatus. . . ."

Speaking on a different subject in another place, Lenin stated: "The gist of the matter is not whether ministries, commissions or specialists, or any other institution will remain in existence—this is totally insignificant." The gist of the matter is that these institutions will no longer command the workers but will be subordinated to the workers, who will supervise their work, their function. In Lenin's words, "The question of control and accounting must not be confused with the question of a scientifically educated staff of engineers, agronomists, and so on. These gentlemen work today, obeying capitalists; they will work even better tomorrow, obeying the armed workers."

The "something in the nature of a parliament," regardless of whether it will exist on the level of the local cell managing transport or be what we at the present time designate People's Commissariat, should be based on the same principles: (1) *electiveness and revocability;* (2) *salary equal to that of a worker;* (3) *gradual transition toward conditions under which any citizen of the R.S.F.S.R. could perform this particular work.*

Our revolution has failed to fulfill the third principle; and that is why we intend to examine it thoroughly. The enumerated principles were fully translated into reality at the beginning of the Russian proletarian revolution. *At their roots* they remain firm even at the present time, but only at their roots. "Something in the nature of a parliament of the workers" runs our administration even at the present time, in all branches of the state, in all departments of national and local government. . . . By passing laws and taking care of their execution, *the workers themselves supervise their own activities.* The stumbling block of our revolution is, however, *the impossibility, at the present time, of bringing about conditions under which any function of the state could be carried out at any time by any citizen of the R.S.F.S.R.* Yet, Lenin indicated quite categorically and frequently that this is a fundamental requirement of the new state and the new society. Thus the question must be raised: "What has made the realization of this principle impossible and how far have we deviated from it?"

According to Lenin, two prerequisites, one economic and the other political . . . , are indispensable for its materialization. The economic prerequisite is that the country must attain a degree of preliminary economic development in which all forms of production, distribution, and satisfaction of the basic material needs of the masses of the population are highly mechanized, like a big capitalist enterprise, and at the same time are technically perfect to the degree that their management *requires neither considerable physical force nor considerable intellectual effort.* The second, political, prerequisite is the availability of human material that is able to manage the state machine without any special difficulties and training. Lenin indicated that both these prerequisites either already exist in capitalist society or should come into existence in the near future.

Concerning the first problem, Lenin stated the following:

At the present the post office is a business organized along the lines of a state capitalist monopoly. Imperialism is gradually transforming all trusts into organizations of a similar type. But the mechanism of social management is here, already at hand. Overthrow the capitalists, crush the resistance of the exploiters with the iron hand of armed workers, break the bureaucratic machine of the modern state—and you have before you a highly technical mechanism freed of "parasites," capable of being set into motion by the united workers themselves, who hire their own technicians, managers, bookkeepers, and pay them all as, indeed, every "state official," with the usual workers' wage. Here is a concrete, practical task, immediately realizable in relation to all trusts; a task that frees the workers of expoitation.

Furthermore, the technique itself, both in production and administration, reduces the function of the worker to the simplest motions. . . . In the ammunition factory a piece of tin which has undergone 121 operations becomes transformed eventually into a ready-made cartridge, whereby . . . the function of the workers has been reduced to placing this piece of metal into one machine and handing it over to the operator of another machine, whose function also has been reduced to the same motions. The application of the same principles of scientific organization of work to administrative functions eventually will reduce them also to the simplest motions, requiring neither specific abilities nor preparation. Lenin wrote about this, and built on this his prognosis of the new state.

Capitalist culture has created large-scale production, factories, railways, postal service, telephones, etc., and *on this basis* (Lenin's italics) the great majority of functions of the old "state power" have become so simplified, and can be reduced to such simple operations as registration, filing, and checking, that they will be quite within the reach of every literate person, and it will be possible to perform them for "workingmen's wages"; this circumstance can (and must) strip those functions of every shadow of privilege, of every appearance of "official grandeur."

Thus, we have arrived at the following principles, which, according to Comrade Lenin, should underlie the construction of the new state: (1) the commune is the fundamental cell of the entire political system; (2) the unification of these communes is based on the principle of a voluntary subordination and the unity of the workers' interests; (3) only some administrative and industrial functions are delegated to the central organs, whereby the latter are organized on the same principles as a commune. The employees of these organs are remunerated equally with wages corresponding to those of average workers.

*The objective possibility of such a form will come only* when economic development has brought about forms of production under which industrial and administrative functions can be reduced to the simplest acts, and when, owing to the general cultural advancement, every citizen of the new society will be capable of performing these functions; or, as Lenin wrote, under conditions "when *all will take turns at management and, therefore, will soon become accustomed to the idea of no managers at all.*" But this is exactly what we have failed to attain.

The attainment of such conditions constitutes a protracted process during which the working class has to resolve a whole series of additional problems, among them the problem of suppressing former exploiters. As pointed out by Lenin,

A special apparatus, a special machine for suppression, "the state," is *still* necessary, but this is now a transitional state, no longer a state in the usual sense, for the suppression of the minority of exploiters by the majority of the wage slaves *of yesterday* is a matter comparatively so easy, simple, and natural that it will cost far less bloodshed than the suppression of rising slaves, serfs, or wage laborers, and will cost mankind far less. . . .

The exploiters are, naturally, unable to suppress the people without a most complex machine for performing this task; but *the people* can suppress the exploiters even with a very simple "machine," almost without any "machine," without any special apparatus, by the simple *organization of the armed masses* (such as the Soviets of Workers' and Soldiers' Deputies, we may remark, anticipating a little).

. . . Finally, only communism renders the state absolutely unnecessary, for there is *no one* to be suppressed—"no one" in the sense of *a class* or in the sense of a systematic struggle with a definite section of the population.

In developing further the same view, Lenin asserted that the resistance of former exploiters will become increasingly weaker and finally will become such a rare exception and "will probably be accompanied by such a swift and severe punishment (for the armed workers are men of practical life, not sentimental intellectuals, and they will scarcely allow any one to trifle with them) that very soon the *necessity* of observing simple, fundamental rules of every-day social life in common will have become a habit." It is on the same basis of habit—which replaces coercion—that the performance of all the remaining functions in the new society will rest. We shall take the liberty of quoting Lenin further, for the purpose of outlining the whole picture of the new society, as it should have been. The problem of why it did not come into being immediately we shall discuss later. Lenin wrote:

Accounting and control—these are *the chief* things necessary for the organizing and correct functioning of the *first phase* of communist society. *All* citizens are here transformed into hired employees of the state, which is made up of the armed workers. *All* citizens become employees and workers of *one* national state "syndicate." All that is required is that they should work equally, should regularly do their share of work, and should receive equal pay. The accounting and control necessary for this have been *simplified* by capitalism to the utmost, till they have become the extraordinarily simple operations of watching, recording, and issuing receipts, within reach of anybody who can read and write and who knows the first four rules of arithmetic.

In another place, Lenin asserted the following: "The specific 'commanding' methods of the state officials can and must begin to be replaced—immediately, within twenty-four hours—by the simple functions of 'managers and bookkeepers,' functions which are now already within the capacity of the average city dweller and can well be performed for 'workingmen's wages.' "

This is the beginning of the second phase in the development of the new society, which manifests itself in a gradual withering away and disappearance of any necessity of command and coercion in the relationships between individual men, though not between whole classes. Furthermore, it manifests itself in the *replacement of the method of suppression and coercion,* which is characteristic of all states, with the *method of habitual activity,* common to each and every citizen and, *therefore, not requiring any kind of coercion.* To quote Lenin again,

From the moment when all members of society, or even only the overwhelming majority, have learned how to govern the state *themselves,* have taken this business into their own hands, have established control over the insignificant minority of capitalists and over the gentry with capitalist leanings, and over the workers thoroughly demoralized by capitalism—from this moment the need for any government begins to disappear, and *every* state begins to wither away more rapidly.
. . . The door will then be wide open for the transition from the first phase of communist society to its higher phase, and along with it, to the complete withering away of the state.
. . . For people *will become accustomed* to the observance of the elementary rules of social life *without force and without subordination* . . . for we see around us millions of times how readily people become accustomed to observing the necessary rules of life in common, if there is no exploitation and if there is nothing that causes indignation or that calls forth protest and revolt which has to be *suppressed.*

The characteristic feature of this period is "equalization."

The means of production are no longer the private property of individual persons. The means of production belong to the whole society. Every member of society, performing a certain part of socially necessary work, receives a certificate from society to the effect that he has done such and such a quantity of work. According to this certificate, he receives from the public warehouse, where articles are stored, a corresponding quantity of products. Deducting that portion of labor which goes to the public fund, every worker, therefore, receives from society as much as he has given to it.

This, however, is not yet full communism. "Until the 'higher phase' of communism arrives, the Socialists demand the *strictest* control by society and by the state of the quantity of labor and the quantity of consumption. . . ." Here, after the indicated deduction, each receives an equal quantity of products for an equal quantity of labor. "However, this is not yet communism, for this does not abolish 'bourgeois law,' which gives to unequal individuals, in return for an unequal (in reality unequal) amount of work, an equal quantity of products." *This is merely the first phase of the socialist society.*

The second phase, according to Lenin and Marx, arrives when, to use Marx's words, the enslaving subordination of individuals in the division of labor has disappeared; when the antagonism between mental and physical labor has disappeared; when labor is no longer a means of living but has become the first necessity of life; when, along with the all-round development of individuals, productive forces too have grown, and all the springs of social wealth are flowing more freely. Only then will it be possible to overcome the narrow horizon of "bourgeois law," and only then will it be possible for society to inscribe on its banners: "From each according to his ability, to each according to his needs." Lenin described this stage in the following way.

The economic basis for the complete withering away of the state is that high stage of development of communism when the antagonism between mental and physical labor disappears, that is to say, when one of the principal [and the last—N.K.] sources of modern social inequality disappears—a source, moreover, that it is impossible to remove immediately by the mere conversion of the means of production into public property, by the mere expropriation of the capitalists. The expropriation will merely make a gigantic development of the productive forces *possible*.

. . . Then there will be no need for any regulation by society of the quantity of products to be distributed to each of its members; each will take freely "according to his needs."

*This is how the second phase of the communist society comes into being.* This is how Marx and Engels imagined this phase. This is how Lenin outlined the further evolution of society.

At this point we shall pass over to the second and last question concerning why it did not happen in our country; for, as we see, the divergence between theory and practice is in fact of extreme magnitude. To comprehend this . . . we shall proceed to an examination of our practical work and in particular to the moment when we committed the first deviation from the theory, namely, the moment when we resorted to *methods* of constructing and administering the state other than those recommended by Lenin. . . . To begin with, Lenin recommended that we start with the abolition of the army. As a matter of fact, we destroyed the old army completely, but in its place we were forced to create a new permanent army, a regular army with all its specific features: peculiar "military" discipline, strict hierarchical subordination, and mechanization of the workers and peasants who were drafted into military service. Indeed, we created a new, Red, revolutionary, class army, linking it closely with the broad popular masses. Nevertheless, the army as such remained in existence.

Marx recommended an immediate liquidation of the police, and following him, Lenin suggested that we "take away from the police all political functions and transform it into the people's militia." As a matter of fact, we abolished and smashed to pieces the political police of the old regime, but at the same time we created in its place our own Soviet police, both secret and uniformed—first *Cheka* and then *GPU*—possessing specific features of a political police, namely, a peculiar form of organization, special discipline and hierarchy. We sought, however, to fill its cadres with the proper new human material—with seasoned revolutionaries—and linked it whenever possible with the broad masses of the people. Nevertheless, we created a police, and by doing so we deviated from Lenin who recommended an organization of militia in which "the entire working population, both males and females, would serve in turn. . . ." ". . . To enlist the organizational abilities of the people for the creation of a militia in which each and all citizens would serve—this is the task that the proletariat carries out with the masses, in the interest of protecting, strengthening, and developing the Revolution." Alas, these words and many others that we have quoted remain the music of the future.

However, the most serious deviation we have committed is connected with an even more basic problem, namely, the problem concerning *the methods of state administration*. To destroy bureaucracy as a special entity, as cadres of men who specialize in administration and because of that assume the position *above society*—this is what Lenin, following Marx, constantly reiterated in his theoretical works. . . . In numerous passages . . . he also pointed out that the administration should be built so as to make the revival of bureaucracy objectively impossible. In a special chapter devoted to a polemic against Kautsky, he wrote the following . . . :

The essence of the matter is not at all whether the "ministries" will remain, or whether "commissions of specialists" or any other kind of institution will exist; this is quite insignificant. The main thing is whether the old state machine (connected by thousands of threads with the bourgeoisie and saturated throughout with routine and inertia) shall remain or be *destroyed* and replaced by a new one.

The quoted words hit the nail on the head and fully correspond to the definition of the Soviet state given by the Twelfth Party Congress six years after the proletarian revolution: "The old state apparatus is still thoroughly permeated with old methods of administration and in terms of its personnel represents the former bourgeois apparatus." Isn't this the most devastating description of existing reality? What did Lenin say on this subject? "We are not utopians to believe that we can do without functionaries during the first periods." *He sought the guarantee against the revival of bureaucracy in the very foundations of the new state.* Thus, he stated,

Marx took the example of the Commune to show that under socialism the functionaries cease to be "bureaucrats" and "officials"—they change *in degree* as election is supplemented by the right of instant recall, when, *besides this,* their pay is brought down to the level of pay of the average worker, when parliamentary institutions are replaced by "working bodies, executive and legislative at the same time."

*Which of those "besides this" have we realized so far? Along with the councils, representing popular masses of individual localities, we erected a bureaucratic system bound to central institutions that possess a considerable dose of discretionary power vis-à-vis their subordinates.* This is what we did first. Then, finally, having destroyed during the first phase of the Revolution the immense inequality of wages which prevailed during the czarist regime and which differentiated the ruling hierarchy of the bureaucratic machine from its lower strata, *we reinstated it fully after the Revolution.* Thus, we have failed not only to translate into reality the fundamental principle— which would have done away with the very soul of a bureaucratic administration, namely, hierarchical and material inequality among the bureaucrats—*but, indeed, we have re-established bureaucracy as a special cadre of men, have made it directly dependent upon the "ruling hierarchs," and consequently have made it again independent of the popular masses. . . .*

The period of the NEP, which gave a special impetus to material inequality . . . , accomplished the rest, which proves the truth of Lenin's words that even proletarian public officials can be bureaucratized. To quote Lenin,

> Under capitalism, democracy is narrow, incomplete, and mutilated by the conditions of wage slavery and the misery of the masses. It is precisely because of the presence of capitalist conditions that public officials in our political and professional organizations became corrupted (or, more exactly, tend to become corrupted) and manifest a tendency toward becoming bureaucrats, i.e., toward becoming privileged persons separated from and standing above the masses.

The quoted views are quite applicable to some of our *workers who under the conditions of NEP became chiefs of the administrative machine.* This is our principal and original sin, an especially great sin, *because, unlike the army and GPU, it was not brought about by political necessity.* This is the fundamental and most essential deviation that we have committed.

Finally, there is another deviation in an entirely different sphere. What was Lenin's view of the first phase of communist society? Here we quote him:

> The means of production are no longer the private property of individuals. The means of production belong to the whole society. Every member of society performing a certain part of socially necessary work receives a certificate from society to the effect that he has done such and and such quantity of work. According to this certificate, he receives from the public warehouse, where articles of consumption are stored, a corresponding quantity of products. Deducting that portion of labor which goes to the public fund, every worker, therefore, receives from society as much as he has given it.
> . . . Every man having done as much social labor as every other receives an equal share of the social product (with the above-mentioned deductions).

What do we have at the present time? What caused us, and to what degree, to renounce our fundamental principles? What could we and what are we able to accomplish now? And, finally, what (within the scope permitted by objective reality) should we do now, this very minute, to come at least a little bit closer to at least the first phase of the communist society outlined by Lenin and Marx?

Prior to answering these questions, we would like to state the following. Objectively, *it is not our fault that the proletarian revolution in Russia stumbled over two objective obstacles that it could not*

178

*overcome by itself, singlehanded.* These two obstacles were the
following: (1) *the belatedness in the coming of the proletarian revolution in the West; (2) the economic structure of our own country.*
. . . . . . .

*There is not even the slightest doubt that at the present time we
cannot fundamentally change our state apparatus so as to be able to
build it on the principles outlined by Lenin. We admit directly and
openly that the objective prerequisites for this do not exist. But we
undoubtedly should be capable of reforming our state apparatus so
as to liquidate its negative features, which have been so vividly manifest in recent times and which we were incapable of paralyzing in
years past. These features are: separation from the masses, bureaucratization, red tape, bureaucratic attitudes toward work, and the
colossal inequality in the material position of workers and public
functionaries.*
. . . . . . .

Other countries—the West European countries, which in comparison to us are far more advanced in the techniques of production
and, consequently, in the techniques of administration—have *by now
already* developed, examined, and applied such methods of production and administration (the so-called principles of scientific organization of production and management) which are not yet available
to us, with which we are not familiar, and with which, at times, we
are even unwilling to become familiar.

This is why our techniques of production and administration are
unusually cumbersome, clumsy, unwieldy, unproductive, hopelessly if
not revoltingly bureaucratic, and expensive. To take everything that
can now be taken in this field from Western Europe—such is the
slogan that . . . Lenin advanced at the time when *no one was thinking
about it.* This slogan is primarily dictated by those considerations of
doctrinal character which we have just exposed and by our views on
the state in general and the proletarian state in particular. Moreover,
in view of our immediate needs, it dictates securing at any price: (1)
simplification of the state mechanism; (2) increasing the productivity
of its work; (3) lowering its cost; and (4), which is dictated by
political considerations, bringing the administration closer to the population.

# A Criticism of Kelsen's Interpretation of the Marxist Theory of State, Anarchism, and Communism*

## ∽ S. Volfson

. . . Never before was the problem of the state as significant to socialist parties as it is in the postwar years. During and after the war, international socialism became confronted with such imperious problems as dictatorship of the proletariat, democracy, participation in governing the state, withering away of the state, liquidation of the state, the state in the transition period, and many other problems connected with the state. Solutions to those problems must be furnished before they get out of hand. The problem of the state has become a demarcation line separating revolutionaries from reformists, Marxism from opportunism. In our epoch the problems of the state are not merely *Zeit und Streitfragen;* they are literally problems of life or death to political parties. In the Preface to his classical work, Lenin stated that "at the present time the problem of the state acquires a special significance both on the theoretical and practical political levels."[1] Now, seven years after these words were written, the problem of the state under socialism has not lost its significance. On the contrary, its significance has become considerably greater simply because of the fact that the Soviet state has entered the historical arena.

It is, therefore, only natural that anti-Marxist literature devotes extraordinary attention to the problem of the Marxist conception of the state. In German literature, which deserves the greatest attention, we find quite a number of voluminous works devoted to our problem. These works may be divided into three groups. The first group is openly against Marxism. Its members are downright enemies of Marxism, attempting to shatter the entire Marxist conception of the state. Hans Kelsen and Friedrich Lenz belong to this group. The second group consists of pseudo-Marxists who destroy the revolutionary essence of the Marxist theory of state. In German literature these opportunist falsifiers of our theory of state are represented by

* *From* "Sovremennye Kritiki Marksizma" [Contemporary Critics of Marxism], *Pod Znamenem Marksizma*, No. 8–9 (1924), pp. 246–61.
[1] *Gosudarstvo i Revolutisya* [State and Revolution], in *Sobranie Sochinenii* [Collected Works] (Moscow, 1921), XIV, Part 2, 297.

H. Cunov and Herbert Sultan. Finally, to the third group belong obliging friends of Marxism, those who defend the Marxist theory of state but who, in defending this theory from the attacks of critics, introduce into it reformist and opportunist elements. This group indulges in the most subtle, and therefore the most dangerous, distortion of Marxism. Karl Kautsky and Max Adler may be identified among such pseudodefenders of the Marxist theory of state.

. . . We shall turn first to one of the leaders of the contemporary anti-Marxist attacks, Hans Kelsen, a professor at the Vienna University. Kelsen is the head of the formal juridical (normative) school. In recent years he has acquired numerous followers among Western jurists. He has published *Sozialismus und Staat,* a big work directed against the Marxist theory of state.

Kelsen's entire work is an embodiment of formal logic, and the starting point of his reasoning is an abstract juridical norm. He is not at all disturbed by the fact that juridical abstraction is in direct conflict with reality. In one of his works, *Hauptprobleme der Staatsrechtslehre,* Kelsen declares the following: "The objections that frequently are raised against the pure formal method (asserting that this method produces unsatisfactory results because it fails to encompass real life and leaves the true legal reality unexplained) are founded on a complete miscomprehension of the nature of jurisprudence, which aims neither at encompassing the true reality nor at 'explaining' life."[2]

Hence the critique advanced by Kelsen against Marxism is, by its very nature, diametrically opposed to our method, to the sociological method, which deals with life in all its manifestations and not merely with a "logical" reality. Kelsen's formal logical schemes, the tools by means of which he attempts to blow up the Marxist concepts of the state, constitute an inimitable example of a metaphysical approach to one of the principal problems of modern sociology. This fact makes discussion between a Marxist and Kelsen difficult: the argument must be conducted on two distinct methodological levels. Although such a task is difficult, it is not impossible.

Kelsen is an enemy of socialism. In the preface to the second edition of his book, he thought it necessary to emphasize most energetically ("mit allem Nachdruck zu betonen") that his work was not directed against socialism. "What I dispute with is merely Marxism and, within it, merely the political theory. It is not the socialist ideal that is questioned but the Marxist contention that it is possible to materialize this ideal without a state."

[2] (Tübingen, 1910), p. 93.

. . . Professor Kelsen takes issue *merely* with Marxism and, within it, *only* with its political theory. This is really a farce. We cannot but laugh when an old scientist, the head of a popular school, naïvely assumes that it is possible to exclude from Marxism its political theory, when he fails to understand that this very theory is an integral, inalienable element of Marxism. Marxism is an integral and harmonious world outlook whose parts are indissolubly connected, mutually supplementing one another, giving meaning to one another. Nevertheless, there are still some hunters who seize one "aspect" of Marxism—philosophy, sociology, economy, "political theory"—and tear it off from the living body of Marx's theory. All critics who attempt to "destroy" Marxism should grasp once and for all that Marxism is an integral, harmonious world outlook. . . .

The starting point of Kelsen's critique of the Marxist concept of the state is a formal juridical definition of the state as a coercive legal order (*Zwangsordnung*). According to Kelsen, the fact that the state is a *union based on domination* (*Herschaftsverband*) is crucial in defining the state. "This means that the social order called state is a *coercive* order and that this coercive order . . . coincides with the legal order."[3] In characterizing the state as a coercive order, Kelsen attempts to stress two points: first, that the necessity of subordination to the state does not depend upon the subjective will of those who constitute this order; second, that the state exercises its authority through coercive acts. Neither the social goal pursued by the state nor its sociological content is of significance to Kelsen's concept of the state; crucial to his concept of the state is merely the juridical norm from the point of view of which the state appears as a legal form of social life. Because of this, it is not surprising that Kelsen is neither willing nor able to grasp the one fact that is crucial for an understanding of the state, namely, the fact that the state pursues a definite social goal—subordination of one class to another. Kelsen declares that he agrees with the Marxist view that a definition of state based on the assumption of solidarity of interests is a fiction. But he cannot accept the view that the state is an instrument of exploitation of one class by another. "The definition of the state as an order expressing a great degree of coercion is not meaningless as is contended by Marxists. On the other hand, Marxist identification of the meaning of the state with exploitative class domination, i.e., with oppression of one class by another for the purpose of exploitation, is completely inadmissible." Why is Kelsen opposed to the Marxist "attribution" of

[3] *Sozialismus und Staat: Eine Untersuchung der politischen Theorien des Marxismus* (2nd ed.; Leipzig, 1923), p. 11.

exploitative tendencies and class oppression to the state? He is opposed for the following reasons: first, there were states whose principal goal was not economic exploitation; second, economic exploitation cannot be recognized as the sole goal of a modern state; third,
a state is conceivable that, instead of promoting exploitation, may
take measures against it; fourth, by introducing labor legislation, protection of labor, etc., the modern state displays tendencies toward a
liquidation of class contradictions.

The above-cited reasons quite clearly demonstrate the fruitless
scholasticism of Kelsenian theory. These reasons may be applicable
to the logical abstraction that Kelsen designated as a state, but they
are completely inapplicable to the real, concrete state, to the state
existing in historical reality and not within a juridical scheme. Kelsen
contends that a state existed that did not pursue economic exploitation. Where and when did such a state exist? Perhaps in the epoch of
primitive communism, in the epoch of classless society, that is, at the
time when the state was not yet in existence? When the state arose,
society was split into classes, one exploiting another. Furthermore,
Kelsen contends that exploitation is not the sole goal of a modern
state. He fails to see that the fundamental and supreme goal of the
state is to secure the possibility of exploitation of one class by the
other, to protect the class division of society. This is the sole social
function of the state. . . . The worn-out contentions of our opponents
that the state takes care of public health, public education, that it
builds railroads for all citizens, protects the security of all citizens,
etc.—that is, contentions that the state performs functions of "general utility"—are completely unjustified. Indeed, the state looks after
sanitation, builds railroads, and by doing this it secures the minimal
prerequisites for its own existence. Without these prerequisites the
state would simply fail to perform its functions. The purpose of these
measures is not to promote general welfare but to secure conditions
under which the state will be able to carry out its principal function
—to be an organization of class domination. The state performs the
functions of "general utility" only if they are indispensable for the
realization of its class tasks.

One of Kelsen's trumps is that a state is conceivable that, instead
of promoting exploitation, would take actions against exploitation.
In connection with this Kelsen had an opportunity to point out the
striking example of the Soviet state. But even in this case the poverty
of Kelsen's logical constructions is quite vividly demonstrated. The
Soviet state is struggling against the exploitative tendencies of the
capitalist class which has been deprived of its ruling position by the

Revolution but has not yet been liquidated. Hence, it follows that this class still exists in Soviet society; it seeks to exploit other classes, but the classes that are subject to the threat of such exploitation hold in their hands the power of the state and take measures against the class enemy. This is the state in a period of transition. The proletariat does not exploit anyone. Indeed, the proletariat is the ruling class in the Soviet state, but the goal of this state is neither exploitation nor enslavement—that is, this state is not a state in the Marxist meaning of the term. The mind of the Viennese professor cannot grasp the fact that Marxists erect their concept of the state not on the principle of juridical normativism but on the basis of a living, dynamic, sociological approach to society and that they are therefore capable of understanding that which Kelsen fails to understand.

As pointed out by Lenin, "Under capitalism we have a state in the proper sense of the word, that is, a special machine for the suppression of one class by another, and of the majority by the minority at that. Again, during the *transition* from capitalism to communism, suppression is *still* necessary; but it is the suppression of the minority of exploiters by the majority of the exploited. A special apparatus, a special machine for suppression—the 'state'—is still necessary, but this is now a transitional state. . . . Finally, only communism renders the state absolutely unnecessary, for there is no one to be suppressed —'no one' in the sense of a class. . . ."[4]

. . . Kelsen is completely puzzled by the Marxist treatment of the problem of society and the state. In his opinion, Marxism opposes society and state, one to another, as good to evil, as altruism to egotism, as general interest to individual interest. To quote him,

> The state becomes an expression of immoral principle, of an egotistic interest, whereas society appears as an expression of the moral solidarity of everyone. The state—the *civitas diaboli*—should therefore be conquered, should "die away," should give way to a classless society free of the state, to some sort of a *civitas dei*. Strictly speaking, the only difference between the concept of St. Augustine and Marxist theory lies in the fact that Augustine quite prudently refers his ideal to the other world whereas Marxism, through application of the causal law of development, applies its ideal to the earthly world.[5]

. . . We stated earlier that Kelsen simply fails to understand the Marxist theory of society and state. Now we shall justify this contention. Kelsen is a classical representative of the type of jurists to whom, as stated by Engels, the juridical form is everything and the

4 *Gosudarstvo i Revolutsiya*, pp. 340–41.
5 *Sozialismus und Staat*, pp. 31–33.

economic content nothing. Because of his juridical statics, he mis-
understood and misinterpreted the Marxist approach to the problem
of society and state, the approach that is based on sociological dynamics. From Kelsen's point of view, Marxism contraposes two
independent categories, two forms of man's social life—*society and
state*. There is no coercion, enslavement, and exploitation in society;
society is a paradise, a paradise that has been lost but will be re-
gained. The state is a receptacle of oppression, suppression, and exploitation; it is a hell—a hell in which humanity lives. All this sounds
good, but it is not "in line with Marx"; it is "in line with Augustine."
According to Marx, society and state are by no means categories in
opposition to each other. The state is nothing but a form of existence
of society, a form determined by economic relationships; it is "a
product of society at a given stage of development," as Engels stated.
At a certain stage in the development of human society, the economy forced society to assume the form of a state, whereas at succeeding stages of development the economy will force society to get rid
of the state. The great merit of Marx and Engels lies precisely in the
fact that they ceased to regard the state as a certain eternal norm;
they converted the state from a *logical* into a *historical* category;
they did not contrapose the state to society but subordinated it to the
dialectic of social development. Max Adler was quite right in pointing out in his polemic with Kelsen that, in addition to destroying the
fetishism of commodity, Marx also destroyed the fetishism of the
state. Kelsen could see this by himself if he would carefully consider
the following famous excerpts from Engels' works:

> The state, then, has not existed from all eternity. There have been
> societies that did without it, that had no conception of the state and
> state authority. At a certain stage of economic development, which was
> necessarily bound up with the cleavage of society into classes, the state
> became a necessity owing to this cleavage. We are now rapidly approach-
> ing a stage in the development of production at which the existence
> of these classes not only will have ceased to be a necessity, but will have
> become a positive hindrance to production. The classes will disappear as
> inevitably as they arose at an earlier stage. Along with them the state will
> inevitably disappear. The society that will organize production on the
> basis of a free and equal association of the producers will put the whole
> state machine where it will then belong: into the museum of antiquities,
> by the side of the spinning wheel and the bronze ax.[6]

> The state is the first ideological power over mankind. Society creates
> for itself an organ for the safeguarding of its general interests against

---

[6] Friedrich Engels, *Ursprung der Familie, des Privateigentums und des Staats*
(22nd ed.; Stuttgart, 1922), p. 182.

internal and external attacks. This organ is the state authority. Hardly having come into being, this organ strives to make itself independent in regard to society; and it succeeds in accomplishing this the more so the more it becomes the organ of a particular class, the more it directly enforces the supremacy of that class. . . . But once the state has become a power independent of society, it produces forthwith a new ideology. It is, indeed, only among professional politicians, theorists of constitutional law, and jurists of private law that the connection with economic facts gets completely lost. In order to receive legal sanctions, the economic facts in each particular case must assume the form of juridical relationships. Thereby, of course, consideration has to be paid to the whole existing system of law. This is why the juridical form appears as everything, and economic content appears as nothing. Public law and private law are treated as independent spheres, each having its own independent historical development, each being capable of and needing a systematic presentation by the thoroughgoing elimination of all inner contradictions.[7]

If Kelsen understood Marx's theory of society and state, he would know that it is inadmissible to draw a demarcation line between these two concepts; then he would not interpret Marx's theory in a St. Augustine-like way. Critics of Marxism are constantly discovering contradictions in our system; by now they have discovered as many contradictions as Marx had hairs in his beard. Hence, it would be strange if such a reputable critic as Hans Kelsen did not also seize upon one of the many "contradictions" of Marx. As a matter of fact, Kelsen seeks to demonstrate a "contradiction" between the political and economic theories of Marx. Since Kelsen has assigned the central place of his book to the disclosure of this contradiction, we shall discuss this problem.

Kelsen's reasoning proceeds from the fact—which is crucial for him—that the ultimate goals of both Marxism and anarchism coincide. In the past we have read a good many pages on Marx's anarchism, for our opponents have done thorough research in this field. Kelsen, too, proclaims that "in principle there is no difference whatsoever between anarchism and the Marx-Engels conception of socialism."[8]

Marxism and anarchism are blood relatives, for both strive for a stateless society, for a free society without authority and coercion. Communism, for which the International fought, under Marx's and Engels' direction, is in fact a genuine form of anarchism. When Marx and Engels struggled against Bakunin, they denounced him for demanding an instantaneous abolition of the state and its replacement by anarchy. On the other hand, they denounced Bakunin because his

---

[7] Friedrich Engels, *Lyudvig Feierbakh* [Ludwig Feuerbach], trans. G. V. Plekhanov, in *Sobranie Sochinenii* [Collected Works] (n.p., n.d.), XVII, 351.
[8] *Sozialismus und Staat,* p. 85.

policy led toward replacement of the existing state with an anarchist organization closely resembling a state. Thus Bakunin was denounced, not because he was an anarchist, but because his anarchism was not consistent enough. Kelsen contends that the strife between Marx and Bakunin was caused by considerations of personal charac- ter. Marx's and Bakunin's world outlooks were quite similar. "Marx, in his political theory, was an anarchist, whereas Bakunin, in his economic theory, was a Marxist."[9] Bakunin's idea of revolutionary state and the Marx-Engels idea of dictatorship of the proletariat are as similar as two drops of water. They were opposed one to another only because of the political fervor of political opponents.

Economic and political aspects of Marxism have nothing in common or, more precisely, they are isolated one from the other. Marx's economic theory leads to a strict, collectivistically centralized economic organization whereas his political doctrine quite clearly strives toward an anarchoindividualistic ideal. These, according to Kelsen, are the fatal contradictions of Marxism. He asserts that men cannot master nature without mastering themselves, i.e., without subordinating themselves to a social organization. This subordination, of course, is not tantamount to exploitation and enslavement. Kelsen demands an answer to the following question: "Is it possible to guide tremendous masses of people—mankind—toward the attainment of certain goals without resorting to external coercion?" The positive answer to this question can be given in only one case, if it is assumed that, owing to the abolition of private property and the subsequent liquidation of classes, the future society will be a solidary society without material contradictions, a society in which only harmless differences of opinion will take place; only in such a case will man willingly subordinate himself to the social order, for then the organs of society would order him to do only what he himself desired. This is the only case that justifies the assumption that man's relationship to society, to its organs, will cease to be a relationship based on domination and will become a relationship of equals, a relationship determined by the equal wills of the comrades constituting this society. This singular case is affirmed by anarchism; the same hypothesis lies at the basis of Engels' view that government of persons will be replaced by administration of things. However, according to Kelsen, this hypothesis is a chimera, a utopia. It is quite possible that communism will furnish society with such obvious economic benefits that any serious opposition to communism would be unthinkable. But communism is not merely an economic order; it is also a cultural organization encom-

[9] *Ibid.*

passing all aspects of social life. Communism will regulate such problems as religion, art, sexual relations, and all this will lead to great conflicts. Even if, in the future society, economic solidarity is attained, it stands to reason that this solidarity will not cover all aspects of social life. This hypothesis is acceptable only to Marxists who, under the influence of an overestimation of economic factors, explain significant historical events exclusively by production relationships.

To quote Kelsen,

> It amounts to an unprecedented shortsightedness to assume that in the future society there will be only the opposition of individual grumblers, that problems of religion, art, and sexual relations will not lead to the creation of distinct groups. . . . The groups that will find themselves in opposition to the system of the communist society will have to be "suppressed" in the same manner as the proletariat is being suppressed today. Consequently, it is questionable whether they will regard the communist society as a solidary society; rather, they will regard it as a coercive order, as an apparatus of oppression, as a "state"; their attitude will be similar to that of present-day "proletarian" sociology toward capitalist society and its system which is based on coercion.[10]

Marxism dreams of replacing the class state with a classless society, but it forgets that a solidary, fraternal society is unthinkable considering the existing nature of man. It is quite possible that it is not capitalism that corrupts man and transforms him into a criminal but, on the contrary, that capitalism exists because its system of exploitation corresponds to man's nature. "Man has a strong instinct to let others work for him and in general to use other men as a means toward attainment of his own goals." Exploitation is a human instinct just as are laziness, stealing, jealousy, honesty. The communist society will have to cope with all these instincts. Hence, the communist social system, too, will be based on coercion; it will be nothing but a *Zwangsordnung,* a state. Marxism is forced to build the future society using the human material from which the present-day states have been created. This makes all Marxist dreams of the future society utopian.

I have attempted to present Kelsen's views on the question of Marx's "contradictions" as accurately as possible. I must admit that I did this not only because I am dealing with an opponent whose views are subject to criticism but chiefly because the presentation of Kelsen's views is in itself their best criticism. Now we shall attempt to take a closer look at Kelsen's arguments.

First of all we shall discuss the problem of the "blood relationship"

[10] *Ibid.,* p. 108.

of Marxism to anarchism, which has led Kelsen to speak of Marx's anarchism and Bakunin's Marxism. Concerning Bakunin, we are not surprised that Kelsen depicts him as a "Marxist." We have had ample opportunity to see how poor and distorted is Kelsen's interpretation of Marxism. Such an expert in Marxism as Professor Kelsen can easily accept Bakunin's economic concept of history as bona fide "Marxism." Plekhanov once characterized Bakunin as a "Proudhonist enlightened by Marxism." But Kelsen should know that to be "enlightened" by Marxism is not tantamount to being a Marxist.

According to Kelsen's authoritative statement, Karl Marx—the sworn enemy of anarchistic theory who never ceased to struggle against all its varieties—"is an anarchist in his political theory."[11] Let us take a closer look at Marxism and anarchism: Marxism rejects the existing state machine. Anarchism rejects it too. Marxism has established that the historical trend leads toward the creation of classless society. Anarchism also strives toward the creation of a classless society.

Do the indicated points of contiguity (or even coincidence) between Marxism and anarchism justify the conclusion: *Marxism is anarchism?* Professor Kelsen says yes. In contrast to his conclusion, we advance the following formula: *Marxism is not anarchism.*

In a letter to Cuno (January 24, 1872), F. Engels quite clearly demonstrated the distinction between Marx's "anarchism" and the theory of anarchism developed by Bakunin:

> While the great mass of the Social-Democratic workers hold our view that the state authority is nothing more than the organization that the ruling classes, landlords, and capitalists have provided for themselves in order to protect their social prerogatives, Bakunin maintains that it is the *state* which has created capital, that the capitalist has his capital *only by favor of the state.* Since, therefore, the state is the chief evil, it is above all the state which must be done away with; then capitalism will go to hell by itself. We, on the contrary, say: do away with capital, with the appropriation of all means of production in the hands of the few, and the state will fall away by itself. The difference is an essential one. Without a previous social revolution the abolition of the state is nonsense.

Lenin's pamphlet *State and Revolution* was available to Kelsen. Had he studied it, he would have found out that the difference between Marxists and anarchists amounts to the following:

---

[11] A similar view has been stated by a Christian Socialist, Fritz Eberstein, in his pamphlet *Die Organization bei Karl Marx* (Essen, 1921). Kelsen is indeed in honorable company.

1. Marxists aim at a complete destruction of the state and maintain that this goal is attainable only after the destruction of the classes by means of a revolution, as a result of the establishment of socialism that leads toward the dying away of the state. Anarchists insist upon the destruction of the state at once; they fail to understand the conditions necessary for such destruction.

2. Marxists maintain that the proletariat must conquer political authority, must completely destroy the old state machine, and must replace it with a new one, with an organization of armed workers, with a commune-like organization. Anarchists, while insisting upon the destruction of the state machine, have not the slightest idea what the proletariat will put in its place nor how the proletariat will use revolutionary authority. Anarchists even reject the utilization of state power by the revolutionary proletariat; they reject revolutionary dictatorship.

3. Marxists call for the preparation of the proletariat for the revolution through a utilization of the contemporary state, whereas anarchists reject this theory.

Anarchists call for an "abolition" of the state; they think that the destruction of the state can be accomplished by means of a decree. According to Marxism, the destruction of the state can take place only as a result of a complex historical process. This process consists of two inevitable phases indissolubly connected one with another. The first phase: replacement of the bourgeois, capitalist state with a proletarian state, the state of the transitional type, born in the fire and storm of the Revolution. The second phase: the replacement of the proletarian state with a classless society which will ensue from the state's gradual loss of its functions—the state's "withering away." This is the tremendous—and principal—distinction between Marxism and anarchism. One who fails to understand it knows almost nothing about Marxism and anarchism.

According to Kelsen, in addition to being an "anarchist," Marx is also a "utopian." Where did Professor Kelsen find "utopia" in the founder of scientific socialism? In Marx's faith in the society of the future, in the society in which the government of persons will be replaced by the administration of things, in a society without enslavement and oppression.

Indeed, it would be strange if such a zealous critic . . . did not mention the "utopianism" of Marx's theory of future society. This "utopianism" is also a target of many of Professor Kelsen's colleagues. In explaining the Marxist "utopia" of the future society, Kelsen asserts that Marxism is "a blind social theory that sees everything in the gloom of economics," incapable of seeing the fact that the existence of the future society will be determined not by economy but by psychology. Before anything else, we would like to note the fact that the extremely logical Professor Kelsen develops an argument that violates some rules of logic: if Marxism is "blind," then how could it see anything, even "in the gloom of economics"? Second, Professor Kelsen is wrong when he thinks that Marxists are complete ignoramuses on the question of psychology. He should have looked at Professor G. I. Chelpanov's *Psychology and Marxism*.[12] Why does Kelsenian psychology give a negative answer to the question concerning the possibility of the existence of a classless society that will replace the state after it withers away? We presented Kelsen's arguments on this problem earlier. Exploitation, laziness, stealing, etc., are human instincts; they are spawned in our nature. As long as we are powerless to change this nature, we cannot even think of a new society. Human nature makes a state organization inevitable, and all dreams about its fall are utopian.

The view defended by Kelsen is in fact his own *testimonium paupertatis*. . . . He contends that exploitation is spawned in man's nature. Exactly the same contention was advanced by earlier Kelsens who lived in the age of slavery; they contended that slavery is spawned in man's nature. Later, the same contention was advanced by serfholders in defense of their right to exploit peasants. In our country, even a primary-school student could sensibly explain to Kelsen that man is neither the exploiter nor the exploited because of his nature, that man does not steal because of his nature but because of existing social conditions. With the change of social conditions those "instincts" that constitute the *ultima ratio* of Kelsen's anti-Marxist criticism will disappear. And we *know*—we do not dream—that conditions are changing. We know this with a strong conviction that only a scientific knowledge of the social process is able to provide.

Indeed, we know that conditions do not change instantly. Hence, we also know that man will not be changed instantly. "We are not utopians. We do not dream of instantly doing away with all government, with all subordination. These are anarchistic dreams, founded on a failure to comprehend the tasks of the dictatorship of the proletariat; these dreams are thoroughly alien to Marxism, and, in fact, they aim at delaying socialist revolution. . . ."[13]

The path toward the society of the future is long. We know that it

[12] (Moscow, 1924).
[13] Lenin, *Gosudarstvo i Revolutsiya*, p. 336.

will be long and agonizing, but we also know in which direction it leads. We cannot foresee the "ultimate goal," for it will be determined by social development itself. As stated in *The Communist Manifesto,* "When, in the course of development, class distinctions have disappeared, and all production has been concentrated in the hands of individuals associated in unions, the public authority will lose its political character. . . . In place of the old bourgeois society, with its classes and class contradictions, we shall have an association in which the free development of each is the condition for the free development of all."

Having crushed the hateful Marxist socialism, Kelsen magnanimously stretches an arm toward the defeated enemy and supplies him with life-saving advice: socialism will be saved if, instead of being oriented toward Marx, it is oriented toward Lassalle. "Zurück zu Lassalle!" triumphantly exclaims Kelsen.

Like Herman Oncken, Bernhardt Harme, and Novgorodtsev, Kelsen urges the working class to discard the great and immortal contribution of Marx, the master of revolutionary activity. Kelsen favors that part of Lassalle's legacy which Marx stigmatized as "the loyal faith of Lassalle's sect in the state." Kelsen praises the political mind of Lassalle, who, in contrast to Marx, contended that the state is not an instrument of the class struggle boiling in the womb of society but a certain moral entity standing above society, an "eternal and sacred fire of civilization."

We have presented only certain of Kelsen's views advanced against the Marxist theory of state. . . . We have concluded that his views are unstable and shaky. In criticizing Kelsen's views, we become convinced that this scientist—one of the leaders of the modern anti-Marxist attacks in the field of the theory of state—chews the old "critical" cud, spiced with normative phraseology and formal juridical scholastics. In place of the Marxist analysis of the social process, Kelsen offers a dead scheme of formal jurisprudence. . . .

# The Proletarian State and Communism*

## ᘓ *V. Veger*

The proletariat, organized as a ruling class, constitutes a state in all respects: economic, moral, and intellectual. It is a state carrying the imprint of the old society in whose womb it originated. Such was the view of Marx. Following this view, Lenin has noted that the proletarian state is a bourgeois state without the bourgeoisie. More specifically, the proletarian state is a bourgeois state without the domination of the bourgeoisie. As a class, the bourgeoisie remains in the proletarian state for a certain period of time. But, in contrast to a bourgeois state, in the proletarian state, the bourgeoisie, deprived of political power, ceases to be a politically dominating class and gradually loses its economic power—the ownership of the means of production. The proletarian state does not liquidate the bourgeois class by means of decrees; such a method is inappropriate in the period of extreme terror. At the same time, however, the proletarian state is drafting into its service specialists, industrial experts, engineers, and officers, and protects them against the attempt on the part of the uneducated strata of the population to liquidate them. The proletarian state adopts an especially cautious attitude toward the masses of peasants; it declares a war only against an insignificant part, namely, against big landowners and kulaks. It renounces the employment of force in commanding the obedience of the overwhelming majority of middle peasants; it seeks to liquidate petty farming gradually, by organizing large-scale state farms, by voluntary communes, and by other methods of an economic and cultural nature. The limitation of economic and political monopoly in the proletarian state is particularly manifest in that the state's activity is subordinated to the directives of the ruling proletarian party and, furthermore, in that each nationality has the right of self-determination, including secession. The latter demonstrates quite clearly the fact that the proletarian state lacks the essential features of a bourgeois state.

But the organization of this society is still far from its emancipation from the narrow horizons of the bourgeois law. Only when these narrow horizons have been overcome, when the division of labor and the

* From *Pravo i Gosudarstvo Perekhodovogo Vremeni* [Law and the State in the Transition Period] (2nd ed.; Moscow, 1924), pp. 52–54.

antagonism between intellectual and physical labor has vanished, will labor become the primary need of life, will individuals attain well-rounded development, . . . will the forces of production provide society with an abundance of wealth. Then the state will wither away.

The difference between the organization of free society and the proletarian state is not less than the difference between the proletarian and bourgeois states. In the higher stage of communism, there will be no need for the apparatus of an organized coercion monopolizing the instrument of coercion, that is to say, there will be no need for political authority. If we judge according to Marx's description of the higher stage of communism, the transition toward the free society will constitute a long process. It is obvious that the construction of a society without any coercion will necessitate the creation of a new psychology by means of which the society would foresee and solve all conflicts without applying organized coercion.

Such organization now is hardly conceivable. The transfer of authority to the hands of the proletariat does not give rise to a new psychology of the classes composing the state. People remain divided into diverse groups, diverse specializations and types of work, with their views and habits, which frequently prevent them from understanding one another.

The reference to a primitive community may give some notion of the state of consciousness in the free communist society. There, man's mentality was characterized by unity. The person constituted a whole. There the enslaving division of labor and the fragmentation of man were absent. Nevertheless, primitive men were poor and miserable beings, all of them resembling one another. The primitive man resembles the man of the higher stage of communism as a newborn baby resembles an adult who is characterized by vigor, mind, will, and feelings. The development of the forces of production will free man from a considerable portion of his work, will shorten the working day, and technology will eliminate rough and hard types of work. William Morris, a visionary of the happy future, was capable neither of renouncing slavery nor of foreseeing that the age of steam, coinciding with the epoch of the bourgeoisie, and the age of electricity, coinciding with the epoch of the proletariat, as well as the future discoveries that we are yet incapable of foreseeing, will bring about a natural transition from the proletarian state toward the future society of communism.

The proletarian state declares work to be a duty of each man, though, in fact, the principle of equal work is absolutely unjust and imperfect. Equal work does not bring about the equality of men. Men differ in their biological needs, in their intellectual abilities, and in their abilities to acquire skills. For an equal quantity of work, they receive an equal quantity of products, and that means, in the final analysis, that inequality among men remains. The requirement of equality will be satisfied with the slogan: "From each according to his abilities, to each according to his needs." The proletarian state is unable to translate this slogan into reality. This slogan will become the foundation of the communist society at the higher stage of its development.

# Revolution, Dictatorship, and Civil Freedom*

## ∽ F. Ksenofontov

"At a certain stage in their development, the material forces of production in society come in conflict with the existing relations of production or with the property relations within which they had been at work before. . . . From the forms of development of the forces of production, these relations turn into their fetters. Then a period of social revolution occurs."[1]

This is a general but, nevertheless, a crucial premise of Marx's theory of revolution. Speaking about the proletarian, communist revolution, i.e., about the revolutionary transformation of capitalism into communism, Marx described the conflict between the forces of production and the capitalist relations of production in the following manner: "The monopoly of capital turns into fetters of the further development of the very mode of production which it engendered and dominated. The centralization of the means of production and the socialization of labor reach the point at which they become incompatible with the entire capitalist membrane, which consequently explodes. Private property approaches its final hours. Expropriators are being expropriated."[2]

Thus, according to Marx, the fundamental cause of a revolution is the conflict between the forces of production and the existing relationships of production—property relationships. The latter are secured, "sanctified," by a system of coercive norms imposed by the ruling class—*by its law*. This system is protected by the entire power of the class, i.e., by state authority.

. . . . . . .

*The essence of Marx's theory, the soul of his teaching, is the recognition and proof that the "class struggle inevitably leads to the dictatorship of the proletariat."* But this conclusion is unacceptable to bourgeois scientists, and it has been factually rejected by the renegades of Marxism—Kautsky and others.

---

* From *Gosudarstvo i Pravo* [The State and Law] (Moscow, 1924), pp. 107–8, 24, 156–59.

[1] See the Preface to Karl Marx, *K Kritike Politicheskoi Ekonomii* [A Critique of Political Economy].

[2] *Kapital* [Capital], ed. Struve (Petrograd, 1899), I, 551.

Marx's theory of the class struggle implies that the class struggle is a political struggle. That is, that in order to establish a new and more perfect form of production, each new social class must destroy the political power (state authority) of the old class which personifies the obsolete economic structure and is hostile to the new class. This is exactly what the "third estate" did to feudal lords, and this is what the proletariat is doing and must do to the bourgeois state, which is a political organization of the capitalist class, an executive committee of the bourgeoisie.

Marx has made it quite clear that the struggle of the bourgeoisie against the feudal lords is different from the struggle of the proletariat against the bourgeoisie. In terms of its exploitative role, the bourgeoisie is a class kindred to feudal lords, for having seized political authority, it utilized it to strengthen and to expand the exploitation of other classes. The role of the proletariat is entirely different. Following the seizure of political authority from the bourgeoisie, it crushes the bourgeois state apparatus and organizes its own proletarian state—the dictatorship of the proletariat, which, according to Marx, "constitutes the transition to the abolition of all classes and to the creation of a classless society," a society without exploitation. Bourgeois society with its classes and class struggles will be superseded by a classless society called communism.

. . . . . . .

The essence of Soviet authority—of the dictatorship of the proletariat—lies in the fact that it is a *mass organization* of the numerically strongest classes in society, the workers and the working peasants. Citizen Kautsky contends that the dictatorship of the Russian proletariat is in no way different from other dictatorships, not even from czarism. To this, our answer is that the dictatorship of the proletariat is indeed similar to the dictatorships of other ruling classes since it serves as an *instrument for suppressing other classes;* but instead of suppressing oppressed have-not classes, it suppresses *yesterday's ruling and propertied classes.*

The essential distinction between the dictatorship of the proletariat and the dictatorships of other classes (feudal lords or the bourgeoisie) is that the latter dictatorships represented a *forced suppression of the majority of the society,* the workers. The dictatorship of the proletariat and its political form in Russia, the Soviet Republic, results in a *forced suppression* of the resisting domestic and international bourgeoisie, obviously a minority in the society. This is the meaning of Marx's statement that the "state is in the service of society." The proletarian state is and must be a class state. As indicated by Engels, "Only when the state becomes representative of the entire society will it become obsolete."

Citizen Kautsky also contends that there is no freedom, no equality, and no democracy in Russia. As a matter of fact, in the Soviet Republic we have more freedom, equality, and democracy than anywhere else. What we do not have is "freedom, equality, and democracy" in Kautsky's meaning of these terms. He uses these terms to mean "political freedom," which Engels characterized as "a deceptive, false freedom."

In the Soviet Republic, freedom, equality, and democracy exist in fact: *the economic and hence political dependence of the workingman upon the capitalist, i.e., the dependence of an overwhelming majority upon an insignificant minority, has been eliminated.* The capital and wealth of the bourgeoisie have been confiscated and transferred into the hands of the workingman. Soviet authority is the broadest authority, an authority that is closest to the people because *only* workingmen participate in elections to the soviets. Election itself takes place in the places of *production:* in factories, plants, workshops, and villages. Therefore, Soviet authority is a labor authority; it is a most expanded labor democracy.

Here, democracy does not appear in its abstract, pure form, as in the bourgeois-democratic state of citizen Kautsky. There, a "pure" democracy prevails, a democracy that can be filled with any content or, more precisely, a democracy the concrete content of which is the bourgeois dictatorship. *Here, democracy has a fixed content which we openly admit, namely, the dictatorship of the proletariat supported by the peasantry.*

It would be both absurd and wrong for the proletariat to introduce a "universal democracy," i.e., to give the right of participation in the soviets, whose task it is to "build socialism and suppress exploitation," to those whom these organs are designed to suppress, the bourgeoisie, priests, kulaks, and their socialist myrmidons. To all remaining classes in society, the workers, peasants, and working intelligentsia, democracy is available, and hereby a most expanded and true democracy.

How should the term "freedom" be understood? If by freedom we mean a true freedom, i.e., freedom for the workingman, freedom for the overwhelming majority of society, then we have the greatest possible scope of freedom. *All material prerequisites* of freedom, i.e., paper, presses, etc., are transferred into the hands of the workingmen

SOVIET POLITICAL THOUGHT

who are "organized in their state." This results in real freedom of the
press, which becomes a powerful instrument for the expression of the
opinion of the workers and peasants.

In suppressing the bourgeoisie, the proletariat destroys its state, its
entire apparatus of material and spiritual coercion of the working
class, including the bourgeois press. It is insane to ask the proletariat
not to deprive the bourgeoisie of this instrument. Equally insane is the
demand that the proletariat should furnish its class enemy, the bourgeoisie, with "freedoms," for example, freedom of speech, assembly,
and political organization. Why should the proletariat do this? Kautsky tells us that we should do this in order to have "criticism." But he
forgets that the proletariat has absolutely no need of bourgeois criticism. *The arms and legs of the enemy must be shackled, and its
mouth must be muzzled with the revolutionary dictatorship.* This is
being done in Soviet Russia.

What does "freedom of political parties" mean? It means freedom
of action for the bourgeoisie since a party is but an advanced part of
its class struggling on behalf of the whole class. Citizen Kautsky, you
should not treat the problem outside of time and space. "Freedom of
political parties" in the Soviet Republic, in Russia, or in any other
country means nothing but freedom of action for the most advanced
section of the bourgeoisie. The working class, "organized in its state,"
has only one party, the Communist party. *As the most advanced and
the most conscious part of the proletariat, the Communist party carries out dictatorship in the name of the whole class.* It has no need of
freedom.

. . . According to Kautsky,

The civil war in Russia has ended, but its result is a victory of
dictatorship, that is, paralysis of political and intellectual life in general.
And dictatorship hinders socialism. . . .
The Russian Revolution is a pure bourgeois revolution. It was never
a proletarian one. What Russia has is not a dictatorship of the proletariat
but the dictatorship of a clique of impostors who call themselves a
worker-peasant government, the dictatorship of a clique that assumed
the reins of government by accident, owing to chance and luck.[3]

This is citizen Kautsky's interpretation of the Russian Revolution.
We leave it up to him, but we would like to suggest that he compare it
with the interpretation of our revolution advanced in his earlier work.
In his *From Democracy to State Servitude,* Kautsky has described the

[3] *Proletarskaya Revolutsiya i Ee Programma* [The Proletarian Revolution and
Its Program] (n.p., n.d.), p. 171.

Russian Revolution in the following manner: "It is pointless to argue whether the Russian proletariat had to take authority into its own hands. Like all revolutions, the Russian Revolution was a spontaneous occurrence. It could not have been prevented nor could it have been engendered artificially."

From the quoted statement, it follows that (1) the Russian proletariat took power into its *own* hands; (2) the Russian Revolution was not engendered artificially but by the whole course of events, or, to use Marxist language, by economic laws. In contrast to this, citizen Kautsky in the previous quotation implied the following: (1) the Russian proletariat *never* took the power into its hands; the authority is in the hands of an *accidentally* successful clique of people; (2) the Revolution came into being purely by chance.

A cheat in any field (as the saying goes, each vice has its own advocate) lies and forgets what he said a few seconds ago.

# Proletarian Justice*    ᴄᴡ    *A. Ya. Vyshinskii*

We are being told that the laws made by the bourgeoisie (which holds the state power in its hands) do not serve its own interests but the general interest; that they do not protect its own good but the general good; that they do not express its own will but the general will. We know, however, that in fact it is not so. All laws in the bourgeois state are bourgeois laws; they are made for the purpose of protecting the bourgeoisie and are applied in a cold and calculated way with the aim of safeguarding its interests.

We know that no judge in a bourgeois state would remain even an hour in his judicial chair if he decided to adjudicate according to his consciousness rather than according to the desires of his masters, the bourgeoisie. And, of course, it is quite natural that the bourgeois spirit reigns in bourgeois courts; that bourgeois judges make decisions in a bourgeois way; that their understanding of law (i.e., legal consciousness) is bourgeois throughout.

The other way around would be incomprehensible. For we know that law is merely an expression of economic relations. In *The Communist Manifesto,* Marx stated that "the ideas of bourgeois society are an offspring of bourgeois production and property relations." In another place (*Critique of Political Economy*) Marx pointed out that "legal relations are rooted in the material conditions of life." Finally, in his famous speech to a jury in Cologne (1847), Marx stated: "Society is not based on law. This is a phantasy of jurists. On the contrary, *law should be based on society.*"

The bourgeois society is bourgeois property. And bourgeois law is the law protecting this property. Whoever fails to grasp this, and thinks of playing childish comedies with so-called universal justice, has also failed to understand the fact that, to a bourgeois, justice signifies his property and his profit. Consequently, the "legal consciousness" on which the bourgeois judiciary is based is nothing but a *bourgeois* consciousness.

For a long time the classes have been opposed, one to another. But only recently the proletariat succeeded in advancing its own law against the bourgeois law, its own socialist legal consciousness against bourgeois legal consciousness. And, having advanced its socialist legal

* *From* "Eshcho Raz o Satsialisticheskom Pravosozanii" [Once Again on the Socialist Legal Consciousness], *Rabochii Sud,* No. 5–6 (1925), pp. 196–200.

consciousness to the forefront of the struggle, the proletariat uses it as an active and creative force. The principle of being guided by the socialist legal consciousness in making judicial decisions was accepted immediately after the creation of the Soviet government and the Soviet Court.

. . . What is the meaning of "the socialist legal consciousness"? As we have seen, neither of our decrees [which referred to "the socialist legal consciousness"—M.J.] provided a definition. But such a definition suggests itself and can be reduced to the following: The Proletarian Court is a court of the proletariat which seized governmental power by means of arms. It seized this power for the purpose of suppressing the resistance of its enemies and for bringing about socialism and communism as soon as possible.

The proletariat is overcoming the resistance by using all the means at its disposal, including such mighty means as the court—court justice. Comrade Bukharin stated the following in "The Communist Program": "In the hands of the working class, the state power is an ax that is being held ready against the bourgeoisie." The blade of this ax is the court, which should act in conformity with the state requirements of the victorious proletariat.

But where do we find the yardstick for judging this interest? How do we know whether a judicial decision is in conformity with that interest? The sole source, yardstick, compass, *is the class consciousness of the proletariat.* The class consciousness of the proletariat has been worked out in the process of the protracted, historical struggle with the bourgeoisie. It has been refined and sharpened on the solid stone of scientific socialism, which revealed to the proletariat not only the secret of its birth but also the secret of its victorious development. The class consciousness of the proletariat, based on the scientific foundations of socialist theories, is pointing out how to conduct the struggle, *what means to use,* and *how* to use them.

. . . The socialist (or communist) legal consciousness is, therefore, the recognition of the necessity to act, when discharging justice, in a way conducive to (1) the revolutionary proletariat dictatorship, (2) with due consideration to the class struggle, and (3) in the name of communism.

Consequently, when a judge says, "I made such a decision instead of another," and adds, "because it is conducive to the dictatorship of the proletariat, to the class struggle, and to communism," then we conclude that his action was guided by the socialist legal consciousness.

Each Communist knows what generates crime in contemporary

society and who (i.e., which class) supplies the offenders. Crime is generated by misery; by capitalist oppression; by corruption and oppression by the capitalist society. The working class also supplies offenders, because it has been plundered and corrupted by capitalism.

Consequently, when an offender from the working class appears before the Soviet Court, the socialist legal consciousness should suggest to the judge both the proper approach and the right decision. For example, the law states that theft is punishable by five years of imprisonment. But, in conformity with the socialist legal consciousness, instead of sentencing the offender to prison, the judge will send him to work in a factory, giving him a suspended sentence.

That is why "the socialist legal consciousness"—as the fundamental principle underlying the Soviet judiciary—does not coincide with the existing codes and statutes and yet will remain in full force and have significance, in spite of the written law.

# Law Is Not a Recipe for Soap Boiling*

## ᚲᚱᚩ I. D. Ilinskii

The problem of law has never been the center of interest in Marxist literature. This is quite natural, for the founders of Marxism thought that the principal science is political economy, the science of the social basis. Furthermore, as a rule, the participation of socialist parties in legislative and administrative organs had been quite limited. Therefore, they were interested in the problems of law purely from the practical point of view. In Russia the Revolution placed power in the hands of a revolutionary Marxist party. One would think that the situation had since changed. In fact, it has not changed. As earlier, the problem of law is in the backyard of the Marxist literature. The books devoted to the general theory of law as well as to individual branches of law are but few. . . . All this, naturally, has its reasons. Law and legality are slogans that smell of antiquity in the epoch of the proletarian dictatorship. The pathos of Soviet construction finds its expression in other slogans; this has been demonstrated by a talented young student of Soviet legality, K. A. Arkhipov.

Nevertheless, we are issuing laws every day . . . , and juridical publishing houses print voluminous commentaries on them. The interpretations of various laws generate hot discussions both among legal practitioners and among legal theorists. On the other hand, in its judicial decisions, the Supreme Court quite frequently delivers lengthy theories of principal juridical concepts. . . . Does this mean that we have law? Indeed, we do. One could claim, as A. G. Goikhbarg and others do, that our law is merely a system of sociotechnical norms, or one could invent other euphonious formulas, but the essence of things is not changed thereby. It is obvious that, in the communist society, law as a coercive social order will not exist. But, *in a class society, even in the transition period, the existence of law is inevitable.* Just to point [this] out, we are concluding international treaties with England, Italy, etc. . . . Furthermore, private property is recognized in our country by law, and legal punishments are provided for violation of property. . . . Our law is a class law, a proletarian law, but nevertheless a law; it is neither an instruction to military

* From *Pravo i Byt* [Law and Existence] (Leningrad-Moscow, 1925), pp. 16–18.

units concerning the shoeing of horses nor a recipe for making cold or hot soap.

. . . Those who participate in building up socialism ought to know the nature and qualities of the law that is used as an instrument in constructing socialism. Merely to assert that law is a superstructure or that law is an instrument of domination, and to triumphantly support these statements with well-known quotations from Marx's and Engels' writings, is tantamount to tramping in the same spot. Our task is to determine the concrete relationship *between law and the economic basis* and, furthermore, to discover quite frequently complex and intricate *class roots of juridical ideology.* Only then could it be shown that Marxism is a valuable method for the cognition of reality and not a nasal drone of quotations similar to the recitation of verses from the Koran.

. . . P. I. Stuchka is a new Marxist theorist of law who is interested in the effectiveness of juridical norms. The state and the legal order appear to Stuchka as inevitable forms of the Revolution. He is attracted by the form of law which appears in real life. Therefore, in contrast to the generally recognized conception of law as an aggregate of imperative and prohibitory norms, Stuchka has developed his own definition of law. He defines law as an order of social relationships advantageous to the ruling class, and supported by its organized power. This is his principal definition, which he with some hesitation supplemented with additional definitions: (1) Law is a system of norms, that is, a system of written laws. (2) The ideology of law, intuitive law, and legal consciousness are also law, which does not yet appear, however, either in a written form or in living reality. P. I. Stuchka has thus arrived at a pluralistic definition of law. In prerevolutionary Russian literature, such a view was expounded by B. A. Kistyakovskii, a writer who accepted some Marxist views but who in general was critical of Marxism.

Being somewhat schematic, the conception of law proposed by Stuchka has significant merits. Its schematism lies in that some legal phenomena combine the characteristics of all three kinds of law described by him. For example, according to the Constitution of the R.S.F.S.R., persons who hire labor for making profit are deprived of the right to elect and to be elected. In this case we have the following: (1) an order of social relationships, namely, the persons who *in fact* are deprived of electoral rights; (2) a legal norm, namely, the text of the Constitution, prohibiting certain persons from participating in elections and ordering administrative organs to prevent these persons from participating in elections; (3) the expression of a "legal ideology," of a legal consciousness, of a class, namely, the proletariat, who regards the order established by constitutional law as *"just."* Such a coincidence, however, does not always take place. In reality the three aspects of law enumerated by P. I. Stuchka are most frequently either entirely separated, or only two of them may be combined, in different proportions and combinations at that.

. . . In some cases, law is able to shape the order of social relationships; whereas in some others, on the contrary, the existing order of social relationships finds its juridical reflection in the mirror of law. The roots of this process lie more or less deeply in the relations of production. But the flow of this process assumes peculiar forms. . . . Quite typical is a situation in which the process under discussion goes through the following stages: (1) Economic necessities bring forth a new form of relationships between men. (2) The interested parties conclude that the utilization of this form is both feasible and expedient. (3) But, since doubts arise concerning the legality of this form, after some struggle its legality is recognized (or not) by law. The trust legislation in the United States is a vivid illustration of such a situation. At first the spontaneous process of capitalistic development resulted in the formation of trusts. Then jurists and the press began to advance the contention that the new organizations were in conformity with "the spirit of the American Constitution," "traditional personal freedom," etc. Finally, after a prolonged social struggle in which the consumers put up resistance to the pressures of organized capital, the Sherman Act and the Supreme Court through its interpretation of this act permitted, with some stipulations and limitations, the existence of the trusts. The line of development in this case is: the order of social relationships, legal consciousness, law.

The second type of development is a situation in which the legislator, leaving behind the consciousness of his contemporaries, issues a law that is met with enmity by the broad masses. This law forcibly breaks up long established and hardened relationships and replaces them with a new one. The social forms (in the broad meaning of the term) that are brought about by this law win the recognition of the population, are recognized as expedient, and the law itself is recognized as just and rational. Quite frequently, although not always successfully, revolutionary legislation takes this path of development. For example, the law separating the Church from the state, which at first was alien and incomprehensible to the broad masses of the Russian population, was put into practice by the apparatus of the Soviet government. The newly created order quite speedily won general recognition and, ultimately, even the clergy was forced to recognize

the reform as expedient and corresponding to "the correctly understood interests of the Church." The line of development in this case
is: law, order of social relationships, legal consciousness.

Finally, a third combination is possible. A demand for a reform
arises in the social consciousness in view of the fact that the existing
order, established by law, hinders the normal flow of life. The legislator, under pressure from social opinion or even under the directly
organized pressure of the interested classes, works out and adopts a
new law which introduces the desired reforms. The line of this development is: legal consciousness, law, order of social relationships.

# A Critical Review of Soviet Theories of Law*

## ⌭ F. D. Kornilov

It stands to reason that the transitional epoch in social develop-ment makes a profound imprint on the ideological content of social thought in general and on scientific thought in particular. One of the features of contemporary transitional times is the *crisis of social con-sciousness,* which is a result of the crisis of social relationships. This is an epoch of struggle between two irreconcilable enemies, namely, between the old, irrational reality and the new, rational reality. It is an epoch of struggle between the old and the new, in *which new forms of social consciousness are being forged and in which new ideas, new thoughts, are engendered.* The contradictions and compromises that arise in the sphere of politics are reflected in the thinking of scientists. Compromises are ugly attempts to "adapt" the old inheri-tance to the recent advancements of revolutionary creativity. These attempts at "adaptation" generate intense contradictions in the think-ing of scientists and lead them to great ideological distortions of reality. In our Marxist literature dealing with law, these attempts are responsible for the great confusion and absurdities in our theory of law. In order to reveal these distortions, we shall analyze the views of several representatives of scientific, Marxist, legal thought.

From the very beginning, two approaches were prevalent in our Marxist literature. The proponents of the first approach identified law with social relationships. The proponents of the second approach could best be described as normativists. In addition to these two ap-proaches, there is a point of view according to which the problem of law is, in the final analysis, a problem of ideology. We shall first dis-cuss the point of view that identifies law with social relationships, for, at first glance, it appears to be a legitimate Marxist point of view. Subsequently, we shall discuss the views of various types of "ideolo-gists."

The main, if not the only, representative of the first approach is P. Stuchka. Stuchka defines law as "a system of social relationships corresponding to the interests of the ruling class and protected by its organized power." He points out that this definition of law was ad-

* From *Yuridicheskii Dogmatizm i Dialekticheskii Materialism* [Juridical Dogmatism and Dialectical Materialism] (Saratov, 1925), pp. 50–70.

vanced by the People's Commissariat of Justice during the preparation of the Guiding Principles of the criminal law. In his opinion, this
definition is not a scientific one; it was a result of the spontaneous
rejecton of the old conception of law; it was merely an instinctive
guess about the forms of social relationships then in existence. We do
not intend to determine the degree to which this definition is an unscientific one. We intend, however, to demonstrate that it is contradictory to the fundamental premises of Marxism. . . .

Initially, we shall answer the question: "What are social relationships?" By social relationships we mean relationships among people[1]
in the process of production, i.e., primarily economic relationships, on
which are erected, and by which are determined, all other relationships, including political and juridical relationships. Therefore, it follows that juridical and political relationships, on the one hand, and
relationships of production (that is, relationships of production, exchange, and distribution), on the other, are two distinct things.
Stuchka seems to accept this view implicitly, since he treats law as an
independent problem, aś a problem separate from that of social relationships. Otherwise, there would be no need to separate law from
society (from social relationships) and to create an independent science of law, a science distinct from both political economy and sociology. And this is exactly what Stuchka intends to do.[2]

Not only is Stuchka interested in studying law as an independent
problem, he even divides law into relationships and norms. Thus, according to Stuchka, "Our point of view does not at all exclude law,
i.e., norms. . . . In our opinion, the system of relationships is a material, *objective* element, i.e., it is law in the objective meaning of the
term. And the legal form of the objective element, that is, the written law, or norm, is a subjective element."[3] This is quite clear, for
Stuchka must know that relationships of production and distribution
existed considerably prior to juridical relationships. He speaks about
this in his *The Revolutionary Role of Law and State*. There he
asserts: "In this tribal community there exists definite, though loosely
organized, economic planning; there is a kind of division of labor,
but there is no law."[4] It follows, then, that law in the modern meaning

---

[1] On this subject see the Preface to Karl Marx, *K Kritike Politicheskoi
Ekonomii* [A Critique of Political Economy].
[2] See Stuchka, "Materialisticheskoe ili Idealisticheskoe Ponimanie Prava?"
[Materialist or Idealist Understanding of Law?], *Pod Znamenem Marksizma*,
No. 1 (1923).
[3] *Ibid.*, pp. 167–68.
[4] *Revolutsionnaya Rol Prava i Gosudarstva* [The Revolutionary Role of Law
and State] (Moscow, 1921), p. 25.

of the term, does not exist in every society; but does this mean that societies without social relationships are conceivable? Stuchka continues in the following way: "In their interrelations, members are guided by habits and customs. . . . There is no written law, no law . . . , there exists a very firm and cohesive society which seems to be regulated only by the laws of nature."[5] To be sure, Stuchka makes a new error by identifying law with the written law, but since discussion of this problem would lead us away from the original theme, we shall examine it later. . . .

The quotations from Stuchka indicate, on the one hand, that law does not exist in every society and, on the other hand, that a society without social relationships is inconceivable. Of course, these statements are contradictory. However, it is up to Stuchka to resolve his own contradictions. We shall dwell on the question of whether these statements contradict the fundamental premises of Marxism.

Earlier, in connection with the problem of the division of law into public and private, we stated that political and legal relationships are conditioned by the relationships of production (by social relationships). Speaking on this subject in his *Ludwig Feuerbach,* Engels . . . indicated that *law is merely the formal reflection of economic (of social, in a very narrow meaning of the term) relationships.*

Economic relationships are preserved in all stages of social development, but the forms of these relationships are constantly changing, and at a definite point (in a society based on private property) they assume the forms of juridical relationships. Consequently, the economic relationships do not become social (production) relationships; on the contrary, they become juridical relationships. They become a formal reflection of those social relationships that assume the form of proprietary relationships. In the process of their development, these relationships give rise to a peculiar legal ideology, to a peculiar pattern of thought, which Engels characterized as the juridical form of thought inherent in a bourgeois society.

In support of our view, we find the following statement in Engels' *Ludwig Feuerbach:* "Since in each particular case the economic facts must assume the form of juridical relationships in order to receive legal sanction, and since, in so doing, consideration of course has to be paid to the whole legal system already in operation, the consequence is that *the juristic form is made everything and the economic content nothing.*"

Therefore, *law is not a system of social relationships but a form of these relationships—a form that finds its concrete expression in the*

[5] *Ibid.*

*juridical norm. Law is not the relationship between people in the process of production but the juridical relationship, which is both formally and concretely expressed in private proprietary relationships, in equivalent relationships.*

We have already indicated that the proponents of the second approach to law in our literature are "normativists." Pashukanis, the author of a highly interesting book, *The General Theory of Law and Marxism,* could be viewed as a representative of this approach. But since Pashukanis, unlike the majority of legal theorists, is not interested simply in searching for the definition of law, we shall critically discuss his views later in connection with the problems concerning norms and relationships. At this point, we would like to discuss the views of those who reject law.

The theory that exerted the greatest influence upon our civil legislation and that is still fashionable is the theory of "social function." The most consistent representative of this theory is Professor Goikhbarg,[6] who, in Stuchka's words, is "the spiritual father of our civil code." We indicated earlier that Goikhbarg's theory is an ideological distortion. Now, we shall try to reveal the social nature of this distortion.

Goikhbarg asserts that "at the present time, both in our state and in bourgeois states, the right to own property is no longer viewed from the juridical point of view, that is, as an unrestricted right of the owner to dispose of his property at will. . . . The view that private property is a social function has been especially stressed in the new German Constitution. . . ."[7] Furthermore, Goikhbarg continues, "Private property is looked upon as a certain good placed in the hands of a person for safekeeping in the interests of society; and, therefore, the person holding private property has *positive* obligations toward society. . . . This view permeates also the construction of the institution of property in our civil code."[8]

These are the principal propositions underlying Professor Goikhbarg's theory, which he regards as the apex of "scientific wisdom," in contrast to the views of the "most backward bourgeois and our jurists."[9] We think that, instead of relying upon the authority of bour-

---

[6] Not to mention such a fumbler as S. Aleksandrovskii, who in his book *Ocherki po Grazhdanskomu Pravu* [Essays on Civil Law] became entangled in contradictions to the degree that we cannot expect anything serious or valuable from him.

[7] *Khozyaistvennoe Pravo RSFSR* [Economic Law of the R.S.F.S.R.] (Moscow, 1924), I, 64.

[8] *Ibid.,* pp. 97–98.

[9] *Ibid.,* p. 58.

geois scientists and even bourgeois constitutions, the honorable professor should make an effort to justify his "scientific wisdom" socio-
logically. But the *shadow of the past is considerably stronger than
the "dream of the future,"* and, therefore, the honorable professor
relies upon the bourgeois dogmatic method in interpreting the law of
the Soviet state. It stands to reason, however, that the "spiritual
father" of our civil code should know what he is doing.

We indicated previously that Professor Goikhbarg's views are not
original. They were discovered (if one can speak of discovery at all)
by an ideologist of finance capital, Professor L. Duguit. Goikhbarg
merely adapted this bourgeois ideology to contemporary Russian reality. According to Duguit, "Neither man nor the collective has any
rights; but each individual must carry out a definite social function.
His social duty is to carry out this function, and to develop his physical, intellectual, and moral personality to the highest possible degree, in order to be capable of fulfilling his function."[10] Furthermore,
"With regard to property, it is no longer treated in modern law as an
inalienable right. . . . It simply exists and must exist. It constitutes an
indispensable prerequisite for the growth of society, whereas all collectivist doctrines are tantamount to a return to barbarism. However,
property is not a right; property is a social function. The proprietor,
or to put it differently, the owner of wealth, shall, because he owns
this wealth, fulfill a social function."[11] This is the quintessence of the
professorial ideology. Professor Goikhbarg should have been capable
of noticing that, according to Duguit, the abolition of property is not
permissible.

Thus, we see that Duguit's theory is an ideology of the bourgeoisie
(of the class of proprietors) which has attained a higher degree of
development in private proprietary relationships. This is an ideology
of the finance bourgeoisie, at the time when the ownership of the
means of production is concentrated in the hands of the trusts, cartels, and joint-stock companies, when society, to use Duguit's expression, is "socializing itself." Since we do not know whether Goikhbarg is familiar with Lenin's brilliant description of the nature of this
ideology, we shall quote Lenin, hoping that Goikhbarg will find a
way out of the impasse.

Private property—says Lenin—is sacred; no one has the right to interfere in the affairs of private property. This is the principle of capitalism.
But capital has already outgrown the framework of private property,

[10] *Obshchee Preobrazovanie Grazhdanskogo Prava* [*La transformation générale du droit privé*] (orig. pub. in Paris, 1912; Moscow, 1919), p. 18.
[11] *Ibid.*

which has led to the creation of joint-stock companies. Hundreds and thousands of stockholders, one unknown to the other, constitute one company. And gentlemen private proprietors have not infrequently burned their fingers when smart businessmen, invoking "the commercial secret," have emptied the pockets of their comrade stockholders. Sacred property was forced to renounce a part of its sacredness; a law was issued, imposing an obligation upon joint-stock companies to utilize proper accounting methods and to publish fiscal accounting figures. Naturally, this measure did not put an end to the deception of the public; deception assumed new forms and became more refined. Big capital, by gradually joining to itself other petty capitals, dispersed all over the world, became even more powerful.[12]

This is the nature of that fashionable ideology to which the Marxist professor, Goikhbarg, succumbed. Duguit's theory does not reject private bourgeois property; it merely disguises it in a new ideological form, in the form of "a social function," in the form of a capitalist's obligation to squeeze surplus value out of his hired labor. This explains why the modern constitutions, which are worshipped by our professor, have imposed restrictions upon property rights and why bourgeois scientists are in favor of such restrictions.

Especially now the bourgeois world is confronted with great social calamities. This is the time when private property, the stronghold of the bourgeois world, is undergoing a crucial test, which it may fail to pass. It is *especially urgent* to inculcate the new ideology into the consciousness of the masses now.

The state, that is to say, the political organization of bourgeois society, stands on the rim of a raging crater. The old forms of wage labor have proved to be useless, and, consequently, the ruling class is searching for new methods of strengthening its domination. Some sort of "compromise" is being conjured up, with the result that the fiction of universal electoral right assumes an acceptable outward appearance, and the capitalist's right to property is disguised within *a new and more perfected fiction*. The right to own private property is "abolished" and is replaced with the "unpleasant duty" of carrying out the *"social function"* of the capitalist slaveholder.[13]

It is evident that the character of contemporary foreign constitutions and statutory laws, as well as of scientific theories, is conditioned by the factual correlation between the forces of production and by the forms of production relationships which correspond to these forces. Their ideological essence is personified in the reformist Social

---

[12] *Sobranie Sochinenii* [Collected Works] (Moscow), XII (1921), Part 2, 136–37.

[13] On this problem, see G. Gurvich, *Nravstvennost i Pravo* [Morality and Law] (Moscow, 1924), p. 19.

Democracy, which has adopted the legal ideas of bourgeois professors.[14] The confusion of our legal theorists stems from the fact that
they ignore this aspect of the problem. In transplanting this new legal
ideology—this product of finance capital—in our contemporary reality, our scientists forget about the socioeconomic peculiarities that
distinguish our reality from the moribund reality of bourgeois society.
They superimpose on our reality ideas that are alien and contradictory to its social nature.

Our constitution has grown up on an entirely different ground; the
principles upon which our constitution is founded are distinct from
the principles underlying the German Constitution or the constitutions of other new bourgeois states. Consequently, our constitution
reflects principles that are entirely different from the ideology of social function.

Speaking of "ideologists," it is indispensable to examine the views
of two somewhat peculiar representatives of Marxist legal theory,
namely, Professors Razumovskii and Reisner. Professor Razumovskii
has stated his essential views on law in an article entitled "Marx's
and Engels' Conception of Law"[15] and in his lecture delivered at the
Socialist Academy.[16] First of all, it should be noted that these two
works comprise views that are mutually contradictory. This could be
interpreted to mean that Razumovskii's theory of law is not yet well
founded and that, for obvious reasons, he is still searching for the
solutions to this complex problem. Nevertheless, we think that some
of his mistakes could have been avoided had he correctly examined
the objective conditions of social development.

Razumovskii's second work, which reflects his theoretical (and perhaps political) evolution, demonstrates that he is already closer to a
correct understanding of the problem, even though his views are still
ambiguous and contradictory. Whereas in his article he adopted the
view that law is an ideology, his later work is based on a more "stable
element," namely the concept of "relationship." Nevertheless, his
second work gives the impression that law is not a reflection of social, economic reality but a product of the ideological activity of legal
theorists (including Professor Razumovskii).

The reader of his work notices instantly the ambiguity of his terminology. It is not at all clear whether he is speaking of law as an
ideology or as a legal ideology. He uses both forms of expression in

---

[14] See Art. 19 of the German Constitution of 1919.
[15] "Ponyatie Prava u K. Marksa i Fr. Engelsa," *Pod Znamenem Marksizma*,
No. 2–3 (1923), pp. 69–97.
[16] Published under the title *Sotsiologiya i Pravo* [The Sociology and Law]
(Moscow, 1924).

the same sense. But, if we agree with him that law is an ideology, then we must deny the existence of those relationships that are regulated by law. Furthermore, we must then conclude that, like religion, law as a "form of consciousness" lacks concrete content. However, we doubt that Razumovskii would accept this conclusion, since, speaking of law in the transition period, he says: "Law ceases to be an ideology and becomes an undisguised expression of the class domination of the proletariat; it becomes a theory of this class domination."[17] The implication is that law does not exist in the bourgeois society, but will exist in the proletarian society. This view is completely contradictory to the views of Marx and Engels cited by Razumovskii. According to Marx and Engels the bourgeois society is precisely a "juridical" society.

If we speak of a legal ideology as some sort of idealistic reflection of *law* (*by law meaning forms of production* [economic] *relationships*),[18] then we infuse into law a concrete content, namely, the relationships of production, exchange, and distribution, instead of that of social consciousness, as is being done by Razumovskii. He maintains that, in addition to being a "superstructure," law is, in essence, primarily a "form of social consciousness."[19] It stands to reason that by accepting this view we may ultimately arrive at the identification of political economy with ideology and, consequently, the identification of economic relationships with the forms of consciousness.

Economic relationships are the relationships of production, which, at a certain point in their development, assume the form of juridical relationships. The bourgeois society is precisely that society in which the juridical form of economic relationships has found its most striking expression. Legal ideology and legal relationships are not one and the same thing, any more than economic relationships and economic ideology are.

It is thus quite obvious that law *is not "a peculiar reflection* of a definite aggregate of economic relationships *within the human consciousness."*[20] *Law is a formal reflection of the relationships of production. Law is not a form of social consciousness but a form of social relationships.*

It remains now to examine the views of another theorist who identifies law with ideology. But since his views do not enjoy great respect at the present time, we shall restrict ourselves to general observations.

---

[17] "Ponyatie Prava u K. Marksa i Fr. Engelsa," p. 96.
[18] Razumovskii seems to accept this view in his *Sotsiologiya*, p. 8, when he states that "relationships of production are reflected in legal form. . . ."
[19] Ibid., p. 6.
[20] "Ponyatie Prava u K. Marksa i Fr. Engelsa," p. 93.

In contrast to Professor Razumovskii, Professor Reisner is not alone in his theory of law, which regards law as a definite psychological phenomenon. Like Goikhbarg, who follows a French bourgeois scientist, Reisner is a follower of the most outstanding Russian bourgeois scientist, Petrazhitskii. As was seen earlier, Petrazhitskii has erected his "theory of law and morality" on his theory of "emotional psychology," at which he arrived through a reconstruction of traditional psychology.[21] Reisner has no need to invent a new psychology; he merely exploited the fruits of his "teacher" and proceeded from the point at which Petrazhitskii had stopped. In full justice to Professor Reisner, we must admit that he carried out his task conscientiously. His eternal, rational, intuitive law is an example of the consistency of his theory.

According to Petrazhitskii, "To the extent that intuitive law increasingly captures the imagination of broad circles, it becomes increasingly more powerful and dominating in the environment. Intuitive law is flexible and diverse; its decisions freely conform to the concrete, individual conditions of a given combination."[22] Continuing Petrazhitskii's line of thought, Reisner asserts: "Law is not cognizant of its birth; it appears to be eternal; it needs no force for its existence, for it seems to be higher and spiritual; it corresponds to life, and goes hand in hand with it; it has an aura of rationality; it has natural qualities; it is normal and is incapable of erring."[23] We would ask Professor Reisner to test the power of his intuition and to find the "eternal, rational" law, were it not for one stipulation he makes. In his opinion, man's social life is subordinated to a process of subconscious psychological emotions. As he puts it, "The subconscious process of life is a fundamental and primary one."[24] "That is why Petrazhitskii dwelt with such painstaking care on the individual psychic aspects of man's emotional life which characterize his activities—primarily his economic activities."[25] Thus, according to Reisner, the lever of economic relationships is to be sought in man's psyche. As a product of man's psychic emotions, law governs social relationships, creates the forms of these relationships, and destroys them. One could hardly outdo this psychological fanaticism.

[21] See his *Vvedenie v Izuchenie Prava i Nravstvennosti* [An Introduction to the Study of Law and Morality] (Petersburg, 1909).

[22] *Teoriya Prava i Gosudarstva v Svyazi s Teoriei Nravstvennosti* [The Theory of Law and State in Connection with the Theory of Morality] (Petersburg, 1909), I, 475–83.

[23] *Teoriya L. I. Petrazhitskogo, Marksizm i Sotsialnaya Ideologiya* [L. I. Petrazhitskii's Theory, Marxism and Social Ideology] (Petersburg, 1908), p. 78.

[24] *Ibid.*, p. 52.

[25] *Ibid.*, p. 53.

# The Supremacy of Law as a Negation of Individualism*

## ◌ *I. D. Ilinskii*

The idea of the individual is merely a point of departure of bourgeois jurisprudence. While proceeding from this idea, bourgeois jurisprudence frequently arrives at conclusions that are contradictory to the interests of individuals. . . . It is not my task to investigate the tortuous road along which juristic thought moves. It must be noted, however, that in the opinion of bourgeois jurists, because of the social contact between individuals, a certain order arises that restricts their arbitrariness and is recognized by them as binding. In Hauriou's view, law creates peace, balances the hostile and conflicting interests of individuals, social classes, and groups.[1] In general, law is the supreme source of social life. Dicey, an English theorist, finds in this also the basic feature of a legal order. Germans are not lagging behind Englishmen and Frenchmen. Kohler thinks that the exclusive and peculiar value of a legal order lies in the fact that, in addition to protecting subjective rights, it also protects cultural values.[2] This is merely a restoration of an old view, which was strongly defended by Trendelenburg: "All human laws originate from a divine source."[3] Even now it is not difficult to find adherents of this view. For example, N. N. Alekseev contends that "in contrast to chaos and anarchy, the value of law and order is an absolute one." All these views are not merely the fruit of pure speculation. Almost the same words were used for the legalization of their rule by the dominant classes. For example, the French Constitution asserted: "The French Republic recognizes those rights and obligations that are prior and superior to the positive law. . . . Family, work, property, and social order are its foundation." Even the basic law of czarist Russia, where the idea of legality had not enjoyed great popularity, thought it necessary to proclaim that "the Russian Empire is governed on a solid basis of laws that are issued by the autocratic authority." The same is true of other constitutions. . . . In all these documents, legal norms appear as imperatives that, to use Professor Hearn's expression, stand by themselves,

* From *Vvedenie v Izuchenie Sovetskogo Prava* [An Introduction to the Study of Soviet Law] (Leningrad, 1925), I, 58–63.

[1] *Les Principes du droit public* (n.p., 1910), p. 6.
[2] *Lehrbuch der Rechtspilosophie* (Berlin-Leipzig, 1909), p. 39.
[3] *Naturrecht auf dem Grunde der Ethik* (Leipzig, 1868), p. 613.

that is, they derive their validity not from an outside . . . but from their inner normative nature. Hans Kelsen developed this view to its logical end in his theory of jurisprudence as a normative science. It is characteristic that the German scientist speaks not of natural law, which he scornfully casts away into the sphere of ethics, but of positive legal norms that come from a state authority.[4]

The supremacy of domination of law is not simply an innocent juridical speculation or an adornment of bourgeois constitutions. One can speak ironically of the idolatry of law, but it would be absurd to deny that respect for the law, cultivated among the masses, is one of the most powerful means for bringing about mass conduct in the interest of the ruling class. Jurists and historians, who carefully study the influence of positive law upon social life, know this quite well. For example, P. B. Vinogradov stated: "The decisive moment in the existence of law is not so much its coerciveness as the psychological *habit* of recognizing the bindingness of norms created by social authority and of subordinating one's self to these norms."[5] The same view was stated by F. F. Taranovskii, who asserts that law, which succeeds in pervading life and becoming a fact of mass conduct, is obeyed as spontaneously as custom. This is the reason law is inescapably conservative. Since old times, law has been one of the most conservative forces of history. . . . The conservatism of jurists is well known. It exerts an influence upon the destiny of societies in which lawyers enjoy a distinguished position. Reflecting on American democracy, Tocqueville, almost a hundred years ago, arrived at the conclusion that the influence of lawyers in the United States was one of the most powerful means against "revolutionary delusion." According to Tocqueville, lawyers, in the spirit of their profession, acquire a taste for a peculiar way of legal thinking. This makes them conservative and quite restrained toward the revolutionary tendencies of democracy.[6] Much time has passed since Tocqueville. Restless Europe since then has had more than ten revolutions and to all appearances has entered into a phase of chronic fermentation, intermittent revolutions, and civil wars. Our neighbors abroad continue as before to enjoy peace under the protection of "the greatest and most perfect constitution." Another question is how long this peace will

---

[4] *Hauptprobleme der Staatsrechtslehre* (Tübingen, 1911), p. 559. Max Adler made an attempt to combine Marxism with Kelsenianism in his "Die Staatsauffassung des Marximus," *Marxstudien* (Vienna, 1922), Vol. 4, Part 2, pp. 67–71.

[5] *Ocherki po Obshchei Teorii Prava* [Introduction to the General Theory of Law] (Moscow, 1915), p. 32.

[6] *La democratie en Amerique.*

preserve its tranquility. It seems that James Beck, a modern student of the American Constitution, has not yet lost his enthusiasm for law, inherited from Hamilton and Marshall. It seems quite clear to Beck that the supremacy of law protects the interests of the minority from encroachment by the majority. It is precisely in the "solemn circle" that outlines the inpenetrable sphere of the individual that the American jurist sees the extraordinary value of law.[7] He even quoted King Solomon in support of his view.

Needless to say, Beck's meditations on the supremacy of law contain nothing new. Plato spoke quite a lot about this problem . . . in his *Laws*. Spinoza, who was convinced that "laws are the soul of the state," even contended that a state with proper laws would exist forever.[8]

. . . In studying recent constitutions, one can easily see that the ideology of the supremacy of law prevails over the ideology of the supremacy of the people. Although the latter is usually proclaimed formally, it is in fact restricted by constitutional law, which transforms the "sovereignty of the nation" into a soap bubble.

[7] James Beck, *The Constitution of the United States* (London, 1922), pp. 131, 155.
[8] Spinoza, *Tractatus Politicus*.

# The Nature of Ideology*  ᘓ  *I. P. Razumovskii*

In the search for the correct way to construct a Marxist critique of the general theory [of law], it is indispensable that a very complicated problem of *ideology* be seriously examined. This problem was introduced by Marx and Engels, and for the most part very little attention is being paid to it in contemporary Marxist literature. The theory of superstructure, and especially the problem of the *forms* of social consciousness, have not yet been adequately examined. This leads to various misinterpretations of the relationship between the ideological form and its economic content. In the field of law, particularly, this fact is responsible for concepts of law as naïve as ideological "reflex," as "social symbolism," as abstract "legal consciousness," etc. . . .

In several letters written in his last years, Engels sought—to use his expression—to correct his own and Marx's "mistakes." To quote Engels: "We all laid and were bound to lay the main emphasis at first on the derivation of political, legal, and other ideological notions, and of the actions arising—through the medium of these notions—from basic economic facts. But in so doing we neglected the *formal side*—the way in which these notions come about—for the sake of content." Furthermore, Engels explains in detail the meaning of the expression "ideology." "Ideology is a process accomplished by the so-called thinker consciously, indeed, but with a false consciousness. The real motives impelling him remain *unknown* to him; otherwise it would not be an ideological process at all. Hence he *imagines* false or apparent motives. Because it is a process of thought, he derives both its *form* and its *content* from pure thought, either his own or that of his predecessors. He works with mere thought material which he accepts without examination as the product of thought; he does not investigate further for *a more remote process independent of thought;* indeed, its origin seems obvious to him, because, as all action is *produced* through the medium of thought, it also appears to him to be ultimately based upon thought." Engels concludes: "This side of the matter, which I can only indicate here, we have all, I think, neglected more than it deserves. It is the old story: *form* is always neglected at first for content."[1]

* From *Problemy Marksistskoi Teorii Prava* [Problems of the Marxist Theory of Law] (Moscow, 1925), pp. 24–35.
[1] Engels, Letter to Mehring (London), July 14, 1893.

Marx is not to be "blamed" though; he simply *lacked the time* to complete the work undertaken. . . . The problem of ideology and, in particular, the problem of law were for Marx and Engels the *starting points* in the development of their historical view. A critical re-examination of Hegel's philosophy of law . . . led them to the material conditions of life in which legal relationships are rooted. The re-examination itself was accomplished in connection with a task that Marx set forth for himself while he was still under Feuerbach's influence: *"To analyze mystic consciousness which is unclear to itself,"* to reveal "man's *self-alienation* in his godless images." The task with which Marx and Engels were confronted, and which they formulated more clearly in their later development, was multilateral. First, they had to uncover the economic content of ideological forms, *their conditioning by economic content, and their connection with this content.* On the other hand, they had to expose all the *peculiarities of the formal side* of ideology, which, in the process of their development, separate themselves from the economic content that conditions them and which, at the same time, constitute *a historically inevitable side* (*a formal affirmation*) of the social process. Finally, they had to determine the *inevitability* of the peculiar development of ideological forms and the inevitability of their *separation* from the economic reality that they express. Marx and Engels succeeded in accomplishing only the first of these tasks; however, they furnished us with an outline of how to resolve the two remaining tasks.

In his letter to Mehring, Engels outlined the following significant peculiarities of "the formal side" of ideology, of "the way in which these notions come about."

1. The real motivating forces behind the thought process are unknown, but the thinking participants of this process assume that both its form and its content are determined by the pure thought of their predecessors.

2. In fact, a remote economic process is taking place, a process independent of thought.

3. The economic process appears to be *based* upon thought, because thought serves as a medium for the disclosure (for the "affirmation") of the economic process, that is, as a medium for producing man's conscious actions which constitute this process.

4. Either false or illusory guiding "notions," ideas, and, in general, historically accumulated thought material lie at the basis of an ideological process.

In a letter to Conrad Schmidt (October 27, 1890), Engels illuminated the problem by pointing out the role played in the creation of ideology by the social *division of labor,* which assumes the form of externally independent spheres. Thus, the external independence of ideology finds its explanation in the relatively factual independence of the sphere of spiritual production, brought about by the social division of labor. "Real distortions" are responsible for the *inverted* character of ideological notions. "Economic, political, and other reflections," Engels states, "are just like those in the human eye. They pass through a *condensing lens* and therefore appear *upside down,* standing on their heads. Only the nervous system, which would put them on their feet again for representation, is lacking."

We shall compare Engels' late views on ideology with earlier ones that were stated by Marx and Engels in the recently published *The German Ideology.* "Almost all ideology," we read, "can be reduced either to a *distorted understanding* . . . of history or to a complete *abstraction* from history. Ideology itself is merely one of the aspects of this history. . . . The fact that conscious expression of the real relationships of these individuals is illusory, that in their representations they place reality on its head, is *a result of their limited material mode of activity.* . . . Only with the introduction of the division of material and spiritual labor, can consciousness really imagine itself as nothing but the consciousness of the existing practice." Jurists, politicians, moralists, etc., Marx then indicates, are involved in an *"objectivization of their occupation, because of the division of labor."* Naturally, the division of labor in this case should be understood not only in the sense of a narrow specialization but in the sense of the general complexities of social production, the diverse social spheres of which no longer appear as a social whole.

Thus, according to Marx and Engels, the "limited material mode of activities" (that is, the conditions of a complex division of labor in which, on the one hand, intellectual labor is differentiated from physical labor, and on the other hand, the awareness of the connection between the diverse branches of social production is lost, and an understanding of the system of social relationships is lacking) is responsible for the fact that intellectual spheres of activity (i.e., thought processes in which representatives of intellectual labor are involved) are *objectivized.* In other words, these thought processes cease to be what they are in reality, namely, socially subjective reflections, that is, reflections in social consciousness of an objective economic process that is independent of thought processes. Thought processes are *abstracted* (isolated) from economic motion and appear to the bearers of these processes as independent, self-sustaining, and therefore as derived from the thought material within which they operate. This objectivization of the thought processes—to the extent that social production loses its organized character and exchange becomes a form of its operation—gradually begins to encompass the ideas of all participants in the production process, the ideas concerning their activity and their social position. It also becomes a characteristic and inalienable feature of social consciousness.

How is the process of the objectivization of the thought processes in social consciousness accomplished from the formal side? Marx and Engels quite frequently asserted that reflection of the real economic process takes place in an "inverted way," by means of "placing it on its head." They used these expressions in order to demonstrate that, in the process of the objectivization of the thought material, *the real relationship between this process and the social reality reflected in it is inverted:* it is not the economic process which gives rise to the corresponding forms of consciousness but the other way around; the thought appears as the real source of social actions. Let us recall the analogy of the condensing lens which was advanced by Engels on several occasions. This analogy should not be interpreted in a narrow physiological or psychophysiological sense. The question under discussion concerns the reflection of already objectivized thought material, that is, the reflection of social reality through the prism ("condensing lens") of those fundamental, guiding notions that appear to be connected with preceding historical thought and that, in their turn, give rise to new logical links in a given sphere of thought. The reflections of fundamental economic relationships in social consciousness (that is, reflections that historically separate themselves from economic relationships and that are regarded as "free ideas") become the point of departure of a further thought process; they become a "condensing lens" and thus give to the new, more particular reflections of social reality *an appearance of deductions made from the fundamental guiding "principles."* Therefore, the thought process carries an imprint of two influences. On the one hand, we encounter a "subjective" (in the social sense) reflection of a more or less remote economic process in various ideological notions and categories. On the other hand, historical "objectivization" of these ideological categories impels them to be deduced one from another, from the preceding thought material; it makes them appear as deductions from the fundamental (preceding) notions of a given ideological sphere. The twofold influence of the economic process and of the accumulated preceding thought material constitutes the basis of the whole process of development of the social consciousness. . . .

Thus, the term "ideology," as used by Marx and Engels, applies first of all to the *formal* features of the modes of thought representations, to the forms of their creation, and to their seeming origin and development from the "idea." Any consciousness, at least from the external side, assumes the *form of ideology,* that is, appears as a development and an expression of certain guiding principles and ideas. However, it is necessary to distinguish a metaphysical consciousness, which separates itself from the reality it reflects and becomes a closed "system," from the dialectical thought of Marxism, in which the dialectic of notions is a reflection of the dialectic of the developing reality itself. The metaphysical element in Hegel's "ideology" is contradictory to its method; his "ideology" is metaphysical in the sense that it became a closed system. The distinctive feature of an ideological view or of a priori thinking in general is that, as stated by Marx in one of his earlier letters, the *"principle remains stationary,"* absolute, and ideas are deduced from it in a *dogmatic deductive* way. On the other hand, the Marxist dialectic deals with a logical development reflecting historical development, that is, not with an abstract logical development of ideas, but, as stated by Lenin, with a "concrete analysis of reality." The exposure of guiding principles—that is, principles that do not possess an absolute meaning and that develop together with the development of social relationships—is not in this case tantamount to "giving birth to ideas" but inevitably flows from the reflection of reality governed by the inner laws of the dialectic. An idea is being disclosed only to the extent that it *reveals itself:* we do not invent connections between phenomena; we find them in the phenomena themselves.[2]

Dogmatic development from abstract reflection of class interest, from "ideas," "principles" (which, by the way, is the most characteristic feature of juridical thinking), and the relative (and to a considerable degree external) independence of this development leads inevitably to the creation of a closed system of ideas, and such are all most significant ideologies. . . .

. . . The development of ideologies usually reaches the greatest force at the time when their basic ideas, that is, their objectivized no-

---

[2] This is what differentiates the proletarian world outlook—"the socialist ideology," to use Lenin's expression—from all preceding ideologies. Or, as pointed out by Marx and Engels in *The German Ideology,* "To us communism is neither a state of conditions that should be brought about nor an ideal to which reality should conform. Communism is a *real* movement which destroys present conditions." *Nemetskaya Ideologiya* [The German Ideology], in *Arkhiv Marksa i Engelsa* [Archives of Marx and Engels] (Moscow-Leningrad, 1924?), I.

tions, *have ceased* to be a relatively objective reflection of the process of material production. The elements of exact knowledge, which continuously accumulate in ideologies, begin to contradict their basic principles, which have become stationary, and, though in the coloring of the earlier ruling ideology, they now reflect the interests of the *new* social class which, in its turn, signifies the conception of the new relations of production.

The above explains why the development of the specific formal features of ideologies is historically inevitable and why their separation from their material roots, that is, "either a distorted understanding of reality or a complete abstraction from reality," is historically inescapable. It is a mistake, however, to see in ideologies merely abstract, ideological reflexes or, to use Professor Reisner's expression, "social symbolism" and "conditional irritants."[3] According to Marx, ideology is at the same time *"one of the aspects of history."* The ideological process, being an abstract reflection of the economic process in social consciousness, constitutes *an inevitable aspect* of this process, that is, it constitutes an "affirmation" of social reality through which the latter manifests itself in social consciousness. The socioeconomic process in its individual phases cannot keep developing (cannot materialize itself) without any participation of consciousness, without any correct or incorrect "knowledge" of its individual phases on the part of producers participating in this process.

Consciousness, even if "inverted," is an indispensable medium for tying the participants of a social process together; *by means* of men's subjective notions and men's volitional aspirations (which, at times, may be going in a completely opposite direction), an objective economic movement, independent of their wills, is accomplished. As stated by Engels, ideological notions are not the ultimate *foundation.* They do not enter into the economic process, into the development of material social relations, as a causal element, but they do serve as a medium for the expression and representation of those of man's activities which constitute this process. Hence, they are an indispensable condition for the development of social relationships.[4]

The idea of causal nexus is frequently understood quite broadly in the sense of all conditions underlying certain effects. It is quite obvious, however, that one must distinguish those conditions that con-

---

[3] "Uslovnaya Simvolika kak Sotsialnyi Razdrazhitel" [Conditional Symbolism as a Social Irritant], *Vestnik Kommunisticheskoi Akademii,* No. 9 (1924).
[4] This problem was misinterpreted by Comrade A. Varyash in his speech on "The Marxist Philosophy of History." See *Vestnik Kommunisticheskoi Akademii,* No. 9 (1924).

tribute merely indirectly to the materialization of the social process from the causal interdependence of the material social relationships that are independent of social consciousness. In social development, only the latter can be viewed as the truly causal, that is, natural, connections. This is exactly what makes ideology a "superstructure" in relation to the real economic basis.

In distinguishing the basis from the superstructure during an examination of the condition of causal dependence, it is necessary at the same time to take into account their *connection* with social relationships. Only such a truly dialectical understanding of the nature of ideology will make it possible to see in it an "inverted reflection" and at the same time an inevitable side of the social process, that is, a form of social relationships. Only then shall we understand why ideology, because of inner contradictions, *abstracts itself* from social relationships and at the same time contributes toward their concretization.

Hence, as correctly stated by Comrade Bukharin in his *The Theory of Historical Materialism,* we should distinguish two distinct sides of the relations of production: first, the time-space distribution of men among the means of production, which forms their *material* relationships; and, second, the reflection of these material relationships in the consciousness of men engaged in production, that is, *ideological* relationships. Material relationships are not fully reflected in the social consciousness. The system of the material relationships in its entirety comes into being in spite of man's will and consciousness. As stated by Lenin, "It was neither true in the past, nor is it true now, that members of society imagine the totality of social relationships in which they live as something definite, *complete,* and *pervaded with a principle.* On the contrary, the masses adapt themselves unconsciously to these relationships, and lack a conception of them as *specific historical social relationships.*"[5] However, *separate* aspects of the process of production (that is, *separate* facts constituting the material process) are accurately or inaccurately, but inescapably, reflected in the consciousness of men and thus bind the consciousness of the participants in the process of production together: as these separate moments of material relationships pass through social consciousness, they produce a socially subjective side of the relationships of production—the ideological relationships. Naturally, the ideological notions of the participants in the process of production do not always

[5] "Chto Takoe 'Druzya Naroda' i kak Oni Voyuyut Protiv Sotsialdemokratov" [What "the Friends of the People" Are and How They Fight the Social Democrats]. [First published in September, 1894, by a provincial group of Russian Social Democrats, in pamphlet form, by hectograph.]

appear in a fully shaped, systematized form. Producers of commodities who are involved in an exchange transaction do not think of themselves as "juridical subjects," although they are considered to be such by their ideologist-jurists. However, they always have one or another, though not necessarily well-formulated, notion of their rights and obligations, of the "freedom" of their actions, etc. Under conditions of a class society these notions assume a more distinct "legal" form because of the awareness that they are protected by state, legislature, judicial institutions, etc.

Having established a connection between ideology and social relationships, the task of the Marxist theory is to comprehend the peculiarity of ideological forms, to study their structure, their component elements, the process of their development, and the causes of their inevitable separation from their economic roots. But what is the task of the general theory of law in connection with ideology? Its task is to approach law—which is a definite historical form of social consciousness—dialectically: to examine the interaction of those of its elements and aspects in which law appears to us as a *social relationship,* as a legal ideology, and as the highest development of the latter—a system of *norms.* This difficult task can be resolved by the Marxist theory only if it adopts the dialectical point of view and the above-stated understanding of the connection between ideology and social relationships.

# Economic Rights under Socialism*

## ᴄᴛᴏ L. Uspenskii

. . . The problem of the socialist system of law has been raised in our literature on numerous occasions. The theories that deserve mention in this connection are those that sought to build socialist law on the expanded principles of subjective rights, namely, those theories that have advanced the concept of the basic rights of man within the socialist society—his basic economic rights.[1] Traditionally, three basic economic rights are distinguished: the right to work, the right to the full product of one's labor, and the right to one's existence.

. . . What is the meaning of the right to work? Menger defines this right in the following way: "Because of the right to work, each able-bodied member of society who fails to find employment with a private entrepreneur can demand from the state or from a public union that he be given ordinary daily employment at a fixed rate of pay."[2] Another student of the right to work, Singer, offers a broader definition: "The right to work, which belongs to every able-bodied citizen, is the right to demand, from the state or from state organs, that he be furnished with an ordinary or a professional job that would secure for him the satisfaction of his needs."[3] Menger thinks that the right to work is a legal measure that merely supplements existing property rights and that it presupposes the existence of private ownership of land and capital.[4] On the other hand, Singer's conception of the right to work, especially the recognition of the right to professional work, calls for the concentration of land, instruments, and means of production in the hands of the state, which is incompatible with private property. Thus, Singer concludes that a full realization of the right to work is conceivable in a socialist, but not in a capitalist, society. But, since under socialism work will become a public, legal obligation of each man, there will be no need to have a special right

---

* From "Pravo i Sotsializm" [Law and Socialism], *Vestnik Yustitsii Uzbekistana*, No. 2–3 (1925), pp. 21–32.

[1] See the excellent work by B. V. Chredin, *Narodnoe Trudovoe Gosudarstvo i Osnovnye Ekonomicheskie Prava* [The People's Labor State and Fundamental Economic Rights] (n.p., n.d.), p. 26.

[2] *Pravo na Polnoi Produkt Truda* [*Das Recht auf den Vollen Arbeitsertrag in Geschichtlicher Darstellung*] (orig. pub. Stuttgart, 1886; Petersburg, 1906), p. 16.

[3] *Das Recht auf Arbeit* (n.p., n.d.), p. 77.       [4] *Pravo*, p. 13.

to work.[5] It follows, then, that the idea of the right to work cannot be realized within the framework of a capitalist system and that it is unnecessary under socialism. Consequently, the idea can be abandoned.

The second economic right is the right to the full product of one's labor. The meaning of this right lies in the principle that a thing should belong to the person who produces it. If something has been produced through the labor of one person, then it should belong to this particular person. If, however, a few persons participated in the production of something, then each of them should receive that part of its exchange value which corresponds to his contribution. According to this principle, the total product of their labor is divided among the workers without any residue. Consequently, neither unearned profit (land rent, capital interest) nor its legal prerequisite (private property) are possible.[6] The idea of the right to the full product of one's labor has enjoyed great popularity in socialist thought. Menger found this idea to be present in the writings of most socialist theorists. Among others, the proposed program of the German Workers' party, 1875 (which challenged Marx to write his excellent critique of the Gotha Program), espoused the right to the full product of one's labor.[7]

Nevertheless, the socialist system of law cannot be based on the idea of the right to the full product of one's labor. If we were to recognize that each worker has the right to the entire product of his labor, without any deduction, then neither cultural nor industrial development would be possible. The demand for the full product of labor is rooted, in part, in the individualistic world outlook, which presupposes that any state is an institution alien to the individual. Concomitantly, it is also rooted in the justified reaction of the exploited, who are dissatisfied with the principle of the distribution of the products of labor in the capitalist societies. Chredin is correct when, speaking about the right to the full product of one's labor, he asserts: "The old proprietary instinct manifests itself in the demands of the working people. The defense of the right to the full product of one's labor is stirred up by the interests of the person who has not yet put an end to the customs and the world outlook of the private proprietor."[8] Therefore, the idea of the right to the full product of one's labor can be recognized to a certain degree in its negative meaning, i.e., in the sense that unearned income is unjust. In no case, how-

---

[5] Chredin, *Narodnoe Trudovoe Gosudarstvo*, p. 34.
[6] Menger, *Pravo*, pp. 6–7.        [7] See Art. 1 of the proposed program.
[8] Chredin, *Narodnoe Trudovoe Gosudarstvo*, p. 39.

ever, can the right to the full product of one's labor, in its positive meaning, become a principle underlying the socialist system of law.

The third basic economic right that should lie at the basis of the new social order is the right to existence. This right has been defined in various ways. For example, Pokrovskii asserts that it is one's right to be provided with the so-called indispensable conditions of existence, that is, with the minimum essentials that the state could and should secure to each man.[9] Menger thinks that the right to existence implies that every member of society has the right to be furnished with those goods and services that are indispensable to his existence.[10] Novgorodtsev speaks of the right to enjoy a dignified human existence, meaning thereby not the positive measures that should be taken in order to bring about the human ideal but merely the removal of conditions that preclude the possibility of a dignified human life.[11]

Novgorodtsev's construction of the right to existence has a pronounced individualistic character; it rests on the idea of a human personality and its dignity.[12] In terms of its content, however, this right is extremely ambiguous, for the very concept of a dignified human existence is indeterminate and expandable. Consequently, this concept is not an appropriate source from which to derive legal norms; at best it can become a source of moral law. Pokrovskii's interpretation of the right to existence is more acceptable. The recognition that every member of society has the right to demand from the state that he be furnished with the indispensable minimum conditions necessary for his existence is not only a feasible principle for a future law but, in part, is being realized in the existing law. . . . Pokrovskii indicates, however, that a complete realization of the right to existence necessitates a specific social system. It presupposes the liquidation of unearned income, which can be attained only through the socialization (more precisely, *Verstaatlichung*) of all means of production, i.e., through the liquidation of private property and capital. Juridically speaking, this socialization would necessitate a legal centralization of economic relationships; instead of being dependent upon the multiple autonomous centers within the state, the entire operation of production and distribution would have to depend upon the state as a single, all-directing and all-regulating center.[13]

[9] I. Pokrovskii, "O Prave Sushchestvovaniya" [On the Right of Existence], *Svoboda i Kultura,* No. 4 (Petersburg, 1906), p. 32. Also see B. A. Kistyakovskii, *Sotsialnye Nauki i Pravo* [Social Sciences and Law] (Moscow, 1916), pp. 583–92.

[10] *Pravo,* p. 8.       [11] Pokrovskii, "O Prave Sushchestvovaniya," p. 4.

[12] *Ibid.,* p. 10.       [13] *Ibid.,* p. 76.

Needless to say, Pokrovskii's conclusions are correct. In any case, leaving aside the question of whether socialism rejects civil law as a matter of principle . . . , the socialist system of law is distinct from a capitalist system, not because it expands the concept of subjective rights, but because it advances a new principle of juridical regulation. It is well known that the very idea of subjective right—as a right presumably prior to and independent of objective legal norms—has the character of natural-law individualism. This idea came into being as a protest against police-state absolutism and found its expression in the theory of the innate and inalienable rights of man.[14] Indeed, the idea of subjective rights is connected with the goods-producing society. And, if this idea were indispensable to the creation of law, then Pashukanis would be quite right in connecting all legal regulations to the relationships of goods producers in a capitalist society. But is it really so? Is the idea of legal regulation in the form of a system of subjective rights the only form of legal regulation? Is not the very principle of subjective rights subject to restrictions? We shall now answer these questions.

. . . In this connection, the theory of Duguit is of special interest. He attempted to eliminate the category of subjective rights from juridical practice altogether. Duguit thinks that the legal norm is grounded in social solidarity, that is to say, in the interdependence of the members of society. . . .[15] In his opinion, the concept of subjective rights is metaphysical; it presupposes the existence of an abstract individual, that is, of a subject of rights.[16] In contrast to the old metaphysical and individualistic conception of law, Duguit advances a new and, in his opinion, realistic concept, namely, the concept of social function. He interprets the meaning of this concept in the following way:

Neither man nor society has any rights. To speak about the rights of an individual or of society, or to speak about the need to bring the rights of an individual into conformity with the rights of the collective, is tantamount to not speaking about anything. Every individual living in society should carry out certain functions, should satisfy certain necessities. He must fulfill these functions because, otherwise, either anarchy or conditions detrimental to society would prevail. On the other hand, acts committed by him in defiance of his function will be suppressed by society. At the same time, all acts that are indispensable to the

[14] See an excellent analysis by Hans Kelsen, *Hauptprobleme der Staatsrechtslehre* (Tübingen, 1911), pp. 567, 592.

[15] *L'État, le droit objectif et la loi positive* (Paris, 1903), p. 161.

[16] *Obshchee Preobrazovanie Grazhdanskogo Prava* [La transformation générale du droit privé] (orig. pub. Paris, 1912; Moscow, 1919), p. 17.

fulfillment of his social function will be protected and guaranteed. The juridical rules will be founded upon the social structure, upon the necessity of keeping the various elements together through the fulfillment of the social functions assigned to each individual and to each group. This truly socialist conception of law will supersede the traditional individualistic concept.[17]

Duguit is not a socialist; his construct presupposes private property. Nevertheless, property, in his opinion, ceases to be a right of the individual and is transformed into a social function. Each individual in society is under the obligation to perform a certain function, a function dependent upon his place in society. . . . Indeed, a number of objections to Duguit's theory could be raised. Nevertheless, his theory represents a complete break with the concept of legal order as a system of subjective rights. Duguit adopts the point of view of capitalist society. However, the relationships existing in a capitalist society in the epoch of finance capital and state capitalism have nothing in common with the relationships of the independent producers of goods, relationships that found their expression in a principle of classic law, namely, in the subjective right and the juridical subject.

Curiously enough, quite a few legal theorists, apart from Duguit, have developed theories according to which law in its subjective meaning is merely an element of the objective law that is superior to it.[18] The theory of law as a social function has also found expression in positive legislation. The war and, subsequently, state interference in economic life have destroyed the old notion of the individual's rights, which were assumed to be prior to and independent of society. It became evident that the rights of an individual person can exist only within the framework of society and that society has the right to impose restrictions and obligations upon its subjects.

. . . The idea of economic rights, which is very popular in modern German legal literature, is to a certain extent based on the theory of social function. . . . For example, according to Hedemann, the principal characteristic of the new economic right is its extreme flexibility. In contrast to the natural-law school—which attributes absolute qualities to legal norms and views them as being eternal and immutable laws, valid for all times and places—the principle of economic rights adopts a diametrically opposed point of view. It asserts that there are

[17] *Ibid.,* p. 31.
[18] See Kelsen, *Hauptprobleme der Staatsrechtslehre,* p. 625; his student, Felix Kaufman, *Logik und Rechtswissenschaft* (Leipzig, 1922), p. 112; and F. Schreier, *Die Grundbegriffe und Grundformen des Rechts* (Leipzig, 1924), p. 148.

no immutable forms and evaluates legal norms from the point of view of their functions, their manifestations, and their lives. The principle of economic rights has modified, in particular, the concept of property. Property is no longer looked upon as an isolated legal concept. It is being recognized that property is affected by public interest. Not the possession but the utilization of property is now of central interest, and a planned regulation of the utilization of property is viewed as the principal task of law.[19]

To a certain extent, our civil code has adopted the idea of law as a social function. Thus, Article 1 asserts: "Civil rights are protected by law, with the exception of when they are used in conflict with their socioeconomic purpose. . . ." Goikhbarg indicates that our code has not approached rights from an individualistic point of view. The factors determining the scope of rights are not individual but collective interests, the interests of the workers' and peasants' state. The rights that we grant are not the innate rights of man; they are rights granted by the state for the purpose of attaining goals that are indispensable to collective preservation. Such a fundamental goal is the development of the productive forces within our country. . . .

The theory of law as a social function is entirely opposed to the concept of law as a system of subjective rights. The principle of subjective rights views man as a subject isolated from society, who sees in himself an independent end. On the other hand, the principle of social function binds the individual to society. Man remains subject to law, but only as he occupies a definite position within society. . . .

. . . The principle of subjective right in its pure form corresponds to the earlier phases of the capitalist society in which the possessors of goods were opposed, one to another, as isolated subjects. The epoch of finance capital has an entirely different character. Here, the feeling of a bond between the individual person and society is much stronger. Indeed, the principle of free disposition of his rights is preserved there, but at the same time the person is restricted by an obligation not to infringe upon existing social bonds. Society in the epoch of finance capitalism is not pursuing one goal and hence has no need to regulate life in its entirety. At the same time, however, it does not conceive of itself any longer as an aggregate of isolated persons, each acting at his own risk. . . .

. . . The problem of the socialist system of law implies the replacement of juridical regulation, based on the principle of subjective

19 W. Hedemann, *Osnovnye Cherty Khozyaistvennogo Prava* [The Basic Features of Economic Right] (n.p., 1924), pp. 27–30.

rights, by the regulation grounded upon the principle of objective law. The juridical system, conceived as a system of subjective rights, did not regulate all aspects of life; it halted before a subject with his rights as before an inviolable sanctuary. On the other hand, regulation in conformity with the principle of objective law implied a thorough mastery of social reality, a complete victory of law over life. Following the translation of such a regulation into practice, the idea of rights and the idea of obligations will blend together. Then, Auguste Comte's precept will be fulfilled: "In the positive state each has duties toward everyone, but no one has any rights. . . . To put it differently, no one has a right other than the right to fulfill his duty."[20]

[20] *Systéme de politique positive* (Paris, 1851), Vol. 1, p. 361. Curiously, the concept of juridical obligation begins to attract the attention of modern jurists. See H. Kelsen, *Hauptprobleme der Staatsrechtslehre*, pp. 318–76.

# Revolution, Law, and Power*  ⟋ *I. Naumov*

. . . According to Marx, "At a certain stage in their development, the material forces of production in society come into conflict with the existing relations of production or—what is but a juridical expression for the same thing—with the property relations within which they had been developed before. From forms of development of the forces of production these relations turn into their fetters. Then a period of social revolution occurs. With the change of the economic foundation the entire immense superstructure is more or less rapidly transformed. . . ."[1]

Marx stated the same view in the third volume of *Capital:*

To the extent that the labor process is a simple process between man and nature, its simple elements remain the same in all social forms of development. But every definite historical form of this process develops more and more its material foundations and social forms. Whenever a certain maturity is reached, one definite social form is discarded and displaced by a higher one. The time for the coming of such a crisis is announced by the depth and breadth of the contradictions and antagonisms that separate the relations of distribution, and with them the definite historical form of the corresponding relations of production, from the productive forces. A conflict then arises *between the material development of production and its social form.*[2]

According to Marx, the development and growth of the material forces of production in society are its content. The relationships of production, or, to use a juridical expression, the property relationships, are its form, engendered by the content, that is, by a given stage of development of the material productive forces in society. This form, in the framework of which the material productive forces are developing, becomes at a certain point too narrow because of a further development of the content, that is, the material productive forces. Removal of the old form and its replacement with a new one becomes the *conditio sine qua non* for the further development of productive forces in society and, consequently, an indispensable condition for the development of the entire social life.

* *From* "Rol i Znachenie Pravovykh Form v Perekhodnyi Period" [The Role and Significance of Legal Forms in the Transition Period], *Sovetskoe Pravo,* No. 5 (23) (1926), pp. 5–8.
[1] Preface to *K Kritike Politicheskoi Ekonomii* [A Critique of Political Economy].
[2] *Kapital* [Capital] (Moscow, 1923), III, Part 2, 423.

Consequently, the revolution, which occurs at a given stage of development of the forces of production, crushes the old, obsolete form of (property) production relationships and creates new forms. And to the extent that new forms of production relations, that is, relations in which men stand one to another as participants in the social process of production, come factually into being—that is, to the extent that new forms or organization of national economy are created *not only in words but in fact*—the old ideological superstructure more or less rapidly changes, giving up its place to the new ideology which corresponds to the new economic structure of society.

But before the broad strata of the population becomes conscious of the new social system or, in other words, before new ideological forms come into being, a more or less protracted period of persistent struggle with the old habits and ideas, which grew up and developed under the conditions of old, prerevolutionary socioeconomic relationships, is inevitable.

Among the ideological superstructures standing above the economic structure of society the legal ideology is most abstract. Its real, visible threads, connecting it with reality, are difficult to see with an ordinary, unequipped eye. This is so, on the one hand. On the other hand, since law protects the real and vital interests of some men, those whose interests it protects endow it with transcendental qualities and refuse to admit that law is a social phenomenon. Hence, it is not surprising that metaphysical, idealist theories of law prevail in the field of jurisprudence. Contemporary bourgeois ideologists—learned jurists and professors of law—poison the souls of young generations with the view that law is a "metaphysical, abstract entity" that stands above men and classes. Some of them do it unconsciously, because of the stagnation of their intellects, but the majority does it consciously.

While opposing law to power, they solemnly proclaim that law is higher than power and that, therefore, power should be subordinated under law. But these gentlemen know quite well that during the entire history of the world not even one state or social order has given away its place to a new state or social order voluntarily. They know equally well that each state and social order creates "its own law," which, in reality, has very little in common with "absolute metaphysical being," a law whose function is to protect the interests of those groups of the population which, having won the victory in the struggle, are stronger than others.

They know equally well that not even one government has ever existed that would not declare officially, or at least pretend, that it represents the interests of the whole people and that the law, which it created in the interests of the ruling class, of the victorious class, protects the interests of the whole people. All this is known to gentlemen, learned jurists, and professors, but they constantly and in different ways repeat that law is "a higher moral value," that the function of law is to safeguard the higher interests of culture and civilization, the interests of the whole society, etc.

But history teaches us that each sociopolitical system creates not only *its own positive law but also its own philosophy of law*. Whereas, in ancient and medieval times, the defenders of slaveholding and feudal systems saw the source of law in religion, the enlightened philosophers and professors, the ideologists of bourgeois systems, are above such medieval prejudices. The reasons for this are clear. In the past it was easy to deceive the people by playing with their naïve religious feelings, by exploiting their ignorance. At the present time, more refined and perfected methods and forms of deception are needed. Since everything flows, since everything changes, the content and the forms of deception are also changing.

Metaphysics took the place of religion. All efforts of bourgeois ideologists are now directed toward idealization of the existing bourgeois system, toward justifying them philosophically. They claim that the bourgeois system is a legal system, a system based on law and not on power, as was the case with the feudal absolutist system, which, presumably, was devoid of a *legal basis* and which was based exclusively on sheer physical force.

In the judgment of the bourgeois ideologists, the democratic state made available the freedom of opportunity for the further perfection of society, and social progress takes place there only within a "legal framework." Therefore, all revolutionary methods for bringing about social and political changes, all violent means for resolving sociopolitical conflicts, are contradictory to the "legal foundations" of society.

Of course, these gentlemen either forget, or pretend to have forgotten, that the bourgeoisie attained power only after a persistent and fierce struggle of the people against absolutism. They forget that bourgeois authority became consolidated only after a complete and final overthrow of absolutism. Nevertheless, they do not hesitate to recognize and to justify the employment of force against the working class by the bourgeoisie. This, in their opinion, is a protection of "legal order" against "anarchistic" acts of the working class.

# Communism and Law* ❧ *I. Naumov*

. . . According to Marx, all law is, in its content, a law of inequality. What does this mean? This means that law arises and operates in conditions of economic inequality. The function of law is precisely to protect economic inequality! This is the historical meaning of law. Everywhere and always law has protected and protects certain advantages and privileges, whatever they may be. This is why Marx designated the law operating in the first stage of communist society as the "bourgeois law."

From this it follows quite clearly that law will disappear only when all economic inequality has disappeared in society or, to put it differently, when society will demand from each "according to his abilities" and will give to "each according to his needs"; that is, in a complete, large-scale communist system. Then, and only then, will the legacy of the old system—the state—disappear with its entire apparatus of coercion.

Since law, which at the first stage of communist society has a bourgeois character, will disappear completely under full-scale communism, it is inadmissible to speak of communist law, communist property, etc. First, this would be a logical fallacy, *contradictio in adjecto*. Second, this would be a false methodological approach, pregnant with unfortunate consequences concerning the meaning of law, its role, and its significance in man's social life.

There is a very popular view which asserts that legal regimen, that is, legal regulation of social relationships, will be preserved in the communist system. Besides "practical" considerations—namely, that man is merely a man with all his weaknesses and deficiencies and that, therefore, "coercion is indispensable"—purely theoretical justifications of this view are being advanced. We are told that law, being an aspect of man's social life, is organically and indissolubly connected with man's social life. Law fully and completely shares the destiny of society and will remain in existence as long as human society exists in this world. Human society is unthinkable without law! From this theory it follows that man is not only a social being but also a legal being, or rather a social being, and, consequently, a legal being.

* *From* "Rol i Znachenie Pravovykh Form v Perekhodnyi Period" [The Role and Significance of Legal Forms in the Transition Period], *Sovetskoe Pravo*, No. 5 (23) (1926), pp. 11–13.

At the first superficial glance, all these theoretical arguments appear to be quite convincing and are presumably based on materialistic considerations. This, however, is merely an appearance. What are the errors of these arguments? It is true that law occupies a very significant sector in social life, that it is organically connected with the structure of society and, therefore, is not artificially invented. It is equally true that man's legal life changes with changes in his social life, with changes in the forms of his social relationships; that is, forms of legal relationships change with changes in forms of social relationships. All this is true. Only one thing is false: the main thing, namely, that law is not an inescapable satellite of the development of human society *at all* stages of its development.

Law appears at a definite stage in the development of human society, namely, when economic antagonism, economic inequality, becomes manifest. Of course, law cannot exist outside and without society, but a society can exist without the law. In a developed communist society—in which not antagonism but cooperation and economic collaboration will be the motivating forces—there will be no law and no legal norms. The legal moment in human relationships will disappear forever. Of course, society will remain in existence and will be developing. A savage, who lives *outside of society* and owns certain tools, is not an owner of these tools in the juridical meaning of the term. His ownership is merely a physical possession and nothing else. A singular fact of possession has no social meaning. Only in society and through society does the savage possessor become a juridical owner. It is not society but the economic antagonism existing in society which gives rise to law and transforms the physical possession into a juridical one. In the classless communist society juridical ownership will be transformed once again into the physical possession of things.

At this point we can outline three moments that are characteristic of law: (1) Law is the social relationship. (2) Law is the social relationship of inequality. (3) Law has a historically limited, a temporary, character.

Of course, from the point of view of the proponents of "communist law," a law is also a social relationship but not a temporary and transitional relationship; law is eternal or, rather, immanent in society. Law, in their opinion, is one of the functions of human society, a function that is indissolubly and organically tied to human society and shares its destiny from the moment of its birth to its very death. From this follows another error of this theory: worship of legal norms and the recognition of norms as the initial, primary moment of legal regulation. From this also follows the traditional definition of law as an aggregate of externally coercive norms, etc.

"Law," according to Marx, "can never be higher than the economic form." What does this mean? This means that law merely expresses, registers economic relationships, but does not create, does not give birth to them. Law merely secures, or protects economic relationships. Only in this limited sense can one speak of law as regulating social relationships. Positive law, therefore, is not the law that appears in a form of written or unwritten norms but the law that operates in real life. Legal norms are law if they do not operate merely on paper but really fix the existing economic relationships.

The recognition of the norm as a primary source of legal regulation is tantamount to its separation from the economic content which it reflects. Furthermore, it is tantamount to a rejection of the Marxist theory of law as a superstructure standing above the economic basis. . . . In order to prevent any misunderstandings and misinterpretations, an additional explanation is necessary. We assert that "law is merely an expression of economic content." An objection can be raised that this view is contradictory to our assertion that law will disappear in a full-scale communist society.

If law disappears, then how will economic relationships be regulated in a communist society? There are only two possibilities: if law is an expression of economic content, then it will remain in existence under a communist system, because under communism there will be an economy; or should we assume that together with law economy will also disappear under communism, which is obviously absurd. Hence, we are told that we should either admit that there will be a legal regime under communism or reject the view that law is an expression of economic content.

All this is not as bad as we are told. No contradiction is involved here. We know that all law is law of inequality, that legal regulations exist only under conditions of economic inequality, and that, consequently, law is an expression of a contradictory economy, that is, an economy founded on antagonism.

# The Last Act of the State: It Withers Away*

## ᐁ P. Stuchka

From our definition of the state as an apparatus of class domination it follows that the existence of the state will come to an end simultaneously with the disappearance of classes, i.e., with the introduction of a classless society. Engels used the expression "withers away" to describe the disappearance of the state. In doing this, he stressed the fact that the disappearance of the state will not be an instantaneous event but a protracted process.

This is simply a logical conclusion of the whole history of class society:

> When at last the state becomes the real *representative of the whole of society*, it renders itself superfluous. As soon as class rule and the individual struggle for existence based on our present anarchy in production disappear, and along with them the collisions and excesses arising from this struggle, nothing more remains to be repressed, and a special repressive force, a state, is no longer necessary. . . . State interference in social relations becomes, in one domain after another, superfluous and withers away of itself. *The government of persons* is replaced *by the administration of things* and by the conduct of processes of production. The state *is not abolished; it withers away* (Engels, *Anti-Dühring*).

Communists are not alone in demanding the abolition of the state. Anarchists, too, demand its abolition. However, as Lenin stated:

> *We do not at all disagree* with the anarchists *on the question of the abolition of the state as an aim.* We maintain that, to achieve this aim, *temporary use must be made of the instruments,* means, and methods of the state power *against* the exploiters, just as the dictatorship of the oppressed class is temporarily necessary for the annihilation of classes. Marx chooses the sharpest and clearest way of stating his position against the anarchists: when they have cast off the yoke of the capitalists, ought the workers to "lay down arms" or ought they to use them against the capitalists in order to crush their resistance? But what is the systematic use of arms by one class against the other, if not a "transitional form" of the state (*State and Revolution*).

From this it follows that there is a great difference between the

* From *Uchenie o Gosudarstve Proletariata i Krestianstva i Ego Konstitutsii* [The Theory of the Proletariat's and Peasants' State and Its Constitution] (5th ed. rev.; Moscow-Leningrad, 1926), pp. 288–91.

"fall" of a bourgeois state and the withering away of the Soviet state. According to Engels, "The bourgeois state does not *'wither away'* but is *'destroyed'* by the proletariat in a *revolution.* And it is *the proletarian state* or semistate *that withers away after that revolution.*"

The question of the inevitability of a transition period between capitalism and communism in a special state of the proletarian type, as well as the question of the transition period itself, etc., was elaborated for the first time by Lenin in his book *State and Revolution.* It is necessary for any conscious man (even a non-Communist) to read this book. I shall, therefore, say only a few words on this subject. Following Marx, Lenin divides the transition into two phases: socialism and communism. "The scientific difference between socialism and communism lies only in that the first word designates *the first stage,* arising from capitalism . . . , while the second word designates its *higher,* further stage."

What is the difference between the first and the second stage in the legal sense? Lenin explains:

In the first phase of the communist society (generally called socialism) "bourgeois law" is not abolished in its entirety but only in part, only in proportion to the economic transformation so far attained, i.e., only in respect to the means of production. "Bourgeois law" recognizes them as the private property of separate persons. Socialism converts them into common property. To that extent, and to that extent alone, does "bourgeois law" disappear. But it continues to exist as far as its other part is concerned; it remains in the capacity of regulator (determinant) of distribution of products and distribution of labor among the members of society. . . . However, this is not yet communism, and this does not abolish "bourgeois law," which gives to unequal men, in return for an unequal (factually unequal) amount of work, an equal quantity of products. . . . To this extent, therefore, the state is still necessary, which, while maintaining public ownership of the means of production, would preserve the equality of labor and equality in the distribution of products.

The withering away of the state and law is possible only in the second stage of development: "The state will be able to wither away completely when society has realized the rule: 'From each according to his ability, to each according to his needs,' i.e., when people have become so accustomed to observing fundamental rules of social life, and their labor is so productive, that they will work voluntarily according to their ability." "The narrow horizon of bourgeois law . . . will then be left behind."

Is it not a utopia? Lenin answers this question in the following way:

From the bourgeois point of view, it is easy to declare such a social order "a pure utopia" and to sneer at the socialists for promising each the right to receive from society, without any control of the labor of the individual citizen, any quantity of truffles, automobiles, pianos, etc. Even now, most bourgeois "savants" deliver themselves to such sneers, thereby displaying at once their ignorance and their self-seeking defense of capitalism.

Ignorance—for it has never entered the head of any socialist to "promise" that the highest phase of communism will arrive; while the great Socialists, in *foreseeing* its arrival, presupposed both a productivity of labor unlike the present and a person not like the present man in the street, capable of spoiling without reflection, like the seminary student in Pomyalovsky's book, the stores of social wealth, and of demanding the impossible.

Until the "higher" phase of communism arrives, the Socialists demand *strictest* control, by society and by *the state*, of the quantity of labor and the quantity of consumption; only this control must *start* with the expropriation of the capitalists, with the control of the workers over the capitalists; and it must be carried out, not by a state of bureaucrats, but by a state of *armed workers*.

. . . For when all have learned to manage and are actually independently managing social production by themselves, keeping accounts, controlling idlers, the gentlefolk, the swindlers, and similar "guardians of capitalist traditions," then the escape from this national accounting and control will inevitably become so increasingly difficult, such a rare exception, and will probably be accompanied by such swift and severe punishment (for the armed workers are men of practical life, not sentimental intellectuals, and they will scarcely allow anyone to trifle with them), that very soon the *necessity* of observing the simple, fundamental rules of every-day social life in common will have become a *habit*.

The door will then be wide open for the transition from the first phase of communist society to its higher phase and, along with it, to the complete withering away of the state.

But could this be the case in our country at the present time, when, after the assumption of power, the proletariat has had to make quite a few, if not many, steps backward; when the duration of the transition period is becoming apparently quite prolonged? Of course, these steps were taken under one condition, namely, that they not lead to the victory of the counterrevolution. Once again I shall use Lenin's words for characterizing this process: "Even such questions are being raised: 'Where are the limits of retreat?' We shall retreat as long as we lack the knowledge and the *preparedness for going over to a solid attack . . . ,* for only if we get hold of something will we be able to go over to an attack. . . ." But "after the victory of the proletariat, though only in one country, there appears something new in the relationship of reform to the revolution. . . . Before the victory of the proletariat, reforms are a by-product of the revolutionary class struggle. After the victory, they . . . become, for the country in which victory is achieved, an inevitable and legitimate 'respite' . . . needed for stopping the retreat at the proper time and for going over once again to an attack."

Since—as Lenin stated in one of his latest articles—under Soviet conditions "all means of production belong to the state authority, the real task remaining for us is only cooperation." Indeed, Lenin did not fail to remind us about the possibility of brutal attack by our enemy. But here the power of resistance depends upon our success and that of the international proletariat.

*After the proletariat's victory,* the idea of "growing into a new society of the future" and the idea of a gradual withering away of the function of political authority assumes, potentially, *a quite real form.* With the growth of the proletariat's power and authority the necessity of real repressions, of the application of violence, decreases. On the other hand, as I have demonstrated in the chapter on electoral law, the number of persons with purely working qualifications increases until, ultimately, the whole population becomes a working population and at the same time acquires electoral rights. Then comes a *true democracy;* then, as Engels stated in the previously quoted passage, *"the state becomes the real representative of the whole of society."* But at the same time it becomes unnecessary, superfluous.

All our People's Commissariats are divided into two groups: economic organs (production and distribution) and organs of coercion (military, internal affairs, and judiciary). . . . It is quite apparent that the latter are gradually withering away and that they undergo atrophy, while the *former,* directing the economic orchestra, are growing. This development may ultimately result even in an "orchestra without a conductor," but this is a matter of the distant future. One thing remains indisputable: *the state, as well as the law in its class meaning, evaporates, i.e., withers away, together with the organs of coercion.*

# Bourgeois or Proletarian Law in the Transition Period*

## ௸ *I. Naumov*

. . . Hardly anyone would deny that as yet we have not reached the stage of the transition period which Marx described in *Critique of the Gotha Program*. We are still in the "preparatory stage." The principal means of production in our country have been almost fully socialized and are the property of the proletarian state, although some means and instruments of production can still be privately owned under conditions provided for by law. . . .

Instead of an *exchange of products* we have the exchange of *commodities* in a monetary form. An economy based on commodities and money, with gold currency, leaves its mark on the entire national economy and determines both the content and the form of law. Therefore, owing to our economic structure, we are closer to the capitalistic society than to the society about which Marx spoke in *Critique of the Gotha Program*. Since law "cannot be higher than economic forms," and since "economic relationships give the content to juridical relationships," our Soviet law cannot be anything but an exact reflection of the economic structure of our society. Judging by the principle on which it is based, our law has a bourgeois character because, like any law, it is a law of inequality. Judging by its content, it is a class law, for it protects the interests of one class—the proletariat.

This, of course, does not mean that all interests and all kinds of workers' interests find protection in the proletarian law. No. Group interests, and other separate interests in general, can be protected only if they are in conformity with the correctly understood interests of the working class as a whole. But, since the interests of the working class as a whole coincide with the interests of social development toward socialism, we are right in saying that proletarian law—as the law of the transition period—protects, and should protect, everything that promotes the development of the productive forces in society aimed at socialism.

Therefore, if at a given moment these interests necessitate giving some "rights and privileges" to the non-proletarian groups of the

* From "Rol i Znachenie Pravovykh Form v Perekhodnyi Period" [The Role and Significance of Legal Forms in the Transition Period], *Sovetskoe Pravo*, No. 5 (23) (1926), pp. 13–15.

population—even to the detriment of the temporary interests of the workers—these rights and privileges must be given and must be protected by the proletarian law. This, of course, will be a right of inequality but a right conceded in the interests of the proletarian class as a whole and, consequently, in the interest of social development —in the interest of communism.

The same is true of bourgeois law in capitalistic countries; it does not protect all interests of the individual bourgeois or bourgeois groups. It protects the interests of the bourgeoisie as a class. In protecting these interests, it very often disregards the interests of individual members of that class. By the same token, it protects the interests of other groups in the population, including those of the working class, *if this is necessary to the interests of the bourgeoisie as a class.* Officially, of course, the bourgeoisie claims to be motivated by the national, social interests or by the interests of "culture," "civilization," etc.

We say that, judging by its principles, contemporary Soviet law is bourgeois law; and at the same time we assert that it is proletarian law. There seems to be a contradiction. We are told that only one of these assertions can be true. Either contemporary Soviet law is by nature a bourgeois law and, consequently, cannot be a proletarian law, or contemporary Soviet law is in fact a proletarian class law and thus cannot have an assertedly bourgeois character.

These objections call for an explanation. First of all, we do not assert that contemporary Soviet law is, *on the one hand,* a bourgeois law and, *on the other hand,* a proletarian law. We reject eclecticism unconditionally.

Bourgeois legal codes comprise norms that protect the interests of the working class, for example, the norms limiting the working day. But, with the exception of hopeless Philistines, no one would assert that bourgeois law therefore begins to lose its class character and becomes gradually "socialized." The same is true of our civil code. It comprises norms that protect even the interests of private owners. This, however, does not mean that our law is losing its proletarian class character. We assert that our Soviet law is *at one and the same time* both proletarian and bourgeois.

Needless to say, we will be told that this is a clear contradiction. Yet, it is a contradiction from the point of view of those who think metaphysically, according to the formula "yes-yes," "no-no," who think that law can only be either bourgeois or proletarian. We employ a different method, the method of the metaphysical dialectic, and arrive at the conclusion that our law is *at one and the same time* both bourgeois and proletarian. It is bourgeois because, like any law, it is primarily a law of inequality. It is an expression of contradictions in our economy and it regulates social relationships based on economic antagonisms. We indicated earlier that one cannot speak of a communist law, for under conditions of large-scale communism law will disappear. During the transition period, law will not be transformed into a special communist law; it will gradually die away.

The same, by the way, applies to the state. What does the state represent during the transition period? It is a bourgeois state without the bourgeoisie. A bourgeois state under the dictatorship of the proletariat is a proletarian state. Judging by the *principles* on which it is based, it is a bourgeois state with the entire apparatus of coercion and, like any state, it is a class state. The only difference between the state of the bourgeoisie and the state of the proletariat lies in their content and their ultimate objectives.

In the hands of the bourgeoisie, the state is an instrument for the suppression and oppression of the classes exploited by the bourgeoisie. In the hands of the proletariat, the state is an instrument for the suppression of the class of exploiters and an instrument for the destruction of the state. In this sense, it is a proletarian state, that is, a state that protects the interests of the proletariat. Exactly the same is true of law in the transition period. Being a bourgeois law in its principle, it protects the interests of the proletariat as a class, whose ultimate objectives are *the destruction of all classes, all law, all states, and the creation of a classless society without law and without a state.*

# A Critique of Legal Nihilism*  ორ  *I. Naumov*

. . . In attempting to find a correct approach to the problem of legal forms during the transition period, we must . . . demonstrate the difference between our approach to law and the approaches that enjoy a great popularity in contemporary Soviet legal literature.

Quite a few very valuable works that adopt the correct Marxist approach to the study of legal problems appeared recently on the literary market. Among them should be noted especially . . . Comrade Pashukanis' valuable work *The General Theory of Law and Marxism* (1924). In this work he makes an attempt to advance a critique of the bourgeois theory of law along the lines of Marx's critique of bourgeois political economy.

It is indispensable also to mention the juridical works of P. I. Stuchka, who is engaged in a persistent struggle with the so-called normativists in law. His unquestionable merit is the establishment, or rather re-establishment, of the fact that law is a social relationship. It is a pity, though, that while being carried away by the struggle with the "normativists" he fails to see the connection of law with other social phenomena.

While recognizing these gratifying events in our juridical literature, it must be noted that at the present time the views on law which constitute an echo from the epoch of militant communism are quite popular. In the epoch of militant communism, the governing trend in law was "legal nihilism." If not in literature, then in the practice of that time, the prevalent view was that law is "a bourgeois prejudice." The popularity of this view in the epoch of militant communism is as easy to understand from the psychological point of view as is the historical meaning of the social trend that in the 1860's, in Russia, was known as "nihilism." Nihilism, which in terms of its content was useless, signified in its time a protest against the then-governing law, morality, customs, and conventions.

"Legal nihilism" in the epoch of militant communism signified also a protest against the previously governing feudal and bourgeois law. A natural, spontaneous protest of the working class against the oppression of bourgeois law assumed the form of protest against law in general. The history of the workers' movement demonstrates that, in

* From "Rol i Znachenie Pravovykh Form v Perekhodnyi Period" [The Role and Significance of Legal Forms in the Transition Period], *Sovetskoe Pravo*, No. 5 (23) (1926), pp. 23–27.

its initial stage, workers resorted to destruction of factories and plants, naïvely assuming that the evil of exploitation is rooted in those neutral instruments of production. It quickly became apparent to them, however, that the causes of their exploitation are rooted in the capitalist mode of production and distribution, that is, in the organization of bourgeois society.

Similarly, at the present time the working class knows that until now law was only for the bourgeoisie, and lawlessness for the workers, because it was a law created by the bourgeoisie for the protection of its interests. Now the working class knows that there can be another law, a law that protects its interests, a law that is directed against the bourgeoisie. Now the progressive strata of the working class know quite well that the "proletarian law" is a class law only in the sense that it aims at an ultimate destruction of the division of society into classes, that is, at the creation of a classless, communist society.

One would assume that five years after the introduction of the "New Economic Policy" the views on law which prevailed during the epoch of militant communism have lost their popularity. The fact is, however, that these views became preserved in one form or another. I have in mind the trend headed by A. G. Goikhbarg, a trend that has quite a few proponents.

In his book *Foundations of the Private Property Law*, A. G. Goikhbarg states the following:

> With the grace of God, the feudal state has been a *religious state*. Religion and law are the ideologies of suppressing classes, the latter gradually replacing the former. Since we must, at the present time, fiercely struggle against religious ideology, we will, in the future, have to struggle against the ideology of law to a considerably greater degree. Any conscious proletarian either knows or has heard that religion is the opium of the people. But only few, in my opinion, know that law is an even more poisoning and stupefying opium of the people. . . .
> . . . Law is more recent than religion, and, therefore, the struggle against the idea of law, the idea that serves the interests of the exploiting classes, is considerably more difficult than the struggle against religious ideas. Since this struggle will be considerably more difficult, antilaw propaganda should become a more pressing task for us than antireligious propaganda.[1]

Following this, Goikhbarg makes a stipulation: "Speaking of the necessity to conduct antilaw propaganda, I naturally intend neither to encourage disobedience of the *rules* established by the Soviet au-

---

[1] *Osnovy Chastnogo Imushchestvennogo Prava* [Foundations of the Private Property Law] (Moscow, 1924), p. 7.

thority, nor to encourage insubordination to what we call the Soviet law. Indeed, it would be very nice if we could do without this expression, if we could replace it with another."[2]

We shall try to determine which of Goikhbarg's views are true and which are false. It is true that bourgeois jurists attribute a specific meaning to the state, designating it as a state *of law,* as a *Rechtsstaat.* Of course, we shall struggle against this view by all means, exposing the real meaning of the contemporary bourgeois state. We spoke about this at the beginning of our article.

It is also true that "with the grace of God" the feudal state was a religious state. However, the practical conclusions that Goikhbarg deduced from these propositions are hardly correct. Indeed, no one with a sound mind would assert that a peculiar "proletarian religion" will exist during the transition period. But, as we have seen earlier, Marx stated quite clearly that there will be a proletarian law in the transition period. All religions are the opium of the people, but not all law will be the opium of the people. The proletarian law is not at all the opium of the people but, on the contrary, . . . is indispensable for the attainment of the final goals of the working class, for the attainment of socialist ideals in society.

Comrade Goikhbarg's mistake is that he proposes to conduct a struggle not against bourgeois law, not against the bourgeois conception of law, and, finally, not against bourgeois legal ideologies. No. He proposes to struggle against all law in general. He proposes to conduct antilaw propaganda in the same way antireligious propaganda is being conducted. In his opinion, legal regulation of social relationships has no place in the transition period: "That which we call Soviet law is not a law *but rules established by the Soviet authority," correct norms, expedient rules, rules realizing the goals for which they have been created.*[3]

To this we can quote only Marx's statement: "In the absence of ideas there are many words," that is, words which explain absolutely nothing. To be consistent, A. G. Goikhbarg should also advocate antistate propaganda. He should also preach that the state is the opium of the people and that it should be destroyed the next day after a social revolution.

In *State and Revolution,* V. I. Lenin proposed to destroy, to smash, the bourgeois state machine, which in the hands of the bourgeoisie serves as an instrument for exploitation and oppression of the working class. But, in contrast to the anarchists, he did not propose to reject the idea of state itself. On the contrary, in his opinion, the

---

[2] *Ibid.,* p. 8.     [3] *Ibid.,* pp. 8–9.

proletariat will be able to suppress the resistance of the exploiters and to open the way for the construction of socialism only by means of the coercive apparatus of state authority.

Hence, the proletarian class state in the transition period is an indispensable instrument for the destruction of class society and for the creation of a classless communist society, and, thereby, for the destruction of the state itself. Comrade Goikhbarg seeks in vain to convince his readers that Marx is fully on his side. In a letter to F. Engels, November 4, 1864, reporting about the statute of the First International Association of Workers, Marx, among other things, has stated the following: "My proposals were all accepted by the subcommittee. Only I was obliged to insert two phrases, one about 'duty' and 'right,' another about 'truth, morality, and justice.' But these are placed in such a way that they can do no harm."

Goikhbarg cites this brief excerpt from Marx's letter to Engels as a proof that Marx regarded both the idea of law and the idea of "right" with great contempt. Among other things, we find the following in the preface to the statute of the International Association of Workers, which was edicted by Marx: ". . . The first International Congress of Workers proclaims that the International Association of Workers as well as all organizations and individual persons belonging to it recognize truth, right, and morality as the foundation of their conduct toward one another and toward all other people, regardless of their color of skin, religion, or nationality."

It is not difficult to see that Marx used the expression "right" not in a narrow juridical meaning but in a broad meaning . . . of "moral, just law" distinguished from a "formal law." Naturally, Marx was opposed to using common phrases and bombastic expressions like "moral rights and duties," which at that time were popular among his political opponents. Commenting on the program of the German Workers' party, Marx took a strong stand against Lassalle's idea of equal law and equal right for the produce of labor, quite rightly assuming that the reconstruction of the existing society is unthinkable on the basis of a juridical norm. Owing to the same considerations, Engels thought it indispensable to take a stand against proponents of "juridical socialism."

The principal defect of A. G. Goikhbarg's views lies in his underestimation of the significance of legal forms in the history of the commodity-producing society, including the modern, highly developed capitalist society. From his point of view, bourgeois law and bourgeois legal institutions are not an inevitable, organic product of the development of bourgeois society but are invented by bourgeois jurists for the purpose of exploiting the working class. Therefore, in his opinion, all that the working class has to do is to seize political power in its hands and—regardless of economic structure of society, regardless of the organization of national economy, regardless of the market distribution, etc.—to decree the destruction of all law, to replace legal norms with "expedient rules, rules realizing the goals for which they have been created." This should be done regardless of the existence of an economy based on commodity-money relationships, for law is independent of economy.

Needless to say, A. G. Goikhbarg commits the same error as one committed by a French socialist, Proudhon, and his followers. As stated by Marx, "Proudhon aims at eternalizing commodity production and at the same time at abolishing the antagonism between money and commodities, and consequently, since money exists only by virtue of this antagonism, at abolishing money itself. We might just as well try to liquidate the pope while retaining Catholicism."

# Determinism, Freedom, and Legal Responsibility*

## ௫ *I. P. Razumovskii*

One of the greater contemporary authors in the theory of criminal law, the well-known representative of German neoclassicism, Wilhelm Sauer, states the following:

> Criminal law is conceivable *only on the basis of the freedom of will.* How could a state impose punishment upon man if freedom of will were nonexistent? How could a state impose upon anyone criminal responsibility for his actions, if he himself is not the cause of his actions? To impose upon him such a great hardship as punishment without presupposing freedom of will would be an injustice, indeed, a gross injustice! If freedom of will is not involved in the case when men become dangerous to the state or society, then, instead of punishing them, one should take preventive measures against them; one should either educate them or make them harmless. Only guilt can be expiated with punishment, and *guilt is conceivable only when there is freedom of will.*

Furthermore, Sauer continues, "Rejection of the freedom of will is tantamount to rejection of man's ability to work on his inner ego, . . . to repudiation of a true morality, religion. . . . Repudiation of the freedom of will and craving for material things can only be interpreted as a decline of the German people and are two of the most serious causes of [Germany's] defeat in the world war."[1]

Such a conception of freedom of will is quite characteristic of many contemporary bourgeois authors. In order to show that Sauer is not the only one to entertain such views, I shall quote a brief paragraph from H. Kelsen's *Hauptprobleme der Staatsrechtslehre.* "Ethics and a science of law," writes Kelsen, *"are unthinkable without presupposition of the freedom of will,* i.e., which is beyond any doubt, without the assumption that the will is independent of causality."[2]

Feihinger—a well-known neo-Kantian philosopher, the founder of *als'ob* philosophy, of the philosophy of so-called fictionalism—thinks that a philosophy of law needs at least a "fiction of the freedom of will." Or, as stated in another place by Sauer, *the three fundamental*

---

* *From* "Determinizm i Otvetstvennost v Ugolovnom Prave" [Determinism and Responsibility in Criminal Law], *Revolutsiya Prava,* No. 6 (1929), pp. 83–94.

[1] *Grudlagen des Strafrechts* (n.p., 1921), p. 504.
[2] (Tübingen, 1911), p. 158.

*principles of modern criminal law are freedom of will, the idea of guilt, and the idea of retribution.*

An entirely different view is advanced by representatives of the sociological school of criminal law. For example, E. Ferry thinks that the physical connection between an act and its resulting effects is by itself sufficient for the appearance of criminal responsibility. He adheres to the point of view of a *complete non-freedom of will.* In his opinion, the motive of punishment is entirely different. At all stages of social development the function of punishment was to protect society from encroachments, to preserve society. This is why Ferry rejects the idea of imputability. The question concerns not the individual but the social responsibility of the criminal, who is responsible for his actions only because he lives in a society.

Angiolini and other representatives of the sociological school of criminal law entertain a similar point of view. Close to them are the conclusions of modern psychiatry dealing with problems of criminal law. For example, Krepelin asserts that "it is quite true that punishment ceases to be such as soon as it becomes purely a measure of social defense; in this we see exactly the great achievement of the new ideas. . . . The idea of retribution is *incompatible with our moral convictions.*"[3]

We have seen that, according to Sauer, morality is unthinkable without the idea of the freedom of will, whereas, according to Ferry and Krepelin, the opposite seems to be true—the idea of retribution turns out to be incompatible with "moral" convictions. The latter point of view exerts a rather strong influence upon authors who, in one way or another, are close to Marxism. Characteristic in this respect are the views of Professor M. Isaev, who believes that "both punishment and measures of social defense are equally expedient reactions to socially detrimental conduct." In other words, guilt is conceived as socially detrimental conduct; no other distinction between the idea of guilt and the idea of socially detrimental conduct is made. From this, of course, the conclusion can be deduced that since, to one degree or another, the possibility of socially detrimental conduct is always present—*even under communism*—criminal law will remain in existence forever.

Whatever the case may be, it is quite obvious that we are confronted with two diametrically opposed views concerning the problem of the freedom of will: an indeterminist view, represented for the most part by authors of the classical school; and a determinist view, represented chiefly by the sociological school of criminal law. Which side should Marxism take? It may seem to be obvious that we can and

[3] *Monatschrift für Kriminalpsychology* (n.p., n.d.), Vol. 3, p. 269.

should be in favor of the determinist "sociologists." Vulgar "Marxists" are so convinced of this that without sufficient criticism they
accept and transplant the ideas of the sociological school, veiled in
"Marxist" phraseology, into Soviet reality. It stands to reason, however, that the "sociological" solution of the problem is clearly *unsatisfactory* from the viewpoint of dialectical materialism. In order to
fully illuminate the Marxist position toward the principal issues dividing "sociologists" from "classicists" in the theory of criminal law,
we shall dwell initially on two questions—the idea of will in contemporary materialist psychology and Marxist views on the so-called
problem of the freedom of will.

The idea of volitional motion as "arbitrary" motion, which prevailed at the beginning and middle of the nineteenth century, was
considerably modified by bourgeois idealist psychology and philosophy at the end of that century. At the same time, a new materialist
idea of the nature of so-called volitional (arbitrary) motion was developed by representatives of objective psychology, reflexology, etc.
The father of reflexology, Sechenov, explained the origin of arbitrary
motions from instinctive motions as a result of their frequent repetition: "The habitualness of arbitrary motions explains to a physiolo-
gist the fact that the external impulses generating them are more difficult to detect as the motion becomes more habitual." This gives rise
to the feeling of freedom of will. But the contrary is also true: frequent repetition transforms arbitrary motions into involuntary motions when they acquire an automatic character. This is how the
constant transition of "necessity" into "freedom" and "freedom" into
"necessity" is accomplished. From the viewpoint of contemporary
objective psychology (Bekhterez, Kornilov) the distinctive feature of
arbitrary reflexes lies in their complete divisibility, in that each arbitrary motion dissolves, so to speak, into its component elements—
thought, recollection, act. The latter two elements constitute the so-
called free will proper.

But this division has a relative character. As pointed out by Kornilov, in reality, when we speak of a volitional process, of arbitrary
motions, we are always confronted with an integral reflectory process.
Even if individual elements of this process can be isolated, their isolation has only a quantitative and not a qualitative character. There is
a definite tie between all of these component elements. The idea of
"free will" comprises not only the resulting element, conduct, but
also two preceding elements, recollection and action. Recollection, on
the other hand, is directly connected with thought, with the idea,
with the consciousness of action. From this it clearly follows that volitional decision—volitional motion, arbitrary act, etc.—is an integral

process in which a significant role is played by thought, recollection, idea—in brief, by consciousness.

This view of the nature of the volitional act is an indispensable prerequisite for a correct understanding of the correlation between necessity and freedom established by Marxism. From the Marxist viewpoint, there exists between the object and subject a dialectical correlation. When we examine the dependence of the subject upon the object, we speak of the subject's activity as inevitable. However, when we examine the same correlation from the subject's point of view, from the point of view of the forms within which the subject becomes conscious of his dependence upon the object, then "freedom" or "arbitrariness" appears as the subject's *form of consciousness.* At this point it is necessary to dwell upon the distinction that is drawn by the Marxist dialectic between arbitrariness and true freedom. Whenever we make a decision, we experience a *feeling of freedom,* of the arbitrariness of our actions. This feeling of freedom is explainable by the fact that the collision of diverse issues, of diverse tendencies taking place in our consciousness makes us temporarily hesitate in making the final decision. Naturally, contrary to our feelings, the choice is not made arbitrarily at all. Sooner or later, these or other tendencies will predetermine our choice, that is, will predetermine it in an absolutely inevitable way. But the clash of diverse tendencies and external stimuli at the moment when the dominating and governing tendency has not yet asserted itself leads to the creation of what may be called a moment of "obstruction" in our consciousness. We do not feel bound by the governing stimulus which has not asserted itself as yet; therefore, in making a decision, we experience a feeling of freedom, of the arbitrariness of our choice. To be sure, the psychic condition in which we find ourselves has some essentially objective roots—the subjective experience of an objective clash of diverse tendencies that affect our consciousness.

Hegel and, following him, Marx and Engels, have taught us to draw a distinction between the idea of arbitrariness as a sensation of "freedom from necessity" and the idea of freedom as constituting *another side of this very necessity.* Bourgeois thinkers do not draw such a distinction; they conceive of the idea of freedom as something "absolute" and contrapose it to the idea of necessity. G. Simmel, for example, contends that freedom implies freedom from anything, freedom from any external constraint: what kind of freedom is it if it is identified with necessity? Plekhanov gave a witty answer to this question in his famous article "The Role of the Person in History." He pointed out that, indeed, one could not say that a pickpocket, who is prevented from stealing valuables from somebody's pocket, is committing an act

free of external constraint. Such "freedom," of course, is not identi-
fiable with necessity. But under conditions of "absolute" freedom
from any necessity we would have no guarantee that our planned
goals would be inevitably realized; such freedom would lead us toward
complete helplessness.[4] The point is that one must distinguish two
things: that which we call arbitrariness, i.e., a tendency to feel free
from any external constraints, which is *alien to the knowledge* of these
external conditions; and that which we call true freedom—when we
feel bound by necessity and at the same time realize that our actions
constitute a definite aspect of this necessity. In this case, the fact that
we are bound by necessity—that the commission of our acts is necessary—does not at all impose upon us any kind of constraint; on the
contrary, it intensifies our aspiration toward such acts and, at the
same time, makes us feel free. Or, as brilliantly formulated by Plekhanov in the above-mentioned article, "A complete subjective and
objective impossibility to act in a different way even when my actions,
at that time, appear to be undesirable—such a complete absence of
freedom is at the same time freedom in its full development." To limit
oneself to the mere recognition that our every act is inevitable is
tantamount to acceptance of the viewpoint of *abstract, mechanical,
fatalistic determinism* which is completely incapable of explaining the
role of the person, the role of the subject, in the social process. The
task of the subject, of consciousness, is to grasp in their *entirety* the
social causes of our actions as well as their possible consequences,
that is, all stimuli and tendencies that clash in our consciousness.
This will make it possible to trace the most essential stimuli—social
tendencies—in the process of humanity's general development.

A *conscious* participation in social necessity is therefore a *specific
form* of the development of this necessity and, like any qualitative
form, it conditions the character of this necessity to a certain extent.
Hence, Marxism does not mechanically reject the idea of "free will";
the idea of "free will" is "removed" and acquires a *new content in the
process of the realization* of necessity. "Freedom of will," declares
the classical Marxist formula, "means nothing other than the *ability to
make decisions when possessing knowledge of the affair"*: the freer a
decision "the more inevitably will its *content* be determined" (Engels).

From the Marxist point of view, "freedom" no longer constitutes

---

[4] Cf. Lenin: "Man's will, his practice, prevents him from attaining his goals
. . . when it is separated from knowledge." "Tetryady po Filosofii: Hegel,
Feierbakh i Drugie" [Notebooks on Philosophy: Hegel, Feuerbach, and others],
in *Leninskii Sbornik* [Lenin's Miscellany] (Moscow), IX (1929), 265. [Published
in English as "Conspectus of Hegel's Book *The Science of Logic*," in V. I.
Lenin, *Collected Works* (Moscow, 1961), Vol. 38.]

an abstract idea. "Freedom" as a conscious form of our activities *always has* a definite, inevitable content. Freedom, determined by necessity or by the totality of social relationships in social life—that is, true freedom—is merely a *subjective expression of real objective relations.* Freedom in this sense ceases to be a naked, abstract category, something that takes place only in our consciousness; it becomes a part of the objective social reality and finds there its *realization.* A contemporary writer, Georg Röber, turns his attention to this aspect of the problem in his article "The Dialectic of Determination of the Will."[5] He argues that the problem of freedom should always be posed concretely. If will is free, then the question is "for what" is it free. If will is constrained, then the question is "what" constrains it. "The problem of will should not be treated in terms of a person separated from society. We approach the problem correctly when we view our goals not as something individual but as supraindividual, social phenomena." As correctly indicated by Röber, in order to define the character of our freedom concretely, historically, as a conscious form of our inevitable acts, it is necessary to examine the relationships between the person and the class and the relationships between his class and society—in connection with the relationships between the classes at a given historical moment, in connection with the general development of the class, etc. This is exactly the way Lenin stated the problem when he said: "freedom for whom, equality for whom?"

Finally, there is another significant element in the Marxist understanding of freedom. The *unity* of freedom and necessity—of object and subject—should not be conceived of as something "ready-made" and "dead" but as a *tendency,* as a living *process.* The "subjectivity," as stated by Lenin, is merely a "state in the development" of necessity. Or, as Hegel stated, "The rational idea of freedom comprises in itself a removed necessity." Man's goal-oriented activity appears, at first, as something external and opposed to the causal connection of phenomena.[6] Only in the historical process of cognition (practice) is their coincidence, their unity, revealed and does the objective character of the subjective ideas of "goal" and "arbitrariness" come to light: "arbitrariness" is transformed into true freedom. This dialectical point of view explains the identity of necessity with freedom as well as their *distinctions.* Furthermore, it explains the validity of a con-

[5] Georg Röber, "Die Dialektik der Willensbestimmungen," *Unter der Bänner des Marxismus,* No. 1–2 (1928).
[6] Cf. Lenin: "In fact, man's goals are engendered by the objective world, and presuppose it . . . , but man *thinks* that his goals originate outside of the world, that they are independent from the world ('freedom')." "Tetryady po Filosofii: Gegel, Feierbakh i Drugie," in *Leninskii Sbornik,* IX, 216–17, 259, and others.

stant historical *contraposition* of the subject to the external objective
world in the process of practical mastering and cognizing of the world.
The development of historical necessity is at the same time the development of freedom which, however, does not coincide *immediately*
and *"completely"* with necessity. In brief, the idea of free will in
Marxism is not only objectivized—is not only filled with a social,
material content—but finds there its *concretization.* At the same time,
freedom of will ceases to be an abstract definition of something that
is everlasting; it becomes a *historical category* and is placed in dialectical dependence upon the changing character of social relationships. . . .

   This idea of freedom implies a corresponding idea of responsibility
which is a specific expression of the knowledge of necessity. The idea
of responsibility in Marxism is also based on the unity of the object
with the subject, necessity with freedom, their identity and distinction,
which constitutes our theory's fundamental dialectical principle of the
relationships between being and consciousness in their historical development. A correct view of responsibility grows together with the
development of a correct view of freedom. . . . Just as freedom of will
at a definite historical stage of development—at the stage of a commodity-producing society—assumes the forms of juridical freedom of
will ("arbitrariness"), so responsibility appears as a juridical responsibility. Even the ordinary view of "responsibility," developed in bourgeois law and morality, comprises a more or less disguised idea of
*consciousness* of the act committed by the person who is subject to
responsibility: the historical practice of humanity leads to this alone.
Historical materialism leads to the rejection of freedom of will—in
the bourgeois meaning—as an "absolute freedom," as "arbitrariness,"
and justifies the Marxist idea of freedom as consciousness of necessity. The idea of responsibility *is not at all eliminated* thereby. Like
the idea of freedom, the idea of responsibility acquires a new *social
content,* becomes concretized; it grows from social relationships and,
at the same time, constitutes a specific qualitative form of their being.

   Responsibility is not an abstract idea, an idea of "duty in general."
In this sense, one must draw a distinction between a general idea of
responsibility and a concrete responsibility in a specific case. Responsibility, as a rule, is always concrete; it is such in relation to a collective, a group, or a class. While representing a historically concrete
social phenomenon, responsibility is always *objective* in its content.
Responsibility is a *specific* expression in man's consciousness of his
social role and of the character of his social conduct displayed toward
class, collective, or society. In terms of its objective social *content,*
responsibility is always a definite *social relationship.* In order to grasp

all the nuances of the diverse forms of responsibility, it is necessary to examine the history of society and, in particular, the history of law.

As is well known, a definite differentiation of social life takes place historically: isolation of social relationships from one another, isolation of superstructures from their bases, isolation of diverse types of superstructures from one another, etc. Particularly dissociated as two distinct spheres are morality and law. In the process of this historical isolation, the general idea of moral responsibility becomes differentiated from what is commonly known as juridical responsibility. Whereas at the foundation of moral responsibility there lies a quite abstract idea of duty—i.e., a social bond embracing all interrelationships among all members of a group—juridical responsibility is connected with the idea of juridical obligation. The latter is always concrete; it constitutes the juridical obligation of a person (subject to law) to a *definite* person or group of persons. Therefore, juridical responsibility is least of all merely a subjective category. It is a definite, *objective legal relationship;* it is a *specific* variety of objective legal relationships, which develops together with the historical development of the entire legal superstructure. Its distinctive feature is that it imposes juridical obligation upon the subject, by means of which a corresponding social relationship is construed. A real *manifestation* of this objective legal relationship, always presupposing juridical responsibility between the subject and contractor, results from its violation by the subject. This manifestation of the objective relationship— assuming a historically determined *legal form*—we call guilt, that is, guilt in a *juridical sense.*

Briefly stated, when we speak of guilt in the juridical sense we should not imagine—as is frequently the case with the popular interpretation of the principles underlying Soviet law—that guilt is a certain moral category connected with theological, religious ideas, with the idea of religious expiation, etc.; that guilt is an idea that originated in the womb of feudal society and that, therefore, it should be discarded, etc. Guilt, as we have demonstrated, is neither a purely moral nor a purely psychological idea, though, naturally, in the field of morality we can speak of moral guilt. But guilt in the juridical sense is neither a subjective nor a "religious" category; guilt is a *real* manifestation of the *objective* relationships of responsibility; it is primarily a definite *objective social relationship* which assumes the appearance of a *legal* form. Historically, the objective content of guilt ("duty," "injury") existed prior to the detection of its connection with the idea of freedom. . . .

Guilt is nothing other than juridical responsibility—responsibility in a juridical form—which comes into being as a result of the violation of a contractor's right by the subject and which therefore assumes the form of a legal relationship in which another party's will is not present. Of course, concealed beyond this legal form is a definite *social content* amounting in the last analysis to the social *danger* of a given act. It would be a mistake, however, to limit oneself to such a "reduction" and not to see the *specific* social *forms* that this social content assumes. When we speak of guilt and its various components —of various "forms" of guilt, intention, etc.—we have a certain historically conditioned category in mind, a certain objective legal relationship that is not reducible to social danger "in general" and that does not exist exclusively in our consciousness, our religious and moral ideas. It should be noted that bourgeois theorists entertain a fairly clear view of the content of guilt. But they fail to grasp the idea of the *unity* of the objective side of guilt with its other side, which they treat as a purely subjective category. Equally, they fail to see that guilt constitutes a juridical concretization of "freedom of will" only at a specific *historical* stage of its development.

The connection between the historical category of guilt and the historical category of legal subject is quite clear. The transformation of responsibility into guilt in the juridical sense and the transformation of the "willing" person into a juridical subject are closely related processes. I do not think that it is necessary to repeat here what has been so well said concerning the origin of criminal law relationships by E. Pashukanis. . . .

In order to confirm our principal views, we shall examine the source of all the bourgeois juridical theories of criminal law of the nineteenth century. We shall demonstrate that in the final analysis there are two diametrically opposed conceptions, two diverse views of guilt, intention, and responsibility, the subjective, a priori point of view and the objective, dialectical point of view. These two diverse views, one connected with idealism, the other complimentary to Marxism, originated with Kant and Hegel.

Quite a number of bourgeois authors contend that in the field of criminal law Hegel is a direct successor to Kant. In a certain sense this view is correct, and, as we shall see later, even Marx indicated that Hegel has given expression to Kant's views in a more systematic and precise form. Nevertheless, despite some similarities, there is a great difference between these two thinkers. . . . At the basis of Kant's philosophy of law lies a distinction that he has drawn between an empirical will and a "pure will," or "free causality," which, as he has stated, "begins the process." According to Kant, the empirical will belongs to an external sphere, to the legal sphere, whereas the pure will exists in the sphere "accessible to the mind." Individual acts of man are subject to the positive law; man's empirical will in his individual acts is subordinated to the law of legality. "Pure" will, on the other hand, is peculiar only to the "general" law, to moral law, to a certain suprasensory moral idea. Kant indicates that only arbitrary actions of individual persons, actions that are mutually coordinated and mutually restricting, belong to the sphere of law. The sphere of formal law is a sphere in which coordination takes place, that is, restriction of the "arbitrariness" of individual persons and their empirical wills. Man's inner freedom, an entirely different phenomenon, is separated from the external sphere. . . . From this there results a constant discrepancy, a constant gap, between these two spheres, between inner freedom and external necessity, between morality, in general, and law.

Kant's philosophy, as we know, is permeated throughout with dualism: the external is separated from the inner, freedom is separated from necessity, knowledge is separated from the external world. Freedom to Kant appears as an inner idea distinct from empirical "arbitrariness," as a subjective, a priori category. Of equally subjective character are all categories connected with the idea of freedom, responsibility, intention, etc. With this, finally, the peculiarly moral Kantian theory of retribution and punishment is connected. According to Kant, punishment should not be viewed as a "means" but as a result of the recognition of man as a moral subject. The law of punishment is a categorical imperative. At its base lies equality as a principle of "pure and strict justice." Punishment, therefore, is reduced to the law of retribution. The latter, like guilt, is interpreted by Kant from the viewpoint of "moral law." In the process of punishment the offender bifurcates into an empirical and "noumenal" man, and, having adopted the latter's point of view, the point of view of "pure legislative reason," the criminal passes sentence upon himself.

Hegel's view on this subject is considerably different. Hegel's point of view is an objective, dialectical one. . . . Lenin has noted that there is an embryo of historical materialism in Hegel's theory. This is also true of the Hegelian philosophy of law. From Hegel's point of view, the philosophy of law, which in his writings goes under the name of "morality," constitutes three stages of development whereby morality is understood as the development of the "objective spirit," i.e., of "morals," *social connections and relationships.* Formal law and morality are viewed by Hegel merely as stages, as "moments," in the development of unity—*objective* social connections, social relationships, and institutions. Thus the Kantian separation of the empirical will and formally restricted "arbitrariness" from inner, subjective freedom is removed. To Hegel, freedom is a realized form of necessity. Kantian constructs of inner moral law became transformed by Hegel into formal moments that are characteristic of the relationships between juridical subjects; the contract became a social relationship. Therefore, in criminal law also, Hegel views the violation of law as an *objective* violation of an *objective social relationship* requiring reestablishment of this relationship. This Hegelian "violation" and "reestablishment" should not be interpreted literally in the spirit of Kantian idealist philosophy to mean that an individual "will" is opposed to the "general will," etc. Their meaning is clearly materialistic. This is why Hegel sees in the punishment of a "law breaker" an "act of his own will." Punishment is an "assertion of law which is engendered by the criminal himself and foisted upon him by force." Hegel viewed crime as some sort of social relationship, as a contract concluded against the will of another party. The criminal cannot be *merely an object* of "corrective" justice; he is *subject to legal relationships that he himself engendered.*

Hegel was not simply "expanding" the Kantian theory of crime and punishment. While developing some of its positive aspects . . . , he furnished this theory with an *objective* basis and a *dialectical* conception of legal relationships. . . . Even the Kantian theory of retribution reflected in an *abstract* way the real forms of legal relationships which were characteristic of a commodity-producing society. Hegel goes considerably further; in his "more precise formulation" (Marx) the "exclusively subjective" moments of guilt and retribution disappear and the "moral" tint, which they had in Kant's writing, is missing. Both the guilt and the re-establishment of the law violated are transformed into an objective legal relationship. The so-called followers of Hegel—right-Hegelians and neo-Hegelians—adopted not the objective dialectical method of Hegel but merely some separate elements from his system and thereby interpret them in an idealistic way. Berner, Kestlin, and other "classical Hegelians" accept merely the idealist peel, and the Kant-like elements, which are of no significance to Hegel, appear to them as fundamental. Meanwhile—and this is extremely significant—Hegel, for example, was against Feuerbach's theory of "deterrence," which was erected on Kantian principles. Hegel's philosophy of criminal law constitutes in this respect a higher stage in the development of the so-called classical school, the stage at which it "closely approaches" (Lenin) a materialistic conception in that it reflects real forms of the existing social relationships characteristic of a bourgeois society. Its deficiency lies only in that it could not elevate itself above these relationships and approach them not only from the viewpoint of *abstract law* but also from the viewpoint of man as an *integral social* being.

Unfortunately, the parts of Hegel's philosophy which to us, to Marxists, have an extraordinary significance are not taken into account by bourgeois thinkers and by authors claiming to be Marxists. In particular, Professor A. Piontkovskii, in his *Marxism and Criminal Law,* quotes a long paragraph from Marx's letter on England, in support of his view that Marx presumably treated with extreme contempt the classical school and Hegel's philosophy of law in particular. Marx presumably valued only Hegel's dialectical method but had no interest in and did not share his philosophy of law. Piontkovskii quotes Marx in a very peculiar way—he skips both the beginning and end of the paragraph! But it is exactly the beginning and end of the quoted paragraph which do not support Piontkovskii's views. . . .

"Generally speaking," Marx writes, "punishment is justified as either a means of correction or deterrence. But what right do we have to punish one man in order to correct or deter another? Both history and statistics have clearly demonstrated that since the time of Cain *no one was either reformed or deterred by punishment.* On the contrary, from the point of view of *abstract law,* there exists only one theory of punishment, which in an abstract form recognizes man's dignity: it is Kant's theory in Hegel's more precise formulation. . . ." Furthermore (having noted that there are many "corrupting" elements in Hegel's theory, that it transforms the criminal from a simple juridical subject into a free, self-determining being, that in this theory German idealism "merely sanctions the law of the *existing society,"* and that Hegel's theory in this respect is also merely a "metaphysical expression of the ancient law of retribution") Marx concludes: "Is it not a self-deception when an individual with his real motives, with his diverse, oppressing occupations, is replaced with an *abstraction* of 'free will,' when the *whole* man is replaced with *one of the many* human features . . . ? In reality punishment is nothing more than *a means for defending society* against any violations of the conditions of its existence. . . ."[7]

What conclusions can be deduced from the quoted views? First, Marx views punishment neither from the viewpoint of deterrence nor from the viewpoint of correction. He says that punishment never proved effective as a means of correction. Second, Marx draws a distinction between the *social* point of view and the point of view of *abstract law.* From the social point of view, in Marx's opinion, punishment is *always* a form of class defense or, as we say at the present time, *a measure of social defense.* From the point of view of "abstract law," i.e., the juridical point of view, Hegel's theory of punishment more than any other "corrupts" and corresponds to the "dignity" of

[7] *Sobranie Sochinenii* [Collected Works] (Moscow, 1921[?]), X, 91.

man as a legal subject. But this theory is also merely an expression of
the laws of the existing society, which, we shall add, are based on
*commodity circulation* and are related to the ancient law of retribution. In addition, taken *in itself,* this theory is inadequate; it substi-
tutes for an integral (social) view of the social individual an abstract,
juridical, *one-sided* view. These are the only conclusions that can be
deduced from the quoted paragraph. . . .

It should be noted that we find confirmation of this point of view in
other, earlier works of Marx. I call attention to the protocols of the
Sixth *Rheinischer Landtag,* to the debates devoted to the question of
stealing wood. There young Marx adhered to the Hegelian view of
punishment. He distinguished a juridical violation from a simple violation of police regulations; he thought it necessary to make punishment a real consequence of violation and found the measure of punishment in an *objective* feature "within the bounds of action."[8]

One could raise the objection that the above-said belongs to the
earlier, idealistic period of Marx, when he still fully adhered to Hegel's point of view. But our view finds confirmation elsewhere also,
for example, in *The Holy Family.* There, Marx draws a distinction
between a "citizen" and a "man." Marx indicates that Hegelian punishment as a sentence passed by man upon himself is, in contemporary (civil) society, *only* an "abstract idea," a juridical interpretation
of the forms of existing relationships. This view can acquire a full
social meaning only in a future society, in a society with "human
relationships." Extremely interesting is Marx's attitude toward the
theories that *abstract* themselves from action—from *violation*—and
examine *merely the individual offender,* subjecting him to corrective
measures. In contemporary bourgeois (civil) society the offender
*cannot* be treated simply as a man, i.e., from a *purely social* point of
view. The latter is possible only in a future society in which the division into man and citizen will be nonexistent. "Punishment, compulsion"—noted Marx—"is opposed to *human* behavior. In addition,
the execution of such a task would prove to be impossible. In place
of abstract law we would have purely subjective arbitrariness, for in
each case it would be up to the official 'honorable and decent person-
alities' to suit the punishment to the individuality of the offender.
Even Plato knew that law must be one-sided and *abstracted from
individuality.* On the other hand, under conditions of human relationships (i.e., under socialism—I.P.) punishment will be nothing
more than a sentence that the offender passes upon himself."[9]

    [8] *Ibid.,* I, 195.
    [9] Karl Marx and Friedrich Engels, *Literaturnoe Nasledie* [Literary Heritage]
(Moscow, n.d.), II, 329.

# Against the Revision of the Marxist Theory of State*

## ᴄᴫᴏ A. K. Stalgevich

The current revision of Marx's, Engels', and Lenin's theory of *state* constitutes a special danger. The validity of Engels' brief paragraphs, in which he discloses the meaning and the nature of the state, is indisputable. In *The Origin of the Family, Private Property, and the State,* he writes:

> The state is, therefore, by no means a power forced on society from without; just as little is it "the reality of the ethical idea," "the image and realtiy of reason," as Hegel maintains. The state is a product of society at a certain stage of development; it is the admission that this society has become entangled in an insoluble contradiction with itself, that it is cleft into irreconcilable antagonisms which it is powerless to dispel. But in order that these antagonisms, classes with conflicting economic interests, might not consume themselves and society in sterile struggle, a power seemingly standing above society became necessary for the purpose of moderating the conflict, keeping it within the bounds of "order"; and this power, having arisen out of society, but placing itself above it, and increasingly alienating itself from it, is the state.

Pashukanis questions the validity of Engels' theory of state. In his work *The General Theory of Law and Marxism,* Pashukanis voices the following doubts . . . :

> Whatever the case may be, Engel's formulation nevertheless remains ambiguous. The state arises because otherwise classes would consume themselves in sterile struggle and thereby destroy society. Consequently, the state arises when neither of the struggling classes is able to attain a decisive victory. In this case one or another follows: either the state secures this relationship and then becomes a supraclass power (which we cannot accept), or the state is a result of the victory of one class, in which case society has no need for the state, for with a decisive victory of one class the balance is re-established and society is saved. Behind all these controversies there is one basic question: "Why does the rule of the class remain not what it is (i.e., factual subordination of one part of the population to another) but assumes the form of an official state authority or, which amounts to the same thing, why is the apparatus of state compulsion created not as a private apparatus of the ruling class, but separate from the latter and assuming the form of an impersonal apparatus of public power, separated from society?"[1]

* *From* "Osnovnye Voprosy Marksistskoi Teorii Prava" [Fundamental Problems of the Marxist Theory of Law], *Sovetskoe Gosudarstvo i Revolutsiya Prava,* No. 10 (1930), pp. 110–13.
[1] *Obshchaya Teoriya Prava i Marksizm* [The General Theory of Law and Marxism] (Moscow, 1924), p. 87.

Strange and absurd are E. Pashukanis' questions. How can one argue that if the state is "a result of the victory of one class" then "society has no need for the state, for with a decisive victory of one class the balance is re-established and society is saved." Hence it follows, according to Pashukanis, that the gist of the question lies not in establishing relations based on class domination and suppression but in establishing "equilibrium." It is well known that, according to Bukharin, the theory of "equilibrium" and coordination of classes removes the necessity of the state or at best reduces its role to a "hoop" of this "equilibrium." This theory also removes the necessity of a proletarian state, for "with the decisive victory" of the proletariat the "equilibrium is re-established and society is saved. . . ." Pashukanis' treatment of this question reveals Bukharin's theory of "blowing up" and "abolishing" the state by the proletarian revolution.

Furthermore, Pashukanis raises the question: " . . . Why does the rule of the class not remain what it is, i.e., the factual subordination of one part of the population to another"? But we ask Pashukanis: What else could it be but a factual subordination of one class to another? Does the form of an *official* domination remove the element of the factual subordination of one class to another? Since Pashukanis shares Bukharin's or rather Bogdanov's (organizational) theory of classes,[2] which fails to see the element of class domination and exploitation of one class by another, he carries this anti-Marxist theory into the theory of the state. Pashukanis' question casts a doubt upon another premise of Engels', which asserts that "in reality the state is nothing but an instrument of suppression of one class by another" and that "this refers equally to both the democratic republic and the monarchy."[3] Of course, according to Pashukanis, only the bourgeois state "assumes the form of an official state authority."

One can see that Pashukanis fails to understand the Marxist theory of state when he raises the question: ". . . Why is the apparatus of state compulsion not created as a private apparatus of the ruling class"? What else could the apparatus of the "ruling class" be but an apparatus of the ruling class, a machine of suppression and class violence, a form of its "public authority separated from the masses of people"? Pashukanis' doubts are obviously superfluous.

It is interesting to ascertain Lenin's views on this subject. Did he doubt the validity of Engels' theory of the state? It is evident that

[2][See E. Pashukanis and I. Razumovskii, *Noveishye Otkroveniya Karla Kautskogo (Karl Kautsky's Recent Revelations)* (Moscow, 1929), p. 43.]
[3] Preface to Marx's *Grazhdanskaya Voina vo Frantsii* [The Civil War in France] (Moscow, 1923), p. 11.

Lenin entertained a different view than Pashukanis. In *State and Revolution,* Lenin wrote the following on the subject that Pashukanis finds controversial: "Here we have, expressed in all its clearness, the basic idea of Marxism on the question of the historical role and meaning of the state. The state is the product and the manifestation of the *irreconcilability* of class antagonisms. The state arises when, where, and to the extent that class antagonisms *cannot* be objectively reconciled. And, conversely, the existence of the state proves that class antagonisms are irreconcilable."

It is evident that Lenin entertained no doubts concerning Engels' theory of state. . . . Pashukanis not only entertains doubts but attacks Engels' and Lenin's theory and defends Bukharin's theory of "blowing up" the state machine. Even recently (May, 1930) he continued to defend this theory of "blowing up." And in 1927, in one of his articles, he eulogized Bukharin, who, in his opinion, "was absolutely right" and who deserved credit for "a profound revolutionary treatment of the question of blowing up the bourgeois state." Here is what Pashukanis wrote:

> First of all, Bukharin was beyond any doubt absolutely right in stressing with all force the necessity of *blowing up* the bourgeois state machine. In this case Vladimir Illich's contention that Bukharin simply restated the views of anarchists, who want to "abolish" the state, is based on a misunderstanding. Bukharin quite distinctly indicated that, while blowing up the bourgeois state, the workers should organize their state authority (dictatorship).
>
> It is quite clear that Bukharin spoke only about blowing up the bourgeois state and not the state in general, not *any* state as anarchists imagine. Therefore, Vladimir Illich's contention that socialists (Engels in particular), in contrast to anarchists, recognize a "dying away of the state," that is, "the state's gradual falling asleep" after the expropriation of bourgeoisie, clearly misses the point. But, having stressed a correct view on the necessity of destroying—that is, blowing up—the bourgeois state machine, Bukharin (as he himself admitted) did not develop adequately in his writings the problem of the dictatorship of the proletariat and of the forms within which this dictatorship would be materialized.[4]

Pashukanis only recently renounced the theory of "blowing up."[5] Indeed, it would be strange even today to defend a theory that long ago was refuted and condemned.

[4] "Desyatiletie 'Gosudarstva i Revolutsii' Lenina" [The Tenth Anniversary of Lenin's *State and Revolution*], *Revolutsiya Prava,* No. 4 (1927), p. 13.
[5] *Sovetskoe Gosudarstvo i Revolutsiya Prava,* No. 5–6 (1930), p. 9.

# The Marxist Conception of Classes and Law*

## ᴄᴧᴩ  *A. K. Stalgevich*

The problem of the *class nature of law* occupies the central place in the Marxist theory of law. But even Marxists reveal a lack of clarity on this problem. The most vivid example of this is the works of Pashukanis. Stuchka quite rightly noted that the defect of Pashukanis' works lies in "negating, ignoring, or at least belittling the class character of law. . . ."[1]

. . . The obfuscation of the class character of law is especially apparent in his conception of *international law.* . . . Here is what Pashukanis writes concerning this problem in his article "International Law."[2]

With the appearance of the Soviet states in the historical arena, international law acquires a new meaning. It becomes a form of temporary compromise between two antagonistic class systems. This compromise is concluded for a period when one (bourgeois) system is no longer able to secure its exclusive domination and the other (proletarian, socialist) system has not *yet* established its domination. In this sense, I think, one can speak of the international law of the transition period. The meaning of this transition period is that an open struggle (intervention, blockade, nonrecognition) is replaced by a struggle within the framework of "normal" diplomatic relations and treaty arrangements. International law becomes an *interclass* law whereby its adaptation to this new function leads through a whole number of conflicts and crises.

Reference to the compromise between "two antagonistic class systems" and to the interclass character of law as a result of this compromise does not tally with Marx's and Lenin's theory of the irreconcilability of class contradictions. Furthermore . . . , Pashukanis' theory . . . is contradictory to the resolution of the Sixteenth Congress of the C.P.S.U.(B.), which asserts that "intensification of all contradictions within the imperialist system is accompanied by an *intensification of contradictions between the U.S.S.R. and the capitalist world* encircling it."

* *From* "Osnovnye Voprosy Marksistskoi Teorii Prava" [Fundamental Problems of the Marxist Theory of Law], *Sovetskoe Gosudarstvo i Revolutsiya Prava,* No. 10 (1930), pp. 104–7.

[1] *Revolutsiya Prava,* No. 2 (1927), p. 13.

[2] *Entsiklopediya Gosudarstva i Prava* [Encyclopedia of State and Law] (Moscow, 1925–30), II, 862.

. . . The question arises: "How did it happen that Pashukanis committed an error which . . . leads to an opportunist revision of Marxism-Leninism?" In order to answer this question it is necessary to uncover the deep roots of Pashukanis' theory. Primarily, attention must be directed to the conception of classes which appears in his works. While criticizing Kautsky's "new" materialist conception of history, Pashukanis appears as an ardent defender of Bukharin and his anti-Marxist conception of classes. To quote Pashukanis:

> While in fact opposed to Engels' view on the origin of class differentiation, Kautsky pretends to be fighting Bukharin. Thereby he resorts to juggling the facts. While quoting a paragraph from *Historical Materialism* that deals with the significance of the division of labor, Kautsky claims that Bukharin fails to see that the relationships to the means of production are the decisive feature in determining the idea of a social class. On this basis he attributes to Bukharin quite a number of absurd conclusions such as, for example, that workers and employees belong to distinct classes with antagonistic interests. In order to see the absurdity of Kautsky's denunciation, it may suffice to quote the following passage from Bukharin's *Historical Materialism:* "The distinct role of the classes in production is based *on the distribution of the means of production among them"* (3rd ed., p. 57). The gist of the problem is that Bukharin, following Marx, views the relations of production, and also the distribution of production, as a dialectical part of the process of production, whereas Kautsky, following Dühring, separates political and juridical elements of property law from the relations of production.[3]

Does Bukharin's conception of classes and his entire "theory of historical materialism" deserve such an unreserved defense? Could one really defend a conception that is being criticized *even* by Kautsky, a conception that stands no criticism? Could one really assert that Bukharin, "following Marx," understands the problem "dialectically" . . . ? For the sake of clarity we shall present Bukharin's conception of classes, which is so zealously defended by Pashukanis.[4] In his *Theory of Historical Materialism,* Bukharin offers the following definition of a class: "By social classes is understood an aggregate of people who play a similar role in production and in the process of production, stand in the same relationships to other people, whereby these relationships are also expressed in things (means of labor). From this it also follows that, in the process of the distribution of products, each class is united by the same source of income, for the

[3] Pashukanis and Razumovskii, *Noveishye Otkroveniya Karla Kautskogo* [Karl Kautsky's Recent Revelations] (Moscow, 1929), p. 43.
[4] Following Pashukanis, A. Angarov also advanced Bukharin's conception of classes as a Marxist one. See*Revolutsiya Prava*, No. 3 (1927).

270 SOVIET POLITICAL THOUGHT

relations of the distribution of products are determined by the relations of production."[5]

In another place Bukharin states that "classes are primarily groups of persons united by common conditions and a common role in the production process, with all the ensuing consequences regarding the process of distribution."[6] Can such a conception of classes be recognized as a Marxist-Leninist one? Indeed not. Lenin, who furnished a classical definition of classes, *did not agree* with Bukharin's conception. Lenin's observation on the margins of Bukharin's *Economy in the Transition Period* are quite characteristic. They reveal a deep difference between Lenin's and Bukharin's views on classes. In opposition to Bukharin's formulation, Lenin writes: "Classes are *first and foremost* 'groups of persons' (stated inaccurately) which differ from each other by the place they occupy in the social system of production, and differ in such a way that one group is able to appropriate the labor of another."[7]

The main divergence between Lenin's and Bukharin's conceptions of classes lies in that Bukharin's definition leaves out the element of *class exploitation* entirely, that is, the exploitation of one class by another, without which the idea of classes turns into a nonpartisan, "sociological," empty shell. This is why Lenin made an additional note: "Stated simply and precisely (theoretically), he left out *the class struggle.*" And we know that "the main evil of right opportunism is that it breaks with the Leninist understanding of the class struggle and slides down to the point of view of *petty-bourgeois liberalism.*"[8]

Without a correct, that is, Leninist, understanding of *class, class society, and the class struggle,* Bukharin could not help but arrive at the most thorough "sociological" treatment of production relations; from vulgar materialism, that is, naturalism, he arrived at idealism. His formulation of the production relations—by which he understands the "labor coordination of men (regarded as 'living machines') in time and space"—is empty and absurd.

[5] *Teoriya Istoricheskogo Materializma* [The Theory of Historical Materialism] (Moscow, 1929), pp. 325–26.
[6] *Ekonomika Perekhodovogo Perioda* [Economy in the Transition Period] (Moscow, 1920), p. 42.
[7] *Zamechaniya na Knigu Bukharina "Ekonomika Perekhodovogo Perioda"* [Notes on Bukharin's Book *Economy in the Transition Period*] (Moscow, 1920).
[8] Stalin, Speech at the Sixteenth Congress of the C.P.S.U.(B.).

# The Relationship between State and Law: A Criticism of Earlier Interpretations*  ✑  M. Lutskii

It is generally (or almost generally) recognized that Marx's and Lenin's ideas on the subject of law have been most *successfully* systematized and *developed* by Comrade Pashukanis. It should be noted that his principal work, *The General Theory of Law and Marxism,* first published in 1924, has played an immense role *not only* in elaborating a Marxist approach to the problems of law but also in *expanding* the Marxist methodology in general. Like any important work, it was and is of great methodological value. Nevertheless, it seems to us that Pashukanis' theory is grossly *deficient* in the case of a cardinal problem—the problem of the relationship of the state to law.

The problem of the state and law is of extraordinary significance to us. Both law and the state are historical *class* categories. They arose at the same time, and constitute a *unity*. [According to Lenin,] "Law is nothing without an apparatus capable of coercing the observance of legal norms," i.e., without the state. Law, that is to say, a developed law, always has the character of a state. Having devoted a special chapter in his work to this problem, Comrade Pashukanis not only failed to resolve it correctly but, in the very *treatment* of the problem, followed in the steps of the bourgeois "science of law." His "failure" is not at all accidental; it was *predicated* by a completely incorrect, non-Leninist understanding of the nature of the state.

The state is an organization of the *ruling class*. In its very nature the state represents a "class matter." Therefore, "the state in the proper meaning of the term" is as old as class society. This is the elementary truth of revolutionary Marxism. But Comrade Pashukanis thinks differently. He thinks that the state (along with law and morality) is a "form of bourgeois society."[1] Only a bourgeois "political" state is a true state. But what about the precapitalist states? We had better listen to Pashukanis himself. He writes: "Engels looks upon the state as a manifestation of the fact that 'society became hopelessly

* *From* "K Voprosu o Vzaimootnoshenii Prava i Gosudarstva" [On the Problem of the Relationship of State and Law], *Sovetskoe Gosudarstvo i Revolutsiya Prava,* No. 11–12 (1930), pp. 189–93.
    [1] *Obshchaya Teoriya Prava i Marksizm* [The General Theory of Law and Marxism] (3rd ed.; n.p., 1927), p. 111.

entangled in class contradictions. In order that these antagonistic classes with their conflicting economic interests might not consume themselves and society in a sterile struggle, a power, *apparently* standing above society, becomes necessary: a power whose purpose it is to moderate the conflict and keep it within the bounds of "order." And this power arising out of society, but placing itself above it, and increasingly separating itself from it, is the state.' "[2]

This explanation is not quite clear at one point . . . , when Engels says that the state power falls naturally into the hands of the most powerful class, "which by means of the state becomes a politically dominant class." This phrase gives ground for thinking that state power is engendered not as a class power but as something standing above the classes and saving them from disintegration, and that only after its rise does the state power become an object of usurpation. Naturally, such an understanding is contrary to historical facts; we do know that the apparatus of power has everywhere been erected through the power of the dominant class. . . . We think that Engels himself would have been opposed to such an interpretation. But, whatever the case may be, *the formula given by him* nevertheless remains ambiguous. The state arises because otherwise the classes would mutually destroy each other in a fierce struggle and would thereby also destroy society. Consequently, the state appears *at the moment when* neither of the struggling classes can attain a decisive victory (?). In such a case, either the state secures this relationship and then is a supraclass power, which we cannot accept, or it is the result of the victory of a class, in which case society has no need for the state, because, with the decisive victory of one class, the balance is re-established and society is saved. Behind all these controversies one basic question is hidden: "Why does class domination fail to remain what it is, i.e., the factual subordination of one part of the population to another, but assumes the form of official state authority, or, *what amounts to the same,* why does the apparatus of the ruling class fail to become a *private* apparatus of the ruling class but separates itself from the latter and assumes the form *of an impersonal apparatus of public* power, separate from society?"[3]

First of all, it is quite incomprehensible why Comrade Pashukanis assumes that there is need for a state only "when neither of the struggling classes can attain a decisive victory," and if one class has attained the victory, "the state becomes unnecessary to society." On the contrary, *historically,* one class becomes victorious, i.e., *dominant.* In order to keep the exploited classes in submission, this dominant

[2] *Ibid.,* p. 93.        [3] *Ibid.*

class *organizes itself* into a state, i.e., into a *special* body of "armed men, separated from the people," into "an institution of public power which is no longer *identical* with the population, organizing itself as an armed power," into a "power alienating itself from society and standing above it."

This seems to be clear: The state, from its very inception, is engendered as a "power alienating itself from society," as a *special* body of armed men, "separated from the population." "The domination of a class does not remain what it is," because otherwise "the antagonistic classes . . . would consume themselves and society in a sterile struggle." Therefore, a "power, standing apparently above society," is necessary. All this is not clear to Pashukanis, because he confuses two problems: the *alienation* of state power (which is characteristic of all state powers), and the *public character* of this alienation (i.e., the specific, concrete manifestation of the alienation within a bourgeois state). This is why Comrade Pashukanis assumes that only a bourgeois state is "a state in the proper meaning of the term." The problem of the state (of the "true" state) in precapitalist social formations disappears because [according to Comrade Pashukanis] only in a capitalist society does "the apparatus of state compulsion . . . assume the form of an impersonal apparatus of *public* power separate from society."

We should note parenthetically that Comrade Pashukanis' train of thought coincides with the thinking of the reactionary jurist Hauriou, who writes as follows: "The phenomenon of state is being viewed as a special, distinct, and limited phenomenon; not every political organization deserves the name of state. By a specific meaning of the term, a state comes into being only when a nation has organized itself into a civil society, i.e., when the political power of domination *separated itself from private property* and assumed the appearance of a public power."[4] In our opinion, however, the oriental despotic states, Roman republics, Athenian democracies, and medieval feudal states were also "states in the proper meaning of the term," i.e., organizations of the dominant class, power "separated from society" and "standing above it."

Comrade Pashukanis' erroneous and opportunistic treatment of the problem of the state and law is connected with the non-Marxist interpretation of the nature of the state. Here, in terms of the treatment of the problem, he simply followed in the steps of the bourgeois science. . . .

. . . . . . .

[4] *Les Principes du droit public* (n.p., 1910), p. 5.

The state and law came into being *at the same time*. From their very beginning they constituted a *unity*. Even in an Asiatic society, which was the first class society in history, law had a clearly defined character (e.g., the famous Code of Hammurabi). This "unity" appears in an especially vivid form during the intensification of the contradictions in a class society. The best example of this is the legal regulation of the imperialist states (particularly during and after the First World War). On the other hand, the active, revolutionary role of the state and law acquires a special significance in a country with a proletarian dictatorship. Although *the Soviet state* is no longer a "state in the proper meaning of the term," it is nevertheless a state, i.e., an organization of the dominant class, of the working class, which, through the instrumentality of its state, builds up a socialist economy. We are not at all inclined to view the state as a "shell" within which the classes cooperate, as does Comrade Bukharin. The Soviet state is *inconceivable without Soviet law,* i.e., without the law, which is qualitatively different from bourgeois law, and which is withering away but, as yet, is not quite dead and still comprises the elements of legal fetishism.

It is well known that in the first phase of communism the "narrow horizon of the bourgeois law" will be preserved. Consequently, only admitted opportunists are inclined to underestimate the immense role of Soviet law, of revolutionary legality, etc. . . .

# Part II ∿ Stalinist Authoritarianism

# Introduction ᓄ

Initial attempts to impose authoritarianism and uniformity in the sphere of Soviet political thought were made in the late twenties. After defeating the "right" and the "left" deviations, Stalin asserted himself as the unquestionable leader of the Communist party. Stalin's idea of the structurally and ideologically centralized party—exercising dictatorship over all aspects of life—called for the introduction of a uniform set of beliefs, binding upon all members of Soviet society.

Stalin stated his intention to bring about ideological uniformity in a speech delivered at the "Conference of Marxist Students of the Agrarian Question," on December 27, 1929. His principal argument was "that theoretical thought is not keeping pace with our practical successes, that there is a certain gap between our practical successes and the development of our theoretical thought."[1] In other words, Stalin was alluding to the conflict between the policy objectives pursued by the Party and the political, legal, and economic theories advocated by Soviet social thinkers. He attributed this conflict to the "bourgeois" influence upon Soviet "theoretical thought" and concluded that only a "merciless struggle" against this influence would assure the victory of socialism.

Following Stalin's pronouncement, several conferences on the theory of law and state were arranged, first in Georgia and the Ukraine, and then on the national level, "The First All-Union Congress of Marxist Legal Theorists," in January of 1931. As officially formulated, the aim of these conferences was to "bring theory into conformity with practice." More specifically, their goal was to ascertain (·1) which theorists were willing to support the Party's policies and ideology, (2) which could be persuaded or pressured into supporting the Party line, and (3) which were determined to oppose the Party line and hence would have to be treated as "class enemies."

The tone of the All-Union Congress was set by Pashukanis—the principal speaker. He subjected his own views as well as the views of other Soviet writers to the "bolshevik criticism," denounced them as "abstract," "formalist," and "bourgeois" deviations from Marxism, and urged the participants of the Congress to adhere strictly to the Party's policy.

The All-Union Congress laid the groundwork for the "principle of

---

[1] *Problems of Leninism* (Moscow, 1954), p. 389.

partisanship." From then on, the leaders of the Communist party assumed a monopoly for determining "the true meaning" of Marxism-Leninism and hence of the Marxist method. The description of social reality advanced by Soviet writers was expected to conform with the standards set up by the political authority. Furthermore, Soviet writers were expected to unconditionally support, propagandize, and justify the Party's policies.

The adoption of the new policy toward Soviet writers led eventually to an almost complete stagnation of social thought. The literature published from then on reveals a remarkable absence of treatment of the basic problems with which it had previously been concerned. Moreover, it is full of mutual denunciations, self-criticism, and confessions of "anti-Marxist mistakes."

However, judging by official pronouncements, the regimentation of Soviet social thinkers was not fully successful. For example, in 1937, Andrey Vyshinskii argued that many writers who "have repeatedly acknowledged their mistakes . . . did it only to continue the advocacy of pseudo-Marxist and anti-Leninist views in a more subtle form."[2] These writers, in his judgment, aimed at "discrediting and undermining the Soviet science of law." Furthermore, by "preaching harmful, anti-Party 'theories' of the dying away of state and law," they sought "to disarm the working class vis-à-vis its enemies and to undermine the state power of socialism."[3]

It was with the purpose of eliminating these and similar deviations from the Party line that "The First Conference of Learned Workers-Jurists" was called in 1938. Vyshinskii, then Deputy Attorney General, acted as the spokesman for the Party at the Conference. With the exception of Stalgevich—who in the name of Marxism contested Vyshinskii's interpretation of law and the state but at the end of the Conference declared himself in agreement with him—there was no opposition to Vyshinskii. The writers who had played leading roles in the twenties and early thirties were not among the participants; most of them had been purged as "enemies of the people." Vyshinskii did not hesitate to admit this by stating that the Conference was called because of "the necessity to make a preliminary summary of the period just passed, during which enemies, wreckers, and traitors were purged from our ranks."[4] The next task, he continued, was "to purge

---

[2] *K Polozheniyu na Fronte Pravovoi Teorii* [On the Situation at the Front of Legal Theory] (Moscow, 1937), p. 5.

[3] *Ibid.*

[4] Akademiya Nauk, Institut Prava, *Osnovnye Zadachi Nauki Sovetskogo Sotsialisticheskogo Prava* [Basic Tasks of the Science of Soviet Socialist Law] (Moscow, 1938), p. 8.

various hostile, anti-Marxist, and anti-Leninist views from our theory of law and to complete construction of the science of Soviet socialist law on the basis of the rich heritage of Marx, Engels, Lenin, and the brilliant works of Stalin."[5]

The purge of "anti-Marxist" views from Soviet political thought failed to be fully successful. Commenting on this subject in 1948, Vyshinskii attributed the failure to "the survival of capitalism in the consciousness of the people, especially in the consciousness of the people who have selected ideological work as their profession."[6] At the same time he introduced a note of pessimism by stating that "these survivals are historically connected with the old society and, unfortunately, are not subject to an easy and rapid liquidation."[7]

On the same occasion, in 1948, Vyshinskii castigated Soviet writers for an excessive use of "the method of 'scientific study' which could be designated as 'quotology.' "[8] By this "method" he had in mind the fact that Soviet writers were restricting themselves almost exclusively to quotations from classics (primarily from Stalin's works) and to making innocuous comments about them. To counteract excessive dogmatism, Vyshinskii urged Soviet writers to familiarize themselves with Western social thought and to utilize the "scientific heritage of the old society."

Adoption of Vyshinskii's suggestions broadened the scope of topics in the years to come. A voluminous literature appeared dealing with Western political, legal, and philosophical thought. This literature was critical of Western thought—at times tendentiously and at times justifiably. Nevertheless, Soviet readers were now able to take at least a limited look at modern Western thought.

Speaking of substantive problems, during the Stalin period, Soviet attitudes toward various social phenomena—but especially toward the state, law, and morality—underwent a complete metamorphosis. The reader will recall that in the early twenties law was viewed as an intrinsically bourgeois and hence evil phenomenon. By the end of the twenties some writers advanced the thesis that Soviet law had a new "socialist content" and hence was not as evil as bourgeois law. In the thirties it became fashionable to argue that in addition to its "socialist content," Soviet law had acquired a "socialist form" and that, consequently, it represented a phenomenon entirely different from

---

[5] *Ibid.*

[6] "O Nekotorykh Voprosakh Teorii Gosudarstva i Prava" [On Some Problems of the Theory of State and Law], *Sovetskoe Gosudarstvo i Pravo,* No. 6 (1948), p. 4.

[7] *Ibid.*

[8] *Ibid.*

bourgeois law. Then, in the late forties, a contention was advanced that Soviet law had lost its coercive character, because it was obeyed voluntarily by the overwhelming majority of the Soviet people. This view led eventually, in the early fifties, to the identification of Soviet law with freedom, with natural law, with universal justice and communist morality.

Another, and perhaps even more significant change that took place during the Stalin period was the revision of "the Marxist method," which was discussed in the Introduction (pp. 15–21). This change came "from above," at the initiative of the political authority. Stalin, who enjoyed a monopoly in the interpretation of "Marxism-Leninism," revised some of its basic tenets beyond recognition. It is fair to say that Stalin did to Marx and Engels what they had done to Hegel, namely, he turned them upside down.

# Georgian Interlude* ∼ Excerpts from a
# Conference on Law

CHAIRMAN BOLOTNIKOV: Comrades, permit me to declare open the Joint Conference of the Georgian Society of Marxist Theorists of State . . . and of the representatives of the Georgian Institute of the Soviet Construction and Law. . . .

[The purpose of the Conference is:] (1) to determine the dislocation, that is, the distribution of forces on the legal front in Soviet Georgia, and (2) to account for the Marxist forces operating here in the legal sector.

. . . Keeping our objective in mind, we shall be able to reveal our own forces and also the forces of our adversaries. At the very beginning I should make the point clear that the various theories to be criticized here are anti-Marxist and hence ideologically harmful. Consequently, we are using the term "adversary" in its literal sense.

We consider the authors of the books to be criticized here to be fully devoted to the Soviet authority; however, while bitterly struggling for the Marxist-Leninist world outlook in all social spheres, we should and will struggle against all manifestations alien to Marxism—against all idealist and pseudoscientific concepts—regardless of their source.

* From *Protiv Idealizma v Pravovoi Mysli Sovetskoi Gruzii* [Against Idealism in the Legal Thought of the Soviet Georgia], Stenographic notes from the discussion of A. I. Gegenav's paper "Legal Thought in the Soviet Georgia," ed. A. A. Bolotnikov (Eku-Tiflis, 1931).

"Georgian Interlude" consists of excerpts from the Joint Conference of the Georgian Society of the Marxist Theorists of State and the representatives of The Georgian Institute of Soviet Construction and Law. The Conference took place on October 25–26, 1930. A similar conference was conducted in the Ukraine in 1930. These two were followed by the First All-Union Congress of Marxist Legal Theorists, which met in Moscow, January 7–14, 1931.

As indicated in the introduction to Part II, these conferences were called at the initiative of the political authority, which sought either to persuade or coerce Soviet writers to adopt the Party line. Initially, many participants in these conferences assumed that they were attending an academic forum for the purpose of impassioned discussions. They soon discovered, however, that the conferences were intended to serve as a "battle-ground" for "the proletariat's struggle against its class enemies." The discussions that followed were conducted "in the spirit of bolshevik criticism and self-criticism." They were filled with passion, drama, and threats. It is hoped that the following excerpts from the Georgian Conference will give the reader some insight into the atmosphere that prevailed during these discussions.

. . . . . . .

GEGENAV: The theory of law is a class ideology. As rightly stated by Engels, juridical world outlook is the classic world outlook of the bourgeois society, and the religious outlook was the classic world outlook of the feudal society. Consequently, in the present epoch of intensified class struggle our class enemies are, naturally, in a favorable position in the field of the theory of law, because this field of ideology has not yet been adequately subjected to Marxist criticism. Hence, Stuchka's thesis that the revolution of law is merely beginning is to a considerable degree valid even at the present time.

[Gegenav continues to trace law to its "bourgeois origin"; he then turns to criticizing Surladze's *Force and Law* (1925), in which the author succumbed to the influence of "the pluralist ontology of Husserl." Gegenav then subjects Vacheishvili's *Kelsen's Theory of Law and State* (1929) to criticism.]

This book is characteristic of the developments taking place in the field of the theory of law in Georgia. . . . Professor Vacheishvili presents Kelsen uncritically and without objecting to his theories. I think that such a presentation of Kelsen can be considered to be nothing but the popularization of Kelsen's views, and his views belong to the arsenal of the bourgeois philosophy of law. In fact, this book . . . is an apology of Kelsenianism. . . .

DZHAPARIDZE: . . . As you know Pashukanis was regarded as the most serious and the most consistent theorist of Marxist law until now. But what do we see now? Against him are a whole number of Marxists—Liberman, Reztsov, and especially Stalgevich, who denounce Pashukanis for his subjectivism which has nothing in common with Marxism. At the same time, Stalgevich denounces Dotsenko for his idealism of the purest type—and so it goes on endlessly. Such is the present condition of the Marxist theory of law. . . . Naturally, Marxist thought in the sphere of law has barely started and it is obvious that its development will require a more business-like and calmer atmosphere. . . .

VACHEISHVILI: . . . I maintain that the bourgeois theory of law is more elaborate at present than the Soviet Marxist theory of law. Anyone who follows bourgeois legal ideology and compares it with the Marxist will agree with me. This is so because the Marxist theory of law is only now in the process of being formulated. Undoubtedly, the founders of Marxism provided the main principles of this system, but as yet we lack a finite system of law. What I am saying is also being agreed to by such representatives of the Marxist theory of law as

Pashukanis and Stalgevich. Marx brilliantly developed the political economy and sociological conceptions, but he did not exhaust all the theoretical problems of law and state. Someone may object to what I am saying: "Please, Marx offers plenty in his *Capital* and in *A Critique of Political Economy.*" Naturally he does; he has shown us the way to construct the Marxist theory of law. I fully agree with this, but this does not mean that we already have a finite system of law. One who sees what is going on in Russian Marxist literature must agree that the Marxist theory of law is in a stage of being formulated at present. The works of Pashukanis, Stalgevich, Dotsenko, Razumovskii, and others are the best proof of this. One must follow and study Russian Marxist literature. I have studied it to the best of my abilities, and I do believe that the Marxist theory of law does not constitute a finite conception. . . .

. . . If Pashukanis, one of the finest jurists in the Marxist camp, is being denounced at present as a thinker who deviates from the Marxist concept of law and who presumably fails to understand the Marxist theory, then what could be said of me—I do not even claim to be thoroughly familiar with the Marxist theory.

Now I turn to . . . the work on Kelsen. In 1929 I had the misfortune to have written a book on him. It was written in the Georgian language. Its name is: *Kelsen's Theory of Law and State.* Why did I select Kelsen? It may appear that I entertained certain sympathies with Kelsen, but that is not true. I do not have any sympathies for Kelsen. I selected him as the most vivid illustration of the trend known as normativism.

Why have I been interested in normativism? Normativism is the best example of the results to which the juridical, or normative, method leads. My book on Kelsen is not simply a presentation of Kelsen or, as Comrade Gegenav said, a popularization of Kelsen. . . . Had Comrade Gegenav read it, and especially had he read the fifth chapter carefully, he would have noticed that there is no popularization of Kelsen. I presented there a comparative evaluation of the sociological and normative methods. I have insisted upon the use of the sociological method during my entire theoretical career and in all my books. . . .

LISOVSKII: . . . Comrade Naneishvili does not pretend to be a Marxist—this is very good. However, this does not give him the right to assert that it is impossible to deduce a picture of the superstructure from the notion of the basis. He gave us the following example: "A house is being built; I see its foundation but I don't know what its superstructure will be." I don't know what an architect would say on this subject but I think that he would say the following: seeing the foundation of a building, I cannot describe all the details of its superstructure but I can say whether it will be a factory or an apartment house; I can say whether it will be a one-floor or a multistory structure, whether it will be made from bricks or concrete. (*A voice from the audience*: Because there is a blueprint.)

In the field of sociology, Marxists regard the fact that the superstructure is fully dependent upon the basis as self-evident, therefore, that it is possible to define the superstructure in terms of its basis. I may not be a musician, but I can determine the character of the music of a society once its [economic] basis has been pointed out to me. (*A voice from the audience*: Correct!)

. . . . . . .

NANEISHVILI: [In response to the denunciation that he succumbed to Kelsen's normative theory of law, which is "a typical fascist ideology of the decaying bourgeoisie."] . . . You spoke the whole time of Kelsen, but you are not familiar with him. You don't know that, speaking of the origin of law, Kelsen published a work—*Wesen der Demokratie*—in which he acknowledges the fact that law is undoubtedly a product of class struggle.

And if you don't believe me, tomorrow I will bring for you the brochure. What I want to say is that you are accusing me of such things that I cannot even speak about, because what you have found in my book is not written there. You are, indeed, a clever man, and you have made the audience laugh, but laughing is not enough! A book must be understood, and you have failed. (*Talakhadze*: But I quoted from it!) Quoting is not enough. Anyone who is literate can quote, but this is not sufficient to understanding the complex problems. I want to tell you one thing: if you want to chase us out of the Institute, then tell us—we'll go.

However, if you want us to collaborate with you . . . , then give us an opportunity to hear *our own* phrases . . . and not the phrases that you attribute to us. For, using your approach, it is easy to destroy not only me but Kant, Hegel, and even Marx himself. If you criticize Marx, not on the basis of what he has said but according to what you attribute to him, then, you must admit, it will be easy to take him apart (*Talakhadze*: Would you perhaps quote any phrase from Marx that could be easily criticized?) You know quite well that the atmosphere of yesterday's discussions is quite different from that of today. Yesterday I listened to papers that were correct in all respects. I factually believed that you invited us here to learn something from a pure academic discussion of various points of view. But, strictly speaking, this has not been the case—you have failed to accomplish this, Comrade Talakhadze. I appreciated yesterday's lecture by Comrade Lisovskii. But today's personal attack upon me by Comrade Talakhadze I consider to be inadmissible in an academic forum. (*Applause.*)

TALAKHADZE: Then it is doubtful that you will learn anything at all, if you adopt such a view.

. . . . . . .

TUMANOV: . . . We Marxists assert that law is carried out in practice by means of coercion and violence, because all law is a class law, and the law of the class without coercion is not a law. . . .
. . . I would like to make Comrade Vacheishvili understand that in our country of proletarian dictatorship, in the epoch of an intensified class struggle . . . , a calm, academic presentation of the view of our enemies is unsuitable. . . . Indeed, we should be familiar with the views of our enemies. . . . But you, [Comrade Vacheishvili] a participant in this struggle, must yourself declare on whose side you are: with Kelsen or with us.

. . . . . . .

BARIGYAN: From the Marxist point of view, everything is historical. Historical is not only the content but also the form. We are frequently being told that Marxism is merely one of the many possible points of view. But this is pure relativism. We are not merely defending Marxism but we consider it to be the only correct and scientific world outlook.

CHAIRMAN BOLOTNIKOV: [Concluding remarks] . . . We hope that the honorable professors will pay attention to our comradely advice. We have no desire to threaten anyone. But we think that our criticism will definitely exert an influence upon them—that it will impel them to acknowledge unequivocally their theoretical errors and to tell us to what extent they adhere to the views subjected to criticism here. If the criticized authors . . . are ready "to die for the last letter of their works," they will remain our enemies, and henceforth we'll be struggling against them mercilessly, resolutely, and everywhere. However, if they admit their errors, if they do not insist stubbornly and dogmatically upon their anti-Marxist positions, we are ready to help them. We are modest people, and although we do not intend in any way to lecture professors, we believe that we are capable of helping some of them to rid themselves of Adam's weakness.
With your permission, the Conference is closed.

# The First All-Union Congress of Marxist Legal Theorists* ☙ *A. Viktorov*

The First All-Union Congress of the workers in the field of the theory of state, Soviet construction, and law (which took place in Moscow on January 14, 1931) and the Ukrainian Conference that preceded it are of tremendous significance. The period of the full-scale socialist offensive against capitalist elements gives us an opportunity to examine the fighting capability of our theoretical front.

During the period of an intensified class struggle and an intense socialist reconstruction of the country, all fundamental political and theoretical questions are stated bluntly. The Party, in the process of struggle, exposes all manifestations of resistance to the large-scale and victorious offensive of socialism in the economic, political, and theoretical sectors. The Party mercilessly exposes all rotten, opportunist, non-bolshevik and anti-Leninist manifestations in the field of theory—all manifestations that, in one form or another, are an expression of the bourgeois or petty-bourgeois influence upon the proletarian ideology; be they assiduously veiled or concealed. (From the resolution of the Conference at the Institute of Red Professors [The section on philosophy and natural sciences], *Pravda,* January 26, 1931.)

This period imposes a series of new tasks upon the Marxist workers in the field of the theory of state, Soviet construction and law. It opens new, broad perspectives and calls for the elaboration of many significant problems. In accomplishing these tasks, we should be guided by the instructions given to us . . . by Comrade Stalin during the Sixteenth Congress of the C.P.S.U.(B.) : "It is clear that we are no longer in the transition period in its old meaning, having entered the period of direct and large-scale socialist construction on the whole front. It is clear that we have already entered the period of socialism, because the socialist sector holds in its hands all levers of the national economy, although we are still far from having constructed a socialist society and from having liquidated class antagonisms." And further: ". . . we are not yet liquidating NEP, because private trade and capitalist elements still remain; but we are certainly liquidating its initial stage, developing its second phase—the present phase— which is its final stage."

* *From* "Pershyi Vsesoyuznyi Zizd Marksystiv-Derzhavnykiv" [The First All-Union Congress of Marxist Legal Theorists], *Revolutsiine Pravo,* No. 1 (1931), pp. 10–12. (Written in the Ukrainian language.)

And that means that the significance and the role of the Soviet state—which is the basic lever used by the proletariat in the process of a bitter class struggle for the reconstruction of the economy and for the realization of the transition to socialism—is increasing enormously. The socialist offensive on the whole front calls for a fundamental reorganization of the ranks and the methods of work by all organs of the proletarian dictatorship. As the reorganization of the organs of the proletarian dictatorship unfolds, new demands are placed upon us: to become more fully armed with the Marxist-Leninist theory; to examine the existing conditions more thoroughly; and to steadfastly adhere to the Party line.

More acute today than ever before are such problems as the necessity to struggle, most bitterly, for the purity of the Marxist-Leninist theory of the dictatorship of the proletariat and to fight against all anti-Marxist and anti-Leninist trends, which have become more active and which aim to disarm the proletariat theoretically and hence politically. In his lecture at the Congress, Comrade Pashukanis cited an entire series of cases dealing with the disguised or obvious advocacy of the bourgeois-democratic views and world outlook. This places the Marxist-Leninist science under an obligation to be more vigilant and prepared to act most forcefully.

However, in order to be able to act against the bourgeois-juridical world outlook, against the representatives of the old, bourgeois professoriate, it is necessary first to eradicate various deviations among Marxists themselves from the Party's general line. We know quite well that all manifestations of opportunism—all rightists and leftists deviationists—utilize theory primarily for the purpose of formulating opportunist platforms.

What is, for example, the difference between the right and the left deviation in the field of theory? It is a rejection of the materialist dialectics, which makes a comprehension of law-governed complexities in the transition period possible. Those who reject materialist dialectics cannot understand the processes involved in the class struggle and, moreover, cannot see the elements, contradictions, and phases involved in it. This results in the loss of the revolutionary perspective and in capitulation if confronted with difficulties. Specifically, in the field of the theory of state and law, the right-opportunist deviation denies that class interests are irreconcilable and advocates the subsiding of the class struggle. This leads to belittling the role of the state, to yielding to market spontaneity, to the theory of the blending of the kulaks into socialism, and to a liberal interpretation of Soviet law and revolutionary legality. Such views—representing the ideology of the kulaks in its pure form—are encountered daily in practical work.

The characteristic feature of the second variety of opportunism— i.e., the methodology of the "left" deviation—is that "leftists" withdraw from the existing reality with all its complexities and objective contradictions and arrive at pure abstractions. Furthermore, their attitude leads to their surrender if confronted with difficulties. . . . Specifically, speaking of the problems of state and law, the "leftist" excesses manifest themselves in relying exclusively upon administrative pressure: in applying violence against the middle peasant; in the slogan to liquidate the Soviets; and, in general, in the condemnation of the Soviet apparatus.

In his speech "Twenty Years of Construction of the Soviet State,"[1] Comrade Kaganovich has brilliantly illustrated how Communists can slide down to the methodological positions of the bourgeois-juridical theory:

There is a book—*The Soviet Constitution*, by Malitskii. Comrade Malitskii uses a bourgeois-juridical method for the purpose of analyzing the Soviet Constitution. His analysis is restricted exclusively to the legal sphere. Consequently, he arrives at the conclusion that "the Soviet republic is a state of law, that it functions within the framework of a legal regime." Furthermore, "The subordination of all organs of the state authority to the rule of law is known as a 'legal regime,' and the state that practices a legal regime is known as a 'state under law.' "

One can hardly fail to see that the non-Marxist thesis advanced by comrade Malitskii is both confusing and harmful. For we reject the idea of a state under law as inapplicable even to a bourgeois state. As Marxists, we regard the bourgeois state—which is disguised in the form of law, democracy, and formal equality—as being essentially nothing but a bourgeois dictatorship. People who pretend to be Marxists and seriously speak about the state under law—and, moreover, who apply the idea of "the state under law" to the *Soviet* state—think like bourgeois legal theorists and deviate from the Marxist-Leninist theory of state.

Comrade Kaganovich's illustration underlines the tremendous need for uprooting such deviations among Marxists themselves, because such views are not restricted to Comrade Malitskii alone. They are entertained by other Communists—Magerovskii, Reikhel, Steklov, and others. Such views obliterate and distort the class essence of the proletarian dictatorship, obfuscate the fundamental difference between the Soviet and the bourgeois states, and seek to transplant to the Soviet soul the bourgeois ideas of "the state under law."

From this background we can see rather clearly the tasks with

[1] *Sovetskoe Gosudarstvo i Revolutsiya Prava*, No. 1 (1930).

which Marxists—that is, workers in the field of state, Soviet construction, and law—are confronted. One could summarize these tasks as follows: to pay careful attention to the distribution of the forces of our class enemies; to study their tactics in the class struggle; and to elaborate—on the basis of the Party's general line—the correct methods to [be used in the] struggle against them.

However, to be able to mobilize the Marxist forces for the fulfillment of these tasks, Marxist theorists must first of all recognize, examine, and overcome their own errors. The Congress quite correctly noted that the criticism and self-criticism of these errors, which at times are very serious, was inadequate on the part of some comrades. Both the All-Ukrainian Conference and the All-Union Congress were conducted under the banner of true bolshevik self-criticism, which gives the assurance that progress will be made in the future. And progress—in conformity with Comrade Stalin's instructions given during the Conference of The Marxist Students of the Agrarian Question—signifies the following: it is inadmissible to separate theory from practice; the struggle against the bourgeois-juridical world outlook and against the idealist trends that are hostile to Marxism-Leninism cannot be relaxed even for a second. Applied to our own ranks, this means that *the struggle must be conducted on two fronts:* against deviations from the correct Marxist-Leninist line and against mechanistic distortions. This struggle must be conducted on the basis of a broad and profound scientific self-criticism.

# Legal Ideology* ⸂⸃ *M. Maryasin*

The great socialist advance on all fronts causes tremendous resistance of class forces hostile to the proletariat. Recently, in *Pravda,* we read about the perfidious assassination . . . of Chepikov, a shockworker and propagandist. This is but one of the manifestations of the vengeance of class enemies against enthusiasts of socialist construction.

Such occurrences are not unique. The intensification of the class struggle and the general activation of the forces that are antagonistic to the proletariat manifest themselves in the popularization of opportunistic trends that seek to distort the revolutionary content of the Marxist-Leninist science. This struggle takes place on the entire ideological front.

In the field of law, and especially in the field of criminal law, we are confronted once again with disguised and frequently even open attempts to revive legal ideology. At the Conference of Marxist Jurists, which has recently ended, Comrade Vinokurov presented his theses, which reflect sentiments that are hostile to us. Proceeding with false theoretical assumptions, Comrade Vinokurov quite naturally arrived at practical propositions that are false, alien, and hostile to us. For example, he asserts that in the field of criminal law we should revert to the theory of free will, guilt, etc.

We shall first dwell on the theoretical presuppositions underlying Comrade Vinokurov's views. In his second thesis, he asserts: " . . . to each form of the relations of production in a class society corresponds a clearly defined form of legal ideology. . . ." Is this assertion true? Is it true that each class society has its own ideology? Is a class society without legal ideology conceivable? Vinokurov answers that it is inconceivable.

In fact, competent and authoritative sources furnish a different answer. Thus, Engels, in his article "Juridical Socialism," which was first published in Russian in 1923,[1] writes the following concerning the ideology of feudal society: "The world outlook of the medieval ages was primarily theological. . . . The church possessed approximately one third of the land in each country. It was a great power in the feudal organization. In addition, the clergy was the only educated

* From "Pravna Ideolohiya" [Legal Ideology], *Revolutsiine Pravo* (Kharkov, 1931), No. 4–5, pp. 235–38. (Written in the Ukrainian language.)
[1] *Pod Znamenem Marksizma,* No. 1.

class. This was responsible for the fact *that church dogma was both the starting point and foundation of all thinking.* Jurisprudence, natural science, philosophy, and all other knowledge were evaluated according to their conformity with the teaching of the church."[2]

We see that the church's dogmas were political axioms as well. Biblical pronouncements were at the same time laws applied in courts. In the hands of priests, politics and jurisprudence, as well as every other science, are merely branches of theology. Hence, we see that there was a class society—feudalism—without legal ideology. Moreover, the world outlook of this society was "primarily theological." How then, could one make assertions similar to those advanced by Comrade Vinokurov?

What is the source of legal ideology? What are the reasons for its appearance? It is well known that an additional power—the bourgeoisie—was developing in the womb of feudal society. At a certain stage of its development the bourgeois class took a stand against big landowners. This class, producing and selling commodities, could not be satisfied with the feudal mode of production which was based on self-consumption. Equally unsatisfactory to the new class was the old religious world outlook that was suitable for feudal lords. There was a need for something else. Thus, "a new world outlook, which became the *classical* world outlook of the bourgeoisie, namely, the juridical world outlook," came into being.[3]

What is the essence of this juridical world outlook or, what amounts to the same, this legal ideology? Earlier, all social and economic relationships were viewed as being deduced from church dogmas. Now, they are based on law and are viewed as having been created by the state. As stated by Engels, ". . . human law replaced divine law; state replaced the church."[4] It follows then that juridical world outlook, that is, legal ideology, appeared on the stage of history *as the classical world outlook of the bourgeoisie* and not at all, as Comrade Vinokurov contends, as an ideology characteristic of all classes.

Gradually, the view arises that law has an independent existence— law at all times and in all countries determines both economic and social relationships. Legal fetishism appears, becomes stronger and more widespread. What is the source of this illusion? Marx, explaining the origin of commodity fetishism in the first volume of *Capital,* demonstrates how in man's eyes social relationships acquire a fantastic form of the relationships between things, in the same way as light from an object is perceived by us as the objective form of something

[2] *Ibid.*, p. 51; my italics—M. M.     [3] *Ibid.*     [4] *Ibid.*

outside the eye itself and not as the subjective excitation of our optic nerve:

> Highly atomized relations between people in their social process of production lead to the fact that their social relations of production, which are beyond their control and conscious individual activity, acquire material character, and therefore all products of their labor acquire the form of commodities. . . .
> This I call the fetishism which attaches itself to the products of labor, as soon as they are produced as commodities, and which is therefore inseparable from the production of commodities.

It follows then that relations between people appear as relations between things. This is the objective source of the mystification of human relations. The autonomy of commodity producers is responsible for the fact that material relations between men become legal relations. Commodity acquires a value only in the exchange:

"Possessors of two commodities must have the desire to exchange their commodities and hence to recognize each other as private owners.

"Possessors of labor power and possessors of money meet on the market and *make a mutual agreement* as two *equal persons,* who differ one from another only in that one buys and the other sells" (my italics—M.M.).

Universality of commodity relations leads to universality of legal form. Commodity fetishism is accompanied by juridical fetishism. In connection with the division of labor, the need arises for professional jurists. To them, "The reflection of economic relations in the form of legal principles is such that it stands on its head. A lawyer imagines that he operates with a priori principles, whereas they are merely economic reflections. Hence, everything stands on its head."[5]

Such is the process of the rise and development of legal ideology. This process will last as long as the mode of material production is restricted, as long as antagonism exists between the forces of production and the relations of production, and as long as capitalism exists. Mysticism will disappear only after the forms of production have been changed. As Marx pointed out in *Capital,* "The whole mystery of commodities, all the magic and necromancy that surrounds the products of labor as long as they take the form of commodities, therefore, vanishes as soon as we come to other forms of production."

The same is true of legal ideology, that is, of legal fetishism. Now, it should be easy to resolve the question of whether or not the prole-

---

[5] Marx, Letter to Conrad Schmidt, October 27, 1890.

tariat needs legal ideology. The answer is that the proletariat does not need legal ideology. The working class, which has no property, cannot find an explanation of its position in the juridical illusions of the bourgeoisie. On the contrary, these illusions obliterate its actual position. The proletariat can acquire knowledge of its social position only if it examines the existing reality without juridical glasses. The new world outlook, which corresponds to the condition of the life and struggle of the proletariat, was furnished by Karl Marx in his materialist theory of history. As pointed out by Engels, "This proletarian world outlook marches triumphantly throughout the world." Hence, the world outlook of the proletariat is not legal ideology; rather, it is a materialist theory of history.

The inexperienced proletariat could seek a means for its struggle in juridical thinking only during the period of its feebleness. Thus, the first organization of the working class and their theorists, who operated on a juridical ground, on the "ground of law," sought to provide the proletariat with a special "legal ground" that was distinct from the legal ground of the bourgeoisie. They sought to expand and supplement juridical equality with social equality; they demanded that the workers be given the full product of their labor—but all this in the framework of bourgeois society!

Quite naturally, *being exclusively on the ground of law* and rejecting political struggle, they rejected the class struggle at the same time. Some of them appealed to a sense of justice, whereas others appealed to a sense of humanitarianism. In defending or rather attempting to defend interests of the working class, they defended themselves from the only conceivable form of action for this class—the class struggle.

Consequently, attempts to impose the juridical world outlook on us, in one form or another, are attempts to put us back into preceding stages; it is a desire to entangle the proletariat in a bourgeois world outlook and to feed it with bourgeois idealism, which means disarming the proletariat. Nevertheless, there are still some people, even under conditions of the dictatorship of the proletariat, who have not yet renounced juridical ideology and who suggest that the proletariat should make use of this ideology. Comrade Vinokurov's theses are an example of such a juridical world outlook. They are an example of clear, pure-will idealism.

Vinokurov, as we have indicated earlier, thinks that each class society has its own legal ideology. From this it follows that the proletariat, under conditions of its dictatorship, also has its own legal ideology, that is to say, the proletariat has the same ideology that was designated by Engels as the classic world outlook of the bourgeoisie.

This is exactly what Vinokurov asserts. In his eleventh thesis we find a conclusion that was implied in the second thesis: "Legal categories —freedom of will, juridical responsibility, intention, negligence, etc., which in the period of monopolistic capitalism were thrown overboard by fascist theories of law—should be revived in Soviet criminal law."

Comrade Vinokurov seeks to transform our open, undisguised dictatorship of the proletariat into an unpretentious lady veiled in legal mist. This, indeed, results in a paradox. Capitalist societies discard freedom of will, etc., as obsolete ideas and we, while being their principal opponents, hastily pick them up.

As another illustration, we would like to quote the views of Fingert and Shirvindt, stated in a very popular textbook on historical materialism. They assert the following: "It is quite obvious that together with the change of property relations are changing legal relations, juridical principles, norms, and laws—in one word, *all that we call legal ideology*" (my italics—M.M.).

It is exactly "in one word, all that . . . ." which is incorrect. Why? Because, if we accept their view, we must conclude the following: if, during the transition period both property and legal relations are changing, then legal ideology is also changing, and that means that existing ideology is replaced by a new ideology. Their fallacy lies in their identification of juridical principles, norms, and law, with legal ideology. Indeed, we do have juridical principles, and these principles are changing. But we do not have legal ideology.

Law and legal ideology are two distinct things. Legal ideology is a fetishist worship of law, a deification of law, an assumption that law is an independent and eternal category. We have law and we assign it a proper and sometimes very great role, but never an independent one. Our laws remain in existence only as long as they correspond to our vital interests, as long as they are conducive to the development of forces of production, to the construction of socialism.

We are not a *Rechtsstaat*. Nevertheless, we know how to force observance of our laws very well. We do not propose to worship our Soviet law in place of bourgeois law; we do not introduce our own new ideology; we liquidate legal ideology entirely. The same thing took place, for example, during the French Revolution, when the bourgeoisie, in advancing the demand to destroy estates, did not aim at preserving itself but aimed, on the contrary, at destroying itself as an estate. Likewise, the proletariat, in advancing the demand to destroy all classes, strives for its own destruction. We do not preserve "all that we call ideology"; on the contrary, we unmask it, defetishize it, that is, destroy it.

Moreover, the crisis of postwar bourgeois rule has led to the rise of fascism in some states, that is, to an open, not even juridically disguised, dictatorship of the bourgeoisie. To put it differently, the intensification of class antagonisms causes the bourgeoisie to throw away its disguise—legal ideology—and reveal its true face. How, then, can one assert that legal ideology exists in the Soviet Union, the country with an open dictatorship of the proletariat, at a time when even the bourgeoisie is forced to discard all juridical illusions?

Comrade Vinokurov's venture proved to be unsuccessful. The Conference rejected his views because they were tantamount to retreating to the past. We will be able to liquidate legal ideology once and for all only if we correctly appraise its meaning and the causes of its existence.

But why do such ventures come into being? Attempts to advance theories reflecting juridical socialism are inevitable under conditions of the dictatorship of the proletariat when commodity relations are still surviving. Petty-bourgeois market relations produce their ideologists. At times, against their will, they become exponents of these interests. They merely reflect the class struggle.

The need to fight against these theories on the basis of Marxism-Leninism becomes even more urgent, for under our conditions ideology plays the most active role in the reconstruction of the entire society on socialist principles. Only a fierce struggle can assure the victory of the proletariat on the ideological front and a further development of Marxist-Leninist science.

# Socialism or State Capitalism in the Soviet Union*

## ൽ *M. Rezunov*

As a result of the great change in urban and rural economy, even the initial years of the struggle for the first five-year plan signified the fact that *the Soviet Union has entered into a new socioeconomic formation—the period of socialism.* In his concluding remarks at the Sixteenth Party Congress, Stalin characterized the basic law of this stage in the following way: "It is obvious that, having entered the period of direct and large-scale socialist construction on the whole front, we are no longer in the transition period in the old meaning of this term. It is obvious that we have entered the period of socialism, for the socialist sector now holds in its hands all economic levers, although we are still far from the construction of socialist society and the liquidation of class differences."

Thus, in mid-1930, the struggle of the proletarian dictatorship for socialism signified the fact that we had left the transition period in its old meaning and had entered the first phase of a communist society. In subsequent years the socialist sector became predominant; *the country of soviets definitively consolidated itself on the socialist path and achieved the decisive victory of socialism.* While the past stages of the transition period comprised, to use Lenin's words, "elements, particles, pieces, of both capitalism and socialism," at the present time the socialist sector holds in its hands all economic levers of the entire economic development of our country.

By definitively liquidating classes and private property for the means of production, by adopting exclusively the socialist method of production, and by making our economy unistructural, the second five-year plan *completed the fulfillment of the tasks of the transition period,* which called for the liquidation of capitalist social relations and the construction of a classless socialist society. This brought the transition period to an end. At the Seventeenth Party Congress, Comrade Stetskii said: "The draft of the second five-year plan signifies that we are completing the second difficult task confronting the proletariat. The first task called for seizing the power, for establishing the dictatorship of the proletariat. The second task is even more com-

* From *Sovetskoe Gosudarstvo i Sotsialisticheskoe Obshchestvo* [The Soviet State and Socialist Society] (Leningrad, 1934), pp. 12–18.

plicated: it calls for bringing about the transition from capitalism to socialism. It is during the second five-year plan—that is, during the years 1934, 1935, 1936, and 1937—that we will complete and resolve the second task of the proletariat, a task of universal historical significance: we will bring the transition period to an end."

Indeed, there will be various types of "theorists" who will start speculations, disputes, and discussions concerning the question on which day of 1937, and at what time—morning or evening—the classless society will come into being. Such talmudists must be driven as far away from our organizations as possible. There is no point in entering into discussion with them; they must be exposed.

We approach this problem politically. We know that, if we succeed in fulfilling the second five-year plan, the task of constructing a socialist society will be realized.

Our class enemies, who cannot ignore the historical successes of the five-year plan, try to deny the fact that the U.S.S.R. has entered the stage of socialism. They are assisted by a clearly anti-Party contraposition of the "dictatorship of the proletariat" to the "epoch of socialism," of the "period of socialism" to "true socialism," etc., which is still frequently encountered in our literature. Some comrades, turning toward the Trotskyite path, attempted to depict "the assertion that the present stage represents the first stage of communism, i.e., socialism," as a "rusty weapon borrowed directly from the right-opportunist arsenal."

Under socialism, Marx and Lenin understood the liquidation of private property for the means of production, their socialization, the liquidation of classes, and the creation of a classless society. They never built empty, abstract, and utopian schemes of socialism. What radically differentiates them from utopian Socialists is that they approached the problem of communism in a strictly scientific way, pointing out concretely how and from what historical elements the new social system would arise. According to Marx and Lenin, socialism was to be built in the transition period. The task of this period is a revolutionary transformation of capitalism into socialism. The founders of Marxism-Leninism spoke of the whole transition period, repeatedly stressing the protracted birth pangs of the new society.

Socialism, as the first phase of the new socioeconomic formation—communist society—does not come ready-made from heaven. It is built and developed in the transition period, in the fire of irreconcilable, fierce class struggle against the overthrown exploiter classes.

. . . Socialism, as the first phase of communism, goes through numerous historical stages, which differ one from another either by

SOVIET POLITICAL THOUGHT

greater or lesser maturity of the new formation or by greater or lesser completeness and plenitude. It is self-evident that the first stage of the socialist society, being the initial phase of the new formation, carries the imprint of the earlier period; we entered socialism, liquidated the basis and the source of exploitation of man by man, but we have not yet liquidated the classes and the class struggle. Moreover, we encounter intensification of furious resistance on the part of parasitic elements that are being liquidated.

The socialist system is born with the birthmarks of capitalism. The proletarian dictatorship will definitely wipe them out in the process of creating the economic basis for the second, higher phase of communist society, not only through liquidation of private property for the means of production, but also through liquidation of antagonisms between town and country and between mental and physical work.

Social Fascists and counterrevolutionary Trotskyites, who claim to be Socialists, distort the Marxist theory in a bourgeois manner. Kautsky, falsely asserting that the idea of a dictatorship of the proletariat was accidental to Marx, propagates the growth of socialism in the womb of a capitalist economy and bourgeois state. By socialism Kautsky means a bourgeois-democratic republic with a social-fascist government at its head. "Socialization," writes Kautsky, "should be systematically prepared by *the democratic state, in which there exists full freedom of political autonomy for all citizens*. Socialization should be accomplished on the basis of democratic administration of enterprises, i.e., on the basis of democratic administration of enterprises with, on one hand, workers' participation and, on the other hand, consumers' participation."[1]

Otto Bauer is preoccupied with similar reactionary fancies. Under socialism, Bauer understands a bourgeois-democratic republic. "Socialism," he writes, "is the self-determination of the people in the productive-economic and labor processes. Concentration of the means of production in the hands of the state is not sufficient for the achievement of socialism. To achieve socialism, it is also necessary that the state authority, which takes care of the means of production, be freely elected by the people and responsible to the people."[2]

On this question, Trotsky is also on the side of the Social Fascists. Denying that the U.S.S.R. has entered the period of socialism, he writes: "Realization of the five-year plan would amount to a gigantic step forward in comparison to the beggarly heritage taken from the

---

[1] *Bolsheviki v Tupike* [Bolsheviks in an Impasse] (Berlin, 1930).

[2] "Die Zukunft der russischen Sozialdemokratie," *Der Kampf*, No. 12 (1931), p. 515.

hands of exploiters by the proletariat. But even after its first victory in the sphere of planned economy, the Soviet Union would still remain in the first stage of the transition period. *Socialism as a system of production, not for the market, but for the satisfaction of human needs,* is conceivable only on the basis of highly developed productive forces."[3] Trotsky replaced Marx's theory of socialism with Lassalle's opportunist theory of socialism. His hostility to the working class was exposed by Marx in the *Critique of the Gotha Program.* Trotsky's view of socialism is precisely the same as that of Adler, Renner, and the whole social fascist fraternity.

The successful fulfillment of the first five-year plan and the transition toward the accomplishment of the grandiose tasks of the second five-year plan demonstrated to the proletariat of the whole world the superiority of the Soviet system over the capitalist system, which found itself in the noose of an international economic crisis. . . . The workers of all countries saw uplift and consolidation in the socialist country and decay, disintegration, and bloody fascist reaction in the capitalist countries. . . . But Social Fascists, who are carrying out the orders of the bourgeoisie, seek, by all means, to deceive the workers in the capitalist countries; they seek to conceal the historical fact that the U.S.S.R. has entered socialism. They contend that the socialism which is coming into being in the U.S.S.R. is state capitalism.

Marx and Lenin wrote that a victorious proletariat organizes a planned socialist economy. A planned economy is possible only under the dictatorship of the proletariat, on the basis of the nationalization of factories, banks, land, means of transportation, and the monopoly of external trade. Without the proletarian dictatorship and the socialist construction, there is no, nor could there be, planned economy. Social fascist propagators of an "organized" capitalism, distorting facts, write:

Marx once pointed out that the feature characteristic of capitalism is that "the worker exists for the production process instead of the production process for the worker." In the Soviet Union the worker also exists for the production process—this feature of capitalism is fully present there. Private capitalism became abolished, but instead of being replaced with socialism it was replaced with state capitalism. "We retreated toward state capitalism," Lenin stated ten years ago, and to Stalin's theory this phrase is even more applicable than it is to the epoch of NEP. To Marx and Engels the transition to a planned economy appeared to be possible only within the framework of a socialist social order. But now we

---

[3] "Entwurf einer Platform der internationalen linken Komminististen zur russischen Frage," *Die Aktion,* No. 314 (1931), p. 79; see also F. Adler, "Der Stalinsche Experiment und der Sozialismus," *Der Kampf,* No. 1 (1932).

discover that socialism is not at all a necessary precondition of a planned economy, that it is merely a negative criterion that is needed for a planned economy, namely, the abolition of the pure-capitalist conception, and that a planned economy is also possible on the basis of state capitalism.[4]

Trotsky echoes Friedrich Adler: "I think that the contention that Russia has already entered the period of socialism, while being only in the third year of the five-year plan, is completely incorrect and disastrous to the reputation of the ruling circles." (Trotsky, the renegade, seems to care about the reputation of our Party?!)

The political meaning of all these Menshevist writings on "state capitalism in the U.S.S.R." and the denial that the U.S.S.R. has entered socialism is . . . one and the same thing, namely, [an attempt] to conceal the growth of sympathy on the part of workers in all countries toward the country of the Soviets; to prevent the mobilization of the working class's forces under communist banners; and, cultivating the so-called public opinion of the capitalist countries with fairy tales about "socialism" in Europe and America and "state capitalism in the U.S.S.R.," to conceal the preparation of war against the Soviet Union.

Marx, Lenin, and Stalin always distinctly differentiated two phases of communist society. Socialism is the first phase. Classes and the sources of class division are liquidated. All means of production are in the hands of society. All possibilities of exploitation of man by man are also liquidated. The socialist mode of production is the only one in existence. Socialist property is the only form of property for the means of production. There "are no class distinctions, because everyone is, like all others, only a worker." At this stage of development, the communist system carries the footprints, "the birthmarks," of the society from whose womb it only recently merged. What are these "birthmarks"?

*First,* society is not yet wealthy enough to satisfy the various, increased needs of the people. At this point of development, society lacks the necessary technoeconomic maturity and the proper level of labor productivity.

*Second,* people have not yet learned to work in such a way as to donate all their forces and abilities to society, without the inevitable legal regulations, according to the principle: "for equal work, equal pay." In view of this, Soviet law and the state are necessary for their protection. In *State and Revolution* Lenin writes:

In its first phase or first stage, communism cannot, as yet, be economically ripe and entirely free of all tradition and of all taint of

[4] Adler, "Der Stalinsche Experiment," pp. 11–12.

capitalism. Hence the interesting phenomenon of communism retaining, in its first phase, "the narrow horizon of bourgeois law." Bourgeois law, with respect to the distribution of articles of *consumption,* inevitably presupposes, of course, the existence of the *bourgeois state,* for law is nothing without an apparatus capable of coercing the observance of legal norms.

Consequently, for a certain time, not only bourgeois law, but even the bourgeois state, remain under communism, without the bourgeoisie!

This may look like a paradox, or simply a dialectical play of words, for which Marxism is often blamed by people who would not make the least effort to study its extraordinarily profound content.

But, as a matter of fact, the old surviving in the new, confronts us in life at every step—in nature as well as in society. Marx did not arbitrarily introduce a scrap of "bourgeois" law to communism; he adapted what was economically and politically necessary for a society emerging from the womb of capitalism.[5]

*Third,* the socialist society will be forced to apply the most resolute measures for a long time (including the liquidation of people who are especially dangerous to the socialist system) against people who are harmful and deliberately destructive to socialist production, i.e., those who seek to undermine the socialist state and to re-establish the capitalist system. This will be especially necessary with respect to those who come from classes that were formerly hostile to the proletariat. It should also be kept in mind that the Soviet state and law will perform the function of a lever in suppressing counterrevolutionary activity among the surviving splinters of the forever defeated system, because the hopes and expectations of those as yet unliquidated survivors of the old world, their hatred and struggle against the classless socialist society, will be nourished and inspired by the capitalist encirclement.

*Fourth,* money and Soviet commerce play, and will play, a tremendous role in the realization of the principle "for equal work, equal pay" (which will serve as a measure of the distribution of labor and of articles of consumption). The strengthening of the Soviet financial system and the development of Soviet commerce prepares the ground for the introduction of a direct exchange of products after the transition to a higher phase of communism. Therefore, Soviet civil law will become of tremendous significance. Its task in this case will be to regulate Soviet commerce and to safeguard the rights of the workers

---

[5] In another place Lenin states: "Accounting and control—these are the *chief* things necessary for the organizing and the correct functioning of the *first phase* of communist society. Here, *all* citizens are transformed into hired employees of the state, which is made up of the armed workers. *All* citizens become employees and workers of *one* national state 'syndicate.' All that is required is that they should work equally, should regularly do their share of work, and that they should receive equal pay."

of the socialist society to the individual articles of consumption which
they acquired with their earned pay.

*Fifth,* the technological and economic level of the first phase of
socialism (the distribution of labor and of articles of consumption
according to the principle "for equal work, equal pay," the methods
of Soviet commerce, and the presence of the circulation of money)
will call forth peculiar forms of relationships among the economic
enterprises in the classless socialist society. Cost accounting and contracts are indispensable instruments for the organization of these
economic relationships in the socialist system.[6] The system of cost
accounting calls for firm, clear legal regulation carried out by the
Soviet state. A scornful attitude toward Soviet law leads directly to
the disturbance of cost accounting and contract discipline.

Finally, . . . capitalist encirclement calls for the maximum strengthening of the power of the socialist state.

[6] This is why it is impossible to agree with the contention of some economists
that cost accounting disappears together with NEP. (On this question see M.
Eskina, "Zakonomernosti Udarnogo Dvizheniya" [Requirements of the Shockworker Movement], *Problemy Marksizma,* No. 8–9 [1931], p. 31.)

# Conditions for the Withering Away of the State and Law: A New Interpretation*      M. Rezunov

Marx, Lenin, and Stalin frequently stressed the great significance of the state and law during the period of socialism. The classics of Marxism-Leninism, in doing this, had in mind the proletarian state and its law. Marx wrote in *Critique of the Gotha Program:*

> What we have to deal with here is a communist society, not as it has *developed* on its own foundations, but, on the contrary, just as it emerges from a capitalist society, which is thus in every respect, economically, morally, and intellectually, still stamped with the birthmarks of the old society from whose womb it emerges. Accordingly, the individual producer receives back from society—after the deductions have been made—exactly what he gives to it.
>
> . . . Here, obviously, the same principle prevails as that which regulates the exchange of commodities, insofar as this is an exchange of equal values. Content and form are changed, because under the altered circumstances no one can give anything except his labor and because, on the other hand, nothing can pass into the ownership of individuals except individual means of consumption.

*Equal obligation of all* to work and *equal rights of all* working people to receive pay according to their work are the principles of the organization of labor and the distribution of the articles of consumption in the epoch of socialism. This was Lenin's view. The same view was also clearly stressed by Comrade Stalin in his speech at the Seventeenth Party Congress.

The problem of law in the epoch of socialism is not an abstract, academic problem. It is a problem of vital importance to our practical work. On this problem, just as on the problem of state, numerous views were advanced, views clearly distorting the theory of Marx, Lenin, and Stalin and capable of bringing great political harm to the proletarian dictatorship. For example, Comrade Liberman, adopting Trotsky's position on the problem concerning the character of the economy in the transition period, intensely propagated the "theory" of the liquidation of Soviet civil law. He wrote: "We have now a new economic policy; we are carrying out the liquidation of relations based on private property. . . . This signifies at the same time liquida-

* From *Sovetskoe Gosudarstvo i Sotsialisticheskoe Obshchestvo* [The Soviet State and Socialist Society] (Leningrad, 1934), pp. 18–32.

303

tion or abolition of relations based on civil law. . . . Thus, the radical change in the socioeconomic conditions in our country leads, first and foremost, to two consequences in the economic-legal superstructure: first, the liquidation of relations based on civil law; and second, the liquidation of relations based on land law."[1]

By liquidating private property for the means of production, the Party and the working class seek to introduce into the whole socialist economy the principle "equal pay for equal work," to develop Soviet commerce as a form of distribution of the articles of consumption during the period of socialism, and to strengthen Soviet civil law, which regulates commerce. The liquidator of Soviet law—Liberman —confuses the liquidation of private property for the means of production with the liquidation of private-property relations in general (i.e., individual property for the articles of consumption, obtained with the wages and income from collective farms), and advances the "theory" of the liquidation of Soviet commerce and Soviet civil law.[2]

Soviet law is one of the most significant forms of policy in the proletarian dictatorship. Soviet law and the revolutionary legality of the proletarian state are the mighty means for suppressing the exploiters' resistance, for strengthening the union between the working class and the peasants, and for the socialist transformation of society. Soviet law and revolutionary legality, as organized powers of the Soviet state, are of special significance during the second five-year plan. Liberman—the liquidator of Soviet civil and land laws—declares that it is impermissible to reduce law to policy (?!); that Soviet civil law, being based on the "relations of private property," is alien and hostile to the socialist system and is subject to immediate destruction.

It is not difficult to see that Liberman's theory on the liquidation of Soviet law (even if only civil law) is directed toward undermining Soviet law and revolutionary legality or, in other words, toward the weakening of the proletarian dictatorship.

The founders of Marxism-Leninism characterized the law in the period of socialism as "bourgeois law." Of course, it is not the law of a capitalist society, safeguarding capitalist property and exploitation. The system of bourgeois law was destroyed by the proletarian revolution together with the bourgeois state. Soviet law—the new historical type of law—safeguards the inviolability and stability of socialist property and the state system of the proletarian dictatorship. It is one

---

[1] "Poslednii Etap Nepa i Khozyaistvennoe Pravo" [The Last Stage of the New Economic Policy and Economic Law], *Problemy Marksizma*, No. 5–6 (1931), pp. 41 and 43.

[2] See criticism of Liberman's opportunist conception in M. Rezunov and V. Undrevich, "Na Putyakh Kontrrevolyutsionnogo Trotskizma" [On the Path of the Counterrevolutionary Trotskyism], *Problemy Marksizma*, No. 1–2 (1932).

of the forms of policy in the socialist state. That is why it amounts to a bourgeois distortion to assert that Soviet law is at the same time the bourgeois law which thrives in capitalist countries.

Marx and Lenin characterized the law in the period of socialism as "bourgeois" (Lenin places the term "bourgeois" in quotation marks), because the equal right of the working people to receive remuneration for their work, according to its quantity and quality, results, in fact, in the unequal satisfaction of their needs. . . .

The right of the producers is *proportional* to the labor they supply; the equality consists in the fact that measurement is made with an *equal standard, labor.* But one man is superior to another physically or mentally and, consequently, supplies more labor in the same time, or can labor for a longer time; and labor, to serve as a measure, must be defined by its duration or intensity; otherwise it ceases to be a standard of measurement. This *equal* right is an unequal right for unequal labor. It recognizes no class differences, because everyone is only a worker like everyone else; but it tacitly recognizes unequal individual endowment and thus productive capacity as natural privileges. *It is, therefore, a right of inequality, in its content, like every right.*[3]

Furthermore, if we keep in mind that one worker is married and another is not, one has more children than another, etc., then it is obvious that in the first phase of communism there could be no full equality, because, with the right of each workingman to receive remuneration according to the quantity and quality of work, one will receive more, another less, one will be richer than the other, etc.

By equality, Marxism-Leninism does not mean general wage leveling under which people would receive an equal quantity of bread, meat, the same cloth, etc. Petty-bourgeois Socialists and primitive "Communists" of the seventeenth and eighteenth centuries were dreaming of such egalitarian socialism. In attempting to discredit Marxism-Leninism, bourgeois publicists and scientists were, and are, producing caricatures of socialist society as a uniform, dull, barracklike society of average men, one as similar to another as two drops of water.

"By equality"—said Comrade Stalin at the Seventeenth Party Congress—"Marxism means, not equalization of individual requirements and individual life, but the destruction of classes, i.e., (1) the equal emancipation of all working people from exploitation after the capitalists have been overthrown and expropriated; (2) the equal abolition of all private property for the means of production after these means have been converted into the property of the whole society;

[3] Karl Marx, *Kritika Gotskoi Programmy* [Critique of the Gotha Program] (Moscow, 1933), pp. 26–27.

(3) the equal duty of all to work according to their ability and the equal right of all working people to receive remuneration according to the amount of work performed (*socialist society*); (4) the equal duty of all to work according to their ability, and the equal right of all working people to receive remuneration according to their needs (*communist society*)."

Consequently, the inequality of distribution of produced goods will remain in the first stage of a communist society. But, at the same time, no one will be able to seize the means of production as his private property and convert them into a means of exploitation.

The elimination of equalization and the introduction of wages based on the principle of the quantity and the quality of the work; the organization of the entire labor supply on this principle; the development of Soviet commerce; the struggle with kulak equalization on the collective farms and the introduction of collective farm calculations based on the quantity and quality of work accomplished—these are the concrete achievements of the "bourgeois law" of the epoch of socialism about which Marx, Lenin, and Stalin spoke. People have not yet learned to work for society without any legal norms because of the survival of capitalist traditions, habits, petty-bourgeois laxity, and the lack of discipline. The "bourgeois law" serves here as one of the most powerful forms of policy of the proletarian dictatorship in the period of socialism.

A fierce class struggle is taking place in our country against the furious resistance of the remnants of the parasitic classes. Proletarian dictatorship suppresses and destroys the anti-Soviet machinations of our class enemies and, by means of revolutionary legality, breaks their attempts to undermine the great edifice of socialist construction. And even after the liquidation of classes during the period of socialism—as long as the economic prerequisites for the application of the principle "from each according to his abilities, to each according to his needs" are not established—there will be need for "bourgeois law" as a standard for the distribution of labor and the articles of consumption, as an instrument for the suppression of counterrevolutionary attempts to harm and hamper socialist construction. But, as long as law is necessary, equally necessary is the proletarian state, which would safeguard law, for law is nothing without the state's protection; a proletarian state, while protecting public property for the means of production, would safeguard equality of labor and equality of the distribution of products.

Complete victory over the surviving traces of capitalism in the economy and in the consciousness of men, the liquidation of all survivors of the antagonism between mental and physical work, and the creation of the material prerequisites for a full communist society, will create conditions for the withering away of the state.

Classes will be liquidated finally by the second five-year plan; however, this does not mean that the Soviet state will begin to die off exactly on January 1, 1938. A firm and strong dictatorship will be necessary, even after the second five-year plan, for the purpose of liquidating all survivors of the class society. "The state is withering away," Lenin said, "insofar as there are no longer any capitalists, any classes, and, consequently, no *class* can *be suppressed*. But the state has not yet altogether died, since there still remains the protection of 'bourgeois law,' which sanctifies actual inequality. For the complete extinction of the state, full communism is necessary."

*Consequently, the law, and the state protecting it, will wither away during the transition from complete socialism to full-scale communism.* This period is far beyond the second five-year plan.

. . . Lenin outlined the path of development and the withering away of the proletarian state and democracy in the following way:

The dictatorship of the proletariat is a political transition period; it is also clear that *the state in this period* represents the transition from state to non-state, i.e., to "no longer state in the proper sense." But, further, Marx speaks of the "future state power (*gosudarstvennost*) of the communist society"!! Thus, there will be state power even in a "communist society"!! Is it not contradictory?

No:  I—In a capitalist society, state      Bourgeoisie needs a state.
       in the proper sense.

       II—Transition (dictatorship of      Proletariat needs a state.
       the proletariat): state of
       transition type (not a state
       in the proper sense).

       III—Communist society: the      A state is unnecessary; it withers
       withering away of the state.      away.

Fully consistent and clear!
In other words:
       I—Democracy, merely by way      Democracy only for the rich
       of exception, never com-      and for a small layer of the
       plete.      proletariat. (Nothing for the
                poor!)
       II—Almost complete democ-      Democracy for the poor, for
       racy, restricted only by the      nine-tenths of the population;
       *suppression* of the bour-      resistance of the rich suppressed
       geoisie's resistance.      by force.

       III—A truly complete democ-      Full democracy, becoming a
       racy, becoming a habit,      habit and therefore withering

and *therefore* withering away. . . . Full democracy is equal to no democracy. This is not a paradox but truth! away, giving in to the principle "from each according to his abilities, to each according to his needs."[4]

Lenin frequently stressed that our state is not a state in the usual meaning of the term, i.e., the state of a small group of exploiters of millions of working people. Lenin characterized the Soviet state as a semistate, "not a state in the proper sense," a state withering away. What did he have in mind by such a characterization of the proletarian state power?

*First,* the Soviet state is a semistate because it is not simply a political superstructure but a mighty economic power, a system of organization of the socialist economy. The proletarian dictatorship holds in its hands the constantly growing . . . national economy (industry, means of transportation, banks, etc.), and exerts a direct influence upon the development of the economy. The bourgeois state, on the other hand, is an executive committee of the bourgeoisie, its political machine for coercive "administration of the people," i.e., the proletariat, in the name of capitalist property and exploitation. "Things," i.e., the economy, in the bourgeois society are administered by individual capitalists and their monopolistic organizations. "The bourgeois state apparatus, bourgeois ministries"—said Comrade Kaganovich at the Seventeenth Party Congress—"do not administer economy. The bourgeois state apparatus plays, chiefly, a police-like regulating role, protecting the interests of capitalists against revolutionary workers while enterprises are directed by the capitalists themselves. In contrast, in our country—in the socialist society—it is the state which gives *unity to political and economic leadership."*

The Soviet state is not only the proletarian political machine "administering the people" but also a mighty, constantly growing system of the administration of "things," i.e., the socialist economy. The sphere of the administration of things by the proletarian state expands in proportion to the growth of socialist industry and agriculture. Hence, the enormous organizational role of the Soviet state in the period of socialism. The liquidation of classes and the remnants of class society, the transition from socialism to full-scale communism—which is impossible without a mighty and strong proletarian dictatorship—will render the administration of the people by the state unnecessary. The activity of a social organization under full-scale communism, that is, a stateless society, will be limited to the administration of things and to the direction of industrial processes.

[4] *Leninskii Sbornik [Lenin's Miscellany]* (Moscow), XIV (1930?), 265–66.

*Second,* the Soviet state is a semistate because it systematically destroys the classes, thus creating preconditions for the transition to the communist, stateless system. By destroying the classes, it destroys the basis of all states forever. What is needed for the destruction of classes, for the liquidation of the sources of class division, and for the liquidation of antagonisms between town and country, between mental and physical work, is a continuous, political and economic strengthening of the proletarian dictatorship. The creation of preconditions for the withering away of the proletarian dictatorship can be achieved only through its strengthening.

This is the law of the development of the proletarian dictatorship. "We are for the withering away of the state. But at the same time we stand for the strengthening of the dictatorship of the proletariat, which is the most vigorous and the mightiest of all state powers that have hitherto existed. The highest development of state power in preparation *for* its withering away—this is the Marxist formula. Is this contradictory? Yes, it is 'contradictory.' But this contradiction is vital and fully reflects Marx's dialectic."

This is beyond the comprehension of some comrades, who advocate the thesis that the withering away of the state takes place *together, simultaneously, along* with the liquidation of classes. And, since the proletarian dictatorship starts the liquidation of classes at the moment of its rise, the beginning of the state's withering away belongs to the first days of the October Revolution.[5] Proponents of this view confuse prerequisites of the withering away of the Soviet state with the withering away of the proletarian dictatorship, which begins *after* the creation of these prerequisites, i.e., after the liquidation of classes and all "birthmarks" of capitalism, in a full-scale socialist

[5] For example, in his "Uchenie Marksa i Ego Istoricheskoe Znachenie" [Marx's Teaching and Its Historical Significance], *Pamyati Karla Marksa, Sbornik* [In Memory of Karl Marx, Symposium] (Leningrad, 1933), Comrade Bukharin, restoring basic assumptions of his earlier mechanist theory of state, writes: "Because the economic development in the transition period is nothing but the ultimate disappearance of the remains of the earlier tenor and economic formations of life, the dictatorship of the proletariat comprises the seed of its own liquidation; its development brings its withering away. . . . This is *the last* historical form of state which, ultimately, immerses itself in society and diffuses in it" (p. 86). Dictatorship of the proletariat "is comprised of the relationship of *domination;* but even this relationship is a disappearing phenomenon, because in the process of class struggle the classes themselves disappear at a given point of development; drawing *everyone* into its direct organization, the state ceases to be itself and, absorbing society, diffuses in it; *the class domination over people* is being transformed into a *classless administration of things"* (p. 87). That is why, in Bukharin's theory, the state withers away "together with the disappearance of classes" (p. 74). See a critique of Bukharin's work in E. Pashukanis, "Na Starykh Pozitsiyakh" [On the Old Positions], *Vestnik Komakademii,* No. 5 (1933).

society. This dangerous confusion on such a significant problem as that of the proletarian dictatorship is capable of causing great harm, for it pours water upon the mill of the bourgeois theories of the weakening of the soviets.

*Third,* the Soviet state is a semistate because, for the first time in history, it draws millions of working people into the administration of the state and, step by step, liquidates all barriers between the state apparatus and the broad masses of workers and peasants. Lenin wrote in *State and Revolution:*

> Here we observe a case of "transformation of quantity into quality"; democracy, introduced as fully and consistently as is generally thinkable, is transformed from bourgeois democracy into proletarian democracy, from the state (i.e., a special force for the suppression of a particular class) into something that is no longer a state in the proper sense. It is still necessary to suppress the bourgeoisie and its resistance. This was particularly necessary for the Commune; and one of the reasons for its defeat was that it did not do this with sufficient determination. But the organ of suppression is now the majority of the population and not a minority as was always the case under slavery, serfdom, and wage labor. And, once the majority of the people *itself* suppresses its oppressors, a "special force" for suppression *is no longer necessary!* In this sense the state *begins to wither away.*

Consequently, our state "is no longer a state in the proper sense," for, being the state of millions of working people, it is no longer a force standing above society. The development of all forms of Soviet democracy, the appearance and boisterous blossoming of the new forms of proletarian democracy during the first and the second five-year plans (such as socialist competition, shock-workers, and technical, industrial, and financial planning, etc.), strengthen tremendously the power of the proletarian dictatorship, make way for the conditions necessary for the withering away of the state and for the fusion of society with the state after the liquidation of classes and their "birthmarks."

This is beyond the comprehension of comrades who propagate the thesis on the withering away of the Soviet state from the moment of its rise. They think that October, 1917, was the beginning of an uninterrupted withering away of the Soviet state. Adhering to such "theories," Comrade Berman advances erroneous views in several of his works: "The withering away of the state is a protracted process. It begins on the first day of the proletarian revolution, on the first day of the seizure of power by the proletariat and the organization of its own state. It comes to an end at a higher phase of the communist society; only then will the complete and final withering away of the state take place."[6] Comrade Berman was struggling energetically against the liquidators of the Soviets, but his formulation of the problem of the withering away of the Soviet state also introduces confusion and error into the political question that is of great significance to our Party.

At the Seventeenth Party Congress, Comrade Stetskii . . . said the following concerning the thesis that the withering away of the Soviet state began in October, 1917:

> During the summer of this year, some Institutes of the Communist Academy were discussing the problem of the state's withering away. These discussions took place after Comrade Stalin's speech at the January Plenum of the Central Committee, in which he stated that the strengthening of our proletarian dictatorship is inevitable. Nevertheless, some "theorists" advanced the view that our proletarian state began to wither away neither later nor earlier but on the second day after the October Revolution and that, consequently, it has been withering away through the past sixteen years. In view of this, one wonders how it could be existing at the present time.
>
> What is the source of such a formulation of the problem? Its source is an incorrect interpretation of Lenin's thesis that our state is already a semistate, that our state is a withering away state. Yes, this is a fact, but it is its ultimate aim; it is the destiny of the proletarian state. To achieve this aim, our state must perform a tremendous task in rebuilding the economy, in liquidating class enemies, in liquidating classes, in drawing the masses into participation in the administration of the state, in promoting self-discipline and the communist attitude toward work.

This is how the problem of the state's withering away stands. Comrades who assumed that the proletarian state begins to wither away on the second day after the October Revolution were quite wrong. They forgot Lenin's thesis that the proletariat needs a state in the transition period, that the state withers away only under communism. They have forgotten Stalin's thesis that the withering away of the proletarian state takes place through its strengthening. All these specu-

---

[6] Ya. Berman, *Diktatura Proletariata vo Vtoroi Pyatiletke* [Proletarian Dictatorship in the Second Five-Year Plan] (Moscow, 1932), p. 49. See a criticism of Berman's errors in M. Mitin, "Priroda Proletarskogo Gosudarstva i Puti Ego Ukrepleniya" [The Nature of the Proletarian State and the Ways of Its Strengthening], *Pod Znamenem Marksizma*, No. 5 (1933). Berman subjected to criticism his erroneous assumptions in "Puti Ukrepleniya Diktatury Proletariata" [The Ways of Strengthening the Dictatorship of the Proletariat], *Sovetskoe Gosudarstvo*, No. 4 (1933).

During the discussion of the problem concerning the ways of further strengthening the proletarian dictatorship (at the Leningrad Section of the Communist Academy, in the spring of 1933) the author of this work underestimated the significance of Berman's errors and treated them in a conciliatory way.

lations concerning the withering away pour water upon the mill of opportunists, upon the mill of those who desire to rest on the results already achieved, those who seek to disarm us in our struggle against class enemies.

. . . Erroneous ideas on an uninterrupted withering away of the Soviet state found their expression also in the literature dealing with Soviet law. In this literature, too, voices began to reiterate that the withering away of Soviet law began in October. For example, Comrade Aleshin wrote: "Just like the proletarian state, Soviet law—the law of the transition period—is a withering away law. The beginning of this 'withering away' dates from the very moment of the proletarian revolution, from the moment of the final victory of the proletariat in the revolution."[7] Arguments about the withering away of Soviet law since October, 1917, are opposed to the Party's Leninist slogan on strengthening and instilling socialist legality.

As proof that their views are correct, some proponents of the "theory" of permanent withering away of the proletarian dictatorship refer to the place in *State and Revolution* where Lenin stated that "the proletariat needs only a withering away state, i.e., a state organized in such a way that it would begin immediately to wither away and could not wither away." Taking these words out of context, proponents of the withering away of the Soviet state from the first day of October interpret them in a metaphysical, formal, and antihistorical way.

In 1917, when we were advancing toward October—Stalin said in a speech delivered . . . on December 2, 1923—we assumed that we would have a commune; that it would be an association of the working people; that we would put an end to bureaucracy and institutions; and that we would succeed in transforming the state into an association of the working people either during the next period or after two to three short periods. However, practice has demonstrated that this is an ideal from which we are still far removed; that in order to save the state from bureaucratic elements, in order to transform Soviet society into an association of the working people, it is necessary to raise the cultural level of the population, it is necessary to have a perfectly secure all-around world situation, so that there would be no need to maintain big military cadres requiring great means and a bulky payroll, whose presence leaves an imprint upon all other state institutions.[8]

---

[7] "Sovetskoe Pravo i Stroitelstvo Sotsializma" [Soviet Law and the Construction of Socialism], *Sovetskoe Gosudarstvo*, No. 5–6 (1932), pp. 81–82. See a criticism of this error in V. Komarov, "Osnovnye Voprosy Teorii Sovetskogo Prava v Svete Istoricheskoi Roli Diktatury Proletariata" [Basic Problems of Soviet Law in Light of the Historical Role of the Proletarian Dictatorship], *Sovetskoe Gosudarstvo*, No. 1 (1934).

[8] Stalin, *Ob Opozitsii* [On the Opposition] (Moscow, 1928), pp. 21–22.

Enthusiasts of the permanent withering away of the Soviet state reject the sixteen years of experience of the socialist construction and the liquidation of classes as well as Lenin's remarks made at the Seventh Party Congress, March, 1918, against Bukharin's amendment to the resolution of the Party program. "When will the state begin to wither away?" said Lenin. "We will be able to convoke more than two congresses before the time comes when we could say: Look how our state is withering away. And this time is still far away. To proclaim the withering away of the state too early is a breach of historical perspective."[9]

*Fourth,* the Soviet state is a semistate, because only a proletarian state can wither away; because a new revolution, directed toward the destruction of this last historical type of state is not necessary; and, finally, because in the womb of the Soviet state there arises an apparatus for the social organization of a stateless system. In the epoch of the dictatorship of the proletariat there arise new, communist forms of labor, new, communist forms of the organization for the process of production, and new, communist forms for the administration of the whole economy.

. . . The strengthening of the proletarian dictatorship reinforces the accumulation of conditions necessary for the withering away of the Soviet state in the future but it does not at all mean that our society is presently being transformed into a stateless one; it does not at all mean that the proletarian dictatorship is presently "gradually atrophying."

. . . At the Seventeenth Party Congress . . . , Comrade Stalin subjected the attempts to revive opportunist ideas about the withering away of the Soviet state at this time to a devastating criticism. He said:

Take, for example, the problem of building a *classless socialist society.* The Seventeenth Party Congress declared that we are heading for the formation of a classless socialist society. It does so without saying that a classless society cannot come of itself, spontaneously, so to speak. It has to be achieved and built by the efforts of all the working people, by strengthening the organs of the dictatorship of the proletariat, by intensifying the class struggle, by destroying classes, by liquidating the remnants of the capitalist classes, and in battles with enemies both internal and external.

[9] Absolutely wrong are Bukharin's contentions that the Soviet state should be developing in the direction of "state-commune." Bukharin wrote: From the state-commune "we are still, unfortunately, very, very far" *(Politicheskoe Zaveshchanie* [Political Testament], p. 27). "We are quite overcentralized. We must ask ourselves: Should we not make a few steps in the direction of Lenin's state-commune?" *(Zametki Ekonomista* [Notes of an Economist] [Moscow, 1928], p. 54).

The point is clear, one would think. And yet, who does not know that the promulgation of this clear and elementary thesis of Leninism has given rise to not a little confusion and to unhealthy sentiments among a section of Party members? The thesis that we are advancing toward a classless society—which was put forward as a slogan—was interpreted by them as a spontaneous process. And they began to reason in this way: If it is a classless society, then we can relax the dictatorship of the proletariat and get rid of the state altogether, since it is destined to wither away soon in any case. They dropped into a state of moon-calf ecstasy in the expectation that soon there would be no classes, and therefore no class struggle, and therefore no cares and worries, and therefore we can lay down our arms and retire—to sleep and to wait for the advent of a classless society.

There can be no doubt that this confusion of mind and these sentiments are as like as two peas to the well-known views of the right-deviationists, who believed that the old must automatically grow into the new and that one fine day we shall wake up and find ourselves in socialist society.

As you see, remnants of the ideology of the defeated anti-Leninist groups can be reanimated and have not lost their tenacity. . . .

It goes without saying that, if this confusion of mind and these non-bolshevik sentiments obtained a hold over the majority of our Party, the Party would find itself demobilized and disarmed.

What, then, is the withering away of the state? It is an atrophy of the organs of class domination, of the apparatus of the class organization of society and economy, and their transformation into organs of classless, communist administration of society and its economic processes. To advocate such a withering away of the state *right now* is tantamount to weakening and undermining the proletarian dictatorship; it is tantamount to preventing the working class from fulfilling its historical task, the liquidation of the capitalist elements and the remnants of class society; it is tantamount to weakening the struggle against the furious resistance of the capitalist elements; it is tantamount to undermining the defensive might of the U.S.S.R.

# State and Law under Socialism: A Reversal of Thought*  ∞  *E. B. Pashukanis*

The completion of the liquidation of the exploiting classes in our country raises the question of the Soviet state as a political superstructure in the classless socialist society. Colossal socioeconomic upheavals have led toward the creation of uniform socialist relations of production in cities and villages and thus toward a new stage in the development of the proletarian dictatorship and Soviet democracy.

The problem of the role of the state and law acquires an especially great theoretical and practical significance at the present time. It is, therefore, necessary to bring to mind several of Lenin's and Stalin's fundamental theoretical premises which should be used as departure points in explaining the significance of the state and law in the period of socialism. It is also necessary to settle accounts with errors and confusions . . . perpetuated by legal theorists.

In *State and Revolution* Lenin quite clearly has resolved the problem of the state under socialism. He draws a sharp line between Communists and the diverse types of anarchist theorists: "We are not utopians. We do not indulge in 'dreams' of how best to do away *immediately* with all administration, with all subordination; these anarchistic dreams, based upon a lack of understanding of the task of the proletarian dictatorship, are basically alien to Marxism, and, as a matter of fact, they serve but to put off the socialist revolution until human nature is different. No, we want the socialist revolution with human nature as it is now, with human nature that cannot do without subordination, control, without 'overseers and bookkeepers.' "

Lenin's *State and Revolution* was directed not only against the opportunist, the reformist, and the Kautskyite distorters of Marxism, who were in favor of appeasing the bourgeois state and against breaking the machine of that state. It was also directed against pettybourgeois and anarchistic "dreamers," who contemplated the abolition of political authority, of state organization, of the organization of force and coercion, "the day" after the proletarian revolution.

Lenin's work was engendered not only by the necessity of settling accounts with Kautsky and his followers but also by the necessity of

* *From* "Gosudarstvo i Pravo pri Sotsializme" [State and Law under Socialism], *Sovetskoe Gosudarstvo*, No. 3 (1936), pp. 3–11.

taking a stand against the anarchistic errors and conclusions of Bukharin. At that time, Bukharin had published several articles in which he developed the anti-Marxist theory of the "blowing up" of the state. He contended that a proletarian party must constantly stress the inappeasable hostility of the working class toward the state.

Lenin's pronouncement concerning law is equally clear: ". . . if we are not to fall into utopianism, we cannot imagine that, having overthrown capitalism, people will at once learn to work for society *without any legal norms;* indeed, the abolition of capitalism *does not immediately lay* the economic foundations for *such* a change."

These condensed premises advanced by Lenin should be thoroughly developed in our theoretical studies of the role of the socialist state and law. . . .

In 1929, at the April Plenum of the Central Committee, Comrade Stalin demonstrated the profound difference between the anarchistic theory of "blowing up," as developed by Comrade Bukharin, and the Marxist-Leninist theory of crushing, or breaking, the bourgeois state machine. Comrade Stalin ridiculed the claim advanced by Bukharin and his students that their confused, non-Marxist theory of "blowing up" was more effective in the struggle against Kautsky than was Lenin's.

At the Sixteenth Party Congress Stalin explained that the road toward the future communist, stateless society would lead through the strengthening of the state's authority in every way possible. He reiterated and developed this thesis at the January Plenum of the Central Committee and Central Control Commission, 1933: "The abolition of classes is not achieved in the subsiding of the class struggle but in its intensification. The state will wither away, not as a result of a relaxation of the state authority, but as a result of its utmost consolidation, which is necessary for the purpose of finally crushing the remnants of the dying classes and of organizing a defense against the capitalist encirclement, which is far from having been done away with as yet, and will not soon be done away with."[1]

Finally, at the Seventeenth Party Congress, Stalin once again took a determined stand against the opportunists, who as a result of the progression toward a classless society attempted to popularize their ideas about the subsidence of the class struggle and the weakening of the dictatorship of the proletariat. "It goes without saying," stated Comrade Stalin, "that a classless society cannot come about of itself, spontaneously, so to speak. It has to be achieved and built by the efforts of all of the working people, by strengthening the organs of

---

[1] *Voprosy Leninizma* [Problems of Leninism] (Moscow, 1934), p. 509.

the dictatorship of the proletariat, by intensifying the class struggle, by destroying classes, by eliminating the remnants of the capitalist classes, and in battles with enemies both internal and external."[2]

On the whole the classless society has been achieved through the efforts of the working people. But only an opportunist could imagine that a further development and strengthening of the socialist system will proceed spontaneously, that the destruction of the classes signifies the obsolescence of the dictatorship of the proletariat and of the state. As stated by Lenin,

The substance of the teaching of Marx about the state is assimilated only by one who understands that the dictatorship of a *single* class is necessary, not only for any class society generally, not only for the *proletariat* that has overthrown the bourgeoisie, but for the entire *historic period* that separates capitalism from a "classless society," from communism. The forms of bourgeois states are exceedingly variegated, but their essence is the same: in one way or another, all these states are, in the last analysis, inevitably *dictatorships of the bourgeoisie*. The transition from capitalism to communism will certainly bring a great variety and abundance of political forms, but the essence will inevitably be only one: *the dictatorship of the proletariat*.[3]

From this paragraph (exceedingly rich in meaning) it follows that the proletarian state will preserve its role during the entire period between the overthrow of the bourgeoisie and the communist society and that, in spite of the possible variety of political forms, the essence and content of this state will be the dictatorship of the proletariat. Soviet authority is the state form of the dictatorship of the proletariat which acquired world-wide significance. However, the Soviet state is not immutable; it develops in connection with the success of the struggle for the destruction of classes.

The creation of a classless socialist society opened a new period in the development of Soviet democracy (new constitution, new electoral law); but, despite the change of political form, its essence remains the same; its essence is the dictatorship of the proletariat. On the whole we have achieved a classless socialist society, but we have not yet attained the higher phase of a communist society. The distinction between socialism and communism, or between lower and higher phases of communism, lies essentially in that, under socialism, where (social) socialist property prevails, distribution takes place according to work, whereas, under communism, with a further strengthening and development of social property, distribution will take place according to needs.

[2] *Ibid.*, p. 580.
[3] *Gosudarstvo i Revolutsiya* [State and Revolution].

The development of the productive forces and of a socialist culture, which will render distribution according to needs possible, signifies the abolition of the antithesis between intellectual and physical work as well as the transformation of work into a vital necessity for man; it signifies those conditions under which people will work without "overseers and bookkeepers," without legal norms, and without compulsory force, without the state. Hence, the process of the state's dying away can begin only after the compulsory character of work has disappeared. This is the fundamental economic prerequisite for the beginning of the process of dying away, for the falling asleep of the state authority.

Speaking of the process of dying away, of the state's falling asleep, in *The Economy in the Transition Period* Bukharin has arranged this process in the following sequence: at first, armed forces will fall away, then instruments of repression (prisons, etc.), and, finally, the compulsory character of work. Lenin inverted this sequence, and that which Bukharin had placed at the end was placed by Lenin at the beginning as a first and fundamental prerequisite without which the beginning of the process of dying away was inconceivable.

Nevertheless, there was a popular theory which asserted that the real process of dying away started with the October Revolution and that this process should be at its height during the period of the liquidation of classes and the construction of a classless socialist society. This was a false, opportunist theory because it did not take into account the fundamental, economic prerequisite without which the state cannot even begin to die away.

The confusion on the problem of the proletarian state's dying away stemmed from the fact that this problem has been fused with that of the nature of the proletarian state as a semistate, as a state which, in contrast to the exploiters' states, does not strive to perpetuate itself but, on the contrary, prepares the conditions and prerequisites for its own destruction. Having overthrown the bourgeois state, the proletariat creates a state of a special type, a state which does not represent a minority exploiting the majority, as in the exploiters' states, but which, on the contrary, is an instrument of the working majority, directed against the exploiters.

The Party's program, which speaks of the gradual drawing of the entire populace into the administration of the state . . . , asserts that "a complete and universal execution of these measures, which constitutes a further step on the road that was taken by the Paris Commune, and the simplification of the function of administration . . . will lead to the liquidation of the state authority." Consequently, the question is how to *prepare the conditions* for the state's dying away. The dying away itself will become possible only in the second phase of communism. The creation of the conditions for the future stateless organization is not a process of weakening the state authority but a process of strengthening, particularly by drawing an increasingly greater mass of the working people into the administration of the state.

There are no barriers in the proletarian state between the state apparatus and the whole mass of the working people; this very state apparatus is, in the broad meaning of the term, the sum of the mass organizations. The peculiar role of mass organization, for example, labor unions and other organizations of the working people, is characteristic of our proletarian state and corresponds to its nature. Of course, these features of our state have existed from the moment of its appearance, that is, since the October Revolution. But the development and strengthening of these peculiarities does not at all signify the falling asleep and the dying away of state authority on account of its uselessness.

In a bourgeois state there exists contradiction, antagonism, between the state and society. Such an antagonism in our country is nonexistent. Our state embraces the mass organizations of the working people, and the activity of the state apparatus is at the same time its social activity. Our state ownership of the means of production is a social ownership. Consequently, the fact that the mass organizations are increasingly drawn into administration and control, the fact that they are entrusted with concrete tasks, should not be interpreted as signifying that state authority is in a process of falling asleep and dying away. On the contrary, this is merely one of the means of strengthening the state. The maximum development of participation of working people signifies the strengthening of the state apparatus, which does not only persuade, does not only exert an ideological influence, but possesses the power and is able to apply force, coercion, and violence.

In addition to governing human beings, the socialist state also governs things in the process of production. . . . The victory of social socialist property in villages and the success of the state planning and administration of the entire national economy increasingly intensify the role and the significance of the organs that manage the economic activity of our society. These organs will be preserved even in a stateless, communist society, for, in conditions in which "work will become man's prime need," organization of this work and of the entire economic life will be necessary. In the present stage, in the stage of socialism, the socialist economy is administered by the state organs; the administration of things in the process of production is inseparable from the government of men, from the function of authority, from state coercion and state law. The increasing role of state planning, the strengthening and expansion of the economic organs, is a process of the strengthening of the socialist state and not a beginning of the state's dying away.

It should be noted also that despite the fact that on the whole the socialist classless society has been built, the class struggle is continuing and the necessity still exists for a further education and re-education of the working masses as well as for the suppression of hostile elements—of those who have not yet surrendered, who continue their struggle with socialism, who continue to resist, who disguise themselves and play dirty tricks. A state apparatus, an apparatus of compulsion, is inevitable for the struggle with the enemies of socialism. Finally, the task of organizing the defense against capitalist encirclement also remains. The defense of the socialist motherland . . . calls for the strengthening of the Red Army and of all other armed forces.

Socialism is a system based on the social ownership of the means of production. Work under socialism is a universal obligation. Distribution is accomplished according to work, its quality and its quantity. This means that nationwide state control and accounting of labor and consumption is inevitable; equally inevitable are legal norms and the apparatus of coercion, without which law would be meaningless.

Socialist society is organized as a state. The socialist state and socialist law will preserve their significance fully to the higher phase of communism. For only in the higher phase of communism will men learn to work without overseers and without legal norms. The view that law dies away under socialism is as much opportunist nonsense as is the assertion that the state authority began to die away the day after the overthrow of the bourgeoisie.

In this connection it is advisable once again to subject to deserved criticism the views that were advanced by the author of this article in his book *The General Theory of Law and Marxism*. This is particularly necessary in order to prevent the repetition of old errors and old confusions in new forms and under new conditions.

Since distribution according to work bears some resemblance to an equivalent exchange of commodities, Marx and Lenin have indicated that under socialism bourgeois law is fully abolished only in respect to the ownership of the means of production. In this case, private property is being replaced by social property. But in the field of distribution a law operates which could be designated, conditionally, in quotation marks, as a bourgeois law, for it represents an application of equal standards to factually unequal men. This law provides for the continuation of the factual inequality between men; it does not take into account differences in physical power, abilities, family situation, etc. . . .

This principle of remuneration according to work is a socialist principle; it is applied in a society in which each can give nothing but his work, in which there is no exploitation, no crisis, and no unemployment, a society in which the principle "he who does not work does not eat" prevails, in which the state guarantees to each a real right to work. Consequently, this "bourgeois" law neither has nor could have anything in common with the class interests of the bourgeoisie. This law, established by the dictatorship of the proletariat, is the law of the socialist state, serving the interests of the working people, the interests of the development of socialist production. A contemptuous attitude toward this law as a "bourgeois" law is becoming only to anarchistic heroes of the "leftist school" and to defenders of the petty-bourgeois wage leveling.

Marx spoke of the inevitability of distribution according to work as a "deficiency" of socialist society. It is self-evident, however, that this expression has a completely relative meaning. Marx spoke of deficiency in comparison with the higher phase of communism. Nevertheless, this problem is completely misrepresented in my book *The General Theory of Law and Marxism*. Law, state, and even morality are declared there to be bourgeois forms that cannot be filled with any socialist content and that must die away during the realization of socialism. In addition to this erroneous view, which has nothing in common with Marxism-Leninism, the meaning of the proletarian state, proletarian communist morality, and, finally, the meaning of Soviet law (which is the law of the proletarian state and serves as an instrument for the construction of socialism) became completely distorted.

The concrete, true history of Soviet law as an instrument of the proletariat's policy . . . was replaced with abstract and erroneous arguments about the withering away of law, about the "disappearance" of the juridical superstructure, etc. Confusing arguments about the dying away of "legal forms," as a phenomenon inherited from the bourgeois world, have led us away from the struggle against bourgeois influence and bourgeois attempts to distort Soviet law.

The concept of law as a form exclusively predicating market exchange was the theoretical premise underlying this anti-Marxist confusion. The relationship between the owners of commodities was declared to be the true, specific content of all law. Naturally, the principal class content, namely, the ownership of the means of production, was thereby neglected. Law was deduced directly from the exchange of commodities whereby the role of the class state, protecting the system of property which corresponded to the interests of the ruling class, was obliterated. The gist of the problem is, however, which class holds in its hands the state authority.

The great October Revolution has inflicted a blow upon capitalist private property and has laid down the foundation for a new, socialist system of law. This is the main point for the understanding of Soviet law, its socialist essence, the law of the proletarian state. . . . The theory which asserted that all law is "bourgeois" was based on the confusion of many distinct things. . . . According to this theory, socialism . . . is opposed to commerce, to cost accounting, and to the control of money. The "leftist" theories about the dying away of commerce and money and about the transition toward a direct exchange of products are logically related to the theories of the "dying away of law" and of "the withering away of the juridical superstructure."

At the First Conference of Marxist Jurists these erroneous theories were subjected to devastating criticism. The great significance of Soviet law was stressed there, a law whose source of power is the dictatorship of the proletariat. ". . . There is no doubt in our minds that despite the fact that Soviet law has to do with diverse economic structures (with all five structures indicated by Lenin), it has at the same time one single source of power, namely, the October Revolution and the dictatorship of the proletariat."

Such facts as "the transformation of the proletariat into a ruling class, the creation of the Soviet state, the nationalization of the principal means of production, the nationalization of land, transportation, banks, and the monopoly of foreign trade impose an imprint upon all Soviet law and give to it a special quality."[4]

After the discussion of 1930–31 the "theory" asserting that the specific feature of law is the fact that it predicates an equivalent exchange was severely criticized and discarded. However, the positive task, that is, a broad, exhaustive study of the system of Soviet socialist law remains unfulfilled so far. Scientific work is still lagging behind in this field. Such crucial decisions as the law of August 7, 1932, regarding sacred and inviolable socialist property, the decisions of the Seventeenth Party Congress on the liquidation of

[4] E. Pashukanis, *Za Markso-Leninskuyu Teoriyu Gosudarstva i Prava* [For a Marxist-Leninist Theory of State and Law] (Moscow-Leningrad, 1931), p. 24.

classes, and Comrade Stalin's directives at the January Plenum of the Central Committee and Central Control Commission, 1933, on new tasks of revolutionary legality, found their expression only in special branches of law (economic, criminal, etc.). The general theory of Soviet socialist law has not yet been worked out in any systematic way. . . .

Now, in the state of victorious socialism, we have entered into a stage in which the Soviet socialist law, on the basis of social socialist property, introduces the same type of production relations to both cities and villages. We have entered the stage of a firm stabilization of socialist relations of production, which encompass both industry and farming. Social socialist property and distribution according to work are precisely the cornerstones on which the system of Soviet socialist law should be developed.

. . . The task of Soviet socialist law is to protect the achievements of the Revolution, the security of our socialist state or socialist social system, to protect social socialist property, to maintain discipline, to defend personal property rights, to defend and to strengthen the Soviet socialist system. This raises the problem of the relationship between Soviet socialist law and socialist morality. In particular, we should stress the close connection between our criminal law and our socialist morality in connection with the role of the courts. The decisions rendered by our Soviet courts on the basis of our law exert moral influence also upon those who are not directly involved in litigation—upon the entire society. Now, the task of education and re-education is of primary significance. The court is precisely the organ that persuades and re-educates while applying coercion and suppression. . . . Our court is an organ of the dictatorship of the proletariat and will remain as such. . . .

# A "New" Approach to Socialist Law*

## ⁘ A. Ya. Vyshinskii

In asserting that law is nothing but a form of capitalist relationships and that law can develop only under the conditions of capitalism (when law supposedly attains its highest development), the wreckers who have been busying themselves on our legal front were striving toward a single objective: to prove that law is not necessary to the Soviet state and that law is superfluous, as a survival of capitalism, under the conditions of socialism. In reducing Soviet law to bourgeois law and in claiming that there is no ground for the further development of law under socialism, the wreckers aimed at liquidating Soviet law and the science of Soviet law. This is the basic significance of their activity as provocateurs and wreckers. Proceeding along this path, they outdid themselves in discovering all sorts of motives, concepts, and "theories" that would facilitate their achieving their criminal purpose. To this is credited the intensified propaganda of the withering away of the law, which we have mentioned above. To this are credited also such distortions as the reduction of law at one time to economics and at another to policy. In each case alike, we destroy the specific character of law as the aggregate of the rules of conduct, customs, and the rules of community living established by the state and coercively protected by state authority. In reducing law to economics—as Stuchka did when he asserted that law is coincident with production relationships—these gentlemen have toppled down into the morass of economic materialism. . . .

. . . During recent years more than a little has been done to purify our science from distortions of every sort, contrary to Marxism and Leninism alike. This work of purification must be continued further, inasmuch as traces of these perversions are still in evidence here and there. Relapses, too, are occasionally noted in this sphere. Our aim must be that at the present time the science of Soviet law and state direct its basic attention to the working out of the problem of the con-

* From "Osnovnye Zadachi Nauki Sovetskogo Sotsialisticheskogo Prava" [The Fundamental Tasks of the Science of Soviet Socialist Law], Sotsialisticheskaya Zakonnost, No. 8 (1938), pp. 12–17.

These are excerpts from Vyshinskii's address at the First Congress on the Problems of the Science of Soviet State and Law, held in 1938. An English translation of the whole address is available in Babb and Hazard (eds.), Soviet Legal Philosophy (Cambridge, Mass., 1951).

tent of Soviet socialist law as an expression of the will of the working class that has triumphed and of the entire Soviet people. Our task is now to provide a positive definition of our Soviet socialist law. The first attempt to furnish such a definition of law was made by the Institute of Law of the Academy of Sciences, which considered and adopted propositions that I presented. That attempt was made—and I emphasize the fact that it is only a first approximation of a definition —in Proposition 24, which says, "Law is the aggregate of the rules of conduct expressing the will of the dominant class and established in legal order, as well as of customs and rules of community life confirmed by state authority, the application of which is guaranteed by the coercive force of the state to the end of safeguarding, making secure, and developing social relationships and arrangements advantageous and agreeable to the dominant class."[1]

Law is neither a system of social relationships nor a form of production relationships. Law is the aggregate of rules of conduct, or norms, yet not of norms alone, but also of customs and rules of community living confirmed by state authority and coercively protected by that authority.

Our definition has nothing in common with normativist definitions; normativism starts from the completely incorrect notion of law as "social solidarity" (Duguit) or as a norm (Kelsen), which is a final integration of the content of law (and with no reference to the social relationships which actually define that content). The error of the normativists is that when they define law as an aggregate of norms they confine themselves to that element, conceiving of the legal norms themselves as something closed in and explained by themselves. Duguit's definition of law as social solidarity contradicts reality, history, and the facts. Law was never an expression of social solidarity. It was always an expression of dominance, an expression of struggle and contradictions, and not an expression of solidarity. Kelsen starts from an objective law that stands above all phenomena and defines all the phenomena of social life. According to him, the state itself is nothing but "the unity of the internal significance of legal propositions," merely the personification of objective legal order—nothing but a norm or an order. The vice in the definitions of Duguit, Kelsen, and other normativists is that they have furnished a definition of a norm which is itself idealistic and abstract and merely the definition of dogmatic jurisprudence. They do not see in law an expression of the will of the classes dominant in society. They do not see in law the ex-

[1] The proposition is set out in its final form to conform with the resolution of the Council.

pression of the class interests dominant in a given society. They do not see that statute and law draw their content from the definite economic or production conditions dominant in society. In the last analysis, production and exchange define the entire character of social relationships. Law is the regulator of those relationships. Our definition starts from the relationships of dominance and subordination expressed in the law. We consider that our definition is in complete accord with Marxist-Leninist methodology. Of course, incompleteness and inaccuracy are possible in our definition—wherefore that definition must be considered and verified from every side and in the most attentive and critical manner. . . .

. . . The problem of the will of the Soviet people as the source of our socialist law possesses extraordinary interest. Our law is the will of our people elevated to the rank of a statute. In capitalist society, allusions to the will of the people served as a screen that veiled the exploiting nature of the bourgeois state. Under the conditions of our country the matter is different in principle: there has been formulated among us a single and indestructible will of the Soviet people, which is manifested in the unparalleled unanimity with which the people vote in the elections for the Supreme Soviet of the U.S.S.R. and the Supreme Soviets of the Union and Autonomous Republics for the bloc of Communist and non-Party candidates. Our Soviet people consist of the working class, the peasant class, and the toiling intellectuals. Our statutes express the will of our people, which is ruling and which is creating new history under the guidance of the working class. Among us, the will of the working class merges with the will of all the people. This provides the basis for speaking of our Soviet socialist law as an expression of the will of the whole people.

# In Defense of the New Definition of Socialist Law*

## ∽ A. Ya. Vyshinskii

One of the more significant problems of the science of socialist law is the definition of . . . law. The first attempt to give such a definition was made by the Institute of Law at the Academy of Science of the U.S.S.R., during the First Conference of Scientific Workers in the Field of Law, July 16–19, 1938.

In making this attempt, the Institute proceeded from the Marxist-Leninist teaching of law. The Institute also recognized the necessity of overcoming the deficiencies then existing in the scientific-juridical works. First of all it was necessary to put an end to the distortions hostile to Marxism-Leninism, to clear our literature on law from the Krylenko-Pashukanis-Stuchka trash, from the Trotskyite-Bukharinist balderdash.

. . . . . . .

In offering its definition of law, on the basis of the Marxist-Leninist theory, the Institute emphasized that it is merely a first approximation of a scientific definition of law, that it calls for further refinement, supplementation, and perhaps even correction.

. . . . . . .

Speaking of deficiencies of the definition of law given by the Institute, some critics see the defect of our definition in the fact that it has a class character and, consequently, that it is not suitable for law in a classless socialist society. Such an objection is groundless. In a classless socialist society, law expresses the will of all people, guided by the progressive part of society, and issues its norms for the purpose of safeguarding, securing, and developing social relations advantageous and agreeable to the workers.

We have entered a new phase in our development—the phase of completing the construction of a classless socialist society and of a gradual transition from socialism to communism. The class differences are wearing out. We are proceeding toward the liquidation of

* From "XVII Sezd VKP(b) i Zadachi Nauki Sotsialisticheskogo Prava" [The Eighteenth Congress of the C.P.S.U. (B.) and the Tasks of the Science of Socialist Law], Sovetskoe Gosudarstvo i Pravo, No. 3 (1939), pp. 6–12.

classes in general and toward the conversion of workers and peasants into the industrious workers of a single communist society. Under such conditions *class* is replaced by *people*—by workers.

It is impossible in such a case to speak of "the will of the ruling class" without the proviso that the will of the class blends here with the will of the people. I have made such a proviso in my report by saying that "our law is the will of our people elevated to law." However, even in a classless socialist society the ruling interests are those which coincide with the interests of the proletariat in a class society.

Consequently, the state policy in a classless society is, in essence, the continuation of the policy of the proletariat in a class society. Therefore, the definition of law as an expression of the will of the ruling class is not contradictory to the fact that "the ruling class" is absent in a classless society.

. . . . . . .

The following definition . . . of socialist law during the transition period from socialism to communism could be given: *Socialist law in the epoch of the completion of the socialist construction and the gradual transition from socialism to communism is a system of the rules of conduct (norms) established in a legislative order by the authority of the workers and expressing their will, the will of the whole Soviet people, guided by the working class at the head of the Communist Party (Bolsheviks), for the purpose of safeguarding, securing, and developing socialist relations and constructing a communist society.*

Comrade Galanza (Minsk) is dissatisfied with our definition of law. . . . Comrade Galanza considers . . . the expression "advantageous and agreeable to the working class" to be one of its deficiencies. He exclaims: "Here the question may arise—"Is the socialist law advantageous and agreeable only to the working class and not to all workingmen in general?" These and similar perplexities reveal the unsatisfactory solution of this question."[1]

Had I said in my report what Comrade Galanza attributed to me, then such a question could, in fact, "arise." But I have said nothing of this kind. . . . Comrade Galanza simply invented this for the sake of polemics.

. . . . . . .

[1] [I am using the uncorrected stenographic notes of Galanza's speech, delivered during the Scientific Conference of the Institute of Juridical Sciences.]

Comrade Galanza's critical remark concerns the question of international law. This remark is restricted to the assertion that our definition provides no "space" for international law. At the same time, Comrade Galanza is dissatisfied with our theses on it.

. . . . . . .

It should be kept in mind that international law is law of a special type. . . . There is no doubt that the principles of bourgeois law find their expression in bourgeois international law, as there is no doubt that the principles of socialist law—the principles of socialism—find their expression in the struggle of the U.S.S.R. for the new principles of international law.

. . . . . . .

The general conclusion is that the definition of law given by the Institute of Law at the Academy of Science and proceeding from Marx's, Engels', Lenin's, and Stalin's great teachings on state and law has, naturally, endured its first test. But it needs further elaboration and refinement.

# Socialist Law and Equality* ∞ *S. A. Golunskii and M. S. Strogovich*

Socialist law is a completely unique type of law, differing radically from all the species of exploiter law (slave-owning, feudal, and bourgeois law). The uniqueness of socialist law lies in the fact that it is the first law in the history of human society which is not exploitive law; it banishes exploitation and expresses the interests and the will of all the toiling people, of the socialist worker-peasant state.

It differs in form and in substance from any law ever existing in any exploiter state. Being the aggregate of norms expressing the will and securing the interests of a people freed from exploitation—operating in a society in which exploiting classes have been destroyed—socialist law is founded not upon private property but upon public socialist property, which constitutes the indefeasible basis of the socialist system. Socialist law is founded on the principles of the proletarian dictatorship that is carrying into effect the state guidance of society. As the interests of the working class in socialist society (in which exploiting classes have been destroyed) reflect the interests of the entire people, the peasants and the intellectuals, so socialist law . . . expresses the will and defends the interests of all the toiling people.

Socialist law consists of the rules of conduct of socialist society, expressing the will of the entire people. The application of these rules (norms) is secured by the coercive force of the socialist state. Socialist legal norms are established either in the form of legislation of the socialist state or in the form of socialist customs and other rules of the socialist communal life, sanctioned by the state.

Socialist law is thus, above all, an instrument with whose aid the socialist state secures the strengthening and the development of socialist social relationships and destroys the survivals of capitalism in the economy, mode of life, and consciousness of human beings.

As the socialist state organizes the future development of socialism in the direction of its higher stage—classless communist society—so socialist law serves the same end.

---

* From *Teoriya Gosudarstva i Prava* [Theory of State and Law] (Moscow, 1940), pp. 204–8. An English translation of this work is available in Babb and Hazard (eds.), *Soviet Legal Philosophy* (Cambridge, Mass., 1951).

Applying the general definition of law to socialist legal norms, one may define socialist law as follows: *Soviet socialist law is the aggregate of rules of conduct (norms) established or sanctioned by the state authority of the socialist state and expressing the will of the working class and of all the toilers; the application of these rules of conduct is secured by the coercive force of the socialist state to the end of defending, consolidating, and developing relationships and orders advantageous and agreeable to the working class and to all the toilers, of destroying completely and finally the survivals of capitalism in the economy, mode of life, and consciousness of human beings and of building communist society.*[1]

. . . . . . .

Wreckers, who at one time operated on the theoretical front of Soviet law, sought to distort Lenin's thought and asserted that Soviet law is, in general, bourgeois law. This was the crudest perversion of the thought of Marx and Lenin. Soviet law is socialist law, not bourgeois law—it merely fails to have attained complete equality in the distribution of products, wherefore Lenin called it "bourgeois law" (in quotation marks). This inequality, however, existing under socialism and completely eliminated only under communism, is already mitigated under socialism; the inequality still remaining has been substantially rectified by such legislation as that relative to pensions, to social security in case of illness, to grants to mothers having many children, etc. Thus, socialist law, while still preserving a certain inequality, is itself a means of mitigating and gradually eliminating that inequality.

Under socialism the equality in socialist law is not yet the higher form of equality which will be attained in classless communist society, where the principle "from each according to his abilities, to each according to his needs" will prevail. But the equality we already have is an equality that is unattainable in an exploiter state; it is an equality that actually guarantees to a citizen a worthy human existence and the development of all his creative forces and capabilities.

In his report to the Seventeenth Congress of the All-Union Communist Party of Bolsheviks, Comrade Stalin furnished an exhaustive definition of equality as the term is understood in Marxism-Leninism. Equality signifies: "(1) the equal emancipation of all working people

[1] The basis of this definition is that proposed by Vyshinskii and considered at the All-Union Congress of Workers in the Science of Soviet Law in July, 1938. (See "The Fundamental Tasks of Soviet Socialist Law," Materials of the First Congress of Workers in the Science of Law, July 16–19, 1938.)

from exploitation after the capitalists have been overthrown and expropriated; (2) the equal abolition for all, of private property in the means of production after it has been converted into the property of the whole of society; (3) the equal duty of all to work according to their ability, and the equal right of all working people to receive remuneration according to the amount of work performed (*socialist* society); (4) the equal duty of all working people to receive remuneration according to their needs (*communist* society)."[2]

[2] *Voprosy Leninizma* [Problems of Leninism] (11th ed.; Moscow, 1939), p. 470.

# The Marxist-Leninist Theory of Truth*

## ᘓ  G. Gak

A classical formulation of the Marxist-Leninist theory of truth was given in Comrade Stalin's work "On Dialectical and Historical Materialism":

Contrary to idealism, which denies the possibility of knowing the world and its laws, which does not believe in the authenticity of our knowledge, does not recognize objective truth, and holds that the world is full of "things-in-themselves" that can never be known to science, Marxist philosophical materialism holds that the world and its laws are fully knowable, that our knowledge of the laws of nature, tested by experiment and practice, is authentic knowledge having the validity of objective truth, and that there are no things in the world which are unknowable, only things which are as yet not known but which will be disclosed and made known by the efforts of science and practice.[1]

This theory of truth has tremendous significance to science and to practical activity. It serves as a theoretical corroboration of the omnipotence of science, of its unlimited possibilities. In affirming that social phenomena are knowable, the Marxist-Leninist theory of truth inflicts a blow upon agnosticism and idealism. Idealists have advanced quite a number of "theories" which deny the possibility of knowing the phenomena of social life. . . . While resolutely refuting idealist concoctions, Marxism-Leninism has brilliantly demonstrated that "the science of the history of society, despite all the complexities of the phenomena of social life, can become as precise as, let us say, biology, and capable of making use of the laws of development of society for practical purposes."[2]

From this follows the tremendous significance of the Marxist-Leninist theory of truth for the practical activity of the working class's party. For, if the world is knowable, if the knowledge of natural phenomena and the knowledge of the laws of social development is authentic, then "the connection between science and practical activity, the connection of theory with practice, their unity, should be the guiding star of the proletariat's party" (Stalin).

What are the features characteristic of the Marxist-Leninist theory of truth? First of all, it is the recognition that *truth is objective*. This theory is directed against idealists who consider truth to be subjective.

* *From* "Marksistsko-Leninskoe Uchenie ob Istine" [The Marxist-Leninist Theory of Truth], *Bolshevik,* No. 17 (1940), pp. 48–59.
  [1] *Voprosy Leninizma* [Problems of Leninism] (11th ed.; Moscow, 1939), p. 543.
  [2] *Ibid.,* p. 544.

Furthermore, Marxism-Leninism teaches that, since our knowledge of the world has the meaning of objective truth, knowledge has no boundaries and leads man toward the absolute truth. The knowledge attained by man at a given historical moment constitutes a historically given stage in an endless approximation of absolute knowledge and, therefore, has the meaning of relative truth. Hence, the *truth* uncovered by human knowledge *is both absolute and relative*. Moreover, the Marxist-Leninist theory of truth asserts that truth is not abstract, that *truth is always concrete*. Finally, this theory defends the only correct, scientific criterion of truth: human practice. The authenticity of human thought is proved through practice. Our task is to examine all these elements of the Marxist-Leninist theory of truth.

Marxist philosophical materialism demonstrates that our views, scientific concepts, ideas, confirmed by practice, have an objective meaning independent of any consciousness. In man's consciousness is reflected the real world: objects, phenomena, as well as their connections and relationships. Objective reality appears not only in man's sensations but also in his thinking. Views and ideas, just as sensations, are a copy, a photograph, of the real world.

Man perceives the world through his sense organs (sight, hearing, touch, taste, smell). While affecting the sense organs, external objects arouse corresponding sensations, the totality of which constitutes the perception of a given object. Naturally, the image of the object and the object of perception are not identical, just as an original and a copy, or an object and its photograph, are not identical. But we can unmistakably recognize an object from its depiction in the photograph.

Skeptics from the idealist camp assert that, since our thoughts do not come in contact with the object itself but only with our sensations, we can know neither the object as it is prior to our perception, nor . . . whether this object exists at all outside of our perception. But can sensation arise without an object affecting our sense organs? It is as impossible as it is for a reflection to appear in the mirror without the reflected object. Consequently, in attempting to explain sensation, subjective idealists—who deny the existence of external objects that affect our sensations—resort to mysticism and devilry.

Not only sensations but also views, ideas, and scientific abstractions have their origins in the material world. In order to see this we shall take a closer look at the mechanism by means of which man cognizes the world surrounding him. Man uses his sense organs actively. While looking at the development of science, we see that progress, in acquiring the knowledge of nature, is connected, among other things, with the development and perfection of the organs of sensory cognition.

For example, the telescope makes possible a deeper and more accurate knowledge of astronomical phenomena; an unequipped eye is unable to see the finest texture of organic and inorganic matter, but this can be done by means of a microscope. Modern photo elements are quite rightly called "electric eyes"; and the thermometer permits us to observe the highest and lowest temperatures.

But even if our sense organs were perfect, sensory knowledge alone would be inadequate for a complete mastery of an object. For example, the cause-effect connection between things cannot be comprehended through sensory perception in the same way we comprehend color, hardness, sound, etc. From this fact agnostics deduced a false conclusion. They argued that since causality is inaccessible to sense experience, we do not know whether it exists in the real world. This conclusion, however, is groundless; it is being constantly refuted by human practice.

Engels wrote:

The activity of human beings *forms the test of causality*. . . . If we bring together in a rifle the priming, the explosive charge, and the bullet, and then fire it, we count upon the effect known in advance from previous experience, because we can follow in all its details the whole process of ignition, combustion, explosion, by the sudden conversion into gas and the pressure of the gas on the bullet. And here the skeptic cannot even say that because of previous experience it does not follow that it will be the same next time. For, as a matter of fact, it does sometimes happen that it is *not* the same, that the priming or the gunpowder fails to work, that the barrel bursts, etc. But it is precisely this which *proves* causality instead of refuting it, because we can find out the cause of each such deviation from the rule by appropriate investigation: chemical decomposition of the priming, dampness, etc., of the gunpowder, a defect in the barrel, etc., so that here the test of causality is, so to speak a double one.[3]

Many examples demonstrate the fact that a phenomenon, existing outside of our consciousness and reflected in man's concepts, thoughts, and ideas, may not be the object of a direct sensory perception. No one has yet seen the earth revolving on its axis—this fact was not established through a direct sensory perception. To be able to see it as directly as we see the traveling of the moon we would have to go to another planet and from there look at the earth. Nevertheless, the view that the earth revolves on its axis reflects an objectively existing fact. We cannot imagine the speed of 270 thousand kilometers per second, but such is precisely the speed of an electron. The value of a commodity has an objective existence, independent of consciousness, although it contains not even a grain of matter that can be seen or touched.

---

[3] *Dialektika Prirody* [Dialectics of Nature] (Moscow, 1936), p. 14.

. . . From this it follows that the instruments of cognition include not only the *senses* but also the *mind*. This, however, should not be interpreted to mean that the mind cognizes an object independently of the senses. According to the materialist theory of cognition, everything that exists in the mind existed earlier in the senses. The mind works on the material supplied to it by the senses.

What, then, is the object of the mind's cognition? In contrast to sensory perception, whose immediate subject matter is a separate, concrete object, the subject matter of the mind is the concrete object in its universality and in its inevitable connection with varied phenomena of the world. The mind discovers the laws of existence and development which are innate in things and phenomena. Such, for example, are the basic laws of dialectic discovered by the founders of Marxism: the law of the transformation of quantity into quality, the law of the unity and struggle of contradictions, the law of the negation of the negation; such is the law of universal capitalist accumulation in bourgeois societies, discovered by Marx; such is the law of an uneven development of capitalism under imperialism, discovered by Lenin; such is the law of universal gravity in physics, discovered by Newton; such are all other natural laws.

These laws—expressing a connection between phenomena, a connection that is universal and inevitable—have an objective existence. The entire history of thought and the history of social practice confirm this conclusion. The progress of human power is parallel to the progress of scientific knowledge, that is, the knowledge of the development of nature and society. It is precisely the knowledge of the laws of the material world that gives man mastery over nature and social relations. Thereby an irrefutable proof is furnished that our knowledge of the world has the meaning of an objective truth.

. . . . . . .

Idealists, who deny the objectivity of truth, arrive at the most absurd conclusions. . . . Idealists of Bogdanov's type assert that truth is something "conditional," something that men deem "convenient" for themselves to recognize as truth. In refuting this idealist nonsense, Lenin noted that by means of such a conception of truth "one can justify any sophistry; one can recognize as 'conditional' the fact that Napoleon died on May 5, 1821; one can, for the sake of man's or humanity's 'convenience,' assume that scientific ideology ('convenient' in one respect) is compatible with religious ideology (very 'convenient' in other respects), etc."[4]

There are some idealists who recognize the objectivity of truth but

[4] *Sochineniya* [Works] (3rd ed.; n.p., n.d.), XIII, 111–12.

interpret it idealistically. Such is Hegel's conception of truth. To him knowledge was the cognition of an objective (absolute) idea that existed prior to and independent of man. Cognition is to be directed toward finding the inner content of a thing, and the inner content, according to Hegel, is a moment of the development of the idea embodied in the thing. To Hegel, truth was that which corresponds to the objective idea. According to Hegel, and in contrast to subjective idealism, truth is no longer something arbitrary and conditional. But Hegel's explanation of the development of objective, absolute ideas was artificial; it was derived from the head and hence cannot be regarded as a real basis of the development of knowledge and determination of truth. Only the material world—which is not a product of any consciousness and which existed prior to and independent of any consciousness—is that to which thought must correspond in order to prove its authenticity. The only correct answer to the question of what is truth is furnished by dialectical materialism: truth is that which correctly reflects objective reality, that which most fully and thoroughly encompasses all connections and interdependences of natural and social phenomena.

But what is the meaning of "correspondence to reality"? At first glance it may seem that this question needs no explanation. But this is precisely the question that raises the central problem of truth.

Human knowledge has been developing through many centuries. Each individual science has its own history. Looking at the history of science, we see that its development on the whole constitutes a progressive motion from lower stages of knowledge toward higher ones. In the process of cognition each new generation depends on the achievements of the preceding generations, continues their work, and advances knowledge further.

Such progressive motion manifests itself in a constantly increasing penetration into the depth of phenomena, that is, in the discovery of basic connections and relations. For example, for a long time man knew nothing about electrons. He acquired knowledge about them as a result of discoveries that were made at the end of the ninteenth and the beginning of the twentieth centuries. Or, for example, let us take Marx's discovery that the mode of production determines all other aspects of social life. From the moment when man began to produce material goods indispensable to his existence, production became the starting point of the entire historical process. Nevertheless, through the ages, man failed to notice the profound tie that exists between production and politics, between production and social consciousness in all its manifestations. Only Marx's and Engels' theory of historical materialism succeeded in demonstrating that the politics and ideology of each social system are conditioned by the mode of production that lies at their base. Another vivid example of a gigantic scientific achievement is Lenin's law of the uneven development of capitalism in the epoch of imperialism, which made a simultaneous victory of socialism in all countries impossible but created an opportunity for the victory of socialism in one country.

. . . . . . .

It is wrong to assume that each new stage of knowledge is related to the preceding one as truth to error. . . . The progress of knowledge necessitates the correction of defects in the earlier-attained knowledge. As noted by Engels, "In all probability we are still approximately at the very beginning of history, and it must be assumed that the generations whose task will be to correct *us* will be more numerous than those whose knowledge we are able to correct, thereby not infrequently displaying a contemptuous attitude toward them."[5]

Hence, truth shall not be conceived of as a complete, universally exhaustive, and ideally perfect image of reality; truth shall not be viewed as something stationary and ossified, for it is constantly in the making; it is a never-ending process. "Cognition"—Lenin pointed out in his notes on Hegel's *Science of Logic*—"is a *process* of immersion in non-organic nature (mind) with the purpose of subordinating it to the subject. . . . Coincidence of thought with object is a *process*. Thought (that is, man) shall not imagine truth as something in a deadly peace or as a simple, pale (dim) picture (image) without tendency, without motion, like a number, like an abstract thought."[6]

Like any process, the development of knowledge constitutes a struggle of contradictions. . . . "Cognition," writes Lenin, "is an everlasting, endless approximation of thought to the object. The *reflection* of nature in man's thought should be understood not as 'dead,' 'abstract,' *motionless and non-contradictory,* but as a perpetual *process* of motion, contradictions, and their resolution."[7]

. . . . . . .

It follows, then, that our knowledge at each given historical stage did not contain truth in its absolute completeness; it was not a knowledge that exhausted the world entirely. Nor, indeed, will it ever become such, for the world is infinite and hence inexhaustible. Our knowledge can increasingly draw closer (as it does) to the absolute, complete knowledge of the world, but it can never come to an end. "Man," Lenin indicated, "cannot encompass, that is, reflect, the *entire* nature, in its totality; he can only perpetually draw closer to it,

[5] *Anti-Dyuring* [Anti-Dühring] (Moscow, 1938), p. 88.
[6] *Leninskii Sbornik* [Lenin's Miscellany] (Moscow), IX (n.d.), 225.
[7] *Ibid.*, p. 226.

creating abstractions, laws, a scientific picture of the world, etc., etc."[8]

. . . The process of increasing knowledge is an endless one; it can never be completed. Therefore, truth, being conditioned by, and restricted to, historical periods, is relative. But each new posterior stage in this process draws man increasingly closer to absolute truth. Absolute truth consists of relative truths. Marxism-Leninism asserts that truth is objective. And "to acknowledge objective truth, i.e., truth not dependent upon man and mankind, is, in one way or another, to recognize absolute truth."

Furthermore, "Human thought . . . by its nature is capable of giving, and does give, absolute truth, which is compounded of a sum total of relative truths. Each step in the development of science adds new grains to the sum of absolute truth, but the limits of the truth of each scientific proposition are relative, now expanding, now shrinking with the growth of knowledge."

Human knowledge, representing an endless number of relative truths, contains at the same time absolute, eternal truths. Truth is at the same time both relative and absolute. Let us give a few examples.

. . . Lenin's and Stalin's discovery of the laws innate in capitalism considerably expanded the knowledge of the capitalist world economy and thereby enriched Marx's economic theory. But an incontestable, absolute truth is the historical tendency in the development of capitalism, which was discovered by Marx. The same applies to the fundamental propositions advanced by dialectical materialism on the universal interconnection of phenomena, on the universality of motion, on the leap-like transition of quantity into quality, and on the struggle of opposites. All these propositions, as well as the proposition of Marxist philosophical materialism on the primacy of matter and the secondary character of consciousness, are absolute truths. This, however, does not prevent dialectical materialism from enriching itself with new propositions. Here we see that truth is both absolute and relative.

To recognize that truth is both relative and absolute is to recognize that cognition proceeds through relative truths toward absolute truth and that, constantly changing and enriching itself, it at the same time also produces knowledge that becomes an everlasting, immutable, and incontestable acquisition of the human mind. The recognition of the absolute and relative character of truth serves as an antidote against both dogmatism, which transforms science into something dead and ossified, and skepticism, which through constant references to the changeability of human knowledge seeks to undermine faith in

[8] *Ibid.*, p. 203.

the truth of human knowledge. Among the enemies of Marxism there were revisionists who, under the pretext of a "struggle against dogmatism," called for freedom of criticism of the foundations of Marxism and sought to "re-examine" and "correct" them; there were also those who sought to ossify Marxism by transforming it into a dead system of hardened dogmas.

The Marxist-Leninist theory of truth, that is, the theory asserting that truth is both relative and absolute, equips us for the struggle against all enemies of Marxist philosophy. From this theory it follows that "mastering the Marxist-Leninist theory means being able to enrich this theory with the new experience of the revolutionary movement, with new propositions and conclusions; it means being able to *develop it and advance it* without hesitating to replace—in accordance with the substance of the theory—such of its propositions and conclusions as have been made obsolete by new ones corresponding to the new historical situation."[9]

. . . A vivid example of the broadening of knowledge, of the discovery of new . . . connections and interrelations between phenomena, is Comrade Stalin's new treatment of the problem of the state under socialism and communism. At the Eighteenth Congress of the C.P.S.U.(B.), Stalin . . . said: "But we can and should expect the Marxist-Leninists of our day not to confine themselves to learning by rote a few general tenets of Marxism but to delve deeply into the essence of Marxism; to learn to take account of the experience gained in the twenty years of existence of the socialist state in our country; and, lastly, utilizing this experience and basing themselves on the essence of Marxism, to learn to apply the various general tenets of Marxism concretely, to lend them greater precision and improve them."

. . . . . . .

The knowledge of the laws of nature and the laws of social development is, therefore, of great significance to both cognition and practice. But it is important to know how to apply these laws in each particular case; to apply them not mechanically, but taking account of the totality of the concretely existing conditions. *History of the C.P.S.U.(B.), Short Course* states: "Mastering the Marxist-Leninist theory means assimilating *the substance* of this theory and learning to use it in the solution of practical problems of the revolutionary movement under the varying conditions of the class struggle of the proletariat."[10]

    [9] *Kratkii Kurs Istorii VKP(b)* [History of the C.P.S.U.(B.), Short Course] (Moscow, 1938), p. 340.
    [10] *Ibid.,* pp. 339–40.

A feature characteristic of the Marxist-Leninist theory of truth is that it regards man's practical activity as the basis of the process of cognition and attainment of truth. The acquired information about the world and its phenomena must constantly be verified in practice, for only practice proves the truth of our views. "Truth," writes Lenin, "is a process. From a subjective idea man arrives at objective truth through practice (and technique)."[11] Moreover, "Life gives rise to a brain. Man's brain reflects nature. Testing the validity of these reflections, by applying them in practice and technique, man arrives at objective truth."[12]

Practice is the criterion of truth and therefore is a constituent part of the process of cognition. But not just any practice draws man closer to the knowledge of objective truth. As stated by Lenin, "Man's will, his practice, hinders itself from attaining its goal . . . in that it separates itself from cognition and does not recognize external reality as truly existing (as objective truth)."[13]

Cognition is not only an activity of the mind—thought; cognition is inseparable from the will of the cognizing subject. The will of reactionary classes and their ideologists often plays the role in history of hindering cognition, at times even resorting to the falsification of science. Examples from the history of the struggle of the Bolshevik party against its enemies demonstrate that the revolutionary mind and the revolutionary will of Bolsheviks carried Marxist science forward toward a constantly increasing mastery of the laws of social development. At the same time, the reactionary will of the opportunists, and their practice, sought in every way possible to prevent the proletariat from utilizing the knowledge of objectively existing opportunities in its struggle for emancipation and from developing faith in its power. The will of the opportunists, which was directed against socialism, gave rise to all sorts of perfidious theories asserting that socialism is a matter of a distant, unpredictable future. These "socialists" did not frighten the Rothschilds and Rockefellers; the latter ranked themselves among those "socialists" who relegated socialism to a distant and unforeseeable future.

Only Lenin and Stalin have brilliantly discerned the new distribution of the class forces, which is in favor of the proletariat and conducive to its victory in the new epoch of imperialism. Lenin's and Stalin's brilliant discovery of the new laws of the imperialist phase in the development of capitalism constitutes a gigantic step forward in the knowledge of the laws of social development; it was born and tested in the fire of revolutionary struggle, in the fire of revolutionary practice, and proved its power as an objective truth.

[11] *Leninskii Sbornik*, IX, p. 237.  [12] *Ibid.*  [13] *Ibid.*, p. 265.

# An Appraisal of Democratic Systems after the Second World War*   ᶜᵛᵔ   *I. P. Trainin*

Interest in the Soviet democracy has never before been as great as it is now after the victorious completion of the war against the German and Japanese aggressors. Now the world attentively follows the methods employed by the U.S.S.R. in resolving and surmounting their postwar difficulties under the conditions of a socialist democracy. On the other hand, our people attentively follow the development of democracy abroad. This article aims to present briefly the peculiarities of both democracies.

. . . . . . .

The ideologists of the bourgeoisie quite frequently reduce the problem of democracy simply to the subordination of the minority to the majority. But, as stated by Lenin, "democracy is not identical to the subordination of the minority to the majority." Democracy, i.e., the specific form of state, is a political authority, an instrument of dictatorship by the ruling class. This is true in the case of both a bourgeois and a socialist state. The crucial distinction is that the bourgeois state exercises dictatorship in the interests of the propertied minority, and the socialist state in the interests of the overwhelming majority of the people. Under conditions of socialism, even the concept of people has a different meaning. The term is interpreted to mean people devoid of exploiters, people consisting . . . of workers, peasants, and the Soviet intelligentsia.

Only those who aim at concealing the class nature of the state, with its attendant dictatorship of a given class, talk of a "pure democracy," contraposing it to a dictatorship. By doing that, they obliterate the problems of *the class content of bourgeois democracy.*

. . . . . . .

Soviet socialist democracy has a number of characteristic features:

1. Soviet socialist democracy is the most *universal democracy*. It opened the way for participation in state government to the broadest

* From "O Demokratii" [On Democracy], *Sovetskoe Gosudarstvo i Pravo,* No. 1 (1946), pp. 12–22.

mass of people. Indeed, without a truly popular democracy, the dictatorship of the working class would have been impossible. Equally impossible would have been the suppression of the workers' enemies within the country . . . without involving the broadest mass of the people in the struggle. The strengthening of the union between the workers, the peasants, and the intelligentsia could not have been achieved without their direct and comprehensive participation in the government of the state. Finally, without the participation and initiative of the broad masses of people, the grandiose economic construction of socialism would have been unattainable. These are the peculiar characteristics of the Soviet democracy.

The organization of the socialist state is based on democratic centralism, which promotes the awakening and development of the broadest independent activity and initiative on the local level. Democratic centralism permits the local organs to have complete freedom to make use of the most suitable . . . means of fulfilling national tasks.

Soviet democracy is a genuine, most consistent democracy. The principle of electing governmental organs from the highest to the lowest levels, the responsibility of the governmental organs to the electorate, the electorate's right to recall deputies who do not justify its confidence, the principle of accountability of the administrative organs to political authority, and, in general, the principle of a true *people's sovereignty* and the identity of the interests of the governing and the governed are most consistently translated into reality in the Soviet state.

The ideologists of capitalism and reformism criticized Soviet democracy because it deprived the former of exploiting the minority of their electoral rights. . . . But the earlier limitations imposed upon the electoral rights in Soviet society were temporary measures, applied only as long as the opposition of the exploiting classes was undefeated. These limitations were definitively removed with the introduction of Stalin's constitution, which established universal, equal, and direct right of suffrage with secret voting for all citizens over eighteen years of age. . . . Only insane persons and those rendered ineligible by a judicial decision are deprived of the right of suffrage.

2. The foundation of the socialist democracy is the social system in which the instruments of production belong to the working people, that is to say, to the state or to the social cooperative organizations. *The economic system of the socialist democracy,* which is developing in conformity with the economic plan, precludes the possibility of an economic crisis, unemployment, etc. The significance of this system has been demonstrated quite convincingly during the victorious war

SOVIET POLITICAL THOUGHT

for the preservation of our fatherland. Its tremendous importance and superiority are being demonstrated at the present time in this postwar period. In contrast to some great foreign powers, unemployment does not exist in the U.S.S.R. With the introduction of the new five-year plan and with the further development of the economy, not only has work been guaranteed to everyone, but in some branches of the economy the scarcity of manpower has been felt. In fact, the Soviet economic system was the only one that secured work for all the demobilized members of its armed forces commensurate with their ability and qualifications.

3. Socialist democracy *does not merely proclaim the rights of citizens formally but guarantees their actual materialization* through material means secured by legislation. The right to work, to rest, to obtain old-age material benefits, to obtain sickness and disability benefits, the right to obtain an education, the right of freedom of speech, press, assembly, etc., are not merely formal but real rights guaranteed by the state.

4. *Soviet democracy is an active democracy.* "In the activity of our numerous labor unions, our industrial, cultural, sporting, and other working organizations, in the creation of the collective farms that unite many millions of the Soviet peasantry throughout the entire vast territory of the Soviet Union, in the steadfast growth of socialist competition in factories and plants, in collective and state farms, in mines and railroads, we see the blossoming of a true people's democracy, which was unknown to us in the old times and which cannot exist in any other state." (Quoted from V. M. Molotov's speech delivered on the twenty-eighth anniversary of the Great October Socialist Revolution.) . . .

5. *Equality,* which is the most significant slogan of democracy, is materializing under socialist conditions in a most consistent way. This slogan means, first, the equality of all members of socialist society in relationship to the means and the instruments of production and, second, freedom from exploitation. Backed by the entire wealth of the Soviet people, socialist democracy guarantees to its citizens an *equal* and *real* right to work, to rest, to receive an education, and to obtain anything that secures and elevates human dignity. It secures the equal rights of women and men, the equal rights for all to receive an income in conformity with the quantity and quality of their work.

6. Socialist democracy is based on the friendship of its peoples. This friendship is the foundation of the political structure of the multinational Soviet state, namely, the foundation of the federal state structure to which the Union republics are subordinated on the basis

of equal rights and which, in turn, unite the people of the autonomous Soviet republics, the autonomous regions, and the national districts. The equality and the friendship of its people have furnished the Soviet democracy, the socialist state, with an indestructible power, so clearly demonstrated in the struggle against the German and Japanese aggressors.

7. Socialist democracy also comprises a *socialist patriotism,* which is distinct from a nationalistic patriotism ("blustering patriotism"). Socialist patriotism expresses the pride of the multinational Soviet people; it thoroughly combines the love of one's people with the respect for other people's rights: this is the principle that constitutes the firm base for the foreign policy of Soviet democracy.

In summarizing these basic features of Soviet democracy, one may conclude that *under Soviet conditions "democracy" means the unlimited sovereignty of the Soviet people. . . .*

We shall now turn to the peculiarities of bourgeois democracy in the contemporary epoch. Leaving aside the well-known concepts of democracy which came into being during the classical bourgeois revolutions at the end of the eighteenth century, we shall note merely that "democracy" signified the people's sovereignty but, in fact, was the sovereignty of the bourgeoisie, which identified its own class interests with those of the whole people. It was a formal democracy that imposed restrictions upon the political rights of the workers and that failed to secure for them the most essential "individual freedom." The worker, who was "sovereign" at the ballot box, was in actuality merely a hired laborer in the capitalist factory without any guarantees or security in his job: ". . . what 'individual freedom' can an unemployed worker have if he is hungry and unable to find work?" (Stalin).

Precisely the same is true of another significant principle of democracy, namely, equality. . . .

. . . . . . .

With the growth of imperialism in the last quarter of the nineteenth century, loud voices resounded on the crisis of the bourgeois democracy. Especially after the First World War, talk on this crisis gained popularity, despite the fact that in the early postwar period quite a number of democratic constitutions came into being, which proved, however, to be short-lived. The class struggle was constantly growing and becoming increasingly intensified; consequently, the bourgeoisie relinquished the old democratic institutions and resorted to an open terror as well as to the fascist method of suppressing the workers. Fascism—which as early as 1923 became established in Italy and was coming into being in Poland, Yugoslavia, and other countries—took a menacing stand against democracy, thus emphasizing its crisis.

Attempts were made to "cure" democracy with capitalistic prescriptions but without consideration of the fact that it was exactly capitalism itself that had caused the ailment of the bourgeois democracy. New theories of democracy were advocated, and in this connection the reformists demonstrated a special zeal.

In contrast to socialist democracy, which became consolidated in the U.S.S.R., the reformists have advanced the idea of "economic democracy." They assumed that, in addition to political democracy—which manifests itself in elections to the parliament and in the parliament itself—private economic interests would be subordinated to social and state interests and that workers would participate in the management of the economy on an equal footing with the industry owners. Indeed, such an illusion (meant for the consumption of simple and credulous workers) found its expression in Germany in the Weimar constitution. . . .

Among the diverse "prescriptions" for the cure of bourgeois democracy in France, the idea of "authoritarian democracy," intensively propagated by Tardieu, became the most important. The decipherment of the meaning of this "democracy" indicates that its essential contents are the following: (1) the elimination of the dependence of executive organs on the legislative, i.e., the strengthening of the privileged role of government (the council of ministers) and the head of government;[1] (2) the right of the head of government to demand the dissolution of parliament if a majority expresses its lack of confidence in it; (3) the bureaucratization of the state apparatus and the deprivation of public officials of their right to join professional unions.

This "authoritarian democracy" aimed at preventing the workers from utilizing democratic institutions, parliament in particular, in the struggle for their interests. It strengthened the reaction in all spheres of social life and became the steppingstone to the fascist state apparatus.

With the growth of the economic crisis in the U.S.A. after the First World War, ideas of technocracy were circulated. According to these ideas, parliamentary representation, in its contemporary form, became obsolete. Life became complicated, and development was de-

---

[1] The same tendency is apparent in De Gaulle's project of the so-called Fourth Republic.

termined by technology. But parliaments are in the hands of professional politicians and lawyers, who have little competence in the technical field. The outbursts of mass dissatisfaction—strikes and revolutions—constitute proof that the existing government does not recognize the significance of technology and is not capable of utilizing its technological achievements for the solution of human problems. The ideologists of "technocracy" thought that they could make the present mode of peacetime life similar to the military life. Who, they argued, would permit idle talk in an army at war? The decisive word would belong to professional militarists and strategists. Similarly, in civilian life the "ship" of state should be in the hands of technicians. . . .

The experience of the socialist democracy confirms the fact that technology is a mighty instrument in raising the welfare of the people; however, only when the contradiction between the social character of production and the capitalist form of appropriation of produced goods has been eliminated will these goods be utilized solely in the interests of the workers.

The idea of democracy has been prostituted in the most insolent way by the Fascists. They attempted to "prove" that the popular masses "rejected" the principle of democracy as the form of the state. Thus, Napoleon I and the "small" Napoleon III contended that they came to power by means of a "democratic" plebiscite. Likewise, Hitler boasted that the leadership of the state fell into his hands as the result of "democratic elections." In his delirious book, *Mein Kampf*, he spoke of "German democracy," which discarded the old democratic concept of "man" and his "individual, inalienable rights" and instead eulogized the principle of the "superman" (*Führer*), who was the living executor of the will of the most reactionary and piratical cliques, and for whom the people were merely a blind, following mass (*Gefolgschaft*). Mussolini, in his turn, "taught" that in contrast to the old democracy, which is based on "arithmetic" (number of votes), a plausible development would be an "accentuated democracy" whose spokesman is the "duce."

The war against brutal fascism was conducted under the banner of democracy. In the process of war, some outstanding statesmen of foreign countries attempted to reformulate the principles of democracy . . . in order to make them adaptable to the new conditions. Outstanding among the various formulations are the principles of democracy advanced by Roosevelt, the deceased President of the United States.

Roosevelt's opponents denounced him as a proponent of "socialism," though obviously he was not implicated in it. On the contrary, they should have been grateful to Roosevelt for his successful guidance of the capitalist boat (the U.S.A.) through the stormy waters of the great economic crisis and through almost the entire Second World War. Being a sensible politician, he knew that, in order to save capitalism under existing conditions, it was necessary to make some concessions to the workers in terms of wages, to demonstrate a greater compliancy to the labor unions, and to render help to the farmers. By doing this, he aimed at preventing a revolution as a means of solving the brewing social problems.

In contrast to the short-sighted "isolationists," Roosevelt knew that fascist ambitions toward world hegemony were threatening the fundamental interests of the United States. He also thought that one should not adhere to the old, worn out phrases about "freedom" and that the concept of "freedom" should be adapted to the psychology of the "average American," on whom the contemporary social and political system of the United States tends to lean.

But what is freedom? The fathers of the American Constitution—who in their strange "obliviousness" had not included the Bill of Rights in the basic law but supplemented it later with various amendments—had stated earlier in their "Declaration" of 1776 that all men are created equal, that they are endowed by their creator with certain inalienable rights, that among these are life, liberty, and the pursuit of happiness. All men were viewed as "equal" and "free": the worker was free to sell his labor or to starve to death; the entrepreneur was free to buy or not to buy his labor; this was the freedom of bargaining and the freedom of contract. Freedom meant: "steal as much as you can." Reactionary American politicians (Hoover and others) have interpreted freedom as "the freedom to accumulate private property," i.e., they overtly advocated the exploitation of workers.

Such a mode of interpreting bourgeois freedom became unsuitable under the conditions of the economic crisis prior to the war, and especially during the war. Roosevelt believed that it was indispensable that the concept of "freedom" be drawn closer to the psychology of an "average" American who is opposed to fascism. At the beginning of the war Roosevelt advanced his "four freedoms," which, in his opinion, should become the basic principles of American democracy.

The first two are individual freedoms, namely, the freedoms of religion and thought. Psychologically, Roosevelt was equal to an "average man" who traditionally associates his American industriousness with an evangelical sermon. Hitler strangled religion because he thought that it was disgraceful for a German to have the same god as people of "lower races." On the other hand, the old puritanism, exported by the first immigrants from England, has defended the "freedom of religion" from absolutism and the Roman popes. This religious principle has also always been advanced as a political principle, and this time it was directed against Hitler. On June 7, 1944, Roosevelt read a prayer on radio for victory over Hitlerism and asked his audience to repeat the words of the prayer; however, as he invoked God's "assistance," he knew that the real victory over Hitler's Germany necessitated a strong army and a large navy. He was deeply engaged in the creation of these, and it was these, . . . not the prayers, which were decisive in victory.

Freedom of thought, as well as other freedoms, is contradictory to American reality, where freedom of thought that is in conflict with the interests of the monopolistic cliques is subject to persecution. It is well known that freedom of thought is limited in the United States; these limitations are as follows:

1. Publishing houses and the press are in the hands of concerns that furnish the people with information that is conducive to their interests; in this respect the best examples are the Hearst and other enterprises, which conduct profascist propaganda, to the detriment of the United States' national interest.

2. The big meeting halls are in the hands of entrepreneurs and reactionary organizations; for example, in 1939 Mrs. Roosevelt resigned from the Daughters of the American Revolution to protest their refusal to permit the singer Marian Anderson to use their hall because she is a Negro. Such examples are many, and, needless to say, labor organizations encounter the same difficulties in procuring meeting space.

3. Deviation from traditional dogmas is subject to persecution in the United States; the best example of this was the "Scopes trial" in the state of Tennessee, during which the proponents of Darwinism were tried for expressing the view that man originates from the ape.

4. The proponents of proletarian internationalism are subject to persecution because their activity is presumably "anti-American."

In Roosevelt's opinion, the first two freedoms cannot exist without economic security. Consequently, they entail additional freedoms. Roosevelt argued that "men at home as well as at the front, both males and females, are concerned with a *third freedom,* namely, the freedom from misery. This freedom means, as far as they are concerned, that after demobilization, when industry is diverted to peaceful pursuits, they will want the right to obtain jobs for themselves as will all able-bodied men and women in America who desire to work."[2]

Finally, Roosevelt has described the fourth freedom in the following manner: "Hitlerism, like any other form of crime or disaster, can grow from any seed of evil, from economic evil or from military feudalism. . . . This entails a struggle for the broadening of man's security here and in the whole world, and in the final analysis it means a struggle for *the fourth freedom*, freedom from fear."[3]

The German aggressor has been destroyed. But there are reactionary cliques in the United States who attempted to prevent the destruction of fascism and who, at the present time, aim at preventing collective efforts from securing peace. These reactionary forces glorify the atomic bomb as an aggressive weapon against people. . . .

The forces of fascism have not been absolutely liquidated yet. They receive support from reactionary cliques in the U.S.A. and England. Consequently, neither "freedom from fear" nor "freedom from misery" exists. . . .

Some leading English statesmen have formulated a concept of democracy in connection with the establishment of democracy in southeastern European countries that had been liberated by the Red Army. Thus, speaking in the House of Commons in August, 1945, Labour Minister Bevan indicated that the conditions which came into being in some countries of southeastern Europe "do not correspond to our meaning of the frequently used term 'democracy.' "

What, then, do they understand by democracy? The answer has been given by the Labourite Prime Minister Atlee, during the Congress of British Trade Unions in September, 1945: "Democracy," Atlee argued, "is not a simple rule of the majority but the rule of a majority that has a proper respect for the rights of the minority."[4]

The nations of southeastern Europe, in particular Bulgaria and Yugoslavia, have, by bitter experience during the German occupation of their territory, become acquainted with the nature of fascism and profascism. They established democratic governments in their countries; but the struggle with fascist elements and traitors, who either collaborated with the Germans or were their agents, continues. The new democratic governments liquidate feudal institutions, introduce land reforms, and distribute land to the landless peasants. This democratic policy is being opposed by a numerically insignificant minority. . . .

. . . The reactionary foreign press seeks to depict the courageous

[2] *Pravda*, January 9, 1943.          [3] *Ibid.*          [4] *Ibid.*, September 30, 1945.

democratic reforms in the countries of southeastern Europe as being primarily the result of the growing influence of the Soviet Union. But, as pointed out by V. M. Molotov, "Such arguments are groundless, since it is well known to everyone that such problems were also resolved successfully in the progressive European countries much earlier." This is especially true of the liquidation of the feudal remnants in land property.

To Marxists, democracy is not a formal, abstract principle, valid for all time. Approaching the problem of democracy, Marxists take into account the concrete historical conditions (primarily economic conditions) as well as the relationship of class forces in each country under these conditions and at each historical stage. Marxists always account for the source and the direction of development in any given society.

In view of historical development, Marxists acknowledge the progressive role of bourgeois democracy in comparison with the regimes existing in the epoch of absolutism and serfdom. Throughout the entire history of class struggle, the working class has . . . been vitally interested in broadening democracy. Without the minimum of democratic rights and freedoms, the working class would have been incapable of preparing itself for the assumption of its historical task, namely, to become a "class in itself," to create its own political party, opposed to all bourgeois parties, and to struggle for the conquest of the government.

In the present historical stage the working class defends all the achievements of bourgeois democracy when the latter is threatened by fascism. . . .

# The Role of Logic and Dialectics in the Theory of Law* ∽ *A. A. Piontkovskii*

The theoretical process of studying positive law involves the analysis of juridical concepts, the systematization of legal norms, the creation of new juridical concepts, and the formulation of juridical constructs. . . . Numerous juridical definitions must be supplied by the jurist. . . . Definitions play a greater role in juridical science than in any other science. The quality of juridical science depends upon the character of the definitions of juridical concepts, juridical institutes, and legal relationships with all their elements. To a great degree, the same is true of the process of applying legal norms.

Bourgeois theory solves the problem of formulating juridical definitions by means of formal logic. . . .

A definition has a theoretically cognitive and practical meaning only when it comprises the *essential attributes* of the concept standing for a phenomenon. Only under these conditions can the definition purport to reflect reality accurately. The formal-logical correctness of classificatory definitions is usually verified by their conversion. For example, the definition of theft as a secret seizure of property is correct because if we interchange its *definiendum* and its *definiens* it remains correct: a secret seizure of property is theft. But the formal-logical correctness of the definition does not prove that it is true. *The truth of juridical definitions depends upon how essential to a given concept are the features indicated in them.* Their significance can be ascertained only by means of a preliminary analysis of the given juridical concept, by determining its elements and their mutual relations, by examining its place and significance in a given legal system, and by explaining its sociopolitical meaning under concrete historical conditions.

Greater difficulties arise in defining the concept of a phenomenon that has more complex and varied features. Such complex phenomena as life, society, state, law, punishment, for example, have been subject to many definitions, each of them comprising merely some of the features of the given phenomenon. Therefore, if the phenomenon is more complex, the theoretical-cognitive significance of its definition

* *From* "K Metodologii Izucheniya Deistvuyushchogo Prava" [On the Methodology of Studying Positive Law], Vsesoyuznyi Institut Yuridicheskikh Nauk Ministerstva Yustitsii SSSR, *Uchenye Zapiski* (Moscow, 1947), VI, 36–56.

is diminished. In this case, the definition becomes merely a preliminary guide; it is not able to uncover the entire concrete content of the phenomenon. This is why Engels stated in *Anti-Dühring:* "From a scientific standpoint all definitions are of little value. In order to gain an exhaustive knowledge of what life is, we should have to go through all the forms in which it appears, from the lowest to the highest. But for ordinary usage such definitions are very convenient and at times even indispensable; they can do no harm, provided their inevitable deficiencies are not forgotten." If a phenomenon is complex and varied, a greater number of its definitions are possible, each indicating some of its characteristic features. From a formal-logical standpoint, each of these various definitions may be correct, because formal logic does not answer the question of which feature of a given phenomenon has to be regarded as the essential one. And, without resolving this question, any definition threatens to be one-sided, superficial, and incapable of encompassing the very essence of the object under scrutiny. While stating certain features of the phenomenon, a definition cannot account for the changes connected with the development of this phenomenon. Long ago Spinoza remarked: "omnis definitio periculosa est."

Juridical sciences always strive to give accurate and clear definitions of their concepts. Our Soviet juridical science should not renounce this tradition. . . . Juridical definitions . . . have a great significance for both the theory and the application of Soviet law. Like any other definitions, to use Lenin's words, they "sum up the essential."

. . . . . . .

Recognition of the fact that the materialist dialectic is the method of our cognition of positive law does not at all imply rejection of the valuable results obtained from a theoretical treatment of positive law through formal logic.

The solution of the problem of relating formal logic and dialectic in the process of studying positive law calls for special examination. Initially, it is indispensable that we clarify the general question of the relationship between formal logic and dialectic in the process of cognition. Naturally, the materialist dialectic does not deny the significance of the laws of formal logic in the development of human knowledge or of its merits in the development of clarity and accuracy in our thinking.

An explanation of the relationship between formal logic and dialectical logic calls for the solution of two problems. First, it is necessary to define the meaning of formal logic as a lower stage of human knowledge, to define the limits of the possible application of its categories for the satisfaction of the elementary needs of our knowledge. Concerning the law of identity of formal logic, Engels has stated in *Dialectics of Nature* that "abstract identity, like all metaphysical categories, suffices for *everyday* use where small dimensions, or brief periods of time, are in question; the limits within which it is usable differ in almost every case and are determined by the nature of the object to which it is applied." Consequently, the limits of application of the categories of formal logic must be determined in each science depending upon its object of study and whether the use of rigidly fixed, constant, immutable concepts in the process of cognition is inevitable. The relationship of formal logic to dialectical logic is quite correctly compared to the relationship of arithmetic to higher mathematics. Just as arithmetic has its own independent sphere of application in which the solution of problems does not require the utilization of the concepts of higher mathematics, so elementary logic has its own independent sphere of application fulfilling the "domestic" needs of knowledge. Such an understanding of formal logic . . . prevents it from being conceived of as an independent theory of cognition. The determination of the limits of the legitimate utilization of the laws of formal logic can be made only by recognizing that dialectical logic is the sole, scientific theory of cognition.

An explanation of the relationship of formal logic to dialectical logic calls for the solution of another question. Dialectical logic rejects formal logic. This, however, should not be interpreted to mean that dialectical logic simply sweeps aside the laws of formal logic. The dialectic comprises, in a "skimmed form," those sections of these laws which are valuable to human thinking. Without observing the rules of arithmetic it would be impossible to take even one step in the field of higher mathematics; similarly, without observing many rules of formal logic one could not have taken even one step in the field of dialectical thinking. . . .

. . . The fact that formal logic is the methodology of bourgeois jurisprudence should not be interpreted to mean that the study of positive law, by its very nature, constitutes the lower sphere of knowledge to which the categories of dialectical logic are inapplicable. Earlier, we demonstrated that the method of study of our socialist positive law is the materialist dialectic. It is only in the process of cognition of the positive law (when we examine individual legal norms by themselves or in their relationship to one another) that the categories of formal logic might be helpful in solving elementary tasks in the study of positive law. However, one must be aware of the limited significance of such a study of law. It is admissible only when it is not in conflict with the study of the sociopolitical meaning of legal norms, when it constitutes an initial state in the general process of a theoretical study of our positive law. We study our positive law for the purpose of explaining the role and significance of its norms in our socialist construction. . . . The materialist dialectic is our theory of cognition, our scientific world outlook, which should permeate the entire study and theoretical treatment of positive law. Thus, in the process of studying our positive law, we give answers to the indicated questions according to the formula "yes-yes," "no-no." This, however, does not at all signify that we renounce the requirements of dialectical logic in the process of studying positive law.

# A Dialectical Solution of the Conflict between "What Is" and "What Ought to Be"*

## ᏋᏤᎧ A. A. Piontkovskii

A view that has acquired popularity in the bourgeois theory of law counterposes the methodology of *legal science*—i.e., a normative science, a science of what ought to be—to *all other sciences* that aim at the knowledge of the world surrounding us (nature and society)— the science of what is. In particular, this Kantian idea has been advanced in theoretical controversies among criminologists. For example, a Russian criminologist, Professor S. P. Mokrinskii, was opposed to treating the discipline of criminal law as a social science: "The object of jurisprudence is not a casuistic evaluation of law as a phenomenon of social life, but law itself—the normative nature of law. The jurist studies law, not as an existential phenomenon, not as a part of social reality, but as something that lies outside reality, as something belonging to an entirely distinct sphere of social consciousness, as a direct expression of what ought to be."[1]

Hans Kelsen has sought to develop these Kantian views most thoroughly. He thinks that sciences should be classified according to their methods of study; he therefore divides all sciences into descriptive and normative. The former explain causal relationships between existing phenomena; the latter do not explain what is, but what ought to be, as determined by a norm—they examine normative connections. According to Kelsen, law can be an object of jurisprudence as a special science only if it employs a special method characteristic of a normative science and fundamentally distinct from the sociological method of studying law, which aims at a causal explanation of legal phenomena. Only dogmatic jurisprudence, in his opinion, is a special science that aims at a purely normative explanation of law devoid of any sociological and psychological aspects of law.[2] Kelsen's goal is to

* *From* "K Metodologii Izucheniya Deistvuyushchogo Prava" [On the Methodology of Studying Positive Law], Vsesoyuznyi Institut Yuridicheskikh Nauk Ministerstva Yustitsii SSSR, *Uchenye Zapiski* (Moscow, 1947), VI, 20–26.

[1] *Sistema i Metod Nauki Ugolovnogo Prava* [The System and Method of the Science of Criminal Law] (1906), p. 4.

[2] *Hauptprobleme der Staatsrechtslehre* (Tübingen, 1911), p. iv.

free dogmatic jurisprudence from all elements of the "descriptive" sciences—sociological, historical, and psychological.

He seeks to justify the methodological peculiarity of jurisprudence as a normative science by the presumed fundamental opposition between "is" and "ought," between "content" and "form." The characteristic feature of Kelsen's work is an attempt to bring his theoretical position to its logical conclusion and to trace its underlying philosophical premises. . . .

In Kelsen's opinion, there exists an insurmountable border line between the "is" and the "ought" on the formal-logical level: "The contradiction between is and ought is a formal, logical one; as long as they remain within the limits of a formal-logical inquiry, there is no way of combining them, for they are separated one from another by an unbridgeable gulf. . . ."[3] According to Kelsen, normatively inevitable connections can never be reduced to causally inevitable connections. The former, however, are no less effective than the causally inevitable connections: "In the sphere of law, of legal reality, delict is connected with punishment as inevitably as the cause is connected with the effect in the sphere of nature, in natural reality. Consequently, the statement 'if someone steals, he ought to be punished' claims not a lesser meaning within the system of positive law than the statement 'if a body is subjected to heat, it expands.' "[4]

The translation of the prescription of "ought" into reality transforms "ought" into "is." Kelsen, however, thinks that this does not invalidate his assertion that, logically, "ought" is diametrically opposed to "is," for only the content of "ought" and not the form of "ought" is transformed into "is": "If 'what ought to be' is accepted in a strict, logical sense as a form thoroughly opposed to 'what is,' then it should not be identified with any content, then one should not pass 'is' for 'ought.' "[5] Hence, the dualism of "is" and "ought" in Kelsen's theory is related to the assumed dualism of "form" and "content."

To be sure, the entire bourgeois dogmatic jurisprudence is founded on the separation of "ought" from "is," on the separation of "form" from "content." The object of the study of bourgeois dogmatic jurisprudence is legal norms as such. This leads to the separation of the legal "ought" from the real world of social relations. . . . Therefore, a criticism of Kelsen's methodological positions is simultaneously a

[3] *Über Grenzen zwischen juristischer und soziologischer Methode* (Tübingen, 1910), pp. 6–7.
[4] *Hauptprobleme der Staatsrechtslehre* (Tübingen, 1911), p. vii.
[5] *Grenzen zwischen juristischer,* p. 7.

critique of the methodological foundations of the entire bourgeois dogmatic jurisprudence.

. . . . . . .

The materialist dialectic resolves the problem of the relationship between "is" and "ought" and between "content" and "form" in a way different from that of the critical philosophy of Kant. . . . The Kantian dualism of "is" and "ought" is founded on a complete separation of action—of man's practice—from human knowledge, on the separation of "practical reason" from "theoretical reason." In Kant's philosophy the "ought" expresses the demand of moral law that man behave in a special way, a demand of the categorical imperative as an absolute command of our reason. . . . These demands of the moral law cannot be scientifically verified; they must be accepted as an article of faith. Bourgeois philosophy—and following it, the bourgeois theory of law—has repeatedly reproduced these Kantian ideas, interpreting them in various ways. Stammler, the neo-Kantian, has found the idea of "ought" which is not reducible to "is" in an absolute principle of justice under which all law is subordinated. Kelsen, another neo-Kantian, found the idea of "ought" which is irreducible to "is" in the logical nature of legal norms.

. . . . . . .

The problem of the relationship between "is" and "ought" has been scientifically resolved by means of the materialist dialectic of Marx and Engels. "The philosophers have interpreted the world in various ways; the point, however, is to change it," proclaims one of Marx's brilliant theses on Feuerbach. The goals of man's activity evolve from the very practice of the historical development of society. One can change the world only if one knows the laws of its development.

The prerequisite for a successful realization of man's goals is acceptance of the idea that practice must be based on the knowledge of objective reality, that "ought" must be based on the knowledge of "is." The materialist dialectic teaches at the same time that "mankind always takes up only such problems as it can solve, since, on closer examination, we will always find that the problem itself arises only when the material conditions necessary for its solution already exist or are at least in the process of formation." Therefore, as long as the goals—which mankind takes up, which an advanced social class takes up in a given historical epoch—have not yet been translated into reality, they appear as an "ought" which is not torn off from reality; they grow out of reality and express the tendency of its development.

Therefore, no unbridgeable gulf exists between "is" and "ought." The "is" and the "ought" are in dialectical unity. The "is" gives birth to the "ought" and the "ought" turns into the "is." The connection of "ought" and "is" in social reality is analogous to the relationship between "possibility" and "reality." The "ought" that is grounded in reality is truly attainable. As a result of man's practical activity, it is turned into a reality.

The solution of the general problem of the connection between "is" and "ought" in social development has relevance for law. Legal norms, expressing definite social relationships, tell man how he ought to behave. This normative "ought" can exist in diverse relationships to concrete, historical reality. Legal norms can secure, protect, and regulate existing social relationships in conformity with the will of the ruling class. Because of the coercive force of state authority, they acquire a stable and firm character. Universally valid legal norms, in the form of a written law, could become, in the hands of the ruling class, an instrument for changing the existing social relationships. In this case, legal norms express truly possible (progressive or reactionary) tendencies of social development and serve as an instrument for transforming these tendencies into reality; the ruling class translates its policy into reality by means of legal norms. The connection of "ought" with "is," its dialectical unity, appears in all its nakedness in the field of law.

The unbridgeable gulf between "is" and "ought," which Kantians and neo-Kantians sought to create, is nonexistent in reality. This unbridgeable gulf is neither implicit in the content of legal norms nor in their logical meaning. Kelsen sought to prove the impossibility of a logical transition from "ought" to "is." But logical categories merely reflect the objective relationships of the external world. They are not at all categories available a priori to our mind, as contended by Kantians. Therefore, it is a fallacy to acknowledge the transformation of "ought" into "is," as is being done by Kelsen, and at the same time to deny the possibility of the logical transition from "ought" to "is."

# The Principal Problems of Legal Theory*

## ୶ A. Ya. Vyshinskii

As a true science, Marxism-Leninism cannot tolerate stagnation, passivity, and backwardness. I cannot help but cite Comrade Stalin's remarkable characterization of theory and the significance that belongs to it in the practical work of constructing socialism. A theory, says Comrade Stalin, "if it is truly a theory, gives the practitioner the power of orientation, the clarity of perspective, confidence in work, faith in the victory of our cause."[1] Such is the role of theory in a socialist society; such is its place in the process of the struggle for socialism. Soviet science would fail to fulfill its task . . . if it were not a science of innovators, supremely struggling for the materialization of their goals.

Soviet science, and this also includes the science of Soviet law, is confronted with the significant task of a thorough utilization of the science and culture of capitalist society. It is wrong to assume that everything has been done in this respect, that nothing can be gotten out of the science and the culture of capitalist countries, that foreign science is unable to offer us anything or, at any rate, something worth the efforts involved in the utilization of this culture for our purposes.

. . . At the present time it is indispensable to seek mastery of those scientific achievements that are being made by foreign science.

. . . But the scientific wealth and the scientific heritage of the old society can be mastered only on the basis of a critical approach to this heritage, especially in the sphere of the social sciences—in the field of ideology. As Lenin said, "One must take the entire culture left by capitalism and build socialism out of it. One must take the entire science, technique, the entire knowledge, art. Without this we cannot build up the life of communist society."[2] This can be done only through overcoming bourgeois methodology, only through the mastery, in full scope, of the solely and truly scientific methodology,

* From "O Nekotorykh Voprosakh Teorii Gosudarstva i Prava" [On Some Problems of the Theory of State and Law], Sovetskoe Gosudarstvo i Pravo, No. 6 (1948), pp. 4–16. (Abbreviated stenographic notes of the speech at the Conference of Jurists evaluating models of textbooks in the theory of state and law, May 18, 1948.)

[1] Voprosy Leninizma [Problems of Leninism] (11th ed.; Moscow, 1947), p. 275.

[2] Sochineniya [Works] (3rd ed., Moscow), XXIV (1932), 65.

360

dialectical materialism, Marxism-Leninism, which, to use Comrade Molotov's pointed expression, illuminates "the general path of historical development, uncovering the meaning of contemporary events."[3]

Lenin and Stalin teach that "without an irreconcilable struggle against the bourgeois theories on the basis of the Marxist-Leninist theory, it is impossible to attain victory over the class enemies," and "only in the struggle against bourgeois prejudices in the theory is it possible to strengthen the positions of Marxism-Leninism."[4] This was said in 1929 in reference to the state of our science of economy. But now it is applicable, in full measure, to our theory of law.

It must be said that there is in our country a quite widespread method of "scientific work" which could be designated as "quotology." The "method" of stringing together as many quotations from the works of great thinkers as possible . . . is still widespread at the present time.

It is clear that the task of science does not lie in simple quoting but in exposition of scientific propositions, in their development, in their practical application. Many of our juridical-theoretical works, however, are deficient in this respect more than in others. Indeed, theorectical discussions are conducted as a rule with the help of quotations. Quotations are, naturally, indispensable, but one cannot conduct a discussion by means of quotations alone. Such an approach will not help, or will help very little, the advancement of science. What is needed is a Marxist-Leninist analysis that enriches understanding; facts and verification of theoretical propositions by factual data are needed. Where those are absent there is no scientific discussion. . . .

. . . . . . .

Soviet law occupies advanced positions in the struggle with class adversaries. Our opponents at the present time have intensified attacks against Soviet law. This is clearly evident in the publications of bourgeois legal theorists and practicing lawyers and in general in the bourgeois . . . press. It is not an accidental occurrence that *The Times,* an English paper, published an article under the title "Laws of nations. Collision with Soviet principles. Challenge to the established order." In this article a view is advanced that Soviet law is different from the law of other "civilized" states. The article says that Soviet authors have arrived at the contention that socialist states,

[3] *Bolshevik,* No. 10–11 (1938), p. 11.
[4] Stalin, *Voprosy Leninizma,* p. 276.

headed by Russia, are the sole true representatives of such principles as justice, equality, and independence. "This daring doctrine," the article says, "is undoubtedly being asserted sincerely." But, the article continues, it involuntarily brings to mind a similar pretense advanced at one time by the apologists of the National Socialist theory of international law.

We shall not dwell particularly on this slanderous declaration. Naturally, it misses the target but it is indicative of the trend of contemporary juridical thought among some representatives of the capitalist countries.

In this article is stated the divergence between the "Western" and the "Soviet" views on the nature of law. The article declares that, to a Western jurist, law should express an extreme impartiality and should be applied to everyone undividedly, and that, apart from these minimal requirements, a Western jurist does not assign to law any definite goals and functions.

"Not so the Soviet jurist," declares freely the author of this article; "to him, law, expressing as he thinks the will of the ruling class, exists for the purpose of safeguarding, strengthening, and developing such social relations and orders as are advantageous to, and desirable for, the ruling class." After perfunctorily giving the content of our definition of law and after naming my work as its source, the author of the article raises objections to the definition, is dissatisfied with it; he is furiously against the definition that varies from the ideas of the "civilized nations"; he reproaches this definition because—in the author's words—it expresses "authoritarian views on law as an instrument serving the interests of only one class within the state."

Thus, *The Times* and its jurists are dissatisfied with our definition of law. In his speech at the conference Comrade Stalgevich declared that he, also, is dissatisfied with this definition, though, in contrast to *The Times,* he does not mention my name.

I did not have the pleasure of listening to his speech but became acquainted with it from stenographic notes, which, however, do not seem to be accurate. Therefore, I cannot assume responsibility for inaccuracies. Why is Stalgevich dissatisfied with the definition of law which was worked out through collective efforts during a conference of jurists in 1938 and which, therefore, is incorrectly attributed to me?

According to Comrade Stalgevich, our definition is normative because it reduces law to the norms of law; in addition, it fails to explain socioeconomic causes of law; it is metaphysically separated from the state; it fails to express the directing role of the Party in the Soviet state; legal norms become transformed into a means of juridical formalism. Not to miss any of the defects, Comrade Stalgevich adds two more: this definition is one-sided and ten years old.

Let's assume that someone asked Comrade Stalgevich how he defines law? Let's say that Comrade Stalgevich did not catch the question, or simply failed to answer it. Perhaps it would be proper to repeat the question and give Comrade Stalgevich an opportunity to answer it? For, one would assume that ten-year remoteness of this definition allowed enough time for Comrade Stalgevich to think out this question (as it behooves a serious scientist) and to discover, finally, his secret to a correct Marxist understanding of law. Such hopes are, however, futile. Unfortunately, Comrade Stalgevich failed to discover his America during these ten years.

In general, he repeated what he had attempted to defend ten years ago during the first conference, but he failed in defending it and, moreover, solemnly renounced it at that time.

I shall cite the declaration concerning the definition of law which Comrade Stalgevich made in 1938: "Having *essentially* no right to change the stenographic notes of my speech, I deem it necessary to declare that, after the debates during the conference, I *wholly and completely agree* with Comrade Vyshinskii's definition of law. At the same time I wholly and completely reject the accusation that I am perpetuating the 'theoretical line' of Stuchka and identifying law with economy. The work of the conference and, in particular, Comrade Vyshinskii's criticism of my speech helped me to free myself of the remnants of some earlier, erroneous assumptions."

Appearing at the indicated conference as the representative of the All-Union Institute of Juridical Sciences, Comrade Stalgevich made several declarations, namely:

1. "In Comrade Vyshinskii's definition is stressed especially the role of written law, the role of juridical norms—of the rules of conduct issued and safeguarded by the state power. The question of written law and its role should be put with special sharpness."

2. "The strong side of Comrade Vyshinskii's definition of law is precisely the fact that the question of written law is put with special clarity. I consider perfectly correct the definition that views law as a system of norms, that is, written laws, definite rules of conduct, and regulations, issued and safeguarded by the state power."

At the present time, however, Comrade Stalgevich points out that the definition of law, worked out in 1938, is normative. Could, in fact, the definition given in 1938 be bad, unsuitable? In 1938 I defended this definition but I cautioned that it was preliminary and that probably it would need some corrections. I do not preclude this at the present time or in the future. It is well known that experience is a better teacher, that theory is nothing but a generalization of experience. I shall remind you that, speaking of the significance of theory for the proletariat, Comrade Stalin wrote: "Theory is the experience of the workers' movement, taken in all its aspects." Quite naturally, the experience of socialist construction accumulated by the Soviet state during those ten years may also call for the modification of individual assumptions in the field of the theory of law.

. . . In view of this experience, it seems to me justifiable to assert that those who qualify the definition of law—given by the Institute of Law and by the first All-Union Conference of Scientific Workers in the field of Law—as normativism have an incorrect notion of what normativism is. Attempts have been made to set this definition off against others; for example, to define law as a system of social relations, as a form of production relations, as a legal order, etc. Those who reject such definitions, who speak of law as an aggregate of the rules of behavior with all the attributes of the definition of 1938, are berated as normativists. But one has only to turn to scientists who in fact are normativists—Duguit, Stammler, Kelsen, and many others— to assure oneself that the label of normativism is being attached to the authors of our definition without reason—out of mere ignorance or dishonesty. What, in fact, are the characteristics of normativism? Defining law as an aggregate of norms, normativists view legal norms as something complete in themselves and try to find an explanation for these norms neither in socioproductive relations nor in international conditions but in the norms themselves. Normativists view even the state as a "unity of the inner meaning of legal principles" or as an expression of "social solidarity." They deny that law is an expression of the will of the ruling classes in society; they do not see and do not recognize that juridical laws derive their content from definite economic or production conditions prevailing in society.

The definition of the Institute of Law proceeds from the fact that the character of social relations is determined by production and exchange and that law is the regulator of these relations, that in law is expressed the relation of domination and subordination. The definition of the Institute of Law presents law as a creative element in the struggle for a new socialist order and ideologically equips the champions of socialism. It has nothing in common with normativism apart from the term "norm" that it contains. Such a vulgarization would be inexcusable. I shall remind you that Lenin—in *State and Revolution,* namely, in the fifth chapter, devoted to the question of phases of communist society—stresses that without falling into a utopia one should not think that after the overthrow of capitalism in the first phase of communism people will at once begin to work for society without any norms of law. . . .

Thus, Marx and Lenin speak of legal norms that regulate "the work of society" and that are indispensable in the first phase of communism. It is not difficult to see that one mention of the term "norm" in the definition and one definition of law as an aggregate of norms—expressing the will of the ruling class and determined by the material conditions of its existence—give no reason to see normativism in the definition. Without going into details, it suffices to note that the definition under discussion is not divergent from the definition of law given by the founders of Marxism-Leninism.

. . . Characterizing bourgeois law, Marx and Engels wrote in the Manifesto of the Communist party: ". . . your right is merely the will of your class elevated to law, a will whose content is determined by the material conditions of the life of your class."

It is precisely this basic Marxist-Leninist thesis that is expressed . . . in our definition. The legal rule is the form in which the will of the ruling class is expressed. The law is not merely one rule but a sumtotal or an aggregate of rules.

Such is the situation with one of the most significant problems—the definition of law. It is evident that there is not even a trace of normativism in it unless one distorts its meaning.

# A Criticism of the "Normativist" Approach to Law*

## ⌘ *A. K. Stalgevich*

We arrived at the conclusion that (1) law in essence is the will of the ruling class elevated to law; (2) the content of this will is determined by the material conditions in the existence of that class; (3) norms, established and safeguarded by the state are the most essential feature of law; (4) the task, materialized by means of law, is the state regulation of social relations in the interest of the ruling class.

. . . . . . .

. . . Taking into account the above-indicated considerations, one may make a general conclusion that *law is the will of the ruling class elevated to law, a will whose content is determined by the material conditions in the existence of that class, expressed in a system of norms established by the state and safeguarded from violation by its coercive power, for the purpose of the state regulation of social relations in the interest of the ruling class.*

. . . . . . .

In the Soviet literature the meaning of law is frequently treated in a normative way. "Normativism" in Soviet jurisprudence manifests itself in the fact that law is being reduced to the norms of law (the rules of conduct); the basic juridical concepts are being formulated in a normative, one-sided way; legal phenomena are examined in a formal, dogmatic way; socioeconomic causes are left unexplained; law is being metaphysically separated from the state; the role of the Party in the Soviet state is left unexplained; legal norms are being transformed into a means of juridical formalism.

A textbook, *Foundations of the Soviet State and Law,* prepared by the Institute of Law at the Academy of Sciences of the U.S.S.R., could serve as an example in this respect. On page 12 of this textbook the following definition of law is offered: *"Law is an aggregate of norms (the rules of conduct) securing the domination of the class and the order that is advantageous and satisfactory to it, issued or sanctioned by the state and depending upon state coercion."*

It should be noted that this definition is a reproduction of the nor-

* *From* "K Voprosu o Ponyatii Prava," [On the Question of the Meaning of Law], *Sovetskoe Gosudarstvo i Pravo,* No. 7 (1948), pp. 57–62.

mative definition of law given in the textbook by Golunskii and Strogovich, *The Theory of State and Law,* where it is said that *"law is an aggregate of the rules of conduct (norms), established or sanctioned by the state authority, expressing the will of the ruling class, whose application is secured by the coercive power of the state."*[1]

The "origin" of this definition is considered to be the definition of law initially formulated during the First Conference of the Scientific Workers-Jurists in 1938. Since then this definition has been considered to be "generally accepted," a starting point and an ending point in deciding fundamental juridical questions; it is repeated, without any changes, as a dogma in the textbooks and educational accessories and serves as a criterion for the evaluation of the people and their scientific and pedagogical work. In conformity with this, in virtue of the existing situation, on the theoretical front of Soviet jurisprudence only works of those scientific workers who unconditionally accept and proceed with this definition are published. That is why it is necessary to speak about this more specifically.

In polemical writings, I, who agreed with the "preliminary" definition of law formulated during the first conference of the scientific workers-jurists, am being reproached for having formulated a different definition of law a year later, in 1938, during the next conference.

I should note that at that time, in 1938, the definition of law was formulated merely in a "preliminary" way or, to use the words of academician Vyshinskii, was offered "only as a first approximation of a definition."[2] Second, the basic task of the conference was not the formulation of the definition of law but the unification of Soviet jurists. . . .

And, if it is discovered afterwards that one or another assumption contains errors or inaccuracies, then it is our sacred duty to re-examine and change outdated concepts and definitions. But in our literature the formal definitions of law—elevated to the rank of primary principles or dogmas—prevail over our science; they restrain and hinder the development of scientific thought and push scientific and pedagogical activities in the direction of formalism.

As a result of this, instead of examination and scientific analysis of the real social phenomena, the textbooks and scientific literature restrict themselves primarily to an analysis of legal norms.

. . . . . . .

[1] *Teoriya Gosudarstva i Prava* [The Theory of State and Law] (Moscow, 1940), pp. 152–56.

[2] *Osnovnye Zadachi Nauki Sovetskogo Sotsialisticheskogo Prava* [The Fundamental Tasks of the Science of Soviet Socialist Law] (Moscow, 1938), p. 37.

The question arises: "What is the source of such normative one-sidedness and formalism?" Under closer analysis it is not difficult to see that its source is a bourgeois understanding of law and the survivals thereof. Thus, for example, a bourgeois professor, Shershenevich, says that law ". . . is a rule of communal life, supported by the state authority."[3]

The idea of law is similarly defined . . . by a white émigré, Professor Taranovskii. "Law," he says, "is nothing but a species of social norms," and "the closest generic concept to law is the idea of social norm." "That means," declares Taranovskii, "that law is a social norm, i.e., a rule of the due behavior of people in a social milieu."

It is equally not accidental that Bukharin—the enemy of the people —and his myrmidons were defining law as a system of coercive social norms, sanctioning and regulating social relations in the interest of the ruling class.

Unfortunately, many of our Soviet jurists in their scientific and pedagogical work repeat in different ways a rehash of bourgeois jurisprudence. Thus, for example, N. G. Aleksandrov is a preacher of the normative conception of law who views law as a species of social norms. *In a way* similar to Taranovskii, law is understood and formulated by him "as such a peculiar variety of social norms, the observance of which could be enforced by the apparatus of the state authority."

The methodological depravity of such a treatment of the idea of law lies in the fact that its champions blow up and elevate one of the forms, aspects, or features of law to an absolute. That is why we reproach the authors of various Soviet juridical works for normative one-sidedness.

It should be noted that the normative deviation or the normative one-sidedness in Soviet juridical literature differs from the bourgeois normativism that, for example, is being developed by Kelsen and his followers.

In Soviet juridical literature normativism is disguised, screened with phrases about Marxism, about the will of the ruling class as the source of law, about the inadmissibility of normativism, etc. In conclusions and definitions it is frequently even stressed that law is not simply a variety of social norms but an aggregate of norms expressing the will of the ruling class. And some . . . equate the definition of law given in *The Communist Manifesto* with the normative definition. In essence, using philosophical language, this signifies identification of

---

[3] G. F. Shershenevich, *Obshchaya Teoriya Prava* [The General Theory of Law] (Moscow, 1911), p. 368.

essence and phenomena, content and form—an identification of the state will of the ruling class with the norms expressing it.

The normativists' train of thought in Soviet juridical literature resembles the reasoning of empirio-critics, who reduced matter to a complex of sensations and, in the final analysis, to ideas and conceptions, while ideas and conceptions are merely peculiar reflections of the objective material reality.

We will be asked about the meaning of the above comparison and allusion. We shall answer clearly that we reproach champions of the normative conceptions of law for distorting Marxist-Leninist methodology in the direction of juridical dogmatism and, consequently, of idealism.

# Elements of Bourgeois Ideology in the Soviet Theory of Law*  ∾  *N. G. Aleksandrov*

A feature shared in common by all bourgeois definitions of law is the rejection of the class-volitional nature of law and the denial that it is conditioned by the material basis of the class society.

However, looking from an external side, bourgeois definitions of law could be divided into two basic types, presumably diametrically opposed, but in fact identical in terms of their exploitive nature.

The first type is represented by the *abstractly normative* definitions, which acknowledge that law consists of norms but at the same time deduce the content of norms not from the material conditions of the class society but from a certain abstract and presumably self-sufficient principle, which has been invented for the purpose of concealing the exploitive nature of bourgeois law. . . .

The second type of bourgeois definition is represented by more recent "sociological" definitions. Definitions of law offered by the representatives of . . . the so-called sociological school are externally opposed to the *abstractly normative* definitions. Representatives of this school assert that law in general is not an aggregate of norms but represents "the factually existing order." To representatives of the sociological school, legal norms are deprived of an active role. They assert that in the best case a juridical norm can express only factually established "legal" relations. The sociological school attributes to legal relations an existence independent of norms. It declares as legal relations even such relations as are not foreseen by norms. To a jurist-sociologist, law is an aggregate of factual "legal" relations, which constitute the factually existing "social order."

. . . . . . .

Unfortunately, some Soviet jurists have erroneously taken . . . the "antinormativism" of the sociological school for a materialist approach to the understanding of law. The advocacy of bourgeois antinormativism was initiated by P. I. Stuchka.

". . . Since the appearance of the sociological trend in the science

* From "K Kritike Perezhitkov Ideologii v Opredelenii Prava" [Toward a Critique of the Survivals of Bourgeois Ideology in the Definition of Law], *Sovetskoe Gosudarstvo i Pravo*, No. 10 (1948), pp. 43–49.

of law," wrote Stuchka, "at least one thing has become certain—that law is precisely a system of social relations."

. . . . . . .

P. I. Stuchka and his students sought in various ways to conceal the fact that normativism does not at all lie in the fact that law is understood as a system of norms, safeguarded by the state from being violated, but in the fact that these norms are not viewed as an expression of the will of the politically ruling class. . . .

If the term "norm" itself is declared a bugaboo, then what happens to the famous formula of law (advanced by the founders of Marxism) as the will of a class elevated to law? For the class will, elevated to law, is nothing but precisely a generally obligatory rule— a norm!

To find an exit from this contradiction, P. I. Stuchka simply declared that Marx "paid a small tribute" to the terminology of "volitional theories of law" insofar as he had been ". . . educated in the conceptions of law of the thirties."

Designating as normativism any idea of law as an *aggregate of norms*, P. I. Stuchka and his students logically arrived at the rejection of the thesis that law is the will of the ruling class elevated to law.

. . . . . . .

Appearing after a prolonged silence, Professor A. K. Stalgevich no longer directly maintains that law is a system of social relations and, at that, relations between "private proprietors."[1] Now, he repeatedly proclaims his agreement with the famous Marxist thesis that law is the will of the ruling class elevated to law, whose content is determined by the material conditions in the life of this class.

However, according to Stalgevich, "the will of the class elevated to law" is one thing and the rules (norms) of social conduct established and sanctioned by the state are another thing—the latter is only "one of the minor features of law," one of the forms of its manifestation. Therefore, Stalgevich accuses . . . in "normativist one-sidedness" all those who understand by law an aggregate of such norms which: (1) express the will of the ruling class, which in the final analysis is determined by the conditions of the material basis of the class society; (2) are safeguarded by the state from being violated; and (3) regulate social relations for the purpose of establishing, securing, and developing orders corresponding to the interests of the ruling class.

[1] "K Voprosu o Ponyatii Prava" [On the Question of the Meaning of Law], *Sovetskoe Gosudarstvo i Pravo*, No. 7 (1948).

According to Stalgevich, a definition of law based on the indicated features is "normativism." We ask: could a class really elevate its will to law without transforming it into the state will, rule, norm, the observance of which can be coerced by the apparatus of state power? Doesn't the "elevation of the will of the ruling class to law" necessarily presuppose a norm-creating activity by the state? Is the role of the state reducible to a mere affirmation, in norms, of the will of the ruling class "elevated to law"? And, finally, is not the norm-creating activity of the state, in particular, one of the means for organizing the will of the ruling class?

It is clear to any Marxist that the ruling class elevates its will to law precisely by means of the norm-creating activity of the state. Therefore, "the will of the ruling class elevated to law" cannot fail to be an aggregate of norms, established or sanctioned by the state authority.

The essence of law does not simply lie in the fact that law is, in general, the will of the ruling class but in the fact that it is the will of the ruling class "elevated to law." ". . . The will, if it is state will, should be expressed as a *law,* established by authority. . . ."[2] The law is precisely "an expression of the will of the classes that gained a victory and hold the state power in their hands."

. . . . . . .

The perniciousness of the ideological remnants of bourgeois sociology lies primarily in the fact that "sociological" definitions of law implant in practical workers a nihilist attitude toward the laws and decisions of the government. On the other hand, if the sociological definition is taken at face value, then it follows that Soviet law is capable of securing only the already existing relations, that it cannot serve as one of the most significant tools for the communist transformation of social relations.

Transference of the views of the bourgeois sociological school to Soviet law is especially pernicious if one takes into account the special significance of ideological superstructures in the socialist, planned society.

Under capitalism, the spontaneously developing economy puts limits on the active intervention of law in social relations. On the other hand, under the conditions of a planned, socialist economy the will of the socialist state (based on a scientific knowledge of objective possibilities) is a factor determining the further development of economic relations.

"The notion according to which the *ideas and conceptions of peo-*

[2] V. I. Lenin, *Sochineniya* [Works] (3rd ed., Moscow) XX (1931), 532.

*ple create their conditions of life,* and not the other way around, is refuted by all past history. . . . Only in the more or less distant future can this notion become a reality insofar as men will understand in advance the necessity of changing the social system (*sit venia verbo*) because of changing conditions and will desire this change before it forces itself upon them in spite of their consciousness and will. The same is also applicable to the conceptions of law and, consequently, to politics. . . ."[3]

"The more or less distant future" of which Engels speaks is a *reality* in the Soviet socialist society, where the people's conditions of life are brought about by translating into reality the policy of Lenin's and Stalin's Party, expressed in particular in the norms of Soviet socialist law.

[3] Engels, *Anti-Dyuring* [Anti-Dühring] (Moscow, 1948), p. 326.

# The Principle of Partisanship*  ᨆ  *M. A. Arzhanov*

The Marxist-Leninist theory of state and law is the only truly and strictly scientific theory of state and law. This means that its approach to the problems that it raises and resolves is a consistently scientific approach. All its principles are based on a solid, scientific foundation. Therefore, it is in all respects diametrically opposed to all, without exception, ever-existing bourgeois "theories" of state and law. All assertions of the Marxist-Leninist theory of state and law rest on authentic, verified, exact knowledge, which has the meaning of objective truth.

In contrast to bourgeois theories of state and law, the Marxist-Leninist theory of state and law is not interested in concealing, disguising, obfuscating, or coloring anything; it depicts the state and law exactly as they are in reality. This theory, consequently, is in full conformity with reality, with facts. The validity of its conclusions, deduced from the scrutinized facts, were and are constantly confirmed by social practice, i.e., by the history of the development of state and law. The Marxist-Leninist theory of state and law acquired this distinguishing feature because it is equipped with the sole scientific philosophy—dialectical materialism. The extension of dialectical materialism to the study of the entire social life resulted in the creation of a real science.

In the bourgeois world a view prevails that knowledge of society and of its laws of development cannot pretend to be authentic, exact knowledge; that this knowledge, by necessity, is and must be relative, approximate, subjective, and inexact; that, therefore, social sciences belong to "non-exact sciences," in contrast to natural sciences, which are "exact." In contrast to this view, Marxism-Leninism has demonstrated that ". . . our knowledge of the laws of social development is authentic knowledge, having the validity of objective truth."[1]

Marxism-Leninism has demonstrated that social science equipped with dialectical materialism can become as exact as, for example, biology.[2] Such an exact science is precisely the Marxist-Leninist theory of state and law, which offers strictly scientific solutions to the

---

* *From* Akademiya Nauk Soyuza SSR, Institut Prava, *Teoriya Gosudarstva i Prava* [The Theory of State and Law] (Moscow, 1949), pp. 11–26.

[1] J. Stalin, *Problemy Leninizma* [Problems of Leninism] (11th ed.; Moscow, 1947), p. 544.

[2] *Ibid.*

problems concerning the rise and development of state and law, their nature and forms, and their roles in the life of society under diverse historical conditions, including the contemporary epoch.

The theory of state and law, founded by genius-like leaders of the working class—Marx, Engels, Lenin, Stalin—is a proletarian theory. It expresses the interests of the working class. These interests are in no way contradictory to the discovered truth, to a scientific, objective knowledge of state and law. On the contrary, these interests are opposed to any deviation from science, from an exact study of reality.

The working class is in need of a strictly scientific knowledge of state and law, in the interest of its struggle against bourgeois systems, in the interest of emancipation of the entire working humanity from oppression and exploitation, and, finally in the interest of constructing a communist society. Its interests coincide with the correctly understood interests of the entire working humanity. The class limitation that is characteristic of other social classes is alien to the working class. The working class needs neither to deceive itself nor others in order to be successful in pursuing its policy, its class line in the field of state and law. On the contrary, its power lies in destroying all and any deceptions, self-deceptions, delusions, and illusions that are deliberately spread and cultivated by the exploiters in order to secure their rule over exploitation.

. . . . . . .

We shall see that other bourgeois theories deduce state and law from human "reason," "will," "justice," and from other abstract ideas that have replaced God but equally lead away from the truth and entangle thought with hazy and false constructions. The bourgeoisie, being a minority in society, suppresses the majority by means of the state and law. Because of its class position, the bourgeoisie, like any exploiting class, cannot do without a deliberate deception of the masses concerning the nature of the state and law and their role and purpose in the life of society. The bourgeoisie is forced to lie, to conceal truth, to spread illusions, in order to "justify" its exploiting state and law in the eyes of the masses and to keep the workers from fighting against the bourgeois system. The bourgeoisie fears more than anything else that the masses will become enlightened, will get to know the real nature of state and law, and that as a result of this a revolutionary attitude toward the bourgeois state will develop. Therefore, the bourgeoisie deliberately confuses the problems of state.

Lenin stated:

This question has been so confused and complicated because it affects the interests of the ruling classes more than any other (yielding in this respect only to the foundations of economic science). The theory of state (Lenin has in mind a bourgeois theory—M.A.) serves as a justification of social privileges, a justification of the existence of exploitation, a justification of the existence of capitalism, and that is why it would be a great mistake to expect impartiality on this question, to approach this question in the belief that people who claim to be scientific can give you a purely scientific view of the subject.[3]

As long as political questions were worked out by representatives or servants of the exploiting classes, the theory of state and law was adapted in an open or a disguised way to the mercenary interests of the ruling classes. *The situation has changed entirely with the appearance of the Marxist theory of state and law. . . .*

. . . . . . .

## PARTISANSHIP IN THE MARXIST-LENINIST THEORY OF STATE AND LAW

The Marxist-Leninist theory of state and law defends openly the principle of partisanship in science and steadfastly carries it into practice. The principle of partisanship, which Marxism-Leninism applies to all spheres of science and to all types of ideology of a class society, requires that in characterizing and evaluating any phenomenon of social life we openly take the consistent class stand, that is, the partisan point of view of the proletariat.

This principle ensues from a recognition of the inevitability of the class and partisan character of social opinions, convictions, theories, etc., in a class society. As long as antagonistic classes exist, there cannot be any theories that would not have a definite class origin and class assignment, that would stand above class tendencies and trends, that would stand outside the contesting parties, and that, so to speak, would be "impartial" and "independent" from a definite class ideology and, consequently, from the interests of a definite class.

In the field of ideology and science under discussion, the principle of partisanship has special significance in connection with the fact that the problems of state and law involve the interests of the classes to a greater degree and more sensitively than any other problem.

From the above-said on the scientific character of the Marxist-Leninist theory of state and law . . . the conclusion follows that partisanship and science are inseparable in this theory. It is characteristic of the proletariat that, as the most progressive class in a society, it resolutely and consistently forwards demands for strict scientific

[3] Lecture "On the State," delivered to the students of Sverdlov University on July 11, 1919.

knowledge. As a true scientific theory reflecting accurately and correctly the objective historical process, the Marxist-Leninist theory of state and law determines that the working class has been destined to become the grave-digger of the capitalist state and that the future belongs unavoidably and everywhere to the proletarian socialist state, which will fulfill the great progressive and noble task of constructing a higher, perfect, i.e., communist, society. Therefore, the proletariat is vitally interested in the development of a real science of state and law. In its turn, this science elevates the working class in its own consciousness and in the consciousness of all working people, but most important, it indicates to the proletariat the correct and safe way in the struggle for the liberation of all working people from oppression and exploitation.

The interests of truth, of science, and the interests of the working class do not contradict one another but, on the contrary, coincide completely. All these and similar assertions of bourgeois theorists, that the science of state and law is an "impartial search for truth," that it is "independent" of political opinions and convictions, and that "objective" judgments on state and law are not based on any class foundation, are false. The hypocritical and sanctimonious character of these assertions as a rule is also well known to those who advance and defend these assertions.

The tendency of bourgeois ideologists to investigate and describe the struggle of different opinions on state and law in isolation from class, political, and ideological struggles in society reduces this struggle to "purely scientific" controversies in which political motives, sympathies, and antipathies shall not play a role. In reality, this tendency pursues a definite political and class aim: to portray the proponents of the exploiters' ideology, the defenders of the bourgeois state and law, as impartial "researchers," concerned only with the seeking of "truth" in the interest of "pure science," in the interest of "all humanity," etc.

Very often bourgeois theorists place themselves in the position of pontiffs of "pure science," as if science were free from any "class prejudices" and "partisan positions." In contemporary bourgeois jurisprudence, a specific reputation in this respect was acquired by Hans Kelsen, who deliberately named his concept of law "the pure science of law" (*Reine Rechtslehre*). Kelsen assures us that his "theory" has a pure juridical character and is in no way related to politics and morality, to classes and class struggle, and that he restricted himself to the special technical and "methodologically pure" problems of jurisprudence, intentionally avoiding socioeconomic and political

questions. In reality, Kelsen introduces ordinary, widespread bourgeois ideas of the "supraclassness" and "eternity" of state and law,
under which he obviously has in mind the imperialistic state and law.

Under the banner of political indifference he propagates the reactionary political ideas of the imperialist bourgeoisie, which are dear
and close to his heart. But even more than that, this preacher of
political indifference and the "pure science" of state and law takes a
strong and malicious stand against the Marxist-Leninist theory of
state and law in his works. Kelsen slanders Marxism rudely, attributing to it vulgar, trivial, and petty-bourgeois views on state and law.
However, he did not find the time to oppose barbarian, misanthropic
fascist "theories." Declaring himself to be an adherent of the notorious "Western," i.e., false and reactionary capitalist, "democracy,"
this priest of the "pure science" does not miss an opportunity to
throw a clod of mud at Soviet state and law and at countries of the
people's democracy.

But if a bourgeois political scientist speaks against partisanship in
science, it does not follow that he is not affiliated with a definite
party, i.e., with a definite political tendency in science. One must
judge in this case not according to words but according to deeds, i.e.,
according to content and the actual class character of the views that
are defended by this bourgeois theorist.

The so-called bourgeois objectivity, advanced as an ideology of
"suprapartisanship," is merely a mask under which bourgeois partisanship is concealed, partisanship that is contradictory to science, to
objective truth. Marxist-Leninist theory tears down this mask of "objectivity." Marxism-Leninism teaches that theories of state and law,
while reflecting certain real relationships of men in a society, participate in one way or another in the class struggle and appear in one
form or another (i.e., openly or behind the scenes, directly or indirectly) on the side of a definite class or a definite stratum of society.
In his "Lecture on the State," Lenin asserted: "When you have become familiar with this question and have gone into it deeply enough,
you will always discern in the question of the state, in the doctrine of
the state, in the theory of the state, the mutual struggle of different
classes, a struggle that is reflected or expressed in the conflict of
views on the state, in the estimate of the role and significance of the
state."[4]

It is not always easy to determine the concrete political tendency—
the socioeconomic roots and ideological source of bourgeois theories

[4] *Ibid.*

of state and law—but this must be done in order to be able to understand these theories and to appraise them correctly.

From the very moment of its appearance, and during the entire period of its development, the Marxist theory of state and law has been a faithful instrument in the struggle against the exploiters' state and law. . . . It is pervaded by a passionate spirit of militant partisanship. . . . It is an effective weapon in the struggle against all bourgeois and petty-bourgeois theories of state and law. . . .

The Marxist-Leninist theory of state and law is incompatible with any, even the smallest, deviations from Marxism-Leninism. . . . As shown by the history of all deviations, any deviation from the Marxist-Leninist theory of state and law inevitably leads . . . to deviations in practice and in politics, is detrimental to the interests of the workers and to the socialist state and law, and gives assistance to our enemies.

# Communism, State, and Law: A Stalinist Interpretation*  ⌒  M. A. Arzhanov

In our earlier exposition we demonstrated that the socialist state . . . and the socialist law . . . represent a completely new historical phenomenon. They are a state and law of a new historical type, earlier completely unknown to human society. Furthermore, we have shown that the socialist type of state and law is not only new but, at the same time, a completely different type, totally different from all preceding types of state and law. Finally, we have seen that the socialist state and law constitute a higher type than all its historical predecessors. It is the highest, the most progressive, type of state and law ever known to history.

Thus, defining the place of the socialist state and law in history, and comparing them to those that existed in the past and are existing at the present, we say that they constitute a new, specific, and higher type of state and law. The above-said, however, is not adequate to fully characterize this historical type. Its full characterization also calls for an explanation of its future, i.e., its direction and point of termination—the ultimate result of its development. Consequently, it is necessary to examine the socialist state and law from a historical perspective.

Marxism-Leninism also illuminated the question of the state and law from the viewpoint of their historical destiny. One of their extraordinarily significant *peculiarities* was revealed, namely, that the socialist state and law represent the highest point of development that could ever be attained by state and law. In contrast to all the preceding types, the socialist state and law *will not be replaced* in the future by a new, subsequent type.

Marxism-Leninism has scientifically ascertained that the socialist type is the *last type* of state and law in history. After complete fulfillment of the tasks imposed upon them, the socialist state and law will become depleted, obsolete, will wither away and disappear. Then state and law will—in general and forever—cease to exist. This will take place after the complete and final victory of communism.

## COMMUNISM AS A HIGHER STAGE OF SOCIAL DEVELOPMENT

A scientific solution of the question concerning the ultimate destiny of state and law could only have been given, and was given, by

* *From* Akademiya Nauk Soyuza SSR, Institut Prava, *Teoriya Gosudarstva i Prava* [The Theory of State and Law] (Moscow, 1949), pp. 493–507.

Marxism-Leninism—by its theory of communist society. Marxism-Leninism teaches that at a higher phase in the development of communism, after its complete and final victory, the state and law will cease to exist. This will happen because society will no longer require them. They will be disappearing—withering away—gradually, in proportion to their becoming unnecessary.

Speaking of the social organization that will be in existence at a higher phase of communism, Marx, Engels, Lenin, and Stalin did not aim at drawing a detailed picture of this organization; they thought that it was possible and necessary to explain only its general, principal features. . . .

What will differentiate communism as a higher phase from socialism as a lower phase?

*In the Economic Sphere:* While the principle of socialism is "from each according to his abilities, to each according to his work," the principle operating under communism is "from each according to his abilities, to each according to his needs."

The materialization of this principle is possible under the following conditions. The economic basis of society is communist property, which in terms of its form is a unique social property for the means and instruments of production. Variations in the forms of social property, still existing under socialism, will disappear under communism. The productive capacity of society attains a level of full abundance of consumer goods, i.e., an abundance through which all the needs of the members of society are fully and regularly satisfied.

Furthermore, the antagonism between city and village completely disappears. Also, the antagonism between intellectual and physical work disappears. Finally, work will cease completely to be only a means for living—it will become a primary and vital need of man. Man will be working in society, giving to it all his abilities, because this will be his organic need. Man will work according to his abilities but will receive—from the total social product—according to his needs, regardless of his own contribution to society (according to his abilities).

It follows from the above-said that under communism such a special organization as the state (which employs coercion) will be unnecessary for the regulation of the economic life of society. There will be no need for law, for juridical norms, the obligatory observance of which is necessarily connected with the coercive power furnished by the state.

*In the Sociopolitical Sphere:* Under communism society knows of no division into classes. Under socialism class division is still in existence, but with the advancement toward communism it gradually loses its meaning: these are friendly classes of workers and peasants. Also, the intelligentsia is still in evidence as a special social group. The remnants of earlier social distinctions disappear under communism. Consequently, political distinctions in society also disappear.

Relationships between men in a communist society lose their political character because political relationships are characteristic only of a society divided into classes. Organizations that will come into existence under communism for the purpose of conducting social affairs will not have a political, coercive character. Engels' famous passage in *Anti-Dühring* says the following about the destiny of the state under communism:

> When ultimately the state becomes truly representative of society as a whole, it makes itself superfluous. As soon as there is no longer any class of society to be held in subjection, as soon as, along with class domination and the struggle for individual existence based on the former anarchy of production, the collisions and excesses arising from these have also been abolished, there is nothing more to be repressed, and a special repressive force, a state, is no longer necessary. The first act in which the state really comes forward as the representative of society as a whole—the seizure of the means of production in the name of society—is at the same time its last independent act as a state. The interference of the state power in social relationships becomes superfluous in one sphere after another and then becomes dormant of itself. Government over persons is replaced by the administration of things and the direction of the process of production. The state is not "abolished," it "withers away."[1]

Phenomena, the struggle against which necessitates coercive organizations and force, will gradually and forever disappear from social life under communism. Crime and antisocial conduct will also disappear. The struggle against individual excesses, which occasionally will take place, will be successfully and effectively conducted in a purely social manner, without a specific apparatus of coercion and without coercive rules of conduct, i.e., without the state and law.

In view of the above-said, in a communist society, misappropriations of social property will disappear. Consequently, the function of the state to protect socialist property from thieves and plunderers will become obsolete. The state organs and the legal institutions, which were necessitated by this function, will also disappear.

Under communism, the organization of communist economy and cultural life is carried out by social institutions, but these institutions and their functions will not have a political, state character. Their functions will assume an organizational and technical character. All members of society, who have been prepared for this as a result of

---

[1] *Anti-Dyuring* [Anti-Dühring] (Moscow, 1948), pp. 264–65. The deficiencies of Engels' views, and the further development of the theory of state under communism by Comrade Stalin, will be discussed in the following pages.

the development of socialist democracy, will participate actively in the formulation and the work of these institutions.

During the higher development of democracy, in the period of transition from socialism to communism, all members of society will be trained and will become accustomed to administering social affairs directly. Thus, democracy will pave the way for its own destruction, for its withering away. Lenin said that only in a Communist society

. . . will democracy itself begin to *wither away,* because of the simple fact that, freed from capitalist slavery, from the untold horrors, savagery, absurdities, and infamies of capitalist exploitation, people will gradually *become accustomed* to the observance of the elementary rules of social life that have been known for centuries and repeated for thousands of years in all schoolbooks; they will become accustomed to observing them without coercion, without compulsion, without subordination, without the *special apparatus* for compulsion which is called state.[2]

In the sphere of the cultural and ideological life of society, communism brings about such a blossoming in the spiritual life of, and such a high level of consciousness to, all members of society that the remnants from the earlier class society will be fully shaken off. Under these conditions the principles of communist morality will firmly and deeply penetrate people's consciousness.

The sense of communist organization and discipline among the members of society rests on a firm and solid foundation. It has become a habit of men, their natural and organic property, which is inherited from one generation to another. The force of habit in the communist way of life, which became a part of man's flesh and blood, is re-enforced by the high communist consciousness of the members of society. The communist society will have communal rules, norms of conduct, obligatory to all its members. However, their obligatory character will be grounded in the inner conviction of the members of society that these norms are correct, moral, useful, and expedient. They will have only a moral, aesthetic, or technical character; they will not require the official sanction of a coercive organization. Their application will not be sustained by any coercive force. Members of society will subordinate themselves to these norms willingly and voluntarily.

It follows, then, from the above-said that communism is a phase in the development of society when internal conditions come into being that are adequate and necessary for the withering away of the state and law. Furthermore, it follows that the socialist state and law will disappear, not as a result of their destruction, demolition, or a revolu-

[2] *Sochineniya* [Works] (3rd ed., Moscow), XXI (1931), 431.

tionary overthrow, but as a result of their "falling asleep," "dying off," and their "diffusion" in society. They will disappear, not as a result of revolution, but exclusively through evolution, not in the way of a leap, but in the way of a gradual transition.

Lenin wrote: "The expression 'the state withers away' is very well chosen, for it indicates both the gradual and the elemental nature of the process. Only habit can, and undoubtedly will, have such an effect; for millions of times we see around us how readily people get accustomed to observing the necessary rules of life in common, if there is no exploitation, if there is nothing that causes indignation, that calls forth protest and revolt and has to be suppressed."[3]

Such are the conditions of life in the future society, under which state and law become unnecessary.

## STALIN'S TEACHING ON STATE AND LAW
## UNDER COMMUNISM ENCIRCLED BY CAPITALISM

These conditions, however, are characteristic only of the *internal* life of the communist society. Engels confined himself to an examination of the conditions of the state's withering away, for he assumed that socialism would be victorious more or less simultaneously in all countries or in a majority of countries. Therefore, Engels did not raise the question of the state under communism in one country. In examining the question of the development of the socialist state, Engels completely abstracted himself from international conditions, i.e., from conditions that are external to a given state.

Is Engels' thesis on the conditions of the state's withering away correct? Comrade Stalin says the following concerning this question:

Yes, it is correct, but only on one of two conditions: (1) *if* we study the socialist state only from the viewpoint of the internal development of the country, abstracting ourselves in advance from international factors, isolating, for the convenience of investigation, the country and the state from the international situation; or (2) *if* we assume that socialism is already victorious in all countries, or in the majority of countries, that a socialist encirclement exists instead of a capitalist encirclement, that there is no more danger of foreign attack, and that there is no more need to strengthen the army and the state.

Well, but what if socialism has been victorious only in one country, and if, in view of this, it is quite impossible to abstract oneself from international conditions—what then? Engels' formula does not furnish an answer to this question.[4]

From this it follows that the thesis advanced by Engels is inade-

---

[3] *Ibid.*

[4] *Voprosy Leninizma* [Problems of Leninism] (11th ed.; Moscow, 1947), pp. 602–3.

quate at the present time, once the possibility of a complete victory of communism in one country encircled by capitalism became clarified. Comrade Stalin says that

. . . Engels' general formula about the destiny of the socialist state in general cannot be extended to the particular and specific case of the victory of socialism in one separate country, a country that is surrounded by a capitalist world, is subject to the menace of foreign military attack, cannot, therefore, abstract itself from the international situation, must have at its disposal a well-trained army, well-organized penal organs, and a strong intelligence service, and, consequently, must have its own state, strong enough to defend the conquests of socialism from foreign attack.[5]

Owing to this, Engels' thesis on the question under discussion had to be made more precise in terms of the new historical conditions. Comrade Stalin points out that Lenin intended to do this . . . , and undoubtedly would have done it, had his death not prevented him. Comrade Stalin, the brilliant theorist, Lenin's continuator, accomplished this task. Comrade Stalin expanded Lenin's teaching on the victory of socialism in one country.

Proceeding with the premise that a complete victory in one country is possible, Comrade Stalin gives a clear and exhaustive answer to the question of perspectives of the development of the socialist state under conditions of capitalist encirclement. Having shown how its forms and functions have changed, and how this state secured the victory of socialism in our country, Comrade Stalin says:

But development cannot stop there. We are moving ahead, toward communism. Will our state remain in the period of communism also?

Yes, it will, if the capitalist encirclement is not liquidated, and if the danger of foreign military attack is not eliminated, although, naturally, the forms of our state will again change in conformity with the change in the situation at home and abroad.

No, it will not remain, it will wither away, if the capitalist encirclement is liquidated and is replaced by a socialist encirclement.[6]

Now, after Comrade Stalin's explanations, it can be assumed that the problem of state and law under communism is resolved. . . .

## TRANSITION FROM SOCIALISM TO COMMUNISM AND THE DEVELOPMENT OF THE SOCIALIST STATE AND LAW

State and law are not withering away in the process of transition from socialism to communism; [they will do so] only after the complete and final victory of communism. Only when the necessary internal and external conditions have already come into being, when

[5] *Ibid.*, p. 603.     [6] *Ibid.*, p. 606.

all prerequisites for the withering away of the state and law have been prepared, will the withering away take place. Naturally, the socialist state and law will not remain unaltered until then. According to Stalin's teaching, changes in their functions and mechanism will be taking place in the course of the development of the socialist society, i.e., in the process of its advancement toward complete communism, depending upon the international situation. However, these changes will lead toward the strengthening and development of the socialist state and law rather than toward their weakening.

Thus, the closer society approaches the moment when the state and law will begin to die away, the stronger they will become. Isn't this contradictory? Well, what takes place ordinarily is that an organism arrives at the end of its life through the utmost weakening and its death is the result of the weakening, of the exhaustion of the vital forces, rather than of the blossoming of these forces.

The problem of this "contradiction" has been formulated and re-solved in a most thorough way in the classics of Marxism-Leninism. The brief, laconic Stalinist formula says: "We are for the withering away of the state. But at the same time we stand for the strengthening of the dictatorship of the proletariat, representing the most powerful and the mightiest of all the state powers that have hitherto existed. The highest development of state power for the purpose of preparing conditions for the withering away of the state power—this is the Marxist formula. Is this 'contradictory'? Yes, it is 'contradictory.' But this is a vital contradiction, and it fully reflects Marx's dialectics."[7]

The strengthening of the socialist state has been taking place, and will be taking place during all phases of the development of our state. The history of the Soviet state and law is a history of continuous growth, strengthening, and perfection. This was, and is being, dictated by the interests of the socialist transformation of society—interests connected with the defense against external attacks.

Without a powerful proletarian state the workers of our country could not have preserved and further developed the conquests of our socialist revolution. The strengthening of the proletarian state signi-fied an acceleration of the process of constructing a new society and a faster overcoming of the difficulties that are inescapable on this path. And this meant an acceleration and facilitation of the process of liquidating exploiting classes, of suppressing the inescapable re-sistance on the part of these hostile classes. Therefore, our Party, under the leadership of Lenin and Stalin, was always taking meas-

[7] *Ibid.* (10th ed.; Moscow, 1938), p. 427.

ures for strengthening and perfecting Soviet law. In a speech, "The Results of the First Five-year Plan," delivered at the Joint Plenum of the Central Committee and the Central Control Commission of the C.P.S.U.(B.), January 7, 1933, Comrade Stalin stated:

A strong and powerful dictatorship of the proletariat—that is what we must now have in order to scatter the last remnants of the dying classes to the winds and frustrate their thieving designs.

Some comrades interpret the thesis on the abolition of classes, the establishment of a classless society, and the withering away of the state to mean a justification of laziness and complacency, a justification of the counterrevolutionary theory that the class struggle is subsiding and that state power is to be relaxed. Needless to say, such people cannot have anything in common with our Party. They are either degenerates or double-dealers, and must be driven out of the Party. The abolition of classes is not achieved by the subsiding of the class struggle but by its intensification. The state will wither away, not as a result of a relaxation of state power, but as a result of its utmost consolidation, which is necessary for the purpose of finally crushing the remnants of the dying classes and of organizing a defense against the capitalist encirclement, which is far from having been done away with as yet, and will not soon be done away with.[8]

Comrade Stalin has repeatedly stressed that incorrect views on the state's withering away are extremely dangerous to the cause of socialism and that they are being disseminated by the enemies of our state. Thus, at the Seventeenth Congress of the Party, Comrade Stalin spoke of Party members who are confused on this question:

The thesis that we are advancing toward a classless society—which was put forward as a slogan—was interpreted by them to mean a spontaneous process. And they began to reason this way: if it is a classless society, then we can relax the class struggle, we can relax the dictatorship of the proletariat and get rid of the state altogether, since it is bound to wither away anyhow in the nearest future. They dropped into a state of mooncalf ecstasy in the expectation that soon there would be no classes, and therefore no class struggle, and therefore no cares and worries, and that therefore we can lay down our arms and retire—to sleep and to wait for the advent of a classless society.[9]

Comrade Stalin armed our cadres . . . with an understanding of the dialectical character of the development of the socialist state— through its continuous strengthening in the direction of the creation of conditions for its withering away after the complete and final victory of communism.

[8] *Ibid.* (11th ed.), p. 394.  [9] *Ibid.*, p. 467.

# Socialist Law as an Expression of the People's Will*

## ↷ Ts. A. Yampolskaya

In recent years Soviet jurists have written a considerable number of books . . . on legal norms and legal relations. However, this theme is so rich in content that one can hardly consider it to have been exhausted. . . . The appearance of Comrade Stalin's brilliant work *Marxism and Problems of Linguistics* illuminates the cardinal problems of the science of society and state and gives us the key to the solution of many not as yet resolved problems. . . .

The definition of law which is generally recognized by Soviet jurists—and which was given by A. Ya. Vyshinskii during the First Conference of Scientific Workers in the Field of Law, in June, 1938—asserts that law is an aggregate of the rules of conduct, i.e., of norms. Proceeding with this definition of law, Vyshinskii explains the character of norms, unveils the content of the notion of norm.

The definition explains the *type of norms* constituting law; it points out that these are norms established by the state, expressing the will of the ruling class, etc. This correct definition of the *nature of norms* offers a correct definition of *law in general,* a definition that is methodologically correct, that has gone through more than ten years of examination and that has fully justified itself.

Under a legal norm Soviet jurists understand . . . a rule of human conduct which expresses the will of the ruling class, which is established by the state or sanctioned by it, and which is protected by its coercive power for the purpose of guarding, securing, and developing social relations and orders that are advantageous and satisfactory to the ruling class.

. . . . . . .

What are the peculiar features that make the norms of Soviet socialist law completely different from the norms of exploiters' law? In essence they are reducible to the following:

1. The norms of Soviet socialist law are established by the authority of the workers, i.e., the Soviet socialist state.

2. The norms of Soviet socialist law express the will of the entire

* *From* "O Pravovoi Norme i Pravovom Otnoshenii" [On Legal Norm and Legal Relation], *Sovetskoe Gosudarstvo i Pravo,* No. 9 (1951), pp. 33–35.

Soviet people, led by the working class headed by the Communist party, and are formulated by the Soviet state in the acts of state organs.

3. The norms of Soviet socialist law—being an active, creative force—exert influence upon the economy, and are directed toward the construction of the communist society and the materialization of the tasks connected with it.

4. The norms of socialist law serve the fulfillment of the functions of the Soviet socialist state.

5. Because the norms of Soviet socialist law express the will of the Soviet people, they are observed voluntarily and with enthusiasm; they are protected from violation by the coercive power of the socialist state.

Thus, the norms of socialist law are rules of conduct, expressing the will of the Soviet people, established by the Soviet state, formulated in the acts of state organs, safeguarded in case of its non-fulfillment by the coercive power of the state, and directed toward securing and developing socialist social relations for the purpose of constructing a communist society.

# Communist Morality* ∽ *M. P. Kareva*

. . . The victory of the socialist revolution created prerequisites for a gradual expansion of the communist morality—of the higher form of morality—among the workingmen. In addition to a new type of state and law, a new system of ethical norms of conduct came into being as a result of the victory of the socialist revolution. . . .

The Soviet socialist system became the basis for the development of our communist morality. And it could not have been otherwise. The Soviet government, the Party of Lenin and Stalin, have only one goal—the welfare of the people—and direct all their actions toward this truly high moral goal.

All the actions of Comrade Stalin confirm his words that for the sake of the people he will give drop after drop of his blood. Is this not a higher grade of human morality? The morality of our Party—the Lenin-Stalin Party—is also the morality of our people. It gives to the Soviet state the power to resist aggressors; it inspires toilers in factories and in fields; it produces mass heroism on the front; it is one of the most significant elements of victory.[1]

. . . The morality that has been consolidated in our society is a form of the socialist consciousness. The aggregate of ethical views of which it consists represents progressive ideas of good and evil, just and unjust, honorable and dishonorable, laudable and shameful. . . .

To understand the superiority of communist morality it is necessary to reveal the content of its norms and basic principles—its criteria for evaluation of human conduct.

This problem was illuminated very clearly, though briefly, in Lenin's speech about the task of the Youth Union. Unmasking the absurdity of the bourgeois accusation that Communists presumably reject all morality, Lenin indicated that, in fact, Communists reject morality only in the sense as it is preached by the bourgeoisie, who derives this morality from God's commandments, "from idealist or semiidealist phrases, which always represent something very similar to God's commandments." Lenin characterized communist morality in the following way:

We say that our morality is fully subordinated to the interests of the class struggle of the proletariat. . . . We say: morality is what contributes to

* From *Pravo i Nravstvennost v Sotsialisticheskom Obshchestve* [Law and Morality in the Socialist Society] (Moscow, 1951), pp. 49–79.
[1] *Bolshevik*, No. 1 (1945), p. 30.

the destruction of the old society and to the unification of all workers around the proletariat, which brings about a new society of Communists. . . . Communist morality is that which serves this struggle, which unites workers against any exploitation. . . . When we are being told about morality, we say: to a Communist, morality is a firm, solidary discipline and a conscious mass struggle against exploiters. . . . The purpose of morality is to elevate human society, to deliver it from the exploitation of labor. . . . At the base of communist morality lies the struggle for the strengthening and completion of communism.[2]

In this remarkable speech of Lenin's is clearly explained the basic, the highest, principle of communist morality, its fundamental difference from all exploiters' systems of morality, the basic criterion for evaluation of human conduct. The struggle for communism, subordination of human conduct to the interests of this struggle—such is the leading principle of communist morality. . . .

We enumerated above merely some basic norms of communist morality. To them belong also such norms as the hatred of enemies; devotion to principles; an honest attitude toward social duties; respect for the rules of socialist communal life; modesty; persistence in attaining goals; care of the woman-mother, of children, the aged, and the sick; respect for human dignity; comradely mutual help. All these norms ensue from the principle of subordination of the people to the interests of the struggle for communism.

. . . . . . .

For the Soviet people the picture of morality, the living embodiment of the highest moral qualities, is the immortal Lenin and his great successor, the architect of communism, Comrade Stalin.

[2] *Sochineniya* [*Works*] (4th ed., Moscow), Vol. 31 (1950), pp. 266, 268, 269, 270.

# The Significance of Stalin's *Marxism and Problems of Linguistics* to Political Theory* ᧡ *S. F. Kechekyan*

Stalin's brilliant work *Marxism and Problems of Linguistics* represents an example of creative Marxism and deepens and develops fundamental theses of dialectical and historical materialism, but in particular the Marxist-Leninist theory of basis and superstructure.

Comrade Stalin ascertains the composition of the superstructure, points out the relationship among its separate parts and some of its essential peculiarities. These instructions have an extraordinary significance to all our sciences, including all juridical sciences. In this article we intend to dwell on only some of the theoretical propositions in Stalin's work, which have especially great significance to the study of political theories and which equip Soviet science with a correct understanding of the active role of political views and ideas, their relationship to the basis, and their interaction with other parts of the superstructure.

While advancing the theory of basis and superstructure, the classics of Marxism have revealed a variety of phenomena belonging to the basis. In the famous Preface to *A Critique of Political Economy* Marx speaks of the relations of production, namely, that their aggregate ". . . constitutes the economic structure of society, the real basis, on which rises a legal and political superstructure and to which correspond definite forms of social consciousness." And, further, he says: "The mode of production of the material life determines the social, political, and spiritual life processes of society." In *Anti-Dühring* Engels speaks of legal and state forms ". . . with their ideal superstructure in the form of philosophy, religion, art, etc."

In conformity with Marx's and Engels' thesis, Comrade Stalin refers to two fundamental elements of the superstructure: views and institutions. He teaches that the superstructure consists of the political, legal, and other views and the political, legal, and other institutions corresponding to them.

The first conclusion that follows from the definition of the superstructure is: the state and law cannot be reduced fully to the phenom-

* From "Znachenie Truda I. V. Stalina 'Marksizm i Voprosy Yazykoznaniya' dla Istorii Politicheskikh Uchenii" [The Significance of Stalin's Work *Marxism and Problems of Linguistics* to the History of Political Theories], *Sovetskoe Gosudarstvo i Pravo*, No. 3 (1952), pp. 6–16.

ena and the forms of social consciousness. The state and law are not an ideology but the institutions corresponding to it, i.e., definite forms or modes of the organization of social relations and of the political rule of one class or another.

The definition of superstructure given in Stalin's work *Marxism and Problems of Linguistics* equips our legal science for the struggle against all types of psychological manifestations in jurisprudence; it strikes at all attempts to depict law exclusively as a phenomenon of social consciousness.

. . . Comrade Stalin teaches us to draw a clear distinction between law and legal views, between state institutions and political views, between legal statutes and political programs.

In the light of Stalin's instructions a legal norm cannot be reduced to legal views. . . . Law secures a definite order of relations which constitutes a definite aggregate of institutions. Defining law as an aggregate of norms, Marxists do not at all intend to reduce it to an aggregate of views—ideology—ignoring norms as a source securing definite orders, ignoring legal institutions that are formed in the process of the operation of legal norms.

. . . . . . .

The second conclusion from the definition of the superstructure given by Stalin is: there exists a correspondence between political and legal views and political and legal institutions.

. . . . . . .

While political institutions are the institutions of authority, the political views are the ideas, theories, views of various classes (struggling among themselves) on the social system, on the nature of state authority, and on the modes of its organization. This defines the scope of political ideas and theories: they are concentrated around the question of state authority, the political organization of society, and the political rule of the class.

A legal affirmation of social and political relations gives rise to legal institutions closely connected to and at times inseparable from political ones, while legal views raise the question of the mode and forms of the organization of social relations and political power by means of legal norms and the legal organization of the economic and political rule of the class that holds the political power in its hands.

. . . . . . .

Stalin's instructions concerning the peculiarities and the role of the superstructure have tremendous significance in the study of the history of political theories. The first feature of the superstructure . . . which is important in the study of political theories is that "the superstructure is the product of the epoch during which a given economic basis exists and operates. The superstructure is, therefore, short-lived; it is liquidated and disappears with the liquidation and disappearance of a given basis."

Similarly, as "the basis is the economic system of society at a given stage of its development," the superstructure is the political, legal, and other views and institutions of society at a given stage of its development. From this follow a number of conclusions. First, in view of the fact that political theories are a part of the superstructure of a given class society, it is inadmissible to depict a political idea as something self-contained that could be explained by itself or in terms of its relationship or interaction with other ideas . . . , etc. Second, there are no, and could not be, "eternal" and immutable ideas. . . .

. . . . . . .

The second significant thesis, advanced by Comrade Stalin and pertinent to the peculiarities of the superstructure, lies in the fact that the superstructure serves the basis, that it cannot be neutral, indifferent, to the fate of its basis, to the fate of the classes, and to the character of the system. It actively assists its basis, actively helps it to rise and to become strengthened. As Comrade Stalin says, "The superstructure has only to renounce this role of auxiliary, it has only to pass from a position of active defense of its basis to one of indifference toward it, to adopt an equal attitude toward all classes, and it will lose its virtue and cease to be a superstructure."

Arising from definite material conditions of social life, the superstructure plays an active, creative role; it exerts a reverse influence upon the basis. Economic development does not flow spontaneously; it is not accomplished, so to speak, by "drifting": it takes place with the active assistance of the superstructure—ideas and institutions—given the basis.

. . . . . . .

Comrade Stalin's work on linguistics inspires all scientists in our country to new creative efforts. Comrade Stalin's enormous contribution to the development of the Marxist-Leninist theory of basis and superstructure equips our science with the most valuable instructions, which should be, and will be, fruitfully utilized also by Soviet science in the study of political theories and ideas.

# PART III ∾ IN SEARCH OF MARXIST IDENTITY

# Introduction ⌘

Stalin's death and the subsequent disclosure of the "cult of personality" resulted in a considerable modification of the relationship between Soviet writers and the political authority. Immediately after Stalin's death, Soviet writers demonstrated a remarkable degree of restraint and loyalty to the Soviet regime. For the most part, they refrained from raising controversial doctrinal issues and restricted themselves to elaborating and justifying the Party's policy. There are reasons to believe that it was a self-imposed restraint, for at that time the political authority either could not afford or deemed it undesirable to exert direct pressure upon social thinkers.

Significant changes began to take place only after the Twentieth Congress of the Communist Party, in 1956. Following Khrushchev's denunciation of Stalin, Soviet writers subjected to criticism the views of Andrey Vyshinskii, who in the past had served as Stalin's faithful spokesman on social questions. In 1938, it will be recalled, Vyshinskii stigmatized the most outstanding social thinkers of the earlier period as advocates of anti-Marxist theories and hence traitors to the cause of communism. Subsequently, some of them were silenced and some liquidated.

After the Congress of 1956, it was pointed out that these social thinkers had been "unjustly accused of harmful, anti-Soviet activity," while, in fact, "apart from a few serious mistakes, they had played a great positive role in the development of the Soviet science of law and Soviet legislation."[1] As a consequence, quite a number of writers of the earlier period (among them Stuchka, Pashukanis, Krylenko, Chelyapov) were rehabilitated.

Another result of the disclosure of Stalin's abuse of dictatorial powers was a change of attitude toward Marxism-Leninism, which constitutes the doctrinal basis of the Soviet regime. Previously, it had been Stalin who assumed a monopoly for the "true" interpretation of Marxism-Leninism and who acted as the final arbiter in ideological disputes. It has been seen in the Introduction to this book that some of the basic tenets of dialectical materialism were revised by Stalin. Yet, under his regime, these revisions were accepted without ques-

---

[1] Editorial, "Za Podlinnuyu Nauchnuyu Razrabotku Korennykh Voprosov Nauki Istorii Sovetskogo Gosudarstva i Prava" [For a Truly Scientific Treatment of the Basic Problems of History of the Soviet State and Law], *Sovetskoe Gosudarstvo i Pravo*, No. 6 (1956), pp. 9–10.

tion and were acclaimed as the greatest contribution to Marxism-Leninism.

After his death, but especially after the Twentieth Congress, Soviet philosophers gradually began to subject Stalin's interpretation of Marxism-Leninism to a searching scrutiny (see, for example, Lebedev's article, 1958, this volume). This led to lengthy discussions involving the basic doctrinal tenets underlying the Soviet state.

A further impetus to these polemics was provided indirectly by West European Marxists. Soviet thinkers have traditionally been sensitive to foreign criticism, especially that stemming from Marxists. However, under Stalin, Western Marxists who failed to accept uncritically the Soviet interpretation of Marxism-Leninism were simply stigmatized as "lackeys of imperialism." Such, for example, was the treatment accorded Yugoslav Marxists and Sartre.

However, after the revelation of Stalin's abuses, Western Marxists who interpreted the views of Marx, Engels, Lenin, and Stalin in a way different from that of Soviet writers could no longer be dismissed easily. Although stigmatized as "modern revisionists," dissenting Western Marxists were given a prominent place in the protracted polemics that appeared during the late fifties in Soviet philosophical, political, legal, economic, and historical journals. (See, for example, the articles by Kammari, 1958, and Platkovskii, 1960, in this volume.)

Another feature of the post-Stalin period is an extraordinary preoccupation with Western "bourgeois" thought. There is hardly any aspect of contemporary German, French, American, and English social thought with which Soviet writers would not be familiar. To be sure, the voluminous literature on Western thought is critical, but not as dogmatically critical as was the case under Stalin.

These new attitudes—the rehabilitation of the Soviet writers of the twenties and the subsequent revival of interest in their views, the reexamination of Stalin's interpretation of Marxism-Leninism, the lengthy polemics with Western Marxists, and persistent discussions of Western "bourgeois" thought—have introduced new dimensions into Soviet social thought. It is no longer confined to narrow topics as was the case under Stalin, when the political authority was using social thinkers primarily for the purpose of legitimizing the Soviet state and justifying its policies. As the reader will see, the scope of the problems it deals with and the depth of their discussion are now even more impressive than they were in the revolutionary twenties.

Amidst the various changes, progressions, and regressions, the one permanent feature that stands out in the history of Soviet political thought is the tendency toward conservativism. Initially, Soviet political thought rejected the traditional, "false" values of bourgeois society with the intention of eradicating them once and for all. Yet, eventually it reverted to these very values and now acclaims them as its own.

The best examples of this conservative trend are the Soviet attitudes toward such social phenomena as law, the state, morality, property, patriotism, and marriage. Originally, all these were viewed as an inevitable product of bourgeois society and hence intrinsically evil. They were to be destroyed during the first stage of socialism. At the present time it is the other way around: Soviet law is depicted as an expression of natural law and universal justice; the Soviet state is described in a rather nationalistic way as "the most progressive state" and the "fatherland of the international proletariat"; morality—for which Marx and Engels had nothing but contempt—has become transformed into a "higher communist morality"; property is now described as "sacred socialist property"; patriotism is depicted as one of the "highest virtues of the Soviet man"; and marriage—which originally was stigmatized as legalized prostitution—is now viewed as a sacred "socialist" institution.

To be sure, the transformation of the original attitude toward various social phenomena into a conservative one did not take place instantly after the Bolshevik Revolution. The process of change from one extreme to the other has gone through various intermediate changes in attitude. Some of these changes have been indicated either in the Introduction or in the part introductions of this book. Others can be traced by the reader as he goes through the original Soviet materials.

# The Relationship of Economic Basis to Political Superstructure* ~ *F. Konstantinov*

Man produces material wealth to sustain life, exchanges and consumes this wealth, and engages in politics, science, the arts, literature, and philosophy. All this constitutes the complex and multiform process of social life, fosters the historical progress of society, its continual development from lower to higher forms.

The philosophers, sociologists and historians that preceded Marx and Engels, vainly tried to find the dividing line in the complexity and multiformity of social life for phenomena that were "important" and "unimportant," substantial and unsubstantial, necessary and casual. And since bourgeois sociologists and historians proceeded (and proceed) from some preconceived and pet idea, all their sociological speculations resulted (and result) in unexampled chaos and subjectivism alien to science.

The great merit of Marx and Engels, the founders of the genuine science of the laws of social development, was that they were the first to ascertain

. . . the simple fact, hitherto concealed by an overgrowth of ideology, that mankind must first of all eat, drink, have shelter and clothing, before it can pursue politics, science, art, religion, etc.; that therefore the production of the immediate material means of subsistence and consequently the degree of economic development attained by a given people or during a given epoch form the foundation upon which the state institutions, the legal conceptions, art, and even the ideas on religion, of the people concerned have evolved, and in the light of which they must, therefore, be explained, instead of *vice versa,* as had hitherto been the case.[1]

Since the production of material wealth necessary for life is a primary, basic and permanent historical fact without which there is no society or social life, it follows that the relations arising between men in the process of production, i.e., the relations of production, are primary and constitute the real foundation, the basis determining political, legal, religious, aesthetic and philosophical views and their corresponding institutions.

In the famous Preface to his *Critique of Political Economy,* Marx gave the following classical definition of the major thesis of historical materialism on the basis and superstructure: "In the social production of their life, men enter into definite relations that are indispensable and independent of their will, relations of production which correspond to a definite stage of development of their material productive

---

* From *Basis and Superstructure* (Moscow, 1955), pp. 3–19. (In English.)
[1] Karl Marx and Friedrich Engels, *Selected Works* (Moscow, 1955), II, 167.

forces. The sum total of these relations of production constitutes the economic structure of society, the real foundation, on which rises a legal and political superstructure and to which correspond definite forms of social consciousness."[2]

Thus, Marx defines the basis as the sum total of production relations corresponding to a definite stage of development of the material productive forces. The political and juridical superstructure, as well as the forms of social consciousness, correspond to, and are determined by, the definite basis of a given historical period.

Lenin held it as Marx's historic merit that in creating the science of society, he drew a dividing line between material and ideological social relations. The latter are a reflection of the first. Material relations are those production, i.e., economic, relations, which, when arising, do not first pass through the consciousness of people, while ideological relations, when arising, first pass through the consciousness of people.

When analyzing the structure of capitalist society and precapitalist social formations, Marx and Engels were guided in all their works by this division of social relations into economic—which are the determinant, and ideological, which are a reflection of the former, and constitute their superstructure. They always considered the ideas of the ruling class to be the dominant ideas of a given society. The basic and chief element in the superstructure is the state, the law and the ideology of the ruling class, which reflect the economic structure of a given society, protect and consolidate it.

The division of social relations into production or economic relations, on the one hand, and ideological relations, on the other, is the keynote of all the works of Lenin. Historical materialism is unthinkable without this division, just as it is unthinkable without the basic thesis that social being determines social consciousness.

The proposition concerning the basis and superstructure makes it possible to explain not only the relationship between ideological phenomena and the economy of society, but also the relationship between the political, legal and other institutions, on the one hand, and the political, legal and other views of the given society, on the other, as well as the relation of these institutions to the economic system of the given society.

The Marxist-Leninist theory of the basis and superstructure has been further developed in the works of Stalin. Stalin's *Marxism and Problems of Linguistics* defines the basis and superstructure, reveals their inner connection and interaction, demonstrates the inevitable elimination of the old, moribund basis and superstructure, and indi-

[2] *Ibid.,* I, 362–63.

cates the inevitable emergence and development of a new basis and superstructure. The work exposes the vulgar, simplifying anti-Marxist views on the basis and superstructure and exhaustively discloses the role of the superstructure in the development of society.

What, then, is the basis of society? The basis is the economic system of society at a given stage of its development. The economic system of society is the sum total of definite production relations at a given historical period, relations that arise between people in the process of the production of material wealth. These relations are determined by the state of the productive forces of society, whose change inevitably brings about a change in the economic basis.

The basis of capitalist society is characterized by capitalist private ownership of the means of production, by the exploitation and oppression of workers by capitalists, and by the capitalist form of distribution of products. The capitalist basis, like the slave and feudal bases, is intrinsically antagonistic, as it is founded on domination and subordination.

In his *Dialectical and Historical Materialism* Stalin gives the following description of the capitalist relations of production, i.e., the basis of the capitalist society: "The basis of the relations of production under the capitalist system is that the capitalist owns the means of production, but not the workers in production—the wage laborers, whom the capitalist can neither kill nor sell because they are personally free, but who are deprived of means of production and, in order not to die of hunger, are obliged to sell their labor-power to the capitalist and to bear the yoke of exploitation."[3]

The three volumes of Marx's *Capital* and a number of other profound works of his are devoted to a comprehensive analysis of the capitalist economic system, i.e., the capitalist basis. The state of the capitalist economic system in its imperialist stage of development was scientifically analyzed in Lenin's *Imperialism, the Highest Stage of Capitalism* and other works, as well as in the works of Stalin.

The capitalist basis has long since become reactionary. The glaring contradictions it has engendered lead to its inevitable doom. The revolutionary class struggle of the proletariat against capitalism proceeds from the nature of the capitalist economic system, and neither decree nor violence on the part of the reactionary ruling circles of bourgeois states can eliminate this struggle.

As a result of the socialist revolution, the capitalist basis in Russia was replaced by the socialist basis, characterized by common socialist ownership of the means of production, the absence of exploitation of man by man, relations of co-operation and mutual help among the

[3] *Problems of Leninism* (Moscow, 1954), p. 738.

free toilers of the socialist society, and by the socialist form of distributing products according to the quantity and quality of labor. . . . The socialist economic system works on the following principle: "From each according to his ability, to each according to his work."

In socialist society the relations of production fully correspond to the state of the productive forces, and the social character of production is bolstered by common ownership of the means of production. The socialist basis is the most progressive basis. It has already demonstrated its vital force and superiority over the capitalist basis. In a brief historical period the Soviet Union has effected a stupendous leap from backwardness to progress. Under the leadership of the Communist Party, the Soviet people have built socialism and are successfully advancing along the road to communism.

The economic basis, i.e., the economic system of a given society, should be distinguished from production, from the process of production. The process of production is the process of interaction between society and nature, while the basis is the sum total of definite production relations between people at a given historical period. The distinctive feature of the basis is that it serves society economically.

What does it mean to serve society economically? It means that in the production of material wealth not only productive forces are required but relations of production as well. Production and, consequently, the existence of society itself, [are] impossible outside these relations of production.

Every new basis supplanting an old, moribund basis, serves society better than the preceding one; the new basis offers greater opportunities and a vaster scope for the development of the productive forces. The economic basis determines the social superstructure. Whatever the basis, such also, the superstructure.

What, then, is the social superstructure? What social phenomena does it comprise? "The superstructure is the political, legal, religious, artistic, philosophical views of society and the political, legal and other institutions corresponding to them."[4]

While it is the specific feature of the basis that it serves society economically, it is the specific feature of the superstructure that it serves society with political, legal, aesthetic and other social ideas and corresponding political, legal and other institutions. The superstructure, like the basis, bears a historical character. The definite superstructure of a given society, born of a definite economic basis of a given historical period, corresponds to that basis. The feudal basis has its feudal superstructure, its social, political and other views and institutions; the capitalist basis—its capitalist superstructure; and the

---

[4] J. Stalin, *Marxism and Problems of Linguistics* (Moscow, 1955), p. 7.

socialist basis—its own, a socialist superstructure corresponding to, and conditioned by, this basis.

Consequently, it is a characteristic trait of the superstructure that it is the product of the one epoch during which a given economic basis exists and operates. The superstructure is, therefore, short-lived; it lasts but one epoch. The definite superstructure of a given historical period is eliminated and disappears with the extirpation of the given basis. The historical necessity of providing full scope for the development of the productive forces of society brings about the elimination of the old, outmoded superstructure and its replacement by a new superstructure.

It is another characteristic trait of the superstructure that its connection with production, with the process of production, is not direct, but indirect, through its economic basis. The changes in the process of production, in the productive forces and in the level of their development, do not directly and immediately influence changes in the superstructure; they act indirectly, through the basis and the changes in the basis.

Dependent on, and in conformity with, the changes in the state of the productive forces, there comes, in the final analysis, a radical change in men's relations of production, a revolutionary replacement of the economic basis. This radical change in the basis leads to a radical change in the social superstructure. In analyzing the process of the revolutionary replacement of the moribund basis and its corresponding superstructure by a new basis and superstructure, Marx wrote: "At a certain stage of their development, the material productive forces of society come in conflict with the existing relations of production, or—what is but a legal expression for the same thing—with the property relations within which they have been at work hitherto. From forms of development of the productive forces, these relations turn into their fetters. Then begins an epoch of social revolution. With the change of the economic foundation the entire immense superstructure is more or less rapidly transformed."[5]

Consequently, the change in the social superstructure lags somewhat behind the change in the productive forces. This sequence is subject, firstly, to the nature of consciousness, ideas, views and ideology, that are a reflection of social being, and, secondly, to the reactionary activities of society's obsolescent forces on guard over the old, moribund ideas, views and institutions.

In class society the superstructure is of a class nature. It is created by the ruling class and serves the needs of the ruling class only, and not those of the whole of society. In this respect the superstructure differs, say, from language, which serves the various classes of a

[5] Marx and Engels, *Selected Works,* I, 363.

given society, which serves alike the bases of various societies and is created by the entire nation, by the given people, and not by one or another class. The language of the Russian people and the languages of the other peoples of the U.S.S.R. served both the capitalist basis and all the classes of bourgeois society, just as they now splendidly serve the socialist basis, socialist culture and all the aspects of life of socialist society.

It is the most important feature of the superstructure that being a product and reflection of the definite basis of a given historical period, it exerts a retroactive influence on the basis that created it.

Unlike the vulgar materialists, the Economists, Mensheviks, Kautskyites, Right-wing Socialists and other followers of the theory of spontaneity, of automatic development, of the peaceful growing of capitalism into socialism, Marxists have always recognized the active role of the superstructure, the great mobilizing, organizing and transforming role of advanced ideas and progressive social and political institutions in the life and development of society.

The superstructure is not passive or neutral to the fate of its basis, to the fate of the classes and the social system. Once begotten, the superstructure becomes a powerful active force that assists its basis to take shape and consolidate. The superstructure helps the new system, the progressive forces of society, to finish off the old basis, the old classes and reactionary forces. ". . . The superstructure is created by the basis precisely in order to serve it, to actively fight for the elimination of the old, moribund basis together with its old superstructure. The superstructure has only to renounce this role of auxiliary, it has only to pass from a position of active defense of its basis to one of indifference toward it, to adopt an equal attitude to all classes, and it loses its virtue and ceases to be a superstructure."[6]

Thus, the superstructure plays an active part in serving the basis that created it. The active nature of the superstructure can manifest itself in the defense and protection of an obsolescent basis, or social system, and its ruling class. This is precisely the function performed by the superstructure in present-day capitalist society, where it shields from ruin the utterly decayed, outmoded capitalist basis. It plays a reactionary role by retarding the development of the productive forces.

As an economic system, capitalism has completely outlived itself. The capitalist relations of production have long since become a major hindrance to the development of the mighty productive forces. Periodic economic crises and devastating imperialist wars are born of the very nature of the capitalist system and manifest the reactionary substance of the capitalist basis.

[6] Stalin, *Marxism and Problems of Linguistics*, pp. 9–10.

The reactionary, capitalist superstructure and, above all, the bourgeois state and bourgeois political and other views, ideas, and theories, are called upon to defend—and actually do defend—the capitalist basis; they protect it, and act as its apologists.

. . . . . . .

The socialist superstructure that arose in the U.S.S.R. on the socialist basis, plays a fundamentally different role. The socialist superstructure and, above all, the socialist state led by the Communist Party, has done everything to finish off the old basis and the exploiting classes, and to ensure the triumph of the new, socialist basis and the new social system.

"In the course of the past thirty years," Stalin wrote, "the old, capitalist basis has been eliminated in Russia and a new, socialist basis has been built. Correspondingly, the superstructure on the capitalist basis has been eliminated and a new superstructure created corresponding to the socialist basis. The old political, legal and other institutions, consequently, have been supplanted by new, socialist institutions."[7]

. . . . . . .

But, in spite of this specific function of the superstructure under socialism in the final analysis the determining role of the basis in relation to the superstructure is also preserved. The socialist state developed and changed its form and functions in conformance to the changes taking place in the economic basis of Soviet society. The strengthening of the socialist basis, of socialist production relations, served as groundwork for the consolidation of the socialist consciousness and the new, socialist outlook of tens of millions of people.

. . . . . . .

When defining the superstructure, Marxism holds political, legal and other views to be primary. Political, legal and other institutions arise from, and depend on, these political, legal and other views. This conforms to the historical course of events.

In the process of social development there first arise new, advanced political, legal and other social views that reflect the requirements of the material life of society, and then appear their corresponding institutions. The contradictions of the capitalist mode of production and the attendant class struggle, as well as the development of scientific thought, nurtured the Marxist idea, the Marxist teaching of the dictatorship of the proletariat; upon gripping the masses, this idea eventually became a material force, and then, as a result of the socialist revolution, the dictatorship of the proletariat and its institutions were established.

[7] *Ibid.,* p. 8.

# Marxism-Leninism as an "Objective Truth": An Argument against Dogmatism and Relativism*

## ⟡ *P. Fedoseev*

The basic premise of the materialist theory of cognition is the recognition of objective reality reflected in man's consciousness. Applied to society, such a reality is social being—the material life of society, which is independent of man's consciousness. . . . As a result of the application of dialectical materialism to social life, objective truth became a property of both the natural and the social sciences that are based on Marxism.

. . . . . . .

. . . It would be incorrect to assume that all premises of Marxism constitute absolute truth—that is to say, ultimate truth that is subject to neither change nor development. But Marxism, like any science, comprises beyond any doubt the elements of the evolving absolute knowledge. Marxism recognizes the historical conditioning of our knowledge, its relative character, but insists that this knowledge constitutes an approximation of absolute truth and that absolute truth consists of the sum total of relative truths.

History shows that communist parties had to struggle against two types of revisionism—against its two forms: dogmatism and relativism. Revisionism often appeared under the banner of loyalty to Marxism and dogmatically preached the inviolability of those principles that had become obsolete and that no longer corresponded to the necessities of economic development, to the new conditions of the proletariat's class struggle. Dogmatists ignore the Marxist premise asserting that truth is not abstract, that truth is always concrete. Mensheviks and Trotskyite-Zinovevite servants of the bourgeoisie clung, for example, to an antiquated view of Marx and Engels—formulated under conditions of premonopolistic capital—that the socialist revolution could be victorious only if it occurred simultaneously in all the civilized countries, that the victory of revolution in one country was impossible. They fought against a creative approach to

* From "Znachenie Marksistsko-Leninskoi Teorii Poznaniya dla Obshchestvennykh Nauk" [The Significance of the Marxist-Leninist Theory of Cognition to the Social Sciences], *Kommunist*, No. 8 (1955), pp. 21–34.

Marxism, against the Leninist conclusion that under new conditions, under conditions of imperialism, the victory of socialism is possible in several or even in one capitalist country.

On the other hand, relativist-revisionists often rejected significant Marxist principles as obsolete on the pretext that the situation had changed and new conditions had arisen. They discarded the fundamental Marxist premises of the class struggle, the dictatorship of the proletariat, relative and absolute impoverishment of the working class, etc. Lenin noted the danger of this revisionism. He asserted that with each change of conditions come amateurs who want to "re-examine" and to "alter" the fundamental premises of Marxism, whereas these changes of conditions can be explained scientifically only from the point of view of the Marxist premises. Lenin's statement, made in "Marxism and Revisionism" and directed against attempts to reject the inevitability of crises under capitalism, is generally known: "Only very short-sighted people could think of altering the foundations of Marx's teachings under the influence of several years of industrial development and prosperity."[1]

Thus, whereas dogmatism leads to stagnation, ossification, and deadening of theoretical thought and practice, relativism is an equally dangerous form of revisionism. In the struggle for the purity of Marxism-Leninism, for its creative development, the Party has always been opposed both to dogmatism, inertness, stagnation of theoretical thought, and to relativist attempts to "alter" the foundations of Marx's teachings.

Revisionist attempts appear at the present time in various fields of the social sciences and constitute a serious danger. It is well known, for example, that under the influence of the events of the last decades . . . some philosophers have renounced the essential Marxist thesis of class struggle as the moving force of history. The Marxist thesis that the history of an antagonistic society is a history of the class struggle was replaced, by them, with the non-Marxist thesis that history is a history of wars. Such an alteration of the essential Marxist formula is unjustified and constitutes a distortion of Marxism. . . .

On the eve of the economic discussion, as well as during this discussion, some scientific workers contended that Lenin's thesis on the inevitability of wars under imperialism had become obsolete. In support of their contention, they argued that after the Second World War new international conditions arose, that antagonism between the camp of socialism and the camp of capitalism was stronger than antagonism among the capitalist countries. Indeed, the fact that con-

[1] *Sochineniya* [Works] (4th ed., Moscow), Vol. 15 (1947), p. 21.

tradictions between capitalism and socialism are stronger is true. . . .
But the changes that took place in the economy and policies of imperialism do not justify renunciation of the Leninist thesis of uneven-
ness in the development of capitalist countries and the inevitability of
intensification of contradictions among these countries!

. . . . . . .

Marxism is an objective truth. The fundamental premises of Marxism have been confirmed by the entire practice of the class struggle.
How could one even suggest replacing those fundamental Marxist
premises, which are the syntheses of world-wide historical practice,
which have been confirmed by practice, upon which is founded the
entire practice of socialist construction, and which illuminate the perspective of communist victory? . . .

Enemies of socialism have often stigmatized loyalty to Marxism,
confirmed by the entire practice of life, as "dogmatism." They have
called for "freedom of criticism," that is, for freedom to revise Marxist theory. Delivering a smashing rebuff to these "critics" of Marxism,
Lenin, almost half a century ago, stated the following:

> Since the criterion of practice—that is, the course of development of
> *all* capitalist countries in the last decades—confirms the objective truth
> of the *entire* socioeconomic theory of Marx, not just a few of its parts,
> formulations, etc., it is evident that the talk about "dogmatism" of Marx-
> ists is tantamount to making an unforgivable concession to bourgeois
> economy. The sole conclusion to be drawn from the opinion of Marx-
> ists that Marx's theory is an objective truth is that by following the *path* of
> Marxian theory we shall draw closer to objective truth (without ever
> exhausting it); but by following *any other path* we shall arrive at nothing
> but confusion and lies.

. . . . . . .

. . . It is well known that absolute truth in any field of science is far
from being exhausted, that knowledge of absolute truth is an endless
process. However, from this does not follow the conclusion that
relative truth is not an objective truth but merely a probable subjective belief. An identification of relative with subjective belief is pregnant with dangerous consequences. For example, scientific workers
in the field of law, such as Comrade Tadevosyan, think that judicial
truth is a probable belief and not an objectively established decision.
"Where," asks Comrade Tadevosyan, "is the criterion by means of
which one could ascertain with certitude the full correspondence of
the material truth to true reality? The sole criterion is the inner belief
of the judges. But this does not make the truth established by a court

identical with the truth that two times two is four. Conscientious judges usually do not think that the truth which they establish is absolute, and those of them who are innerly convinced of this frequently commit an error just like any investigator."[2]

Such an understanding of truth in judicial practice can lead to gross violations of socialist legality. Such theoretical reasoning, calling for rejection of the authenticity of judicial truth, justifies subjectivism and arbitrariness in imposing sentences and opens loopholes for lawlessness. Marxism-Leninism is incompatible with such forms of the subjectivist understanding of truth. The scientifically authentic is only a proposition that corresponds to objective processes, to historical facts. One would think that this is clear to all our scientific workers. However, in different fields of the social sciences there is a tendency to treat facts arbitrarily, to conceive of history as policy projected into the past, to treat it from the point of view of the present day.

. . . Speaking of the relationship between social science and politics, the aim of social science is not to project contemporary political relationships into the past, but rather, proceeding from an objective analysis of occurrences and their meaning, to determine correctly our political attitude toward them by openly adopting the point of view of the working class, being guided in scientific work by Marxism-Leninism, that is, by the policy of the Communist party.

[2] *Sovetskoe Gosudarstvo i Pravo,* No. 16 (1948), p. 68.

# The Unity of Contradictions under Socialism*

## ᲚᲔ *V. P. Rozhin and V. P. Tugarinov*

It is necessary, in resolving theoretical questions, to keep in mind the political implications of these solutions. The discussion of contradictions in a socialist society should demonstrate the superiority of the socialist system over the capitalist one.

. . . In this connection we intend, above all, to subject to criticism a view (which some authors consider to be indisputable and settled once and for all) that contradictions are the only source and the driving force of all development and that this is precisely the meaning of Lenin's thesis concerning the absolute character of the struggle of contradictions. Such a meaning is attributed by some discussants to Lenin's statement: "There is not, and could not be, any development without contradictions." The mentioned comrades, and many of our philosophers, entertain such a view. To express doubt about the validity of this view appears, at first glance, as a revision of the very foundations of the Marxist dialectic, as an attack upon the law of the unity and struggle of contradictions.

The law of the unity and struggle of opposites, which is one of the fundamental laws of the materialist dialectic, represents above all a theoretical construct—a generalization and a copy of contradictions in capitalist society. Nevertheless, this law is at the same time a universal law of the development of both society and nature. Of course, this law operates also in a socialist society. It would indeed be a deviation from Marxism to deny the presence and the enormous significance of contradictions in the development of a socialist, and in particular the Soviet, society. However, the classics of Marxism-Leninism do not assert that the development (of whatever it might be) takes place only on the basis of contradictions. The development takes place on the basis of the operation of all dialectical laws. Furthermore, correctly understood, the law of the unity and struggle of opposites comprises the moment of the unity of opposites, their correspondence, not only their struggle and their mutual exclusiveness. This aspect of the law under discussion acquires, in our opinion, a specific significance in the development of the socialist society.

* *From* "O Protivorechiyakh i Dvizhushchikh Silakh" [On Contradictions and the Driving Forces], *Voprosy Filosofii*, No. 3 (1957), pp. 136–38.

The capitalist system develops on the basis of inner contradictions that tear it apart. The most obvious superiority of a socialist system over a capitalist one—a superiority that was demonstrated even by the utopian socialists—is its harmonious character, which is constantly increasing during the process of development of this system. In the socialist society, parallel to, and in dialectical unity with, the forces of contradictions, there are operating and developing the forces of harmony, unity, and the commonness of people in all spheres of life; these forces are moving the socialist society forward.

It is well known that the moving forces of our society are: the moral-political unity . . . , the friendship of peoples . . . , Soviet patriotism . . . , etc.

We are being told that it is impossible to fully free oneself of contradictions. This, of course, is true. By resolving one set of contradictions and freeing ourselves from them, we create prerequisites and conditions for the rise of new contradictions, for contradictions are as absolute as motion itself. But does this mean that man, after freeing himself from one set of contradictions, is powerless to prevent the rise of others? Everything depends upon the type of contradiction. Naturally, neither under socialism nor under communism is man able, for example, to suspend the growth of necessities which may outstrip the growth of production.

On the other hand, due to the destruction of class antagonism, in the Soviet Union there takes place a further strengthening of the moral-political unity of Soviet society: the unity of the working class with the peasants and the friendship of the peoples. Consequently, one should not look fatalistically upon the rise of new contradictions. Knowing the laws of social development, one can restrict the sphere of activity or even completely free oneself of one set of contradictions, weaken the operation of others, and avert still others.

Soviet society is free of the antagonistic contradictions that are characteristic of capitalism.

Stepanyan and other participants in the discussion assert that the contradiction between the growing needs and the attained level of development in production is, under socialism, the chief contradiction and moving force of the socialist society. . . . We think it is wrong to elevate contradictions in the development of socialist society to the rank of motive forces. In our socialist society such motive forces as the unity of the working class with the peasants, the moral-political unity of Soviet society, friendship of the peoples, Soviet patriotism, criticism and self-criticism, socialist competition, etc., operate. These are social forces that assist our society to satisfy the rising needs, to overcome contradictions, difficulties, and deficiencies in work; and in doing this they move and push our society forward. These forces do not manifest themselves by themselves but through the activity of millions of Soviet people.

Taking into account objective contradictions, the Party and the Soviet government organize the people's struggle for the purpose of resolving and overcoming contradictions. . . . Contradictions alone do not move our society forward; this is being done by the Soviet people directed by our Party.

# Objective and Subjective Rights*

## ⚭ *A. A. Piontkovskii*

In its resolutions, the Twentieth Party Congress pointed out to state, Party, and social organizations the necessity of vigilantly guarding Soviet laws, of exposing all those who encroach upon the socialist legal order and the rights of Soviet citizens, of sternly suppressing manifestations of arbitrariness and lawlessness. The Communist party considers safeguarding the rights and freedoms of Soviet citizens to be one of the fundamental tasks of the socialist legality. For the purpose of carrying out this policy a number of significant legislative acts have been issued in recent years, acts that are directed at strengthening socialist legality and creating conditions that would make violations of the socialist legality which took place in the past impossible. . . .

. . . A theoretical elaboration of the problem of subjective rights of the citizens of socialist society has special political significance at the present time. . . .

The problem of subjective right . . . , and in particular the question concerning subjective rights of citizens in relation to the organs of the socialist state, has received clearly inadequate treatment. . . .

. . . It seems to us that the indispensable prerequisite for the successful elimination of this gap is an unequivocal recognition that subjective right has the quality of law. Therefore, one could have misgivings about the success of the treatment of the problem of subjective right if one proceeded on the assumption that the very expression "subjective right" should be relinquished. Let us remind the reader that in an editorial, "On the situation of the Juridical Sciences," published in 1953 in the journal *Voprosy Filosofii,* the idea of subjective right was declared as non-corresponding to socialist relations, and the preservation of this idea in Soviet juridical literature was looked upon as the result of the influence of bourgeois jurisprudence.[1]

In the article "Problems of Content and Form in Law," L. S. Yavich declared the term "subjective right" archaic ( ! ) and suggested that it should be completely given up and replaced by the term "legal competence" (*pravomochie*).[2] The authors of a new textbook, *The Theory of State and Law,* selected the same path. Without giving any

* *From* "K Voprosu o Vzaimootnoshenii Obektivnogo i Subektivnogo Prava" [On the Problem of the Relationship between Objective and Subjective Rights], *Sovetskoe Gosudarstvo i Pravo,* No. 5 (1958), pp. 25–28.

[1] No. 1 (1953), p. 105.

[2] *Uchenye Zapiski Tadzhikskogo Gosudarstvennogo Universiteta* [Scientific Reports of the Tadzhik State University], Issue 3 (1955), p. 61.

justification, they renounce the very idea of subjective right and, in its place, speak of legal competence of the subject to juridical relations.[3] Hence, it is not surprising that the problem of subjective right, and in particular the question of subjective rights of citizens, could not find proper illumination in that work.

In the article "On the Question of the Meaning of Law," I. E. Farber expressed himself against our proposal to consider as law not only objective right (the legal norms) but also subjective right and, following L. S. Yavich, declared himself in favor of renouncing the idea of subjective right. It would be a mistake to view all these declarations as involving merely a terminological problem. They are connected with an understanding of the relationship between objective and subjective right. Thus, I. E. Farber wrote: "Consequently, subjective right should by no means be referred to as law, because only legal norms are law, that is, norms expressing the state will of the class that carries into practice dictatorship and its authority."[4] I. E. Farber's position is consistent in its own way: if law is merely an aggregate of legal norms, then subjective right is not law. . . .

I. E. Farber's denial that subjective right has the quality of law is closely connected with the dogmatic treatment of the conception of law which was formulated by A. Ya. Vyshinskii in 1938.[5] While he correctly focused the attention of Soviet jurists upon the need to systematically study the legal norms of active Soviet legislation (this played a positive role in the struggle against legal nihilism), his general approach to the understanding of socialist law nevertheless arouses serious objections. The point of the matter is that in defining the nature of socialist law he proceeded merely "from the relations of domination and subordination expressed in law."[6] Such a one-sided approach fixed attention upon only one aspect of law—as a definite obligation emanating from the state. Such an understanding of law made it necessary to view legal norms themselves in a one-sided way, merely as imperative norm-prohibitions. What were overlooked thereby were the "permissible" norms, which found wide expression in Soviet legislation and which establish, precisely, the subjective rights of citizens.

Such an understanding of law was definitely connected with the generally mistaken proposition of Stalin about the intensification of the class struggle in the period of socialism, which he advanced dur-

[3] M. P. Kareva, S. F. Kechekyan, A. S. Fedoseev, and G. I. Fedkin, *Teoriya Gosudarstva i Prava* (Moscow, 1955), p. 418.

[4] *Sovetskoe Gosudarstvo i Pravo*, No. 1 (1957), pp. 43, 47.

[5] *Voprosy Teorii Gosudarstva i Prava* [Problems of the Theory of State and Law] (Moscow, 1949), p. 83.

[6] *Ibid.*, pp. 84, 415.

ing those years. The view of the socialist law as expressing a relationship of domination and subordination reflected merely the militant side of the dictatorship of the working class, its attitude toward the enemies who sought to undermine the power of the workingmen. But, as Lenin taught, the dictatorship of the working class is at the same time an unprecedented expansion of democracy for the working masses—drawing them into the administration of state affairs. In uncovering the nature of socialist law it is inadmissible to ignore the socialist democratic character of the dictatorship of the working class, which is reflected in law. . . .

. . . The reduction of right to legal norms alone is contrary to actual reality. Law is a considerably more complex social phenomenon than mere legal norms—than rules of due conduct—which are safeguarded by the coercive force of the state.

The definition of law as "an aggregate of norms" fixes attention merely upon the aspects in which jurists are directly and primarily interested. Dialectical logic is opposed to such a limited approach in cognizing law. In studying law, we should take into account the dialectical connections of all its sides; we should reveal its nature as a unity of opposites—of objective and subjective right. In actual reality an effective legal norm always produces legal relations corresponding to it. Objective law exists, therefore, always in unity with subjective rights and the legal obligations corresponding to them. One without the other is nonexistent. . . .

We reject the theory of natural law and the inalienable rights of a person. The existence of subjective right is connected with the norm of objective law. Yet, at the same time, the creation of subjective rights, in conformity with the norm of objective law, cannot be viewed as an arbitrary action on the part of the legislator. It expresses the material conditions in the life of society. The subjective rights of the citizens of a socialist society are created in conformity with objective necessity in the development of the socialist society, in which the welfare of the toilers of the socialist society constitutes the highest law of the state's policy. Socialist society creates material conditions for the thorough development of the person and a thorough satisfaction of his material and cultural needs. The subjective rights of citizens of a socialist society are the legal conditions for the satisfaction of these needs of a person. Subjective right is not an archaic and useless idea for socialist law. On the contrary, in conformity with the objective necessities in the development of socialist society, it acquires actual and fullest significance. The problem of subjective rights of citizens in a socialist society is a juridical aspect of a general problem concerning the relationships between a person and the socialist state.

# A Reappraisal of Stalin's Interpretation of Dialectical Laws* ∽ *S. P. Lebedev*

Textbooks on dialectical materialism, individual articles, and pedagogical practice are still lacking adequate clarity on the question of the classification of the fundamental laws of materialist dialectics. Chapters on the Marxist dialectical method are written in textbooks in such a way that one gets the impression that four rather than three fundamental dialectical laws operate in nature, society, and in thought as well.

This happens because textbook authors treat the four features of the Marxist dialectical method as the fundamental laws of dialectic.[1] Taking into account the fact that in these textbooks the law of the negation of the negation is not included among the fundamental dialectical laws, it is clear that such a classification of the fundamental dialectical laws differs substantially from the views of the classics of Marxism-Leninism on this subject. It is well known that the founders of the materialist dialectics . . . formulated three fundamental laws thereof: the law of the unity and struggle of opposites; the law of the transformation of quantity into quality and vice versa; and the law of the negation of the negation.

In the textbooks these propositions were revised without any factual substantiation. Simply a new structure of the fundamental dialectical laws was advanced, corresponding to the four basic features of the Marxist dialectical method. A few articles appeared, which attempted to substantiate theoretically the necessity for a new classification of the fundamental laws of the materialist dialectic. Characteristic in this respect was S. Ya. Kogan's article "On the Classification of the Elements of the Dialectical Method" in which he sought to justify such a necessity.[2]

The basic thought in this article is that "there is no . . . basic feature of the Marxist dialectical method that would not be a reflection

* *From* "K Voprosu o Klassifikatsii Osnovnykh Zakonov Dialektiki i Ikh Vzaimosvyazi" [On the Problem of the Classification of the Fundamental Dialectical Laws and Their Interconnections], *Vestnik Moskovskogo Universiteta*, No. 2 (1958), pp. 79–89.

[1] See, for example, *Dialekticheskii Materializm* [Dialectical Materialism], ed. G. F. Aleksandrov (Moscow, 1953), pp. 69, 107.

[2] "O Klassifikatsii Elementov Marksistskogo Dialekticheskogo Metoda," *Izvedeniya Odesskogo Gosudarstvennogo Universiteta imeni I. I. Mechnikova* [Abstracts of the I. I. Mechnikov State University of Odessa], II, Issue 1 (Odessa, 1949).

of the fundamental law of the objective dialectic."[3] Kogan seeks to prove that the classification of the fundamental dialectical laws advanced by Engels was essentially incorrect because he included among the fundamental laws of the materialist dialectic neither the universal principle of interrelation nor the principle of development. Kogan points out that the division of the materialist dialectic into two groups of elements—initial basic principles and the fundamental dialectical laws—was unfounded. He thinks that the universal interrelationship of phenomena, motion, and development should be included among the fundamental dialectical laws:

> The unification of the first and second group of elements of the dialectic should have originally resulted in a theory of five basic features or laws of the materialist dialectic. But the exclusion of "the negation of the negation" from the fundamental features or laws of dialectic resulted in a theory of four basic features of the dialectical method which correspond to their classification advanced by Comrade Stalin: (1) universal connection and interdependence—the unity of natural and social phenomena; (2) motion and development in nature and society; (3) development as a transformation of quantitative changes into qualitative; (4) development as a struggle of opposites.[4]

We dwelt to some degree upon Kogan's article because it reflects clearly enough the revision of the classification of dialectical laws that has been accomplished tacitly in other articles and textbooks. Did this revision have an adequate scientific basis? We do not think so. Engels was right in not including the principles of universal connection and development among the dialectical laws. To be sure, while giving a *general* description of dialectics as a science, Engels frequently emphasized that the materialist dialectic is a science of universal connections and development.

Engels knew quite well that this proposition should be verified by discovering the laws of this universal connection and development of phenomena. For this reason precisely, Engels provided a verification of dialectic as a science of universal connections[5] and formulated the fundamental objective laws of the dialectical development of the world. Having pointed out that dialectic is a science of universal connection, Engels spelled out the principal dialectical laws. He wrote: "Dialectics as the science of universal interconnection. Main laws: transformation of quantity and quality—mutual penetration of polar opposites and transformation into each other when carried to extremes—development through contradiction or negation of the negation—spiral form of development."[6] Engels did not assert that the

---

[3] *Ibid.*, p. 7.      [4] *Ibid.*
[5] *Dialektika Prirody* [Dialectics of Nature] (Moscow, 1950), pp. 1, 38–43.
[6] *Ibid.*, p. 1.

universal interconnection of phenomena is a dialectical law. He clearly stated that his task was to demonstrate the main laws of universal interconnection or motion of phenomena.

Such an approach to the analysis of the materialist dialectic and the classification of its laws has a basis in the objective world itself. The infinitely multiform connections, motions, and changes in the objective world constitute merely a sphere and a condition for the operation of the fundamental laws of dialectic. The fundamental laws of dialectic express, from different points of view, the essence of the universal connection and change of phenomena. In contrast to metaphysics, dialectic regards all laws as laws of motion and development. Each law of dialectic, while expressing an *inevitable relationship, defines* some aspect of the process of development and interconnection of phenomena. The law of the unity and struggle of opposites expresses an inevitable relationship between opposites, their inner connection and struggle, which is the source of motion and, at the same time, the source of the interconnection of phenomena. The law of the transformation of quantitative changes into qualitative expresses an inevitable relationship between quantitative and qualitative changes, which, together with the law of the unity and struggle of opposites, determines the transformation of one phenomenon into another. The law of the negation of the negation, while expressing an inevitable relationship and inner connection between qualitatively different stages of development, determines the movement from lower to higher forms in the process of development.

These three laws are the fundamental laws of dialectic in the proper meaning of the term, for they *determine the movement, the development,* and, consequently, the interconnection of the phenomena of the world. Hence, the universal interconnection and the development of the phenomena of the world, while representing a sphere and a precondition for the operation of the fundamental laws of dialectic, are at the same time a result of their operation. Therefore, the inclusion of universal connection, motion, and development among the fundamental dialectical laws is completely unfounded.

. . . Stalin has neither indicated anywhere that universal interconnection is a law of the materialist dialectic nor sought to give a new classification to the fundamental laws of dialectic. He sought to outline the general, the most basic, requirements of the dialectical method which must be observed in the study of reality and in practical activity.

The attempts of some of our philosophers to depict the universal connection of phenomena as a dialectical law were largely due to a dogmatic and erroneous interpretation of Stalin's view that "the multifold phenomena of the world constitute different forms of matter in motion; that interconnection and interdependence of phenomena, as established by the dialectical method, are a law of the development of moving matter; and that the world develops in accordance with the laws of movement of matter and stands in no need of a 'universal spirit.' "[7]

Only by approaching the quoted statement dogmatically and literally could one deduce from it the conclusion that universal connection and interdependence is a dialectical law. In fact, however, Stalin's statement implies no such conclusion. In formulating the *first feature of Marxist philosophical materialism,* Stalin sought to emphasize the view that, since the connections between phenomena are objective, the world develops in accordance with its own laws and not in accordance with the will of a spirit or consciousness.

. . . It should be noted that some of our philosophers interpret too broadly the universal laws that are studied in Marxist philosophy. Occasionally one encounters assertions that the basic features of Marxist philosophical materialism are at the same time the fundamental laws of Marxist philosophy. In fact, however, they should be regarded only as the basic principles of philosophical materialism. A scientific principle—which asserts that the world is material in its very nature and that matter is the sole objective reality existing independent of our consciousness—should not be regarded as a law. Comrades who regard this basic principle as a law assume that it has an indispensable property of law, namely, the universality expressed in the statement that all phenomena of the world are material. They forget, however, that a law in the precise meaning of this term is an essential, inevitable *relationship.* If this relationship in a given realm of phenomena is universal, we have a law. This is not the case with the first feature of Marxist philosophical materialism, which describes the universal property of all phenomena—their materiality—and not the essential relationship between these properties. Therefore, statements that reflect or outline the general properties of certain objects should not be regarded as laws in the proper meaning of the term. . . . For example, V. P. Tugarinov regards as a law the statement "all elephants have proboscises."[8] Elephants as a species of animals have thousands of additional specific properties, but statements expressing these properties are not laws, for they do not express essential, inevitable rela-

[7] *Dialekticheskii i Istoricheskii Materializm* [Dialectical and Historical Materialism] (Moscow, 1953), pp. 10–11.
[8] *Zakony Obektivnogo Mira, Ikh Poznanie i Ispolzovanie* [The Laws of the Objective World: Their Knowledge and Utilization] (Moscow, 1954), p. 133.

tionships between properties, aspects, or processes. Consequently, while all laws are expressed in the form of a general, affirmative judgment, not all general affirmative judgements express a law. Naturally, the assertion of Marxist philosophy that matter is primary and consciousness secondary should not be treated as a law. It may seem at first glance that we are dealing with a law since this assertion does concern the *relationship* of consciousness to the material world. However, this specific relationship, which has been stated by all materialist philosophies, actually lacks the character of a law because it does not express an inevitable relationship between two phenomena, a relationship that determines their mutual development or even their existence in general, as is the case with a law.

Matter is the real content of everything in existence. Matter is the objective reality that exists and develops independent of consciousness. Consciousness, on the other hand, is not a material phenomenon, not a material property. The content of consciousness, which is a property of highly organized matter, constitutes the very relationship to matter. It is expressed in reflection, in knowledge, of the material world. There is actually no inevitable relationship between the material world and consciousness, for, as previously indicated, matter exists and develops outside and independent of consciousness. From the statement "consciousness is secondary and determined by being" only the conclusion that the laws of material being are primary can be deduced, whereas the laws of any science, philosophy included, are secondary and reflect the laws of the material world. There are no intermediate laws existing within the relationship between the world and consciousness.

. . . It is equally inadmissible to regard as a law of Marxist philosophy the proposition that our consciousness is able to reflect correctly the surrounding world. This proposition also lacks the qualities of the Marxist-Leninist conception of laws. This proposition speaks merely of *a characteristic feature of one property—the ability of consciousness* to know the surrounding world.

The view that parallel to the laws of the Marxist dialectic there also exist laws of Marxist philosophical materialism found its expression in V. P. Tugarinov's book. He writes: "The laws of the Marxist dialectic have operated and will operate forever. The same is true of the laws of Marxist philosophical materialism, which reveal the most general relationship between being and consciousness."[9] From this it follows that the relationship between consciousness and matter was always in existence and that, consequently, consciousness always

9 *Ibid.,* p. 108.

existed and operated as a special force. In fact, however, consciousness is secondary—derivative—and hence could not always have existed and operated.

Stalin's cult of personality and a dogmatic approach, particularly to his *Dialectical and Historical Materialism,* did serious damage to the realization and elaboration of the Marxist dialectical method. The presentation of Stalin's formulation of the basic features of the Marxist dialectical method as an ultimate and complete theory is responsible for the fact that our philosophers limited themselves primarily to selecting illustrations of these basic features instead of developing the problems of dialectical materialism creatively. . . . We indicated earlier that Stalin's aim was to expound the most general characteristics of the dialectical method's main requirements, which must be observed in examining natural and social phenomena. To be able to comprehend them correctly, it is necessary to examine them in their interrelation and motion. Supported by the view of Marxist-Leninist classics, Stalin quite correctly emphasized this requirement. But he furnished merely a very general scheme of the scientific dialectical method. He did not attempt to break it down into components as had been done in a detailed way by Lenin in *Philosophical Notebooks,* where he spoke of sixteen elements of the dialectic. The general character of the dialectical method's first feature, as formulated by Stalin, is expressed in the fact that it fails to indicate the necessity of analysis as the first and foremost task of scientific investigation. Indeed, it is true that one cannot comprehend a phenomenon unless it is studied in connection with the surrounding phenomena. It is well known, however, that an explanation of the causes and laws of phenomena calls for exposing individual phenomena—for dissecting the entity. In this connection, Engels said that one cannot understand even one phenomenon without examining it in isolation from others in the process of experimentation. Consequently, the initial dialectical approach to a scientific investigation of phenomena has a two-sided, contradictory character; it comprises a unity of analysis and synthesis. This is why, in his description of the elements of dialectic, Lenin assigned the first place to the unification of analysis and synthesis, side by side with objectivity of the examination of phenomena. Marx, who brilliantly applied the dialectical method in *Capital,* indicated that the point of departure of a scientific investigation (for example, in political economy) is the society as a closely connected and concrete totality of its diverse components. But, in order to comprehend a capitalist society, it is not enough to argue that its parts are interconnected. To know it, the concrete whole must first be divided into its parts: the simplest but essential relationships (such as labor, commodity, value, etc.) must be educed. An explanation of the essential relationships—of fundamental causes—is the first condition of a scientific investigation of all the world's phenomena. This aspect of the problem was not mentioned by Stalin in his formulation of the first feature of the Marxist dialectical method.

Marx emphasized that in examining capitalist society the division of the whole into its parts is merely the first, preliminary, stage of a scientific investigation. The second stage of a scientific, dialectical investigation of capitalist society consists of ascending from simple, basic, abstract definitions, which express the essential relationships toward that which is concrete. At this stage, the law-governed historical development of all of capitalism's essential economic relationships come into view. As a result of this investigation, a concrete, well-rounded understanding of such a phenomenon as the capitalist society is obtained in the form of an aggregate of numerous scientific notions. Consequently, the dialectical method should not limit itself merely to recognition of the principle of the world's development but should examine the development of the world's phenomena in their essential, law-governed relationships.

In such a dialectical investigation of capitalist society, Marx applies a logical mode of presenting its development. He examines the basic, material processes, separating and isolating them from the accessory, nonessential conditions. This method of scientific investigation, which examines given processes in their "pure" form, was used by Marx on the basis of the dialectic. The examination of phenomena in their "pure" form, by educing essential, simple, basic relationships by means of dividing the complicated whole into parts, and, then, the ascendency from these simple, essential relationships toward presentation of the concrete object with all its complexities were component parts of Marx's dialectical approach to the study of capitalism.

The fundamental laws of dialectic are an organic part of Marx's dialectical method. Their objective unity and interrelation were shown in the methodological significance of the philosophical categories of essence and phenomena, content and form, necessity and spontaneity, etc. In this way, Marx thoroughly revealed the content of the dialectical method. His profound analysis of this problem should be reflected in our textbooks and articles devoted to analysis of the Marxist dialectical method and methodology of investigation.

The last question that should be examined is one concerning the interrelationship of the fundamental laws of dialectic. Both in textbooks and in many articles, the interrelationship of the fundamental laws of the materialist dialectic is presented in a one-sided, incorrect way. Authors of many textbooks and articles assert that only one law—the law of the unity of opposites—expresses the essence of development, while other laws are merely its concretization.

Such incorrect views were stated in a most obvious way by M. F. Vorobev in an article in the *Vestnik Leningradskogo Universiteta*. He writes:

The principal law among the fundamental laws of the materialist dialectic is the law of the unity and struggle of opposites. This law—this principle—is the constitutive kernel of the materialist dialectic. *Its object is the essence of development*. It discloses the essence of development, i.e., the unity and struggle of opposite tendencies, not only in the source of development, but also in the transformation of a phenomenon from one qualitative state to another, and indeed opposite, qualitative state (a leap), and in the process of development, from its beginning to its end, with the contradictory tendency—of moving away from the starting point and appearing to be returning to it—inherent in this process.[10]

All the basic, universal aspects of development that are also expressed in other laws are included by Vorobev in the law of the unity and struggle of opposites. "The object of the second law of the materialist dialectic," writes Vorobev, "is the *form* of development."[11] He also views the law of negation as a "law of the form (tendency) of a progressive motion."[12] Furthermore, Vorobev states explicitly that the law of the transition of quantity into quality indirectly ensues from the law of the unity and struggle of opposites and that "the law of the negation of the negation is derivative from the law of the unity and struggle of opposites and the law of the transition of quantitative changes into essential, qualitative ones."[13] At first glance everything seems to be well, for it is established where the difference and the subordination of the laws lie. In fact, however, this excogitated, speculative construction fails to establish the active interaction of the fundamental dialectical laws; what it does is to establish a subordination of the laws in such a way that the law of the interpenetration of opposites appears as the single, unconditional cause of development. The quoted propositions do not correspond to concrete phenomena and processes, which reveal an interaction among these laws, that is, the fact that they *jointly condition* (*determine*) *the content of the process of development and the operation of one another as well.*

Any laws—and this includes the dialectical laws—express one or another universal aspect of the essence of the process of development, because "law" and "essence" are concepts of the same order.

[10] No. 23 (1956), p. 57.     [11] *Ibid.*, p. 58.     [12] *Ibid.*     [13] *Ibid.*, p. 66.

It is inadmissible to view other laws as merely a passive result of the law of the unity of opposites and to assume that they do not *determine* anything in the *content* or essence of the process of development. For example, if we look at the facts, we see that quantitative and qualitative changes in the development of the means of production play an active role in the formulation and development of contradictions in the production of any formation and in its transition into a new society. These quantitative and qualitative changes in the means of production are not a simple result of an intensification of contradictions; in a definite sense they are the cause of the intensification of contradictions between the forces of production and the relations of production. It is impossible not to recognize that the law of the transformation of quantity into quality—accumulation of quantitative changes in temperature—is responsible for the transformation of water into another qualitative state. In this case, it is impossible to contend that the transformation of water into steam or ice is determined only by the interaction (development) of the opposite forces of attraction and repulsion of molecules. What takes place here is an active interaction whereby quantitative and qualitative changes play a definite role in the intensification of the development of the forces of attraction and repulsion of molecules during the transition from one quality to another. . . . If one examines broader spheres in the development of the world—instead of only separate facts from social life, for example, revolution, which is a result of intensification and expansion of contradictions—it becomes apparent that it is impossible to view the law of the transformation of quantity into quality always as a form of the manifestation and concretization of the law of the unity and struggle of opposites. The law of the transformation of quantity into quality is organically connected with the operation of inner contradictions, but at the same time it has a relatively independent role in the process of development and change and together with other laws determines the essence and the content of changes taking place in the world. In non-organic nature—where inner contradictions play an even greater role—the law of the transformation of quantity into quality has especially great significance in determining the content of the development.

The view that the two other laws are merely derivative forms of the manifestation of the law of the unity of opposites leads in essence to a denial of their active, independent operation. Proceeding from such a point of view, Vorobev arrives at the following logically consistent conclusion concerning the law of the negation of the negation: "Taken by itself, this law equally fails to explain anything and has a purely descriptive character."[14] The first part of this statement is quite incorrectly formulated, because taken by itself, in separation from other laws, none of these laws can operate, exist, and explain anything. Apart from the unnecessary reservation "taken by itself," it follows that the law of the negation of the negation merely describes the operation of the law of the unity of opposites—that it is merely the passive registrant. Consequently, the law itself is inactive. It is incomprehensible why, after stating all this, Vorobev speaks of the law of the negation of the negation as one of the fundamental laws. Could this law be a fundamental one without expressing one or another aspect of the essence of the content in the process of development? The view stated by Vorobev has a definite number of proponents among Soviet philosophers, who also think that this law is a form of describing the operation of the law of the unity and struggle of opposites. . . . Therefore, they either reject the universal dialectical law or they do not recognize it as a fundamental one. . . .

Lenin's comparison of the law of the unity of opposites to the kernel of dialectic is so treated by some philosophers that other laws of the materialist dialectic appear merely as external forms of the manifestation of this kernel. Such a simplified treatment does not permit us to understand that the operation of the law of the interpenetration of opposites is, in its turn, conditioned by the operation of the law of the negation of the negation and the law of the transformation of quantity into quality.

[14] *Ibid.*

# A Rejoinder to "The Revisionist Myth about the Liberation of Science from Ideology"*

## ↫ M. D. Kammari

One of the revisionist attacks against Marxism is directed at its very foundations—the materialist dialectic. Revisionists endeavor to separate historical materialism, the Marxist theory of history, political economy, and scientific socialism from the philosophy of dialectical materialism. Bernstein and other late-nineteenth-century revisionists also attacked Marx's revolutionary dialectic. They sought to draw Marx's dialectic closer to Kant, attempting to "supplement" Marxism with gnosiological neo-Kantian scholasticism. Kautsky contended that historical materialism could be combined with any philosophical system, even with neo-Kantian philosophy, with Machism, and with diverse positivist schools of philosophy. Such "unification" of Marxism with the idealist philosophy signified not only rejection of the philosophical foundations of Marxism but also a distortion of the Marxist theory of history and of the Marxist economic and political theories. Furthermore, it implied a revision of the policy, strategy, and tactics of the working class.

The Machian school (Bogdanov, Bazarov, Yushkevich, Valentinov, Adler, and others) has revised Marxist philosophy and has sought to combine Marxism with empirio-criticism, the philosophy of Machism. On the other hand, ideologists of Trotskyism and right-opportunism (Bukharin and others) have distorted the materialist theory of history along the lines of mechanical materialism and subjective idealism.

Nevertheless, all revisionist attacks against Marxist philosophy have suffered complete defeat. Marxist philosophy has gained a victory over revisionism, expanded its sphere of influence, and conquered the minds of many millions of people. In view of this, it would seem rather paradoxical that revisionist ideas are being revived, that there are still people who pretentiously seek to "free" Marxist sociology from "a definite world outlook," that is, dialectical materialism, and who endeavor to diffuse Marxism with bourgeois philosophy

* From "Revizionistichestkii Mif ob 'Osvobozhdenii' Nauki ot Ideologii" [The Revisionist Myth about the "Liberation" of Science from Ideology], Voprosy Filosofii, No. 7 (1958), pp. 3–19.

and sociology. A classic example of this new trend is an article by Kolakowski which appeared in the Polish weekly *New Culture*[1] and which was subjected to criticism in an earlier issue of *Voprosy Filosofii*. Another example of this trend is an article written by J. Wiatr and Z. Bauman which appeared in the Polish journal *Myśl Filozoficzna*[2] under the title "Marxism and Modern Sociology."

The principal aim of Wiatr's and Bauman's article is to "liberate" science from ideology. To justify their aim they advance the following historical argument: "The subordination of science to ideology is most constant and most persistent in the field of social sciences. Whereas natural sciences freed themselves from the tutelage of ideology relatively early, social sciences entered this path only in the nineteenth century, and as yet they have failed to free themselves completely."

In Wiatr's and Bauman's opinion, the aim of sociology and other social sciences is to free themselves from the "tutelage" of all ideologies, which they characterize as "a class-distorted (deformed) reflection of social reality." Needless to say, anyone who is familiar with the history of philosophy cannot fail to notice that we are confronted with a new type of the old positivist endeavor to free science from all ideologies, from all philosophies, but primarily from the Marxist philosophy.

It is well known that positivists have stigmatized the principal problem of philosophy—the relationship of thinking to being—as unscientific, and that they designate anyone who studies this problem as a metaphysician. They assert that philosophy and ideology must be entirely separated from science. Marxism has amply demonstrated the failure of positivist myths to liberate science from philosophy. In view of this, revisionist ventures once again disclose the misery of their philosophy.

Marxism asserts that no scientist is free from the influence of one or another philosophy. The point is whether he is under the influence of a philosophy that leads toward scientific knowledge or has succumbed to the influence of a philosophy that leads him into a maze of scholasticism, fideism, and theology. The history of science demonstrates that materialist philosophy alone makes it possible to perfect the scientific methods of cognition, while idealism leads to unscientific, prescientific, false, and vicious methods of cognition.

According to Wiatr and Bauman, Marx's merit lies in his discovery of "the fact that social sciences are subordinated to ideology," in his disclosure of the causes underlying this subordination, and in his

[1] No. 4 (1957).          [2] No. 1 (1957).

discovery of the power that will free science from ideology. This power is the working class. "The ideology of the proletariat," they argue, "was meant to be a specific type of ideology, one which would be a negation of ideology in the traditional meaning of the term, one that would be a science." Consequently, they conclude that Marxism is not an ideology but a science. Needless to say, such a contraposition of science and ideology is inadmissible. . . .

Marxism does not struggle for the liberation of science from all ideologies. It struggles only for the liberation of science from the false, unscientific, idealist, reactionary ideology and from the influence of fideism and religion. Marxism struggles for the triumph of the progressive, revolutionary, proletarian ideology in science, for the triumph of the ideology of scientific communism. Only persons entangled in positivism could advance the slogan of freeing science from all ideologies. In its very nature, the Marxist philosophy as a science of the most general laws of development of the objective world and cognition is incompatible with the nature of positivism.

To be sure, neither Wiatr nor Bauman openly opposes dialectical materialism. Moreover, they claim that they are creative Marxists, true materialists, and true dialecticians. But their concept of freeing science from ideology is permeated with the idea of reconciling Marxist and bourgeois social sciences, Marxist and bourgeois sociology, that is, a reconciliation of materialism and idealism in social sciences. Like the views of other revisionists, those of Wiatr and Bauman, which are advanced in the name of the creative development of Marxism, are directed against incorrigible "Stalinists" and "dogmatists." But their own concept is an example of the fusion of dogmatism with the revision of Marxist foundations. Since their conception is based on an incorrect interpretation of Marx's and Engels' views on ideology, we think it necessary to restate the views of the founders of Marxism on this subject.

Marx and Engels in their works (directed against the idealist German philosophy and in general against the idealist theory of history which asserts that self-developing ideas give rise to a material world, nature, society, state, and history) have characterized this ideology as false, illusory consciousness, reflecting reality in a distorted way. Engels uncovered the gnosiological and sociological roots of this distorted reflection of reality in a letter to Mehring (July 14, 1893). There he stated the following:

Ideology is a process accomplished by the so-called thinker consciously, indeed, but with a false consciousness. The real motives impelling him remain unknown to him; otherwise it would not be an ideological process at all. Hence, he (Paul Barth—M.K.) imagines false or apparent motives. Because it is a process of thought, he derives both its form and its content from pure thought, either from his own thought or from that of his predecessors. He works with mere thought material, which he accepts without examination as the product of thought; he does not investigate further for a more remote process independent of thought. Indeed, its origin seems obvious to him, because as all action is produced through the medium of thought it also appears to him to be ultimately *based* upon thought.

Furthermore, Engels discloses the gnosiological roots of this erroneous, false, illusory, idealistic concept, stressing the role of causal succession in the development of ideology (political, juridical, philosophical, moral, and theological ideology). Indeed, even idealists at times note the fact that the development of ideas is affected by external, material relations, by the facts and events of real life, but these facts and events are regarded by ideologists as a product of preceding ideas, as a result of the process of thinking. . . .

. . . He who has read Engels' letter to Mehring carefully and who has compared Engels' views with the concrete history of the development of ideology cannot fail to notice that Engels had in mind neither all ideologists (all thinkers) nor all ideologies. He had in mind "the so-called thinkers," that is, the ideology of the idealists, of people with a false, idealist world outlook, as well as all those who think along the idealist line. (Such outlooks were prevalent in the domain of ideology prior to the scientific upheaval in the understanding of the history of society accomplished by Marx and Engels.) It is self-evident that Engels regarded neither himself nor the founder of scientific communism, Karl Marx, as "ideologists" of this type, although both of them were ideologists beyond any doubt, ideologists of the most advanced and revolutionary class in bourgeois society, ideologists and leaders of the working class.

In the essay "What is to be Done?" Lenin has uncovered the incompatability of the Marxist ideology with bourgeois ideology. He has shown that the scientific ideology of Marxism came into being and developed in a way distinct from that of the workers' consciousness. Furthermore, he has shown that the Party introduced the theory of scientific socialism into the workers' movement, into the consciousness of the masses.

Only a hardened dogmatist could deduce from Marx's and Engels' criticism of the idealist understanding of history that they were against ideology in general, against all ideology, and that they regarded all ideologies as "distorted reflections of reality."

. . . . . . .

. . . Scientific ideology is a result of scientific cognition. It is not passive; it plays an active role in its further development. It exerts an influence, not only upon the development of knowledge (upon the organization of observation, experience, experiments, the creation of scientific hypotheses, and upon the verification of these hypotheses through practice), but also upon the development of man's social practice. The ideas of the class struggle, of the socialist revolution, of the dictatorship of the proletariat, of the construction of socialism and communism, the ideas of socialist patriotism, internationalism, international friendship, and the struggle for peace, reflect objective necessities in the present stage of social development. This is why these ideas govern the minds of hundreds of millions of people, and why they constitute a tremendous material force in history.

Only people who are hopelessly lost in the labyrinth of positivism can contrapose science and ideology as two hostile and incompatible things; they alone can be against ideology "in general"; only they can depict all ideologies as distortions, as disfigured reflections of social reality. Sensing the weakness of their standpoint, Wiatr and Bauman qualify their view by asserting that, strictly speaking, Marxism is not an ideology any longer but a science. First, instead of drawing a distinction between scientific and unscientific or antiscientific ideologies, their assertion implies a positivist contraposition of science and ideology in general. Second, Wiatr and Bauman acknowledge that along with science, Marxism has preserved and revived ideology; specifically, "ideology in the traditional meaning of the term." In his article "Interpretations of Historical Materialism"[3] Wiatr attempted to set himself apart from the revisionists by stressing that, in Marxism, science and ideology are blended together. But this does not change the nature of his position; it remains positivist and hence directed against the philosophical foundations of Marxism. Wiatr and Bauman seek to free "Marxist sociology" from ideology, from Weltanschauung, that is, from the Marxist philosophy, in order to be able to develop it "together with the modern world sociology" of which bourgeois sociology is a part. They fail to see that modern, natural and social sciences (which are developed by bourgeois scientists) are "blended together" with the idealist, bourgeois Weltanschauung and with ideology in general. . . . Lenin called for grounding modern, natural science on solid philosophical, dialectical-materialist foundations, without which it could not withstand the pressure of bourgeois ideology, the pressure of idealism, fideism, and mysticism. On the other hand, in conformity with positivist philosophy, modern revisionists call for freeing social sciences from "genetic ties" with the Weltanschauung, with the philosophy of dialectical materialism. Why? Be-

[3] *Studja Filozoficzne*, Nos. 1–4 (1958).

432                                      SOVIET POLITICAL THOUGHT

cause they want to weaken the beneficial influence of the scientific
Marxist ideology and philosophy upon the development of science in
all countries, but especially in the socialist countries.

The positivist contraposition of science and ideology constitutes an
attempt to obliterate the fact that the materialist and the idealist
world outlooks, the scientific and the antiscientific ideologies, are diametrically opposed. According to Wiatr and Bauman, all ideologies,
at all times, are alien and hostile to science and scientific cognition
and therefore must be removed from its sphere. In their opinion, "The
social function of ideology as a class-distorted reflection of social
reality primarily lies in devising symbols, stereotypes, and social
myths, uniting society around the ruling elite (or around the elite that
strives to rule), and securing the voluntary subordination of society to
this elite."

From this they deduce the conclusion that the proletariat has no
need "of the social function performed by ideology." In speaking of
ideology in general, they obliterate and disregard the fact that the scientific, socialist, Marxist-Leninist ideology is indispensable to the proletariat.

According to Wiatr and Bauman, the working class is not interested "in the revival of ideology." It is the struggle among diverse
groups within the working movement which has led to the formation
of a new type of ideology "in the traditional meaning of this term." In
their opinion, the mythological character of this ideology and its
monopolistic claims to be superior to social sciences are connected
with the fact that, within the working class, groups have arisen that
are interested in subjecting the entire class to their will; groups that
pursue a policy that conflicts with the interests of the whole class,
and that, therefore, instead of using rational and logical argumentation, resort to emotional, ideological argumentation by means of
symbols and stereotypes. In other words, groups have appeared in the
midst of the working class that are hostile to scientific knowledge; in
"the previous historical period," these groups have assigned to Marxist philosophy a religious ideological function. Instead of freeing social science from the blinkers of faith, instead of destroying the "institutions of social taboo," instead of exposing symbols and stereotypes,
philosophy itself was used during Stalin's period as an instrument for
strengthening new taboos and new ideological symbolism; Marxist
philosophy was subjected to a falsification!

We have stated Wiatr's and Bauman's conceptions almost in their
own words. The ideological and social aims of their concepts are quite
evident. Their enemy is neither reformist ideology, nor reactionary
bourgeois philosophy; their enemy is the Marxist-Leninist philosophy,

which has been converted by communist parties into a sharp and mighty ideological weapon in the class struggle. The struggle of the communist parties for the purity of the Marxist-Leninist ideology, their struggle against revisionist attempts by diverse, ideologically unstable elements in the working movement, is depicted by Wiatr and Bauman as dogmatization and canonization of the Marxist premises, as the establishment of the principle of primacy of faith over science!

The defense of the Marxist principles, which have been verified and confirmed in the fire of class struggle and revolution, is depicted by revisionists as the strengthening and expansion of "new social taboos." The defense, by Marxist philosophy, of the principles of proletarian internationalism, the dictatorship of the proletariat, the unity of the working class and peasantry, the unity and solidarity of the communist parties, their revolutionary discipline, the defense of the social ownership of the means of production, and the prohibition of the violation of these principles—all of this is merely the "strengthening of new taboos" to which all anarchistically minded revisionists are opposed, using the pretext of the "creative development" of Marxism.

According to eclectics, who have no firm principles, who jump from one position to another, who change principles like gloves, all firm convictions and their passionate defense are "religious fanaticism (faith)," whereas eclectic doubts, ideological hesitations, switching from one to another ideological camp, naked relativism, and the denial of objective truth are symbols of the "creative" development of science.

## ATTACKS ON MARXISM AND THE PROPAGANDA OF BOURGEOIS IDEOLOGY UNDER THE BANNER OF REJECTING PARTISANSHIP IN SCIENCE

Wiatr and Bauman began their article with an attack upon ideology in general. They alarmed the reader with the fear of the revival of ideology within Marxism and with the danger of "ideological pressure on social sciences." But . . . their criticism is directed against the Marxist ideology, against the philosophical foundations of Marxism, instead of against idealism and the reactionary bourgeois ideology.

If one believes Wiatr and Bauman, it is not the imperialist, reformist, and revisionist ideology, but the ideology that is revived and defended by . . . the leading cadres of the communist parties that threatens social sciences. Looking from the revisionist point of view, a favorable attitude toward colonialism is not as injurious to the social sciences as are, for example, the Marxist-Leninist theory of two principal classes in bourgeois society and the theory of society in the period of transition from capitalism to socialism. Wiatr and Bauman regard this theory as "scientifically primitive" and contend that it should be replaced with a bourgeois theory of "social stratification." To quote them: "The problem of social stratification under socialism cannot be supplanted with an interpretation of Stalin's scientifically primitive thesis on the division of society into two non-antagonistic classes and intelligentsia; this thesis itself is in need of verification or at least refinement."

. . . We cannot fail to notice the cowardly manners that are characteristic of revisionist attacks upon the foundations of Marxism. They conduct these attacks under the pretext of advancing a criticism of the individual representatives of Marxism and in silence pass over all their accomplishments. In this specific case, they neglect the fact that Marxists, including Stalin, have furnished not only a profound, concrete analysis of the nature of "two principal classes" in all antagonistic formations and societies and an analysis of the transition period from capitalism to socialism, but also an analysis of the diverse, intermediate social strata and of the diverse groups within the classes.

The appeal to free science from ideology logically leads to an attack on the principles in Marxist philosophy and sociology. Revisionists call for a "positive" definition of such expressions as the "Marxist social science" and the "Marxist sociology." They are categorically opposed to Lenin's assertion that only a person who accepts and translates into reality all essential premises of Marxism, who brings the class struggle toward the dictatorship of the proletariat, toward the construction of socialism, and toward the liquidation of all classes, can regard himself as a Marxist. Revisionists draw a distinction between two parts of Marxism:

> On the one hand, a definite world outlook and a social program; on the other, a general theory of society which constitutes a program of scientific sociology. The first part contains a definite evaluation of the capitalist society, a plan for the transformation of existing societies, and an outline for the future society. The second part contains two postulates. According to the first, social studies should concentrate on the material, social relationships that are the ultimate cause of the entire social life. Furthermore, the causes of social dynamics should be sought in conflicts that are the results of the diverse strata existing in society. The second postulate asserts that social science should be systematically freed of the distorting influence of class ideology.

In the opinion of revisionists, the demand that a scientist should accept both parts of Marxism is unreasonable, for this would mean that such a scientist would have to evaluate a given system of social science from the viewpoint of his relationship to "the current political course of the communist parties," which would be tantamount to recognizing the "primacy of ideology over social science." The latter implies the subordination of science to ideology, which is "in principle contradictory to the basic premise of Marxism." They do not tell us, however, to which specific premise it is contradictory.

"Marxist sociology cannot find the proof of its validity in the fact that it is genetically related to a specific world outlook," that is, dialectical materialism. Marxist sociology should aim at neither justifying nor "illustrating" "the axiomatically accepted ideological premises or postulates of a political program." Such are the decrees of the revisionist sociologists concerning social science. They resort to a cheap demagogery by asserting that the validity of scientific propositions should not be sought in their compliance with a world outlook but, rather, in their compliance with the reality that these propositions "describe." But is it not the criterion of the truth of a theory, which the Marxist philosophy and the Marxist world outlook accept? Is the materialist dialectic, as a science of the most general laws of the development of society and knowledge, not a faithful reflection (an analogy) of reality? Does not the Marxist philosophy teach how to determine the correspondence of theory with reality through social practice? Is the policy of the communist parties, including the "current" policy, not based on Marxist social science? Or is it as subjective and emotional as a "sociological study" of socialism, capitalism, feudalism, etc., which refrains from *evaluating* these phenomena both from a scientific and an "emotional-mythological" point of view?

. . . While opposing the Marxist principle of partisanship in social science in a class society, Wiatr and Bauman quite "peculiarly" interpret the class character of social sciences. In their opinion, social sciences (which in themselves are presumably free of class character) acquire a class character because of the influence exerted upon them by the "class ideology," which is alien to all sciences. Under this influence, "Propositions that are not subject to a scientific, logical-experimental verification but that are subject to an ideological criterion of social utility" are introduced into science. An impression is created that social sciences do not express the interests, world outlooks, and needs of the classes that are struggling in society. Then it follows that, for example, the sociological theories of Comte, Spencer, Tardaou, Durkheim, Rickert, Bogardus, Ross, Bernheim, and Toynbee, are not bourgeois and idealistic in essence; that they do not express the social and political philosophy of the bourgeoisie but are extraclass and supraclass theories; that they comprise only a few unscientific ideological propositions, which could easily be eliminated from these sociological theories without impairing their social nature.

436                                  SOVIET POLITICAL THOUGHT

From this it follows that both Marxist and bourgeois sociologists can put aside their ideological principles, can osculate, and begin to produce a general, single, new, and modern sociology in place of the old, class sociology.

For the sake of clarity we would like to stress that, from a Marxist point of view, objective truth is independent of the consciousness, will, and interests of the classes. Objective truth in science is always the same; truth in mathematics, geometry, history, philosophy, political economy, cannot be different for different classes (this Marxists do not deny when they speak of partisanship in philosophy and natural sciences or when they speak of the class character of social sciences). But, first, objective truth is not found *ready-made;* it is discovered in a complex, contradictory process of cognition, which is always *socially* conditioned, and which, in a class society, is inevitably strongly influenced by the ideological struggle of the classes. Second, all sciences always serve definite *social forces,* classes; the primary *social* function of science is to serve the interests of the ruling class, its needs and necessities. Third, science is a product of men who belong to diverse classes in society, who approach the object of cognition from different points of view, from the viewpoint of their social interests, whose attitude toward objective truth is different, and who deduce different theoretical, methodological, and ideological conclusions from the same discoveries. All of this must leave a specific class imprint on the *content* of social sciences, not to mention their utilization. Natural sciences, which study natural phenomena, involve the interests of the classes to a lesser degree; they can be used in the production of material goods by all classes; owing to this, the class structure of society does not leave such an imprint on them as on the social sciences. Hence, it is absurd to speak of feudal, bourgeois, or proletarian mathematics, geometry, physics, chemistry, and biology. But the ruling classes in society determine the manner and the purpose of the utilization of these sciences, either for the purpose of enriching a clique of exploiters and oppressing the exploited masses or for the purpose of liberating the suppressed and exploited masses, either in the interest of war and the destruction of peoples or in the interest of peace.

In the field of natural sciences a bitter struggle takes place between materialism and idealism concerning the interpretation of the meaning of scientific discoveries. On the one hand, it is conducted in favor of idealism, fideism, and theology, with a view to justifying the bourgeois world outlook. On the other hand, it is conducted in favor of materialism and atheism, with a view to justifying the proletarian, socialist world outlook. Even a sharper ideological struggle permeates all social sciences. In view of this, what should a Marxist do? He can do only one thing—defend materialism, atheism, and objective truth in science against idealism, fideism, religion, and bourgeois lies.

Is the modern bourgeois sociology idealistic? Wiatr and Bauman contend that the "main trends in modern sociology are not idealistic." (To be sure, Wiatr and Bauman have in mind non-Marxist, bourgeois sociology, for, in their opinion, Marxist sociology is merely in the stage of inception; it lacks its own scientific apparatus, its own theoretical system, and its own methodology.)

. . . Wiatr and Bauman contend that the *majority* of bourgeois sociologists have adopted the materialist position, that is, in a sense, that they have failed ideologically. As a confirmation of this thesis, they indicate that quite a number of bourgeois sociologists assume that economic factors are determinant in social development. Such, for example, is V. Ogborn's concept. In Wiatr's and Bauman's opinion, he should not be criticized for idealism but for a "one-sided exaggeration of the role of technological changes," that is, for vulgar materialism. Furthermore, the recognition of "the determining role of the social structure, with respect to the diverse social forms of human thought, is almost a universal and indisputable principle." This is Wiatr's and Bauman's argument and it is followed by two "conclusions":

1. "During the period following the formulation of its foundations by Marx, Marxist sociology failed to perfect the scientific apparatus necessary for the development of a scientific theoretical system; it is still not far removed from the original, though quite significant, principles." It has failed to produce its own methodology and, therefore, it should go begging to, and learning from, bourgeois sociology.

2. "At the same time, individual Marxist sociological premises have been adopted by, and utilized in, diverse sociological theories, even in those theories that pretend to have nothing in common with Marxism." These theories became Marxist, materialist, and dialectical in essence; they call for . . . "a dynamic examination of the object of study," for the study of interconnections between quantitative and qualitative changes, and for a search for the source of social dynamics in the collision of antagonistic forces, etc.

But if it is true that there are more problems that unite them than divide them, and especially if it is true that "the impassable gap that splits two philosophical trends has become, at the present time, quite old-fashioned," then we ask why all these disputes, discords, and struggles between Marxists and non-Marxists? The fact is . . . that the gap between Marxism and idealism, between Marxist and bourgeois sociologies, is impassable; in reality the struggle goes on with full force as before.

The obliteration of class contradictions and class struggle in the field of sociology is genuine idealist charlatanism. It was known long ago that bourgeois scientists—historians, sociologists, economists—have used, and are using, some premises of the Marxist philosophy, of its dialectical method, of Marxist sociology, to their own benefit. Engels, Lenin, Plekhanov, as well as other Marxists, spoke of this but at the same time they criticized eclecticism, hopeless confusion, the absence of consistency, idealism, and metaphysics in the theories of bourgeois scientists. It was Lenin himself who so profoundly demonstrated that such bourgeois ideologists as Struve, Sombart, or such reformists as Bernstein, had adopted only *those parts* of Marxism *which are acceptable to a bourgeois,* but rejected the *essentials.* They have even recognized (true, only ostensibly) the class struggle, but they rejected its logical implications—the dictatorship of the proletariat and the liquidation of the exploiting classes as well as classes in general. Every Marxist knows that many bourgeois theorists and reformists have recognized the "significance" or even the supremacy of the economic factor in the development of society but, at the same time, have denied the determining role of material production, of the material conditions of life, in the development of society and the determining role of social existence in the development of consciousness. Every Marxist knows that bourgeois theorists and reformists have developed a confused, eclectic theory of the interaction between diverse but equal factors. A majority of positivist sociologists adhere to this theory.

In a polemic against Struve in 1894, Lenin demonstrated that the theory of a supraclass and non-class science of society is an expression of the ideology of bourgeois objectivism, which is diametrically opposed to the Marxist ideology. Marxist materialism comprises proletarian partisanship, that is, an obligation to take the position of a given class, namely, the position of the most progressive and revolutionary class of society, the working class, and to study and evaluate from this position diverse social phenomena. Later, in 1905, in the struggle against the political ideology of Cadets and bourgeois liberals, Lenin demonstrated that the idea of *nonpartisanship,* which bourgeois ideologists advanced in science and politics, is a *typical bourgeois* (and petty-bourgeois) idea. The ideology of nonpartisanship is an ideology of those social strata and classes that, owing to their social position, are interested in obliterating class contradictions, antagonisms, and contradictory class interests. This is why their ideologists do not speak openly in the name of the class they belong to but disguise their views under the hazy ideology of "impartiality," "nonpartisanship," and the "supraclassness" of their class policy. Of course, this does not make their policy and ideology, philosophy and science impartial, nonpartisan, and supraclass. On the contrary, disguised by nonpartisanship, these ideologies serve the bourgeoisie much better than they would if they were advanced openly as the expression of its class interests.

Naturally, bourgeois ideologists and—lagging behind them—revisionists refuse to admit this. They persistently contend that discussions and scientific disputes in sociology, as in all other sciences, are not, and should not be, understood as "a manifestation of the struggle of political conceptions." To be sure, no Marxist has ever contended that all disputes in science are a manifestation of the struggle of political conceptions; Marxism asserted and asserts that, in a society split into antagonistic classes bitterly struggling against one another, there can be no "impartial" or "nonpartisan" science, one that is neutral toward the antagonistic classes. As stated by Lenin: "To expect science to be impartial in wage-slave society is as silly and naïve as to expect impartiality from manufacturers on the question of whether workers' wages should be increased by decreasing the profits of capital."[4]

In spite of their efforts, revisionists conceal the fact that bourgeois social science, in one way or another, defends the capitalist system and wage slavery and that it identifies the capitalist system with the "free" world and slanders socialism. Marxism has declared merciless war against this wage slavery and, employing the only correct method —the class struggle and the construction of a classless communist society—it leads the working class toward liberation.

History develops in conformity with Marx's and Lenin's outline! And the fact that bourgeois sociologists, reformists, and revisionists direct furious attacks against the Marxist ideology, its philosophical foundations, its sociological theory, and, in particular, against the *political conclusions* deduced from this theory once again confirms the validity of the Marxist-Leninist theory of class struggle. As stated by Lenin: "The dialectic of history is such that the theoretical victory of Marxism forces its enemies to *disguise* themselves as Marxists."[5]

Recent Marxist successes gave rise to attempts to revive the rotten, bourgeois liberalism, which assumes the form of modern revisionism and pretends to be acting in "defense" of a creative Marxism. Its aim is either to choke Marxism entirely to death or at least to smother some ideologically unstable Marxists in "liberal" embraces. At the

---

[4] *Sochineniya* [Works] (4th ed., Moscow), Vol. 19 (1948), p. 3.
[5] *Ibid.*, Vol. 18 (1948), p. 546.

same time, other detachments of bourgeois ideologists quite openly "refute," criticize, and slander Marxism. Such an approach to "criticizing" Marxism has been known in the past, and only those who are inexperienced in the ideological struggle can fail to notice it. Wiatr and Bauman relied upon just such people when they stated the following: "We think that we must reject the view that conceives of world sociology as a theater of war, with trenches from which the enemy positions are systematically fired upon!" But is it not hypocritical to make such a statement after they themselves have subjected the positions of the "official" Marxist social science and the Marxist theory of the class struggle to open fire, after they have showered praise upon the main trends in bourgeois sociology!

Immediately preceding the praise of bourgeois sociology, Wiatr and Bauman restated the bourgeois lie regarding "the decline of social sciences during the era of the Stalinist terror." We should bear in mind that these attacks on social science in the socialist countries were made immediately after the fascist *Putsch* in Hungary. In all probability these attacks contributed to the joy of all bourgeois critics of Marxism, who at that time were rejoicing over the "crisis" of Marxism and world communism.

The revisionist myth about the liberation of science from ideology and their rejection of partisanship in philosophy and sociology leads logically toward a separation of science from practice. . . .

. . . Marxism assumes that practice is *the basis* of all knowledge and that it is an objective criterion for judging the validity of a theory. Practice determines the direction of the development of cognition, its tasks and problems, and furnishes the instruments as well as the material means for cognition. Practice is "higher" than theory in the sense that it possesses the knowledge of "immediate reality." It transforms theory into life!

. . . Lenin's view, which is now axiomatic to Marxists, is that he who separates Marxist philosophy, dialectical materialism, from revolutionary practice, from politics, strategy, and tactics, disfigures materialism and makes it deadly and one-sided. It is precisely the unity of the Marxist theory with the revolutionary practice, with the policy, strategy, and tactics of the proletariat, that makes Marxism irreconciable with—and hostile to—dogmatism and scholasticism. As a result of this unity, the revolutionary theory remains eternally alive, developing, and creative. Marxism does not belittle the role of theory. By uniting it with practice organically and indissolubly, it gives a meaning to theory that no other philosophy is capable of giving; it transforms theory into the paramount instrument for the revolutionary transformation of the world by man.

# A Reply to Western Critics of "Socialist Democracy"*

## ∽ M. Z. Selektor

. . . The economic foundation of socialist democracy . . . is the socialist economic system based on the social ownership of the means of production. . . .

. . . The contention of bourgeois propagandists that socialization of the means of production kills individual initiative is nothing but a malicious falsehood. Socialism has liquidated the freedom of capitalist enterprise, the freedom of capitalist exploitation, but, at the same time, it has provided unlimited opportunity for the creativity of the popular masses, thus enabling each workingman to develop his abilities to the fullest. . . .

. . . Owing to the objective conditions existing during the formation of a communist society, public property under socialism exists in the form of state property. Bourgeois and reformist enemies of the socialist system interpret this fact as the enslavement of the individual by the socialist state because it presumably concentrates in its hands both political and economic power. Such a hideous distortion of socialism is being promoted by revisionists who . . . contend that the regulation of the economy by the socialist state constitutes a survival of state capitalism and gives birth to an "étatist bureaucracy," thus "limiting the freedom of work and the freedom of a direct producer."

Only one who intentionally shuts his eyes is unable to see that the relationships between the socialist state and an employee of a state enterprise are not the relationships between the proprietor of the means of production and the individual who is deprived of these means and who, consequently, is subjected to exploitation by the state. State property in socialist countries is the property of the whole people. This means that in the socialist state each direct producer, i.e., each worker, appears as a co-owner of the public wealth as he participates in the administration of this wealth through the state organs. He is, therefore, an equal master of socialist production, free from exploitation.

Under socialism, the presence of social ownership of the means of production renders a planned development of the national economy both possible and indispensable. This development is put into practice

* *From* "Sotsialisticheskaya Demokratiya i Lichnost" [Socialist Democracy and the Person], *Voprosy Filosofii*, No. 9 (1958), pp. 29–33.

by the state's planning of the socialist economy. Once again, the enemies of socialism see in this the destruction of personal freedom. Thus, a declared defender of "free" capitalist enterprise, F. Hayek, in his book *The Road to Serfdom* states the following: "If the 'dictatorship of the proletariat,' even democratic in form, resorts to a centralized administration of the economic system, it destroys individual freedom as thoroughly as any autocratic government. . . . The more 'planning' being done by the state, the more difficult becomes the planning for an individual."[1]

But, in fact, socialist planning does not restrict man's freedom. On the contrary, it constitutes an indispensable prerequisite of the latter. Capitalist anarchy in production and competition transforms the individual into a toy in the hands of social spontaneity, upsetting all individual plans and calculations. Capitalism with its "free" enterprise is a system in which man proposes and market spontaneity disposes. On the other hand, a planned organization of social production signifies the end of spontaneity in the historical development and its replacement by man's domination over the forces of production and social relationships. Under the conditions of socialism, man ceases to be a victim of crises, unemployment, and the fear of tomorrow. The planned development of the socialist society opens clear vistas for the activity of each individual; it makes man truly free, permits him to plan his activity rationally, and enables him to attain his intended goals. . . .

. . . Whereas the material, economic basis of man's freedom in the socialist society rests on the social ownership of the means of production, its spiritual basis . . . lies in socialist ideology, the theoretical foundations of which rest on the teaching of Marxism-Leninism. Champions of the bourgeois pseudofreedom are very much opposed to the fact that the Marxist-Leninist world outlook is dominant in the Soviet Union and they stigmatize it as "conformism" or "totalitarian thinking." But to denounce the Soviet people as being "totalitarian thinkers" because they reject the distorted idealist conception of reality and adhere to the scientific, dialectic view of the world is as "justified" as to reproach modern bourgeois humanity for "conformism" because it rejects alchemy but recognizes chemistry. The socialist ideology liberates man from the fetters of mysticism and superstition and gives him real freedom of thought based on knowledge. . . .

. . . In their attempts to accuse the socialist system of suppressing human freedom, bourgeois and right-socialist "critics" point out that

[1] Cited by Columbia College, Contemporary Civilization Staff, *Man in Contemporary Society* (New York, 1956), Vol. 2, pp. 341, 343.

only one party exists in the U.S.S.R., namely, the Communist party. They contend that political freedom is inconceivable in a country with only one party, and that the one-party system deprives the individual of the opportunity to express his opinions freely and hence precludes the competition of opinions. But, if we judge the degree of democracy in a political system . . . by a criterion as formal as the existence of several parties, then the czarist regime would appear as a "picture" of democracy because czarist Russia had more parties than other bourgeois democracies. . . .

. . . Unipartyism and multipartyism are merely political forms. Consequently, they should be examined and appraised concretely, in close relationship to the conditions that brought them about and in terms of the content comprised in their forms. Under conditions of imperialism, which aggravate class antagonism in a capitalist society to the extreme, unipartyism means the rejection of democracy, the imposition of a fascist social and political system, and the imposition of totalitarianism. Unipartyism represents—as it has been shown graphically by fascism in Germany and Italy—an attempt of the imperialist bourgeoisie's most reactionary circles to suppress all progressive forces—primarily the revolutionary movement and the organizations of the working class. Under socialism, i.e., conditions without antagonistic classes, unipartyism signifies a complete unity of the economic and political interests of all members of society—a society that consists exclusively of the working people. . . .

. . . The moral and political unity of Soviet society and the solidarity of the Soviet people with the Communist party does not preclude competition of opinions among Soviet men. . . . The Soviet people's popular and effective form of free expression is criticism and self-criticism, which constitute the moving force of development in socialist society. . . .

. . . Naturally, speaking of the superiority of socialist democracy over bourgeois democracy, one should not neglect the difficulties and contradictions in the development of the socialist society. The Soviet socialist society is not a "ready-made paradise." The development of socialist democracy does not take place smoothly and evenly but has to overcome deficiencies, mistakes, and distortions. . . .

# The Unity of Individual and State Interests under Socialism*  ᨆ  *M. Z. Selektor*

Socialist relationships have created for the individual a new position in the state and have placed him in a new relationship to it. . . . As a tool of domination in the hands of exploiters, the bourgeois state constitutes a force hostile to the working masses, and, consequently, the workingman is impelled by the conditions of his existence to struggle against the state.

On the other hand, the relationship of each individual capitalist to his state is characterized by duplicity. As a member of the capitalist class, each capitalist is interested in strengthening the bourgeois state. He strives to keep the exploited masses in obedience and to subjugate and plunder other countries and nations. At the same time, however, each capitalist or capitalist monopoly disregards the general interest of the state when it is to their own interest, namely, to gain greater profit. A bourgeois hypocritically extols the sanctity of civil obligation and seeks to imbue the workers with deference for the law of the bourgeois state; but he himself ignores his obligations to the state if they interfere with his personal enrichment. It may suffice to note, for example, the knavish machinations resorted to by capitalist monopolies in the United States to avoid paying the requisite taxes.

By contrast, the relationship between the individual and the state has an entirely different character under socialism. Irreconcilable contradictions between the individual and society which are characteristic of all social formations based on private ownership of the means of production have been removed by socialist relationships. Because the individual well-being of each socialist toiler depends upon the strengthening and development of social property and upon the increase of the material and spiritual riches of the socialist society, socialism unites the private interests of the individual and the interests of society into one whole.

The socialist system has also changed the interrelationship between society and the state. In contrast to an exploiting state—which represents the interests of one segment of society, the propertied minority —the socialist state expresses the will of the whole society, of the

* *From* "Sotsialisticheskaya Demokratiya i Lichnost" [Socialist Democracy and the Person], *Voprosy Filosofii*, No. 9 (1958), pp. 33–36.

whole people. Under conditions of socialism the state's interest coincides with social, public interests, and, conversely, social, public interest appears as the state's interest. From this it follows that unity of individual and social interests under socialism constitutes at the same time unity of the interests of the citizen and state interests.

This unity is reflected in Soviet law. Since private ownership of the means of production has been liquidated in the socialist society, there is no need for the existence of private law or, consequently, for the division of law into public and private. This, of course, does not imply that state rights supersede individual rights. The norms of all branches of Soviet law combine the protection of social, state interests and the private interests of citizens.

The unity of individual and state interests under socialism neither implies that they are indistinguishable nor precludes the existence of certain contradictions between the state's interests and the direct interests of an individual citizen. But these contradictions do not affect the foundations of the socialist system, because the entire social system of socialism, the whole activity of the socialist state, is directed toward serving man's welfare, and, consequently, such contradictions are successfully surmounted by the consolidation and development of socialist relationships and by the growth of communist consciousness among the workers. The growth of the might of the socialist state serves as a guarantee for the flourishing of the whole society and of the individual personality as well. Therefore, the Soviet people provide their state with support and love and display the greatest concern for state interests.

Socialist democratism has given a new meaning to, and has enormously elevated the significance of, the concept of civil duties and has created a new attitude of the people toward them. In contrast to capitalism—where the officially prescribed civil duties conceal the selfish interests of the bourgeoisie—the concept of civil duty in socialist society incarnates the interests of the whole society, the nation, the socialist fatherland, and, consequently, the interests of man himself. Soviet men are legitimate masters of their state, and this fact creates in each Soviet citizen a sense of individual responsibility for the conditions of state affairs and dictates the high civil consciousness of Soviet man, who views the fulfillment of his obligations to the state as his own self-fulfillment.

The socialist state has liquidated the gap between the rights and obligations of its citizens—a gap characteristic of the entire exploiting state in which rights are a privilege of the propertied classes whereas the workers are bound primarily by obligations. Socialist democratism

has brought about equality and unity of the citizen's rights and obligations. While providing its citizens with broad rights and freedoms in
all spheres of sociopolitical life, the socialist state lays upon them
definite obligations. The Constitution of the U.S.S.R. demands of each
Soviet citizen the following: to defend the socialist Fatherland; to
take care of and to strengthen social socialist property; to observe
labor discipline; to discharge honestly all civil duties; and to respect
the rules of communal life. The constitutional rights of Soviet citizens
as well as the obligations laid upon them by the socialist state correspond equally to the interests of the citizens. Consequently, the more
accurately and conscientiously Soviet men fulfill their obligations to
the socialist state, the more successfully will socialist society progress,
and the more extensive will the realization of democratic rights and
freedoms by Soviet citizens become. Freedom in the scientific, Marxist-
Leninist understanding has nothing in common with the negation of
any discipline. The Marxist-Leninist world outlook rejects the phraseology of anarchists advocating man's "absolute" freedom and interpreting freedom as a complete arbitrariness on the part of an individual who is free to do anything, who obeys no one but his own will,
who determines his own rights, and who refuses to acknowledge his
obligations to other people. Marxism-Leninism teaches that social
organization is inconceivable without a certain degree of discipline.
The interrelationship of discipline and freedom depends upon the
character of the discipline, who creates it, and whom it serves. . . .

. . . Socialist society does not renounce discipline in general. On the
contrary, the role of social discipline in all its manifestations increases
considerably under socialism. The highly concentrated and highly
mechanized character of socialist production, the direct social character of work under socialism, and the objective necessity of the planned
development of the whole national economy, which is translated into
reality by the socialist state through its planning activity, necessitates
an incessant strengthening of socialist discipline in production, labor, planning, and government. The strictest discipline of the workers and the highest possible unity of their will and action are indispensable for the successful completion of the grandiose tasks of
communist construction.

At the same time . . . socialist discipline is, in its very essence, opposed to the discipline of an exploitive society. Socialist discipline is
not imposed upon the workers by the exploiters but is established by
the people themselves in the interest of all the people, of society as a
whole. Hence, it has a conscious and voluntary character.

The transition from a system of private ownership of the means of production (which cultivates egotistical stimuli in man's behavior) to the socialist social organization (which is based on the unity of private and social interests, with the social interests playing the leading role) is accomplished in a relentless struggle against the habits and traditions generated by private ownership. These habits and traditions are still apparent even after the victory of socialism; they manifest themselves particularly in the contraposition of private interests to social and state interests. The Communist party of the Soviet Union, the Soviet state, and the whole Soviet society surmount the survivals of capitalism in the consciousness of workers by means of persuasion or, if the case necessitates it, by applying measures of state coercion against the antisocial elements; they educate the Soviet people in the spirit of deference toward social and civil duties, loyalty to which is the guarantee of personal freedom. Socialism transforms not only the economic and the political systems of society but also the spiritual face of men. The entire structure of socialist life implants in workers a deep understanding of the indissoluble connection between their personal interests and the interests of socialist society as a whole and strengthens the new motives stimulating men's activities. Increasingly, a public problem becomes a personal problem to each Soviet man. At the same time, the struggle for greater social interests elevates personality and promotes its spiritual growth.

To a bourgeois, who looks at the world through the prism of money and who is motivated exclusively by profit, such an attitude of the Soviet people toward social and state interests appears to be unnatural. Apologists of capitalism interpret this attitude as the enslavement of the individual by the state; they charge that socialism transforms the individual into "construction material" in the hands of the state. But that which bourgeois blind men and slanderers seek to depict as the enslavement of the individual by the socialist state is, in fact, an unlimited devotion of the Soviet man to his state. In this devotion are reflected the idealistic features of Soviet men, their service to the noble social ideals that have been translated into reality by the Soviet state, and the unity of the interests of all citizens of our country with those of the socialist state.

# A Rejoinder to Bourgeois Critics of Marxist Dialectics* ❧ *G. M. Shtraks*

Since the appearance of the Marxist philosophy, its opponents from the camp of bourgeois philosophy have never ceased in their attempts to "refute" dialectical and historical materialism. However, never in the history of Marxism have bourgeois reactionary philosophers published as many books intended to refute Marxist philosophy as during the postwar period and especially in recent years. . . .

The object of the most frequent attacks on the part of representatives of contemporary bourgeois reactionary philosophy is the law of the unity and struggle of opposites. Their class sense evidently prompts them to conclude that this law represents the central point of all Marxist dialectics. In attempting to undermine it, they seek to destroy the whole edifice of the materialist dialectic.

The most popular method of contemporary critics of the law of the unity and struggle of opposites is the denial of the objective and universal character of contradictions. Carrying on Dühring's tradition, they assert (in different ways) that only logical contradictions are possible and that the recognition of contradictions in things is pure nonsense. Thus, M. Merleau-Ponty, in his *Les aventures de la dialectique*,[1] finds that the main sin of the Marxist philosophy is the fact that it assigns dialectic . . . to objective reality, that it "places dialectic in the object, in the being, where it least belongs."

Marxist philosophy does not need to "place" dialectic in objects. Each progressive step taken by contemporary science brings to light objective contradictions in reality. . . .

. . . Present-day bourgeois critics of Marxism make frequent attempts to advance "concrete arguments" in favor of their denial of objective contradictions. They devote special attention to the criticism of the many examples of contradictions, which were given in the classics of Marxism-Leninism and which brilliantly reveal the objectivity and universality of contradictions. Significant in this respect is the work of a professor of the Vatican Eastern Institute—Gustav Wetter. This work is devoted to the criticism of dialectical materialism.[2]

In advancing his attacks against the law of the unity and struggle of opposites, he asserts that contradiction is not intrinsic to an object,

---

* *From* "Yadro Dialektiki i Ego Sovremennye Kritiki" [The Kernel of Dialetic and Its Modern Critics], *Voprosy Filosofii,* No. 4 (1959), pp. 74–83.

[1] (Paris, 1955), pp. 88–89.

[2] *Der dialektische Materialismus—Seine Geschichte und sein System in der Sowjetunion* (2nd ed.; Vienna, n.d.).

for mutually exclusive relations are peculiar only to distinct objects or distinct conditions of one and the same object and, consequently, they cannot constitute a unity of opposites but, on the contrary, are in a state of mutual exclusiveness—struggle.

. . . . . . .

Wetter quite openly explains why he so persistently struggles against contradictions: because the recognition of inner contradictions as the source of self-motion of matter leaves no place for God. Such an openness is indeed commendable. Nevertheless, it should be kept in mind that two hundred and fifty years ago Bishop Berkeley was refuting the existence of matter on the "ground" that it is incompatible with the will of God.

While Wetter writes in a popular way, addressing himself to a broad audience and invoking God in the struggle against dialectics and the law of the unity and struggle of opposites, another critic of Marxist philosophy, an American pragmatist, Sidney Hook, seeks especially to influence men of science, with the purpose of diverting them from dialectical materialism. For this reason, he asserts that the dialectical method is incompatible with a scientific approach to phenomena, that the recognition of objective contradictions is antithetical to the basic principles of scientific investigation, and that such a method cannot even be consistently formulated.[3] He seeks to give this claim a semblance of truth by analyzing the examples of contradictions given by Engels and questioning the presence of contradictions in them.

First of all, Hook denies that contradiction is intrinsic to mechanical motion. He asserts that Engels' famous proposition on the contradictoriness of mechanical motion violates the formal-logical law of contradictions and, therefore, is incompatible with a scientific approach. Furthermore, he asserts that motion can be described "in a relatively consistent way" without reference to contradictions of any type. To account for the fact that the position of a particle in a space at a given moment is a constant function of time is all that is needed. And the idea of a constant function does not require the existence of infinitesimally small intervals of space and time.[4]

Without offering any convincing arguments, Hook replaces the idea of "the motion of a particle" with the idea of its "position in space," which is not one and the same thing. Many generations of scientists struggled with the problem of motion which Hook declares, with one

[3] *Dialectical Materialism and the Scientific Method*, A Special Supplement to the Bulletin of the Committee on Science and Freedom (Manchester, England, 1955).
[4] *Ibid.*, p. 8.

stroke of the pen, to be nonexistent but which, however, does not cease to exist. According to Hook, the motion of a particle is simply the sum of its positions in space, each of which is described by means of the constant function of time. Thus, the contradiction of motion is set aside, or curtained, as Lenin said in his criticism of Chernov's similar metaphysical view of motion. But what is at stake is precisely the demonstration of how the motion comes into being and how, in time, the position of a particle in space is changed. The true solution of this problem was given by Engels and Lenin, who discovered the contradictory connection between space and time in the process of motion.

"Even a simple mechanical change of position can come about only through a body's being at one and the same moment of time in one place and in another, being in one and the same place yet also not in it. And the continuous origination and simultaneous solution of this contradiction is precisely what motion is."[5] Concretizing and further developing Engels' analysis of the contradictoriness of motion, Lenin wrote: "Motion is the essence of space and time. Two fundamental concepts express this essence: (infinite) continuity (*Kontinuität*) and 'punctuality' (= denial of continuity, *discontinuity,* of time and space). Motion is a contradiction, a unity of contradictions."[6]

Lenin's thesis demonstrates that in a contradiction there is expressed contradictoriness of both space and time—continuity and discontinuity, which are characteristic of all forms of existence of matter. . . .

. . . The recognition of a contradictory nature of motion, space, and time lies at the basis of the most significant divisions of mathematics and modern physics. Consequently, in being opposed to the Marxist philosophy, Sidney Hook—the "defender" of the scientific method—finds himself in the ludicrous role of subverting science in general.

As could have been expected, Hook fully rejects contradictions intrinsic to knowledge and takes up arms against Engels on this question. He questions Engels' thesis that the cognition of truth is a process in which contradictions are constantly overcome. . . . In Hook's judgment, "strictly speaking, what are being resolved are problems, mysteries, and difficulties, but not contradictions."[7] It is not difficult to see, however, that in the field where science encounters "problems, mysteries, and difficulties" there are always serious contradictions present, waiting for their resolution, for example, contradictions between old theories and new facts that were not accounted for by these theories, etc.

5 Engels, *Anti-Dyuring* [Anti-Dühring] (Moscow, 1957), p. 113.

6 "Filosofskie Tetradi" [Philosophical Notebooks], *Sochineniya* [Works] (4th ed., Moscow), Vol. 38 (n.d.), p. 253.

7 *Dialectical Materialism,* p. 10.

To "refute" Engels' thesis on the cognition of truth as a contradictory process, Hook attributes to the author of *Anti-Dühring* views that did not belong to him nor could they have belonged to him. He suggests that, according to Engels, the ideal of scientific knowledge is presumably absolute, real knowledge. But one who entertains such an ideal must assume that there are absolute, certain truths that make it possible to appraise truths that are not absolutely certain.[8] Hook contends that, from a Marxist point of view, absolute truth appears as an immutable standard for judging relative truths. At the same time, he passes in silence over the fact that Engels as a dialectician-materialist was interested not in a confrontation of one truth with another but in reflection of the objective reality, which can never be exhaustive, because of the inexhaustiveness of the very object of cognition—the endlessly developing nature. From this ensues the inescapable contradiction between the limitless possibilities of cognition and its limited realization in each epoch. . . .

The significance of the Marxist teaching on contradictions, both to science and practice, was demonstrated long ago. Seeking to undermine, among men of science, the increasing influence of the materialist dialectic, its critics contend that the recognition of contradictions in all objects precludes the possibility of formulating a scientific approach to them and their true knowledge.

Thus, a Catholic critic of the Marxist dialectic, a professor at Freiburg University, J. M. Bochenski, in his book *Der Sowiet-Russische Dialektische Materialismus* (*Diamat*),[9] declares that it is impossible to deduce any methodological conclusions from the recognition of inner contradiction in all objects, for, according to dialectic, in each individual case one encounters other contradictory factors. In other words, the specific character of a contradiction precludes its universality and thus any possibility of formulating a valid, general approach to all contradictions.

But such an argument can deceive only those who want to be deceived. For it is well known that each particular contradiction contains certain general features expressing a law: for example, the relativity of unity, the absoluteness of the struggle of contradictions, the development of contradictions, definite forms of its movement and overcoming, etc. These are precisely the features that constitute an objective basis for the formulation of a general approach to all contradictions; and this is being done by dialectical materialism.

In the judgment of a popular West German "critic" of dialectical materialism, M. Lange, the recognition of contradictions hampers cognition of concrete reality. In his work *Marxism-Leninism-Stalinism* Lange asserts that Soviet philosophers make the single structure

---

[8] *Ibid.*, p. 11.     [9] (2nd ed.; Bern, 1956).

of a social formation hardly distinguishable by pointing out contradictions in social life.

This peculiar assertion calls for rejection of the knowledge of the nature of historical process. Contrary to what Lange says, the type of contradictions peculiar to one formation differentiates it from other formations. In disclosing contradictions of one or another formation, Marxist science discovers the laws of its origination, development, and transformation into another, higher formation. The contemporary reactionary bourgeoisie fears the operation of objective contradictions in society and therefore questions the very fact of their existence. Lange and other "critics" of the law of the unity and struggle of opposites merely express the position of the bourgeois class.

To search in contemporary bourgeois philosophy for a unity of views on dialectics in general and contradictions in particular would be futile. Even within the framework of one and the same philsophical school different viewpoints on this problem are encountered. It has been seen that Wetter—a German neo-Thomist—rejects contradictions in God's name. A French neo-Thomist, Andre Marc, in a collection of essays, *Aspects de la dialectique*,[10] accepts contradictions but interprets them so that they become transformed into a means for the justification of the existence of God and of the universal harmony in the world, thus excluding any true contradictions.

. . . . . . .

An attempt to create a counterpoise to the law of the unity and struggle of opposites is characteristic of bourgeois philosophers. The most exponential in this respect is a book by Freiherr Bella von Brandenstein, *Der Aufbau des Seins—Systeme der Philosophie*.[11]

Brandenstein advances new, presumably philosophical categories, behind whose very abstract definitions is concealed well-known class interest. Degrading contradiction, and in effect "banishing" it from the field of philosophy, Brandenstein introduces as a counterpoise to the category of contradiction a category of "order" which is one of the highest concepts of his philosophy. As a definite philosophical category, "order" signifies a universal formal dependence, which generally exists between the "higher condition" and the "lower dependents."[12] Depicting the "order" in nature, the author finds it in the fact that natural causes represent spiritual forces; that man is a corporeal-spiritual being; that an immortal soul gives a peculiar essence to the body—its ego, its acts and state, and the objective content of its consciousness; that the processes of nature represent an interaction of the spiritual forces in matter; that variable reality springs from the

[10] In *Recherches de philosophie, II* (Paris, 1956).     [11] (Tübingen, 1950).
[12] *Ibid.,* p. 63.

latter condition and from the immutable reality, that is, from God.[13] Brandenstein needed the category of "order" for the purpose of "substantiating" an age-old idealist and religious thesis on the dependence of matter upon spirit, of nature upon God, and for the purpose of refuting the existence of contradictions.

The exploiting classes have always seen a higher order in the fact that they exploit the working masses. . . . That is why they are bent on identifying "order" with the absence of contradictions and the presence and intensification of contradictions as the disturbance of "order." The bourgeois philosopher who elevates "order" to the rank of a higher philosophical category is only expressing the viewpoint of the exploiting classes.

The Marxist dialectic does not at all deny the existence of a certain order in nature. Nature does not represent a chaotic agglomeration of phenomena. There is an order in nature, expressed in the material unity of the world, in the law-governed process of the development of matter. But an order is not an antipode to contradictions. The order that exists in nature is precisely an expression of the operation of objective necessity and hence of objective contradictions that determine the development of the entire sphere of reality. Objective necessity in the motion of matter, contradictions as an inner source of development—this is the objective basis of the order of nature.

Being aware of the inability to refute any proposition of Marxist teaching on contradiction, its critics resort to a direct falsification of the pronouncements of the classics of Marxism-Leninism on the law of the unity and struggle of opposites.

Thus, speaking about the Leninist theses on the universality of contradictions and their presence in all spheres and phenomena of reality, Lange asserts that these are "accidental declarations." But anyone who has read Lenin (as well as Marx and Engels) knows that the recognition of the universality of contradictions is the most significant feature of Marxist-Leninist thought.

. . . . . . .

A special place in the struggle against the Marxist understanding of contradictions (which is the only scientific one) belongs to the so-called tragic dialectic (J. Wall and others), which insists that "eternal conflicts" are absolutely unresolvable. In terms of theory, this view represents a denial of the active role of contradictions, for, if contradictions cannot be resolved, then it follows that the preservation of the earlier, old quality is inescapable and the rise of a new quality is impossible. But it is precisely in the transition from an old quality to a new that the active role of contradictions is most clearly visible.

[13] *Ibid.,* pp. 241, 246, 252.

From the practical viewpoint, "tragic dialectic" performs a definite social function: by insisting that antagonism in a capitalist system is unresolvable, it "eternalizes" capitalism.

In reality, there are no unresolvable contradictions. In spite of the forces that may oppose the resolution of contradictions, contradictions will ultimately and inevitably be overcome, for the overcoming of contradictions is prepared for by their entire earlier development, which cannot be halted. This conclusion is fully applicable to contradictions under capitalism, for they are inevitably resolved through a socialist revolution, which takes place when the indispensable objective and subjective prerequisites come to maturity. In contrast to the everlasting "tragic dialectic," which distorts objective reality and expresses the bourgeoisie's fear of the future, fear of its inevitable end, the Marxist dialectic can be characterized as an optimistic dialectic that correctly reflects the objective world and expresses the confidence of the working class, and all progressive forces, in their ability to overcome all matured contradictions in social development.

A peculiar variant of "tragic dialectic"—which is but a parody on dialectic—is the denial of some bourgeois philosophers that dialectic operates under conditions of socialism. Thus, the previously mentioned . . . Max Lange asserts that the acknowledgment of the moral-political unity of socialist society, Soviet patriotism, and the union of workers and peasants constitutes a denial of dialectic.

Another French theological philosopher contends that, with the conquest of power and the destruction of capitalism, the Bolsheviks also destroyed dialectic—the foundation of Marxism—because the liquidation of antagonistic classes presumably leads to the termination of historical development.[14] On this basis "Soviet socialism" is declared to be an "end of history."

. . . . . . .

Marxism has proved, and historical experience has fully confirmed, that contradictions manifest themselves in countlessly varied ways and that under conditions of socialism many new elements appear in their operation, elements that were not encountered in mankind's prehistory period; these contradictions come into being and are overcome on the basis of a moral-political unity of society, the friendship of peoples, and socialist patriotism. A true history of mankind begins only with socialism; it finds its expression in the non-antagonistic character of contradictions—contradictions of continuous growth and all-round social flourishing.

[14] Henri Denir, Roger Garaudy, George Cogniot, and Guy Besse, *Les marxistes répondent à leurs critiques catholiques* (Paris, 1957), pp. 61–62.

# Religious and Communist Morality*

## ⚭ V. I. Prokofev

Like other forms of social consciousness, religion is a reflection of man's social being. Religion gives a fantastic form to its reflection of the material conditions of man's life. Even in *The German Ideology,* Marx and Engels emphasized that in religion "men transform their empirical world into an abstract, imaginary substance which confronts them as something alien. An explanation of this cannot be extracted from other conceptions, from 'self-consciousness,' but from the entire mode of production that existed up until now. . . ."[1]

In addition to the real world, religion recognizes the existence of the heavenly, unearthly, supersensory, and unknowable world and insists that man has the ability to have contact with this world. The believers are induced into believing that man is dependent upon unknown, secret, "superhuman" forces. Religion is inconceivable without a mystical element, without faith in supernatural forces that must be worshipped because man's health and happiness depend upon their disposition or wrath.

When man was helpless vis-à-vis the powerful forces of nature and depended upon elemental laws of social life, his tendency to personify the material world surrounding him led to fantasy, to the idea of the supernatural. Needless to say, religion is not just any fantasy; it is fantasy concerning the supernatural. Engels writes in his *Anti-Dühring:* "In the beginnings of history, it was the forces of nature which were first so reflected and which in the course of further evolution underwent the most manifold and varied personifications among the various people." This tendency toward personification, according to Engels, created gods everywhere.

Deification of the forces of nature increased under the conditions of man's highly limited social experience and the low level of development of the forces of production. With the division of human society into hostile classes—the exploited and the exploiting—the class forces were added to the forces of nature which dominate man. The belief was spread that social life, like nature, is dependent upon Divine Providence, which presumably stands above society and governs man's life. Thus, conditions were created under which the oppressed

* From "Antigumanisticheskii Kharakter Religioznoi Morali" [Antihumanist Character of Religious Morality], *Voprosy Filosofii,* No. 9 (1959), pp. 29–42.
[1] *Sochineniya* [Works] (2nd ed.; Moscow, 1955), Vol. 3, p. 146.

456                                    SOVIET POLITICAL THOUGHT

and dominated toilers sought oblivion and comfort in religion. Religion is "always and everywhere a form of the spiritual oppression of the popular masses who are condemned to poverty, to loneliness and to working for others. The helplessness of the exploited classes in their struggle with the exploiters inevitably gives rise to the belief in a better life in the next world, just as the helplessness of a savage in his struggle with nature gives rise to the belief in gods, devils, miracles, etc."[2]

Like an ideology, religion is a very complex social phenomenon. It encompasses various elements of the believer's consciousness; it interacts with other forms of consciousness, reacts upon them and in turn is affected by them. It has pervaded both literature and art. Through the course of many centuries, it has utilized the ruling classes as an instrument for moral indoctrination of the oppressed.

In any more or less developed religion we find elements of morality, with norms that seek to encompass all aspects of man's life, to regulate his entire existence, and to determine his conduct and actions from the cradle to the grave. In appealing to a believer's personality, the church seeks to rule his deep and intimate feelings. Even at the present time we encounter devotees who go to a church or house of prayer with the hope of obtaining answers to various questions about life!

It is natural for a man who ponders over the questions of life to arrive at his own ideals. An ideal plays a great role both in the life of an individual man and in the life of society. But, there are different ideals. A high ideal exerts an ennobling influence upon man and makes him more conscious and active in the struggle to improve terrestrial life. A religious ideal is fantastic and antisocial; it enslaves man's consciousness. As stated by Lenin, "Religion gives man an ideal. Man needs an ideal, but a human ideal, an ideal corresponding to nature, not a supranatural ideal."[3]

Religion creates a fantasy of an ideal world, that is, a "divine kingdom" in which the pious man is promised a full reward for the deprivation experienced by him during terrestrial life. For its purposes, the church has cleverly utilized the ardent dreams of the oppressed about justice, equality, good, and fraternity and has shaped them into fantastic hopes for "life after death," for life in "the other world." The Gospel preaches love, mercy, and justice: "Come unto me, all ye that labour and are heavy laden, and I will give you rest. For my yoke is easy, and my burden is light."[4]

Religion and the morality preached by it promise comfort to men. But religion brings about a false and illusory comfort. It propagates

[2] V. I. Lenin, *Sochineniya* [Works] (4th ed., Moscow), Vol. 10 (1947), p. 65.
[3] *Ibid.*, Vol. 38 (n.d.), p. 64.        [4] Matt. 11:28, 30.

the fantastic view that all men are equal before God and urges man not to attribute any significance to the factual inequality between the poor and the rich, the exploited and the exploiters, the oppressed and the oppressors. That is why Marx characterized religion as a general theory and system of the moral sanctions of the false world, as a universal basis of comfort. But, as stated by Lenin in his "The Fall of the Second International," "He who comforts a slave instead of preparing him for revolution against slavery is helping the slave-holders." A true comfort, a true satisfaction can be attained by people who suffer under economic oppression and lawlessness only through a revolutionary struggle for the reconstruction of life.

In seeking to provide people with illusory comfort, religion makes extensive use of emotional appeal to the believers. In analyzing the religious emotional experiences of believers, we find not only distorted reflections of the elemental forces of nature and social being but also religious feelings corresponding to these reflections. It is impossible to free oneself of these feelings without breaking with religion altogether. . . . It should be noted that in recruiting their flock ecclesiasts have always sought to appeal not so much to man's reason . . . as to his senses. They cleverly catch the man at moments of joy or suffering, skillfully stupify him with the splendor of church decorations, the flavor of frankincense, prayers, and songs. One should not underestimate the power of the emotional effect of temple art, confession, and divine service. It is not an accident that most religions seek an ally in the aesthetic senses. They make constant and extensive use of architecture, pictures, music, and other types of art.

. . . Religious ideas are presented not in an abstract logical form but in a pictorial concrete form. Although these ideas are false, they are made an object of visual contemplation and are expressed symbolically in the rites of the divine service. Unfortunately, our comrades who conduct atheist propaganda or organize cultural leisure for the youth frequently display a lack of proper inventiveness in the struggle with the emotional influence of the church for they think that this influence deserves no attention. The emotional aspects of religious beliefs should not be ignored in atheist propaganda and in cultural educational work. Verbal explanations alone are inadequate for the reindoctrination of people who are entangled in a religious maze. The struggle with religion is not only a struggle with a harmful ideology but a struggle for the purification of human senses from religious opium.

According to this very significant proposition for scientific atheist propaganda, propagandists should study people's lives, feelings, and thoughts thoroughly and should display a penetrating sensitivity toward their feelings. Quite recently the author of this article attended a propaganda seminar at which he was told that several workers from a plant located in a suburb of Moscow had begun to participate actively in church services. Among those new believers was even a locksmith-progressivist. In the process of discussion it was revealed that the worker, who had never before attended a church but who became an active churchgoer, had been struck by a personal misfortune with which he had been unable to cope, and social organizations had not helped him in time.

Very often ecclesiasts are successful in their work simply because our social organizations do not pay adequate attention to the cultural and educational work of those citizens who do not participate in social life and who live in a world of narrow self-interest. In overcoming religious feeling, a greater role should be assigned to realistic art, literature, and skillful organization of people's leisure. Due to the efforts of the Party and the state, Soviet people have acquired more free time in recent years. In the new seven-year plan the time for rest and leisure will be even greater. Our people now live better. They can and want to conduct their family celebrations in a more attractive and interesting way. Ecclesiasts noticed this quite quickly; the cases of ritualistic weddings and christenings have increased. Should we not begin to think about the introduction of broad-scale amusements and good, fascinating festivals and outdoor feasts? Our task is to supplant religious celebrations with vivid popular festivities. It would not be out of place to think about Soviet wedding rites, wedding songs, bridal attire, thereby accounting for the rich local and national customs and traditions.

Present-day propaganda of religious ideology and religious morality is conducted by means of refined methods. The preachings of contemporary ecclesiasts deal primarily with questions of morality whereby religious morality is pronounced to be an absolute standard of man's conduct. The source of this morality, according to ecclesiasts, can only be a single, absolute God. They persuade believers that the image of God is an inborn, indelible quality of human nature: God's image can be distorted but cannot be eliminated. And since, according to ecclesiasts, morality and religion are indissolubly interconnected, the existence of morality is inconceivable without religion. Hence, they attribute a supranatural, divine origin to moral laws. Those who want justice to triumph on earth must believe in the existence of the all-mighty God who punishes men for evil deeds and rewards them for good conduct. They assert that, if this consolation, or incentive, disappears, our world will be transformed into an actual hell. Presumably only religion can restrain man's "animalistic instincts"; the very moment man is given freedom from religious ties morality perishes.

. . . In attempting "not to be behind the times" and in being afraid to appear before people as ignoramuses, ecclesiasts glorify the successes of modern science in all possible ways. At the same time, they seek, quite persistently, to prove that moral values and goals cannot be founded on science and cannot be deduced from the objective reflection of the world. The knowledge acquired by science is presumably by its very nature too indefinite to sustain moral convictions.

According to the preachers of religious morality, the sphere of science and mind is limited to the study of existing reality. Morality, on the other hand, is and should be preoccupied with what ought to be, not with what factually exists, but what ought to exist in conformity with our convictions and desires. There is presumably an insurmountable wall between what factually exists and what we think ought to exist. The task of both science and the mind is to establish the truth of facts, that is, to disclose the essence of the world surrounding us and to reflect it faithfully in concepts. But only morality, not science, can answer the question of whether the world is good or evil, whether it is immersed in good or evil, whether it is improving or worsening in its development. Without a moral consciousness man would simply be a cognizing subject, indifferent to the entire world. If man had only a cognizing intellect, he would know neither evil nor good. This moral consciousness, according to the Christian teaching, is the voice of God's will. We are being told that the solution to the mysteries of human life is to be sought not in science but in the great religious systems.

While hypocritically eulogizing science and technological achievements, ecclesiasts glorify the human mind only as "God's gift." In their opinion, although science broadens man's intellectual horizons, develops his power, and increases his mastery over nature, it cannot elevate man morally, for this can be done only by religion.

. . . One can easily see the unsoundness of the ecclesiasts' endeavors to separate morality from science with an insurmountable wall. Like any ideology, morality can be either scientific or unscientific; that is, its norms can reflect objectively existing human relationships either in a distorted, false way or in a more or less accurate way. Communist morality can be recognized as scientific in the sense that it is grounded in the principles of Marxism-Leninism and its philosophical basis is dialectical materialism. Scientific morality objectively reflects the interests of the working class and of all progressive humanity. The working class is the bearer of progressive morality, not because it enjoys a special God's grace, but because of its place in social production, because of the collective character of labor, and because of the tradition of revolutionary struggle. One of the peculiar features of morality as a form of social consciousness lies in the fact that it reflects existing reality in the concepts and ideas of conscience, honor, duty, good, evil, etc.

Different moral systems interpret the relationship between what is and what ought to be in different ways. The "ought" contains ideal motivation, motivation which is objectivized, conditioned, and not arbitrary. It also contains something else: the will necessary for the materialization of the "ought." Therefore, science and morality are not contradictory but are united, closely bound, and interacting.

The aim of science is the betterment of man's life. The struggle for a better life, for the construction and strengthening of communist society, constitutes the basis of communist morality. As stated by Lenin: "At the foundation of communist morality lies the struggle for the strengthening and completion of communism."[5]

## MORALITY IS NOT INBORN

The history of the ethical sciences offers numerous examples of brilliant criticism advanced by philosophers, long before the appearance of Marxism . . . , against religious morality. But pre-Marxian philosophers could not destroy it finally, because they held positions of idealism and inconsistent materialism.

Masterfully revealing the inescapable tie between idealist and religious views, Marx and Engels wrote: "All idealists, both philosophical and religious, old and new, believe in inspirations and revelations, in saviors and miracle workers, and whether their belief assumes a vulgar, religious form or an enlightened, philosophical form depends only upon the degree of their education. . . ."[6]

The norms of religious morality are deduced from revelations, through which God presumably announced his commandments and desires. Thus, Jewish and Christian religions assume that the religious and moral commandments were received by Moses directly from God on the mountain of Sinai.[7] The Bible narrates how . . . God appeared before Moses and handed him commandments that primarily demand obedience from the people. It is significant that all of God's commands are accompanied by a threat of punishment in case of violation and by a promise of reward for obedience. Almost all the commandments begin with the expression "thou shall not."

The first four commandments speak of man's relationship to God and demand from man an absolute recognition of one God as the creator of man and the universe. The tenth commandment pronounces the sacredness of private property. Whereas ecclesiasts were and are deducing the norms of man's conduct from God's commandments,

[5] Sochineniya [Works] (4th ed., Moscow), Vol. 31 (1950), p. 270.
[6] Sochineniya, Vol. 3, p. 536.       [7] Exod. 20:12–26.

the idealist philosophers deduced them from different sources. What they have in common is that both ignore the influence of social being upon the creation of norms. That can easily be seen by looking at the answers given by diverse idealist moral systems to the question concerning the source of morality. Some of them see the source of morality in the "voice of Socrates," others in "absolute reason" or in a "higher law of humanity," in the "dictates of the heart," in "inborn egotism," etc., etc. But all of them fail to see the source of morality in the revolutionary, practical activity of men.

Marxism-Leninism teaches that men are not born with ready-made moral ideas and feelings. The source of morality is not God's commands, not animal instincts, but the social conditions of man's material life. We shall not forget Marx's remarkable thought: social being determines social consciousness.

For example, religion teaches that conscience is something eternal, immutable, that it is God's voice and will within us. In fact, an eternal conscience is nonexistent. Conscience is nothing but a reflection of life's picture, social forces, in man's moral consciousness. Like man's moral convictions, conscience does not speak only of what is good or bad but it also obligates man to do good and to avoid evil. In reflecting man's picture of life, conscience assumes diverse forms. Since members of different classes have a distinct consciousness and picture of life, their ideas of conscience are different. "A proprietor's conscience is different from that of a poor man's, an intellectual's different from that of one who is incapable of thinking."[8]

Religious teaching attributes a supranatural origin to the conscience of duty. According to ecclesiasts, man's conscience of duty is inborn. The idea of duty necessarily implies the idea of obligation toward authority that exists outside of and above us. This authority is God.

To be sure, the conscience of duty is one of the highest moral senses and it is a phenomenon conditioned by history. It constitutes an expression of man's principal obligations toward other persons, collectives, and society. With the development of society, the sense of duty is transformed into a conviction and helps man fulfill his duty to the very end, even if such a fulfillment is connected with unbelievable hardships and costs man his life.

Thus, the root of all social customs and morals should be sought not in religious tenets but in the conditions of the material life of society, in the character of economic relations. Morality existed and will exist independent of religion. Morality was the earliest form of social conscience. Its rise and formation belong to the initial stage of human history. The stage in which religion arose was preceded by hundreds of thousands of years of human history during which even

---

[8] Marx and Engels, *Sochineniya*, Vol. 6, p. 140.

the slightest traces of religious beliefs were absent. Customs and morals existed prior to the rise of religion.

With the rise and further development of the religious cult, religion usurped the customs and morals that arose in primitive society and transformed moral norms into decrees of gods. The idea of oughtness begins to assume a religious character. The ideas of sin and sanctity come into being. Religion becomes the buttress of social injustice, and he who violates the moral dogmas of the church is censured and convicted as an enemy of the divine world order.

Religious fear begins to play a significant role—fear of man's and God's vengeance for the disobeying of religious rules. The sense of fear and of responsibility to the collective ultimately gives rise to the idea of retribution, requital for sins. This idea begins to encompass the most diverse elements: violation of taboo; punishment for a violation of the customs and morals of the tribal community. Any moral violation is regarded as an offense against God. The requital that follows is either good or bad, depending upon man's deed.

All ancient religions sought to resolve the question of good and evil. Persians assumed that there are two gods: the god of good and the god of evil, Ormazd and Ahriman. In other religions we find gods who are creators and protectors as well as gods who are destructive. Titans, who inhabited Olympus, and Prometheus, chained to a cliff for stealing fire from heaven, illustrate an attempt to explain the struggle between good and evil, between order and disorder in nature and in human society. Pantheists asserted that evil is nonexistent, that everything is good—god.

The image of gods entertained by the ancient Greeks was that of their own heroes, who, as human beings, had not only perfections but also defects, human passions, and even vices. The deity was viewed by the Greeks as the essence of man himself and, therefore, Greek gods, like real human beings, lacked moral austerity. Human passions and vices became the passions and vices of the gods. Envy and hatred, cunning and slyness, adultery and jealousy, were characteristic of both men and gods. Greek gods were capable of cruelty, bloody violence, and outbursts of wild passion.

Aside from peoples and states, Roman conquests also brought into contact and amalgamated religions. This resulted in a mixture of different faiths: Egyptian, Judaism, Hinduism, Buddhism, Greek polytheism, and mysticism, witchcraft, and spiritualism. In the Roman slave-holding society, the gods were the gods of war, victory, and were representatives of useful things. Roman gods were not idealistically minded; they were gods of cold reasoning, concerned with the immediate and common needs of man's life.

## THE ANTIHUMANISM OF
## RELIGIOUS MORALITY

All ancient religions (Egyptian, Greek, Roman, and others) arose under conditions of tribal systems. Born in a preclass society, they were not suited for the sanctification of a class system. New conceptions of the world, morality, and law were needed, conceptions which would correspond to the slave-holding relationships that were coming into being in the ancient states. In order to adapt itself to new conditions, the Church had to assume a new shape. The result was monotheism. In the Roman Empire the monotheistic religion became Christianity. In the center of Christian morality lies the teaching that suffering is a natural part of human life. The essence of Christianity is the idea of the victory of good over evil through the suffering of the good. . . . According to Christian theologians, suffering has great moral significance, for it is conducive to man's deliverance from vices and evil, makes him responsive to the misfortune of others, and strengthens cosuffering in him. There is no perfection without suffering; God suffers, and so did Jesus Christ. One should not search for those who are responsible for human sufferings, because sufferings are inevitable and only through them will man attain future blessedness.

The teaching about suffering is also a principal part of Buddhism: birth—suffering, old age, illness—suffering, death—suffering. To live means to suffer, for there is no other road to man's salvation but universal suffering. Life itself is a great evil from which all other tribulations ensue. Evil is inherent in, and inseparable from, life; hence, the destruction of evil is inconceivable without the destruction of life.

Because Buddhism proceeds from false assumptions, it is not difficult to see that it disarms man, paralyzes his ability to act and to improve reality, and pronounces as futile all his efforts directed toward the attainment of happiness on earth. While urging the masses to be meek, Buddhism condemns them to suffering and deprivation on this earth, promising them, at the same time, great happiness after death.

Christian teaching also inevitably leads to complete despair and a lack of faith in the possibility of the victory of good on earth. The teaching of passive long-suffering reveals the reactionary nature of the moral principles of all religions. The perfidy of all these religious teachings constitutes a serious danger, for they are advanced under the banner of humanism. Their unsoundness and pernicious influence is most apparent in their blessing of the most monstrous humiliation and insult of man, i.e., his sufferings, as the only possibility of the "purification" of the world from evil.

Christian humanism asserts the independence of man's inner

world from the social environment. Therefore, the morality of suffering is the morality of appeasement of social evil. The most powerful and real weapon in the struggle against Christian "humanism" is communist humanism. The latter subverts the "theoretical" justification underlying the idealization of suffering—the conception of "inner law" which denies social environment a role in formulating man's conscience.

Christian morality teaches that the suffering existing in this world is a result of sin. Suffering is the best means of purification from sin. No man on earth is righteous by birth; all are sinners. . . .

. . . What must be done to put an end to evil, to destroy the realm of sin? Christian theologians teach that in order to be delivered from original sin and to find salvation, it was necessary to satisfy God through a great propitiating sacrifice. Since men could not provide such a sacrifice because of their natural depravity, they needed assistance from above. God himself decided to provide such a sacrifice; that sacrifice was God's Son, Jesus Christ.

The teaching of atonement for man's sins by the Son of God is one of the central parts of Christian morality. . . . Christ has atoned for the sins of everyone who believes in him. Although sin was deprived of its enslaving power, it still lives in man's flesh; and Satan, although condemned, is still not destroyed and continues to tempt people. Therefore, the final atonement will take place during the Second Coming of the Savior, when the atonement of flesh will be added to moral atonement.

The Christian teaching of atonement reflects the impotence, feeling of doom, and helplessness of the oppressed working masses. The helplessness of the enslaved masses in their struggle with exploiters aroused in them faith in a miraculous savior, in a "Messiah" who will appear on earth and will free all those "suffering and burdened." Faith in Christ—the Savior—weakens people's will toward the struggle and undermines confidence in their own power. This faith breeds a feeling of worthlessness and submissiveness on the part of religious people. Servants of the Christian Church urge people to submissively wait for the general good that will be brought by the Savior.

The Christian theory of sin and atonement is the main object of present-day church propaganda. Under the conditions of bourgeois society this theory is quite suitable for the ruling classes because the idea of atonement and salvation helps the bourgeois ravage and plunder people daily and make capital from the blood and sweat of the workers.

By its very nature, the theory of atonement is antihumanist. It disarms man of his ability to cope with the difficulties of his life and it considers the struggle for a revolutionary transformation of an unjust capitalist system fruitless. A significant element of Christian morality are the commandments that deal with the love of God, neighbor, and one's self. Man is created to serve God and that means to love him and have faith in him. In love, Christianity sees a principle of the relationships between men and a foundation of all moral laws and all justice. But, in the final analysis, the love of man is absorbed by the love of God. Man should be loved only in God for the sake of God; and human society as a whole finds its justification in the divine principles.

In Christian morality, man's love of God is always fused with a fear of God. Fear is the central element in religious teaching. Fear is an integral part of the idea of authority, and education in bourgeois society is grounded in it.

For the sake of the divine kingdom, a Christian should renounce his father and mother, wife and children; in general, he should renounce everything earthly in order to devote his total life to the love of God. The stern words of the Gospel, attributed to Christ, do not sound like the spirit of "love of neighbor." "If any man come to me, and hate not his father, and mother, and wife, and children, and brethren, and sister, yea, and his life also, he cannot be my disciple."[9] "He that is not with me is against me."[10] Either with Christ or against him! No interpretation can modify the exclusiveness and intolerance of Christian teaching.

The request to love Christ, without which man is presumably condemned to eternal suffering, also contains enmity toward non-believers and members of other faiths. In the Gospel we find the following paragraphs: "But those mine enemies, which would not that I should reign over them, bring hither and slay them before me."[11] Or, "He that gathereth not with me scattereth abroad."[12] This means that a Christian should regard everyone who does not share his views as an enemy.

Soviet society, that is, communist ideology, frees human beings from one of the most repulsive features implanted by religion—religious and nationalistic hatred of people of another faith or nationality. There is no place in our country for religious enmity between men, a feature characteristic of the bourgeois system.

Applying their own standards to others, defenders of the church seek in every way possible to convince people that, owing to their ideological views, Communists suppress freedom of religion and hate and persecute believers. N. S. Khrushchev . . . gave a convincing an-

[9] Luke 14:26.    [10] Matt. 12:30.    [11] Luke 19:27.    [12] Matt. 12:30.

swer to these tales related by enemies of communism: "As atheists, we by no means inculcate enmity toward believers. We have never called for hostility between peoples on religious grounds or for wars between states on ideological grounds, as we never shall. We treat religious people not merely with tolerance but with respect. We struggle against religion only when it is being used to harm people."[13] Indeed, we are not indifferent to harm inflicted by religion upon the growing generations. . . . But we struggle with this harm by means of a patient explanation of the falsity of the moral precepts of religion.

According to Christian faith, the relationship between God and man is based on the principle of subordination and service. There is not even a hint of equality. On the contrary, absolute inequality prevails. The inequality between God and man, which corresponds to the inequality between master and servant, is called "love of God" by Christianity. One must be meek; one must regard oneself as a beggar before God. This spiritual misery is the first step toward salvation, and that is why the Gospel considers it a most significant condition of moral development.

In addition to the love of God, Christian morality considers the love of neighbor as one of its significant principles. According to this principle, everybody should live in love with everybody else, for all have one God who loves with one love and will judge all in one court. As stated by Pius XII, "Love of an enemy is higher than heroism." Or, as pointed out in the *Journal of the Moscow Patriarchate:* "In worshiping God, thou shall worship each man regardless of his shortcomings."[14]

All these contrivances amount to nothing but preaching a class world, based on the following precept from the Gospel: "But I say unto you, love your enemies, bless them that curse you, do good to them that hate you, and pray for them which despitefully use you and persecute you."[15] The Soviet people reject this religious morality, for it has a definite reactionary character. A true humanism, that is, a true love of men, presupposes hatred of the enemies of humanity, hatred of imperialist plunderers and the exploiters and oppressors of the workers.

Like all false constructions, Christian morality is quite contradictory. Along with the principle of an "eye for eye" it calls for "nonresistance to evil" and commands one to turn the left cheek to him who hit the right one. . . . This moral-religious, all-reconcilable prin-

[13] "Za Ukreplenie Mira mezhdu Narodamy" [For the Promotion of Peace among Nations], *Pravda*, May 17, 1959.
[14] *Zhurnal Moskovskoi Patriarkhii*, No. 7 (1956), p. 41.
[15] Matt. 5:44.

ciple, seeking to extol a passive Christian humanism, is diametrically opposed to communist humanism. Our morality teaches the following: he who withdraws from evil and does not offer resistance to evil, objectively supports its existence. In order to bring about good, it is necessary to destroy evil, fighting it with all means and power.

Like other principles of our Soviet morality, communist humanism is distinguished by a militant, fighting spirit. In addition to an irreconcilable hatred of the enemies of humanity, it requires a merciless struggle against them. Our humanism is neither an abstract idea nor a hypocritical love of mankind; rather, it is a true love of those who struggle for the happiness of nations, peace on earth, and the victory of communism. Only a life that possesses a great and deep love for the working people, a life devoted to humanity, brings true happiness.

Our life refutes the Kantian contraposition of duty and interest; it also refutes the religious path of ennobling man through suffering. The various theories that oppose personal and social happiness are equally unacceptable to the Soviet people. In bringing about his own happiness, the Soviet man quite rightly sees its basis in the successful application of his power for the sake of social good. The happiness of the Soviet man lies in his awareness of his full social value, in serving the great national cause, that is, in the awareness that a true good lies in his utmost promotion of the materialization of the great ideals of humanity, through his labor and thought. Communist humanism finds vivid expression in the titanical struggle being waged by the nations against instigators of a new war.

For twenty centuries, Christianity preached love of one's neighbors. But these preachings did not help prevent mankind from frequent entanglements in bloody battles. Only during the last forty-five years imperialists unleashed two world wars. . . . Representatives of various churches blessed these wars and many ecclesiasts have sought to morally justify the crimes of the imperialists. In countries occupied by Nazies during the Second World War, the Vatican and its agents furnished all possible help to the fascist oppressors. Today, the Vatican places the Catholic Church in the service of an aggressive, reactionary policy of American monopolies.

The hypocrisy . . . of bourgeois ideologists who conceal themselves behind a religious shield has been revealed by N. S. Khrushchev . . . : "Adenauer is the leader of the Christian Democratic party. It would seem that he should be guided by evangelical precepts, which the people in his party are so fond of enlarging on. Yet this 'Christian' has a cross in one hand and wants to take an atom bomb in the other. Indeed, he relies on the bomb more than on anything else, though such an attitude neither conforms to evangelical precepts nor promotes the solution of the German people's national problem."[16]

. . . Soviet humanism manifests itself in love toward man, in respect for his personality, and in aspiring to assist those who are in need. But it is impossible to love men indiscriminately; and while loving, it is impossible to suffer submissively, to forgive everything, and to appease everything. Such humanism is alien to us. Soviet humanism comprises love toward the working humanity and hatred toward those who encroach upon the freedom of the workers, who cultivate man-hatred, who prepare new wars and seek to perpetuate colonization and exploitation of man by man.

An optimistic and bright view of man lies at the foundation of Soviet humanism. Everything new and progressive is being grown and cultivated in our country. Man has wide opportunities for developing his creative individuality and all of his physical and spiritual qualities. Prejudice and a pessimistic view of the future are alien to him. We educate Soviet people in the spirit of courage and cheerfulness, in the spirit of a profound confidence in the righteousness of our worthy cause.

Khrushchev described the difference between the hypocritical Christian morality and the true morality very well in his conversation with a reporter for *Figaro:*

Frequently, plenty of nonsense is being told about us Communists; we are being told that men who do not believe in God, whom even believers cannot clearly imagine, cannot be guided by the high feeling of humanism. But Communists are the most humane people, because they do not wage the struggle for their own good life only. . . . We think that each man has the right to work, the right to a good life which human society can create for all men. We are for the true equality of men and peoples. Is this not an expression of humaneness? Concern for a living man, for the society in which he lives, concern for the life of the people—these are our ideals, these are our convictions. I think that this is much better than to believe in God and to plunder the workers, to throw them out into the streets from the factories and plants, as is being done by capitalists who believe in God.[17]

Communist morality, expressing the progressive and humane aspirations of Soviet society, is a tremendous force promoting a successful construction of communism. It elevates man, makes him a fighter and a reconstructer of life, one who utilizes the objective laws of nature and society to the benefit of all mankind. To be moral is to give all power and energy to the cause of the struggle for a communist society.

[16] *Kontrolnye Tsifry Razvitiya Narodnogo Khazyaistva SSSR na 1959–1965 Gody* [Control Figures for the Development of the National Economy of the U.S.S.R. for 1959–1965] (Moscow, 1958), p. 87.

[17] *Pravda,* March 27, 1958.

# The Clerical Apology of "People's Capitalism"*

## ∽ L. N. Velikovich

The apology of private capitalist property is the main concern of the social theory of modern ecclesiasts. Clerical apologists of the capitalist system pronounce private property to be sacred and inviolable. In the encyclical *Rerum Novarum* Pope Leo XIII wrote: "The socialist theory of social property, which replaces private property, must be totally rejected. . . . Let the inviolability of private property be an immutable law to all those who sincerely seek the happiness of the people. In this connection it is significant that the law should promote the spirit of property, should cultivate and develop it to the utmost among the popular masses."[1]

Catholic social doctrine asserts that the aspiration for private property is a necessary manifestation of human individuality—a spiritual need of man. But now, since socialist property has become firmly established in the Soviet Union and other socialist countries, capitalism's apologists have even greater difficulty in justifying the existence of capitalist private property. Ecclesiasts resort to anything possible to prove that private property in the modern capitalist world does not involve exploitation of man by man.

One of the arguments used by ecclesiasts in justifying private property is the contention that it involves definite obligations toward society. Ecclesiasts argue that one must distinguish the possession from the use of private property. In their opinion, modern capitalists are merely managers of the wealth granted to them by God. They presumably carry the "burden of property" in fulfilling their Christian duty. The deputy of the Vatican's Secretary of State, Acua, wrote that "proper ordering of life requires recognition and respect of private property." At the same time, he emphasized that "material wealth is not given for the unlimited and exclusive enrichment of a few but for the satisfaction of everyone's needs. A proprietor should use the wealth that is at his disposal in a way beneficial to all members of the collective."[2]

Catholic sociologists' reasoning about the social function of private

* From "Klerikalnaya Apologetika Sovremennogo Kapitalizma" [The Clerical Apology of Contemporary Capitalism], *Voprosy Filosofii*, No. 3 (1960), pp. 79–86.
[1] *The Basic Social Encyclicals* (New York, 1953), p. 19.
[2] *Vita Economica e Ordine Morale XXIX Settimana Sociale Dei Cattolici d'Italia,* Bergamo, September 23–30, 1956, p. 13.

property is a classic example of social demagoguery. . . . Ecclesiasts assert that the liquidation of private property will lead toward lethargy, toward society's stagnation; for development of the human personality, in their opinion, is conceivable only on the basis of private property. "Therefore," wrote Messineo, a Jesuit, "any action against capitalist private property is an action against man's freedom."[3]

Capitalism's clerical defenders seek to prove that an individual has no opportunity for demonstrating his initiative in a socialist system. It is well known, however, that, through suppression of exploiters, the socialist system has created all the conditions necessary for development of the initiative of millions of people—for an all-round development of their abilities. The experience of socialist countries irrefutably demonstrates the fact that only social ownership of the means of production secures a harmonious development of the personality. The liquidation of capitalist private property creates real opportunities for the transformation of every worker into a creative person.

. . . Clerical defenders of capitalist private property have become increasingly aware of the fact that they cannot limit themselves merely to a sanctification of private property. It became fashionable among the ecclesiasts to speak about a "positive solution" to the problem of private property. This solution is nothing but propaganda for a "people's capitalism."

Clerics assume the leading role in propagandizing the theory of "people's capitalism." They claim to be the originators of this theory. In fact, the current view that is widely propagandized by "people's capitalism" theorists—that is, the theory of social partnership—appeared as early as 1891 in the encyclical *Rerum Novarum*. Thus, the Church's social doctrine provides the theoretical basis for the reactionary propaganda of "people's capitalism."

Clerical propagandists speak about the workers' participation in the management of enterprises and about their joint responsibility with capitalists for management. This erroneous theory seeks to justify the possibility of class cooperation between workers and entrepreneurs. In justifying the significance of the principle of joint responsibility for the capitalist economy, an Irish journal stated the following: "From the socioeconomic point of view, the advantage of joint responsibility lies in that it promotes industrial harmony, increases the employees' personal interest in the business, and lowers the number of industrial conflicts."[4]

The true meaning of all this talk about joint responsibility is an

---

[3] *Civilta Cattolica,* September 17, 1957, p. 348.
[4] *Studies,* Spring, 1956, p. 119.

attempt to tie the workers to the interests of entrepreneurs. The Church recommends for this purpose the utilization of "people's shares," which are regarded as the principal instrument of "people's capitalism." The apologists of capitalism's dissertations about the workers who possess a few shares as co-owners of enterprises is a vulgar demogoguery. First of all, the number of such workers is very small. An American publicist, C. Wright Mills, in his *The Power Elite*, reports that 98.6 per cent of the workers in the United States do not own any shares. Furthermore, even if a worker owns a few shares, he cannot exert any influence upon the management of the enterprise. Capitalists seek to exploit "people's shares" to weaken the workers' class self-consciousness.

While widely propagandizing the thesis about transformation of the workers into co-owners, clerical theorists at the same time emphasize that they are against an infringement of capitalists' interests. In advancing the slogan "property for all," clerics do not cease to defend capitalist property, which, as previously, they pronounce to be sacred and inviolable. Clerical apologists of capitalism propagandize an idea according to which the workers should invest a considerable portion of their wages in the acquisition of shares. Thus, at the expense of reducing the part of their wages which goes for consumption, the clerics propose that workers acquire shares and, by doing this, place a part of their wages at the disposal of the capitalists. Therefore, it is not an accident that clerics urge the workers to economize more and spend less.

Noel Breuning, a Jesuit and a principal commentator on papal social encyclicals in West Germany, asserts that a division of capitalist property would fail to bring about positive results. In his opinion, "From the moral, cultural, and political points of view, a belated enrichment of people with property acquired in such a manner would never have the same meaning as property has to a genuine proprietor. This would only prove the old truth that a granted property is no property."[5]

At the basis of the importune propaganda of "people's capitalism," conducted by clerical apologists of capitalism, lies a thesis on social reconciliation of the antagonistic classes. Ecclesiasts propagate intensively the theory of "social partnership," which asserts that under the existing conditions the struggle against capitalists is no longer necessary, because we have entered a period of cooperation between the proletariat and the bourgeoisie. Hence, the propaganda of the "social partnership" is tantamount to asserting a possibility of the existence of capitalism without a class struggle.

[5] Cited by Otto Reinhold, *Ein Dritter Weg* (Berlin, 1959), pp. 45–46.

The West German and Austrian bishops have demonstrated a special zeal in propagandizing "social partnership." An Austrian bishop stated the following in his pastoral message: "What we are concerned with nowadays is a responsible collaboration of social partners. The system of partnership corresponds to the nature of man and entrepreneur."[6] But how can one speak about a partnership when the capitalist is the owner of the means of production and the workers possess only labor power that they must sell to capitalists in order to secure the means of subsistence?

The capitalist can at any time fire the worker whom the ecclesiasts depict as a social partner of the capitalist. Such phrases as "people's capitalism," "social partnership," etc., cannot change the exploitive nature of capitalism. Clerical preachers of "people's capitalism" seek to replace the class struggle with class peace while preserving exploitation, which is an impossible task.

What currently disturbs the Church hierarchy is the intensification of the class struggle in capitalist countries. This is why clerical ideologists are making utmost efforts to demonstrate that the Marxist-Leninist theory of classes and class struggle is obsolete. Catholic theorists also seek to make a contribution toward the "refutation" of Marxism and its theory of the class struggle in particular.

They assert that, while it is true that the class struggle existed in the past, there are no reasons for such a struggle in the modern capitalist world. With what evidence do they support this thesis? First of all, they contend that the working class is no longer an exploited class, that crucial changes have taken place in its position. For example, the Catholic Archbishop of Los Angeles, McIntyre, declared: "It is painful even to recall the injustices perpetrated in the early industrial era. Fortunately, we hope, this will never happen again."[7] This declaration seeks to induce the believers into believing that the time of social conflict has passed and that an epoch of social harmony has come into being.

West German clerics maintain that the workers have no need to fight against capitalists because . . . the earlier existing antagonism between labor and capital has lost its significance to a considerable degree.[8] Adenauer in one of his speeches contended . . . that "socialism today is obsolete because in the Federal Republic the workers are no longer exploited."[9]

. . . It should be noted that the ecclesiasts merely repeat the elements of bourgeois propaganda. For example, they entertain the

[6] *Weg und Ziel,* No. 2 (1957), p. 141.
[7] *Vital Speeches of the Day,* Vol. 22, No. 6 (1956), p. 166.
[8] *Die Welt,* May 15, 1957.        [9] *Novoe Vremya,* No. 46 (1958), p. 21.

view that a process of de-proletarianization of the proletariat is taking place in the capitalist world. Abbot Zaniewski, in his dissertation *The Origin of the Roman and Modern Proletariat,* asserts that, in spite of Marxist prognostications, the misery of the masses did not increase with the development of industry, but, on the contrary, the masses have gained the opportunity to raise their standard of living. Furthermore, he contends that in the capitalist world a "social transformation" is taking place that raises the worker to the level of the former bourgeois. Such a transformation, in his opinion, is presumably particularly noticeable in the United States, where the de-proletarianization of the proletariat is almost an accomplished fact.[10] By means of such assertions, the reverend-economist seeks to "refute" the universal law of capitalist accumulation discovered by Marx.

An obvious refutation of the "theory" of de-proletarianization of the proletariat in the United States is the 117-day strike of half a million steel workers in 1959. Only under government pressure, which applied the reactionary Taft-Hartley Act, did the strike come to an end. Abbot Zaniewski . . . ignores the fact that in the capitalist countries, including the United States, there are millions of unemployed. In the country in which the proletariat presumably disappeared, the average annual family income in 1956 was $4,237. According to United States official statistics, in 1956 the income of 34.5 per cent of American families was below $3,000, that is, below the living minimum, which, according to the United States Department of Labor, is $4,400 for a family of four. To this should be added the fact that the average income of Negro families in 1956 amounted to only $2,289.[11]

. . . A Catholic professor, Vito, in his paper on "Classes and Social Stratification,"[12] maintains that capitalist society knows of no division into antagonistic classes; that it represents a joint, complex, and rich social structure. Catholic ideologists seek to convince the believers that Italy is a country of social mobility, that is, a society in which each man can move from one social group into another, from the bottom to the top of the social ladder. And this is being said about Italy, a country that has approximately two million unemployed and in which the living standard is one of the lowest in Europe!

. . . In fact, not even one capitalist country succeeded in relaxing

[10] Romuald Zaniewski, *L'origine du proletariat romain et contemporain: Faits et theories* (n.p., 1957), p. 327.

[11] See Herbert Aptheker's article "O Klassovom Soznanii v Amerikanskom Obshchestve" [On Class Consciousness in American Society], *Novoe Vremya,* Nos. 44 and 47 (1959), p. 19.

[12] *L'osservatore Romano,* September 22–23, 1958.

the class struggle, despite the active assistance of clerics and right-socialists. The facts show that the capitalist world is an arena of a constantly intensifying class struggle. According to official statistics furnished by the International Labor Organization, the number of working days lost as a result of strikes was 49.0 million in 1954, 58.1 million in 1955, 73.5 million in 1958. According to preliminary statistics, in the United States in 1958 there were approximately 3,400 strikes in which 2,200,000 workers participated. This resulted in the loss of approximately 23.5 million working days.[13]

. . . In view of these facts, the assertions of an Austrian Catholic professor, Messner, that strikes are survivals of the nineteenth century are absurd.[14] This is precisely why the ecclesiasts have intensified the propaganda on behalf of class peace and class collaboration. It is by no means an accident that Pope John XXIII devotes a great deal of attention to this question. For example, in April, 1959, he was persuading Catholic workers not to be guided by the theory of the class struggle, because an ideology that advocates enmity and spreads hatred between classes is an erroneous one. He supported this view by asserting that all employees in industry are fulfilling socially useful functions and, consequently, they should be inspired by the spirit of charity and cooperation instead of by the spirit of class struggle. He expounded the same views on May 1, 1959, by asserting that . . . social problems should be resolved not through social conflicts but on the basis of the principles of the Gospel.[15]

. . . What should be done to improve the position of the workers? Judging by the encyclical issued by John XXIII, capitalists should not only evaluate the worker from an economic point of view—they should not limit themselves to the recognition of the worker's right to just wages—but they should also respect his dignity and treat him as a brother.[16]

Thus, a view is thrust on the believers that it is not capitalism in itself that is the cause of their tribulations but that subjective defects of individual capitalists are the cause, and that this cause could be removed easily if capitalists were guided by the Catholic social doctrine. Capitalists are extremely interested in spreading such illusions among the workers. But increasingly wider strata of workers are beginning to realize that it is impossible to liquidate exploitation through prayers and appeals to capitalists; they are beginning to

[13] *International Politico-Economic Yearbook,* 1959, p. 44.
[14] *Wort und Wahrheit,* No. 10 (1959), p. 590.
[15] *Pilot,* April 13, 1959; *L'osservatore Romano,* May 2, 1959.
[16] *Civilta Cattolica,* July 18, 1959, p. 122.

realize that exploitation can be liquidated through the liquidation of capitalist ownership of the means of production, which is defended so intensely by capitalism's ecclesiastical apologists.

What is characteristic of the clerical apology of capitalism is an attempt to reduce social problems to moral problems. Clerics justify their right to participate actively, or even decisively, in the solution of social problems by asserting that these problems are primarily moral problems. Of course, economics and morality are mutually connected, but they are not identical. Clerical ideologists identify economics with morality because this gives them the opportunity . . . to interfere in the economic and political life of society with the aim of supporting the exploiting classes. In view of these attempts, the exhortations of the imperialist bourgeoisie's ideologists toward a moral self-perfection of various strata in capitalist society become fully understandable.

"The capitalist system is not inherently bad," writes A. Desqueyrat, "because collective bargaining, which draws entrepreneurs and employees closer, is not unlawful or, rather, is in itself not contrary to morality. Hired labor is an ancient tradition of man, a tradition that involves nothing amoral."[17]

Thus, the system of exploitation existing in capitalist society is justified by references to religious morality. At the same time, in the judgment of modern clerics, any action against capitalism is deeply amoral. The problem of the relationship between labor and capital is viewed by clerics as an ethical problem. Therefore, it is not surprising that they appraise class conflicts as deviations from the norms of Christian ethics.

The ideologists of capitalism maintain that . . . each man should be conscious of his personal and social responsibilities. But what is the workers' social responsibility? This question was answered in part by Cardinal Tisseran. In his pastoral letter in 1957, he spoke about the violation of God's commandment "thou shalt not steal" by the workers who do not work diligently enough to justify their wages. This ecclesiastic hierarch reminded the believers that employees who do not work conscientiously and waste working time are violating God's commandments.[18] Indeed, the ruling classes are anxiously waiting for the workers to be pervaded by this "feeling of responsibility."

Clerical identification of economic and moral problems is one of the forms of apology for the capitalist system. Clerical theorists seek

---

[17] *Bilan spirituel de capitalisme* (Paris, 1955), p. 25.
[18] *L'osservatore Romano*, June 28, 1958.

to persuade the workers that the cause of all evils inherent in a bourgeois society is not the capitalist mode of production but the workers' deviation from God and religion. They argue that the cause of social conflicts is not the antagonism between the class interests of the workers and capitalists but the departure from God of both classes, their violation of moral norms prescribed by Christianity. At the same time, Christian morality has never condemned capitalist exploitation. The enrichment of monopolists at the expense of the workers was never condemned by the Church—was never regarded as contradictory to Christian morality.

The aim of the moralization of social problems is to divert the workers from the struggle to change the relations of production, to liquidate the capitalist system. In stressing that social problems are in their very nature moral problems, clerical defenders of capitalism seek to persuade the workers that all economic problems can be resolved, not through a revolutionary struggle, but through moral self-perfection.

From the viewpoint of capitalism's clerical apologists, the antagonisms between labor and capital can be resolved within the framework of the capitalist system. All that is needed is that the capitalists should renounce immoral exploitation of the workers, and the workers, in their turn, should renounce the "immoral" class struggle in order to resolve all antagonisms in the spirit of Christian love toward one's neighbor. Such appeals to morality aim at confusing the workers, that is, at persuading them that exploitation can be liquidated by means of prayers and admonishment of capitalists. . . .

# Modern Capitalism and Economic Crisis*

## ๛ *Collective Authorship*

Bourgeois propagandists, reformists, and revisionists depict state-monopoly capitalism as a new social system that is basically different from the old capitalism. For this purpose, they deliberately equate this form of monopoly domination with those state-capitalist measures that the working people by their class struggle have succeeded in wringing from the capitalist class. They also claim that the capitalist state is now able to control economic development and to rid it of crises and that the present-day bourgeois state stands above classes. The old exploiting capitalism, according to them, has now given way to a "universal welfare state," and predatory imperialism has become "people's capitalism."

The theories of the British bourgeois economist John Maynard Keynes, which he developed as far back as the thirties, provide the "theoretical basis" for such views. In contrast to other bourgeois economists, he recognized that capitalism was seriously ailing and had lost the capacity for economic self-regulation. Keynes, however, would not, and could not, agree that the illness was incurable. Moreover, he took upon himself the role of "healer" of capitalism, advancing a whole series of measures for its "rehabilitation" by means of government controls and the development of state-monopoly capitalism. Keynes and his followers attach particular importance to special measures for maintaining capital investment in production at a proper level, government control of credit (regulating the rate of interest), and money circulation ("controlled" depreciation of money in order to decrease the real wages of workers). Keynes's teaching is, in essence, an apology of capitalism, for it is based on the illusory assumption that it is possible to perpetuate the capitalist system by eliminating a number of its shortcomings and some of its disastrous effects on the working people.

At present, not only most bourgeois economists, but considerable numbers of right-wing Social Democrats, base themselves on Keynes's theories. Many right-wing Socialist parties in their programs have

* From *Osnovy Marksizma-Leninizma* [The Foundations of Marxism-Leninism] (Moscow, 1960), pp. 288–97.

officially renounced Marx's economic theory in favor of that of Keynes. A very open call for the replacement of Marxism by Keynesianism was sounded by the British Labour leader John Strachey in his book entitled *Contemporary Capitalism*. He asserted that Keynes, although an open defender of capitalism and an enemy of socialism, proposed, without himself being aware of it, methods for achieving a *gradual* evolution from state-monopoly capitalism . . . to socialism. Keynes called upon the state to encourage the investment of capital in production in every way possible and to establish a control over those possessing money that would make them spend it instead of hoarding it and thus maintain effective demand at a high level. Strachey asserts that this compels the bourgeois state to equalize incomes by increasing taxes on profits. According to him, the British state, adopting Keynes's advice, is in fact already carrying through a redistribution of the national income and is "planning" the economy, with the aim of maintaining a high level of effective demand and "full employment."

Strachey considers that the nationalization of several industries and the establishment of a national system of social insurance and health service by the Labour government, has already made Britain socialist. However, he admits that "oligopoly," i.e., cliques of big monopolists, dominates the economy of Britain. Not in the least embarrassed by this, he assures us that Britain has "passed over the class conflict," that relations between workers and employers have entered a "peaceful phase," etc.

Certain French Socialists, e.g., Georges Bourgin, the historian, and Pierre Rimbert, the economist, also seek to depict the growth of state-monopoly capitalism as the gradual transformation of capitalist society into a socialist one.

What are the fallacies in such views of present-day capitalism? First, the right-wing Social Democrats lump together state-*monopoly* capitalism and all other forms of state capitalism without making any distinction between them. They then substitute one term for the other, concealing the *monopoly* nature of present-day capitalism and depicting it as a form of state capitalism in which there is no place for capitalist monopolies. In other words, they embellish present-day capitalism by completely effacing its essential features—the yoke of predatory monopolies, militarism, parasitism, crises, and unemployment. In reality, however, precisely these constitute the *basic features* of present-day state-monopoly capitalism.

Second, the right-wing Social Democrats distort reality by claiming that the monopolies are subordinate to the state, which is supposed to stand "above classes." In actual fact, the state is controlled by the capitalist monopolies. Under state-monopoly capitalism, the decisive power in society is concentrated in the hands of the very big corporations, with the top few hundred richest families exercising a direct or indirect dictatorship.

Third, the right-wing Social Democrats attempt to slur over the class character of ordinary *state capitalism,* depicting state-capitalist measures as steps in building *socialism.* As long as power remains in the hands of the bourgeoisie the nationalization of individual enterprises and other state-capitalist measures do not eliminate the capitalist relations of exploitation, even in those countries where such measures at present have a progressive character, e.g., in India and Indonesia. Socialist production relations cannot arise in the midst of capitalism; only the material preconditions for socialism can be created there. To begin the building of socialism on the basis of these preconditions, however, is impossible as long as the state remains in the hands of the capitalists, i.e., as long as power is not transferred to the working people.

In scientific socialism, as well as in the minds of many generations of participants in the working-class movement, the idea of socialism has always been closely associated with social ownership. Present-day right-wing Social Democrats, however, are now also contesting this scientific view. For example, the declaration of the Socialist International states: "Socialist planning does not presuppose the establishment of social ownership over all the means of production. It is compatible with the existence of private ownership in the basic branches of the economy." Guided by this view, the British right-wing Labour Party leadership has declared itself against further nationalization measures. . . .

A careful examination of the programs of present-day right-wing Social Democrats cannot fail to disclose that their portrayal of "socialism" is in essence merely a copy of existing state-monopoly capitalism. Their vision of the future does not go further than this social "ideal," i.e., the ideal of the Morgans and Rockefellers.

Some *revisionists* in Yugoslavia have also followed in the footsteps of the right-wing Social Democrats in their embellishment of present-day capitalism. The draft program of the League of Communists of Yugoslavia declares that in capitalism today there appear more and more "new *elements in the economy* which are *socialist* in their objective tendency" and "exert *pressure* on the capitalist mode of production"; "the rights of private capital are being restricted" and more and more of its economic functions are being turned over to the state.

Thus, they say, "a process of development toward socialism" is taking place in the capitalist world.

This revisionist idea coincides, in essence, with the claims of right-wing Social Democrats that capitalism is growing over into socialism. However, it was, of course, more difficult for Edvard Kardelj to "convince" Communists in Yugoslavia of the likelihood of such a "miraculous transformation" than for Mr. Strachey to convince Labourites in Britain. When Kardelj called this capitalism "state capitalism," many Yugoslav Communists suggested that it be called by its real name—state-monopoly capitalism. Kardelj, however, in his speech before the Congress of the League of Communists of Yugoslavia, insisted on using the term "state capitalism," explaining that the term "state-monopoly capitalism" merely expresses the "origin of state capitalism." Thus, like a clever conjurer, he transformed reactionary state-*monopoly* capitalism into an embryonic form of the less offensive *state capitalism*. He then manipulated state capitalism as well as transformed it into *"socialist elements"* that finally purge present-day capitalism of its foulness. . . . This, indeed, is real "sleight of hand and no swindle!"

Such a justification of the revisionist program of the League of Communists of Yugoslavia was, of course, amusing, but not very convincing. In opposition to the reformist and revisionist program of state-monopoly capitalism "growing over" into socialism, the Marxist-Leninist parties advance a program of resolute struggle against the capitalist monopolies, against their domination, and for the overthrow of the dictatorship exercised by a handful of families comprising the monopolist aristocracy.

Marxist-Leninists strive to utilize in the interests of the working people all possible reforms under capitalism, including reforms of a state-capitalist nature. At the same time, they hold that the replacement of the capitalist by the socialist mode of production can take place only as a result of a socialist revolution.


IS CAPITALISM GETTING RID
OF ECONOMIC CRISES?

After the 1929–33 world economic crisis, and particularly after the Second World War, monopoly capital with government assistance established a whole system of anticrisis measures. These measures are a characteristic feature of the machinery of state-monopoly capitalism.

The major anticrisis measure consists of huge government orders for, and purchase of, armaments and strategic materials, which provide many big monopolies with a considerable and steady demand. Of great importance, too, is government control in the sphere of credit and banking, where previously the stormy development of crises generally began. In order to prevent panicky withdrawal of deposits, which led in the past to the failure of large banks, the imperialist states have in effect taken upon themselves the role of guarantor of these deposits. Moreover, government regulation of stock exchanges and issuance of securities has been introduced almost universally in one form or another. To prevent crises, the state also undertakes various measures to restrict or curtail production, e.g., by raising the interest on bank credits and granting premiums for reducing the area under cultivation. Simultaneously, the state seeks to influence the economic situation by regulating consumer credit (the sale of cars, television and radio sets, furniture, etc., on credit or hire purchase).

Supporters of state-monopoly capitalism widely advertise such measures, alleging that their adoption has succeeded (or almost succeeded) in curing capitalism of its crises and that they ensure the steady growth of production. The road is now said to be open to perpetual "prosperity" and deliverance from unemployment.

But how do matters really stand? By way of example, let us take the United States, where the big capitalist monopolies have achieved the greatest freedom of action, the strongest influence over the state, and where the ravages of war have least affected economic development.

Despite the highly favorable postwar conditions for the United States in domestic and foreign markets, anticrisis measures have not had the desired effect. Instead of a steady growth of U.S. industrial production, three slumps in production occurred in the single decade 1948–58. The first took place in 1948–49, when the drop in production, according to official data, amounted to 10.5 per cent. The second developed four years later (1953–54), the decrease amounting to 10.2 per cent. And the third occurred three years later (1957–58), with production falling 13.7 per cent.

The crisis character of these production slumps is indicated by the fact that mass unemployment in the United States not only has not disappeared but has actually increased. With each succeeding production slump, the number of those registered as fully unemployed grew sharply. Thus, in 1949 unemployment rose by 1.3 million over the 1948 level; from 1953 to 1954 it rose by 1.6 million; and in mid-1958, unemployment was 2.4 million higher than the 1957 average. At the beginning of 1959 about 5 million fully unemployed

were officially registered. Moreover, it should be kept in mind that
official production figures include armaments and strategic materials,
for which government orders during crises increase rather than decrease. If war production is excluded, the curtailment of civilian
production will undoubtedly prove to be much greater than that
which appears from an examination of available U. S. statistics.

These are indisputable facts regarding the recent period. It would
be incorrect, however, to conclude that state-monopoly capitalism
can in no way influence the nature and form of economic crises by
means of anticrisis measures. As a matter of fact, they can achieve
some success in this respect.

State-monopoly capitalism can undoubtedly influence the form,
sequence, and nature of a particular crisis. The big monopolies are
in a position to utilize the enormous financial power of the state as a
shock absorber, which in many instances weakens the spontaneous
explosive force of a crisis at its outbreak. Moreover, there are now
more possibilities than before for big capitalists to avert bankruptcy
by stabilizing their position at the cost of the bankruptcy of medium and small capitalists. Furthermore, in time of crisis the big
corporations can often prevent spontaneous decreases in commodity
prices from taking place and, at times, can even raise certain prices.
They can also take advantage of huge war orders from the state, so as
to ensure themselves high profits even during periods of economic
crisis.

This, however, reveals only one aspect of the matter. The other
aspect is that the anticrisis measures used for the enrichment of
monopolies inevitably sap the economic strength of a country and
worsen the material conditions of the overwhelming majority of the
population. Insofar as the bourgeois state, by increasing taxation
and depreciating the currency, plunders the people in order to finance
a frantic arms race, effective demand inevitably decreases. Thus, the
stage is set for new acute outbreaks of the incurable ailment of capitalism—economic crises. The more the monopolies succeed in preventing price decreases—previously an accompaniment of crises—
the greater become the obstacles to the disposal of commodity sur-
pluses. In the final analysis, this makes it more difficult to emerge
from the crisis and to create the conditions for a new economic upsurge. Furthermore, to the extent that the capitalist state succeeds,
through its intervention, in saving the big corporations from bankruptcy and in absorbing other shocks produced by the crisis, it interferes with the redistribution of capital among the various branches
of production by means of which the necessary proportions between

them are established. Thus, state-monopoly capitalism, although exerting a certain influence on the course of a crisis, does not eliminate its causes but, on the contrary, only makes the illness more deep-seated, thereby creating the basis for new crises.

To conceal the crisis nature of the frequent postwar production slumps in the United States, bourgeois economists euphemistically refer to them as "recessions." Changing the label, however, does not change the contents. The crisis nature of such production slumps stems from the nature of their causes, which are basically the same as those of all other capitalist crises of overproduction. In other words, the anarchy of production prevailing under capitalism and the capitalists' incessant pursuit of maximum profits periodically bring about a sharp discrepancy between the growth of production and the lag in effective demand. The expansion of markets cannot keep pace with the rise in production. It is precisely the objective function of economic crises to temporarily overcome this discrepancy.

Changes seen in the character of recent crises, particularly in the United States, do not, of course, provide sufficient basis for the claim that all economic crises under state-monopoly capitalism will henceforth have these features. The future will undoubtedly reveal diverse forms of economic crises in capitalist countries, and, in particular, in due course much more violent economic shocks may occur in the countries of state-monopoly capitalism. One thing is quite clear: as long as the contradiction exists between the social character of production and the capitalist (private) form of appropriation, i.e., as long as capitalism exists, economic crises will inevitably recur. Anticrisis measures and all attempts at economic regulation by present-day state-monopoly capitalism do not stabilize capitalist economy but, on the contrary, increase its instability.

"The continuous alternation of crisis slumps and feverish uptrends," said Comrade N. S. Khrushchev at the Twenty-first Congress of the C.P.S.U., "demonstrates the instability of the capitalist economy. Neither the arms race nor any other measure can ever rid the economy of the United States and the other capitalist countries of overproduction crises. Whatever the capitalist states do, they will never be able to eliminate the cause of crises. Capitalism is too weak to break the death grip of its own contradictions; they keep growing in size and scope, threatening new economic upheavals."

Despite the facts, bourgeois theorists and revisionists seek to show that it is nonetheless possible to eliminate crises and preserve capitalism. As evidence, they frequently point to the favorable postwar economic situation in the major European capitalist countries.

Up to 1957–58, it is true, there were no clear indications of production crises in these countries (disregarding crises in some industries—coal, textile, etc.). However, only those who wish to deceive themselves or others can, on this basis, proclaim the advent of an era of "crisis-free capitalism."

The favorable economic situation in Western Europe, even more so than in the United States, resulted from certain transient, historically determined causes bound up with the aftermath of war. These countries suffered considerable destruction and devastation during the war. This applies especially to Germany, Italy, and France and also to Japan (the sole Asian country of monopoly capitalism). Obviously, there could be no overproduction in these countries as long as the destruction due to war had not been made good. This took, however, more than just a year or two.

No sooner was this achieved in the main than serious signs of crisis began to appear. Thus, beginning with 1958, production was cut down in Britain, Belgium, Holland, Norway, and Japan; while in West Germany, France, and Italy only small increases in industrial production were recorded. In 1958 the volume of industrial production and foreign trade of the capitalist world declined for the first time since the end of the war.

Thus, history has once again discredited the pseudotheorists who specialize in whitewashing capitalism. Confronted by undeniable facts, they seek to excuse themselves by pointing out that Marxists, too, have erred in regard to crises, that the entire postwar course of the cycle and of crises did not resemble the pattern previously described by Marxists. As a matter of fact, Marxists have never contended that one cycle must parallel another, and that the established periodicity and features of crises are not subject to change. In 1908, for example, in answering the revisionists who challenged Marx's theory of crises, Lenin wrote in *Marxism and Revisionism:* "Facts very soon made it clear to the revisionists that crises were not a thing of the past: prosperity was followed by a crisis. The forms, the sequence, the picture of the particular crisis changed, but crisis remained an inevitable component of the capitalist system."

Communists, of course, do not gloat over the fact that capitalism has not succeeded in eliminating crises. Despite the assertions of bourgeois propagandists and reformists, the communist movement does not pin its hopes for the victory of the socialist revolution on the outbreak of economic crises. A destructive economic crisis, to be sure, increases the wrath of the working people against capitalism.

But as history has shown, it simultaneously promotes reaction and fascism and increases the danger of war.

Moreover, Communists cannot welcome economic crises, for they are fully aware of the great misfortunes involved for the broad masses of the working people. And that is why Communists have always exposed the unfounded illusions of the crisis-free development of capitalism. For only after the working people—onto whose shoulders the monopolies seek to shift the entire burden of crises—succeed in freeing themselves from these illusions will they be able to fight properly for their vital interests.

The best way to abolish crises is to replace capitalism with socialism. It would be a most serious mistake, however, to consider that under capitalist conditions all struggle against the onerous consequences of crises is futile. Communists believe that such a struggle is indispensable and can yield important results for the masses of people.

The communist parties, therefore, organize the working people to fight for such government measures that would in any way alleviate the conditions of the masses. These measures include higher wages, the extension of mutually advantageous trade relations with the socialist countries, which have eliminated crises forever, the organization of large-scale public works, the construction of housing, schools, and hospitals, improved unemployment insurance, lower taxes, and controlled rents.

# Repudiation of the Revisionist View on Dictatorship, Democracy, Communism, and the State*

### ༒ V. V. Platkovskii

In developing and implementing Marx's and Engels' views on the state, Lenin stated quite clearly that historical development inevitably leads to the fall of capitalism and to a transition to communism. With equal clarity Lenin answered the question on the destiny of the state. First, in a capitalist society the state exists in the proper meaning of the term, for it is indispensable to the bourgeoisie. Second, in the transition from capitalism to communism the state is preserved, for it is indispensable to the proletariat; however, it is a special transitional type of state, or a "non-state in the proper meaning of the term." Third, in a communist society the state is unnecessary and will wither away.

The replacement of a bourgeois state by a proletarian state can be accomplished only through a socialist revolution. Only the new state that comes into being after the revolution is *capable* of withering away and is constructed so that it *can* wither away. As stated by Lenin, "Dialectic is both concrete and revolutionary; it draws a distinction between the 'transition' from the dictatorship of one class to the dictatorship of another class and the 'transition' from the democratic proletarian state to non-state ('withering away of the state')."[1]

Anarchists attempted to interpret the Marxist view on the inevitability of the demolition of the bourgeois state as a demand for an immediate "abolition" of the state, including the state of the proletarian dictatorship, and as an immediate renunciation of any statehood. In unmasking anarchists, Lenin demonstrated that the proletarian revolution does not aim at destroying the state immediately. Moreover, not even all aspects of the bourgeois state are subject to destruction; only the military-bureaucratic apparatus, created by the bourgeoisie, must be destroyed, must be crushed. Lenin referred to Marx's views, stating that "workers replace the dictatorship of the bourgeoisie with their own revolutionary dictatorship . . . ; they

* *From* "Leninskoe Uchenie o Sotsialisticheskom Gosudarstve i Sovremennost" [Lenin's Theory of the Socialist State and Modern Times], *Voprosy Filosofii*, No. 4 (1960), pp. 15–29.
[1] *Sochineniya* [Works] (4th ed., Moscow), Vol. 28 (1950), p. 30.

give to the state a revolutionary and transitional form, instead of laying the weapons aside and abolishing the state."[2]

Class-conscious workers flatly reject these anarchist views; they know that after the overthrow of the bourgeoisie and the destruction of the bourgeois state the revolutionary proletariat cannot at once renounce the state. The primary reason for this is that there is no other organization able to replace the state at once; no other sociopolitical organization of the workers commands the universality of the state organization to carry out state functions. Without a universal organization possessing the authority to govern, society would fall inevitably into a state of anarchy which would lead to the restoration of the power of the overthrown exploiters.

The historical necessity of the proletarian state lies in the fact that the conquest of authority by the working class is merely the beginning of the socialist revolution, not its culmination. The proletariat needs the state organization for the purpose of ending the revolution —for the creation of a classless society. Nevertheless, almost forty years after the necessity of creating the socialist state was quite clearly demonstrated, modern revisionists once again raise the question of whether the proletariat needs its own state. They accuse Leninist Communists of "idolatry" and "superstitious faith in the state." They contend that the proletariat needs a dictatorship instead of a state, that the dictatorship of the proletariat should not be converted into a state, that dictatorship in general is a political and not a state order, and that the dictatorship should not manifest itself in the state power but "in an unconditional directing role of the proletariat." Paradoxically, revisionists justify all this absurd gibberish by references to Lenin!

These wise theorists fail to notice their delicate position. First, the political organization in the case under discussion is a state organization. Second, the "unconditional directing role of the proletariat" would be meaningless if leadership in the form of a state is excluded. During all phases of the revolution the proletariat uses different forms to carry out its leading role (hegemony) vis-à-vis the peasants and other strata of workers. The state leadership—that is, the dictatorship of the proletariat—is a higher form of the manifestation of the directing role of the proletariat in society. Third, and most significant: what are the revisionist goals in demanding the renunciation of the state organization of the proletarian dictatorship? Is the dictatorship of the proletariat, that is, the state authority of the proletariat,

[2] Karl Marx and Friedrich Engels, *Sochineniya* [Works] (1st ed.; Moscow, 1933), XV, 88–91.

conceivable without adopting the form of a state? It is well known that in 1918, German opportunists advanced the slogan of "independence for the working class from the state." It is equally well known that in 1918, in his pamphlet *The Dictatorship of the Proletariat* Kautsky contended that a class can merely "rule but not govern" and that, therefore, Russian soviets should not be turned into state organizations. In essence, modern revisionists advance the same idea.

Lenin took a stand against Kautsky, pointing out that his views have nothing in common with Marxism and socialism and that he takes the side of the bourgeoisie, "which is ready to allow anything with the exception of converting the organizations of the class it oppresses into a state organization."[3] Lenin demonstrated that opposition to the organization of the working class into a state signifies either the renunciation of state authority in general or the recognition of the possibility of the working class utilizing the old state machine.

Nowhere have the founders of Marxism-Leninism admitted the possibility that the dictatorship of the proletariat could exist in an amorphous, diffused, disorganized form. They have always stressed that the dictatorship of the proletariat is a form of the state. Thus, in *The Communist Manifesto,* Marx and Engels defined the dictatorship of the proletariat as a state, that is, the proletariat organized into a ruling class. In the *Critique of the Gotha Program* Marx stated: "Between the capitalist and the communist society lies the period of the revolutionary transformation of the former into the latter. To this also corresponds a political transition period in which the state can be nothing but the *revolutionary dictatorship of the proletariat.*" This proves that Marx designated the dictatorship of the proletariat as a state without any qualifications.

The same idea of the dictatorship of the proletariat as a state organization was systematically elaborated by Lenin. He consistently emphasized that the dictatorship should be a specific organized power, namely, a state power, and that the slogan of the dictatorship of the proletariat should not be profaned with a jelly-like concept of authority. Lenin indicated repeatedly that the dictatorship of the proletariat is a form of the state. He wrote: "The proletarian state, the dictatorship of the proletariat, is not a 'form of government' but a *state of a different type. . . .*"[4] The dictatorship of the proletariat "is a new type of state organization."[5] Hence, contrary to revisionist claims, it follows from Lenin's observations that the concept of a socialist state and the dictatorship of the proletariat should not be op-

[3] *Sochineniya,* Vol. 28, p. 239.        [4] *Ibid.,* p. 88.
[5] *Ibid.,* Vol. 29 (1950), p. 345.

posed. This is why Lenin always spoke of the Soviet state as a dictatorship of the proletariat.

Revisionists contend that the state organization can be replaced at once with diverse forms of non-state organizations, for example, labor unions. But it was indeed Lenin who opposed such ventures, designating such views as anarchosyndicalism. Speaking on this subject in April, 1917, Lenin stated . . . : "The Council of Workers' Deputies is not a professional organization as the bourgeoisie would like it to be. The people see differently and correctly; the people see in it an authority. . . . This is the type of state which can lead toward socialism."[6]

Historical development leads, in the final analysis, to a point where the state organization is replaced with social self-government. But this will not take place in the near future—only under full communism. The demand to replace the state with other forms of social organization and self-government is tantamount to renouncing the state, the dictatorship of the proletariat.

In their violent attacks on the socialist state, the revisionists advance an argument borrowed from the bourgeoisie. According to this argument, the state precludes democracy. They assert that, as long as the state exists, there can be no true democracy and that the state must be superseded by democracy. The revisionist theory of the immediate "dying away" of the state is based on this thesis. But such a view is absurd. Lenin demonstrated that "democracy is *also* a state and that, consequently, democracy will disappear after the disappearance of the state."[7] Lenin emphasized . . . that opportunists "constantly forget that the destruction of the state is at the same time the destruction of democracy, that the dying away of the state is the dying away of democracy."[8]

Democracy is a historical, transitional phenomenon. In the course of millenniums, starting with the embryo of democracy in antiquity, forms of democracy have been changing with the change of the ruling classes. In his work *Marxism on the State*,[9] Lenin stated the following: "The dialectic (course) of development is as follows: from absolutism to bourgeois democracy; from bourgeois democracy to proletarian democracy; from proletarian democracy to non-democracy." This concise statement indicates quite accurately and clearly the trend in the development of the forms of democracy, the principal periods of transition from bourgeois democracy to proletarian democracy, and from the latter to a social system under communism.

---

[6] *Ibid.,* Vol. 24 (1949), p. 119.    [7] *Ibid.,* Vol. 25 (1949), p. 369.
[8] *Ibid.,* p. 428.
[9] *Marksizm o Gosudarstve* (Moscow, 1958), p. 43.

Hence, democracy is merely a form of the state and consequently can neither set it aside nor replace it as is contended by revisionists. On the contrary, democracy will die away together with the state. Thus, we can speak of a thorough and increasingly greater development of the socialist democracy as merely the preparation of political conditions for the dying away of the state. In this sense, at the Twenty-first Congress of the Communist Party, Khrushchev asserted that the main goal in the development of a socialist state is the full-scale development of democracy, drawing the broadest strata of the population into the administration of domestic affairs and encouraging all citizens to participate in directing the economic and cultural construction.

The principal thesis, the *idée fixe,* of modern revisionists is an immediate dying away of the state, specifically, the socialist state. Whenever they speak of the state, they reduce all questions to its dying away and assert that the struggle for this end is the immediate, decisive, and principal task of socialist countries. This leads to weird results: in every possible way revisionists extol the modern bourgeois state as a supraclass state, as an instrument for the "transformation" of capitalism into socialism, as favoring the working class. Speaking logically, the bourgeois state should be strengthened, but at the same time they are horror-stricken at the thought of strengthening the socialist state and demand its dying away.

What are the arguments advanced by revisionists in favor of the immediate dying away of the state? Primarily they refer to Marx's and Lenin's pronouncements which state that the proletariat gives to the state a "transitional"—that is, temporary—form and that "the proletariat will only temporarily be in need of the state. . . ." The crux of the problem, however, is that revisionists fail to answer the question: "How long will the proletariat be in need of the state?" From the Marxist-Leninist view of the temporary, transitional character of the proletarian state, they hastily deduce that the state is merely "an elementary form of the struggle of the working class for socialism," that the state is necessary only in the first stage of a socialist revolution (and not in all countries at that, but only in the most backward), and that in any case the state should die not under communism but in the transition to socialism.

Revisionists must know that Marxism solved this question long ago. Thus, in his review of Bakunin's *State and Anarchy*[10] commenting on Bakunin's view that "dictatorship will be temporary and brief," Marx stated the following: "Non, mon cher (No, my dear)!

[10] *Gosudarstvennost i Anarkhiya* (n.p., 1873).

*The class rule* of the workers over the resisting elements of the old world shall last until the economic foundations necessary for the existence of classes have been destroyed." This statement indicates quite clearly that the dictatorship (state) of the proletariat is necessary not merely for a very brief time, and not only in the *initial stage* of the struggle for socialism, but for a *lengthy period*—for the entire transition period from a class society to a classless society, from capitalism to communism.

In full conformity with Marx, Lenin also indicated that the dictatorship of the proletariat will inevitably be protracted. According to Lenin, "The essence of Marx's theory of state is comprehensible only to one who realizes that the dictatorship of *one* class is indispensable not only for a class society in general, not only for the proletariat, which has overthrown the bourgeoisie, but for the entire *historical period* that separates capitalism from the 'classless society,' from communism."[11] Modern revisionists are neither able nor willing to comprehend this essence of Marxism. Pretending to be as innocent as lambs, they seek to create the impression that they are not opposed to the above-quoted Marxist-Leninist views. They assert that the dictatorship of the proletariat can be protracted, but the state—that is a different matter. But we have already discussed the premise held by the falsifiers of Marxism, who oppose the socialist state to the dictatorship of the proletariat.

To prove their views, revisionists refer to Lenin's *State and Revolution,* especially to the statement that the proletariat will need the state only temporarily, that ". . . the proletariat needs only a dying away state, that is, a state that is built in such a way that it will begin to die away at once, and could not fail to die away."[12] However, in the very same work, Lenin indicated that "the determination of the moment of future 'dying away' is completely out of the question, especially since it certainly will be a protracted process."[13] Furthermore, he indicated that "only communism will render the state completely useless" and that, "under conditions preceding the 'higher' phase of communism, socialism calls for the *strictest* control of work and consumption. . . ."[14] From this, it quite clearly follows that revisionists commit a shameless juggling and falsification of facts. Lenin stated that the state is temporarily necessary to the proletariat, but that it is impossible to determine the moment of its dying away because it will certainly be a protracted process. Revisionists interpret these statements as a call to the *immediate* dying away of the state.

[11] *Sochineniya,* Vol. 25, pp. 384–85.     [12] *Ibid.,* p. 374.
[13] *Ibid.,* p. 429.     [14] *Ibid.,* p. 441.

Revisionists, who pretend to be dialecticians and "creative" Marxists, fail to conceive the dying away of the state as a dialectical process; they approach it metaphysically as a mechanical act of abolishing the state. The dying away of the state is a gradual and protracted process, during which the state, as well as its functions and organizational forms, are changing gradually. These changes correspond to the specific stages of the socialist revolution and communist construction. According to Lenin, "After the 'transition stage' of *the revolution,* the 'transition stage' of the gradual dying away of the proletarian state will take place. . . ."[15]

. . . At any rate, it is indisputable that the socialist state is indispensable to the proletariat as long as it has not yet fulfilled its universal historical task of building communism. Lenin indicated that "the state authority, a centralized organization of power, is indispensable" to the working class.[16] This statement describes the role of the socialist state as the broadest all-embracing centralized organization of the workers' power. As a centralized organization of power, the socialist state serves as an instrument for the construction of socialism and communism.

Theoretical problems of scientific communism—among them the problem of the state—have acquired special significance under the conditions of the large-scale construction of communism within our society. What will be the role of the socialist state in the creation of a material-technical basis for communism, in the communist education of the workers, and in the communist construction in general? What changes will take place during the transition to communism in the basic functions of the socialist state? In which direction will the political forms of the organization of society, the organs of state administration, and the social organizations develop? What are the methods and practical steps leading toward the dying away of the state under communism? All these questions are of vital practical significance. The correct solution to these problems is indispensable if the program of communist construction developed by our party is to be successfully realized. Such a correct, scientific, Marxist-Leninist solution to all these problems was given in Khrushchev's speech delivered at the Twenty-first Congress of the C.P.S.U.

It must be noted, however, that in our publications one occasionally finds a somewhat simplified, limited interpretation of the problem of the development of the state in the transition to communism. It is stated simply as a problem of the state's dying away. But the Twenty-first Party Congress does not in any way reduce the problem of the state merely to the problem of its dying away. In both

[15] *Ibid.,* Vol. 28, p. 300.          [16] *Ibid.,* Vol 25, p. 376.

Khrushchev's speech and in the resolutions of the Congress the problem of the state is treated in a broad, all-inclusive way, as a problem that involves: the *development* of the socialist state in the new stage of communist construction; the *role* of the socialist state in the construction of communism; the development of the political organization of society, of the state system, and of the administration, which will culminate in the complete dying away of the state and in the transition to a communist social self-government.

Frequently the question is raised as to whether our state is or is not yet dying away. Khrushchev stresses that one should not conceive of the process of the dying away of the state in a simplified way, as the falling of leaves in autumn, when, as a result of shedding their foliage, only the naked branches remain. The process of dying away is a complex and protracted one. It does not depend upon the wishes of individual persons or organizations; it is determined by objective conditions—the course of the development of the socialist society and the nature of the socialist state. In answering a question on the dying away of the state submitted by an American correspondent, Khrushchev stated the following: "Strictly speaking, this process is taking place now. The functions of the state government, as well as some of the organs of coercion, are undergoing changes in the course of the development of the Soviet state."[17] Khrushchev always stresses that the process of dying away is a protracted and gradual one, and that it should be neither precipitated nor hindered.

It is well known that, in speaking of the dying away of the state, Engels used the term to "fall asleep," stressing the gradualness and protractedness of this process. This gradualness and protractedness of the process of the dying away of the state has also been indicated by Engels in his introduction to Marx's *Civil War in France,* where he states that only "generations born in new, free social conditions . . . will be capable of throwing away the rubbish of statehood." The founders of scientific communism in their examination of the dying away of the state as an objective, natural process have resolutely rejected subjective arbitrariness and haste. Hence the reason Lenin wrote: ". . . we can speak only of the dying away of the state, stressing the protractedness of this process, its dependence upon the speed of the development of the *higher phase* of communism, and leaving the question of the time and the concrete forms of the dying away entirely open, because the materials for answering these questions are unavailable."[18]

[17] *Za Prochnyi Mir i Mirnoe Sosushchestvovanie* [For a Durable Peace and Peaceful Coexistence] (Moscow, 1958), p. 246.
[18] *Sochineniya,* Vol. 25, p. 440.

The Marxist-Leninist view, which asserts that the socialist state has a specific nature and is essentially distinct from the exploiters' state, is crucial for the correct understanding of the process of the dying away of the state. A strict differentiation of the diametrically opposed socialist and bourgeois states is a fundamental prerequisite of Marxism-Leninism. Reformists and revisionists fail Marxism precisely on this fundamental and principal question. They select and stress only those elements of the socialist state which make it similar to other states and which justify calling it a state. At the same time they obliterate the nature of the socialist state, that is, the aspects and features that distinguish it from the exploiters' state and that make it a nonstate in the strict meaning of the term. This reformist and revisionist position is alien to Marxism-Leninism and hostile to the working class. It aims at confusing the masses of workers and at preventing them from knowing that they should treat the socialist state *in a way entirely different* from the treatment of a bourgeois state.

In terms of its class nature, its aims, its tasks, and its functions, the socialist state is a state of a specific type. This state was designated by Marx, Engels, and Lenin as "not quite a state," as "not a state in the full meaning of the term," as a "semistate," or as a form of transition from state to non-state, a form of a dying away state. At the same time the socialist state still preserves features common to all states, which makes it possible to speak of it as a state. The dialectic of development is the following: with the advancement of the socialist society toward communism, the features of our state (which characterize it as a state) will disappear, will die away, whereas the non-state features, the non-state aspects of the political organization of society, will become more fully developed. Furthermore, to understand correctly the process of dying away it is necessary to bear in mind that the socialist state is not stationary, that its tasks and functions are subject to constant and gradual changes in the course of constructing a communist society.

. . . . . . .

The development and change of the functions of the socialist state pursue a significant tendency—a continuous perfection of the state system and a strengthening of the state's role in the communist construction. This is an objective, natural tendency in the development of the socialist state, a tendency leading to its dying away. No form of life disappears before it has been entirely exhausted. The same is true of the state.

But the Marxist-Leninist thesis on the inevitability of the strengthening of the socialist state in every possible way throws revisionists into panic. They characterize this thesis as a "Stalinist revision" of Marxism and contend that, on the contrary, the path toward the state's dying away lies in its weakening. Why? Because they contend that the preservation and the greater strengthening of the socialist state inevitably leads toward its bureaucratization, toward its elevation above society, and toward the enslavement of society by the state. To escape this danger, one must, in their opinion, deliver oneself from the state, take measures for implementing its instant dying away.

. . . . . . .

The social meaning of the revisionist demands for an immediate dying away is quite clear: It is a petty-bourgeois prejudice inherited from the past. During the course of many centuries the oppressed people have seen in the state an alien and—to them—a hostile power; they were imbued with hatred toward it. This was legitimate and just because the state was oppressive and hostile to the workers. But after this state was destroyed, and after the workers and peasants themselves had created their own state, the old hatred toward the state remained in the form of prejudice on the part of a petty bourgeois who became accustomed to seeing merely evil in the state and who was incapable of comprehending the difference between the new, socialist state and the old, exploiters' state.

Having relinquished the Marxist class positions in evaluating the state, and having confused the socialist state with the bourgeois one, revisionists are fiercely opposed to the strengthening of the socialist state and are in favor of its immediate dying away. They advance their views as Marxism. This, however, is not Marxism; this is anarchism, expressing the petty-bourgeois nature of the revisionists, their inability to discipline and organize themselves, and their unwillingness to take into account the objective laws of the socialist revolution and of the construction of communism. Marxism-Leninism sees in the strengthening—instead of the weakening—of the state the only correct path for preparing the conditions for the dying away of the state, the objective natural necessity for the transition from state to non-state.

There is another problem that is constantly by-passed by our ideological opponents who disguise themselves as Marxists; this problem concerns the prerequisites and conditions necessary for the dying away of the state. Lenin called for the consolidation of both domestic and international prerequisites for the state's dying away. In his brilliant *State and Revolution* he devoted a special chapter to an analysis of the economic conditions necessary for the state's dying away. Lenin regarded the economic prerequisites to be the principal, decisive ones, without which it would be inconceivable to speak of the dying away of the state.

Under socialism the forces of production are not yet adequately developed, and society is forced to distribute products in conformity with the principles "he who does not work does not eat" and "for an equal quantity of work an equal quantity of products." Yet these principles do not eliminate the factual inequality in distributing products, for men's abilities are not equal: one is stronger, another is weaker; one has a large family to support, another has none. Hence, material inequality still remains, but the exploitation of man by man becomes impossible. So long as society is forced to apply the principle "from each according to his abilities, to each according to his work" the state remains inevitably as the means of securing the equality of work, the equality of the distribution of products, and for the purpose of protecting social property, i.e., the means of production.

The economic basis for the state's dying away is the development of the production forces to the degree that will create an abundance of material goods and will permit the application of the communist principle "from each according to his abilities, to each according to his needs." Such conditions are attainable because of modern scientific and technological achievements, the all-round development of the people, the transformation of work into the first vital need of man, and the bringing about of a higher labor productivity by comparison with capitalism. As stated by Lenin, "The state will be able to die away completely when society has realized the rule: from each according to his ability, to each according to his needs, i.e., when people have become accustomed to observing the fundamental rules of social life, and their labor is so productive that they voluntarily work *according to* their ability."[19]

The development of the economic basis of communism leads to profound social changes: overcoming the existing difference between intellectual and physical work, the difference between a village and a city, and a gradual disappearance of class distinctions between members of society. The liquidation of these distinctions which are the source of social inequality, will create social prerequisites for the dying away of the state.

Some political prerequisites are also necessary for the dying away of the state, namely, the complete development of democracy. Lenin has indicated that the development of socialist democratism is a

[19] *Ibid.*

*condition* that permits the state to die away.[20] When people have gradually become accustomed to observing the rules of social life, when they have become accustomed to observing these rules voluntarily, without any compulsion, only then will the state (that is the special apparatus of compulsion) be unnecessary. According to Lenin, "Only Soviet, or proletarian, democracy" leads to the destruction of the state, "for, by drawing the mass organizations of the workers toward constant and indispensable participation in the administration of the state, it immediately begins to prepare the dying away of the state."[21]

Lenin's notes on Bukharin's *Economy in the Transition Period* are of special significance for a correct understanding of the process of the state's dying away. As is well known, Bukharin has asserted that "the growth curve of the proletarian state begins to fall down abruptly. First the army and the navy—which are the most coercive instruments—will die away, then the system of punitive and repressive organs, and finally the compulsory character of work, etc." In the margins of this book Lenin has written the following: "Is it not vice versa? First 'finally,' second 'then,' and finally 'first.' " What is the meaning of this observation?

Revisionists interpret it in their own way and conclude that the "growth curve" of the state should begin to fall down with the abolition of the state's economic functions. Revisionist theorists support this view with references to Lenin. They do this in order to "condemn" Soviet Communists who presumably disregard Lenin's view and are preoccupied with a "bureaucratic revision" of Marxism. But this is either a misunderstanding or a deliberate falsification. Whatever the case may be, we are confronted with the usual revisionist method, which aims to distort, juggle, and falsify the views of the Marxist-Leninist classics to which they refer.

In fact, the gist of Lenin's observations is entirely different. He stresses the creation of *economic prerequisites* as a crucial condition for the state's dying away. Lenin indicates that the dying away of the state begins not with the abolition of the organs of compulsion but, on the contrary, with the transformation of work into a habit, into voluntary work, without compulsion. But this requires the creation of the proper economic conditions. Lenin has emphasized that "Without falling into utopianism, we cannot imagine that, having overthrown capitalism, people will at once learn to work for society *without any legal norms;* indeed, the abolition of capitalism *does not immediately lay* the economic prerequisites for *such* a change."[22]

---

[20] *Ibid.,* Vol. 27 (1950), p. 242.     [21] *Ibid.,* Vol. 28, p. 444.
[22] *Ibid.,* Vol. 25, p. 439.

What are these economic prerequisites? Revisionists think that the constant diminishing of the state's interference in the economic life of society is the economic prerequisite for the dying away of the state. But this is like beginning at the end. By economic prerequisites Lenin meant something entirely different, namely, the attainment of a level in the production of material goods that would make the regulation of labor and the distribution of products unnecessary. When work is transformed into the first necessity of life, when society becomes able to distribute products according to the rational needs of each man, only then will the inevitability of controlling labor and consumption fall off, and only then will there be no need for a special apparatus of control, for the state. To be sure, not the weakening, not the dying away, of the state's economic functions, but their strengthening and intensification are necessary for the preparation of such economic prerequisites.

. . . A full dying away of the state is possible only under full-scale communism and only if there is no danger of a military invasion from outside. . . . Communism is a society without the state. This is a generally known truth. However, petty-bourgeois theorists interpret this to mean that after the disappearance of the state no organization will remain in society, that a realm of anarchy will prevail. The conception of society as a shapeless, unorganized, anarchistic mass of people is narrow and unscientific. Society would inevitably disintegrate if each of its members behaved in his own way without consideration of the interests of others, if egotism and anarchism prevailed. Quite on the contrary, the communist society will be a highly organized and harmonious commonwealth of working people.

The high level of development in production, science, and technology under communism will necessitate a systematic and organized distribution of labor in diverse branches of industry and a social regulation of working time taking into account the peculiarities of the industrial processes. The distribution of material and spiritual goods according to need, the social education of children as well as other social affairs under communism, will call for definite forms of social organization. But the organizations that will be created for conducting social affairs will lose their political, state character; these will be social organizations.

Hence, the dying away of the state does not imply the abolition of all social organizations. Society will pass from the state, not toward "nothing," but toward *non-state,* that is, toward an organization that will lose its political character. What does this mean? What will the future organization of the communist society be like? What features will differentiate it from the state?

In characterizing the future communist society, Marx raised the following questions in his *Critique of the Gotha Program:* "To what transformation will the state in communist society be subjected? In other words, which social functions, analogous to the present-day state functions, will still remain? This question could be answered only scientifically. . . ." Marx is interested in the *dying away* of the state in connection with the problem of the *development* of a communist society, that is, he explains to what transformation the state will be subjected under communism and in what direction it will die away. In handling this question Marx remains true to his dialectical method. Instead of guessing and inventing the form of the future social organization that will replace the state, he formulates the question in a strict scientific manner: What social functions that are analogous to present-day state functions will remain under communism? To reword it, present-day *state* functions will die away, but social functions analogous to them will nevertheless remain. What type of functions will they be? In what respect will they be different from state functions? Marx raised these questions merely in a general theoretical manner, providing an opportunity for their future solution after further practical experience.

In the works of the Marxist-Leninist classics we find theoretical premises that explain the principal essence of the transformations to which the state will be subjected under communism. In *The Communist Manifesto* Marx and Engels have indicated that the public, that is, the state authority, will lose its *political* character. What does this mean? In his *Anti-Dühring* Engels defined this premise in greater detail. He stated that (after the state had concentrated in its hands the means of production and after it had become a true representative of the whole society) "the state interference in social relations becomes little by little superfluous and withers away of itself; the government of persons is replaced by the administration of things and by the conduct of the processes of production." In an article "On Authority" Engels returned once more to this problem by stating that ". . . social functions will lose their political character and will be transformed into simple administrative functions." In developing the same thought, Lenin stated: "At a certain point of its dying away, the dying state can be designated as a non-political state."[23]

Thus, the state is a political organization, a political authority, regulating social relationships. Under communism, political authority dies away, the state no longer interferes in social relationships. The life of society is no longer regulated by the legal norms

[23] *Ibid.,* p. 410.

of the state; it is regulated by high moral principles, by the consciousness and collective interests of the people, by their active participation in the administration of social affairs. The State loses its political character. At the same time the specific organs of state authority which support social order and regulate relationships between men disappear. Social order is supported by a voluntary observance of the rules of social life, which become a habit, by self-discipline, and by the organization-mindedness of the people. However, social functions that are analogous to present-day state functions still remain in existence in the communist society, namely, such functions as the direction of the processes of production, the education of children, the security of social order, etc. But this is no longer state government; this is social government, self-government.

Thus, the dying away of the state is a dialectical process of transition from state to non-state, is a development of the socialist state into the communist social self-government. As stated by Khrushchev . . . , "We say that under communism the state will die away. But what organs will be preserved? Social organs! Regardless of whether they are to be known as the Communist League of Youth or Labor Unions, they will be social organizations through which society will regulate its relationships. One should make the way clear for this now by teaching people so that they can develop the habits for such conduct."

Such is the general tendency of the development of a political organization, of the state, in the transition to communism. Revisionists are opposed to these fundamental premises of the state's dying away. They contend that Soviet Marxists bypass or ignore the problem of the state apparatus and that this is in conformity with their "bureaucratic" concept of the state. Revisionists reduce the concept of state to an apparatus and think that the most significant problem is that of abolishing it. Needless to say, we are confronted with a complete confusion of the diverse types of states—the bourgeois and the socialist states. Like all other types of exploitive states, the bourgeois state is in fact a military-bureaucratic apparatus. In describing the diverse types of exploitive states, Lenin said that "the state is precisely an apparatus of government, detached from human society."[24] The case of the socialist state is entirely different. Owing to its nature, its tasks, and its functions, it cannot be reduced merely to an apparatus of government; it is an immeasurably broader system of state authority and administration.

The political organization of society under socialism is the dicta-

[24] *Ibid.*, Vol. 29, p. 437.

torship of the proletariat, which constitutes a highly thought-out, harmonious, and proved through experience system of state and non-state institutions, embracing all aspects of life in Soviet society. This "mechanism" of political organization comprises the following main component units: first, the organs of state authority, that is, the soviets, which constitute the most popular and all-embracing organization of all workers; second, the organs of state government, which constitute the proper state apparatus and which include executive and regulatory organs of state authority as well as administrative organs for the state administration of economy and culture; third, the workers' mass social organizations—labor unions, cooperatives, youth leagues, and other organizations that unite Soviet citizens in diverse branches of industrial, cultural, scientific, sporting, etc., activities. The leading and directing force of all these state and social organizations is the Communist party of the Soviet Union—the vanguard of the workers in our country.

Each of these component units of the political organization of Soviet society performs its definite tasks and is of great significance in the life of society. Hence, the question is, in what direction will all these units, these elements of political organization and government, develop in the transition to the communist, social self-government.

The existing reality furnishes tremendous material, and our Party has accumulated a wealth of experience in the construction of the state so that it is possible to definitively answer the question. The resolution of the Twenty-first Congress of the C.P.S.U. states that "under existing conditions the principal trend in the development of the socialist state is the full-scale development of democracy, drawing all citizens toward participation in the guidance of economic and cultural construction and in the administration of social affairs. It is indispensable that the role of the soviets as a mass organization of the workers be increased. Many functions, which at present are executed by state organs, should gradually be transferred into the hands of social organizations."

Thus, the general tendency in the development of the political organization of society lies in the full-scale development of socialist democracy, but primarily it lies in increasing the role of the soviets as mass organizations of the workers and in increasing the role of social organizations in the administration of state affairs. Insofar as the apparatus of state government is concerned, this system will be subject to change in the course of the development of the socialist society toward communism. At a given stage and under definite internal and external conditions the organs of coercion will die away, will disappear completely. The organs of the administration of national economy will remain, but they will no longer be state organs; they will be the organs of social self-government.

In this context it is significant to emphasize that communism is not a society that will come in a ready-made form and will remain stationary and frozen. One must not think metaphysically by assuming that, after the advent of communism, the state, with all its attributes, will be left behind somewhere. The communist society is a living society, a constantly changing society; its principles will be constantly developed and perfected. In conformity with this, the diverse aspects, functions, forms, etc., of the state organization will gradually die away. At present it is impossible to foretell when this process will be completed. At any rate, it will not be completed immediately after entering the higher phase of communism. One must not imagine, in view of this, that the existing political organization will immediately die away and be replaced by social self-government. Social organizations, which in the future should supersede the state and its organs, will not come in a ready-made form under communism. Naturally, this will be a protracted and gradual process, in the course of which the organs of government and the social organizations (which exist at the present time) will be developing and changing, and new social organs and organizations (to which the function of the state organs will gradually be transferred) will be able to come into being.

Lenin stated that, "prior to the attainment of full communism, no form would be final."[25] To be able to solve the constantly increasing complex and gigantic tasks of economic and cultural development, the socialist society . . . will create the most expedient forms of administration in correspondence to the arising necessities or will transform, reorganize, and perfect the existing forms. The main trend, however, is clear: the present-day political organization of Soviet society—as well as of all its component elements and links—will gradually be transformed into a social, communist self-government.

[25] Ibid., Vol. 28, p. 195.

# Historical Necessity and Man's Conscious Activity*

## ᘐ Collective Authorship

The development of society is a process governed by laws and subject to a certain historical necessity that does not depend on the will and consciousness of men. The most important aim of the social sciences, the prerequisite for the application of objective laws in the interests of society, is to discover the nature of this necessity, to find out what laws determine the development of history and how they operate.

The Marxist thesis of history as a process governed by laws is directly opposed not only to the subjectivist conceptions of history as an agglomeration of accidents but also to fatalism, which denies the significance of the conscious activity of men and their ability to influence the course of social development.

The fatalist point of view is organically alien to the materialist conception of history. The laws according to which society develops do not operate automatically, of their own accord. Formed as the result of men's activity, these laws determine in their turn the general direction of human activity. There can be no social laws without people, outside their activities.

This conception of historical necessity fundamentally distinguishes Marxists from opportunists, who, for example, from the correct proposition that the victory of socialism is determined by laws, arrive at the completely false conclusion that there is no need to fight against capitalism, that it is only necessary to wait for the time when the "laws of history" themselves will bring about the replacement of capitalism by socialism.

In fact, historical laws themselves, without people, do not make history. They determine the course of history only through the actions, the struggle, and the goal-oriented efforts of millions of people.

The bourgeois critics of Marxism try to accuse it of a contradiction on the grounds that, on the one hand, Marxists speak of the inevitability of the replacement of capitalism by socialism and, on the other, create a political party to fight for socialism. It would never occur to

* From *Osnovy Marksizma-Leninizma* [The Foundations of Marxism-Leninism] (Moscow, 1960), pp. 138–49.

503

anyone, they assert, to create a party for bringing about an eclipse of the sun, if it were already known that such an eclipse was bound to occur.

This argument arises from the failure of bourgeois "critics" to think things out and shows their inability or lack of desire to understand the theory of Marxism and the course of history. Unlike an eclipse of the sun, which takes place without any human participation, the transition from capitalism to socialism is a change of the social order, which takes shape as a result of men's activity and which cannot change of its own accord. Conscious human activity is itself an indispensable component part of the law-governed movement of society toward socialism. When people say that objective laws will ultimately take effect, they do not mean that certain necessary changes will occur in society by themselves but that sooner or later social forces interested in the realization of these laws will arise, and these forces will by their struggle put these laws into effect.

Marxism-Leninism, which regards social laws dialectically, sees that they operate in the form of a dominating tendency of development in given social relations. This means that a law determines the general direction of movement necessarily ensuing from certain objective conditions. But social development is contradictory, and the concrete course of events depends not only on general laws but on the actual correlation of class forces, on the policy of the warring classes and many other specific conditions. When Marxists assert that capitalism will inevitably be replaced by socialism, they have in mind the following: the objective laws of capitalist society inevitably lead to the sharpening of its economic and political contradictions; this gives rise to a constantly intensifying struggle of the working class and all the working people against the capitalist system, which will culminate in the downfall of capitalism and the triumph of socialism. The struggle of the working class expresses historical necessity, but its success at any particular moment is influenced by many circumstances—the level of class consciousness and organization of the working class, the degree of influence of the Marxist parties, the policy of the socialist parties, the policy of the bourgeois state, and many other things. The effect of some of these factors may be to hasten the ultimate success of the struggle of the working class; the effect of others may be to delay it. In the final analysis, however, the triumph of the working class and the victory of socialism are inevitable. Therefore, by promoting the development of the struggle for emancipation of the working class and all the working people, by encouraging the growth of their political consciousness and organization, the

Communists and their allies accelerate the natural course of history and alleviate the "birth pains" of the new society.

Thus, while acknowledging the necessity, that is, the law-governed nature of the historical process, Marxist theory at the same time emphasizes the decisive role of the active struggle of people, of the progressive classes. "Marxism," wrote Lenin, "differs from all other socialist theories in the remarkable way it combines complete scientific sobriety in the analysis of the objective state of affairs and the objective course of evolution with the most definite recognition of the importance of the revolutionary energy, the revolutionary creative genius, and the revolutionary initiative of the masses—and also, of course, of individuals, groups, organizations, and parties that are able to discover and exercise contact with various classes."[1]

The fact that the laws of history are manifested in men's conscious activity involves recognition of the enormous role of social ideas. Bourgeois critics of Marxism contend that historical materialism belittles or even wholly denies the role of ideas in history. This is shown, so they think, by the fact that Marxists consider the spiritual life of society a reflection of its material being. But to indicate the source of origin of social ideas certainly does not mean denying or belittling their significance. In fact, Marxism by no means denies the significance of ideas, social ideals, human passions and aspirations, man's inward motives in general. Communists would contradict themselves if, on the one hand, they tried to give the working people a scientific, communist ideology, a feeling of class solidarity, internationalism, and so on, while on the other, they denied the importance of the subjective factor, i.e., of conscious human activity in history.

Marxism merely states that people's ideas and sentiments are not the ultimate causes of historical events, that these ideas and sentiments themselves have their roots in the conditions of people's material life. But Marxism at the same time emphasizes that the conditions of material life can stimulate people's actions only by passing through their consciousness and being reflected there in the form of definite views, ideals, aims, etc.

[1] *Sochineniya* [Works] (4th ed., Moscow), Vol. 25 (1949), pp. 358–59.

# Marxism-Leninism as a Philosophy and a World Outlook* ∽ Collective Authorship

To master the fundamentals of Marxism-Leninism requires serious and thoughtful study and, consequently, much work and time. What are the fruits of such a study? Stated briefly, the answer is that it gives us an integral world outlook, the most progressive outlook of our time, one in which the cardinal components of the great teachings of Marx and Lenin are blended in a harmonious, integral system.

. . . . . . .

Marxism-Leninism has great merits that distinguish it from all other philosophical systems. It does not recognize the existence of any supernatural forces or creators. It rests squarely on reality, on the real world in which we live. It liberates mankind, once and for all, from superstition and age-old spiritual bondage. It encourages independent, free, and consistent thought.

Marxism-Leninism accepts the world as it actually is, without adding to it an invented hell or paradise. It proceeds from the fact that all nature, including man himself, consists of matter with its different properties. And nature, as well as all its individual phenomena, is in the constant process of development. The laws of this development have not been ordained by God and do not depend on man's will. They are intrinsic in nature itself and are fully knowable. There are no inherently unknown things in the world; there are only things that are still unknown but that will become known through science and practice. The Marxist-Leninist world outlook stems from science itself and *trusts* science, as long as science is not divorced from reality and practice. It develops and becomes richer with the development of science.

Marxism-Leninism teaches that not only the development of nature but the *development of human society,* too, takes place in accordance with objective laws that are independent of man's will. By revealing the basic laws of social development, Marxism raises history to the level of a genuine science capable of explaining the nature of every social system and the development of society from one social system to another. That was a tremendous victory for scientific thought.

* From *Osnovy Marksizma-Leninizma* [The Foundations of Marxism-Leninism] (Moscow, 1960), pp. 5–19.

506

Bourgeois representatives of social sciences (sociology, political economy, historiography) could not refute the materialist conception of history nor oppose to it a theory acceptable to the majority of bourgeois scientists. Yet many bourgeois scientists obstinately repudiate historical materialism. Why? Because it refutes the faith in the "eternity" of the capitalist system. For if the transition of society from one system to another takes place in conformity with natural laws, then it must follow that the capitalist system is bound to give way to another, more progressive social system. And this is something not only the capitalists but the scientists dependent on them materially and spiritually find it hard and bitter to acknowledge.

Never in the history of class society has the ruling class believed in the inevitable doom of its system. The slave-owners felt sure their system would last forever, for they believed that it was established by divine will. The feudal lords who superseded them likewise believed that their system had been established by divine will and for all time. But they were forced to give way to the bourgeoisie, and then it was its turn to seek comfort in the illusion that capitalism was "eternal" and "immutable." And many learned sociologists and historians, reluctant to break with capitalism, try in every possible way to refute the fact that the development and change of social systems follow intrinsic laws that do not depend on the will of the ruling classes and their ideologists. Hence, bourgeois ideologists wage war on the Marxist conception of history not because it is wrong but precisely because it is true.

By revealing the laws governing the operation and development of the forces of nature and society, genuine science can always foresee the new. The Marxist science of the laws of social development enables us not only to chart a correct path through the labyrinth of social contradictions but to predict the course that events will take, the direction of historical progress, and the next stages of social development.

Thus, Marxism-Leninism gives us an instrument that enables us to look into the future and see the outlines of impending historical changes. This "time telescope" has revealed to us the magnificent future of humanity freed from the yoke of capitalism, from the last exploiting system. But when progressive science invites bourgeois scientists (who claim that "nothing can be predicted") to apply the Marxist "time telescope," they simply shut their eyes—they are afraid to look into the future.

Marxists never fear to look into the future. They represent the class to which the future belongs and have no use for illusions, which are shattered the moment they come into contact with the facts, with science. Headed by Lenin, the Russian Marxists foresaw the socialist revolution in Russia as a task that history had matured. Accordingly, they rallied the working class for decisive struggle against the exploiting system, organized the storming of its bastions, and achieved complete victory.

. . . . . . .

Marxist-Leninist theory provides a scientific basis for revolutionary *policy*. He who bases his policy on subjective desires remains either a futile dreamer or risks being thrust into the background by history. For history does not conform to man's wishes if these are not in accordance with the laws of history. That is why Lenin emphasized the need for a sober scientific analysis of objective situations and of the objective course of evolution as the basis for defining the political line of the Party and for subsequently carrying it out with all revolutionary termination. Marx said: "We must take things as they are, that is, uphold the revolutionary cause in a form that corresponds to the changed circumstances."[1]

. . . . . . .

The Marxist-Leninist world outlook is also a true compass in every sphere of *scientific endeavor,* not only in the social but also in the natural sciences. For is it not true that a correct understanding of the world and its general laws, interrelations, and processes greatly helps the natural scientist in his creative research? That understanding is provided by Marxism-Leninism. It is no accident that their research experiences are now leading many eminent scientists either to accept Marxism fully or to tacitly adopt some of its elements, in order to gain a more profound knowledge of the secrets of nature and be in a better position to serve the interests of humanity.

Furthermore, the Marxist-Leninist outlook opens up splendid prospects to workers in the *arts and literature.* It directs their creative efforts toward a deeper and richer reflection of reality through artistic media. Without the beneficial influence of a clear, progressive world outlook, the work of contemporary writers and artists is at best anemic. In our day, Marxism-Leninism offers the artist a full and clearcut conception of the world.

Whereas bourgeois literature is more and more succumbing to moods of hopelessness and unrelieved pessimism, the work of pro-

[1] Karl Marx and Friedrich Engels, *Sochineniya* [Works] (1st ed., Moscow), XXV (1936), 475.

gressive writers and poets is imbued with a life-asserting optimism. Their artistic creation is inspired by faith in a brighter future and calls for the building of that future. Whereas Western bourgeois ideology is caught in a desperate crisis of disbelief in man and the future of civilization, the Marxist-Leninist world outlook inspires a desire to work for noble social ideals.

Thorough mastery of Marxism-Leninism gives one a profound conviction not only of the correctness of the workers' cause but of the historical inevitability of the coming triumph of socialism throughout the world. Marxism-Leninism is a source of strength, even to the weak; a source of steadfast political principle. It instills the unshakable ideological conviction that enables one to withstand all trials and ordeals.

. . . . . . .

The indestructible foundation of the whole edifice of Marxism-Leninism is its philosophy—dialectical and historical materialism.

. . . . . . .

Unlike spontaneous or naïve materialism, philosophical materialism *scientifically* substantiates, elaborates, and consistently applies materialist conceptions based on the findings of progressive science and social practice. Materialist philosophy is an effective weapon against the pernicious influence of spiritual reaction. It provides a guide throughout life, showing the correct way of solving the philosophical problems that agitate men's minds.

. . . . . . .

The idealists often calumniate materialism, presenting it as an "uncanny, a sinister, a nightmare view of life" (William James). Actually, it is idealism, especially its latter-day versions, which is a philosophy of gloom. It is idealism, not materialism, which denies man's ability to acquire knowledge and preaches distrust in science. It is idealism, not materialism, which extols the cult of death. It is idealism which has always been a receptive soil for the most abhorrent manifestations of antihumanism—racist theories and fascist obscurantism. Philosophical idealism refuses to recognize the reality of the external material world, repudiating it and proclaiming it unreal and advancing instead an imagined, non-material world.

In contrast, materialism gives us a true picture of the world without any superfluous additions in the shape of spirit, God, the creator of the world, etc. Materialists do not expect aid from supernatural. forces. Their faith is in man, in his ability to transform the world by his own efforts and make it worthy of himself.

Materialism is in its very essence an optimistic, life-asserting, and radiant world outlook, entirely alien to pessimism and *Weltschmerz*. That is why, as a rule, materialism is the world outlook of progressive social groups and classes. Its supporters fearlessly look ahead and are not tormented by doubts of the justice of their cause. The advocates of idealism have always sought to slander materialism, maintaining that materialists have no moral values and lofty ideals, these being the prerogative only of supporters of idealist philosophy. In point of fact, the dialectical and historical materialism of Marx and Engels, far from rejecting progressive ideas, moral principles, and lofty ideals, lays great emphasis on them. It considers that successful struggle for progress, for a progressive social system, is impossible without noble ideals that inspire men in struggle and bold creative work.

The struggle of the working class and the Communists convincingly refutes the stupid idealist lie that materialists are indifferent to ideals. For this struggle is being waged for the highest and noblest ideal of all—communism—and it produces legions of intrepid fighters supremely devoted to that ideal.

# On Communist Society: Its Immediate and Future Prospects* ∽ Collective Authorship

Communism is a society that puts an end to want and poverty once and for all, assuring the well-being of all its citizens. The working-man's age-old dream of abundance comes true under communism. The way to this is opened up by the socialist reconstruction of society, which puts an end to private ownership of the means of production, to the exploitation of man by man, and to unjust social orders. It removes the barriers that hampered the development of the productive forces and makes it possible in time to create the solid material and technical basis essential for the achievement of an abundance of the good things of life.

. . . . . . .

The achievements of modern science and technology, and the discoveries that they are on the threshold of making, provide tangible and real prospects of satisfying all the needs of the members of society, not only as regards prime necessities, but also as regards goods and services that are considered as luxuries today.

. . . . . . .

By regarding large-scale modern production, technical, and scientific progress as the only possible basis for the creation of abundance, Marxism-Leninism by no means makes the solution of this problem dependent only on production, on technology. No, this problem has a no less important *social* aspect. Its solution is simply impossible without the social conditions formed after the victory of socialism. No technical or scientific progress under capitalism can ensure abundance for all members of society. A vivid example is furnished by the United States, the richest and most developed country in the capitalist world, where the high level of production, it would seem, could ensure a comfortable life for the entire population, but where, despite this, there are millions of people who are undernourished, live in bad conditions, and lack the bare necessities of life.

This means that it is only in combination with the principles of socialism that a high technology of production can provide genuine abundance for all the people. It is only after the social system and the

* From *Osnovy Marksizma-Leninizma* [The Foundations of Marxism-Leninism] (Moscow, 1960), pp. 735–53.

production and distribution of material and spiritual values have been remade along socialist, and then along communist, lines that this abundance begins to yield its fruits for *every* member of society.

## FROM EACH ACCORDING TO HIS ABILITY

Under communism, as under any other social system, human labor remains the sole source of all values. "Communism will bring man not a lordly life in which laziness and idleness prevail, but a life of labor, an industrious, cultured and interesting life!"[1]

Hence, whatever the development of technology, whatever the victories of science, the slogan "from each according to his ability" will remain the immutable principle of the communist system. It is well known that this principle already prevails under socialism, proclaiming the duty of all members of society to work to the full measure of their abilities. Communism, however, introduces deep changes into the content of the formula "from each according to his ability."

First, by ensuring the all-round development of the individual, the conditions of the communist system lead to the flowering of all the abilities of man and thereby make the labor performed to the full measure of his ability much more productive. Second, the fulfillment by each person of his duty to work according to his ability is ensured under communism by different methods than under socialism. In socialist society, material stimuli (payment according to work), operating in combination with moral stimuli, are of decisive significance. Under communism, all members of society will work, prompted solely by moral stimuli, a high sense of consciousness. In other words, this will be labor without payment and the satisfaction of all the needs of the workers without payment.

"Communist labor in the narrower and stricter sense of the term," Lenin wrote, "is labor performed gratis for the benefit of society, labor performed, not as a definite duty, not for the purpose of obtaining a right to certain products, not according to previously established and legally fixed norms, but voluntary labor, irrespective of norms, labor performed without expectation of reward, without the stipulation of reward, labor performed out of a habit of working for the common good and out of a conscious realization (which becomes a habit) of the necessity of working for the common good—labor as the requirement of a healthy organism."[2]

---

[1] Statement of N. S. Khrushchev taken from *XIII Sezd Vsesoyuznogo Leninskogo Kommunisticheskogo Soyuza Molodezhi 15–18 Aprela 1958 Goda* [The Thirteenth Congress of the Lenin Young Communist League, April 15–18, 1958], Stenographic Report (Moscow, 1959), p. 277.

[2] *Sochineniya* [Works] (4th ed., Moscow), Vol. 30 (1950), p. 482.

It is clear that labor can become a habit, life's prime want of each person, not only when the consciousness of people reaches great heights, but also when the very nature of labor itself changes. One of the prime conditions for this exists already under socialism: the exploitation of man by man disappears. Other conditions are created in the period of transition to communism. Human labor is replaced by machines wherever excessive physical exertion is required, wherever work is monotonous and exhausting. The time spent working in material production is steadily reduced. Lastly, there is abolished the old division of labor which crippled man, chained him for life to one trade, barring the road to the development of his capabilities and inclinations.

Thus, the labor activities of people are transformed on the basis of the technical re-equipment of industry and the wide application to it of the achievements of science, that is, on the basis of the social and cultural progress of the new society. Under communism, human labor will be entirely freed from everything that made it an onerous burden for thousands of years. It will become not only free but also genuinely creative. In the automated production of communist society, the functions that no machine is capable of performing, i.e., primarily the creative functions associated with the design and improvement of machines, will assume an ever greater place in the work of man.

An approximate picture of what labor will be like under communism can be drawn by bearing in mind its main features, which are as follows: (1) each worker, both as regards skill and the nature of his labor, performs functions for which a trained engineer is required in present-day production; (2) people work 20–25 hours a week (i.e., approximately 4–5 hours a day) and, in time, even less; (3) each person can choose an occupation in conformity with his inclinations and abilities and can change it at will; (4) all talents and abilities inherent in people are fully developed and applied, either in the process of their production activities, or in their free time; (5) while working, a man does not have to think about his livelihood, or how much he will get for his labor, because society has assumed all responsibility for satisfying his needs; (6) labor enjoys the highest respect in society and becomes, in the eyes of all, the chief measure of man's worth.

Under such conditions, labor naturally turns into a free, voluntary matter, into an inner urge and habit of all members of society, because creative labor is liked by every normal human being and is, as Engels put it, "the highest enjoyment known to us."[3]

[3] Karl Marx and Friedrich Engels, *Sochineniya* [Works] (2nd ed.; Moscow, 1955), Vol. 2, p. 351.

For labor to give people happiness, it need not be converted into a sort of entertaining game that requires no exertion of physical or mental effort, as some utopian Socialists imagined. Polemizing against such naïve views, Marx wrote that "free labor, for example, the labor of the composer, is at the same time a devilishly serious matter, a most intensive strain." No less serious a matter is the labor of a designer, inventor, or writer, in a word, every genuinely creative labor. But does the exertion that it involves make such labor less attractive?

Free, creative labor under communism will give the members of society such deep satisfaction that the conception of leisure will not be associated in their minds with the conception of complete idleness. Most probably, besides their main production activities, which will take up only a small part of the day, many people will engage in science, invention, art, literature, etc. The general cultural level and the special knowledge of millions of people will be so high that all these forms of "amateur" activities will represent a constantly growing contribution to the development and prosperity of society.

Communism will gradually make the supreme joy of free and creative labor available not only to a few but to all; the time spent working, which throughout the centuries was considered lost by the millions, will become time that makes life fuller. That will be the great achievement of communist humanism. Its results will be felt in all spheres of society's life, giving rise to new relations between people, creating prerequisites for the unprecedented development of the personality, and ensuring conditions for the firm establishment of the new, communist mode of distribution.


## TO EACH ACCORDING TO HIS NEEDS

Communism introduces a mode of distribution of material and spiritual benefits that is based on the principle of "to each according to his needs." In other words, each man, irrespective of his position, of the quantity and quality of labor he can give society, receives from society, gratis, everything he needs.

It is easy to understand that this means not only a paramount revolution in views on labor, which, as shown above, ceases to be a mere means of earning a livelihood. Together with the disappearance of the need to control the amount of labor and consumption, together with the abolition of money and the disappearance of commodity-money relations, the very nature of the connections between man and society are radically changed. These connections are completely freed from selfish considerations, from everything introduced into them by the quest for an income, for material gain.

The opportunity to obtain from the public stocks at any time, gratis, everything needed for a cultured and carefree life will have a wholesome effect on man's mind, which will no longer be weighed down by concern for the morrow. In the new psychology and the new ethics there will be no room for thought of income and private property, the quest for which constitutes the entire meaning and purpose of life for many people under capitalism. Man, at long last, will receive the opportunity to dedicate himself to lofty interests, among which social interests will take a foremost place.

Distribution according to needs is introduced under communism, however, not only out of humane considerations, not only out of a desire to free all members of society from concern for the morrow. It takes place also owing to a direct *economic necessity,* which arises at this high stage in the development of social production. Distributing material and spiritual benefits in conformity with the needs of people, the communist system thereby creates the best conditions for the further development of its main productive force, the workingman, for the flowering of all his abilities. This will benefit both the individual and society in equal measure. Pointing to this circumstance, Engels wrote that "distribution, insofar as it is governed by purely economic considerations, will be regulated by the interests of production and that production is most encouraged by a mode of distribution which allows *all* members of society to develop, maintain, and exercise their capacities with maximum universality."[4]

Some none-too-clever critics of Marxism try to prove the unfeasibility of the ideals of communist society by raising various "tricky" questions. If all benefits are distributed gratis, will not everyone want to get every day not only a new suit of clothes but also a new automobile? And what if each member of society demands for himself a palace with scores of rooms or wants to obtain a collection of jewelry and unique works of art?

The authors of such absurd suppositions slander the citizens of the future communist society, to whom they ascribe their own failings. The communist system naturally cannot undertake to satisfy all whims and caprices. Its aim, as Engels stressed, is the satisfaction of the reasonable needs of people in an ever-increasing measure.[5] Does this mean that instead of money relations some other forms of a forcible regulation of consumption will be needed? No. Under communism, it should be expected, there will in general be no need to determine which needs are reasonable and which are not. People themselves will be sufficiently cultured and conscious not to make

[4] *Anti-Dyuring* [Anti-Dühring] (Moscow, 1957), p. 188.
[5] Marx and Engels, *Sochineniya* [Works] (1st ed.; Moscow, 1933), XV, 421.

obviously unreasonable demands on society. As Lenin wrote in 1917, communism "presupposes not the present productivity of labor *and not the present* ordinary run of people, who, like the seminary students in Pomyalovskii's stories,[6] are capable of damaging the stocks of public wealth 'just for fun' and of demanding the impossible."[7]

Naturally, a certain amount of time will be needed to develop in all citizens a reasonable attitude toward consumption, but the society of the future, with its abundance of material and spiritual benefits and the high level of consciousness of its citizens, can fully measure up to this task. And if, nevertheless, there are some people with unjustifiably high claims, they will not be able to disorganize the communist system of distribution. Society will be able to give people with an inordinate appetite . . . a double portion,[8] Engels wrote. But in communist society this will only place such people in a ridiculous light before public opinion. After this, hardly anyone would want to repeat such an experiment.

It will be all the easier for people to get used to communist forms of consumption since they do not require of them any artificial self-restriction or asceticism, or an austere way of life. In general, the preaching of asceticism is alien to scientific communism, which sees the aim of social production precisely in the full satisfaction of the material and spiritual requirements of all members of society. Moreover, communist society itself from the very beginning will be sufficiently rich to satisfy generously all the needs of the citizens in food, clothing, shelter, and other prime necessities and also to place at their disposal everything an intelligent and cultured person needs for a full and happy life.

Undoubtedly, under communism, consumption itself will rise to a higher level, the tastes of people will develop and become more refined. Communist social relations will create a man who will organically abhor depraved tastes and requirements characteristic of past epochs in which possession of things and the level of consumption were the primary criteria of man's position in society. Instead of luxury, the main criteria of the value of things will become convenience and real beauty; people will cease to see in things an object of vainglory and a measure of success in life, will cease to live for the sake of amassing things, and thereby will restore to things their real purpose—to ease and beautify man's life.

It may be assumed that the laws governing mass production—and

---

[6] [N. Pomyalovskii, a Russian writer of the nineteenth century, described the strict regime that prevailed in seminaries and the coarse customs of their students.]

[7] *Sochineniya*, Vol. 24 (1949), p. 441.        [8] *Anti-Dyuring*, p. 325.

the production of all main articles will be such under communism—will operate in the same direction. Of course, in time, communist society will become so rich that it will be able to satisfy the highest requirements of people. But it will also be so rational that it will not waste human labor and public wealth. More rational and worthier application will always be found for both. It will involve, of course, not the lowering of aesthetic demands but the rise of new, higher aesthetic criteria, corresponding to the entire pattern and way of the new life.

All this shows that the realization of the communist principle "to each according to his needs" will be a tremendous achievement of mankind. There is no point in trying to guess what concrete form these needs will take. One thing is clear—they will be much higher and more diverse than at present. Human needs are neither stationary nor immutable; they are developing and growing all the time. Under communism, this process will be particularly rapid. That is why the communist system sets itself the task of satisfying the *constantly rising needs* of all members of society.

## THE FREE MAN IN A FREE SOCIETY

Communism is the most just social system. It will fully realize the principles of equality and freedom, ensure the development of the human personality, and turn society into a harmonious association, a commonwealth of men of labor.

Equality and freedom have always been the dream of the progressive part of mankind. Many social movements of the past developed under this banner, including the bourgeois revolutions of the eighteenth and nineteenth centuries. But in a society founded on private ownership of the means of production and divided into classes of exploited and exploiters, oppressed and oppressors, this dream remained unrealizable.

It is only when the means of production become public property and the exploitation of man by man is made impossible that a way is opened to actual, not simply formal, equality of people, to their real emancipation. This historic task is fully accomplished by communism. *Universal, actual equality of people* is one of its main social principles.

Equality is achieved in the first place by the fact that communism is a classless society in which the last remnants of the social distinctions and attendant inequality still preserved under socialism are liquidated, including the distinctions between town and country, between manual workers and brain workers. The disappearance of these distinctions in no way signifies a leveling of individualities, a uniformity of human capabilities and characters. Communism is not a barracks inhabited by persons who lack individuality. Such a caricature of the future can be painted only by incorrigible vulgarizers or deliberate slanderers. In reality this society opens up a boundless scope, which has never existed in the past, for the all-round development of the human personality in all its limitless diversity.

Communist equality presupposes the eradication not of all distinctions between people but only of such distinctions and such conditions as would give rise to a difference in the social position of people. Irrespective of the origin and position of man, irrespective of his contribution to social production, under communism he will receive equal opportunities with all others to participate in deciding common affairs, will receive opportunities for self-improvement and the enjoyment of all the good things of life. It is one of the salient features of communism that it ensures that highest degree of equality under which, as Marx said, even *"distinction* in activity, in labor, does not involve any *inequality,* any *privilege,* in the sense of possession and consumption."[9] Herein lies the great social significance of the mode of distribution of material and spiritual values which the communist system introduces.

At the same time, communism also brings with it the final triumph of *human freedom.* Already in the first, socialist phase of development of the new society, people receive the most important of all the freedoms, freedom from the need to work for exploiters. The fact that the working people are at the helm in socialist society gives true meaning to democracy, i.e., the principle of rule by the people. Communism goes further, creating for the first time the conditions under which all need for coercion disappears.

Why does this become possible under communism, although in past history no society could even dream of renouncing coercion? The point is that for thousands of years social conditions prevailed that made irreconcilable contradictions, the clash of interests of individuals and entire classes, inevitable. It is this division of society which gave rise to coercion, bringing into being a special machine of class violence and also a system of legal norms imposed on people by a force concentrated in the hands of the ruling classes.

Such division of society is abolished already with the victory of socialism. Communism, transforming production, distribution, and labor, at the same time ensures the full fusion of the social and economic interests of all members of society. As a result, the grounds for any measures of coercion disappear. The relations of domination and

---

[9] Marx and Engels, *Sochineniya* (2nd ed.), Vol. 3, p. 542.

subordination are finally replaced by free cooperation. There is no need for the state. The need for legal regimentation withers away. For cultured people imbued with lofty ideas and high moral standards, as people will be under communism, the observance of the rules of human behavior in the community becomes a habit, second nature. Under these conditions, Engels wrote, "the government of persons is replaced by the administration of things and by the guidance of processes of production."[10] The disappearance from public life of all compulsion will transform not only the social conditions of future society but also man himself, who in everything will act freely in accordance with his convictions, his consciousness, and his moral duty.

The supreme goal of communism is to ensure *full freedom of development of the human personality,* to create conditions for the boundless development of the personality, for the physical and spiritual perfection of man. It is in this that Marxism sees genuine freedom in the highest meaning of this word.

Universal sufficiency, an improved system of hygiene and public health services, and a rational mode of life in communist society will ensure man's health, longevity, and physical perfection. The mode of distribution inherent in communism will free people forever from concern for their daily bread. Free, creative labor, far from suppressing, will, on the contrary, develop man's manifold, inherent capabilities.

Leisure time will increase greatly. Let us recall the great significance that Marx attached to this. He said that under communism the wealth of society would be measured not by the amount of working time but by the free time of its members. Leisure means not only time for rest, the restoration of man's strength, but also, to use the words of Marx, the space for the development of his personality.

The members of the new society, cultured people of versatile development, will undoubtedly find rational and worthy ways of filling this "space." Study will become just as much an integral element of each man's way of life as work, rest, and sleep. The enjoyment of all kinds of cultural benefits will rise immeasurably. Society, becoming richer, will be able to assign ever more resources and labor for the production of these benefits.

The development and improvement of the individual will also be facilitated to a great extent by the fact that communist society will ensure boundless opportunities for the display of all man's abilities, and, as is known, talents need to be used in order to flourish and become perfected.

[10] Karl Marx and Friedrich Engels, *Izbrannye Proizvedeniya* [Selected Works] (Moscow, 1955), II, 141.

With the creation of all these prerequisites the full power of the human intellect will be developed. The cultivation of people's characters and sentiments will also attain immense heights. The new conditions of life will develop to the full new moral stimuli: solidarity, mutual good will, and a deep sense of community with other people—members of the single human family. All this will open before mankind boundless opportunities to enjoy life, to partake of its pleasures in full.

At the same time, the all-round development of the personality will be a powerful factor in the further rapid progress of communist society. For the intellect, talents, and abilities of people are the greatest of all the riches any society possesses. But in the past, owing to social conditions, this wealth was utilized only to a minimal extent. What boundless prospects will open up when the abilities and talents of each man are fully developed and when they are utilized fruitfully and not wasted!

The freedom that communism gives man will not mean the disintegration of society into separate communities and, still less, into individuals who do not recognize any social ties. Such a conception of freedom is entertained only by the followers of anarchism and petty-bourgeois individualism. For them, freedom implies the rupture of all social ties and the abolition of any social organization. But such "freedom" cannot be of benefit to people.

Society needs some form of organization for social production to function normally and develop, for culture and civilization to flourish, ensuring all people well-being and a free and happy life. That is why the place of the state is taken not by the reign of universal anarchy but by a system of *public self-government*. It is pointless to guess at the definite forms this system will assume, but some of its general outlines can be discerned with a considerable degree of certainty.

Social self-government under communism is an organizational system embracing the *entire population,* which will *directly administer its affairs* with the help of this system. New forms of organization will be needed for the establishment of such a system, forms that enable the common will to be revealed correctly and in good time and to be effectively applied, uniting many millions of people for the accomplishment of the tasks confronting society.

Communist social self-government will in the first place be a ramified system of mass organizations and collectives. Only in this way will it be possible to ensure the constant participation of all members of society in administration, to mobilize their energies, experience, and creative initiative.

The methods of administering social affairs also will be correspondingly altered. In the economy, the main sphere of social self-government, these will be methods of scientific planning, the organization of voluntary ties and cooperation between production collectives and economic zones. In deciding other affairs, methods of public influence, the influence of public opinion, will be utilized. Under communism, public opinion will become a mighty force, capable of bringing to reason those individuals who might not want to follow communist customs and rules of behavior in the community.

The atmosphere in which the activities of social self-government will be carried on will also be fundamentally new. Social self-government presupposes not only full publicity and knowledge of society's affairs but also a very high degree of civic activity by the people, their deep interest in these affairs. Most likely a public discussion of society's affairs will involve disputes. This, however, will not be an obstacle but, on the contrary, will help to find the most correct solution of problems. Insoluble contradictions, as experience shows, arise on the basis of irreconcilable interests and ignorance. These causes will be ruled out under communism; consequently, only differences in experience, in degree of knowledge, in approach to some particular questions, will remain. But it will not be difficult to resolve such divergencies in the conditions of a deep-seated community of interests, aims, and world outlook.

All these features of communist social self-government will be wholly in accord with the nature of the relations between people in the future society, relations of cooperation, brotherhood, and fellowship. The communist man is not an egoist, not an individualist; he will be distinguished by conscious collectivism and deep concern for the common good. The mainspring of the morality of this man is devotion to the collective, his readiness and ability to observe sacredly the social interests. It is these qualities of the free and equal citizens of the new society that will make communism a highly organized and harmonious community of people, real masters of creative communist labor.

## PEACE AND FRIENDSHIP: COOPERATION AND RAPPROCHEMENT OF THE PEOPLES

Communism means new relations between the peoples. They will arise as a result of the further development of the principles of socialist internationalism, which today constitute the basis of relations between the countries of the socialist world system.

The victory of the socialist revolution liquidates the social and economic causes that give rise to wars between states and makes peace and friendship the basis of relations between the peoples who are building the new society. Communism reinforces these relations still further, a result that follows from the very essence of the communist system. ". . . In contrast to the old society, with its economical miseries and its political delirium," Marx wrote prophetically about communism, "a new society is springing up, whose international rule will be *peace* because its national ruler will be everywhere the same—*labor!*"[11]

We see that today, too, the principle of equality of nations, irrespective of their size and level of economic and cultural development, prevails in relations between the socialist countries. The victory of communism raises this principle to a new, higher level, ensuring the *actual equality* of countries where the new system has been established. Already during the transition to communism all of them have been brought up to the level of the advanced ones, and they will more or less simultaneously enter the communist era.

The creation of a world socialist system has brought with it the close cooperation and mutual assistance of the liberated peoples. Communism means the further consolidation and advance of this cooperation. It opens the way to an unprecedented drawing together of the economies and cultures of all the peoples, the aim being their most rapid and successful development.

All these changes are an inalienable part of the communist remaking of society, which will result in the disappearance of all traces of disunity and isolationism in the relations between peoples. Nations and, consequently, national cultures and languages will, of course, exist for a long time after the victory of communism as well. But life and the relations of various peoples will be freed from everything that gives even the least reason for enmity and discord, isolation and estrangement, national egoism and exclusiveness.

This will be a colossal gain for mankind. The abolition of only one such wasteful, savage, and bloody form of international "relations" as war, even at the present level of economic development, would make it possible to accomplish gigantic tasks. It has been calculated, for example, that the resources swallowed up by the Second World War were enough for building a five-room house for each family in the world, a hospital in each town with a population of over 5,000 people, and for the maintenance of all these hospitals for ten years. Thus, the resources wasted on one world war would be enough for radically solving the housing and the health problems that today are so acute for the majority of mankind.

[11] *Ibid.,* I, 449.

What treasures could be created by employing for constructive purposes the funds now spent on the arms race, the energies of tens of millions of people now serving in the armed forces or working in war industries! The economic drawing together of the communist countries, the development of their economies along the lines of a world communist system, will also bring tremendous benefits to the peoples. Broad cooperation and specialization will open up new opportunities to save human labor and increase the output of all goods. On this basis, rates of economic growth will be accelerated to an unprecedented degree.

Boundless possibilities are opened up under communism for the cultural advancement of mankind as well. The cultures of different peoples, national in form, will be increasingly imbued with the same communist content. Their drawing together on this basis will provide a mighty stimulus to the mutual enrichment and development of national cultures and in the long run will lead to the formation of a single, deeply international culture that will be truly the culture of all mankind. The rate of scientific progress will be greatly accelerated because it will be possible to coordinate the efforts of scientists on an international, and then on a world-wide, scale. The contacts of people of different countries and nationalities will attain an unusual scale. They will know each other better, learn from each other, and increasingly feel that they are members of one human family. It may be said that communism will impart a new, lofty meaning to the very concept of "mankind," turning the human race, which for thousands of years was torn asunder by discord, quarrels, conflicts, and wars, into one world-wide commonwealth.

## FUTURE PROSPECTS OF COMMUNISM

So far we have discussed primarily the immediate prospects of communism, the prospects in store for the first generations of people who will have the good fortune to live in that society. Even its general contours show that the communist system from its very first steps realizes the most cherished aspirations of mankind, its dream of general sufficiency and abundance, freedom and equality, peace, brotherhood, and cooperation of people.

This is quite natural because the ideal of communism goes back deep into history, into the very depths of the life of the masses. Dreams of this ideal can be found in folk tales about the "Golden Age" which were composed at the dawn of civilization. The liberation movement of the working masses in antiquity and in the Middle Ages put forward many demands that were communistic in their substance.

At the boundary between the two epochs, feudal and capitalist, the outstanding thinkers of those days, the utopian Socialists, made the communist ideal the cornerstone of their doctrine of the perfect society. True, those thinkers could not divine the secret of the laws of social development, could not give a scientific justification of the possibility and historic necessity of communism. Only Marxism turned communism from a utopia into a science, while the merging of scientific communism with the growing working-class movement created that irresistible force which is moving society to the next stage of social progress—from capitalism to communism.

By merging with the working-class movement, communism did not lose its great, general, human content. Engels was profoundly right in pointing out that "communism is a question of humanity and not of the workers alone."[12] The victory of communism will mean the realization of the dream of all working mankind. For the communist system signifies the triumph of humanity, the complete victory of *real humanism,* as Marx said.

What makes communist humanism practicable is not only the fact that the creation of an interesting, happy, and joyous life for all becomes a mighty, all-conquering motive of human activity. Of decisive significance is the fact that under communism society will at long last have the full opportunity of attaining such a goal. A powerful basis for production, greater power over the forces of nature, a just and rational social system, the consciousness and lofty moral qualities of people—all this makes it possible to realize the most radiant dreams of a perfect society.

It is with the victory of communism that the real history of humanity in the loftiest meaning of this term begins. Man differs fundamentally from all living creatures in that his intellect and labor save him from the necessity of passively adjusting himself to his environment and enable him to remake this environment in conformity with the interests and needs of mankind. And, although mankind has existed for many thousands of years, it is only communism which ushers in the era of its full maturity and ends the prolonged prehistory when the life of each man individually and the life of society as a whole were shaped by alien forces, natural and social, that were beyond man's control. The victory of communism enables people not only to produce in abundance everything necessary for their life but also to free society from all manifestations of inhumanity: wars, ruthless struggles within society, and injustice, ignorance, crime, and vice. Violence and self-interest, hypocrisy and egoism, perfidy and

12 Marx and Engels, *Sochineniya* (2nd ed.), Vol. 2, p. 516.

vainglory, will vanish forever from the relations between people and between nations.

This is how Communists imagine the triumph of the genuine, real humanism that will prevail in the future communist society. But even after attaining that summit, people will not stop, will not be idle, will not give themselves over to passive contemplation. On the contrary, their energies will multiply tenfold. Solved problems will be replaced by new ones; in place of the attained goals, new ones, still more entrancing, will arise. The wheels of history will continue to revolve.

Herein, if we think of it, is the greatest good fortune for mankind, a pledge that it will never be deprived of the supreme satisfaction and happiness resulting from creative labor, active endeavor, and the bold overcoming of obstacles. Exceptionally rapid, practically boundless development is indeed a salient feature of communist society. Even after the victory of communism, life will confront people with ever new problems, the solution of which will require the creative effort of each succeeding generation.

First of all, it is clear that the development of social production will never come to an end. What factors will stimulate its continuous progress? These are: the constant rise in the needs of the people of communist society, . . . a very rapid rise; furthermore, the growth of population, which naturally causes an expansion in the production of both material and cultural goods. The social need to reduce further the working time of the people and to increase their leisure is a factor acting in the same direction. It is not difficult to foresee that the development of production itself will call for the solution of many, very complex problems connected with the improvement of production organization, the training of highly skilled personnel, the invention and application of all kinds of technical innovations.

. . . . . . .

Nor will man ever cease his efforts to perfect the structure of the society in which he lives, the forms of social self-government, the way of life, the norms of human behavior and relations in the community.

What a boundless field of activity will be open before communist society in the development of the abilities and personality of all its members, in achieving the physical and spiritual perfection of the people themselves!

The advance to the shining heights of communist civilization will always engender in people unusual power of will and intellect, creative impulses, courage, and life-giving energy.

# A New Type of Man under Socialism*

## ⟿  V. P. Tugarinov

Contemporary bourgeois culture, devoid of any significant social ideas, promotes the lowering of moral ideals, a passion for the external aspects of life, the "automobile civilization," the cult of primitive entertainment, and the dissipation of life. A decadent ideology and psychology, degrading man, is being developed. The philosophy of existentialism, fashionable in the circles of the Western intelligentsia, advocates the idea of an eternal and insurmountable antagonism between the person and society, the rejection of personal obligations to society, man's helplessness in the world surrounding him, and the senselessness of personal goals and of existence in general. With the "advance of technology"—which presumably replaces the person and renders him obsolete—man is declared superfluous. The ideas of man's "loneliness" and "lostness" in a hostile world are being spread.

. . . . . . .

Under conditions of socialism and communism, the human personality develops on a qualitatively new basis—not on the basis of alienation of the person from society, which is the case in the antagonistic socioeconomic formations, but on the basis of *the unity and the harmonious correspondence of personal and social interests*. The economic, political, and spiritual development of all society is the fundamental and main condition of the prosperity, freedom, and spiritual development of each individual. Therefore, in socialist, but even more in communist, society, the antagonism between personal and social interests, between egotism and altruism, becomes devoid of its objective roots.

Man in a socialist society is neither an egotist, thinking exclusively of his own prosperity, nor an altruist, who takes care of others but not of himself. He should be imagined neither as a mercenary acquirer nor as a victim, though voluntary, on the altar of social interests. The man of the new society does not renounce his personal interests in favor of social interests, because this society will not demand from him constant self-sacrifice and self-denial—with the excep-

* *From* "Sotsialisticheskoe Obshchestvo i Lichnost" [Socialist Society and the Person], *Kommunist*, No. 18 (1960), pp. 27–34.

tion of some extraordinary cases, like war, or other moments that call for self-sacrifice. . . .

The harmonious union, the drawing together of the interests of the person and society, is taking place in conformity with the law of social progress under socialism. The process of converging personal and social interests signifies that man's life increasingly depends upon social interests, that man freely, voluntarily, and gladly gives himself to the service of social progress because he sees in this act not "sacrifice" but the fulfillment of his life.

At times, our opponents argue in the following way: socialist society furnishes social justice but not personal freedom, whereas in the "Western world" the person is free without social justice. In fact, however, the person is incomparably freer in a socialist society than in the so-called free world. . . .

Marx and Engels have connected personal freedom with the liquidation of classes. More than a hundred years ago they knew what is unknown to our opponents today, namely, that freedom is inseparable from social justice, i.e., from the liquidation of classes. Freedom without social justice, without the liquidation of class exploitation, is inconceivable in a modern society. Freedom of the person and freedom of "all" are nothing but the liberation of workingmen from capitalist exploitation. . . .

Freedom from misery in socialist society is both material and spiritual freedom. Spiritual freedom liberates man from oppressive fears and anxieties, from the opium of religion, and becomes the source of optimism, of inspiration, and of social activity—a source of all the features characteristic of the population of socialist countries. . . . All the remaining forms of socialist spiritual freedom of the person are determined and secured by the fact that in socialist society the people themselves determine and control all forms of social life. Let us take, for example, freedom of speech. For the broad masses, freedom of speech manifests itself in the freedom of business-like, constructive criticism of the deficiencies in the performance of the state apparatus and economic organs. It is opposed to the "freedom," so much appreciated by the bourgeois intelligentsia, to write and publish whatever one feels, including the release of gangster films, pornographic albums, and decadent readings. An American publicist, D. Marion, speaks quite pointedly about "freedom" of the press in the "free world": "The paper on which the Constitution has been published should be reinforced with the paper on which money is printed; only then would your right of freedom of the press become a real freedom." The same is true of other freedoms. Money, the secret of bourgeois freedom, is its starting point and its end.

Socialism destroys the power of money, of capital, and creates conditions for the true freedom of man. The following is significant for a correct understanding of the new forms of personal freedom. The scope of personal freedom under capitalism is determined by the degree to which men succeed in achieving relative independence from society. Under socialism and communism personal freedom depends upon man's ability to see that his interests and the interests of society coincide—upon his ability to make social interests his own. To put it differently, personal freedom under socialism is materialized not on the basis of the separation and alienation of the person from society but on the basis of the unity, of the correspondence, of personal and social interests, on the basis of a complete blending of person and society in the process of approaching communism.

Both freedom in general (that is, freedom on the philosophical-historical level, as activity based on the recognition of necessity) and freedom on the personal level (that is, freedom as an ability to act in conformity with one's will) can be attained only under the conditions of socialist and communist society. Personal freedom is unattainable for the workers in a society with antagonistic classes because the conditions of an exploitive system are contradictory to their interests and needs. Under socialism, on the other hand, as a result of the objective correspondence of personal and social interests, a level of man's development is being attained in which man ceases to perceive the social requirements imposed upon his behavior (i.e., norms of social discipline and morality) as external coercion but sees them as an expression of his own motives and desires. As man accepts these norms as internal regulators of his conduct, he ceases to feel state and moral "coercion" and fulfills these norms in conformity with his own convictions and desires and in conformity with the social will.

Thus, in comparison with the bourgeois personality, a complete transformation of man's character takes place under socialism.

# A Critique of the Theory of the "Synthesis" of the
# Socialist and Bourgeois Systems* ҩ S. L. Zivs

At present the anticommunism of modern bourgeois social science and propaganda is undergoing a deep and insurmountable crisis. One of the many manifestations of the crisis is the complete inability of the ideologists of imperialism to counteract the bright ideals of communism with any positive ideas. Bourgeois ideologists have already given up the dream that their political ideas can attract and captivate the masses. Their basic aim is somehow to oppose the dissemination of the Marxist-Leninist ideology.

This situation can explain such phenomena as the constantly growing eclecticism in contemporary bourgeois social sciences and the increasing number of opportunist conceptions that, at times, are contradictory to the traditional theses prevalent in one branch or another of the bourgeois social sciences. An example of this is the appearance of a reactionary, utopian conception of the "synthesis" of socialist and bourgeois legal systems and a theory of "transformation" of socialist law. These theories seek to prove that socialist law is undergoing a fundamental transformation and that there is a gradual leveling of the differences between the legal systems of the capitalist and socialist countries.

The concept of the transformation of the legal system of socialist countries is a by-product of a more general theory of "evolution" of the socialist economic and political systems, a theory asserting the possibility of "hybridization" of social antipodes—socialism and capitalism. This theory of evolution of the social system of socialism was an object of frequent speculation by bourgeois ideologists who dreamed of a transformation of socialism—of its *"evolution in a pragmatic and pluralist direction."*[1]

. . . What is the meaning of the formula of evolution in a *pragmatic* direction? Pragmatism—that is, opportunist inconstancy, or more

* *From* "Reaktsionno-Utopicheskaya Kontseptsiya 'Sinteza' Sotsialisticheskoi i Burzhuaznoi Pravovykh Sistem" [Reactionary-Utopian Conception of a "Synthesis" of Socialist and Bourgeois Legal Systems], *Sovetskoe Gosudarstvo i Pravo*, No. 6 (1960), pp. 53–64.

[1] Arthur M. Schlesinger, Jr., "Varieties of Communist Experience," *Encounter,* January, 1960, p. 56.

precisely, the non-adherence to principles, and narrow-mindedness —is opposed to the adherence to principles and clearness of purpose. When speaking of the pragmatic revolution, ideologists of imperialism endeavor to create the impression that the practical policy of the Soviet state can develop in a form of zigzag-like fluctuations and pragmatic compromises.

It is not difficult to see that this theoretical fantasy is connected with the method, favored by bourgeois propaganda, of depicting concrete measures, proposals, and actions of the Soviet Union as "tactical" measures based upon opportunist considerations. Such, for example, is the assertion—which distorts historical truth—that the policy of peaceful coexistence is a "tactical" measure of Soviet diplomacy, a pragmatic and temporary deviation from the basic course of foreign policy, from the plans for the "permanent export of the revolution."

. . . It is hardly necessary to present many arguments to illustrate the fallacy of both the propagandist reasoning on the opportunist-tactical actions of the Soviet state and the "theoretical" thesis on pragmatic evolution. Both of them seek to portray the implementation of general communist goals—which are being materialized by the Communist party of the Soviet Union on the basis of profound knowledge and the utilization of the materialist laws of social development—as actions that are not in accord with the ideas underlying scientific communism.

In doing this, the spiritual advocates of capitalism hope to prove that the concrete achievements of socialist countries (for example, their scientific, technical, or social achievements) are not linked together by a single chain of causal connections—that is, that they are not the result of the victory of the Marxist-Leninist ideology which became transformed into the principal force of human progress.

To be sure, the theory that attributes an evolution in a pragmatic and pluralist direction to the Soviet system also contains a second element. In speaking of the *pluralist* revolution, bourgeois ideologists endeavor to prove that . . . the ruling ideology in Soviet society is breaking up into multiple ideological centers, undermining the unity, that is, the monolithic character, of the socialist social system.

According to the conjectures of an American professor, Von Mehren, socialist society possessed a "monolithic quality" during the "revolutionary stage." In Von Mehren's judgment, it is "very significant," at present, to determine "whether socialist societies are moving away from the monolithic quality that characterized them during their revolutionary stage toward a more pluralistic community."[2]

Only an ill-intentioned and distorting mirror can deform the reflection of Soviet reality in such a way as to deny the constant strengthening of the monolithic character of the socialist society, as to deny such manifestations of its monolithic character as the moral-political unity of the peoples of each socialist country. . . .

Despite the fact that the meaning of evolution in a pluralist direction is clear, we would like to make a few additional comments concerning some nuances of this fashionable invention of bourgeois social science. The point is that the thesis on the evolution of socialist society toward pluralism is interwoven with an equally antiscientific and equally false thesis on the leveling of the main differences between socialist and capitalist societies. One of the principal advocates of the "relativity of differences" between the social systems of socialism and capitalism is a famous American author—historian, sociologist, and former diplomat—George Kennan. His formula, asserting that the differences have "a relative rather than an absolute character," has been picked up by various organs of the bourgeois press.[3]

In spite of our complete disagreement with the thesis of the "relativity of differences" (this thesis, to be sure, is one of the assumptions underlying the conclusion of the hybridization of opposed social systems), we cannot fail to note that its inclusion in the arsenal of scientific and propagandistic ideas of the bourgeoisie constitutes in itself quite a characteristic phenomenon. This thesis, in part, reflects the bourgeois ideologists' forced acknowledgment of the vital crisis facing the spiritual rule of the imperialist bourgeoisie. Troubadours of the bourgeoisie themselves have recognized the fact that bourgeois ideology has lost its former hypnotic power and is no longer capable of competing. Bourgeois ideologists more frequently recognize the fact that the social and political systems of capitalism have lost their power of attraction in the arena of ideological struggle. "The small enthusiasm that our political institutions arouse raises serious problems for us," declares a French publicist, B. de Jouvenel.[4]

To be sure, it would be incorrect to assume that the appearance of

[2] Arthur T. von Mehren's views are quoted from the materials of the Warsaw Conference on the Problems of Socialist Legality held in 1958.

[3] M. Laski, "Ein Gespräch mit G. F. Kennan," *Der Monat*, January, 1960, p. 15.

[4] L'influence de la révolution industrielle sur les institutions politiques," *Le Monde*, October 1, 1959.

concepts of the "relativity of differences" between the opposed social class systems has completely forced out of the market of ideas (which serves the bourgeoisie) those theoretical constructions that, in a more primitive and direct form, condemned the socialist system as "satanical" and "antinatural." It would amount to an exaggeration to assert that they became the ruling conceptions. One thing, however, is certain—those conceptions are a characteristic product of the time when, under the pressure of reality, a considerable number of the ideologists of the imperialist bourgeoisie were being forced to give up the justification and propaganda of the views that held capitalism to be the only legitimate social system—a natural, perpetual, and immutable political regime. It is precisely Kennan who, in connection with his thesis on "the relativity of the differences," admits that "the events of recent years compel us (i.e., bourgeois ideologists—S.Z.) to re-examine the point of view" according to which "the Anglo-Saxon type of liberal democracy represents the most finished product of political thought and has universal significance."

Propagandists of the concept of the "leveling" of principal differences contend that the further development of socialist and capitalist social systems will lead to an evolutionary transformation of their character. Such an evolution will result in an even greater "leveling" of the differences and ultimately in "hybridization."

It is not difficult to see that the theory of easing the antagonism between the major present-day social systems merely represents a variation on the standard reformist myth of evolutionary change in the nature of capitalism, the bourgeois state, and the "autotransformation" of the social structure of capitalism. The class character of reformist schemes—for evolutionary change in the political system of capitalism and for the "transformation" of the political rule of monopolies into a "universal welfare state"—is well known to us.[5]

Enthralled with linguistic "equilibristics" . . . , ideologists of the imperialist bourgeoisie have made an attempt to apply the theory of "social evolution" to the development of socialist society.

Indeed, the socialist society, state, democracy, and law are developing in conformity with the dialectical process of drawing closer to communism. But, while developing, they do not change their character, their class content. On the contrary, their character—their class content—becomes even more distinct. But it is precisely the quality of the socialist state-legal superstructure which bourgeois ideologists

[5] See V. A. Tumanov, "Burzhuazno-Reformistskaya Teoriya 'Gosudarstva Vseobshchogo Blagodenstviya" [The Bourgeois-Reformist Theory of the "Universal Welfare State"], Sovetskoe Gosudarstvo i Pravo, No. 11 (1959).

seek to refute and distort. The law-governed development of socialist society is interpreted by bourgeois ideologists as the advancement of socialism toward capitalism. "The goals and tendencies of Russian communism are turned in the same direction as the goals and tendencies of the liberal industrial West," declares the afore-mentioned Kennan.[6]

What is the purpose of this invention about the similarity between capitalism and socialism? What is its specific propaganda role? First of all, its purpose is to depict the development of a socialist society, in particular Soviet society, as a supplication to the historical course of a capitalist society. An impression is being created that, in the long run, the Soviet society will become merely a communist variant of the "universal welfare state." As a matter of fact, bourgeois ideologists have coined a special expression—"the communist welfare state." This expression has been coined by the editors of an official publication of the United States Information Agency—*Problems of Communism*—in order to stress that the direction of Soviet society does not constitute anything original in comparison with the development of the "welfare state" in the West.[7] If, in the process of its "development," the Soviet state can become only a variant of the welfare state (presumably existing in the West), why then should millions of simple people throughout the world look with hope and love toward the socialist reality and the real communist future? The exploited masses should then simply be satisfied with the "welfare" provided for them by a system of social relationships based on the private ownership of the means and instruments of production. Ultimately this is the meaning of the imperialist apologists' reasoning on the "communist welfare state."

. . . Against the background of these general sociological considerations a special pseudoscientific juridical theory came into being, a theory on the evolution of the legal systems of the socialist countries and on the easing of differences between socialist and bourgeois law. . . . The world-wide, historical victories of the socialist system compel bourgeois jurists to change their tactics in explaining the nature of socialist law. Instead of ignoring Soviet law, bourgeois jurists now prefer to depict the historical course of development of socialist democracy and legality as an adaptation of the traditional institutions of bourgeois law. In bourgeois legal literature one encounters frequent references to the possibility of a synthesis between bourgeois and socialist law.

[6] *L'Express*, October 15, 1959, p. 15.
[7] See the special issue of *Problems of Communism*, IX, No. 1 (1960).

According to bourgeois authors, the symptoms of such a synthesis are to be found in the adaptation of the forms and institutions of bourgeois law to socialist law. In the new codification of Soviet law —which is taking place in conformity with the decisions of the Twentieth and the Twenty-first Congresses of the C.P.S.U. and which represents an organic development of Soviet democracy and socialist legality—some bourgeois jurists are willing to see a "forced acceptance" of the legal forms of bourgeois states.[8] An Austrian jurist, Marcic, went even further by declaring that "the East has entered the path of accepting the forms of the West."[9]

The law-governed process of the further strengthening of socialist legality . . . is depicted by bourgeois ideologists as evidence of the "evolution" of the socialist system and of its "approximation of Western ideals." Such a declaration was made by Professor A. Ross at the 1958 International Conference on the Problems of Socialist Legality in Warsaw.

An analogical declaration was made by Professor John Hazard of Columbia University in a paper presented in 1958 at the Fifth International Congress of Comparative Law in Brussels. Hazard declared that, whether or not Soviet jurists recognize it, there is nothing in Soviet law to prevent it from accepting the principles that are viewed by Western jurists as elementary to a functional conception of the rule of law.[10]

In reality, what Ross is willing to see as a deviation from the principles of socialism, and what Hazard declares to be the beginning of a synthesis with Western law, constitutes a further development of the progressive, revolutionary character of socialist legality.

. . . Bourgeois legal theorists make an attempt to demonstrate that the immutable, eternal, and universal juridical elements and institutions (which have already found their perfect realization in bourgeois law) increasingly find their way into Soviet law as a result of its "evolution." In doing this, bourgeois legal theorists make extensive use . . . of two theories: (1) the theory of the "continuity" of legal forms; and (2) the theory of the universality of legal principles.

Both these theories are used with the aim of proving that the formation and development of a legal system is determined not by socio-

[8] *The Federal Criminal Law of the Soviet Union,* Russian text with an English translation, Introduction by J. M. Van Bemmelen (Leyden, 1958), p. 25.

[9] R. Marcic, *Vom Gesetzstaat zum Richterstaat—Recht als Mass der Macht,* (Vienna, 1958), p. 15. It is characteristic that such a "prognosis" received favorable comments in the pages of the juridical press. See H. Klecatsky, "Der Staat von Morgen," *Juristische Blätter,* October 1, 1959, p. 15.

[10] "The Rule of Law: Some Problems Fundamental to the Ultimate Synthesis between Soviet Law and Western Concepts," p. 4.

economic factors but by an arbitrary combination of legal institutions.
. . . Proponents of this conception view a legal system as the result . . .
of a combination of immutable legal principles.[11]

The concept of . . . the "continuity" of law is one of the most dangerous theories. It seeks to prove that legal forms are independent and sociopolitically neutral. The gist of this concept is a thesis . . . on the "migration" of legal forms that presumably have an abstractly neutral character and that remain so, regardless of the change in sociohistorical conditions.[12]

Applied to the law of socialist countries, the idea of historical continuity leads bourgeois jurists to search for concrete, historically immutable elements on which Soviet law and the law of the People's Democracies are presumably based. A Polish *émigré*, Grzybowski, serving American propaganda aims, asserts that . . . a society of the "Soviet type" is in no position to function without the "elements of non-socialist law."[13] An American professor, Berman, who detected in Soviet law (!) a Byzantian and Mongolian legacy as well as the elements of Western law, declares that the Soviet legal system contains "in a general form the entire apparatus of concepts and institutions of the Western legal system."[14]

. . . . . . .

We shall now examine the role played by the theory of the "universality" of legal principles in the propaganda of the conception of a "leveling" of differences between the legal systems of "West and East." The gist of this theory is the view that the fundamental principles of any legal system have a universal, immutable character, independent of concrete sociopolitical conditions. The leading role among the proponents of the universality of legal principles belongs to representatives of the natural-law doctrine in bourgeois jurisprudence. However, theorists who are not natural-law proponents also make extensive use of the idea of cosmopolitan universality of fundamental legal principles.

The principal function of the natural-law doctrine has always been

[11] This view was originally developed by G. Jellinek . . . and expanded by an American theorist, S. Finer. . . . See G. Heckscher, *The Study of Comparative Government and Politics* (London, 1957), p. 34.

[12] A recently deceased West German legal theorist, H. Mitteis, compared the immutability of legal forms with the technical means of expression in art. See his *Die Rechtsidee in der Geschichte* (Weimar, 1957), p. 669.

[13] K. Grzybowski, "Continuity of Law in Eastern Europe," *The American Journal of Comparative Law,* Winter, 1957, p. 73.

[14] H. J. Berman, "The Comparison of Soviet and American Law," *Indiana Law Journal,* Vol. 34, No. 4 (1959), p. 563.

to justify the immutability and sacredness of the legal systems of the exploiting states. Under present-day conditions the specific tasks of the natural-law doctrine stand out quite distinctly: (1) the task of proving that the principles underlying the legal systems of "civilized nations" stem from a single source; and (2) the task of promoting the idea of a cosmopolitan "integration" of law into a single world system of law.

It is no accident that the most famous representatives of the natural-law doctrine, for example, Del Vecchio and Coing, are actively promoting the cosmopolitan "unity of the legal systems of civilized nations." . . . According to Coing, a West German Professor, "a true world system of law," as a system of the "civilized world," should not depend upon national codification; it should be based on suprapositive principles.[15] Del Vecchio, who two decades ago published a special work on the natural-law origin of general legal principles,[16] is at present engaged in a study of the role of natural-law sources in "coordinating organs and institutions" for the purpose of bringing about a "cosmopolitical unification."[17] Contemporary bourgeois legal theorists hope to utilize natural-law doctrines as a basis for creating a universal cosmopolitan theory of law. For example, Hall, an American professor, visualizes the possibility of transforming natural-law jurisprudence into a universal philosophy.[18]

Bourgeois legal theorists endeavor to prove the existence of general principles and institutions that presumably have universal validity. Consequently, they reject the class meaning of law and evaluate socialist law from the viewpoint of immutable, abstract categories. . . . While approaching Soviet law from the viewpoint of such universal, natural criteria, Hall hypocritically and demagogically raises the question: "Is it a law from the natural-law point of view?"[19] He finds "The communist philosophy of law . . . obviously irrational." Indeed, it would be naïve to expect that such a "rational" compass as natural-law philosophy (which is quite strongly diluted with the philosophy of pragmatism, behaviorism, semanticism, and neorealism in

[15] H. Coing, "Geschichte und Bedeutung des Systemgedankens in der Rechtswissenschaft," Österreichische Zeitschrift für Öffentliches Recht, No. 3 (1957), p. 269.

[16] G. Del Vecchio, "Les principes généraux du droit," Recueil d'études sur le source du droit (Paris, 1934).

[17] G. Del Vecchio, "Européisme et cosmopolitisme," Revue générale de droit internationale public, No. 2 (1957), pp. 208–9.

[18] Jerome Hall, "The Progress of American Jurisprudence," The Administration of Justice in Retrospect (Dallas, 1957), p. 38.

[19] Ibid., p. 39.

its American edition)[20] could lead him to any other appraisal of the Marxist materialist theory of state and law.

. . . Kiralfy, a lecturer at the University of London and the author of an article on the rule of law in "communist Europe," views legality and communism as two distinct phenomena between which an equilibrium can at times be established and at times disrupted: "If it is necessary for the Communists to choose between communism and legality, there is little doubt that legality will go by the board, but it is equally clear that they hope for an equilibrium between the two."[21]

. . . Concerning socialist legality, it is an integral element of socialist democracy, that is, an organic part of it. Legality represents one of the most significant instruments of the peoples' struggle for a revolutionary reconstruction of society. Socialist legality is one of the methods for state guidance, one of the levers for the construction of a communist society. Communists maintain that one of the indispensable conditions for the construction of a communist society is a strict observance of the laws that express the true will of the people.

. . . The lively interest displayed by Soviet legal theorists in the problem of legality is interpreted by some bourgeois jurists as a "promising" basis for the establishment of a "genuine *Rechtsstaat.*" Such a view was expressed by M. Rigin in *Ost Europa Recht* in his review of my book *The Crisis of Bourgeois Legality in Contemporary Imperialist States.*[22] Unfortunately, the nature of this article does not permit discussion of some additional questions raised by Rigin. But speaking of his "hope" for establishing a *Rechtsstaat* in the Soviet Union, we shall merely note that the bourgeois and socialist interpretations of the idea of a *Rechtsstaat* represent two diametrically opposed ideas in terms of their class content.

In the final analysis, the sociological conception of leveling the differences between social systems and the juridical theories of the evolution of socialist law reflect the hopes of the ideologists of the imperialist bourgeoisie that peaceful coexistence between states with distinct social systems will lead to ideological concessions on the part of the Communists.

Ideologists of the imperialist bourgeoisie who count on the "evolution" of the socialist political system do not even hide their hope that

[20] This applies especially to Jerome Hall's *Studies in Jurisprudence and Criminal Theory* (New York, 1958).

[21] A. Kiralfy, "The Rule of Law in Communist Europe," *The International and Comparative Law Quarterly,* Vol. 8 (July, 1959), Part III, p. 465.

[22] *Ost Europa Recht,* No. 2 (1959), p. 135.

peaceful coexistence will be a factor capable of exerting ideological pressure upon socialism. Ideologists of imperialism declare that the lessening of tension in international relations will provide an opportunity for "the forces of social pluralism to perforate the dogmatism of the Soviet social system."[23] These calculations on the part of the proponents of "creative coexistence" are based on the assumption that the policy of capitalist countries will influence the "evolution" in the Soviet Union. In another article, Schlesinger discusses the question of the degree to which "Western policy can promote such an evolution in the Soviet Union."[24] Such arguments demonstrate quite clearly the true class nature and the great political danger of the thesis on the inevitability of an "ideological truce."

The requirements of the class struggle arising in the period of transition from capitalism to socialism preclude the possibility of any concessions in the ideological sphere. A reconciliation of ideologies is as impossible as leveling the differences between social systems or "synthesizing" the legal systems of socialist and capitalist states.

[23]Arthur M. Schlesinger, Jr., "Chancen eines liberalen Kommunismus," *Der Monat,* February, 1960, pp. 51–52.

[24] *Harper's Magazine,* February, 1960, p. 76.

# A Repudiation of "Ethical Socialism"*

## ⤳ *I. Gorina*

The achievements of socialism arouse fury and spite on the part of its opponents. A united front of reaction does everything possible to slander socialist countries and to undermine the revolutionary spirit of the workers. Rendering assistance to the imperialist bourgeoisie are the renegades of the working movement—the leaders of right-socialism of all colors and shades. Among them not the least place belongs to the representatives of so-called ethical socialism.

Advocates of "ethical socialism" regard socialism not as the result of a law-governed development of society but as a realization of eternal, immutable, moral norms that are intrinsic in all men. Men presumably possess an inborn sense of equality, justice, and universal solidarity. These eternal qualities, being presumably an inalienable part of human nature, compel each individual to act in the name of humanity and social justice. From this quality inherent in all men, that is, from the tendency of man's will toward an ideal social organization, is deduced "ethical socialism."

The attempts to justify socialism by means of ethics are publicized as the last word of socialist thought. In fact, however, these attempts are not new. Just like the designation "ethical" socialism, most of the arguments on behalf of such a socialism are borrowed from neo-Kantians of the second half of the nineteenth century. Declaring Marxism to be merely an economic theory, the neo-Kantians proposed to combine Marx with Kant, to supplement Marx's economic theory with Kant's moral theory, to give Marxism an "emotional tint," and to save it from "one-sidedness."

This idea was caught up and developed by the pillars of opportunism: E. Bernstein, K. Kautsky, Austrian Marxists, "legal" Marxists, and by anyone who wanted to dilute revolutionary Marxism with sweet talk about good, truth, moral ideas, etc. . . . At the present time "ethical socialism" is widely advocated in France, England, the U.S.A., West Germany, and other capitalist countries. It constitutes an ideological weapon of Right-Socialists in their struggle against Marxism and the communist parties.

* *From* " 'Eticheskii Sotsializm' — Ideologicheskoe Oruzhie Reformizma" ["Ethical socialism" — An Ideological Weapon of Reformism], *Kommunist*, No. 18 (1960), pp. 76–84.

The barrenness of the ethical theory of socialism can be seen singularly in the fact that its point of departure is the rejection of the objective laws of history and, consequently, the rejection of the objective necessity of socialism. This thought stands out in all the newly adopted programs of the socialist parties of Austria, Switzerland, and West Germany. At the Vienna Congress of the Austrian Socialist party (May, 1958), where the new platform was discussed, its authors and defenders indicated that one of the positive aspects of the program is the absence of any ideas that would even remotely remind one of the historical necessity of socialism. A Socialist, Christian Broda, stated at the Congress: "A tremendous step forward since the Linz Program is the recognition that there is no necessity in history and that everything happening in the world is man's creation." The speeches of other participants of the Congress had the same meaning. The late Benedict Kautsky, the faithful guardian and expounder of his father's opportunist traditions, emphasized his special merits in developing new principles of socialism which presumably have forever put an end to the Marxist interpretation of socialism as a historical necessity.

Likewise, the Godesberg Program of the Social Democratic party of West Germany—which calls itself a party of "free spirit" and proclaims Christian ethics and classical philosophy as the ideological sources of its socialism—entirely rejects socialism as a system diametrically opposed to capitalism and as a historical necessity. The leaders of this party surrendered to Adenauer's policy.

The Right-Socialists see the true meaning of freedom in the rejection of objective historical necessity. To them, as to all subjectivists, freedom and necessity are mutually exclusive ideas. The recognition of objective necessity in the development of history is interpreted by them as fatalism; they depict their socialism as a society in which man's "good will" is considered a higher law of life. Such a position leads to the renunciation of socialism as a real socioeconomic system and turns the struggle for socialism into fruitless complaint about "moral evil," into a Platonic hope for the victory of "higher moral principles."

In attempting to divert the masses from the revolutionary struggle, Ethical Socialists, in addition to rejecting the law-governed, historically objective character of socialism, also reject the existence of classes and the class struggle under conditions of contemporary capitalism. Their moral program for the transformation of society is opposed to the Marxist theory of classes and class struggle. Such, for example, is the view of English Labourites. In 1956, a group of

Labourites, who had been advocating the idea of "moral socialism" for several years—Allen Flanders, Rita Hinden, and others—published a collection of essays under the title *Socialism of the Twentieth Century*. The main task of this book was to justify a kind of socialism which is attained without the class struggle and without dictatorship and which presumably stands above narrow class interests. The class struggle is removed as something vulgar and amoral.

Equipped with ethical phraseology, Right-Socialists contend that the contemporary capitalist world is classless; the social forces that would hinder the realization of socialism are presumably absent there. Furthermore, shamelessly and in disregard of obvious facts, some Right-Socialists cite the United States as an example of an "earthly paradise" without classes and class struggle. Thus, in 1950, a former leader of the French Socialist party, A. Philip, stated quite openly . . . that his "socialist ideal" is the American way of life.

. . . Right-Socialists explain and justify their rejection of the Marxist theory of classes and the historical role of the proletariat by the fact that the working class in most capitalist countries does not, and will not, constitute a majority of the population. Therefore, it is senseless to lean upon it in the struggle for socialism. But this argument misses the point. Marxism did and does assert that the power of the proletariat as a class lies not only in its growing numbers but chiefly in the position that it occupies in the system of capitalist production. It is well known, for example, that in Russia—the first country to have accomplished a socialist revolution—the proletariat did not constitute a majority. Neither did it constitute a majority in Greater China or in some other socialist countries. Nevertheless, it was precisely the working class of these countries which headed the victorious struggle for socialism; and it is precisely the working class of the capitalist countries which constitutes a fighting vanguard of all progressive movements.

The "obsolete" Marxist theory is replaced with another scheme of social differentiation. Attempts are made to demonstrate that classes, class struggle, contradictions between capital and labor, and exploitation are in the process of destroying themselves. For this purpose, a claim is advanced that socialism is not connected with the interests of any particular class. Furthermore, it is claimed that the class of entrepreneurs has disintegrated, that a new, independent middle class has come into being, that the proletariat has become differentiated into a great number of independent groups. The fundamental contradiction of bourgeois society, we are told, is the contradiction between various social groups. This contradiction is presumably connected not with capital but with the size of income and its mode of distribution.

The theoretical error of this conception lies in the fact that it ignores a very significant scientific criterion of defining class membership—one's relationship to the means of production, that is, a man's place in the system of social production. This conception is politically harmful because it leads to dispersion of the working class's power, slurs over the crucial contradictions between the proletariat and the bourgeoisie, and disarms the revolutionary movement.

Apostles of ethical socialism fail to bring the ends together when they speak about private property. They deny the existence of classes but defend the rule of private property. Since it is impossible to prove that, let us say, Rockefeller, Morgan, Du Pont, and others stand in the same relationship to the means of production as the proletariat and all workers, advocates of ethical socialism deny that there is any connection between the classes and private property and assert that the latter is not a hindrance but an asset to socialism. Agreeing with Leon Blum, a leader of the French Socialist party, Jean Tixier, wrote: "Socialism is something entirely different from the destruction of capitalist property."

In brief, socialism is a classless society in which private property rules. This is the most recent discovery of the Right-Socialists, who deem it their duty to serve the interests of the bourgeoisie!

Having finished with classes, advocates of ethical socialism turn to the question of world outlook. It makes no sense to speak about "class consciousness" in a society in which classes do not exist. The previously mentioned representative of ethical socialism, A. Philip, has taken some pains to prove that a "universal world outlook" of the proletariat, which would arouse in it hopes and excite it to struggle, cannot exist in contemporary bourgeois society.

The falsification is quite obvious. Indeed, at the present time, as a result of right- (ethical, democratic, etc.) socialism, the working class is split. A definite part of the workers still have faith in the leaders of social democracy. But from this it does not follow that a proletarian world outlook, based on an objective unity of the essential economic and political interests of the working class, is nonexistent. . . .

Thus, the originators and advocates of ethical socialism renounce socialism as an objective, historically determined social system. They advocate a socialism which, in the economic sphere, does not call for the abolition of private property, exploitation, and material inequality; which, in the political sphere, denies the existence of classes and class struggle in contemporary capitalist society; and which, in the philosophical sphere, rejects the need for any philosophical credo—any world outlook. These theoretically erroneous and politically harmful views are the starting point of additional falsifications of scientific socialism.

We are told that "socialism is an immutable moral ideal." Furthermore, "socialism is a political choice made in the name of a universal moral ideal that cannot be found in an analysis of social phenomena." While advancing their antiscientific, idealist interpretation of socialism—according to which socialism has no roots in real life, is connected neither with the past nor with the future, but represents a purely moral ideal—theorists of such socialism fail to answer the question of whose ideal their socialism is and upon whom it counts.

It is well known that a dream of a socialist system—based on justice, equality, and freedom—was engendered in ancient times. The history of socialist theories produced famous names of great utopians who courageously and fearlessly exposed the evils and vices connected with private property. In their writings they expressed the hopes and aspirations of the oppressed classes. Therefore, apart from its immaturity and chimerical character, their socialism constituted a progressive and highly moral phenomenon. But the true love of mankind and the moral meaning of socialism as a social system with its profound emancipating nature were uncovered in the theory of scientific socialism, the founders of which transformed the great dream of socialism into a science.

. . . . . . .

In the contemporary world two systems exist—socialist and capitalist—and if Ethical Socialists attack real socialism, they are defending capitalism. They fail to propose a concrete plan for the transformation of society. Their socialism cannot be translated into reality because it is devoid of an objective historical basis. It stands to reason that ethics, morality, and any other phenomenon of the spiritual life of society are in no position to become the foundation of a social system, for it itself depends upon the economic system of society—is conditioned by the latter. Socialist morality does not lead to socialism; on the contrary, a new socialist morality comes into being as a result of the victory of socialism. In addition, a system that would correspond at the same time to the moral ideals of antagonistic classes is inconceivable. A genuine, nonfictional socialism—one that corresponds to the moral ideas of the working class and all workers—is incompatible with the rule and morality of the bourgeoisie.

Therefore, ethical socialism is not common to all mankind, as is being claimed; it is a petty-bourgeois socialism. Disguised under slogans of "universal fraternity" and "justice," it defends the inviolability of the bourgeois relations of production.

. . . The Right-Socialists who appear under the banner of ethics have transformed socialism into an act of pure will, connected with neither the laws of history nor classes, confronting humanity as an eternal task of moral self-perfection. Like Kant—who relegated freedom and "good will" to the other world, which is inaccessible to man, to a world in which there is no causality and no necessity but only the realm of purpose—apostles of ethical socialism relegated the materialization of socialism to infinity and transformed it into an unattainable utopia. . . .

The problem of man, that is, the problem of "respect of human dignity," became converted by Right-Socialists into one of the fundamental principles of the ethical justification of socialism. But they are not concerned with a real historical man. They regard man as a being isolated from and independent of external conditions. In his conduct, man is guided exclusively by abstract moral laws. Since man himself prescribes his norms of conduct, he should not be viewed as a means but as an end. This is the essence of the "most recent" appraisal of man, asserting that, since man is a bearer of moral law, since he is a self-contained unit, he should be universally respected. It is true, of course, that man, person, people, should not be a means as they are under capitalism. However, the solution of this problem should not be sought in individualism but in the proletarian class solidarity. The defense of extreme individualism—to which bourgeois subjectivist sociology has always adhered—is presented by Ethical Socialists as a most recent conception of man and is being used in the struggle against Marxism, against socialist countries.

Thus, Benedict Kautsky . . . advanced, as a principal argument against Marxism, the principle of a "new" socialism, based on an ethical world outlook, with man as its cornerstone. The program of the Swiss Social Democratic party speaks about man as "an end of history and an end in himself." Such views are also expounded in other programs.

What is the meaning of these assertions? Is it not well known that it is precisely scientific socialism which serves man, which leads the class struggle in the name of man, freedom, and justice? The founders of ethical socialism purposely distort this question and seek to replace scientific socialism with pseudosocialism, truth with lies.

While advancing demands for man's freedom and autonomy, justice and equality, they have in mind not economic equality; not property equality; not an equal relationship to the means of production; not the emancipation of millions from misery, oppression, and exploitation; but merely a spiritual self-perfection of man. Therefore, the struggle for socialism is transferred from the material and political spheres into an illusory spiritual sphere. . . .

Supported by historical experience, Marxists think that social equality, that is, destruction of the classes, secures an unlimited development for each individual and creates a truly free society. Any other interpretation of this question is false and hypocritical. As stated by Lenin, "Freedom is a deception if it contradicts the interests of the emancipation of labor from the oppression of capital."[1]

Right-Socialists see the true humanist nature of socialism in the fact that it presumably offers people a free choice of the mode of consumption, place of work, etc. Under conditions of contemporary capitalist society, such a declaration seems to be bad irony. The Right-Socialists themselves leave no doubt concerning their understanding of freedom of choice. The program of the West German Social Democratic party . . . states: "Socialism struggles for a free market in which true competition rules always. . . . Free enterprising initiative and free competition are significant elements of the Social Democratic economic policy." But this quite frank statement of the socialist ideal concurs neither with the idea of socialism nor with the idea of man's freedom. Such "freedom" constitutes a paradise for capitalists. True socialism and man's true freedom are incompatible with "free competition." Socialism is moral only insofar as it is opposed to private property, which cultivates the spirit of personal profit, money-grubbing, and egotism. West German Socialists pass off capitalism for socialism while in fact renouncing the struggle for true socialism.

The problem of man as a higher end of history . . . is resolved by contemporary Ethical Socialists in the spirit of neo-Kantianism as well as in the spirit of existentialism. While expounding Kantian assumptions, they reduce the struggle for socialism to a struggle for the materialization of the eternal moral principles inherent in man. Similarly, existentialists substitute for the problem of social reconstruction the problem of an internal emancipation of man, that is, his moral perfection.

Repeating existentialist arguments, contemporary Ethical Socialists regard man as an isolated being, "free from society." "There is no

[1] *Sochineniya* [Works] (4th ed., Moscow), Vol. 29 (1950), p. 324.

determinism," they declare; "man is free, man is freedom." Such an interpretation of "freedom of will" constitutes a defense of bourgeois individualism, according to which each individual has his own morality, which is not subject to any social laws or rules.

In fact, however, such an isolated man and such a morality are nonexistent. Man is a social being, closely tied (in the past as well as in the present and future) to other men; those ties condition his conduct, his views, and his moral principles. "Even when I carry out *scientific*, etc., activity—activity that I can seldom conduct in direct association with other men—I perform a *social* act because I act as a *man*. It is not only the material of my activity which is given to me . . . , but *my own social existence is* a social activity. For this reason, what I myself produce, I produce for society with the consciousness of acting as a social being."[2]

Viewing man independent of historical and social conditions, Ethical Socialists assert that excepting good will—excepting man's moral will—there is nothing that can serve as a foundation of socialism. In attacking Marxism from these subjective-idealist positions, they accuse it of regarding man as a means instead of an end of history. In this respect Ethical Socialists are not original; they are merely reiterating bourgeois criticism of Marxism. For example, a contemporary critic of Marxism, Victor Antolin, declared that Marxism is incapable of resolving the problem of the relationship between personal and social interests. This Catholic theorist wants to drive a wedge between Marx and contemporary Marxists. In contrast to Marx, who thought that personal and social interests will blend together under communism, he contends that contemporary Marxists revise their theory and assert that under communism society will dominate the individual. In doing this, contemporary Marxists presumably give up the epoch of universal and final emancipation of man—the epoch of a complete unity of social and personal interests. Man becomes morally and spiritually impoverished. Marxism presumably ignores the spiritual nature of man and transforms him into an element of production.

Indeed, Marxism regards man as an "element of production." The workers are the most significant and decisive element of the production forces in any society, not only in a socialist one. The recognition of man's labor as an element of production neither diminishes his dignity nor restricts his freedom. Everything depends upon the question: "To whom does production belong and whom does it

[2] Karl Marx and Friedrich Engels, *Iz Rannikh Proizvedenii* [From Early Writings] (Moscow, 1956), p. 590.

serve?" Not participation in the production of material goods but "freedom" from production—that is, unemployment—is the plague of mankind under conditions of capitalism. That is what restricts freedom and oppresses and degrades man morally. . . .

From the Marxist point of view, the forces of production are in the final analysis the main basis of the historical process—of the entire progressive development of mankind. The recognition of the workers as a production force does not at all imply a reduction of the human personality to the role of an instrument of production. On the contrary, Marxists—Communists—regarded and do regard their principal task to be the emancipation of the workers from that degrading position into which they were placed by capitalism, where the workers are reduced to the position of the instruments of production, appendages to machines, a source for exploitation.

. . . Critics of Marx and communism distort the true communist conception of man, personality, and people. Marxists regarded and do regard man as a higher link of the universe—a higher flower of nature. Marxists fight for man's domination over things, machines, and nature, not for the domination of things, machines, instruments of production, and social relations over man. A true domination over nature is possible only when man becomes the master of his own social relations, that is, under conditions of socialism. Only under socialism does the workingman represent a higher value, and does the all-round development of man become a real and conscious goal and condition of historical progress.

Under conditions of capitalism a man's value depends upon his bank account, his wealth, the amount of money he has. Under conditions of socialism a man is valued by his abilities, gifts, talents, and his work for the good of society. Not even one world outlook, not even one society, has elevated man as high as has Marxism—socialism. No other society has oppressed, suppressed, and exploited man as mercilessly as has capitalism.

. . . Socialism establishes a direct tie between production and consumption. That which man gives to production, he gives in the interest of the entire society and of each man. The development of production here is dictated not by profit and personal gain but exclusively by the interests of the entire nation. Production is developed for the purpose of satisfying all the material and cultural needs of the workers.

. . . Communists, the faithful students and followers of Marxist-Leninist theory, are fully convinced that man's personal freedom is attained primarily through the creation of a high living standard for the whole nation, which calls for a persistent and gigantic effort on the part of all men. The communist parties and the governments of all socialist countries deem their principal task to be the development of all branches of industry. Such a development will become the foundation of the spiritual development of men—the foundation of their true freedom. Only under such conditions, "in place of the *wealth* and *poverty* of political economy, we have the *wealthy man* and the plentitude of *human need*. The wealthy man is at the same time one who *needs* a complex of human manifestations of life."[3]

Such a freedom and fullness of spiritual life is unattainable in a capitalist society, where there are whole armies of unemployed, where personal qualities and talents do not eliminate the threat of unemployment and poverty, where society stands vis-à-vis man as an elemental and hostile force, and where, finally, there exists an unresolvable conflict between personal and social interests and man's freedom is brutally suppressed.

[3] *Ibid.*, p. 596.

# The Idea of Historical Change and Progress*

## ⌀ I. S. Kon

Following the idealist philosophy and sociology, modern bourgeois historiography refrains from mentioning historical progress or evolution, and gives preference to a more "refined" idea of "social change." According to H. Barnes, a famous American sociologist, the idea of "change" is more precise than the idea of "progress," for it does not contain value elements and lends itself to factual verification. In his opinion, the question of whether certain changes are progressive or regressive always instigates controversy on the criterion of evaluation while such is not the case with the idea of "change." "Even the destruction of civilization through the technological facilities of the electronic age will be a social change, even if it is the last in the series."[1]

The repudiation by bourgeois science of the idea of progress is a reflection of its reactionary character. . . . In attempting to discredit historical optimism, which is characteristic of Marxism-Leninism, Rothacker asserts . . . that the idea of historical development is organically connected with the Christian eschatology and Messianism.

The ancient Greeks' world outlook, which was directed toward the cosmos, did not contain any hope for the future but rather an orientation toward the past. On the other hand, according to Rothacker, the biblical world outlook assumes that in the process of history God reveals himself to man and that this is the basis of the faith in ultimate salvation. Accepting the view of a German existentialist, K. Löwith, Rothacker asserts that Marxism-Leninism also constitutes an eschatology. Furthermore, while distorting Marxism-Leninism, Rothacker makes an attempt to identify the theory of communism with biblical myths and prognostications.[2]

There would be no need to refute this nonsense if it were not presented in the open discussion of an international congress. Indeed, the idea of progress was factually alien to ancient thinkers. But this was not due to the "cosmic" orientation of their world outlook; it was due to slow historical development. The political history of the ancient

* *From* "Burzhuaznaya Filosofiya Istorii v Tupike" [The Bourgeois Philosophy of History in an Impasse], *Voprosy Istorii*, No. 12 (1960), pp. 43–47.

[1] Harry E. Barnes, "Historical Sociology," *Readings in Contemporary American Sociology*, ed. Joseph S. Rouček (New York, 1958), p. 265.

[2] XIth congrés international des sciences historiques, Stockholm, August 21–28, 1960, *Rapports*, Vol. 1, p. 22.

world was saturated with exceptional drama: the changes of reign, the fall of empires, the appearance and disappearance of nations. All this had its influence. At that time the material basis of human existence remained relatively unchanged, and the cumulative character of the historical process remained unnoticed by its contemporaries. Naturally, the combination of the stormy changes in politics with the stability of the material basis of men's lives could not bring forth the idea of progress but rather produced skepticism and pessimism. Hence, the majority of ancient authors viewed history either as a regressive process, moving along a descending line from the ancient "Golden Age," or as a simple alternation of certain cycles. The idea of progress factually arose only in modern times, with the acceleration of social development, particularly with the development of science and technology. This is why during the Enlightenment the theories of progress were pervaded with vivid rationalism.

It is quite absurd to trace the idea of progress to Christian eschatology and even more absurd to see anything in common between the religious philosophy of history and Marxism. First of all, Christian eschatology is profoundly antihistorical. Engels indicated that Christians, "having manufactured a special 'history of God's kingdom,' deny that true history has any inner meaning and recognize only their own abstract, and in addition fabricated, history of the other world as meaningful. Asserting that mankind will attain fulfillment in Christ, they attribute to history an imaginary ultimate end, which presumably was achieved by Christ. They break history in midstream, and, therefore, if only for the sake of consistency, they should interpret the subsequent eighteen centuries as wild absurdity and complete insipidity."[3]

The "meaning of history" about which the religious philosophy of history speaks, the "order" that it finds in human actions, are theological concepts connected with the idea of the "divine rule" of history. In the words of the leader of modern Thomism, Jacques Maritain, "The forces of nature and culture are directed, illuminated, and supported by the trans-natural and trans-cultural forces" of divine grace.[4]

On the other hand, Marx's theory of history rejected once and for all everything transcendental and "non-historical." As though foreseeing an attack by modern "critics," who denounce Marx's "deification" of history as presumably being a replacement of the old God, Engels wrote:

[3] Marx and Engels, *Sochineniya* [Works] (2nd ed.; Moscow, 1955), Vol. 1, p. 592.
[4] C. Journet, "D'une philosophie chretiénne de l'histoire et de la culture," *Jacques Maritain: Son œuvre philosophique* (Paris, 1949), p. 42.

*History* does nothing; it "does *not* possess immense riches," it "does not fight battles." It is *men*, real, living men, who do all this, who possess things and fight battles. It is not "history" which uses men as a means of achieving—as if it were an individual person—*its* own ends. History is *nothing* but the activity of men in pursuit of their ends.[5]

The religious philosophy of history looks pessimistically upon real history and connects "salvation" with its termination. As stated by N. Berdaev, whose writings are popular in the West at present, "He who believes in eternal life should treat terrestrial life soberly and should know that it is impossible during this life to overcome the dark, irrational forces and that suffering, evil, and imperfection are inevitable in this life."[6] Maritain joins Berdaev in asserting that the ideal "Christian freedom" will be attained "only after the completion of human history" and that "it will arise neither from history nor from the world, but from the Living God."[7] On the other hand, according to the Marxist-Leninist theory, the communist system comes into being in conformity with objective laws as a result of historical development and the struggle of the working masses. Furthermore, the communist system does not constitute the "end" of development and the end of history; on the contrary, according to Marx, it is the beginning of true human history freed from the yoke of exploitation. Finally, the communist system is not an abstract, ethical ideal but a real, historical movement. We have already built up socialism and have entered the period of the large-scale construction of communism. It is not a dream but the real life of hundreds of millions of people. . . .

The idea of progress, which Rothacker considers to be dead, expresses not only the historically substantiated optimism of the communist movement but also a deep, scientific meaning. It is only meaningless and antihistorical when interpreted idealistically or metaphysically. If the historical process is viewed from the idealist viewpoint as a process of the self-development of the spirit or as a simple aggregate of individual actions, then it is in fact difficult to find an objective criterion for the evaluation of events and changes. Thus the problem of progress can be raised only on the moral, ethical plane: Is man improving himself and feeling happier in the course of history? No simple answer can be given to this question, for in the process of historical development humanity is constantly confronted with new tasks, and it is ridiculous, therefore, to search in history for complacency. The criterion of historical progress should be sought in

[5] Marx and Engels, *Sochineniya*, Vol. 2, p. 102.
[6] *Smysl Istorii* [The Meaning of History] (Berlin, 1923), p. 121.
[7] *Scholasticism and Politics* (New York, 1941), pp. 140, 248.

the sphere where fundamental laws of social life come to light. Such a sphere is that of material production. Lenin viewed the development of the forces of production as the most reliable criterion of the historical process.[8]

Naturally, material production is not the sole criterion. Historical process unfolds unevenly, contradictorily, and the rate of development of the diverse spheres and aspects of social life is far from being the same. The determination of the historical role of a phenomenon necessarily calls for a concrete analysis of the class structure in an existing formation, the level of its development, the role played by the classes at each historical stage, etc. The Marxist-Leninist principle of historicism requires an examination of any phenomenon of the past or present—first, in its ascent, development, and change; second, in its relationship with other phenomenona and conditions at the given stage; third, in its relationship with the concrete experience of history which permits the establishment not only of the immediate, but also of the remote, effects of the investigated process or phenomenon. This principle finds its expression in the concept of a socioeconomic formation in its application to world history.

The socioeconomic formation is a historically determined stage in the development of society; its basis is the mode of production characteristic only of this stage.[9] The concept of the socioeconomic formation generalizes the specific features that distinguish one historical epoch and one social organism from all others. At the same time, it establishes the features held in common by various countries undergoing the same stage of social development. At the same time, the idea of formation encompasses the specificity of the fundamental periods of world history and serves as a criterion of the repetitiousness of significant historical phenomena. Each antagonistic formation represents a definite cycle in the development of society; it undergoes periods of inception, development, decline, and death. At the same time, the rotation of socioeconomic formations is not a simple circular rotation but a progressive movement. Marx wrote: "The country that is more developed industrially only shows to the less developed the image of its future."[10]

The theory of the rotation of socioeconomic formations, which lies at the foundation of the Marxist-Leninist periodization of world history, is not an abstract scheme under which historical facts are subsumed. It is a general theory of historical process. But individual nations in their historical development can escape some antagonistic

[8] *Sochineniya* [Works], Vol. 13 (1947), p. 219; Vol. 32 (1950), p. 212.

[9] For details see G. E. Glezerman, *O Zakonakh Obshchestvennogo Razvitiya* [On the Laws of Social Development] (Moscow, 1960), pp. 116ff.

[10] *Kapital* [Capital] (Moscow, 1955), Vol. 1, p. 4.

formations. In addition, historians face the complex problem of combining the general historical periodization with the periodization of the history of the diverse aspects of social life—political forms, art, philosophy, etc. In their works dealing with both "world history" and specific studies, Marxist historians, guided by the Marxist-Leninist theory, resolve these problems by proceeding from the specificity of the phenomenon or period under study. . . .[11]

What is the attitude of the bourgeois historians who do not recognize the progressiveness of the historical process? They break up the historical process into multiple independent, self-contained cycles, "cultures" (Spengler), "civilizations" (Toynbee), or, to use Rothacker's expression, "styles of life." . . .

The meaning of any historical event or phenomenon is immanently contradictory. Some of its aspects are directed toward the past and express the inertia of the historical process whereas others constitute an embryo, a trend, a possibility for the future. Whether the historian wants to or not, he cannot escape this fact. However, if he sees in history nothing but "changes," and does not understand their character, he inevitably arrives at absolute relativism with all its implications.

Such is the irony of history. Like Dilthey, Rothacker claims to be against relativism. He asserts frequently that "nothing is further from a true historicism of the German historical school than 'destructive' relativism," that his concept is a "pluralist and not a sceptical" one.[12] He disavows the "one-sided and narrow" concept of the tasks of history characteristic of presentism.[13] But his postulates inevitably give rise to an insoluable contradiction. Rothacker admits that the interest in historical and social problems has, in general, a prescientific, practical origin and that it is determined by the necessities of historical life. But if objective progressiveness is not a part of historical reality, if each new "present" is not genetically higher than those preceding it, then the historical perspective he offers is inevitably relative, and the rewriting of history by each new generation adds nothing to the knowledge of truth. Then each generation and each historian has an inalienable right to his own image of the historical past, and history itself is then based on an "article of faith," as was contended by C. Beard and H. Marrou. Such a conclusion is unavoidable.

[11] See, for example, N. I. Konrad, " 'Srednye Veka' v Istoricheskoi Literature" ["The Middle Ages" in Historical Literature], *Iz Istorii Sotsialno-Politicheskikh Idei* [From the History of Sociopolitical Ideas] (Moscow, 1956), pp. 75–96.

[12] *Logik und Systematik der Geisteswissenschaften* (Bonn, 1948), pp. 149, 150.

[13] *Rapports*, Vol. 1, pp. 12–13, 23.

# A Soviet View of "Pluralist Democracy"*

## ⟋ *V. E. Guliev*

The development of state-monopolist capitalism, the intensification of its socioeconomic and political contradictions, the intensification of the state's interference in social life, and, consequently, the augmentation of the exploiting and reactionary role of the imperialist state which represents and expresses the omnipotence of the monopolist bourgeoisie, compels apologists of capitalism to devise theories that aim at disguising the true class nature and antiproletarian attitude of the bourgeois state. There is an obvious tendency in Western "political science" to present the state power of the capitalist class as collective power, shared by a great number of both bourgeois and workers' social organizations. There is another purpose to this: to convince the labor movements that workers' organizations (trade-unions, syndicates, etc.) are already participating in the administration of social affairs and that, consequently, they have, in principle, attained their ideal; what now remains is merely the proper coordination of the efforts of all social associations and the adjustment of their collaboration.

. . . . . . .

Such ideas are encountered in works representing various trends and schools of contemporary bourgeois and social-reformist political and legal thought and are advanced under the fashionable name of "pluralist democracy." The aim of this article is to elucidate some of the fundamental aspects of the indicated views, to discover their ideological class roots, and to reveal their complete scientific worthlessness.

The meaning of the idea of "pluralist democracy" is as follows. Contemporary society (i.e., capitalist society in the period of imperialism) represents a conglomeration of "social strata," or "layers," that unite individuals of similar material position, profession, type of occupation, age, religious conviction, place of living, etc. The interests of each "stratum" are opposed to the interests of other "strata," and, consequently, the entire society appears as a jumble of the clashing interests of various social collectives. It is precisely as a

* *From* "Nesostoyatelnost Burzhuaznykh Idei o 'Pluralisticheskoi Demokratii'" [The Worthlessness of Bourgeois Ideas of "Pluralist Democracy"], *Sovetskoe Gosudarstvo i Pravo,* No. 8 (1961), pp. 83–94.

result of the clash and subsequent reconciliation of various interests that "social welfare" is achieved and "social interest" maintained.

According to the theory under discussion, numerous social organizations ("pressure groups," "interest groups"), which comprise all members of society and represent their group interests, are created for the purpose of formulating, expressing, and carrying out sociogroup interests. There is no agreement among theorists of "pluralist democracy" concerning the standards to be used in determining what constitutes an "interest group." . . . A Swedish professor, G. Heckscher, discusses the history, composition, and activity of the following organizations functioning in Sweden: professional unions of industrial workers, associations of manufacturers, professional unions of white collar workers, cooperative associations of farmers, associations of "free churches," temperance league, cultural, and sport associations.[1] An English professor, S. Finer, enumerates a different set . . . of "interest groups," namely, employers unions, big trade-unions ("the big six"), cooperative movements, unions of persons from "free" professions, "civil organizations" (unions of government employees), organizations of specific layers of the population (war invalids, pensioners, and . . . bicyclists!?), church, evangelical, and other religious associations, cultural societies (among them, societies for the purpose of amusement and leisure).[2]

It is indicative that Heckscher and Finer, as well as a majority of other theorists of "pluralist democracy," do not include political parties in the category of "interest groups." Heckscher, for example, fails entirely to analyze the activity of parties in his work.[3] In Finer's opinion, political parties are merely instruments in the hands of various "pressure groups" that control and direct the activity of parties or, when necessary, exert pressure upon them.[4] At an international conference of scientists . . . engaged in a study of the activity of "interest groups" (U.S.A., fall, 1957), the opinion was stated that these groups, "perhaps even to a greater degree than parties, at the present time represent a central phenomenon" in sociopolitical life.[5]

Heckscher regards the activity of "interest groups" as being deci-

---

[1] "Pluralist Democracy: Swedish Experience," *Social Research,* Vol. 15, No. 4 (1948), pp. 417–61.

[2] *Anonymous Empire: A Study of the Lobby in Great Britain* (London, 1958).

[3] At times he mentions Social-Democratic and Communist parties but does not include them in the circle of "democratic associations" that are the objects of his study.

[4] *Anonymous Empire,* p. 23.

[5] H. Ehrman (ed.), *Interest Groups on Four Continents* (Pittsburgh, 1958), p. 231.

sive in determining the political physiognomy of society and the
character of social relationships within it.[6] Finer describes "groups"
as being "so ubiquitous and so numerous that they are common-
place," and "their day to day activities pervade every sphere of
domestic policy. . . . They are an empire—but an anonymous empire."[7] Their activity in England is "a tremendous factor; they
pervade the whole of British political life."[8]

. . . . . . .

Theorists of "pluralist democracy" dwell primarily on that activity
of "interest groups" which aims at achieving goals by exerting influence upon the various links in the state apparatus, mainly upon
parliament and the government. . . . Voluminous works are devoted
to a theoretical justification of the methods and forms of such influence and pressures.[9]

Other theorists pay more attention to questions dealing with the
activity of "groups" outside and apart from the state apparatus—
activities that involve negotiations with "competing" groups or the
exertion of pressure upon them. The state appears here merely as
an arbiter in cases of particularly strong conflict between "groups"
with diametrically opposed interests. Representatives of the former
and prevalent trend are, for example, Ehrman, Finer, and many
others.[10] The latter and less popular trend is represented by
Heckscher.

It is not difficult to comprehend the causes responsible for the
appearance of these two principal trends in the theory under discussion. The differences in evaluating the main forms of activity of
"interest groups" flow, naturally, from the difference in opinions
on the role of the contemporary imperialist state—of its apparatus.
Authors who favor intensification of the state's interference in the
sphere of socioeconomic and political relations, . . . that is, who
adopt the conception of the "maximal state," see the key to the success of "pressure groups" primarily in their exertion of pressure on
the proper state organs. On the other hand, authors who adhere to a
"neoliberal" trend, that is, who are in favor of restricting the state's
authority in socioeconomic life, set their hopes essentially on the in-

[6] "Pluralist Democracy: Swedish Experience."
[7] *Anonymous Empire*, p. 17.        [8] *Ibid.*, p. 94.
[9] In the Soviet literature on this question see the following: P. Romashkin,
"O Formakh i Metodakh Podchineniya Monopoliyam Gosudarstvennogo
Apparata Kapitalisticheskikh Stran" [Forms and Methods for Subordinating the
State Apparatus to Monopolies in Capitalist Countries], *Kommunist*, No. 9
(1958); A. Arzumanyan, "Lenin i Gosudarstvenno-Monopolisticheskii Kapital-
ism" [Lenin and State-Monopolist Capitalism], *Kommunist*, No. 7 (1960).
[10] Ehrman (ed.), *Interest Groups*.

dependent activity of "interest groups." However, they are not opposed to the state's intervention in the struggle against "subversive activities" on the part of progressive organizations. . . .

. . . . . . .

According to proponents of this view, in the sphere of the relationships between the "groups," the state can assume one of two functions: either that of an arbiter, coordinating and conciliating the interests and demands of diametrically opposed social organizations; or that of an organ sustaining social order and security, that is, an organ defending "the interests of society as a whole."

It may seem that these views fully coincide with those of "classical liberalism" and the "state's non-interference" school. Apart from the fact that the actual position and role of the bourgeois state has substantially changed in the era of imperialism, it should be noted that the contemporary views of theorists of "moderate state interference" differ considerably from the views and ideas of their predecessors. Whereas in the period of industrial capitalism and free competition bourgeois liberals stood for the state's non-interference, at the present time, Heckscher and others like him prefer "limited interference." Previously the state occasionally arbitrated the relations between labor and capital. Now the creation of permanent state organs for arbitrating the "conflicts" between labor and capital is being extolled.

The hypocrisy of nineteenth-century liberals did not, as a rule, go beyond the assertion that the state protects equally the interests of the hired workers and entrepreneurs. Today the state is openly praised as an organ that protects mainly the interests of the working class. . . .

The myth about "pluralist democracy" did not develop in a vacuum. Even a cursory familiarity with earlier bourgeois conceptions of state and law gives reason to conclude that their underlying assumptions appeared during the period of capitalism's transition to the imperialist stage of its development.

The basic ideas underlying the division of state sovereignty among numerous social associations were stated in the works of Leon Duguit, who promoted the view of state as "an institution of institutions" and spoke about the materialization of sovereignty "fully shared" by social institutions.[11] Similar ideas were advanced by Morris Hauriou, the founder of the theory of institutionalism. In his

[11] *Sotsialnoe Pravo, Individualnoe Pravo, i Preobrazovanie Gosudarsva* [Social Law, Individual Law, and the Transformation of the State] (Moscow, 1909), pp. 34–38.

558 SOVIET POLITICAL THOUGHT

opinion, the main requisite for a "stable" society (that is, a capitalist society) is a "balance" among the various institutions, including church and labor unions. Among other "institutions," Hauriou lists corporations, "which possess internal freedom that permits them to pursue their own goals and to exercise their functions. . . ."[12] While speaking of labor unions, and even recognizing their "economic sovereignty," Hauriou at the same time . . . calls on workers and their associations to exercise "moral discipline and self-restraint."[13]

"Institutionalist" views were further developed by a French jurist, G. Renard. Advancing the dogmatic slogan "freedom through organization,"[14] Renard claimed to be a proponent of socialism, the embryo of which, in his opinion, is engendered in the womb of capitalism in the form of various economic, political, and cultural social associations comprising representatives of all classes and social groups.[15]

One cannot fail to notice a definite affinity between "institutionalism" and Laski's right-socialist views on the political organization of capitalist society. According to his "pluralist conception," the capitalist state shares power with the social organizations of the workers, primarily with labor unions. Laski places the group interests of workers in various labor unions above their class interests.[16] He thinks that the collective efforts of the workers, united along professional lines, are changing capitalist society[17] and signify "a revolution of professions against the standards of capitalist democracy."[18] The activity of social organizations that presumably share power with the state in capitalist society, according to Laski, is precisely the path that leads toward overcoming the crisis of bourgeois democracy.[19]

Laski's successor, who developed further his "pluralist conception," is John Strachey—a theorist of contemporary laborism. Strachey seeks to prove that a "diffusion of power" among all classes and their organizations is taking place in capitalist society. In his opinion, the contemporary imperialist state became transformed into a "state of universal welfare." One of the decisive causes of this transformation was the "balancing influence" exerted upon the state by the monopolies, on the one hand, and by the trade-unions

[12] *Osnovy Publichnogo Prava* [Les principes du droit public] (orig. pub. 1910, n.p.; Moscow, 1929), p. 114.
[13] *Idea Dyugi* [Duguit's Idea] (Yaroslavl, 1914), p. 24.
[14] *Mysli o Budushchem* [Thoughts on the Future] (orig. pub. Paris[?], n.d.; Moscow, 1906), p. 29; French title not available.
[15] *Sotsialisticheskii Stroi* [Le régime socialiste] (orig. pub. Paris, 1898; Petersburg, 1906), p. 57.
[16] *Democracy in Crisis* (London, 1933), pp. 60–61.
[17] *Ibid.,* pp. 200–1.    [18] *Ibid.,* p. 60.    [19] *Ibid.,* pp. 60, 206.

and farmers' organizations, on the other hand. The feature that differentiates Strachey's position from that of Finer, Heckscher, and other bourgeois authors, is a formal one: Strachey lists a smaller number of organizations that presumably make the realization of the notorious "pluralist democracy" possible.[20]

It is imperative to compare the theory of pluralist democracy with the true picture of the political organization of capitalist society. This political organization represents, on the one hand, a system of the class dictatorship of the bourgeoisie and, on the other hand, a system of the class resistence of the working class and some nonproletarian layers of the population against the rule of the capitalists (and in many countries landowners). To be sure, life is more complex and more contradictory than this scheme. Its complexity and contradictoriness is due to, first, the presence of the so-called middle strata, whose organizations apparently occupy an "independent" position. Second, individual state organs (usually representative institutions) include, in part, representatives of the working classes. Finally, the bourgeoisie, seeking to expand the social basis of its rule, draws to its side individual layers of the workers (the labor aristocracy, the trade-union bureaucracy, civil servants, and others) and through them exerts decisive influence upon some social organizations of workers. Such organizations, being under the pressure of a hostile influence, become pseudoproletarian.

All these circumstances create an appearance of popular sovereignty, give rise to belief in the supraclass character of the bourgeois state and other illusions that are zealously propagated by bourgeois politicians and theorists of "pluralist democracy." In reality, political power belongs to the economically dominant class—the bourgeoisie—which rules society by utilizing two types of organization: bourgeois and pseudoproletarian, the latter being in fact also bourgeois but including some categories of workers and civil servants.

The bourgeois organizations are primarily associations of manufacturers, bourgeois political parties,[21] and the state. The entire sys-

[20] *Contemporary Capitalism* (London, 1956). A critique of this work is presented in V. I. Gantman's article, "Novyi Variant Reformistskoi Teorii Burzhuaznogo Gosudarstva" [A New Variant of the Reformist Theory of Bourgeois State], *Sovetskoe Gosudarstvo i Pravo*, No. 7 (1958). Strachey returns once again to the problem of the relationship between bourgeois democracy and social organizations in his *The End of Empire* (London, 1959), pp. 101–11.

[21] In terms of their composition these parties are not purely bourgeois; at times they encompass a fairly good number of proletarians and semiproletarians, but in terms of their aims and place in the system of the bourgeois dictatorship they are "thoroughly bourgeois"; the right-socialist parties are also numbered among them.

tem of bourgeois power is directed by the national associations of manufacturers through their main levers of political power, the bourgeois parties, which in turn direct the state apparatus.

These associations guide the activity of the state apparatus mainly through bourgeois political parties; but they also provide direct guidance (bypassing parties) through their representatives in the state apparatus, through lobbyists and other media.[22] It stands to reason that no "pressure group" can compete with the all-powerful associations of capitalists who wield economic and political power. The activity of these associations proceeds under conditions of strict secrecy, causing irritation and opposition even on the part of some bourgeois politicians and theorists.[23] Capitalist organizations, especially the associations of big business, employ a special staff of workers to maintain a liaison with the government; they possess special knowledge of domestic and international events and do not hesitate to use any methods for the attainment of their goals, including blackmail, bribery, etc.[24]

Speaking of the role of bourgeois political parties in the system of capitalist dictatorship, it is necessary to note that, as pointed out earlier, the majority of "pressure group" theorists does not include parties as one of these groups. Moreover, these theorists seek either to disregard or to distort the position and significance of parties. An explanation for this can be found in the very role played by bourgeois political parties as direct instruments of capitalist associations[25] vis-à-vis the state apparatus. While distorting the true state of affairs, some Western scientists contend that parties themselves are under the pressure of "interest groups." In fact, the parties—with their alluring demagogical slogans aimed at attracting voters and with their internal discipline also binding upon the deputies who vote in parliaments in conformity with the directives of their party leaders—constitute a significant and handy instrument in the hands of the bourgeoisie, primarily of its monopolistic factions. Indeed, some bourgeois parties express the group interests of the various factions of the capitalist class,[26] but to the proletariat and to the workers they represent a power that is hostile and opposed to proletarian organizations.

An unseemly role is being played by the leading centers of right-

[22] See Ehrman (ed.), *Interest Groups*, pp. 100, 101, 118–20, 125.
[23] See Finer, *Anonymous Empire*, p. 133; he writes that secrecy constitutes a "parody on democracy and a genuine plot against democracy."
[24] *Ibid.*
[25] See R. Titmus, *The Irresponsible Society* (London, 1960).
[26] See W. Schaber, *USA — Koloss im Wandel: Ein Amerika-Bericht* (Darmstadt, 1958), p. 31.

socialist parties. The purpose of this link in the bourgeois dictatorship is to deceive separate layers of the proletariat and workers and
to compel them to follow either the bourgeois policy or one that
pleases the bourgeoisie. At times the schismatic official policy of the
right-socialist parties is explained as the result of the venality of the
leaders of these parties. But, without for a second excusing the
traitors of the working class's cause, one should bear in mind that,
"however strange these words may sound, in a capitalist society the
working class can carry on a bourgeois policy when it forgets about
its goal of emancipation, when it reconciles itself to hired servitude
and becomes absorbed in collaboration with one or another bourgeois party for the sake of a seeming 'improvement' of its slavish
position."[27]

Lenin's thought offers the key to understanding the position of
the leading organs of rightist labor unions, which constitute what we
have previously designated as pseudoproletarian organizations in
the system of the bourgeois dictatorship. The position of these labor
unions is quite contradictory. On the one hand, under the direction of their yellow leaders they pursue a probourgeois policy of deceiving the workers; on the other hand, the objective course of events
pushes even the most rightist labor unions into an economic struggle
with capital. Therefore, insofar as they politically represent essentially probourgeois organizations hostile to the unions that are members of the International Federation of Trade Unions, they are an indirect (and at times a direct) instrument in the hands of the capitalists and their state. In this sense Sidney and Beatrice Webb . . . were
quite right in calling the yellow trade-unions "a part of the social
machine" of the bourgeoisie.[28]

However, if these labor-union associations organize strikes and
the picketing of enterprises and demand improvement of working
conditions, etc., they then objectively . . . express the interests of
the proletariat and receive support and approval from the leftist labor
unions and communist and workers' parties.[29]

Events demonstrate that a growing process of the emancipation of
the proletariat from the influence of the "bourgeois-ized" labor aristocracy and the rightist labor unionist leaders is taking place. This
arouses fear on the part of capitalists, who, consequently, adopt

[27] V. I. Lenin, *Sochineniya* [Works] (4th ed., Moscow), Vol. 36 (n.d.), p. 179.
[28] Quoted in *Marxism Today*, Vol. 4, No. 1 (1960), p. 1.
[29] The bourgeoisie, for its part, extols the schismatic activity of the rightist
labor unions. . . . See N. Chamberlain, *Labor* (New York, 1958), p. 41; M.
Vincent and J. Mayers, *New Foundation of Industrial Sociology* (Princeton,
1959), p. 279. . . . On the growth and activization of the working movement
. . . , see R. Roberts, *National Wages Policy in War and Peace* (London, 1958),
p. 176.

antilabor laws and intensify legal and illegal repressive measures against the labor unions that are opposed to rampant monopoly capital and the arbitrariness of the imperialist state.

The above shows how hypocritical and false are the contentions of contemporary followers of "institutionalism" (such as preachers of "pluralist democracy") that the labor unions share power with the state—possessing part of its sovereignty or at least exerting upon the government, parliament, and other links of the imperialist state apparatus the same influence as the associations of the capitalists. . . .[30]

Indeed, the working class movement organized in trade-unions is able to wrench numerous concessions from the ruling bourgeoisie and its state. But these concessions . . . do not mean that the proletariat has any share in state power.

If such is the case with the "power" of the labor union, then the profuse talk about the "power" of cooperative associations, about the "sharing of sovereignty" between the state and the farmers organizations, between the state and the cultural societies, etc., is a thin, pitiful lie. All of these and similar associations either represent subsidiary levers of the dictatorship of the bourgeoisie or join the workers' and democratic movements, thus becoming targets of attack on the part of official authorities and diverse reactionary organizations like the Ku Klux Klan, "white citizens' committees," etc.

The attitude of the theorists of "pluralist democracy" is extremely negative toward the activity of the communist and workers' parties, leftist labor unions, unions of the communist youth, and other organizations that do not enter into the system of the dictatorship of the bourgeoisie and are directly opposed to it. These organizations represent significant component parts of the political organization of society in the period of transition from capitalism to communism. Being the kernel, the vanguard, of those forces that sooner or later will liquidate bourgeois dictatorship and break up its state machinery, the proletarian and in part semiproletarian organizations constitute an embryo that will develop into a system of the dictatorship of the working class the day after the socialist revolution.

Realizing this, the bourgeoisie . . . persecutes and even drives the communist parties and their subsidiary organizations underground. . . . The faithful myrmidons of reaction devise theories that seek to justify the persecution of progressive social organization by the ruling circles. An American professor of political science, Horn, seeks to

---

[30] By means of such lies bourgeois professors seek to justify an illegal application of the "antitrust laws" against the labor unions. . . . See W. Leiserson, *The American Trade Union Democracy* (New York, 1959).

convince his readers that the government of the United States is both under an obligation and has the right to take preventive measures against the harm brought to "society and its institutions" by the so-called subversive organizations. By "subversive organizations" Horn has in mind the Communist party of the United States and other democratic organizations.[31]

The most powerful and most effective instrument of bourgeois class rule is the capitalist state, whose role within the mechanism of bourgeois dictatorship is not diminishing (as is contended by some proponents of "pluralist democracy") but, on the contrary, is constantly growing. A number of factors are responsible for this growth. First, with the development of state-monopoly capitalism (a process visible in all imperialist countries), the state's interference in the economy increases, mainly in the interest of large monopoly capital. Second, the aggravation of the class struggle in the capitalist world gives rise to the intensified activity of the imperialist state in the politicoideological domain as a means of suppression and deceit of the workers. Third, the imperialist state—its military, intelligence, diplomatic, and propaganda apparatuses—serves as the principal instrument of the imperialist bourgeoisie in its struggle against the world socialist system and against the national liberation movements of colonial peoples and independent countries.

The subordination of imperialist state apparatus to monopolies[32] strengthens its antiproletarian tendency. The songs of the preachers of "pluralist democracy" sound especially false when the voices of monopolists and leading state employees burst into their dissonant chorus, demanding the complete subordination of the state apparatus to big business. For example, objecting to suggestions not to tie business with politics, C. Randall, a big American entrepreneur and a former special assistant to the President of the United States, has declared that, in his opinion, one should not separate the problems of business from governmental policy—"they should be decided jointly and by one and the same person."[33] This is quite an admission!

In view of the above, the theory of "pluralist democracy"—asserting that a "division of the state's sovereignty" between the state and various "interest groups" is taking place—seems to be worthless at its very basis. . . .

[31] A. Horn, *The Group and the Constitution* (Stanford, Calif., 1956).
[32] On the control of American monopolies over the government of the United States, Congress, and diplomatic and propaganda apparatuses, see I. Joesten, *Öl regiert die Welt: Geschäft und Politik* (Düsseldorf, 1958).
[33] *The Communist Challenge to American Business* (Boston, 1959), p. 198.

# A Critique of Western Ethical Relativism*

## ౪ *K. A. Shvartsman*

No other trend in contemporary bourgeois philosophy expresses its nihilistic attitude toward a scientific solution of ethical problems more openly than neopositivism.

. . . . . . .

Representatives of neopositivism assert that different people, groups, and classes in society evaluate the same facts differently. But they refuse to define the character of these evaluations and to explain which of them are true and which are false. Ayer and Carnap think that it is impossible even to raise the question of truth and falsity, of justice and injustice, of moral evaluations, and of norms. They contend that moral evaluations "have no source of truth, natural or supernatural, from which they can be deduced."[1] Neo-Positivists assert that it is impossible to determine either the validity of moral positions or the validity of the evaluation in which these positions are reflected, for we do not possess the satisfactory criteria for the solution of these questions. This, in their opinion, is the basic difference between moral norms and scientific laws.

Ayer has quite rightly noted the fact, established long ago by Marxist ethics, that it is impossible to determine the truth of a moral evaluation if we use as a criterion purely subjective factors (personal approval, personal utility, etc.). . . .

. . . . . . .

In essence, Ayer has demonstrated that subjective criteria used in evaluating ethical judgments lead toward relativism in the field of morality.

But it would be wrong to assume that Ayer is interested in furnishing an objective criterion for the evaluation of ethical judgments. The proof of the invalidity of the criterion advanced by subjective ethics is utilized by Ayer as an argument in support of his

* *From* "Neopozitivizm Unichtozhaet Etiku" [Neopositivism Destroys Ethics], *Voprosy Filosofii*, No. 1 (1961), pp. 64–75.
[1] A. J. Ayer, "The Claims of Philosophy," *Reflection on Our Age* (London, 1949), p. 63.

thesis that ethical judgments are devoid of scientific meaning. He goes even further than subjectivists, than the ethical systems criticized by him. Thus, fully agreeing with subjective ethics that an objective criterion for an analysis of moral evaluations is impossible, he severely criticizes subjective ethics for its recognition of the possibility of true and false ethical judgments. In Ayer's opinion, "The whole dispute about the objectivity of values, as it is ordinarily conducted, is pointless and idle."[2]

Is it really so? An analysis of moral views and feelings, norms of conduct, and mores that existed at various stages and were entertained by different classes convinces us that these views, feelings, etc., express objective social relationships existing independent of the will and consciousness of men. Moral views, norms, etc., either correspond to the objective necessities of social progress (i.e., express the interests of the progressive social forces) or they do not correspond to them (i.e., they express the necessities of the forces that are opposed to social progress). In the former case they are true and in the latter they are false. Precisely the task of ethics as a science of morality is to grasp the objective foundation of moral norms and evaluations and to show, in terms of the necessities of social progress, which class is the incarnation of the moral truth of the epoch. In our time, morality is inseparable from the struggle for peace, for the emancipation of humanity from exploitation, from wars, from any type of suppression; it is inseparable from the struggle for conditions that will secure the all-round development of man and that will emancipate his consciousness from the habits and prejudices of a private proprietor. Such a struggle is being conducted by millions; this struggle is in conformity with historical necessity, with social progress. By means of this objective criterion we are able to determine what is just and unjust in the contemporary world. The activities that are conducive to the materialization of the matured historical necessity and that serve social progress are truly moral and just. On the other hand, the activities that hinder progressive social development are immoral and unjust.

If ethics deduces moral norms not from life, not from history, but from a non-historical source, then it naturally does not contain even a grain of science. But ethics can and should be based on facts that are part of a law-governed development. Ethics, in view of its character, is not different from other sciences. Any true science, while studying facts, formulates certain principles that are generaliza-

2 "On the Analysis of Moral Judgments," *Philosophical Essays* (London, 1954), p. 242.

tions of facts and that aid in further investigation. At any rate, as Engels stated, "The principles are not the starting point of investigation but its final result; they are not applied to nature and human history, but abstracted from them; it is not nature and the realm of humanity which conform to these principles, but principles are only valid insofar as they are in conformity with nature and history."[3] All this applies also to moral principles, ideas, norms, categories, etc. . . .

. . . C. Stevenson, an American emotivist, sought to moderate Ayer's and Carnap's skepticism regarding ethical value judgments and the amoralism inescapably stemming from it. While stressing his solidarity with the principal position of Ayer and Carnap, Stevenson states openly that he "seeks merely to qualify their views . . . and to free them from any seeming cynicism."[4]

In contrast to Ayer and Carnap, Stevenson acknowledges that ethical judgments have a definite social meaning. Emotional meanings, he says, are by no means vague or unclear, and, therefore, ethical judgments deserve no less attention than those that, according to logical positivism, have a cognitive meaning. . . .

. . . It would seem that Stevenson's statement . . . implies an attempt to move away from subjectivism in the field of morality and to recognize the objective content of ethical categories and judgments. This, however, is not the case. Stevenson stands firm on the position of subjectivism. His definitions of such ethical categories as "good," "evil," "justice," etc., are the best evidence of this. He thinks that the motives underlying the approval or disapproval of a value judgment depend entirely upon man's feelings and perceptions. *"Any* statement about *any* matter of fact which *any* speaker considers likely to alter attitudes may be adduced as a reason for, or against, an ethical judgment."[5] This means that Stevenson, like Ayer and Carnap, does not recognize the objective content of moral judgments and reveals that he is a man without moral principles.

Stevenson seeks to correct Ayer's and Carnap's proposition that ethical value judgments can be neither true nor false. He admits that this proposition "leads into error" and thinks that "ethical judgment can be either true or false."[6] Stevenson seeks to substantiate this with his proposition about existing differences in men's convictions and positions. Differences in convictions, in his opinion, have a place in science. They are determined by the different attitudes of men toward facts and can be overcome by an appeal to facts. In

---

[3] *Anti-Dyuring* [Anti-Dühring] (Moscow, 1957), p. 34.
[4] *Ethics and Language* (New Haven, Conn., 1944), p. 267.
[5] *Ibid.,* p. 114.          [6] *Ibid.,* p. 267.

the realm of morality, he says, there are differences in the position of men, that is, differences in terms of goals, aspirations, and interests. Stevenson notes that men belonging to different classes and societies differ more often on ethical questions than on those of fact. At the same time, he indicates that since the differences in men's positions, as distinguished from the differences in their convictions, are rooted in the inner state of the subject—in differences of feelings, aspirations, etc.—they cannot be overcome through an appeal to facts; they are insurmountable. No one, says Stevenson, can prove the validity of his attitude. Each seeks to change the attitude of another without furnishing the evidence. Stevenson does not see any connection between convictions and men's attitudes. He emphasizes that "it is a disagreement in attitude that chiefly distinguishes ethical issues from those of pure science."[7]

What does Stevenson mean when he asserts that "an ethical judgment can be either true or false"? Since, he says, an ethical judgment contains the descriptive element, it is at times possible to determine its truth empirically, that is, by the verification of the described facts. But since, according to Stevenson, the predominant part of an ethical judgment consists of "emotive" elements, since the "descriptive part may be inadequate to emphasize its emotional meaning," he concludes, like Ayer and Carnap, that on the whole it is difficult to solve the problem of the truth of ethical value judgments.

Like Ayer and Carnap, Stevenson arrives at this conclusion because he fails to see the objective factors that determine the moral position of different men, classes, and society. He fails to see that the diverse positions of men and classes are determined by the diverse economic and social conditions in which they live. . . . Like other proponents of "emotive" ethics, he consequently adopts the position of moral subjectivism and relativism.

What is the social meaning of the neopositivist ethical theory? What practical conclusions follow from it?

We have seen that to deny the objective character of moral norms and evaluations, to reject the possibility of solving the question of their validity, leads to a moral unscrupulousness. Many representatives of emotivism see in this unscrupulousness the superiority of their conception over other schools of ethics. According to Ayer, the fact that some schools of ethics consider ethical judgments as inescapably true or false leads to the rise of conflict between men. Neopositivism, on the other hand, having deprived moral evaluations of objective meaning, leaves no place for disputes and antagonisms

[7] *Ibid.,* p. 13.

between men of different moral views. Ayer says that, if two men are in agreement concerning certain facts but at the same time are in complete disagreement in their evaluation of these facts, there can be no contradiction between them. "No one's desire"—writes the American emotivist, Asher Moore—"can be unjust; it can only be incompatible with my own. . . . As a consistent emotivist, I can have no ground for giving my own inclinations preference over his and therefore none for calling his judgments wrong. All ideals, provided only they be true expressions of the passions which prompt them, are equally legitimate and equally arbitrary."[8] From this it follows that each man is free to choose any moral norms, is free to follow any pattern of behavior, for "no pattern of behavior is better or worse than another,"[9] "for two different courses of action cannot each be preferable to the other."[10]

This reasoning expresses the desire of Neo-Positivists to escape from the solution of burning problems and from the intense, present-day social conflicts. Even some bourgeois philosophers assert that the neopositivist skepticism "represents an escape from many vital problems of our time."[11]

. . . . . . .

. . . As rightly stated by an English Marxist philosopher, Lewis, neopositivist ethics deprives men of the principles guiding their lives, "of the norms, by means of which they can give preference to one pattern of behavior over another."[12] In the "best" case, it prompts people to be indifferent toward life and toward significant social problems that are the center of the struggle.

The Neo-Positivists' ethical relativism and their aspiration to escape from solving social problems practically leads to moral cynicism and furnishes a justification for the most monstrous crimes committed by the reactionary social forces. If any pattern of behavior is equally right, then how can we condemn colonial oppression, or the imperialist attempts to suppress national liberation movements, or the recent mass murders in the Union of South Africa? To these and other questions neopositivism cannot give an answer that would be

[8] Emotivism: Theory and Practice," *The Journal of Philosophy*, Vol. 55, No. 9 (1958), p. 376.

[9] Ayer, "The Claims of Philosophy," p. 62.

[10] Ayer, "On the Analysis of Moral Judgments," p. 247.

[11] F. Mayer and F. Brower, *Patterns of a New Philosophy* (Washington, D.C., 1955), p. 9.

[12] *Science, Faith and Scepticism* (London, 1959), p. 37.

satisfactory to honest men and, in particular, to those who suffer under suppression.

. . . . . . .

. . . Millions of people in our time have become convinced that Marxist ethics, which is the truly scientific theory of morality, aids people in choosing a way of life and in determining their attitude toward social questions. It serves as a mobilizing force in the struggle for a new society. Marxist ethics successfully fulfills this task, for it is in full conformity with life, with the matured necessities of social development. Among the broad masses of the workers everywhere, there grows the recognition that the struggle for peace, democracy, and the socialist system is just. The working masses, guided by the communist and the workers' parties, actively struggle against modern imperialism and against its morality for the victory of the new system and a truly human morality.

# Science and Morality: A Marxist Interpretation*

## ∾ A. F. Shishkin

At first glance it may seem that there is no connection between morality and science, that science is far removed from morality. Science studies the objective laws of development of the material world—nature, society, and human thought. In doing this, it makes possible a scientific prediction of events. Morality, on the other hand, deals with the norms of human conduct, that is, with an evaluation of human behavior. The former deals with the problem of how and why (that is, in conformity with what laws) certain phenomena come into being whereas the latter formulates definite requirements for human conduct. Let us take, for example, a scientific law that expresses the interdependence of mass and energy, and a moral law, "You ought to carry out your obligations honestly." In the former we deal with a law, the content and form of which do not depend upon human will; in the latter the very formulation of the law, or of the rule, expresses the requirements of society, or of a definite class, while the concrete historical content of these requirements is quite distinct at the different stages of its social development.

Because of this, bourgeois scientists frequently conclude that science and morality are absolutely opposed. Science frequently challenges morality; confronted with such a challenge, morality, even the highest morality, is powerless. Is that so? Is it really true that scientific laws are in themselves hostile to morality, humaneness, and that they make morality obsolete?

A careful study of these questions reveals that the assertion that science and morality are incompatible is only true when the scientist operates with pseudoscientific "laws" or when he confuses the question of scientific achievements with their utilization in a given society. Speaking of the first case, for example, morality advances the demand to ease sufferings, to comfort the sick, to prevent diseases, etc., whereas science tells us that there is a natural law according to which a part of humanity is doomed to death because of a scarcity of the means of existence. Consequently, if science is guided by morality, it will find itself in conflict with its own laws. In

* From "Nauka i Moral" [Science and Morality], *Voprosy Filosofii*, No. 4 (1961), pp. 134–41.

570

attempting to hinder the effectiveness of this law, science can only increase misery and degeneration, for it seeks to prolong man's life in conditions under which, according to natural law, the population grows considerably faster than the means of existence. What do the "scientists" conclude from this? Being in the captivity of a thoroughly false, misanthropic conception of Malthus, they conclude that science cannot be guided by moral considerations and that science has nothing in common with morality. One should not struggle against diseases and epidemics, hunger and degeneration, for it is contradictory to the natural law of things.

In fact, such a law is nonexistent. Blinded by bourgeois prejudices and pseudoscientific theories, scientists cannot grasp the fact that the roots of the misery and suffering of the masses are to be found in the social system of capitalism and not in the fantastic natural law of overpopulation, that, consequently, one cannot deduce from such a scientific "achievement" the conclusion that morality and science are opposed as a matter of principle.

Let us take an example from literature. *The Disciple,* a novel by the French writer P. Bourget, speaks of a scientist who is engaged in the study of psychological problems. This scientist seeks to prove that man's inner world, his character, is subject to the iron laws of necessity, that all the features of man's character are manifestations of inevitability; that good and evil are merely social labels that cannot in any way affect the mechanism and the manifestation of human passions. The scientist does not consider the possibility that his ideas can exert any influence upon men, especially a destructive one. Only after learning that one of his admirers committed a crime under the direct influence of his ideas does he succeed in understanding that ideas can corrupt and distort. Although the hero of the novel (and its author) do not arrive at the correct conclusions regarding the relationship of science to morality, the objective meaning of the conflict presented by the author is that it is not science which is opposed to morality but false theories, pretending to be scientific, which conflict with morality.

The laws of nature and society, discovered by science, are not related to morality in the sense that they operate independent of the will and consciousness (including the moral consciousness) of men. Men know of no laws of nature and society which would "prohibit" them from living in a society (as long as the necessary conditions for life exist on our planet) and, consequently, from entertaining definite social opinions, moral principles, norms, rules, customs, etc. It is obvious that the laws of capitalist exploitation and competition comprise not even an element of morality. Moreover, while ruling men, these laws are hostile to the moral development of men. It is well known that science discovers these objective laws not for the purpose of perpetuating the conditions within which they operate but for the purpose of changing these conditions. Following the discovery of the laws of the development of capitalism, the Marxist science of society has demonstrated that the development of bloody, predatory capitalism . . . creates the prerequisites for the fall of capitalism and for the victory of socialism. It furnishes the suffering and exploited class—the class that is struggling against capitalism—with a clear purpose and with the methods for the struggle. And that means that a moral factor is introduced, a factor the significance of which cannot be underestimated.

From the above it follows that one cannot speak of any absolute opposition between science and morality. The aim of science is to assist men in transforming nature and society. This is precisely why the progressive social forces always strive to advance science. On the other hand, those social classes interested in the perpetuation of prejudices and superstition have seriously obstructed the development of science.

The history of class society demonstrates that the development of world knowledge was allowed and encouraged by the ruling classes only when it promoted their interests. The laws and theories of natural science which were in conflict with the foundations of the official ideology were declared immoral and subject to persecution on the part of the moribund classes—beginning with stakes and tortures in the Middle Ages and ending with the "monkey trials" in the age of bourgeois "civilization."

It is well known that men of science had to defend Darwin's theory from accusations of immorality. . . . It is common knowledge that one of the characteristics of the contemporary bourgeoisie is "the fear of a science, the fear of a scientific analysis of modern economy."[1] Bourgeois ideologists willingly replace such an analysis by appealing to religion and universal morality, which justify the yoke and exploitation of the workers. In the old society, the finer scientists always fought against transforming social science into the maidservant of the exploiting regimes; they have looked upon it as a means for popularizing the ideas of reason and humaneness. According to V. O. Kluchevskii, a famous professor of history at the University of Moscow, T. N. Granovskii "taught the science of history in such a way that his students would carry out of his lecture a faith in their future, a faith

[1] V. I. Lenin, *Sochineniya* [Works] (4th ed., Moscow), Vol. 20 (1948), p. 117.

that served as their guiding star during the gloomiest nights of our life."[2] As far as the Marxist science of society is concerned, it first determined the laws of social development and discovered the inevitability of replacing capitalism with socialism and then it advanced the slogan of struggle to the class that is both the material and moral bearer of this transformation.

Bourgeois social science fails to recognize that it is possible to deduce objective goals, ideals, etc., from real movement, that is, from real facts. Bourgeois philosophers and scientists see in such a deduction a confusion of "facts" and "values," "is" and "ought," an inadmissible conversion of science into politics or morality. They assert that the slogan of *The Communist Manifesto*: "Proletarians of all countries unite!" has nothing in common with science but merely expresses the desire of certain persons, parties, etc. Such a delimitation of "facts" and "values," "is" and "ought," stands no criticism. Values are inseparable from objects possessing values; values are not something independent, belonging to a different world, "just as color does not belong to a sphere of objects which is distinct from the colored objects."[3] The exchange value cannot be separated from the commodity exchanged, of which the value is a part. Likewise, the sphere of "ought" cannot be separated from reality if this "ought" is not something fantastic. On the basis of an analysis of facts and phenomena, of the laws of their development, science can arrive at conclusions concerning both what is and what ought to be. One cannot deny the fact that science (including the entire sphere of natural sciences) constantly formulates propositions concerning what *should* be done, what is and is not possible, how definite laws should be expressed, which means are better than others, etc. In other words, science makes normative or value judgments. It cannot be isolated from the "world of values," especially where its aims are concerned. Science can never be separated from the goals it pursues nor from the question of which social forces its achievements serve. In view of this, science is never free of moral considerations, particularly in conducting its experiments. It sees to it that there is no risk of human life in conducting experiments (for example, the experimental examination of a new means of medical treatment, the examination of the performance of the living organism in cosmic flights, etc.).

Science attaches a value to man's life, looks after his welfare, seeks

[2] V. O. Kluchevskii, "Pamyati T. N. Granovskogo" [In Memory of T. N. Granovskii], *Sochineniya* [Works] (Moscow), VIII (1959), 390.

[3] Mario Bunge, "Nauchnyi Podkhod k Etike" [A Scientific Approach to Ethics], *Voprosy Filosofii*, No. 1 (1961), p. 83.

to increase his power over the forces of nature and to help him to rationally organize his social life. Therefore, it cannot but seek close ties with the forces struggling for peace and progress, for human happiness. It is apparent that the contradiction between facts and values is not a real one, that it does not correspond to the existing state of things.

So far we have examined only one aspect of the question concerning the relationship of science to morality: Can science pursue social, moral goals—is it free of moral considerations in utilizing its results? There is, however, another aspect to the question of the relationship of science to morality: Can moral judgments and evaluations be scientifically true? To this question bourgeois scientists, who seek to create a gap between science and morality, as a rule give a negative answer.

Such a negative answer is given and even "scientifically" justified by contemporary Positivists. In their opinion, the world of science is a world of logical concepts and relations. Morality lies outside this world and, consequently, outside the realm of science. For example, Bertrand Russell wrote that deciding the differences between one value and another is not, and cannot be, the function of science. "The difference is one of tastes, not one as to any objective truth."[4] Science cannot decide the question of values, for the latter lie outside the realm of truth and error. Therefore, questions concerning ethical values "may be ignored in their intellectual form, though in emotional forms they retain political importance."[5] In other words, morality belongs to the sphere of emotions and not to reason; it has nothing to do with truth.

A Positivist, R. Carnap, also asserts that only self-evident truths of logic and mathematics, as well as the truths of empirical sciences, insofar as the latter deal with experiential facts that can be verified through sensory observations, possess a real scientific meaning. Philosophy is urged to discard all "metaphysical" problems . . . as lying outside its realm of experience. It is engaged in a logical analysis whereas empirical sciences deal with experiential facts. Since ethics is simply describing moral situations, it belongs to the field of empirical psychology. However, if it deals with "values," that is, if it contains judgments of what is good and evil (norms of conduct and

4 *Education and the Social Order* (London, 1932), p. 220. [The quoted statement does not appear in the source indicated by Shishkin. It does appear, however, in Russell's *Religion and Science* (New York, 1935), p. 250.]

5 B. Russell, *Religion and Science*, p. 250. [The statement quoted by Shishkin does not appear in the source indicated. It appears, however, in Russell's *Education and the Social Order*, p. 220.]

evaluation), it belongs to metaphysics. Normative or regulatory statements with which ethics deals are deprived of any meaning.

"A value judgment," says Carnap, "is a command made in a misleading grammatical form. It can exert an influence upon human conduct, and this influence can either be or not be in conformity with our desires, but it is neither true nor false. It asserts nothing, and can neither be proven nor disproven."[6]

Ayer and Wittgenstein argue along the same lines. Like Carnap, they deny that ethical judgments have any meaning since these judgments do not aim at stating facts but at evaluating them. Moral norms and evaluations express nothing but our feelings and desires. Moral judgments can be neither true nor false. They add nothing to the facts. Attempts to find the rational foundations of morality are fruitless.

Let us examine these constantly repeated positivist assertions. Where does their theoretical fallacy lie? It lies in the denial of the fact that moral ideals, principles, and norms are connected with man's social life, that is, with the social relations that are developing in conformity with objective laws and that find their ideological expression in diverse forms of social consciousness and hence also in moral "values." It has been seen earlier that a study of the moral "values" of each historical period and each class makes it possible to see their dependence upon the material conditions of social life, upon men's social being, upon the interests of definite classes. This dependence is a fact, and, for this reason alone, moral ideas, norms, and evaluations have a definite social meaning. They express the demands of a definite society, or a class, vis-à-vis human conduct. The point in question is whether or not these demands correspond to the objective needs of the development of society and man. In the first case they promote social development whereas in the second they hinder it (although, naturally, they accommodate a definite social class, namely, the class departing from the scene). In the first case they promote the real public good whereas in the second they protect the privileges of a few to the detriment of society as a whole, that is, to the detriment of society's objective needs. In the first case they have the quality of truth whereas in the second they do not. Consequently, moral ideas can be either true or false. They are true when they are based on the knowledge of the developing reality and express its future. "An idea is both *knowledge* and aspiration (desire) [of man]," wrote Lenin.[7] This, too, applies to moral ideas, which can also be a result of knowl-

[6] *Philosophy and Logical Syntax* (London, 1935), p. 24.
[7] *Sochineniya*, Vol. 38 (n.d.), p. 186.

edge, that is, truth about human conduct, which becomes a will, an aspiration, and a desire of the champions for a better future for society and man.

The bankruptcy of logical positivist views is manifest in another respect. They contend that morality is an expression of emotions. In fact, moral judgments are something more than emotions. Moral judgments (norms, principles, evaluations) express the interests of large groups of the population—of entire classes and entire nations. Therefore, they cannot be examined in the framework of empirical psychology. They constitute a part of the social psychology and ideology of definite groups of the population or classes. But, as indicated earlier, the progressive classes, who are the standard-bearers for historical progress, have an ideology different from the ideology of the *moribund* classes, who hinder social development. To a lesser or greater degree (depending upon the concrete historical conditions), the former strives to be scientific (though it is not always free of illusions); the latter is antiscientific from the very beginning. The former is capable of developing, and is developing, while overcoming the opposition of reaction; the latter is incapable of developing and therefore perishes sooner or later. The stated theoretical proposition, confirmed through historical experience, sufficiently demonstrates the fact that it is impossible to reduce moral judgments to an expression of the *"emotive position"* of the person making these judgments.

Finally, even if man's moral judgment expresses simply his feelings, these are not at all meaningless. The task is to find out their social meaning. Man does not live outside society. When masses of people express a feeling of just indignation about a certain social system, this indignation has a fully determinable social meaning. It is a symptom of the decay of this system. Likewise, such human sensations as the feeling of social obligation, comradeship, personal dignity, etc., have an equally determinable social meaning in the conditions under which people struggle against exploitation and oppression. These sensations are inseparable from man's moral consciousness, from his opinions; consequently, they have a definite rational foundation, irrespective of whether or not they are clearly perceived by man. To create a gulf between man's sensations and his mind is tantamount to a metaphysical dissection of human consciousness. In practice, man's mind and his sensations are inseparable and are equally determined by social conditions. In an exploiting society, man's moral feelings and views are in the captivity of vulgar practical needs, which frequently thoroughly engulf the consciousness of the workingman. On the other hand, they are suppressed or distorted by the greed and craving for profit on the part of their exploiters. Communist society is a real arena for the development of truly human moral feelings, views, and principles, in which the exploitation of man by man is nonexistent and in which man is not the means of production but its end. In such a society, a true human morality—the communist morality—asserts itself. It is the morality of that class which, in contrast to all other classes, seeks happiness not only for itself but also for all workers, for all the oppressed. "A victory of the new social system brings gains to all strata of the population, with the exception of a clique of exploiters," says the Declaration of the Conference of the Representatives of the Communist and Workers' Parties. In the militant demands of the working class, the finest aspirations of the workers—for peace and fraternity among nations, for the liquidation of oppression in all its manifestations, be it class, national, racial, or of one sex by another—find their fullest expression. That is why, while examining the various types of morality operating in a bourgeois society, Engels answered the question of what true morality is in the following way: "That morality contains the maximum elements promising the permanence that presently supports the overthrow of the existing regime, represents the future, and that is proletarian morality."[8] This view is even more timely now than it was eighty years ago when it was formulated.

Communist morality, the highest criterion of which is the struggle for communism, is stripped of the dogmatism that is particularly characteristic of theological moral systems. At the same time it has absolutely nothing in common with moral relativism, which regards all norms to be equally good, which asserts that objectivity is inapplicable to the domain of morality, that each class has its own morality, and that each is right in its own way. Since the development of morality takes place in conformity with objective laws, the relativist reduction of moral norms to subjective tastes, commands, and successes and the denial of the possibility that moral judgments could have the meaning of objective truth are out of place.

What are, at the present time, the practical consequences ensuing from the separation of science and morality and from the refusal to see a rational meaning in moral judgments? In separating science (the domain of "facts") from morality (the domain of "values"), some bourgeois scientists refrain from passing any judgment concerning the employment of atomic and nuclear weapons. They assert that it is not the purpose of science to explain whether or not the use of such weapons is good or evil. Science, in their opinion, should be free

[8] *Anti-Dyuring* [Anti-Dühring] (Moscow, 1957), p. 88.

of moral considerations, for the idea of good and evil lacks an objective meaning.

Need it be said that a scientist who argues in such a way is an accessory to the imperialists' crimes? A scientist, like any other intellectual, cannot free himself of questions raised by social life; he cannot be indifferent to the problems of who utilizes scientific discoveries and for what purpose: do they promote progress or reaction, war or peace, the oppression of men or their liberation. . . . The problem of the utilization of the laws discovered by science directly affects the consciousness of scientists; they cannot escape from this problem by hiding behind the screen of "objectivism," "pure science," etc. On the other hand, the problem of consciousness, that is, morality, is not a purely subjective matter. It has been stated earlier that morality can express the objective needs of social life—that is, universal historical truth—for example, the idea of peace among free nations or the happiness of people. At the present time, progressive scientists in the capitalist world resolutely protest against the utilization of the great discovery of our time—atomic energy—for the purpose of the mass destruction of people; they protest against the utilization of scientific discoveries for criminal purposes and against the militarization of science.

According to an atomic scientist, P. Young (*Brighter Than a Thousand Suns*), prior to the First World War, scientists as a rule thought it irrelevent to consider the moral consequences of their discoveries. The situation has changed drastically. After the First, but more especially after the Second, World War the connection between the laboratory and war became so apparent that the problem of consciousness, that is, of the moral responsibility for the utilization of scientific discoveries, imperiously entered the lives and activities of scientists.

Life itself leads them to the single correct answer, which was given by the famous physicist F. Jolie-Curie. "Scientists," he wrote, "cannot form a group of a select few, far removed from other people and from practical needs. As members of a great collective of toilers, they should be concerned with the application of their discoveries. The discovery of atomic energy and the consequent creation of dreadful weapons compels scientists to act, for the stakes of the game bear threat to the future of mankind."

"We should join the ranks of those who think that a nuclear war would be an unheard of horror and that, therefore, people who insist upon continuation of tests (whose danger defies description), should be held guilty for the crime against humanity," noted B. Russell.[9] "I believe that there is a greater power in the world than armies and nuclear bombs—there is the power of good, of morality, of humanitarianism," wrote the famous American scientist and champion of peace L. Pauling.[10]

. . . Soviet scientists share N. S. Khrushchev's view that "man's mind and consciousness cannot tolerate the menacing threat of nuclear war" and that remarkable scientific discoveries "can bring about prosperity and happiness to mankind if they are directed toward peaceful aims."[11]

The true assignment of science, that is, its true aim, lies in serving the people, in improving man's life. It is a highly human aim. A genuine scientist should be a champion of truth, an enemy of any kind of deception and prejudice spread by the ideologists of the ruling, exploiting classes. The struggle for science, for the utilization of its achievements for the benefit of man, calls for courage, fortitude, self-sacrifice, and faith in the victory of reason, that is, in those moral qualities that are characteristic of the fighters for a new social system, those who are against the obsolete, old system. In other words, the only way science can develop now is by joining those forces that struggle for the liberation of mankind from the yoke of capital, for the liberation of science from serving capitalists, from the bourgeois ideology and morality.

Socialism is inseparable from science. Socialist society organizes the production and distribution of products on a scientific basis for the purpose of increasing the material well-being and cultural level of the masses. Only socialism liberates science from bourgeois ideology and morality and gives it a new assignment—to serve labor, the people. Only socialism transforms scientists into free intellectuals. . . .

---

[9] Preface to a collection of essays, *Chem Grozyat Ispytaniya Yadernogo Oruzhiya* [The Threat of Nuclear Testing] (Moscow, 1958).

[10] L. Pauling, *Ne Byvat Voine* [No More War] (Moscow, 1960), [In Pauling's original work *No More War!* (London, 1958), the sentence reads as follows: "I believe that there is a greater power in the world than the evil power of military force, of nuclear bombs — there is the power of *good,* of *morality,* of humanitarianism" (p. 193).]

[11] Letter to Bertrand Russell, March 5, 1958.

# Dictatorship and the State during the Transition from Socialism to Communism*  ∞  *A. I. Lepeshkin*

The most significant tasks of the Party for the period of the construction of a communist society in our country are clearly formulated and scientifically well-grounded in the program of the C.P.S.U. The program of the C.P.S.U. assigns the greatest attention to the questions of the political organization of society in the period of the construction of communism. It contains a number of new theorectical propositions.

. . . . . . .

In our judgment, from these new . . . propositions, contained in the Party's program, ensue the following three significant theoretical questions, directly related to the theory of the Soviet *state and law: (1) the relationship of the dictatorship of the proletariat to the socialist state; (2) the directing role of the working class of Soviet society; (3) the character of the social changes that have taken place in the nature of the state—in its political basis—in connection with the transformation of the state of the proletarian dictatorship into a state of the entire people.*

It is stressed in the Party's program that the experience of socialist construction in the U.S.S.R. fully confirms the Marxist-Leninist thesis that peoples can arrive at socialism only as the result of a socialist revolution and the establishment of the dictatorship of the proletariat, i.e., through the establishment of the political rule of the working class.

The working class needs the dictatorship of the proletariat, not only for the purpose of suppressing the resistance of the exploiting classes, but mainly for the purpose of organizing the construction of socialism and for securing not only complete but final victory, for establishing peace and friendship among the peoples and attaining a complete sociopolitical and ideological unity among them, for

* *From* "Programa KPSS i Nekotorye Voprosy Teorii Sovetskogo Sotsialisticheskogo Gosudarstva" [The Program of the C.P.S.U. and Some Problems of the Theory of the Soviet Socialist State], *Sovetskoe Gosudarstvo i Pravo*, No. 12 (1961), pp. 3–10.

preparing the conditions necessary for the country's entry into the period of the direct construction of communism. The working class in our country utilized its political rule for the purpose of materializing these and other historical tasks. The working class is the only class in history which does not seek to eternalize its political rule but utilizes it for solving the tasks imposed upon it.

In connection with the fundamental changes in the country's economy, in the class structure of society, and in the national relations among the peoples of the U.S.S.R., which secured the victory of socialism, substantial changes have taken place also in the very nature of the dictatorship of the proletariat—in its basic tasks. It was in this period that the process of a gradual growing over of the state of the dictatorship of the proletariat into an all-people's political organization of the toilers of socialist society began. The dictatorship of the proletariat itself creates the conditions necessary for its own withering away prior to the withering away of the Soviet state. The socialist system of economy and socialist property completely dominate all sectors of the country's economy; class antagonism and all forms of the exploitation of man by man have been done away with forever; the final victory of socialism is secured. The construction of communism now becomes the practical task of our people. All this demonstrates that the time has come when the dictatorship of the proletariat, having fulfilled its historical mission, ceases to be necessary in the U.S.S.R. The dictatorship of the proletariat disappears, but the state remains as the main tool for the building of communism.

Thus, while the presence of the dictatorship of the proletariat is necessarily connected with the existence of antagonistic classes and their remnants, the existence of the socialist state is necessary to the workers even after all capitalist classes have been destroyed.

It is well known that in the *Critique of the Gotha Program* Marx drew a distinction between the dictatorship of the proletariat and the "future statehood of communist society." Consequently, Marx thought that the state remains preserved even after the dictatorship of the proletariat is no longer needed. In his famous work, *State and Revolution,* Lenin wrote that "the state withers away, since there are no more capitalists, no more classes, and no *class* can therefore be *suppressed*. But the state has not yet withered away completely. . . ." Lenin indicated, therefore, the necessity for the existence of the state even after the exploiting classes have been liquidated, even when society is composed of friendly classes and there is no more political suppression of one class by another.

As far as the historical destiny of the Soviet state is concerned, the solution of this question is ultimately closely connected with the solution of the question concerning the victory of socialism on the international plane.

Thus, the dictatorship of the proletariat is a historically transitional institution, connected only with the execution of definitive, historically conditioned tasks—securing not only the complete but the final victory of socialism—while the existence of the Soviet state is connected not only with these tasks, but also with the construction of a complete communist society.

As Khrushchev said in his address on the Party's program, during the public discussion of the program of the C.P.S.U. some comrades suggested inserting into it the view that the dictatorship of the proletariat must be preserved up to the complete victory of communism. Regarding such proposals, Khrushchev said that they are advanced "from the positions of a dogmatic rather than a creative approach to the processes taking place in life," that

such comrades fail entirely to take into consideration the objective conditions that have arisen in our country and operate with quotations arbitrarily snatched out, losing sight of Marx's, Engels', and Lenin's teaching of the state of the dictatorship of the proletariat as a state of the transition period from capitalism to socialism—of the first phase of communism. They fail to take into consideration the fact that in our socialist society there are now only the working classes, which are engaged in socialist production and are the only classes in a sociopolitical and ideological respect. After the complete and final victory of socialism there is no ground in our country for the dictatorship of one class. Indeed, in respect to which class could we have a dictatorship? We have no such classes.

And furthermore, Khrushchev emphasized that the thesis—formulated in the Party's program—on the growing over of the state of the dictatorship of the proletariat into an all-people's state fully corresponds to what has taken place in the sociopolitical life of our country, in the political system of the Soviet state. The all-people's Soviet state is the result of the deepest social transformations engendered by the entire course of communist construction; it is engendered by life, by the practice of the construction of communism, and it "expresses our line in the political organization of society—the all-out development of democracy."

With the examination of the question of the relationship between the dictatorship of the proletariat and the state is organically connected the question of the preservation of the leading role of the working class in Soviet society after the dictatorship of the proletariat ceases to be necessary from the viewpoint of internal tasks of the communist construction in our society.

What are the historical causes producing the leading position of the working class in the Soviet society, and what are the organizational forms in which it will be further materialized? To begin with, it seems to us that the Party's program introduces some clarifications of the notion of "the leading position of the working class," which is not identical with the notion of the dictatorship of the proletariat. While earlier, in our literature, the question of the leading position of the working class . . . was being identified with the notion of the dictatorship of the proletariat, now, in light of the program of the C.P.S.U., it is apparent that they are not identical notions. The difference between the notion of the dictatorship of the proletariat and the notion of the leading role of the working class lies in the difference of the historical frameworks embraced by these notions.

It is well known that the working class begins to concretize its leading role in the revolutionary struggle of the workers considerably prior to the victory of the socialist revolution and the establishment of the dictatorship of the proletariat. The Russian working class exercised a hegemony over the revolutionary forces of the people during all three revolutions in Russia, but only as a result of the Great October Socialist Revolution was the dictatorship of the proletariat established.

The leading position of the working class is being preserved also in the present period, when the dictatorship of the proletariat has ceased to be necessary from the viewpoint of the tasks of the internal development of our country. The Party program says that the role of the working class as the leader of society will be completed with the construction of communism, with the disappearance of classes. Consequently, the leading role of the working class at the present time is not only being preserved but, even more, it will be developing and growing stronger in the period of the large-scale construction of communism. This new theoretical thesis, advanced by the program of the C.P.S.U., has great significance for a thorough understanding of the social character of the state power, carried out by the all-people's state in the period of a large-scale construction of communism.

. . . . . . .

In what organizational forms will the leading position of the working class in Soviet society be secured? The forms and means of securing the leading role of the working class in the social and state life of the country will be extraordinarily diverse. The main one, in our judgment, will be the following: the strengthening of the leading role of the C.P.S.U. in the entire state life of the country, which will signify also the strengthening of the role of the working class in the building of communism. Although the C.P.S.U. has become a party of the whole people, its kernel, as before, is the representatives of the working people—of the most progressive and organized class in Soviet society. And as long as the influence of the Party is growing, the role of the working class in the life of society will also be growing and getting stronger. And this means expansion of the role of social organizations and unions in communist construction, but primarily of the professional unions, uniting the working class; this means the activization of all other organizations and unions of the working class to which a number of functions of the state organs are now being gradually transferred. Thus, for example, in recent years permanently functioning industrial conferences have been introduced, uniting by now more than 4.5 million workers and employees, through which the working class increases considerably its influence over the organization of the direct administration of socialist production.

The Party's program says that the Soviet state, which arose as a state of the dictatorship of the proletariat, became converted into an all-people's state—into an organ expressing the interests and the will of the entire people. Indeed, the expression "people's state" was used earlier in Marxist-Leninist literature, but the notion of "the Soviet all-people's state" is one of those new theses in the Marxist-Leninist science of the socialist state that is advanced in the Party's program.

It is well known that in *Anti-Dühring* Engels was strongly opposed to the slogan of German Social Democrats about the "free-people's state" and considered it to be "scientifically inconsistent." Referring to this view of Engels, Lenin wrote that "all states are 'a special force for the suppression' of the oppressed class. Therefore, *all* states are *non*-free and *non*-popular. Marx and Engels were repeatedly explaining this to their party comrades in the seventies."

Asserting that "*all* states are *non*-free and *non*-popular," that they are "a special force for the suppression" of the oppressed class, the classics of Marxism-Leninism, of course, had in mind primarily the experience with the activity of the bourgeois states, which in terms of their nature, tasks, and functions have never been, and, as long as they exist, could not be, free and popular states. The bourgeois state has been and remains an instrument in the hands of the ruling classes—the exploiters—for the purpose of suppressing the exploited workers.

The proletarian state of the transition period from capitalism to socialism occupies a special place. The main feature of the dictatorship of the proletariat in the U.S.S.R. is its organizational work in rallying the toiling masses around the working class and in mobilizing all their creative efforts for the creation of a new system— socialism and then communism. Not the method of coercion, but the method of persuasion, is the fundamental and principal one in the activity of the state of the dictatorship of the proletarian class. The dictatorship of the proletariat represents a true proletarian democracy, securing the political rule of the proletariat, which, in union with other toilers, exercises the state power. Therefore, Lenin emphasized that the dictatorship of the proletariat "is no longer a state in the proper sense."

The new thesis in the program of the C.P.S.U. on the Soviet all-people's state represents a further step in the creative development of the Marxist-Leninist theory of state in general and of the socialist state in particular. It reflects a totally new period in the development of socialist society and the state, when the state ceases to be an instrument of one class in society and becomes an embodiment of the single public will—an expression of the interests of the whole society, when the proletarian socialist democracy is converted into an all-people's democracy, into a political form expressing the sovereignty of the people.

. . . . . . .

While all states hitherto known have been, and are, in terms of their nature, dictatorships of the ruling class, now a state has arisen that ceases to be an instrument of class domination. The all-people's state is a political association of the whole people, expressing its sovereignty in full scope and without any restrictions.

The feature distinguishing the social nature of the all-people's state from the state of the dictatorship of the proletariat is the liquidation of the political rule of one working class and the establishment of the rule of all classes and social groups in Soviet society, i.e., political rule of the people. Consequently, in terms of its nature, the all-people's state is a new type of socialist state, unknown before in the history of human society.

The prophetic words of *The Communist Manifesto,* that the proletariat, having become the ruling class, "abolishes the old relations of production . . ." and, having abolished class antagonism, abolishes "thereby also its own rule as a class," have become reality.

# War and Revolution*  ⌖  A. Butenko

When a society accomplishes the transition from one historical phase to another, the defenders of the receding system flood the world with numerous fictions and excogitations about the "misery" and "sufferings" presumably to be expected by mankind on the new path. . . . In this respect contemporary bourgeois ideologists differ little from their predecessors. . . . To frighten workers, the outspoken bourgeois press has sought for decades, and is seeking, to identify the path to socialism with war and bloodshed, to depict Marxism as a theory viewing the world-wide victory of socialism as the result of a destructive war.

Communists have repeatedly exposed such falsifications. However, bourgeois ideologists remain undistrubed by the fact that the "horrors" associated by them with the transition to socialism do not exist in reality, that their caricature-like depiction of the Marxist theory is as similar to Marxism as a scarecrow is to a beautiful human body. Striving to arouse a distrust of the communist movement and of its ideology, the imperialist reaction even now keeps insisting that Communists need interstate wars to overthrow capitalist systems and establish socialist orders. A new, shattering blow was dealt all these excogitations by the Declaration of the Conference of Representatives of the Communist and Workers' Parties of eighty-one countries, in which this slander was resolutely repudiated. "Marxist-Leninists," says the Declaration, "have never held that the path to social revolution goes through wars among the states."

Contemporary bourgeois ideologists are pursuing far-reaching goals by identifying the transition to socialism with bloodshed and by insisting that the path to social revolution goes, as a rule, through a world war; they are trying to appeal to the most sensitive feelings of millions of people—to their love of peace and their hatred of a world-wide nuclear war. They try to direct these feelings against revolution—against socialism.

The slanderous fabrications of our enemies have nothing in common with life. The working class—the most progressive class at present—has been longing, and is longing, for the least painful (to society) resolution of both international and domestic problems of

* *From* "Voina i Revolutsiya" [War and Revolution], *Kommunist*, No. 4 (1961), pp. 49–55.

social development. To Communists, peace among nations has always been the most significant condition of social progress, and a peaceful transition to socialism has been the most desirable form of the revolutionary transformation of capitalism. . . .

Since the bourgeois ideology . . . confuses completely different social phenomena—revolution with war, unjust wars with just wars, wars among states with civil wars—we shall examine the nature of, and the actual relationship between, war and revolution.

## WAR BETWEEN NATIONS AND REVOLUTION

Among various bourgeois, reformist, and revisionist attempts to tie or to identify revolution with war, one of the central places belongs to the thesis that for Marxists the path to social revolution must go through *interstate wars*—that world war is a necessary condition of social transformation, a prerequisite for the transition to socialism. In attempting to "substantiate" this slanderous fiction, the enemies of Marxism most frequently use two types of arguments: "factual" and "theoretical."

*First Argument:* Referring to historical facts, but primarily to the fact that both world wars ended with socialist revolutions, the falsifiers of Marxism assert that, from the Marxist viewpoint, such a path to social revolution is the only one possible. Bourgeois ideologists argue that communism can count, and is counting upon being successful only under conditions of calamities and privations, which are generated especially by world wars. Under different conditions, they contend, the success of revolution would be impossible. Thus, E. Schieweck, a West German anti-Marxist, in his book *Outdated World Revolution*,[1] writes that at present, in view of the "transformation" of capitalism and of the growth of general prosperity, the idea of revolution has lost ground and that the transition to socialism on a world-wide scale through a natural-historical process has become impossible. He finds that one of the chief causes of international tension is the attempt, attributed by him to "Soviet socialists," to "bring about reality in conformity with Marxist prognostications" through artificial means. Contemporary revisionists also seek to depict the revolutionary consolidation of the dictatorship of the proletariat as a result of war.

All these clever constructions are absurd, because the references

[1] *Die überholte Weltrevolution: Neue Perspectiven für die Beziehungen zwischen Ost und West* (Düsseldorf, 1959).

588                                       SOVIET POLITICAL THOUGHT

to history on which they are based create merely an appearance of
argumentation while in fact obfuscating the point of the matter.
What are the facts? It is true, indeed, that both the First and the
Second World Wars ended with socialist revolutions that resulted in
the creation of the Soviet Union and of other socialist countries in
Europe and Asia which today constitute the world system of socialism. However, this fact does not at all signify the presence of a certain necessary, law-governed connection between revolution and
war, that is, it does not affirm that which is attributed to it by anti-
Marxists. "The fact," states the Declaration of the Conference of
Representatives of the Communist and Workers' Parties, "that both
world wars, unleashed by imperialists, ended with socialist revolutions does not at all mean that the path to social revolution necessarily goes through a world war, especially in our epoch when a
mighty world system of socialism is in existence."

The tricky method of the enemies of Marxism to depict revolution—frequently following a war—as a phenomenon caused by war
is aimed at concealing the real, irremovable causes generating revolutions; it is directed toward obliterating the principal difference
between war and revolution. However, in reality, war and revolution—though in the final analysis generated by general conditions
in an antagonistic society—are distinct social phenomena, brought
about by distinct causes.

What is war? A war between states is the result of the operation of
the laws of an exploitive society; the begetting of the exploiters'
policy; the continuation of the policy of a given class by means of
armed forces, bloodshed, and violence. There are different kinds of
wars: world wars and local wars, national liberation wars and civil
wars. As stated by Lenin, "There are wars and wars. One must consider the historical conditions that gave rise to the war—which
classes are conducting it, and in whose name."[2] The wars under discussion, namely, the world wars of 1914-1918 and 1939-1945, were
prepared and unleashed by international imperialism—the monopolistic bourgeoisie. Both world wars, being a striking manifestation
of the decadence of capitalism, were not accidental; they were
peculiar . . . results of the operation of the inner necessity of
capitalism.

A proportional and even economic growth of individual economies and states is impossible on the basis of private-capitalist property. Therefore, the whole development of a capitalist society is
subject to the law of uneven development. The operation of this

───────────────────────────

[2] *Sochineniya* [Works] (4th ed., Moscow), Vol. 24 (1949), p. 363.

law constantly changes the existing power relations in the capitalist world, gives rise to new forces, which disturb the earlier equilibrium, and, in doing this, intensifies all contradictions of capitalism, intensifies its antagonisms, and generates instability, wavering, in the whole capitalist system. The restoration of the periodically disturbed equilibrium can be accomplished under imperialism not only by means of economic shocks and crises (which clear the way for those most powerful) but also by means of a forcible, military readjustment of the world, of its markets, and of spheres of influence in conformity with the real correlation of forces. Objectively, world wars are the most radical means for the adaptation of imperialist policy to the law of the uneven development of capitalism.

All imperialist wars have served, and do serve, to enrich a clique of war profiteers, arms merchants, and suppliers of the means of destruction. At the same time, they bring countless disasters and sufferings to the workers. . . .

The causes and aims of revolution are different. Revolution is the result of the conscious creativity of the people, a natural transition from one social system to another—from a lower historical phase to a higher one. Growing ripe on the basis of objective contradictions—as the popular masses (because of their own experience) become convinced of the necessity to change the existing system—revolutions are of different types: bourgeois, popular-democratic, and proletarian. The social revolutions that came at the end of the First and Second World Wars (October, 1917, Revolution in Russia, and the revolutions in various countries of Europe and Asia) are a proof of the decadence or, even more, of the decline of capitalism. They were generated by the laws operating within capitalism. However, the operation of these laws is not necessarily connected with the conditions created by war, and, therefore, war itself is not at all necessary on the path to socialist revolutions.

At the basis of the development of human society lies the development of the modes of production, which is subject to the law of the correspondence of the relations of production to the character of the forces of production. The operation of this general sociological law is the determining element of the necessities inherent to a given formation. In the end, all socialist revolutions are the result of the operation of this general sociological law. With the development of the forces of production, an irreconcilable contradiction comes into being between the capitalist character of the process of production and the private-capitalist appropriation of its results. From a certain point on, a further successful development of production is possible only if the private-capitalist property (capitalist relations of production) is forcibly abolished, which cannot be accomplished without an active revolutionary action of the masses. The masses become necessarily more active because the preservation of the old relations of production leads toward the destruction of the forces of production—toward the disorganization of production, which affects the situation of the working masses, who, sooner or later, but unavoidably, arrive at the conclusion that the revolutionary change of the existing system—i.e., the replacement of capitalism with socialism—is necessary. In brief, in contrast to war, a socialist revolution is the result of the activity of the workers and of their conscious utilization of the general, sociological law of the correspondence of the relations of production to the character of the forces of production.

All this shows that wars between nations and revolutions are distinct social phenomena, that there is no necessary connection between them, and that they are engendered by different causes. However, while the path of a revolution does not necessarily go through a war between nations, the fact that both world wars ended with socialist revolutions calls for an explanation. The gist of the matter is that the very same law of the uneven development of capitalism exerts an influence upon both the rise of wars and revolutions. The uneven development of capitalism gives rise to a general disturbance of the existing equilibrium and thus weakens capitalism in some of its links. In the cases under discussion this has led to the following: having unleashed the world war, the bourgeoisie not only failed to strengthen (by means of war) the weakened position of imperialism but achieved the very opposite result. The war brought the poverty of the masses to an extreme, intensified contradictions, and thus heightened the revolutionary activity of the masses against capitalism. Therefore, the socialist revolution—prepared by the entire history of the development of capitalism—was not generated, but was precipitated, by war. Writing on this subject, Lenin stated: "It would be impossible to put an end to the rule of capitalism if the whole economic development of capitalist countries did not lead to this. War precipitated this process and hence made capitalism even more vulnerable. No power could destroy capitalism if it were not undermined by history."[3]

The imperialist nature of capitalism remains unchanged at the present time: as before, the law of the uneven economic and political development operates in the bosom of capitalism; and the corre-

[3] *Ibid.,* pp. 381–82.

lation of forces between imperialist states is changing. But such a course of events does not mean that humanity must necessarily live through another imperialist world war before the world-wide victory of socialism. . . .

Under present conditions, the operation of the law of the uneven economic and political development of capitalism does not necessarily lead to military solutions, because nations are now able to avert war. There is, however, no power in the world capable of preventing the operation of the general sociological law of the correspondence of the relations of production to the character of the forces of production, which necessarily leads to revolution because no means short of revolution can resolve the constantly aggravating contradictions between the social character of the process of production, brought about by capitalism, and the private-capitalist appropriation of its results.

*Second Argument:* Snatching scraps of phrases from Marxist literature, contemporary distorters of Marxism endeavor also to convince the masses that communism is an expansionist system—that Marxists view the victory of the world revolution as the result of a military clash between the socialist and the capitalist camps, a consequence of victory in a world war. The slogan of world revolution —declares E. Williams—bears witness to imperialist intentions of communism. "Their language," others slanderously declare, "is a language of total war. They aim at world revolution with a consistency and purposefulness unprecedented by any dictatorship in the past." In other words, imperialist propaganda seeks to prove that the peaceful coexistence of two systems is merely a tactical communist maneuver—that it is contrary to the Marxist-Leninist theory of socialist revolution. For example, speaking at a session of NATO, F. Strauss, Defense Minister of the G.F.R., declared: "Lenin never spoke of the peaceful coexistence between states with distinct social formations. . . ." Strauss contended that, according to Lenin, capitalism will perish "as the result of a revolutionary uprising of the working class against the ruling classes in conjunction with the last great war of the socialist camp against capitalist states." Revisionists and renegades echo the bourgeois distorters of Marxism on this question; they, too, for example, P. Herve, contend that revolution "is being exported from Moscow in the vans of the Soviet Army."

There is, however, not even a grain of truth in such reasoning. First, aggressiveness is alien to the very nature of socialism. It is not the first time that Communists have been subjected to the pseudoaccusations of "Red imperialism" and "Red militarism." Even during the first years of Soviet rule—when world reaction took up arms to choke socialism in its cradle—the ideological servants of the counterrevolution were blessing, with one hand, the military invasion of the stranglers of the revolution and, with the other, were scribbling declarations in which any military effort on the part of the bleeding Soviet Republic was stigmatized as "Red militarism." In answer to this hypocrisy, Lenin wrote: "There are silly people who scream about Red militarism; they are political swindlers who create an appearance of believing in this silliness and throw such accusations right and left, utilizing their lawyers' ability to invent false evidence and to litter the eyes of the masses with sand."[4]

The enemies of socialism will not succeed in affixing to it the vices under which capitalism is suffering. For even before socialist states came into being, imperialist wars were consuming millions of lives. Socialism is peace. Under socialism there are no exploiting classes interested in the arms race, in the acquisition of new markets, and in an additional sphere for capital expansion. Already, today, millions of people living in the capitalist world know that it is not the socialist state and its foreign policy which represent a threat to peaceful coexistence; they know that the danger of a new war lies in the aggressive nature of contemporary capitalism.

It is precisely finance capitalism—possessed of a craving for profit—which creates the danger of a new world-wide conflict, because of its predatory, extortionist policy. Preparing a new world slaughter, imperialists increase their profits by means of an arms race and line their pockets with enormous sums of money collected from taxpayers by the bourgeois state. According to the reports in the American press, capitalist states that participate in various aggressive blocks annually spend 63 billion dollars for military purposes—more than half of the annual income of underdeveloped countries.

Second, waging wars for the sake of "making happy" other peoples is quite alien to the communist ideology; it is opposed to the Marxist view of revolution as an inescapable phenomenon, generated—in conformity with natural-historical necessity—by the internal developments in each capitalist country, that is, by the extreme aggravation of social contradictions. There is no need to go far for evidence: the Great Socialist October Revolution became

[4] *Ibid.,* Vol 29 (1950), p. 48.

victorious at the time when socialism was yet nonexistent in the world. The overwhelming majority of bourgeois ideologists realizes perfectly well that deadly danger threatens the capitalist system not from the outside but from the inside. However, only the most honest of them dare to admit this. Thus, J. Warburg, in *The West in Crisis,* states: "The deadly danger to Western civilization stems not from external but from internal enemies. The political and economic system of the West is eroding from within."

Since the socialist revolution is primarily the product of the internal development of each country, it cannot be imposed from outside; it can be accomplished only by the people of a given country, who are convinced of the necessity to change the existing system. The choice of one or another social system—states the Declaration of the Conference of the Representatives of the Communist and Workers' Parties—is an inalienable right of the people of each country. This sovereign right cannot be taken away under any pretext, and the Communists sacredly honor it, being against any "export of revolutions." But, while proclaiming (together with all other democrats) this sovereign right of the people, the Communists do not stop here. They deem it their duty to do whatever may be necessary to secure this sovereign right for all peoples. They have never been, and cannot be, indifferent observers of the counterrevolutionary intervention into the internal affairs of a country that has taken the revolutionary course. They declare their readiness to repulse, with all means, the aggressors who, by exporting counterrevolution, seek to deprive the people of any country of their lawful right to change their social system. As stated in the Declaration, "The communist parties, led by the Marxist-Leninist theory, have always been opposed to the export of revolution. At the same time, they resolutely struggle against the imperialist export of the counterrevolution. They deem it their international duty to call on the peoples of all countries to unite, to mobilize all their inner forces, to act effectively, and, leaning upon the might of the socialist world system, to prevent, or to resolutely rebuff, imperialist interference in the affairs of the people of any country who rose to a revolution."

The transformation of socialism into a decisive factor of social development, and its increasingly effective influence upon the international situation, open new perspectives for the working class in capitalist countries: a considerable preponderance of socialism over capitalism can become the beginning of the period of socialist revolutions without interventionist wars—without external intervention.

SOVIET POLITICAL THOUGHT

Indeed, capitalism may try—by means of war between countries, by means of a new world war—to prevent the world-wide victory of the socialist revolution, but such an attempt is inevitably doomed to failure: the forces of socialist revolution will inevitably destroy the forces of imperialist war, because the laws of history are more powerful than the laws of atomic artillery. A new world war, if imperialists were to succeed in unleashing it, would precipitate revolutionary upheaval to an even greater degree than previous wars and would result in the destruction of the entire capitalist system.

Contrary to the slander of bourgeois ideologists, the road to world-wide victory through a war between countries—through a nuclear world war—is not at all the ideal of the working class, because its ultimate goal is not simply the overthrow of capitalism at any price but the construction of communism. And communism cannot be built quickly on ruins. A world war, while precipitating the destruction of capitalism, would at the same time lead to the destruction of hundreds of millions of people and would delay the advance toward communism for a long time. At the same time, a world war would do tremendous damage to social wealth. All material and spiritual values of the world were produced by the labor of the popular masses. Communists cannot permit the exploiters to destroy, by means of a world-war conflagration, all these values that rightly belong to the people—to communism, which can be brought about only by utilizing all the achievements of human civilization.

Therefore, the struggle for peace between countries and the struggle for a revolutionary transition to communism are inseparable. Protecting the world from the conflagration of a new world war, Communists are confident of the inevitable victory of socialism in all countries, because the socialist revolution is an inevitable law of the internal development of a capitalist society, and wars between states are not needed for its victory.

# Name Index

596

598

# Subject Index

Abstractions: made by man, 338–39

Abundance, material: under communism, 511; social and technological prerequisites of, 511, 512

Accounting and control: simplified, under communism, 172–73; necessary for first phase of communism, 301$n$, 302

Action, social: motives behind, 21, 411–13, 512, 514, 520; and purpose, 22–23, 82–83; and "false" motives, 32, 219. *See also* Causality; Dialectical laws; Freedom; Free will; History; Natural laws; Necessity

Activism: in history, 22–23, 82–83. *See also* History

Administration, public: replacing legislation, 62–63; lack of knowledge of, 162, 170, 178; measures against bureaucratization, 162–63, 168, 169, 173, 178; bureaucratization of Soviet, 162–78 *passim*, 495; principles and requirements of, 163–68, 169–70, 171; deviations from principles of, 168, 170, 175–76, 177, 178; on local and national levels, 168–69; simplified, under communism, 171, 173, 318; government of persons replaced by, of "things," 186, 189, 309$n$, 382, 519; organs of, remain under communism, 319–20, 502; of "things," inseparable from men, 320; non-political character of, under communism, 382, 499–500. *See also* Authority, political; Bureaucracy; Communism

Agnosticism: and Marxism, 333; denies causality, 335

Agrarian Question, Conference of Marxist Students of, 277, 289

Alienation: of self, 220; of state power, 273, 495

"American way of life": ideal of Right-Socialists, 541

Anarchism: and collectivism, 58–62; and attitude toward law, 74–75, 247–48, 372, 415; economic centralization spurned by, 160; and Marxism, 160–61, 185–86, 188–89, 190, 240; advocates immediate abolition of state, 486

Aristocracy: and class war, 158; labor, 561

Army: abolition and re-establishment of, 175

Asceticism: alien to communism, 516

Authoritarianism: initial attempts to impose, in late 20's, 277

Authority, political: no need for, under communism, 82–83, 191, 193, 382–83, 499–500, 502; administrative organs subordinated to, 343; and subjective right, 414–16; replaced by self-government, 489, 500, 502, 520, 521; dies away, under communism, 499

Authority, public: no need for political, 82–83, 191, 193, 382–83, 499–500, 502; loses political character, 82–83, 191, 499, 502. *See also* Authority, political; Communism; Law; Socialism; State

"Automobile civilization": and bourgeois culture, 526

Autonomy: individual, advocated by anarchists, 160

Barter: sanctioned by dominant class, 101–2, 108–9

Basis: and superstructure, 26–30, 99, 103–4, 400–6; mode of production as, 27 and $n$, 158, 337–38, 392, 589; relations of production as, 27, 103, 158, 392, 401, 402, 403; determines superstructure, 27, 225, 283–84, 400, 403; interaction between superstructure and, 28, 84–85, 104, 107, 108, 392, 394, 401; and superstructure as figurative expression, 99, 106; confusion of superstructure with, 104, 105; of capitalist society, 402, 405–6; of socialist society, 403, 406; historical duration of, 403–4; serves society economically, 403–4. *See also* Superstructure

Beauty: as criterion of value under communism, 516

Being: social, and consciousness, 27, 76–77, 401, 421; and disorganized thinking, 76; overcoming dichotomy between thinking and, 80. *See also*

601

606

"tragic," 453–54; "optimistic" Marxist, 454. *See also* Dialectical laws; Dialectical materialism

Diarchy: after March Revolution, 109–10

Dichotomy: of thinking and being, 79–80; of "is" and "ought," 357–59, 459–60, 573; of science and morality, 570, 571, 572, 574, 577–78, 579

Dictatorship of the proletariat: as result of class struggle, 39, 195; *vs.* division of power, 75; should exploit science of law, 86; in transition period, 94, 161, 195–96, 486–87, 488, 491; inconceivable without state, 94, 487–88; opposed by anarchists, 161, 189, 486; bureaucratization of, 162–78 *passim*; difference between bourgeois dictatorships and, 196; democratic character of, 216; opposed to "true" socialism, 297–98; "theory of permanent withering away" of, 312–14; remains in classless society, 317; will be protracted, 491; ceases to be necessary in U.S.S.R., 581; "growing over into all-people's political organization," 581–82; necessary for complete victory of socialism, 582; role of working class after disappearance of, 582–83; Party's role after disappearance of, 583–84

Discipline: sense of, under communism, 383; and freedom under socialism, 446

Division of labor: and ideology, 33, 221–22

Dogmatism: and "quotology," 279; and truth, 339

Domination: and subordination, overemphasized, 416; and subordination replaced by "free cooperation," 519

Dualism: of thought and matter, 5–6; of being and thinking, 80; of "ought" and "is," 357–59, 459–60, 573

Duties, civil: new attitude toward, 445; unity of rights and, 233, 445–46

Ecclesiasts: justify private property, 469–70; propagate theory of "peo-
ple's capitalism," 470–72; seek to liquidate exploitation through prayers, 474, 476; reduce socioeconomic problems to moral, 475–76

Eclecticism: in bourgeois social sciences, 438, 529

Economics: interaction between ideology and, 84–85; and politics, 94–95; gloom of, 190; influenced by superstructure, 394. *See also* Basis; Superstructure

Economy: political, as a science, 47; unistructural, after second five-year plan, 296; planned, and dictatorship, 299; planned, on the basis of state capitalism, 299–300; crisis in, precluded, 343; wealthy man replaces wealthy, 548

Egotism: under capitalism, 514, 592; and altruism, in socialist society, 526–27

Election: to soviets, 197. *See also* Electorate; Suffrage

Electiveness and recall, principle of: in state-commune, 163, 165, 168, 170

Electoral right, universal: rejected, 148–49; since 1936, 343. *See also* Suffrage

Electorate: government's responsibility to, 343; limitations on rights of, 343; right of, to recall deputies, 343

"Elementary principles of law": stealing bourgeois property contrary to, 129; stealing worker's time and labor in conformity with, 129

Emotions: legal, and class interests, 145

Emotivism: and subjectivism in ethics, 564–68 *passim*

Encirclement, capitalist: and strengthening of state, 316, 320; and communism in one country, 384–85

Equality: incompatible with law, 96–97, 111, 115; as deception, 118; political, fraud, 120; under socialism and communism, 305–6, 331–32; in socialist democracy, 344; universal, under communism, 517–18; "actual," among peoples under communism, 522; social, 545

Equilibrium theory: of classes, 14–15, 265–66; of state, 265–67

Equivalent exchange: presupposes law and state, 135–36; 209–10

616

pression, 456; morality in, 456,
458; brings illusory comfort, 456–
57; equality before God compatible
with social inequality, 457; and
deficiency of atheist propaganda,
457, 458; appeals to aesthetic sense,
457–58; and punishment, 460;
morality preceded, 461–62; function of fear in, 462, 465; and
suffering, 463–64; function of
atonement in, 464; love and hate
in, 465, 466–67; promotes meek-
ness, 466
Remuneration. *See* Wages
Responsibility: for social conditions,
124; criminal, 137, 252, 253; and
freedom of will, 252–53; juridical,
258, 259–60; moral, 259
Retribution: social determinism and
principle of, 71; incompatible with
morality, 253
Revisionists: distorting Marxist philosophy, 427; blending Marxism
with bourgeois philosophy and
sociology, 427–33 *passim*; in favor
of idea of "social stratification,"
433–34; pretends to defend Marxism, 439–40; on socialist elements
in capitalism, 479; denounce Soviet
communists in "idolatry" of state,
487; misinterpret dying away of
state, 491–92; obfuscate nature of
socialist state, 494; on "Stalinist
revision" of state in transition, 495;
denounce Soviets in "bureaucratic
revision" of Marxism, 497
Revolution: as natural phenomenon,
11, 18; from above, 20; law and
court, 52–56, 72–75; aims of proletarian, 57–68 *passim*; difference
between proletarian and bourgeois,
59–66, 72–75; English, and elements of feudalism, 134; forthcoming, in Germany and America,
134; abolishes parliamentarianism,
167; causes of, 195, 234–35, 589–
90; character of Russian, 198–99;
and retreat, tactical, 242; socialist,
and human nature, 315; "permanent," and peaceful coexistence, 530;
no necessary connection between
war and, 588; war and, distinct
phenomena, 588–90; wars merely
precipitate, 590; bourgeois ideologists distort Marxist theory of,
591–92; social, cannot be imposed

from outside, 593; communists
opposed to export of, 593–94. *See
also* French Revolution
Rights: legal, a sham, 25; and might,
55–56; "true," ideology of Social
Revolutionaries, 121–22; Marx's
aversion to idea of duty and, 122,
250; idea of, to be replaced with
neutral term, 122–23; Lenin's use
of term, 123; and idea of justice,
128; equal, verbal rubbish, 130; private property, as stimulus of economic activity, 133; economic, 227–
33; idea of obligation blending with,
233; objective, 233; electoral, 343;
unity of, and obligations under
socialism, 445–46
—inalienable: derived from "natural-
law individualism," 230; discarded
by Hitler, 347; not included in
U.S. Constitution, 348; rejected by
Soviets, 416; choice of social systems and, 593
—subjective: and capitalist society,
231; idea of, denounced, 414–15;
and objective law, 416; concerns
man's relationship to state, 416;
useful for socialist law, 416
Right-Socialism: rejects historical
necessity, 540; hopes for victory of
"higher moral principles," 540; accepts "American way of life" as
socialist ideal, 541; deceives workers, 561
Rotation: in public office, 168, 170;
in management, 171–72; failure to
attain, 176–77
Rule of law: a deception, 74; "the
state under law," criticized, 121,
249, 288; and Soviet law, 534. *See
also* Legality; *Rechtsstaat*
Rules: observance of, under communism a habit, 172, 173, 241, 242,
383, 500, 519; new character of,
under communism, 382–83

Science: and politics, 3–4, 39; and
theological assumptions, 6; of laws
of motion, 9; historical materialism as, of society, 21–22; and
partisanship, 39–43, 374–79, 435–
40; of law as instrument in class
struggle, 85–86; social life mystery
to bourgeoisie, 142; descriptive,
356; normative, 356; and problem

*Designed by Gerard A. Valerio*

*Composed in Times Roman by Monotype Composition Company, Inc.*

*Printed offset by Universal Lithographers, Inc.*
*on 50 pound Old Forge F*

*Bound by Maple Press in Columbia Fictionette*